AF760909

Settlement, Nesting Territories and Conflicting Legal Systems in a Micmac Community

Settlement, Nesting Territories and Conflicting Legal Systems in a Micmac Community

Daniel P. Strouthes
Department of Geography & Anthropology
University of Wisconsin–Eau Clair

Yale University Publications
in Anthropology
number eighty-nine march 2010
Department of Anthropology, Yale University
Division of Anthropology,
Peabody Museum of Natural History
New Haven, Connecticut

Yale

Yale University Publications in Anthropology Number 89
Settlement, Nesting Territories and Conflicting Legal Systems in a Micmac Community
by Daniel P. Strouthes

The *Yale University Publications in Anthropology* series, published by the Peabody Museum of Natural History at Yale University and the Yale University Department of Anthropology, is supported by the Theodore and Ruth Wilmanns Lidz Endowment Fund for Excellence in Scholarly Publications, dedicated to the dissemination of scholarly research and study of the world and its cultures.

Richard L. Burger *Curatorial Editor-in-Chief*
Lawrence F. Gall *Executive Editor*
Rosemary Volpe *Publications Editor*
Index by Aardvark Indexing

The *Yale University Publications in Anthropology* series embodies the results of researches in the general field of anthropology directly conducted or sponsored by the Yale University Department of Anthropology and the Yale Peabody Museum Division of Anthropology. Occasionally, other manuscripts of outstanding quality that deal with subjects of special interest to the faculty of the Department of Anthropology may also be included. Issues range in size from brief papers to extensive monographs and are numbered consecutively as independent contributions published at regular intervals.

For submission guidelines send inquiries to:

Publications Office
Peabody Museum of Natural History, Yale University
P.O. Box 208118, New Haven, CT 06520-8118 U.S.A.
Phone: (203) 432-3786 • Fax: (203) 432-5872
E-mail: peabody.publications@yale.edu
URL: http://www.peabody.yale.edu/

Distributed by Yale University Press, New Haven and London | www.yalebooks.com

© 2010 Peabody Museum of Natural History, Yale University. All rights reserved. This book may not be reproduced, in whole or in part, including illustrations, in any form or media without the written permission of the Peabody Museum of Natural History, Yale University.

Cover: The 74 Street subdivision on the Eskasoni Reserve, Cape Breton, Nova Scotia, Canada. Photograph by Daniel P. Strouthes.

Library of Congress Cataloging-in-Publication Data

Strouthes, Daniel P.
Settlement, nesting territories and conflicting legal systems in a Micmac community / by Daniel P. Strouthes.
p. cm. -- (Yale University publications in anthropology number ; v. 89)
Includes bibliographical references and index.
ISBN 978-0-913516-25-6 (trade pbk. : alk. paper)
1. Micmac Indians--Land tenure--Nova Scotia--Eskasoni Region. 2. Micmac Indians--Legal status, laws, etc.--Nova Scotia--Eskasoni Region. 3. Micmac Indians--Nova Scotia--Eskasoni Region--Government relations. 4. Eskasoni Region (N.S.)--Race relations. 5. Eskasoni Region (N.S.)--Politics and government. I. Title.
E99.M6S77 2010
971.5004'97343--dc22

2010005191

ISBN 978-0-913516-25-6
ISSN 1535-7082
Printed in the U.S.A.

∞ This paper meets the requirements of ANSI/NISO Z39.48-1992 (Permanence of Paper).

Contents

FIGURES AND TABLES

List of Cases

Page numbers are in italics.

Continued

Real Property Cases by Type of Law

Preface

Judging by the amount of attention from the media, scholars, governments and nongovernmental organizations, many in today's world are searching for new ways to reduce or prevent conflict. In the 20th century, the Eskasoni band of Micmac Indians of Cape Breton Island, Nova Scotia, Canada, invented just such a novel means of conflict control. In fact, this new method, involving territorial defense, became so valuable that the band even changed its land tenure system to strengthen it. Although based on aspects of traditional culture, it is in fact new, developing after the settlement of the people in the early 20th century. But as remarkable as this invention is, it is but one of several ways in which the Micmac adapted to a settled life.

The data I present here bear on current discussions of cultural change. In his popular work Modernity at Large, Arjun Appadurai (1996b) provides an account of cultural diffusion in the world today. It is a gloomy picture of Western culture invading non-Western societies, bounding across sociopolitical and geographic boundaries without pause and eagerly embraced by individuals throughout the world. Anyone who has visited, even briefly, some of these societies can immediately recognize and understand what Appadurai describes.

I cannot help but wonder whether this is the whole of the story. Appadurai chooses for his examples the most easily observed phenomena, among them consumer goods, sports, mass media and major religions. Does the process of diffusion affect all parts of the culture equally? Even the diffusion studies of an earlier era did not make this claim. To put the question another way, in talking with other students of North American Indian societies, this very subject sometimes comes up by way of noticing that North American Indian people usually dress as do European Americans, live in the same kinds of houses, enjoy the same music, cinema and sports, worship at the same churches, and fight in the same armies. Yet we all notice profound differences in other less overt parts of the culture, including moral values, etiquette, language, and political systems. Many of these parts of the culture remain from pre-Columbian times despite centuries of foreign domination.

Furthermore, for Appadurai and others (for example, Sanders 2003), the modern world opposes the traditional one, hence the term "modernity." In this framework, innovation should not and does not come from local, indigenous non-Western people such as the Micmac, but rather from the centers of cultural innovation, such as the United States.

The aim of this book is not to describe how a group of North American Indian people have maintained a tradition, but rather to describe and analyze how such a group has invented a legal system that is neither traditional nor borrowed from the dominant European American culture. By examining law and social control mechanisms, two less obvious aspects of culture, I will show that not all culture change in today's world originates from diffusion and globalization. Rather, some very important parts of culture change as a result of internal social dynamics and a conscious desire for improvement.

This book has two purposes. First, it describes and analyzes the land tenure law of a band of Micmac Indians living on the Eskasoni reserve on Cape Breton Island in Nova Scotia, Canada. Second, it describes and analyzes the effect of settlement on the band by examining changes in the modern indigenous Band Council land tenure system.

The land tenure law of this band presently occupies three legal levels, which can be found in many legal systems, each with its own body of law; in the past, there were as many as five legal levels in the legal systems that applied to the band. Today, the Canadian Indian system, Canada's federal real property laws applying to Indians, has the widest geographical and social jurisdiction. The next level of jurisdiction belongs to the Eskasoni Band Council, an indigenous legal authority, which dates from 1957. Although the Band Council consists of bureaucrats employed by the federal government of Canada, it is made up entirely of Micmac members, elected by Micmac people, who make laws for their own purposes and not those of the federal government. The smallest jurisdictions belong to the descent group or family. Each descent group or family has its own legal system for real property. Thus, several hundred separate legal systems exist at this lowest legal level.

In addition, there were until recent decades two other legal systems, each occupying their own legal levels. The earlier of these was the aboriginal Grand Council, the unified body of political leaders and legal authorities of the Cape Breton Micmac, which applied to most of the Indian people of Cape Breton. The second, of brief duration (1942–1978), was one that Indian Affairs, a federal agency, imposed on the people of Eskasoni.

"Indian Affairs" is the popular name for the federal agency that has administered matters pertaining to North American Indians in Canada since the country became a Dominion in the 19th century. Its official name and bureaucratic affiliation have changed several times since then, and so I will refer to it by its popular name. I also use the popular term "Indian Agent" to refer to the Indian Agency Superintendent, a federal employee who dealt directly with Indians until the position became obsolete in the 1970s.

This book will describe and analyze the real property law of each of these systems, and put forth an analysis of why the Grand Council's legal system included no land tenure system. In analyzing the Band Council's land tenure system, I place especial emphasis on the effects that settlement of the Micmac population has had on it. Transition from mobile to settled life requires first and foremost a change in the use of land, and once changes in land use patterns take place, changes in the social relationships of people as users of land inevitably follow. Land supplies resources humans use and, as discussed below, can hold even greater importance for social control. If the supply of land does not meet demand, conflicts over access to land inevitably arise, in turn affecting social relationships. As land use patterns change, so too do the conflicts of interest that affect social relationships. Very often, although not universally, these conflicts, especially the most common and dangerous ones, must be regulated by law. In short, to arrive at an understanding of the changes in social relationships brought about by settlement, a study of change in land tenure provides an obvious and effective means to analyze some of the most pivotal changes. Strangely enough, despite this obvious empirical and theoretical link between the subjects of settlement and land tenure, I am aware of only one short article (Galaty 1980) that uses land tenure to analyze settlement (often known as "sedentarization").

The focus of this article leads me to mention a relevant point. It describes a land tenure system imposed by a state government, and not the indigenous system, if one exists. Legal systems that the state imposes on culturally distinct peoples rarely fulfill the needs of those small indigenous societies who must endure them. In other words, there may be little functional relationship between the self-perceived needs of the people in a small and culturally separate society and an alien and externally imposed legal system. To understand the conflicts crucial to a society, and how these change over time, one must study the indigenous legal system.

For this reason I have focused on indigenous law: the Band Council's legal system, the Grand Council's system, and the descent group and family systems. I also studied the Canadian Indian land tenure system, since it forms part of the overall land tenure system and incorporates a legal authority with whom the Micmac must contend. The study of the Canadian Indian system also provided the opportunity to study a crucial aspect of the Band Council's system, namely, how the Band Council legal system manages and limits the operation of the federal system within its jurisdiction.

So far as I am aware, this work represents the first study of the indigenous land tenure system of a settling people and the first study of the development of a North American Indian legal system. My interest in this subject developed during fieldwork in the summers of 1980 through 1984, and the fall of 1982, during my studies of the whole of Micmac culture. I became aware that people were using territorial control to circumvent and ease social friction. This differed from the situation of the previous nomadic period, during which mobility had allowed antagonists to maintain a physical distance from one another. Later, I concentrated on the collection of legal cases, especially those concerning real property.

I collected most of the material for this book during these periods, and also from June 1985 through August 1987, a total of 41 months. Subsequent fieldwork took place in the summers of 1994 to 1999, and 2002 to 2009, totaling just over another 16 months. In 1987, I undertook several more months of archival research and research on Canadian court decisions on Indian real property rights. In my fieldwork I relied on participant observation techniques and, especially, the interview of Micmac informants. Though only a few Micmac individuals are unable to speak fluent English (and many speak better English than Micmac), and though much of my fieldwork was conducted in English, it proved extremely advantageous to understand the Micmac language. Though I never became perfectly fluent speaking the Micmac language, by 1986 I was able to understand the Micmac spoken by others in conversation without any difficulty. In addition, I learned to read and to write Micmac using the five most common orthographies, and so to understand texts printed in the Micmac language.

I conducted my research primarily on the Eskasoni reserve, located on Cape Breton Island, though I also did brief research on all of the other five Cape Breton reserves as well as on Micmac reserves on the mainland of Nova Scotia, and New Brunswick and Quebec. I used several hundred informants, though most of the significant information presented here I obtained from approximately 80 individuals with whom I became well acquainted over the years. That my research took place over a period of 19 years proved invaluable. This book would not be possible without my knowledge of the language and the perspective brought by exposure to Micmac society for this length of time. Not only did a long fieldwork period allow a study of the culture in its entirety, it permitted the collection of a variety of legal cases as they occurred.

Throughout this book I use a definition of the term "law" devised by Leopold Pospisil (1971:8), a definition with the following four criteria:

1. Law is a principle manifested in a decision made by a political authority.
2. It contains a definition of the relation between the two parties to the dispute (obligatio).
3. It has a regularity of application (intention of universal application).
4. It is provided with a sanction.

My primary data consist of trouble cases themselves. I present these in the text, as well as citations of the relevant Canadian court decisions that have been published in various court reporters. I include four types of Micmac cases in the text: legal cases (defined by the criteria above); political cases (cases which meet criteria 1, 2 and 4 above); dispute cases (cases in which no individual takes part as an authority); and legal–political cases, which combine legal and political elements in their decisions. These types of cases are identified as such. I analyze real property legal decisions in terms of the legal principles that may be abstracted from them, a method of analysis developed by Pospisil (1958a, 1958b).

As much as possible, data are arranged chronologically so that the reader may have a better understanding of the causal relationships between historical social progression and legal change. I present discussions of the various legal systems in order of the systems' initial historical appearances.

My research would not have been possible without the assistance first and foremost of the friendly people of Eskasoni; knowing them has made me a happier person. I am also indebted to the Eskasoni Band Council and Band Office staff, the staff members of the Public Archives of Canada, Public Archives of Nova Scotia, and of the Department of Indian and Northern Affairs; to them I extend my appreciation and thanks. In the preparation of this work, I am most grateful for the helpful comments of Rebecca French, Ward Goodenough, Floyd Lounsbury, John Middleton, Jerry Offner, Thomas G. Poulette, and especially those of my graduate school adviser and mentor, Leopold Pospisil. I also thank Victoria Giannola, Kyran Hamill, and Bradford Roman for their assistance with the maps. I gratefully acknowledge the support of the American Philosophical Society, the Canadian Embassy, the Jacobs Research Funds of the Whatcom Museum Society, the University of Wisconsin–Eau Claire, the University of Wisconsin System Institute on Race and Ethnicity, Wesleyan University, and Yale University.

A Note on Micmac Orthography

The orthography that I use in this work, shown below, is adapted slightly from the Francis–Smith system. The consonants l, m, n, w and y are sonorants, the others obstruents, and all may be syllabic. Stress is indicated by a vertical tick (‘) preceding the stressed syllable.

Micmac	International Phonetic Alphabet equivalent
a	ɔ/a
a:	a:
e	ɛ
e:	e:
i	ɪ/i
i:	i:
ɨ	ə
j	dz
k	k/g
l	l
m	m
o	ʌ/o
o:	o:
p	p/b
q	x
s	s/z
t	t/d
u	u/ʊ
w	w
y	j

On the Use of the Spelling "Micmac"

I have chosen to retain the traditional spelling "Micmac" because there is not yet a consensus among the Micmac people about the appropriate term of reference or spelling to use. Most in Nova Scotia now prefer the spelling Mi'kmaq. However, many in Québec prefer Mi'gmaq, a spelling which itself represents an innovation and contrasts with another spelling they had used until recently. Many in New Brunswick prefer Miigmaq, also a change from the spelling used there until recently. Some older people continue to use Micmac. There is also a serious movement by many native speakers to use the word *Lnu* or *Ulnoo* (however spelled), which is the autonym meaning "the people." No one alive today can state with certainty either the origin or the meaning of the word "Micmac." Even though the orthography I use for other Micmac terms in this work is essentially that of Francis-Smith, the choice of the appropriate term of reference and its spelling is probably best left to the people themselves. For me to choose one spelling over another would be to favor one side over another, in a debate I have no interest in joining.

Part I:

Ethnographic Introduction

CHAPTER ONE

History and Environment

Prehistory and Early History

The patrilineal Micmac speak an Algonkian language, and at contact inhabited what is now the Gaspé Peninsula of Quebec, Nova Scotia, Prince Edward Island, and eastern New Brunswick in Canada. Archeological evidence suggests that the Micmac did not inhabit the region originally. Rather, the ancestors of the modern Micmac migrated from the Canadian Shield to replace the Maritime Archaic people at approximately 1000 B.C. (Tuck 1978:34). Until well into the 20th century, they subsisted by migratory hunting, fishing, and gathering, although beginning in the 19th century most also began to raise potatoes and to sell or barter wooden handicrafts while on their travels.

Although they had early encounters with Basques, the first colonial people with whom the Micmac had prolonged contact were the French. They traded furs for French manufactured goods, and later adopted the Roman Catholic faith.

Before their association with the French, the Micmac sometimes fought with their rivals the Beothuks and the Maliseet. "Maliseet" is a Micmac term that the Micmac use to poke fun at a people they know properly as *'Etjemin*; *Mal'i:sit* translates as "he/she speaks poorly (or lazily)," a reference to their vocabulary, very similar to that of Micmac, with the exception that many Maliseet words have fewer syllables than their Micmac cognates.

When the French began to fight the Beothuks, the former encouraged the Micmac to become their allies, and together the French and Micmac virtually exterminated the Beothuk people (Reynolds 1978:106–107). Later, the Micmac colonized Newfoundland, the Beothuks' home, especially in the 19th century (Pastore 1977). In the 1980s, the Micmac of Conne River, Newfoundland, were granted Indian status, defined in Canada's *Indian Act* (the federal statute containing the rules by which the federal government administers Indians and reserves; R.S.C. 1985, c. I-5, s. 2) as a person registered with the federal government as an Indian, and a reserve (federal land set apart for the use of a band of Indians) was established for their newly created band (a band, by definition of the *Indian Act*, is a group of Indians for whom reserve lands have been set apart; a band has a unique and exclusive membership and legal identity; R.S.C. 1985, c. I-5, s. 2).

During the intermittent hostilities between the French and the English, the

Micmac fought alongside the French against the English and their allies, the Iroquois. The long-standing enmity between the Micmac and the Mohawk, whom the Micmac know as *Kwetej*, predated the French and Indian War (1754–1763), but became even more heated during that time. The Micmac and their Algonkian allies, the Penobscot, Passamaquoddy, Maliseet, and several smaller tribes, formed the Wabanaki ("eastern") Confederacy in the late 17th or early 18th century to oppose the Iroquois. Later on, some members of the two sides concluded a peace. Between 1713 (the Treaty of Utrecht) and 1763 (the Treaty of Paris), when Cape Breton Island remained the last significant French possession on the Atlantic seaboard, many Micmac moved there for protection from the British. During the American Revolution, Micmac allied themselves with the Americans against the English, who defeated them previously and who had afterwards persecuted them.

The 19th century saw a great influx of English and Scottish settlers to the Maritime Provinces. Unlike the French, who only sparsely settled coastal areas to fish and to trade, the English and Scottish settled the land as farmers. To protect the Indians from being completely excluded from any rights to land, and fearful of their extinction, provincial governments set aside lands for their use. The Eskasoni reserve, for example, was surveyed in 1832 and officially set aside as land reserved for the exclusive use of Indians in 1834. Unlike the usual practice in the United States, the Canadian provincial governments created reserves out of lands that Indians frequently visited. When Canadian Confederation, the union of the British colonies of North America into the Dominion of Canada accomplished by the *British North America Act,* took place in 1867, control over the reserves and governmental responsibilities for the Indians transferred to the federal government. Initially, Micmac used reserves as home bases, but largely settled on them for much of the year by the early part of the 20th century.

By provision of federal statute through the *Indian Act,* the Micmac were organized into federally recognized bands in the 1940s and 1950s. I use the term band in this sense to discuss the Micmac after the mid-1950s, when the provisions of the *Indian Act* were enforced; otherwise, the term is used in its anthropological meaning. Each band member has a band number; until age 18, children share their father's band number. A woman acquires her husband's band number and band affiliation on marriage. The government has assigned to each Micmac band at least one reserve, a few of which are uninhabited. Cape Breton has five bands, each one with a reserve where their members reside.

The Indian Agency Superintendent and the Centralization Program

The federal Centralization Program stands as the most significant event in Nova Scotia Micmac history since the end of the colonial era wars. Begun officially in 1942, it did not get into full swing until after World War II. The program ostensibly intended to convert the Nova Scotia Micmac from semi-migratory hunters, fishermen, and handicrafts peddlers into fully settled agriculturalists, pastoralists, and industrial workers, thereby moving them gently but pointedly toward assimilation and acculturation. To facilitate the administration of the project, the Micmac popu-

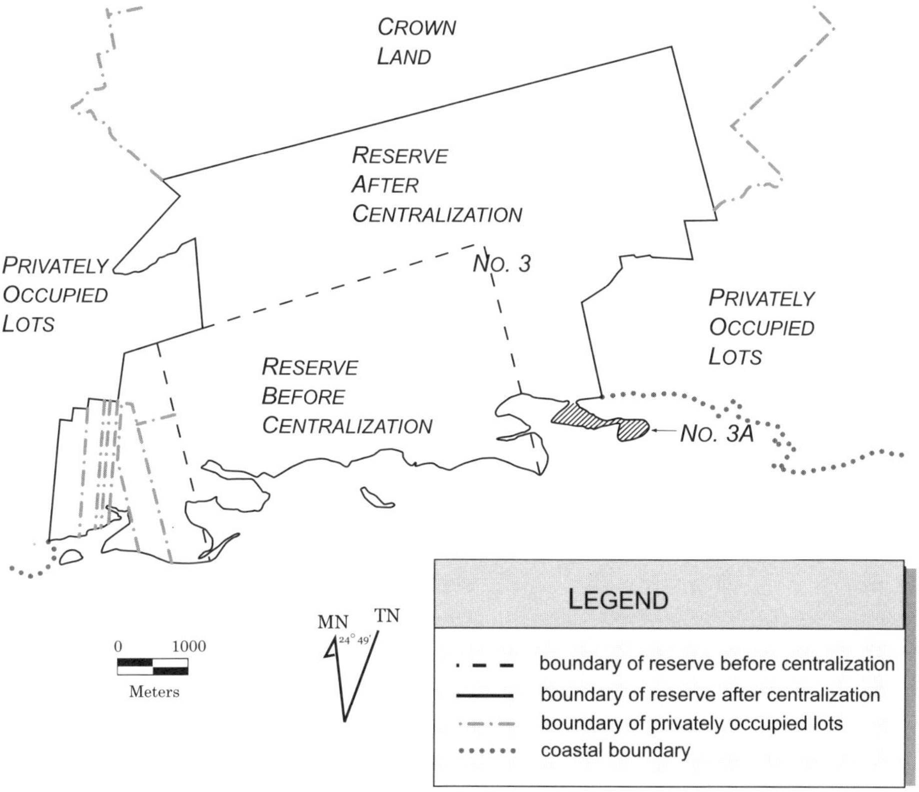

Figure 1. Map A: Eskasoni reserve boundaries before and after centralization.

lation was to be "centralized" on the Eskasoni reserve on Cape Breton Island and the Shubenacadie reserve on the mainland. The genuine reason for the Centralization Program, which caused a considerable amount of suffering for the Micmac people, turns out to be less noble than the publicly stated one: white people in Nova Scotia had complained about the temptations posed to their sons by Micmac girls and women (Upton 1979:175). Hence the choice of Shubenacadie and Eskasoni, which sit at a distance from white towns. In addition, a group who had long been living in North Sydney, although not on a reserve, was moved to Eskasoni. To accommodate the newcomers, the federal government enlarged the Eskasoni reserve (Figure 1). A major portion of the enlargement consisted of the area known as Castle Bay, a former non-Indian settlement, where most of the Micmac newcomers settled.

During the 1940s Centralization Program, the Indian Agent's primary function was to move people living in places other than Eskasoni and Shubenacadie to those two reserves and to encourage them to farm. Indian Affairs enticed people to move with offers of employment and new houses. The Indian Agent courted the *'Saqmaw* (at first a headman, but at this time a chief, usually known in recent years as *'Kji:saqmaw*, or "great *'Saqmaw*") of the Micmac Grand Council to lend support to the Centralization Program. Believing that the experiment would lead to a higher standard of living for his people, the *'Saqmaw* gave it his blessing, thereby encouraging many followers. The Indian Agent rewarded his compliance by giving him the best farmland on the Eskasoni reserve. The *'Saqmaw*'s approval of Centralization later cost him the support and respect of some of his followers.

Many of those who initially moved to Eskasoni eventually returned to their reserves of origin, or moved to yet other reserves. Some went back because there were no houses waiting for them in Eskasoni when they arrived. This was especially true for the people from Whycocomagh. Furthermore, there was tension between some of the Whycocomagh people and some of the Eskasoni people almost from the start of the Centralization Program because some Eskasoni people felt that the Whycocomagh had earlier stolen the office of the *'Saqmaw* from them. When the *'Saqmaw*'s office left the Denny family's line of descent, the Grand Council chose a Whycocomagh man (Gabriel Sylliboy) for the office. The Denny family, traditional heirs to the office, have long lived in Eskasoni.

Centralization brought hundreds of new faces to the enlarged Eskasoni reserve. One Eskasoni resident disparagingly called the new people "drifters*ik*" (drifters). Resistance to the new settlers sometimes led to fistfights, and the strain created by mixing the newcomers with Eskasoni residents also manifested itself for a period in youth gangs. Teenaged boys from Castle Bay, the new arrivals, would travel to other parts of the reserve to assert their presence, sometimes forcefully. The teenaged boys in other areas of the reserve responded by organizing their own gangs to meet the threat. The gangs fought each other, and some later caused a considerable amount of vandalism, particularly to the school. The Indian constables proved unable to disband these gangs until the mid-1970s.

In an effort to prevent immigrants from returning to their homes on other reserves, the Indian Agent burned down several of the empty houses at Whycocomagh and had a Micmac man who had once lived there raze the school, as well as the school on another reserve, in return for the salvage lumber. Other Micmac had no houses to which they could return, having sold them to non-Indians who removed them from the reserves. The Indian Agent required that those who had sold their houses pay him the money that they had received as partial payment for the new houses that had been built for them. The destitute, who constituted the vast majority, were not required to pay for their new houses.

Although many of the people remained at their new homes at Eskasoni and Shubenacadie, the Centralization Program failed in its key goal of moving the entire Indian population of Nova Scotia to the two reserves. The bold Indian Affairs experiment also failed from the perspective of the Nova Scotia Micmac. Few Micmac did more than a little farming, and of the five inhabited Cape Breton reserves slated for abandonment only one, Malagawatch, was entirely depopulated (and is today in the process of being repopulated). The experiment took place once, only in Nova Scotia, and ended in 1949.

In 1956 the federal government decided that the people living at Eskasoni should become a federally recognized Indian band, as provided by the *Indian Act* (R.S.C. 1985, c. I-5, s. 2). In that year, the band's first chief and band councillors were elected according to *Indian Act* regulations, taking office in 1957. A Band Council is the legislative and administrative authority of most Canadian Indian bands, and exists by authority of the *Indian Act* (R.S.C. 1985, c. I-5, s. 2). It includes one chief and at least two, but no more than twelve, councillors, all elected by adult band members according to rules set forth in the *Indian Act* (R.S.C. 1985, c. I-5, s. 74). Members of the Band Councils are paid employees of Indian Affairs. The chief's office compares with that of a municipality's mayor, rather than a chieftain's. This individual's importance derives from a unique duty in the band to deal directly with the federal government. Micmac speakers also refer to this person as *'Saqmaw* (headman or chief).

Since the Indians living on the other Cape Breton reserves were supposed to have been relocated to Eskasoni under the Centralization Program, they were not organized into bands until 1958 through 1962. Micmac presently live in 29 bands in five provinces, ranging in population from fewer than 50 persons to more than three thousand. Quebec has four Micmac bands, New Brunswick nine, Prince Edward Island two, Nova Scotia thirteen, and Newfoundland one. The Micmac population has grown rapidly in the past four or five decades. In 1970, the Micmac population was fewer than ten thousand, but now exceeds twenty thousand people. Approximately one-half or fewer of these people speak the Micmac language at present, and this fraction grows steadily smaller.

Physical Description of Cape Breton Island and Eskasoni Reserve

Cape Breton Island

Cape Breton is located roughly at latitude 46° north and longitude 61° west. Lying to the northeast of the Nova Scotia mainland, it occupies 10,828 square kilometers. Bras d'Or Lake, a saline tidal body located in the south-central region of Cape Breton Island, covers 1,153 square kilometers. The island's terrain is hilly, rising to 450 meters north of Bras D'Or Lake and to 200 meters south of it. Cape Breton lies at the southern reaches of the polar air mass, which affects it intermittently throughout the year, although the Atlantic Ocean and the Bras D'Or Lake greatly moderate the climate. The prevailing winds are westerlies throughout the year.

Eskasoni Reserve

Eskasoni is between latitude 45°54′N and 45°59′N, and between longitude 60°35′W and 60°41′W. The reserve is on the north shore of the east bay of Bras d'Or Lake, 48 kilometers from Sydney, North Sydney, and Glace Bay, an urban region of approximately 60,000 people.

The reserve itself occupies 35.8 square kilometers (8,846 acres), although this figure is currently under review for accuracy. It has a narrow coastal plain, north of which are hills rising to more than 200 meters, and on top of these hills lies a large peat bog. All settlement occurs on the coastal plain and at the foot of the hills on the southern side of the reserve (Figures 4 and 7).

The Demography of the Eskasoni Micmac

The demographic data on the Eskasoni Micmac (Appendix I) indicate several important trends. The first of these is that the population is growing rapidly. The figures for 1949 show many children aged zero through five years. This is undoubtedly the start of the tremendous growth that the Micmac have experienced since the late 1940s. The end of Centralization in 1949 meant that no more people would be moving to Eskasoni from other reserves, and in fact some of the number represented here would later return to their reserves of origin. Even given that, the fact that there were 692 people at Eskasoni in 1949 and 2,043 in 1985 means that the population grew by 295% in a mere 36 years. Between 1972 and 1985, the population of Eskasoni rose from 1,289 to 2,043. By 1996, the population stood at 2,865 (Mi'kmaq Resource Centre 1998; this collection of short sketches of Micmac communities in Nova Scotia was written by Micmac students at the University College of Cape Breton), and by 2000, 3,356, of whom 502 live off the reserve (DIAND 1997–2004). This high annual growth rate of 3.09% between 1949 and 2000 results from both high birth and fertility rates; although both rates were high before World War II, infant and childhood mortality rates also stood correspondingly high. The data also show that, because of the relatively high proportion of children in the population, the high birth rate is likely to continue; 55% of the population was below the age of 20 in 1996 (see Mi'kmaq Resource Centre 1998).

As a general rule, the Micmac population of Nova Scotia suffers from low employment rates, low levels of formal schooling, and low earnings (see Appendix I). Thus, in these respects, the Micmac are similar to other Indians across North America.

Finally, the data show that nearly all of the small numbers of Eskasoni band members who live off of the reserve are of working age, indicating that the few people who do leave the reserve leave to work, and then return on retirement.

Principles of Justice

To understand legal ideals and legal behavior, it is helpful to discuss the basic principles of justice that the Micmac believe should underlie all legal actions. These principles, moreover, ideally guide all daily behavior.

1. An authority should curtail an individual's behavior only if it causes harm to the community at large.

2. Disputes within the family should be adjudicated solely by family authorities.

3. Preservation of maximum individual rights and responsibilities should receive top priority in the making of any judgment.

4. All cases should be treated strictly uniformly; favoritism, discrimination, and prejudice have no place in the legal process.

Rules and Principles

Indian Affairs Rules

INDIAN AFFAIRS RULE 1
All natural resources harvested or mined on a reserve are property of the Crown and must be purchased to be used. The proceeds from the sale of these are credited to the band, for use by the Band Council.

INDIAN AFFAIRS RULE 2
The Indian Agent may not evict a resident of a house unless there is another house waiting for the evictee to occupy immediately.

Indian Agent Rules

INDIAN AGENT RULE 1
Families and individuals may claim exclusive rights only to land that they themselves have cleared of forest.

INDIAN AGENT RULE 2
Indians living on the Eskasoni reserve may alienate their individual interests in real property to one another, without the need for lawful possession.

Eskasoni Real Property Behavioral Rules

ESKASONI REAL PROPERTY BEHAVIORAL RULE 1
An individual acquires ownership of free (unoccupied or unused) land by being the first to reside on that land or the first to use it. Free land consists of land that was never occupied or that was abandoned by a previous owner. Micmac people usually describe free land as "land that no one owns." This rule applies to all forms of land, including residential sites, wooded areas, logging roads, waterfront and beach land, and natural meadows.

ESKASONI REAL PROPERTY BEHAVIORAL RULE 2
Ownership rights over land include rights of alienation, possession, and usufruct, as well as the right to prevent its occupation, possession, or use by others.

ESKASONI REAL PROPERTY BEHAVIORAL RULE 3
Ownership rights terminate on the abandonment of the land, as when one's wigwam is moved to a different location and residence is established there or, in the case of woodlots, cessation of both use and intent of continued use.

ESKASONI REAL PROPERTY BEHAVIORAL RULE 4
The builder of a house has ownership of the house until alienating it, and each subsequent owner has the right of ownership until alienating it.

ESKASONI REAL PROPERTY BEHAVIORAL RULE 5

In the case of intestacy, the real property of the deceased is to go to the surviving spouse. If there is no surviving spouse, it is to go to the eldest surviving offspring, regardless of sex, so the recipient can use it to care for the younger offspring.

ESKASONI REAL PROPERTY BEHAVIORAL RULE 6

The band as a whole owns reserve land that is unowned by individuals.

ESKASONI REAL PROPERTY BEHAVIORAL RULE 7

In cases in which the marital house is built on a Family Home Territory, it will be owned by the spouse whose lineage owns the Family Home Territory where the house is built, after a divorce or separation.

Band Council Real Property Rules

BAND COUNCIL REAL PROPERTY RULE 1

No one awarded a new house by the Band Council may enter that house until construction is completed.

BAND COUNCIL REAL PROPERTY RULE 2

The Band Council prohibits the use of the band's funds to purchase housing from individuals (with the exception of expropriations ordered and paid for by Indian Affairs).

BAND COUNCIL REAL PROPERTY RULE 3

Non-band members may reside on the reserve, subject to the conditions set forth in Band Council Legal Principle 12, but may own neither houses nor land on the reserve (no cases recorded).

BAND COUNCIL REAL PROPERTY RULE 4

A house may not be destroyed or dismantled except when decrepit and then only under the special permission of the Band Council.

BAND COUNCIL REAL PROPERTY RULE 5

The Band Council will not expropriate real property owned by band members.

BAND COUNCIL REAL PROPERTY RULE 6

All individuals receiving a new house in their own name from the Band Council for the first time must have their houses built in one of the new subdivisions (no disputes recorded).

BAND COUNCIL REAL PROPERTY RULE 7

Band members living off the reserve may not own property on the reserve.

BAND COUNCIL REAL PROPERTY RULE 8
The band owns all the houses on the reserve that were built at band expense; only those who built or extend their houses at their own expense or have lawful possession have ownership of those houses.

BAND COUNCIL REAL PROPERTY RULE 9
Unmarried individuals who possess houses and who frequently have drunken, unruly parties in their houses will lose possession of their houses.

Grand Council Legal Principles

GRAND COUNCIL LEGAL PRINCIPLE 1
Anyone who causes significant damage, loss, or injury to another party is guilty of a criminal offense, unless such damage, loss, or injury is due to accident or insanity (abstracted from Legal Cases 5, 6, 8, and 9).

GRAND COUNCIL LEGAL PRINCIPLE 2
Activities and behavior that promote a positive image of the Micmac people to the outside world must flourish and failure to promote these activities constitutes a criminal offense (abstracted from Legal Cases 10, 13, and 15, and Dispute Case 8).

GRAND COUNCIL LEGAL PRINCIPLE 3
Civil disputes that cause social disruption to more than a few people constitute criminal offenses (abstracted from Legal Case 13).

Indian Agent Legal Principles

INDIAN AGENT LEGAL PRINCIPLE 1
All, and only, uncleared reserve land is open to settlement and to the building of private housing.

INDIAN AGENT LEGAL PRINCIPLE 2
Subject to Indian Agent Legal Principles 1 and 4, and the *Indian Act* provision that only Indians may occupy reserve lands, the Indian Agent may direct the use of reserve lands and the siting of all occupancy and houses, as he wishes.

INDIAN AGENT LEGAL PRINCIPLE 3
An individual who damages a building or any other federal government property on the reserve is liable to federal prosecution for that damage.

INDIAN AGENT LEGAL PRINCIPLE 4
No person may be evicted from a house unless there is another house waiting for the evictee to occupy immediately.

Family/Descent Group Legal Principles

FAMILY/DESCENT GROUP LEGAL PRINCIPLE 1
Owners of houses may license their use by others without compromising their ownership rights. Behavioral conditions attached to these licenses may be used to control the behavior of younger members of the family/descent group.

FAMILY/DESCENT GROUP LEGAL PRINCIPLE 2
Owners may control the interests of other members of the family/descent group in real property within the Family Home Territory.

FAMILY/DESCENT GROUP LEGAL PRINCIPLE 3
The lineage patriarch or matriarch may control the settlement of people and building siting on his or her Family Home Territory.

FAMILY/DESCENT GROUP LEGAL PRINCIPLE 4
The patriarch or matriarch may control the initial settlement of people and building construction on his or her Family Home Territory, but may have limited authority over the ownership, possession, and alienation of houses on the Family Home Territory once other parties have acquired ownership.

Band Council Legal Principles

BAND COUNCIL LEGAL PRINCIPLE 1
In the event of divorce, the parent awarded custody of the couple's children by the provincial courts will be allowed possession and ownership of the matrimonial house.

BAND COUNCIL LEGAL PRINCIPLE 2
Primary residence in a house confers on the primary resident a right of ownership to the house against the Band Council that the Band Council will not normally alter.

BAND COUNCIL LEGAL PRINCIPLE 3
House and land ownership is subject to any contractual agreements made between an individual and the Band Council.

BAND COUNCIL LEGAL PRINCIPLE 4
The Band Council will rent a house or apartment on behalf of an indigent Indian tenant only in cases in which the rental property is lawfully possessed.

BAND COUNCIL LEGAL PRINCIPLE 5
No one awarded a new house by the Band Council may enter that house until construction is completed.

BAND COUNCIL LEGAL PRINCIPLE 6

The politically privileged may own houses in which other people reside, so long as they remain politically privileged.

BAND COUNCIL LEGAL PRINCIPLE 7

The Band Council may halt woodcutting operations that deface the natural beauty of those parts of the reserve easily visible from settled areas and roadways, to the point that band members complain publicly.

BAND COUNCIL LEGAL PRINCIPLE 8

The Band Council decides civil cases between private parties to preserve the ownership rights of the primary resident and maintain the status quo.

BAND COUNCIL LEGAL PRINCIPLE 9

No contracts made between private individuals have any bearing on Band Council decisions.

BAND COUNCIL LEGAL PRINCIPLE 10

Only the fact of primary residence gives the right of ownership to a house; ownership of land by itself gives no right to own or possess housing on it. Housing may thus be legally personal property in situations in which the land where it is located belongs to another individual.

BAND COUNCIL LEGAL PRINCIPLE 11

The primary resident on a plot of land owns it, no matter who later builds on it, so long as residence is maintained. Ownership of a house and the land on which it is situated are thus divisible.

BAND COUNCIL LEGAL PRINCIPLE 12

The chief allows non-Indians on the reserve at his sufferance and may use this sufferance to control offensive behavior, which includes proselytizing and repossession of property.

BAND COUNCIL LEGAL PRINCIPLE 13

The Band Council ignores lawful possession when no party insists on rights under the provisions of lawful possession; it will give the lawful possessor possession of property owned by another party by primary residence in cases in which the primary resident will not lose possession of a dwelling; and it will preserve by political means either possessory or ownership rights to dwellings acquired by primary residence against the lawful possessor of the same property.

BAND COUNCIL LEGAL PRINCIPLE 14

A person who receives a new house supplied by the Band Council must return ownership of the old house to the Band Council, subject to individual contractual conditions.

BAND COUNCIL LEGAL PRINCIPLE 15
Any unbuilt reserve land owned by individual private band members may be expropriated by the Band Council for the construction of development projects ordered by the Band Council.

BAND COUNCIL LEGAL PRINCIPLE 16
The Band Council may expropriate any unbuilt reserve land for construction projects ordered by the Band Council, except in those cases in which owners present powerful political opposition to expropriation.

BAND COUNCIL LEGAL PRINCIPLE 17
The rights of ownership of structures is subject to public safety and community appearance concerns, and the Band Council may order the razing or removal of housing that it deems poses a hazard to public safety or is an eyesore.

BAND COUNCIL LEGAL PRINCIPLE 18
Band members may own housing in which others reside.

BAND COUNCIL LEGAL PRINCIPLE 19
The ability to rent real property to the Band Council depends on one's level of political privilege.

BAND COUNCIL LEGAL PRINCIPLE 20
Unmarried house owners who frequently have drunken, unruly parties in their houses will lose possession of their houses.

BAND COUNCIL LEGAL PRINCIPLE 21
Those who commit arson will be prosecuted for the crime in federal criminal court.

CHAPTER TWO

Behavioral Ideals and Extralegal Social Control

Understanding Micmac Behavioral Ideals

As is the case with all human cultures, that of the Micmac is integrated. Hence an understanding of the Micmac land tenure system requires an appreciation of social control generally, and of Micmac ideals of justice. In turn, to understand Micmac social control, and to understand why legal mechanisms accomplish rather little of it, we must first have an understanding of Micmac behavioral ideals. An appreciation of these behavioral ideals is further necessary to understand the essential characteristics of Micmac law and legal change.

These influences themselves have depended on the physical, technological, and economic conditions which Micmac experienced up until the past few decades. Before the 1940s, the Micmac lived a physically demanding existence. The climate of the region is adverse, their technology was rudimentary by today's standards, and food and cash reserves were usually small. Because these factors forced them to disperse and migrate, Micmac frequently lived as isolated groups of nuclear families, and even single nuclear families, who had to fill their own needs. It is no wonder at all, then, that self-reliance assumed utmost social and cultural importance. Further, those who worked hardest, were intelligent, and had the ability to think innovatively succeeded materially and garnered the greatest authority and prestige. People still idealize these qualities and seek them in potential leaders and mates, praising hard and creative workers as *sama:tewi:t* ("smart").

Regular social isolation once constituted the norm, and this, combined with the need to make all the decisions necessary to survive, have made Micmac people highly independent, and possessed of great pride and self-respect. In fact, Micmac have developed self-respect to such a degree that virtually no one makes apologies. During all of my time in the field, I can recall hearing only four apologies from one Micmac to another, and all of these were clearly insincere (*meske:i:* or "I apologize").

Perceptions of Superiority

Along with highly independent behavior goes an unwillingness to accept authority. Of course, there are various types of authority in Micmac society, ranging from parental authority to that of the *'Saqmaw* ("headman"), and of course some submission to authority must exist for groups to form and to function. But, on the whole, Micmac are loathe to admit or even to discuss the existence of authority or submission to it, or even that differences in social status exist. This contributes to a tendency toward the kind of social atomism that Barnouw (1950, 1961) observed for the Chippewa. To be sure, differences in individual personal qualities, such as ability, persistence, and appearance, make for topics of discussion, but to suggest that one person is superior to another is not done, especially publicly. It is considered rude, boorish behavior to make statements that insinuate superiority or inferiority on the part of any person, group, or class.

Perhaps naturally in such a social environment, many people attempt to distinguish themselves from other members of the community. In most cases, it is acceptable to demonstrate ability in a particular pursuit. Many Micmac choose sports, such as softball or hockey, to prove superiority. Others buy the first snowmobile, satellite dish, or other such technological innovation in the community to show eminence. Election to public office, owning a business, having prowess as a lumberjack or a speaker of the Micmac language, or working as a police officer also serve to distinguish. These all represent socially acceptable means of displaying superiority. The public at large cannot easily claim that people do these things primarily for self-aggrandizement. Nevertheless, some people do make such claims. Several times I have heard people who entered contests of one sort or another accuse the winner of entering solely for the purpose of making the losers appear inadequate, even when such claims obviously have no merit.

Only actions that clearly show a disdain for others imply superiority in an unacceptable way, and these stimulate criticism. Take, for example, the following account of a softball player's actions. A young man was one of the better players on the reserve; he had a good reputation and was the object of envy because of this. He felt, however, that because his abilities exceeded those of his teammates and of the members of the Micmac teams he faced, he would derive more pleasure and improve his skills by playing with a better, non-Indian team. His decision to play with a non-Indian team was widely interpreted as a condemnation of Indians as inferior people. Many members of the community criticized and ostracized him for his decision to join a non-Indian team, an association he ultimately abandoned.

One great difficulty in showing off is to do so in a way that is strictly positive, that is to say, does not diminish or take away from the efforts or chances of others. The Micmac are quite clever in this. Take, for example, big-game hunting. In the first half of the 20th century, megafauna were not numerous, for a variety of reasons. Micmac could, and apparently did, believe that to take deer meant the loss of opportunity to another hunter. Therefore, the situation common among so many hunting and gathering peoples — in which the good hunter gains political power by supplying food to the other members of the band — did not apply in the usual form among early 20th-century Micmac. Anyone who piled up many deer carcasses with the goal of impressing other band members would have been regarded as a lunatic, older Micmac tell me. Rather, the leading men relied on farming, as well as fishing and snaring rabbits, because fish and rabbits were then plentiful. In sum, these men were givers and could be in no sense considered to deprive anyone else of anything.

Those who act in such a way as to suggest that they think themselves superior (*wel'amsit*) can be publicly castigated, but people also denigrate those who are not self-sufficient. For example, those who fail to provide their families with the material necessities of life usually experience a great deal of shame. In the past, before the advent of relief (a government social welfare program that provides cash payments and, in earlier times, purchase orders directly to recipients), this problem occurred more commonly. Those who needed food were so ashamed that they would send their children rather than go themselves. Even in today's Eskasoni reserve, with its social welfare government, the stigma of asking for help, even when entitled to it by federal regulations, remains. One only has to look at terms commonly applied to those who request housing assistance, for example, from members of the modern reserve's Band Council. One might say *'sukholiwa:len* ("you suck-hole him [or her]") to an acquaintance who asks for help, which also implies a greatly subservient role for the benefactor. One might more gently say *pustemi:n* ("you cry [for your help]"). This too represents a stigmatized position, even though many people ask for assistance.

Public and Private Behaviors

Those in the community who work productively are expected to share their wealth and so avoid the perception that they work only to increase their own wealth and prestige, while caring nothing for the well-being of others. However, to preserve self-esteem in others, they are expected to share in a way that neither demeans the poor nor promotes self-aggrandizement. In other words, one should not be stingy, giving to those in need, but giving without calling attention to either the plight of the poor or one's own magnanimity. Usually this simply means giving help privately. In return for largesse and discretion, the giver gains prestige and followers. These followers support their benefactor in political matters and disputes, and seek his or her advice. They also request help when in trouble, although, again, usually privately. In this way individuals often become political leaders and legal authorities. At the very least, recipients should not speak ill of their benefactors, and many people give help merely to avoid being the target of gossip or sorcery.

Before World War II, those who did hunt deer developed a clever means of distributing both meat and prestige that avoided the stigma of charity. In many hunting societies, the successful hunter simply presents meat to others. Since the Micmac would regard such public displays of superior–inferior social relations with distaste, they preserved the fiction of equality by allowing each man to acquire a share of the catch by earning it. The hunter would kill and bring back the carcass. Another man or two would clean it, another man or two would skin it, and another man or two would butcher the animal, dividing it up into as many equal portions as there were men involved. They then drew numbers (obviously an idea of European origin) to determine the order of selecting the portions of meat, with the man drawing number one choosing his portion first, and so on. The hunter had a chance equal to that of the others of selecting the best portions, and thus had a status no different from that of his co-workers, on the face of it at least.

People also preserve others' pride by avoiding involvement in their disputes. To defend a friend involved in a dispute indicates that that friend is inferior and incapable of handling his or her own affairs; this loss of face thereby assists the friend's opponent in the dispute. It is also interpreted as an obvious ploy to turn the friend from an equal into a subordinate follower in a public, and therefore embarrassing, way. Thus, the kind of loyalty that European and many American friends expect of one another, coming to each other's defense, the Micmac usually regard as dishonorable. Several times friends of mine advised me to stay out of all disputes, even friends' disputes, for to do otherwise would without doubt always bring trouble.

Of course, Micmac individuals privately regard some in their community as inferior, as lazy, stupid, immoral, or mentally disturbed. As a matter of etiquette they never say so publicly and maintain a fiction of equality in their interactions with everyone, even those whom they consider inferior or dislike for whatever reason. The ideal of social equality therefore finds expression in Micmac etiquette in the uniform treatment of social contacts: one should behave toward the least socially prominent visitor the same as toward the highest status person. Although an ideal, it is one nearly always met in actual behavior. People still very commonly brag that "I treat all people the same, rich or poor." I have even seen those who would beat or kill one another, if they thought that they could escape punishment or retribution, sitting down together to drink beer and swap stories. Leaders, or those who wish to be, must adhere to this norm scrupulously. Although such behavior might strike the non-Micmac observer as incredibly insincere, even two-faced, it does in fact provide enormous benefit: those who observe this behavioral norm can readily go to another person, even an enemy, and request assistance. This must have had great survival value in the past.

A further concession to this principle of etiquette can be found in conversational norms. To preserve a fiction of equality, even mere disagreement is considered in poor taste, since it involves the contradiction of the ideas of another person. Another person's ideas are a part of his or her person and to attack them is to attack the individual, even if the ideas are ridiculous. It is better to allow people with wrong ideas to be disabused of them through personal experience.

Methods of Social Control

In a society that considers the uniform treatment of all the ideally correct behavior, how do members of the community deal with thieves and those who destroy private property? The victim of a relatively minor breach of proper behavior alters his or her behavior not at all and makes no mention of the incident. It is left to the conscience of the perpetrator to enforce proper behavior. Individuals are expected to know which of their actions are improper and, through self-realization, cease to perform them. A victim of theft, for instance, would say generously and ideally — and I have heard this on more than one occasion — "he must've needed it."

Micmac leaders face an important obstacle in that Micmac people generally react negatively to accusations of guilt and to lectures on how they should behave. In Micmac society, the more an individual tries to have another do something, the more the other individual may react contrarily (conversely, the Micmac say that one should grant a favor requested four times). This kind of behavior is to be expected if coercive measures are used. The Micmac term for this behavior is *'ki:kalsit* ("he [or she] acts contrarily and/or petulantly"). For example, a creditor is more likely to receive payment of a debt by making no mention of the debt to the debtor; to speak of it implies that the debtor is trying to evade his or her responsibilities. A Micmac man once advised me that the best way to collect payment of a debt is to "just keep bumping into the people who owe you money; it doesn't always work, but it is the best way."

One should ideally remain silent on the subject of another's wrong. For example, in two instances men who were deeply hurt by their wives' infidelity never mentioned to their wives their opposition to their behavior. "She knows that she's not supposed to see other men," one man told me of his wife (on the other hand, the wife defended her infidelity, saying of her husband that "he never told me not to do it"). In two other instances, theft victims who knew the identities of the thieves refused either to confront them or to complain to the police. The victims were saddened over their losses, but refused to pursue the matter. Again, it was left to the consciences of the thieves to enforce proper behavior. Anticipating the actions of a thief or of one who destroys private property can render justice by causing that person to suffer by his or her own improper behavior. The following two true accounts were considered humorous because of the cleverness shown by the intended victims.

During Centralization, men worked hard every day to cut timber to provide lumber for the new houses that Indian Affairs was building. One worker had a trick that he liked to play on his co-workers, who during work breaks frequently took their gloves off and put them down on any nearby stump. Likewise, axes were thrown into stumps until the break was over. The worker would walk over to a fellow to make conversation and plunge his axe into the nearby stump, ruining the co-worker's gloves, as if by accident. One day a man came to work sporting a brand new pair of leather gloves. When lunch break was called, he placed them prominently in view on a stump. The worker saw them, strode over, and struck them with his axe. To his chagrin the axe bounced from the gloves — the owner had placed a 6d nail into each of the fingers of the gloves. The worker spent the next two hours trying to resharpen his axe.

The trickster in this account is also the intended victim in the next story.

TABLE 1. Micmac ideals of social behavior.

Principle	*Ideal behavior*
Behavioral Postulate 1	Work hard and productively.
Behavioral Postulate 2	Never do anything that causes another grief or loss.
Behavioral Postulate 3	Avoid behaving in such a way as to suggest that you think yourself superior and others inferior, and this means that you should treat all others as uniformly as possible.
Behavioral Corollary A	Share the results of your productive work with those who do not or cannot produce as much, so as to prove that you does not think of yourself first and others second.
Behavioral Corollary B	With the results of your productive work, help support those who have little, but do so in a way that avoids positive publicity for yourself, and preserves the dignity of the recipient.
Behavioral Corollary C	Ignore the improper actions of others as much as possible.
Behavioral Corollary D	Avoid conflict in any form, including argument.
Behavioral Corollary E	Never involve yourself in a conflict in which you are not one of the disputants.

This man used to keep gasoline in a gas can next to his house to fuel his machinery. Often he found the can empty, however. He also noticed that a young man with a car frequently drove by. Knowing that the young man had no job and could not afford to buy gasoline, he decided to stop the thievery. He acquired a second gas can, and put about a gallon of gas into one, and into the other three or four gallons. He also poured some sugar into the can with more gas. The next morning the can with the larger amount of gas was empty and the other can was untouched. A couple of days later, the young fellow's car became inoperative. The man told the young man, "that's what happens when you are greedy."

Principles of Ideal Behavior

When subtle means such as the ones described here fail to stop improper behavior, individuals may resort to stronger, less desirable approaches. In addition to occasional legal sanctions, Micmac make extensive use of ostracism and revenge, which, because they are intimately linked with the subject of this study, are discussed at a later point. Neither revenge nor ostracism are considered ideal forms of behavior, since they involve disdain and the discriminatory treatment of others.

From the foregoing we can distill principles of ideal behavior (Table 1) that will be expressed as behavioral postulates and behavioral corollaries.

Part II:

Government

CHAPTER THREE

Micmac Political and Governmental Systems

This chapter outlines the various political and legal systems that have governed the Micmac, given in the order of their creation. It begins with a discussion of early political systems, continues on to describe the Grand Council, a form of traditional government unique to Cape Breton, and then discusses the imposed Indian Affairs governments, the Indian Agent, and the Band Council.

Micmac legal authorities function as political leaders first and foremost, and Micmac political systems greatly influence Micmac legal systems. An understanding of Micmac land tenure thus calls for the analysis of the political system in some depth. As we will see, the changes in the political system discussed in this chapter influenced profound changes in Micmac legal systems.

The aboriginal Micmac called their informal headman leader and authority *'Saqmaw*, a term that Micmac today translate as "chief." With the exception of Cape Breton, each band usually had only one *'Saqmaw*, who led as the primary authority, although others often had power as well. As individuals and groups migrated, they fell under the authority of different *'Saqmaq* (the plural form of *'Saqmaw*) when they joined other bands. Many groups have been, for a time at least, without a *'Saqmaw*, and individuals, families, and descent groups have frequently lived apart from groups that had *'Saqmaq*. In such cases, the family/descent group patriarch or matriarch formed the ultimate political and legal authority; on occasion these small group authorities were known as *'Saqmaq* as well. Because of the imposition of the Canadian *Indian Act*, the *'Saqmaw* no longer exists in traditional form.

Early Political Systems Outside of Cape Breton

This section on Micmac political systems as they existed outside of Cape Breton is presented here for two reasons. The first is to give a picture of early political systems, which were observed by missionaries outside of Cape Breton. The data collected by these observers give a general portrait of Micmac politics as it probably existed before the creation of the Grand Council and its migration to Cape Breton. The second reason for presenting data on Micmac politics outside of Cape Breton is to show that the Cape Breton Grand Council represents a unique body of leaders and authorities whose laws and leadership principles differed from those of Micmac politicians elsewhere.

Men served as *'Saqmaq*, and the size of a man's extended family translated directly into political power and status. Father Christien Le Clercq, a late 17th century missionary among the Micmac of the Gaspé and Miramichi regions, observed that even when no longer obeyed, a *'Saqmaw* with a large lineage did not always lose his position:

> We had among us, at the River of St. Joseph (now known as the Restigouche), one of these old chiefs whom our Gaspesians (the natives of the Gaspé Peninsula of Quebec, or Micmac) considered as their head and their ruler much more because of his family, which was very numerous, than because of his sovereign power, of which they have shaken off the yoke, and which they are not willing any longer to recognise. (Le Clercq 1910:235)

Father Pierre Biard, a Jesuit missionary among the Micmac of the Port Royal Nova Scotia region in the early 17th century, also noted: "There is the Sagamore (*'Saqmaw*) who is the eldest son of some powerful family, and consequently also its chief and leader" (Thwaites 1897:87). Biard also noted that polygyny helped the ruler maintain power:

> In order to retain their authority and power by having a number of children; for in that lies the strength of the house, in the great number of allies and connections. (Thwaites 1897:101)

In addition to kinship connections, the *'Saqmaw* gained authority through his ability to produce material wealth, which he distributed among his followers. Le Clercq gave the following account of a man who wished to take the place of the established *'Saqmaw*, an account which shows that having numerous kin stood by itself as an insufficient condition for leadership:

> It happened that a stranger wished to dispute his right of command, or at least to share with this ruler that government, with its imaginary grandeur, for which he had as much regard as if it were the greatest empire of the world. The competitor arrived well provided with axes, with guns, with blankets, with beavers, and with everything which could give him some prominence and some entrance into the sovereignty which he claimed was properly due him by right of hereditary succession, because his father had been formerly head and chief of the Gaspesian nation. "Very well," said our Indian, "show that thy heart is a true chief's heart and worthy of absolute empire over the people whom I rule. There," continued he, "are some poor Indians who are wholly naked; give them thy robes of otter and beaver. Thou seest, again, that I am the worst dressed of all, and it is through this that I wish to appear chief — though despoiling and depriving myself of everything in order to aid my Indians. Therefore, when following my example, thou shouldst be as poor as I. Let us go a-hunting when the time is right, and the one of us who kills the most moose and beavers shall be the legitimate king of all the Gaspesians." The stranger accepted this challenge with spirit. In imitation of our chief, he gave away everything he had, and kept back nothing except the bare necessaries. He went hunting, but he was so unfortunate as to do it very badly, and consequently he was obliged to abandon the enterprise which

> he had formed of commanding our Gaspesians, who did not wish to recognize any other head than their old and brave chief whom they obeyed with pleasure. (Le Clercq 1910:235–236)

In short, families and individuals often followed the traditional *'Saqmaw* out of material self-interest. Biard made the same observation of a *'Saqmaw* he knew:

> All the young people of the family are at his table and in his retinue; it is also his duty to provide dogs for the chase, canoes for transportation, provisions and reserves for bad weather and expeditions. The young people flatter him, hunt, and serve their apprenticeship under him, not being allowed to have anything before they are married, for then only can they have a dog and a bag; that is, something of their own, and do for themselves. Nevertheless they continue to live under the authority of the Sagamore, and very often in his company; as also do several others who have no relations, or those who of their own free will place themselves under his protection and guidance, being themselves weak and without following. (Thwaites 1897:87)

Wisdom, or at least intelligence, also often seemed requisite for effective leadership and authority, for Le Clercq noted of one *'Saqmaw*: "But, in fact, all his power and authority are based only upon the good will of those of his nation, who execute his orders just in so far as it pleases them" (Le Clercq 1910:234–235). Consequently, some *'Saqmaq* held power only so long as those over whom they ruled believed that such authority benefitted them personally.

But not all *'Saqmaq* ruled in such a highly democratic way. Some *'Saqmaq* became autocratic rulers who used fear of punishment to rule. A 17th-century trader made the following record of his observances of a group of Micmac at Richibuctou, in what is now New Brunswick:

> The Chief at Rechibouctou, named Denis, is a conceited and vicious Indian. All the others of the Great Bay (of St. Lawrence) fear him. He has upon the border of the basin of this river a rather large fort of stakes, with two kinds of bastions; inside is his wigwam, and the other Indians are encamped around him. He has a great piece of wood placed upright to the top of a tree, with large pegs which pass through it in the manner of an estrapade and serve as steps for ascending to the top. There from time to time he sends an Indian to perceive anything along the coasts. From this place one can see far out to sea. If any vessels or canoes are seen, he has his entire force brought under arms with their bows and arrows and their muskets, places a sentinel on the approach to ask what persons they are, and then according to his whim he makes them wait, or has them come immediately. Before entering it is required that they make a discharge of their guns, as a salute, and sometimes two. Then the leader enters, and his suite after him. He never goes out from his wigwam to receive those who come to visit him. He is always there planted upon his haunches like an ape, his pipe in his mouth if he has any tobacco. He never speaks first. He expects that he shall be paid a compliment; and sometimes he replies with the gravity of a magistrate. If he goes to the wigwam of some Indian, on arriving he has a musket discharged to inform the other Indians, who come out from their wigwams, and go to meet him with their muskets. Then they accompany him to the wigwams, (and) when he goes inside they again fire each one a shot from his musket. Such is the manner in which he makes them receive him, more through fear than through friendship. They all wish for his death; he is not liked by a single one. If they are delinquent in their duty he beats them,

> but not when they are together, for in this case he could not do it with impunity. But when he catches them alone he makes them remember their duty. If the Indians make a debauch, he is never of their number, (but) he hides himself; for in drunkenness they are as great chiefs as he, and if he were to say something which made them angry, they would murder him. At such times he is wise and never speaks of his greatness. (Denys 1908:195–196)

The most famous of all Micmac *'Saqmaq* is Membertou (*'Mempltu*), who became the first Micmac to be baptized and led other Micmac to become Roman Catholics. He ruled through the use of fear, including fear of the supernatural. Membertou was a *pu'oin*, a sorcerer or shaman. According to Biard: "It happens sometimes that the same person is both *Aoutmoin* [*pu'oin*] and *Sagamore*, and then he is greatly dreaded. Such was the renowned Membertou" (Thwaites 1897:89). To this day many fear the *pu'oin*. Moreover, Membertou was a *pu'oin* without peer, according to Marc Lescarbot, a French writer and attorney who lived in the Port Royal area from 1606 to 1607 (Thwaites 1896a:75). A *pu'oin* casts spells on adversaries to cause illness, injury, accidents, damage, or death, and uses a *puoin'oti* (fetish bag or stick) to increase his or her power. Today, the *pu'oin* takes pains to hide the casting of spells, as well as the *puoin'oti*, which stands as proof of magical activities, because to cast spells openly invites retaliation either in the form of spells or physical aggression. Membertou wore his *puoin'oti* openly on his body (Hoffman 1955:461), indicating such strength of authority that he feared no revenge.

Membertou also had great personal physical prowess and used his strength and fighting ability to cower his adversaries. According to Biard, Membertou was "the greatest, most renowned and most formidable savage within the memory of man; of splendid physique, taller and larger-limbed than is usual among them" (Thwaites 1896b:23). Lescarbot mentions that "he has been a very great and cruel warrior in his youth and during his life" (Lescarbot 1928:354). A perquisite of his position was that he did not have to work for material necessities. Whereas some of those Micmac leaders mentioned above hunted for their followers in return for loyalty, according to Lescarbot (Thwaites 1896a:75–77), Membertou did "not impose taxes upon the people, but if there are any profits from the chase he has a share of them, without being obliged to take part in it" (Thwaites 1896a:75).

Membertou's style of government obviously gave offense to other Micmac. Again, Lescarbot: "Therefore rumor runs that he has many enemies, and is well content to keep close to the French, in order to live in safety" (1928:354–355). It may also very well have been that Membertou became a Catholic to enhance his relationship with the French, or perhaps to acquire even greater supernatural powers; his motivations in this regard have not survived.

Authority Derived from Non-Indian Governments

The *'Saqmaw* often had a virtually impossible task in leading people so self-reliant and independent. Often throughout the recorded history of the Micmac those who followed their leaders did so only as long and as far as they desired. After losing two wars to the British, Micmac leaders, if unhappy with their new masters, at least made political use of them from time to time by requesting from the British letters or medals as evidence of official recognition of their positions. The *'Saqmaq* used these pieces of evidence to increase their authority over their own people. Perhaps they reasoned that the weight of authority of the British would thus be transferred to themselves (see Upton 1979, pl. 12; Hamilton 1984:4). These medals and letters were often passed on from one *'Saqmaw* to the next like badges of office, as the Grand Council's *'Saqmaw* passes on his British-minted medal today.

The British commissions as chiefs may have aided the *'Saqmaq* in the short term, but certainly politically damaged many in the long term. In one instance, the misdeeds of a New Brunswick *'Saqmaw* caused him to "lose Perley's confidence and respect in 1841, and that crippled him drastically as a political force" (Hamilton 1984:27). Perley was the New Brunswick Indian Commissioner.

Whereas, notwithstanding the *'Saqmaw's* medal, the Cape Breton Grand Council avoided British and later Canadian interference in Micmac internal affairs until forced to relinquish most of its power in the period from the 1940s to the 1960s, other *'Saqmaq* used British and Canadian authority to bolster their own power. Once under that authority they were obliged to accept the rules governing the election of chiefs in the 1868 *Indian Act* (R.S.C. 1985, c. I-5, ss. 74–78). Several Micmac bands outside of Cape Breton ostensibly practiced the election of chiefs by these rules well before 1900.

The *Indian Act* contains provisions whereby Indian Affairs can remove officials elected under the terms contained within the act (R.S.C. 1985, c. I-5, s. 79). This allowed a host of such removals and new elections. Official calls for removal came from Indian Agents, but usually originated as petitions from Micmac themselves, as seen in the Legal Case below (Hamilton 1984:46). (As I use the term, Legal Case refers to a trouble case that is decided by a legal authority in conformity with a legal principle and that embodies the four attributes of law listed earlier; see Chapter 1.)

LEGAL CASE 1

First party: Charles Cloud, chief of the Red Bank New Brunswick band.
Second party: Several petitioners, members of the Red Bank Band.
Authority: Indian Affairs.
Date: November 6, 1906.

Location: Red Bank reserve, New Brunswick. (Unless otherwise noted, all trouble cases, whether legal, political, or dispute cases, took place on the Eskasoni reserve.)

Facts: Charles Cloud had been elected chief in 1905. After the election, he paid little attention to his duties as chief and drank heavily. His followers complained to Indian Affairs.

Outcome: Indian Affairs found the charges of neglecting his duties and excessive alcohol consumption well founded, removed Cloud from office, and prohibited him from serving as chief for three years.

Two decades later, an almost identical set of circumstances led to a similar decision against the chief of the Sydney band, the only Cape Breton band outside of Grand Council control.

Micmac band members from all over the Maritimes sent many petitions concerning improprieties on the part of chiefs and councillors to Indian Affairs. Many of these allegations would later prove false, having been motivated by spite or political considerations, as in the following petition made by several members of the Eelground band in 1936:

> We the members of Eelground, County of Northumberland, wish to inform the Department how the reserve is situated also the maladministration by our chief Peter J. McKay within the last four years. First. Trespassing cutting lumber by the White people, not dealt with under the [illegible] of the *Indian Act*. Second. The condition of the public roads, never seen the like within the last four years. Third. Our chief is appointed by the Department as bailiff to keep the white people from trespassing but instead of that he permission for the white people to cut. Fourth. On the 7th of March our chief was heavy under the influence of liquor, also attempting bodily harm Dan Paul and Peter J. Barnaby also using profane language to two women on the Public Road. Fifth. Our last election in the year 1935, Peter J. McKay was defeated by the members of the Band, but the department confirmed him as chief, so in that matter we are not getting justice. Sixth. Within the last four years there is no account of any stumpage that was collected from the lumber cut on our reserve, although there was a lot of lumber cut during that period. Seventh. Our chief neglected to look after Joan Hare in building dwellings on our reserve at Big Hole. Eighth. Our chief held three different picnics for the benefit of our church but never any account was shown by our chief where the proceeds went. Honourable Sir: we the members pray that the Department dismiss our Chief Peter J. McKay and grant us another election so that we could get another man that could read and write and handle our affairs more to the satisfaction of all. (Public Archives of Canada, RG 10, vol. 7935, file 32-55-4)

In reply to an Indian Affairs query on the petition, Indian Agent Charles Hudson made the following report on April 4, 1936:

> In reply I beg to inform you that I have looked into this matter and I cannot find where these Indians have any grounds for complaints. There are two factions on the reserve and the complaint comes from the one against the chief, and they are trying to make things as disagreeable for him as possible. The most important of the complaints against the chief would be that he is letting white people trespass on the reserve. This is not correct. The next would be that there was no stumpage collected for timber cut, and the department demanded no stumpage as the records will show. The stumpage dues were waived as a measure of relief. In regard to the complaint that the chief was under the influence of liquor, and tried to do harm to Dan Paul and Peter J. Barnaby, it was made in retaliation for the chief having one of the band taken to court and prosecuted for assault for which he is serving a 60 day term in the County jail. This assault was an attack on the Chief by one Alex Ward Jr., of the reserve. Ward's sympathizers are the ones who are making all the complaints against Peter J. McKay. In regard to the conduct of Peter J. McKay as chief of the Eel Ground Band, I have to say that it appears to me to be satisfactory, and he is doing as well as can be expected in carrying out his duties. (Public Archives of Canada, RG 10, vol. 7935, file 32-55-4)

The Secretary of Indian Affairs responded to the barrister hired by the complainants that he intended to abide by the Indian Agent's report and would not investigate the matter further. This petition shows that Micmac band members have attempted to manipulate Indian Affairs to accomplish their own political goals.

Finally, the institution of the *Indian Act*'s system of electing chiefs and councillors did not always stem from the chiefs' acceptance of outside authority to increase their own, nor from coercive pressure by Ottawa. Many of the Micmac *'Saqmaq*, before governmental influence, held their inherited positions for life. John N. Julian of the Eel Ground, New Brunswick band, was one such man. By the time he died in 1888, he had so alienated the members of his own band that all 48 eligible voters in the band, including members of his own family, petitioned Indian Affairs for a system of electing chiefs (Hamilton 1984:36).

Some bands had no taste for any federally recognized leader, either life-term or elected, though it is unclear whether this was because they had had unfavorable experiences, or because they simply had no use for one. The following is taken from a letter by Indian Agent G. L. Carm to Indian Affairs in Ottawa, dated October 26, 1938:

> I have mislaid your letter of recent Re Indian Chief of the Yarmouth Indians. But in reply I beg to state upon enquiry that there is no chief now and never has been. The Indians tell me they are satisfied with conditions as they now exist because when there is any trouble they can call on the R.C.M.P. [the Royal Canadian Mounted Police, a federal law enforcement agency]. Hoping this is the information you require. (Public Archives of Canada, RG 10, vol. 7936, file 32-64, part 1)

Interestingly, the main function of the chief, as the members of the Yarmouth band expressed it, was law enforcement. After leading and adjudicating, the leader's role as policeman was the one considered most important by Cape Breton Indians and by the members of the Grand Council themselves.

In the modern era, some elected leaders continue to use Indian Affairs for their own political purposes. In the mid-1980s a Cape Breton chief used Indian Affairs and the Royal Canadian Mounted Police (RCMP) to investigate the criminally fraudulent misdeeds of a former chief who had attempted both to regain power and to reduce the chief's power. Ultimately, the former chief received a large fine and lost standing in the band as a result.

Micmac Government on Cape Breton

This section introduces the legal systems that exist or have existed on Cape Breton Island at various times at five different legal levels since the latter part of the 19th century. These are, in order of initial appearance: the family/descent group, the Grand Council, the Canadian courts, the Indian Agent, and the Band Council. With the exception of the family/descent group level, each of these levels pertains to a single legal system. The family/descent group level is associated with as many families or descent groups as compose in the band. The legal systems existing at the level of the family/descent group, the Grand Council, the Indian Agent, and the Band Council are covered generally here. I omit a general discussion of Indian law at the Canadian federal level because of this subject's great size and complexity, as well as because it has already been well addressed by several authors (see, for example, Morse 1985; Woodward 1990; Elliott 2000). I begin with a brief description of Micmac legal terminology and basic ideas, before examining the four legal levels themselves.

Micmac Legal Terminology

The Micmac of today, with the exception of a few students of the language, use no Micmac term to refer to the concept of law; they use the English term instead.

Many legal terms are still known to at least some present-day Micmac. The Micmac verb *il'suteket* ("to decide") refers to all decisions, including legal ones. By adding the prefix *nuji-* ("one who"), we have the Micmac term for a legal authority, *'nujilsuteket* ("one who decides"). This refers to anyone who has legal authority, whether a *'Saqmaw*, a Canadian court judge, or someone who has special authority in a particular circumstance. The related word *ilsu'taqn* ("a deciding") refers to a trial. There are also the terms *'tepɨlutaqn* ("final decision") and *kok'wojiey* ("justice"). Rand (1888) gives the lexeme *ut'plutaqn*, but I have never heard this word used. He also gives *tepɨlute'kimkewey*, which may be translated as "the essential property of a final decision (decision for which there is no appeal)," or "legal principle of a final decision," but this too seems to be outside the ken of the modern Micmac.

The Micmac term for one who makes rules is *ele'ke:wit*, probably a Basque loan (Bakker 1989:260). Micmac also translate this term as "king." A variant of this term, *ele'ke:wuti*, refers to a rule itself. There are several other synonymous terms given by Rand (1888), such as *'takumowuti*, which are no longer in use.

The fact that the Micmac have a legal terminological system indicates that law has long held considerable social significance and was probably systematized aboriginally.

The Progression of Legal Cases

Interestingly, once an alleged offense is brought to their attention, Micmac legal authorities typically have little difficulty acquiring knowledge of the legally relevant facts to any case. Often, the injured party presents the facts to petition the legal authority's help. After the request for help is made, the authority typically confronts the alleged offender with the plaintiff's understanding of the facts of the case, at which point the alleged offender will correct what he or she feels to be any misstatement by the accuser. Alleged offenders, of course, never volunteer any incriminating evidence, but they rarely attempt to deny the truth or to prevaricate. Attempting to deceive the authority could not easily succeed because the details of the case usually become widely known in the small band community. Therefore, attempting to lie can do no good, but only harm (see, for example, Legal Case 55).

Though the accused usually readily admits to the true facts of the case, the usual strategy is to argue that the actions were justified by interpreting the facts in a beneficial light, and claiming that a legal principle other than that given by the plaintiff is the decisive one (see, for example, Legal Cases 57, 68, 69, and 112). The accused often argues that the allegedly injured party has unclean hands, and makes an accusation against the allegedly injured party in return (see Legal Case 66).

The ease with which the Micmac legal authority can collect the true facts of a case allows for quick legal decisions, often on the spot (see Legal Cases 7, 57, 91, and 108). However, politically difficult decisions can lead to months of deliberation (see, for example, Legal Case 96).

Law and Government at the Family/Descent Group Level

Undoubtedly family/descent group legal systems appeared first, though these original legal systems and their laws differed from those of even 50 or 100 years ago. The legal systems at this level constituted the only ones applying to those Micmac who lived as separate and independent nuclear or extended families, rather than in larger bands under the authority of a *'Saqmaw,* as many did from time to time even as late as the end of the 19th century.

Here I briefly touch on law at the family/descent group level as it exists today. An important legal level, its legal systems decide most of the cases adjudicated on the reserve. However, the picture of general law at this level is also very complex owing to the sheer number of legal systems and laws involved: one for each family or descent group, several hundred at Eskasoni.

Most commonly, senior adults make decisions that apply to their offspring. Authority extends outside of the patriline only rarely. Further, men and women seldom have legal authority to make unilateral decisions concerning their spouses; there is usually no law, only political dispute and compromise, in these instances. In fact, arguments often occur between spouses over the punishment of children or the use of money; as a result of the latter, married couples frequently have completely separate finances, including separate savings and checking accounts. Also, the Band Council will issue husbands and wives separate relief checks. In cases in which one spouse offends the other, the injured party may take whatever appropriate steps he or she wishes in retaliation. In the case of infidelity, both men and women will customarily bar the other spouse's entry to the matrimonial house, as in the following Dispute Case (a trouble case in which no authority makes a decision).

DISPUTE CASE 1

First Party: AD (husband).
Second Party: BD (wife).
Date: 1987.

Facts: AD had been having an affair with another woman for some time, and finally decided to leave his wife for the other woman.

Outcome: When BD discovered that her husband had left her for another woman, she threw all of AD's personal property out onto the lawn and barred his entrance to the marital house.

Distinctions between legal systems at this level are much the same as in other societies and involve rules, principles, and sanctions for violations, which are applied to offspring. Some parents exercise very little legal control over the behavior of their children, as in the following examples.

DISPUTE CASE 2

First party: GY.
Second party: Grandchildren of GY.
Date: 1986.

Facts: GY, living with most of her children and their own nearly two dozen offspring, had spent the day washing the grandchildren's clothing and putting it away. Later that evening, the grandchildren took every one of the hundreds of articles of clothing and threw them all over the floor. The grandmother did nothing to the children whatsoever, but only complained to other adults.

DISPUTE CASE 3

First party: TF.
Second party: Children of TF.
Date: 1986.

Facts: TF's children covered the inside walls of the house with crayon markings.

Outcome: TF said nothing to them. He explained, "It's my fault because I didn't get them coloring books."

Another father said that he rarely punishes his children, who are infamous in their neighborhood for their bad manners, because, he says, "I want them to be my friends when they grow up." Other parents, on the other hand, expect their children to adhere to a high standard of behavior, as in the following case.

LEGAL CASE 2

Defendant: A five-year-old girl.
Authority: Her mother.
Date: 1987.

Facts: The girl was in a bad mood and whined continuously for 10 or 15 minutes.

Outcome: The mother repeatedly told her daughter to stop whining, but she continued to do so. Finally, the mother slapped her daughter on the face, and the child stopped.

Law at the family/descent group level usually makes use of relatively mild sanctions. The following case, however, is an exception to this rule.

LEGAL CASE 3

Defendant: JW, a young man.
Authority: BW, his father.
Date: 1987.

Facts: JW, a fellow who often angered those around him, stole his father's chainsaw and sold it to another man on the reserve.

Outcome: BW discovered the theft, lectured his son, and pressed theft charges against him in the Canadian court system.

Comment: The harshness of the punishment, having one's own son prosecuted in a federal court, was popularly considered unjust (Micmac usually prefer that the non-Indian courts remain uninvolved in all but the most violent disputes), and thus an improper way to encourage the son to behave properly.

The Grand Council

Introduction and History

After introducing material on the structure and function of the Grand Council, I here describe the Grand Council authority and leadership as it existed from the 1870s through the early 1960s, at which time Band Councils mandated by the federal *Indian Act* became politically and legally predominant. This is followed by a description of how the Grand Council authority has declined since the 1950s, a short discussion of how the Mission priest recently took control of behavior at the Mission, a section showing how the Grand Council recently attempted to increase its own political power, and a final summary.

Although the Grand Council shares several traits with those of the other aboriginal Micmac political systems described earlier, it is unique in that it is made up of several people who work together under a *'Saqmaw* to govern several bands, rather than just one. Therefore, the Micmac of Cape Breton formed a true tribe in the anthropological sense. The Grand Council members occupy offices, making them chiefs, unlike the *'Saqmaq* outside Cape Breton, who were headmen. They also differ from some other Micmac leaders in that they work not for self-aggrandizement, but instead use traditional and Christian behavioral principles to raise the standards of morality and behavior among their followers.

Though it traditionally governed primarily through legal means, the Grand Council also had many political functions. Some of these endure today, including leading the Micmac of Cape Breton and dealing with external political entities, although in these the Grand Council is secondary to the Band Councils. The Grand Council remains the cynosure of the St. Anne Mission, a week-long celebration of the feast day of St. Anne, the Micmac patron saint. In the Micmac language the Grand Council is known as *'Sante: 'Mawiomi*, which may be translated as "the group who meets on Sunday" (in particular, Pentecost Sunday). The Grand Council discusses its most important concerns, decides the group's future course of action, and plans the schedule of the upcoming St. Anne's Mission on Pentecost Sunday.

Although some Micmac today claim that the Grand Council has been around as long as the Micmac themselves, the Grand Council in fact originated during a historical period of conflict. Documents indicate that it arose, in greatly different form, during the French and Indian War as part of the Micmac response to the hostilities (Hoffman 1955:569–572). Also, the Micmac, along with the Penobscot, Passamaquoddy, Maliseet, and several smaller groups, made up the Wabanaki Confederacy, which allied itself with the French against the British and the Mohawk. At that time many of the Micmac united under a man by the name of Denys. Denys and others represented the Micmac at Wabanaki Confederacy meetings. After their defeat in the French and Indian War, Denys and many of his followers retreated to Cape Breton Island (known then as Isle Royale), the only remaining French territory in the region after the Treaty of Utrecht in 1713. Denys made his home in Eskasoni, where his descendants (who now spell their name Denny) still reside. Tomah Denys later led the Micmac against the British in the Battle of Quebec in April 1760. Sometime afterward the Wabanaki Confederacy made peace with the Caughnawaga Mohawk, a peace renewed each year until 1872.

As a result of the British expulsion of the French from Acadia, the Micmac endured a 200-year period in which they were left almost completely without the services of priests because of their inability to pay for them (Upton 1979:156). Grand Council members undertook to preach the weekly sermons and to lead prayers and hymns in the Micmac language. For this reason an ability to read prayers and hymns in Micmac (in script or in hieroglyphic form), and to memorize many of them, remained a requirement for membership until recently.

The Micmac hieroglyphic script writing system developed from the introduction of the Christian gospel to Micmac people. To more accurately remember what the missionary Le Clercq taught them, some Micmac invented symbols, which they wrote on birch bark. LeClercq later standardized these symbols, and added some that he invented to make the system able to express more fully the lessons he taught. Still later, the missionary Antoine Pierre Maillard published hymnals and prayer books that used the hieroglyphs (Wallis and Wallis 1955:23).

Attributes

Members of the Grand Council elect their new members, usually on the basis of the following attributes:

1. The member must be Micmac.

2. The member must be religious.

3. The member should be physically strong. This attribute was important in the Grand Council member's function as a political leader and legal authority, since a Grand Council member should be able to resist physical intimidation that would

interfere with the position's functions. For this reason women did not become members of the Grand Council until very recently, and then only in auxiliary positions and roles.

4. The member should be wise. Intellectual ability, knowledge, and experience are prized attributes for membership in the Grand Council.

5. The member should be literate in the Micmac hieroglyphic script, to be able to read the prayer books written in the script. This qualification, however, is no longer necessary.

6. The member should have memorized prayers and hymns in the Micmac language, to be able to lead the parishioners in weekly prayer and to present lectures. This too is unimportant today.

7. The member, and particularly the *'Saqmaw*, should show model behavior. One expectation is to never become visibly angry, no matter what anyone may say.

8. The member should be (although is not always), a son of a previous Grand Council member. Frequently, a man will be elected to the office his father held.

9. Neither the Grand Council nor its members distribute personal wealth, or redistribute wealth from band members to one another, as did *'Saqmaq* outside of Cape Breton. Rather, its members often impoverished themselves in fulfilling their functions. These duties, including attending many political meetings, frequently interrupted efforts to earn a living

Structure

The Grand Council's influence and leadership has traditionally been limited to the Micmac population of *Una'ma:ki* (Cape Breton Island), sometimes known as the "head district" of the Micmac because the Grand Council is located there. The historical strength of the indigenous leadership here is undoubtedly one reason why Catholic religious leaders have noticeably less influence than they have had at Restigouche (as noted by Bock 1966:38, 55–64). Outside of *Una'ma:ki*, the normal arrangement is for each Micmac *mimaje:winu'e:katik* (literally, "people of a place where there are people" or "group," "settlement," or "band") to have a *'Saqmaw* who represents them and keeps the peace among them. On Cape Breton traditionally there was one *'Saqmaw* for the entire island, and one *'Keptin* (Captain) for each band; however, since the Centralization Program of the 1940s there have been more captains than bands because of the confusion brought about by some captains moving to Eskasoni. The *'Saqmaw* of the Grand Council is known to English speakers as the "Grand Chief." He is a chief in the anthropological sense of the word, occupying an office. To him belongs the greatest amount of authority in the Grand Council. Directly below the *'Saqmaw* in the Grand Council hierarchy is the *'Kji:keptin* (Grand Captain) whose primary duty is to directly oversee the captains, his direct subordinates, as well as to render advice to the *'Saqmaw*.

The captains traditionally functioned as leaders and authorities of the various individual bands, acting on their own initiative as well as the commands of their two superiors. The final traditional office in the Grand Council is that of the *Pu'tu:s* ("one who orates"). His original responsibility was to read the Micmac wampum at the St. Anne's Mission, Caughnawaga, and Wabanaki Confederacy meetings, and any other occasion that called for it. This wampum dated from the time of the Wabanaki (*Wapa'na:ki:k)* Confederacy wars against the Mohawk, and the peace agreement made at Caughnawaga in the 18th century. The wampum was last seen publicly in the 1960s. The *Pu'tu:s* now acts primarily as an advisor to the *'Saqmaw.*

The derivation of the term *'Keptin,* or "Captain," is uncertain. It may have been derived from *capitaines des sauvages,* as the colonial French called those Micmac men who were the offspring of French trappers and Micmac women. These *capitaines* were intermediaries between the two societies and held considerable power as a result (Upton 1979:26–27). A native Micmac speaker with some university-level training in linguistics supplied another analysis to me. He argues that the term derives from the Micmac *kep'tinin,* which translates as "holy of body." This certainly agrees with the role of the Captain, which was, for 150 years or more, to replace the absent Catholic priests in the delivery of sermons, leading prayer and the singing of the Catholic hymns, teaching the catechism and Gospel, carrying out burials, and many of the other functions that priests normally perform. Barring resignation or dismissal by the *'Saqmaw,* all Grand Council members hold their offices for life.

The office of the *'Saqmaw* passed down within the Denys–Denny lineage, usually from a father to one of his sons, often the eldest. That is, until 1918, when *'Saqmaw* John Denny, just before his death, told his son not to take the office. At the next St. Anne's Mission, the other members of the Grand Council prepared to install John Denny's son as *'Saqmaw,* but the son said that he did not want to hold the post. The priest who was there to administer the Mission agreed that all people should obey their parents and sided with the son. Since that time there have been three successive *'Saqmaq,* all of whom had been captains and won the office of *'Saqmaw* by vote of the other members of the Grand Council. The most recent of these, Ben Sylliboy, was installed in 1992 after the death of Donald Marshall Sr. in 1991. None of these men belong to the patriline that produced John Denny, although Grand Council members have kept men of the lineage in mind as possible successors to the office ever since 1918. Chute (1999:494) claims that the line of succession may have been broken before 1918 as well.

Although members of the Grand Council normally keep their offices for life, the *'Saqmaw* may remove any other officer as he wishes, and as nearly happened to one member in the 1980s.

LEGAL CASE 4

Party: Grand Captain Alex Denny.
Authority: 'Saqmaw Donald Marshall.
Date: 1980s.

Facts: The Grand Council is a very conservative political and legal body, not given to bold, radical changes. Grand Captain Denny, on the other hand, wished to make the Grand Council a potent international force for the benefit of the Micmac people. In his zeal, he made some claims to foreign governments and to the United Nations that were simply untrue.

Outcome: When Donald Marshall discovered that the Grand Captain had exceeded his authority, he warned him that another such mistake would cost him his office in the Grand Council.

The *'Saqmaw* takes an oath on assuming office to the effect that he will serve for life; all *'Saqmaq* have thus far in history left office only in death. The Grand Council traditionally had no female members. Recently, however, the Grand Council elevated the members of the Micmac Choir (which includes women) to membership in the Grand Council, but at an auxiliary rank.

Functions

In the 20th century, at least, the Grand Council's overall goals were to make the Micmac as morally upstanding as possible, and to unify them as a political force for their own benefit. To this end, it fulfilled the following functions:

1. To provide political leadership for the Micmac of Cape Breton (shared with the Band Councils since the latter's inception).

2. To police criminal activities (until Centralization in the 1940s).

3. To adjudicate crimes committed by Micmac of Cape Breton (until Centralization).

4. To administer the annual St. Anne's Mission in July.

5. To represent Micmac people and their interests to federal, provincial, and local governments (shared with the Band Councils, and secondarily to the Band Councils).

6. To lead prayer and hymns, bury the dead, teach the catechism, and deliver sermons in church on Sundays (from 1762 until Centralization).

Among the Micmac, an individual's ability to lead rests in large part on his ability to convince others through verbal argument, to lead by example, to remain personally unbiased and uninvolved in any kind of civil law, to maintain high moral standards in oneself and one's family, to be knowledgeable, and to possess exceptional intellectual and physical ability. In short, the *'Saqmaw*, as the supreme Micmac leader, is supposed to embody the ideal qualities of a Micmac man. Their leadership depended, largely, on the probity of its members, and the respect that they garnered.

The people paid the Grand Council members great deference because of their moral probity, and for this reason Grand Council members had great authority within the community. For example, before the 1940s, a St. Anne's Mission participant who first entered Chapel Island (which gives the Chapel Island reserve, of which it is a part, its name) crawled on hands and knees from the shore all the way to the church. There, the participant asked a member of the Grand Council for permission to enter the island and partake in the activities of the Mission. Although largely a formality, this supplication illustrates the respect once given to the authority of the members of the Grand Council, as well as to the behavioral institutions of the Mission.

Although *'Saqmaw* Gabriel Sylliboy had made some unpopular decisions, notably his agreement to the Indian Affairs Centralization Program (see Dispute Case 4), he is otherwise described in the highest terms by the Micmac people even today, four decades after his death in 1964. He is the only person whom I have heard Micmac people describe as *Nis'kamewey* (literally, "of God" or "holy"). He earned fame throughout the Micmac world for his oratorical ability. As the head of the Mission, he gave a long speech on the Sunday each year when St. Anne's Day is celebrated, in which he discussed proper Micmac behavior and ethics as well as the political situation of the Micmac people. He stressed defense of hunting and fishing rights. Part of his assessment of the Micmac political situation always included the idea that the Micmac are too few to have their voices heard in Halifax and Ottawa, and therefore during his speeches told his audience that they should have more children.

In addition, he lectured each newlywed couple, often for hours, on the subject of how husbands and wives should behave toward each other to ensure a successful marriage, as well as on more general topics of proper Micmac etiquette and responsibility. All Micmac newlyweds in Cape Breton visited him for this obligatory lesson.

'Saqmaw Sylliboy took an active role as leader and legal authority in community affairs. With the assistance of the Grand Captain, he oversaw the leadership and authority of the captains of the other Cape Breton reserves. That is, the captains, who exercised authority over their own individual bands did so on the instructions of the *'Saqmaw* himself, although they enjoyed latitude in their interpretations of the facts of a case, and in their actions.

This is not to say that the *'Saqmaw*'s every command was slavishly obeyed, nor that the captains could not rebel against the *'Saqmaw*. Ideally, this latter should never happen, although just such a situation did occur in the following case.

DISPUTE CASE 4

First party: 'Saqmaw Gabriel Sylliboy.
Second party: Two Grand Council captains.
Date: Mid-1940s.
Location: Cape Breton Island.

Facts: Indian Affairs sought to gain Micmac support for its Centralization Program by first getting the support of Micmac leaders. Indian Affairs held out material benefits and technical advancement as inducements for the Micmac people to relocate to Eskasoni; specifically, new housing and farming assistance, a priest, and employment.

The *'Saqmaw* saw the program as a chance for the Micmac to advance themselves economically, and endorsed it.

Two of the Grand Council's captains viewed Centralization differently. They felt that the people on their own reserves were better situated for economic advancement, residing as they did in a city and near a town, respectively, than in Eskasoni, which sits well away from a town of any size. Further, they knew that interband rivalries would create frictions that could cause social disruption. They also questioned the sincerity of Indian Affairs in administering this program and imputed various nefarious motives to it. Finally, they saw Centralization as ultimately assimilative in its future impact and reacted against this as well.

One of these captains, Noel Marshall of *'Potlotek* (Chapel Island), told the *'Saqmaw* that he did not have the authority to approve the Centralization Program on behalf of the Micmac people, that it was a matter for individuals to decide for themselves. Popular resentment began to rise against the program and against the *'Saqmaw* as more and more people moved to Eskasoni and found that they did not like living there. The highly democratic *'Saqmaw* reacted to this resentment by removing his (British-minted) medal of office and throwing it to the ground, thereby symbolically abdicating. When Pentecost Sunday arrived, Captain Marshall told the *'Saqmaw* that he should not put on his medal until he asked for forgiveness from the Micmac people, and the *'Saqmaw* agreed. Further, he stated that only a priest might replace the medal. He noted that a priest installs the *'Saqmaw* in office, and because he had left it he needed a priest to regain that office. At the St. Anne's Day Mission, Sylliboy begged for the forgiveness of the people. He also agreed to a request of Marshall and others that he would never again involve himself with the policies of the federal government (Johnson 1982). He thereupon resumed the office of *'Saqmaw*.

Outcome: The two captains, with some other people, met several times to discuss Centralization. They then counseled the members of their reserves against moving to Eskasoni. One of the captains was very successful in keeping his band from moving; only three people went to Eskasoni and two of those ultimately returned to their home reserve. On the other reserve, the captain did not succeed so well, for many, if not most, of his band left the reserve never to return.

Donald Marshall Sr. succeeded *'Saqmaw* Gabriel Sylliboy on the latter's death in 1964. Marshall, whom the Micmac praised for his decency and high personal moral standards, led primarily by example, and continued his predecessor's later policy of avoiding much interaction with the Canadian and other state society governments.

However, the 1970s saw the installation of a dynamic new leader, Alex Denny, as Grand Captain. Largely on his own initiative, Denny has returned the Grand Council to a focus on extra-Micmac political relations. One part of his strategy has been to bring in new members from outside of Cape Breton Island, including mainland Nova Scotia, Quebec, New Brunswick, and Newfoundland. Thus, it can truly be said that the Grand Council presently constitutes the only pan-Micmac political body.

A major part of the Grand Council's new strategy has been to research and revive old treaties that the Micmac signed with external powers. Among these is the 1776 Treaty of Watertown with the Colony of Massachusetts (Appendix D). The Grand Council, in combination with provincial Micmac representative bodies, has also managed to force the Canadian federal government to recognize provisions of the treaties of 1725 and 1752 (Appendix B), in particular the establishment of hunting and fishing rights outside of reserves. In this regard, the Grand Council has taken a leading role in increasing aboriginal rights in Canada generally.

The Grand Council's Legal System

The Grand Council acted as the Cape Breton Micmac legal authority from its founding in the 18th century until the 1940s. As exemplars of the ideal Micmac legal authority, the Grand Council members behave in a dignified and reticent manner and impose harsh sanctions reluctantly. They further allow those private parties who disagree with each other to sort out their own difficulties themselves, and interfere only when the parties cannot resolve the case on their own, when the problem looks to be growing, or when the public as a whole takes sufficient offense. The Grand Council accomplished this by adjudicating only criminal cases, never civil ones. Micmac socialization stresses the importance of individualism, and therefore jurisprudence stresses that the individual should learn of his or her wrongdoing by facing the direct consequences of offending others. If this means a bloody nose, or hurt feelings, or avoidance by others, so be it; a valuable lesson has been learned. On the other hand, such a process may create a bully. But so long as there are bigger, stronger people around who are right-minded, the bully does not get very far, perhaps only as far as terrorizing his or her own family, whose members typically escape if they can.

Ordinarily, the Micmac expect everyone to adhere to accepted behavioral ideals (see Table 1). However, for a Micmac authority to abide strictly by Behavioral Postulate 3 and Corollaries C, D, and E would mean an inability to render legal or political decisions. Members of the Grand Council overcame this obstacle because the people allowed and expected them to disregard those ideals in the performance of their duties as authorities, and because they were so circumspect in their personal behavior that others followed their examples and usually welcomed the imposition of their leadership and authority. The Grand Council preference for psychological sanctions along with mild physical sanctions has much to do with this. It used no coercive sanctions, but instead relied largely on the ostracism of the offender by other band members to make its primarily psychological sanctions effective.

In rendering legal justice the members of the Grand Council, and in particular *'Saqmaw* Gabriel Sylliboy, usually acted as follows: The Grand Council member would happen on a Micmac person in the act of breaking the law, weigh the facts of the case and the legal issues involved, and deliver a judgment and sanction on the spot (see, for example, Legal Case 7).

Moreover, the members of the Grand Council wielded authority in much the same way as does a parish priest. Like the parish priest, the *'Saqmaw*, Grand Captain, and captains saw fit to lecture the people of the community on matters of morality, and sometimes to intercede directly when breaches of morality became serious. Second, the

Grand Council members resembled the priests in that they used the Sunday sermon to discuss proper behavior, discouraging certain acts and encouraging others.

Grand Council members most often used as a sanction verbal admonition, a psychological punishment. This might take the form of an impromptu lecture to a drunken man whom a captain or the *'Saqmaw* passed on the road, a special visit to the house of a married couple who neglect their children, or an oblique reference in the weekly church sermon to the wrong of committing a particular sort of offense, omitting the names of those involved, but with the realization that offender and offense were known to all. In most cases, the shame involved in receiving the verbal admonition caused the offender to improve his or her behavior. Moreover, having one's infraction aired in church often led to ostracism by other members of the community. As the following case shows, however, words were sometimes not enough.

LEGAL CASE 5

Defendants: A married couple with children.
Authority: 'Saqmaw Gabriel Sylliboy.
Date: Circa 1930.
Location: A Cape Breton reserve.

Facts: This couple had been drinking for several days without becoming sober and, as a result, did not feed or clothe their children properly. After the *'Saqmaw* learned of the situation, he went to the family's home and implored them to stop drinking and start behaving responsibly toward their children. This lecture did no good.

Outcome: After another lecture failed to cause the couple to change their behavior, the *'Saqmaw* directed the reserve's constable, an Indian man employed by the Royal Canadian Mounted Police, to take the children away from the couple. The Grand Chief placed the children temporarily with the families of Grand Council members. When this happened, the couple's shame drove them to stop drinking and resume a sober style of life. Shortly thereafter, the Grand Council returned the children to their parents.

Comment: There are several interesting aspects to this case, which is similar to others of that era. The first is that the policeman who was charged with upholding federal and provincial law acted under the direction of the *'Saqmaw*, instead of the Royal Canadian Mounted Police. Rather than charging the couple with illegal manufacture, possession, and consumption of alcohol, as he might have done, he assisted the *'Saqmaw* in a different and probably far more effective strategy to alter the couple's behavior. The second aspect of this case that draws attention is the goal of the Grand Council's judicial decision. The *'Saqmaw*'s decision was primarily intended to improve the care of the children, and only incidentally to stop the parents from drinking. Had the case gone to the court system, the couple might have been punished for drinking with a jail term (the usual sanction then), and the children's care would have suffered; they would have been cared for by another Micmac couple if one could have been found. The Grand Council's solution fit Micmac standards of justice better than the Canadian court's likely decision would have done.

The Grand Council relied primarily on psychological sanctions and, of these, lecturing, often in public and therefore also inducing shame, was the most frequently used. However, it also used relatively minor physical penalties, whose effect was primarily psychological, as well as economic restitution (both to the injured individual and to the community) as sanctions, as in the following case.

LEGAL CASE 6

Defendants: Three teenaged boys.
Authority: '*Saqmaw* Gabriel Sylliboy.
Date: 1950s.

Facts: Three teenaged boys broke the window of a man's house, and the '*Saqmaw* investigated the offense.

Outcome: The three boys received the sanction of a lecture from the '*Saqmaw* on the wrongfulness of their action. The '*Saqmaw* also required them to replace the window and to provide labor for the community by supplying firewood to the elderly.

LEGAL CASE 7

Defendant: An intoxicated man.
Authority: '*Saqmaw* Gabriel Sylliboy.
Date: 1950s.

Facts: While walking down the road one day, Gabriel Sylliboy came across the intoxicated man, who was also walking down the road.

Outcome: Sylliboy lectured the man in public on his public drunkenness, saying that it set a bad example for the community.

The '*Saqmaw* also had a clear and very Christian idea of the responsibility of the individual to the group and acted on it in much the way many priests of the era did. At his insistence, for example, a church was built at Eskasoni, being completed in 1910. During the several years of construction, the '*Saqmaw* would ask men to help him cut timber, take it to the sawmill, and bring the lumber back to the building site, all without pay. If the men he chose expressed aversion to doing this hard work without remuneration, the '*Saqmaw* browbeat them until they changed their minds.

For serious infractions of the Canadian *Criminal Code*, those Grand Council members who lived on reserves without constables often acted as policemen or witnesses. When a captain decided that a member of his community had committed a serious offense, such as murder or assault (usually involving alcohol use, thus a breach of the *Indian Act* as well), he would remove the offender to the nearest Royal Canadian Mounted Police station. Otherwise, the captain would allow the reserve constable, a Micmac man and RCMP employee, to arrest and confine the offender. The RCMP would then handle the investigation, the Crown would handle the prosecution, and the court the trial and sanction. According to the captain of one pre-Centralization Cape Breton band, assault involving alcohol use made up the vast majority of the problems he encountered.

However, in all cases involving the infraction of the *Criminal Code* or the *Indian Act*, the Grand Council member acted as a legal authority in that he determined, to his own satisfaction, that the accused individual was guilty of an offense before turning him or her over to the federal authorities. In the following cases, a Grand Council member decided that no offense had been committed and the accused were thus never turned over to the RCMP for arrest and prosecution under federal law.

LEGAL CASE 8

Defendant: A Micmac man.
Authority: A Grand Council captain.
Date: 1930s.
Location: A Cape Breton reserve.

Facts: The defendant had gone hunting with another man, and shot and killed him. He claimed that the shooting was accidental. So-called hunting accidents were not unknown as a means of killing personal enemies (and sometimes public ones) in Nova Scotia, for non-Indians and Indians alike.

Outcome: Publicly, at least, the captain accepted the defendant's claim that the shooting was accidental and took no further action.

LEGAL CASE 9

Defendant: A Micmac woman.
Authority: A Grand Council captain.
Date: 1940s.
Location: A Cape Breton reserve.

Facts: The defendant was mentally ill and on two occasions left her newborn child outside in the middle of winter to die.

Outcome: The captain decided that because of her mental condition she committed no crime and took no action.

The Grand Council had sufficiently formidable power in the 19th century that a decision the *'Saqmaw* once made caused a schism within the Micmac population of Cape Breton. The following case deals with this historical occurrence and shows the traditional Micmac means of handling what were considered unjust legal decisions.

LEGAL CASE 10

Defendants: Several Eskasoni families who did not wish to comply with a directive issued by the *'Saqmaw* John Denny.
Authority: *'Saqmaw* John Denny.
Date: 1870s.
Location: Cape Breton Island.

Facts: In the 1870s the Grand Council decided that Chapel Island must have an exemplary new church for the annual Mission to replace an older, more modest building. The Micmac at the time were short of cash with which to build the church, so the *'Saqmaw* decreed that each Micmac family in Cape Breton contribute a man to work on the church at Chapel Island (we do not now know whether by "family" (*nikmaq*) he meant a nuclear family, extended family, or descent group). For this reason, many families moved to '*Potlotek*, the reserve that includes Chapel Island. If a family did not wish to send a man, then the '*Saqmaw* expected it to pay a cash fine for each day that it supplied no worker.

Outcome: Some of Eskasoni's families vehemently opposed the decree. The '*Saqmaw* could not force them to surrender either a worker or the amounts of their fines. The rebellious families responded to these orders in a traditional Micmac way: they left the Eskasoni reserve and went to live in Sydney and in North Sydney, where they sold handicrafts and took jobs in the area's factories and coal mines. They avoided the '*Saqmaw*'s decision by leaving his jurisdiction, thereby forming at least two new bands on Cape Breton independent of the Grand Council.

One of these bands, the Sydney band, as it became known, followed the advice of the Indian Agent to elect *Indian Act* chiefs. The first such elections did not comply precisely with the *Indian Act*, and so there was no bona fide band or Band Council in Sydney until 1958. The people of the Sydney band nevertheless regarded the men they elected as their legitimate leaders. The '*Saqmaw* John Denny Jr. never ceased attempts to regain control over the Micmac of the Sydney and North Sydney groups (both part of the Sydney band under Indian Affairs reckoning). In 1906, Denny wrote two letters to a D. K. McIntyre, Indian Agent for the Sydney band (Public Archives of Canada, RG 10, vol. 7936, file 32-61, part 1). In these letters Denny attempted to influence McIntyre's selection of the chief and councillors of the band. Apparently, Denny did not know that the members of the band were by then electing their own leaders, and that McIntyre's role in the matter extended only as far as ensuring that the elections proceeded fairly. In later years, the rift between the Sydney band and the '*Saqmaw* healed somewhat and '*Saqmaw* Gabriel Sylliboy selected Captain Ben Christmas from the band to represent it to the Grand Council. Christmas was at the time the *Indian Act* chief, a post he held for several decades. He continued as captain until his death, long after he left the office of chief. Nevertheless, the Sydney band never relinquished their practice of electing chiefs to return to the system of having the '*Saqmaw* appoint a captain as their sole leader.

In other matters, the '*Saqmaw* and his captains worked more closely to control the behavior of the Cape Breton Micmac and to represent the Micmac people to the federal and provincial governments. Most members of the Grand Council sought to correct what might be considered flaws of character, low moral or ethical standards, and peccadilloes. The socially deleterious use of alcohol, swearing, vandalism, public argument, adultery, and child neglect were some of the offenses that they sought to control. They treated these as crimes that reflected badly on the entire Micmac community.

Until the 1950s or so, the Grand Council appointed a man called the *Nujjikl'apteket* ("he [or she] who watches over them") to control behavior at the annual St. Anne's Mission. The *Nujjikl'apteket* enforced the following rules: no one may fight, swear, argue, drink alcoholic beverages, or allow their children outside after 9:00 p.m. while on the island. It was also understood that no one was supposed to engage in sexual activity while on the island, though this was not an offense against man, but rather a religious taboo. The *Nujjikl'apteket* sometimes punished an offender by sending him or her to *'Mintuakij* (literally, "place of devils") or, rendered in English, "jail island," a tiny island some 180 meters (200 yards) distant from Chapel Island itself. The *Nujjikl'apteket* left the prisoner there until he felt that the prisoner had been sufficiently punished, or until sober. In addition, the *Nujjikl'apteket* delivered a lecture on proper Mission behavior.

LEGAL CASE 11

Parties: Two intoxicated women arguing with each other.
Authority: Nujjikl'apteket.
Date: Pre-1940s.

Facts: Two intoxicated women had a loud argument while at the Mission. The *Nujjikl'apteket* apprehended them.

Outcome: Both were taken to *'Mintuakij*. One escaped by swimming to the mainland.

The following case involves the last instance of the use of *'Mintuakij*.

LEGAL CASE 12

Defendant: A non-Indian relative of a non-Indian man married to an Indian woman.
Authority: 'Saqmaw Gabriel Sylliboy.
Date: 1940s.

Facts: The defendant was inebriated when he arrived by boat at Chapel Island.

Outcome: The defendant was immediately taken by some of the people who were there near the landing to another boat and taken to *Mintuakij*. After several hours, during which time he became sober, a member of the Grand Council sent for him. When the offender returned to the island, a member of the Grand Council lectured him, telling him to never enter the island drunk again.

The following case shows the function of the Grand Council as a body of authorities that judges a particular range of criminal cases, but one that passes no judgment on torts, or that does so only by way of deciding criminal cases.

LEGAL CASE 13

Parties: Two factions of a Micmac baseball team.
Authority: The Grand Captain.
Date: 1930s.
Location: The *'Potlotek* reserve.

Facts: In this case, a disagreement created two factions in the reserve's only men's baseball team. The dispute was over who should be able to join the team, whether or not members of the band should be able to play on non-Indian teams outside of the reserve, and who among the team members should have the right to make these decisions. As time went by the factions grew further apart, to the degree that they would no longer play together as the same ball team. The dispute simmered some time longer without resolution.

Outcome: The Grand Captain, who lived on the same reserve, called the people involved together. In front of most of the rest of the band, he chastised the team members for most of the day for acting so disputatiously. He lectured about the responsibility of all Micmac to work together toward common goals and to advance the Micmac people, so that the outside world would judge them more favorably. The lecture was intended not only to decide the issue of the ball team, but to instruct the band membership as well. The Grand Captain decided the case, rather than the captain who would normally do so, because he happened to be living there and because his office and authority are superior to those of captain. He decided that all Micmac should play on Micmac teams only, so that the teams, which represented the bands and reserves, could benefit from the talents of all Micmac and create a better impression of Micmac ballplayers, and of the Micmac as a people, among the people of the outside world. Further, the Grand Captain appointed one member of the team as an authority to decide all future questions and disputes pertaining to athletic teams and events; all who want to play must follow his rules or they would not be allowed to play. A major object of this judgment was to prevent future dissent and disharmony.

Comment: The settlement of the point of the dispute was secondary to the punishment of the crime, which was the act of disputation itself. Decisive evidence that this case was criminal rather than civil is that the judge summoned the offenders before him. The disputants did not seek him out as an authority to render a decision to solve their own private disagreement.

Perhaps the most interesting aspect of this case is that the Grand Council took decisive legal action in a case that many might consider trivial (a dispute internal to a ball club), while on the other hand it took no action on homicides (Legal Cases 8 and 9), which many in other societies would regard as more properly deserving of serious attention and response. While this point of view has merit, it neglects an essential function of law, that of maintaining social order. In the ball club case, the dispute actually caused considerable conflict within the community. The homicide in Legal Case 8 apparently did not, perhaps because the victim may have been a troublesome person whom the community was happier without; those in Legal Case 9 constituted neither willful, and therefore criminal, nor socially disruptive acts.

The Grand Council's Legal Authority Declines

The Grand Council's political and legal power fell off in the 1940s and afterward for three basic reasons. First, the Catholic priests returned, therefore the captains no longer delivered the Sunday sermon and could no longer use this forum to rally public opinion and ostracism against legal offenders in the community. Second, and most important, the Indian Agent came to live on the Eskasoni reserve and exercised strict control over the reserve constable. The constable greatly increased legal vigilance over drinking, assault, and truancy (Steen 1951). The Grand Council's gentler, noncoercive handling of problems became ineffective beside the harsh measures of the Indian Agent, police, and the Canadian court system. When people began to fear the federal legal system, they had less interest in the moral admonitions of the Grand Council members, which relied greatly on voluntary compliance for effect. One Micmac man characterized them by saying that "all they had was church power." The third significant factor was the death in 1964 of *'Saqmaw* Gabriel Sylliboy, who had vigorously investigated and adjudicated crimes, and single-handedly kept the Grand Council an important legal authority until then (see, for example, Legal Cases 5, 6, and 7).

The Grand Council has maintained a measure of legal authority at the St. Anne's Mission, although by the early 1960s, at least, behavioral standards at the Mission had begun to fall. Further, it seems that the Grand Council had already by that point given up its role of policing the Mission's rules of behavior. If the following case recorded by Howard (1965:7) is any indication, the priests who said Mass at the Mission policed behavior out of their own willingness to do so.

LEGAL CASE 14

Defendants: Several Micmac teenagers.
Authority: The Mission priest.
Date: 1962.
Location: Chapel Island.

Facts: The priest caught several teenagers outside after curfew.

Outcome: The priest chased the teenagers into their wigwams and tents and told them to go to sleep.

Comment: As soon as the priest left, the teenagers came out of their lodgings. Apparently, the young peoples' curfew, universally respected in the 1940s, was well on its way to being a thing of the past.

Though the power and scope of the authority of the Grand Council were waning, it remained the supreme authority at the Mission, as seen in the following case.

LEGAL CASE 15

Defendants: James Howard and Steven Gluckman, two visitors to the Mission.
Plaintiff: The Mission priest.
Authority: The Grand Council.
Date: July 1962.
Location: Chapel Island.

Facts: The defendants, one of whom described the case (Howard 1965:6–7), came to the Mission and set up their tent. The Mission priest came by and asked some questions. When he discovered that neither of the men was Catholic, the priest ordered them off the island. The men went to the *'Saqmaw* for adjudication of the dispute.

Outcome: The *'Saqmaw* and his assistant, Ben Christmas, captain and chief of the Sydney band, agreed to allow the two men to remain.

While the Grand Council retained authority, the events of the 1960s saw other changes in the legal system applied at the Chapel Island Mission. Two closely timed events have had radical and lasting effects on the administration of the Mission.

One of these was Vatican Council II. Micmac opposed this easing of the rules Catholics were expected to observe, including the removal of the prohibition against the consumption of meat on Fridays. In their eyes, Vatican II cheapened the faith. The Grand Council enforced the pre-Vatican II rules by withdrawing official permission to visit the island from those who did not observe these rules. As a result, some people, especially the younger ones who came primarily to enjoy themselves, camped on the Cape Breton mainland, directly across the strait from Chapel Island. This constituted an open rebellion against the authority of the Grand Council. While the people who camped on *qam'e:k* (or "the other side," the mainland of Cape Breton Island), as it is known, experienced some public ridicule and shame, they did place themselves outside of the Grand Council's jurisdiction, which by then for most intents and purposes extended only as far as Chapel Island's coastline. To have broken Catholic dietary laws, for example, while on Chapel Island would have been to risk great public censure and possibly to provoke the Grand Council to take action.

The second important event occurred shortly after Vatican II, and this was the death of *'Saqmaw* Gabriel Sylliboy and the installation of his successor *'Saqmaw* Donald Marshall in 1964. By that time, the captains had largely relinquished their function as legal authorities to the Indian Agent, the Band Councils, and the Canadian courts. Marshall had little interest in exercising legal authority. The change of the Grand Council's function as a result of Sylliboy's death shows that the Grand Council's legal authority was informal and depended on the personality of the officeholder. Because Micmac law and politics rely so greatly on the character of authorities and leaders, it is always a potentially crucial event when officers change. Such was indeed the case in this instance.

An authority must exercise its power from time to time to curb the spreading of abuses of the rules. This is how the leadership of *'Saqmaw* Marshall (who died in 1991) faltered, many Micmac say. While all agree that his heart was in the right place, people generally maintain that he simply did not exercise power when and as he should have, but instead left the decision of whether or not to follow the Mission rules to the judgment of those attending. One Micmac woman put it bluntly: "he doesn't have balls."

Without forceful leadership and authority from the Grand Council, behavioral standards at the annual Mission fell to a low that most Micmac found unacceptable. By the early 1980s, virtually the only control over behavior was public censure and parental control over offspring, in whatever forms the latter took, as in the following case.

LEGAL CASE 16

Defendant: A Micmac woman 24 years of age.
Authority: Her mother.
Date: 1982.
Location: Chapel Island.

Facts: The woman's mother had come across her while she was under the influence of alcohol.

Outcome: The mother verbally reprimanded her daughter and told her never to drink while at the Mission. The daughter refrained from drinking while at the Mission for the remainder of her stay.

Verbal admonitions from parents and others have little or no effect on some, however. In the early 1980s, I observed many people drinking, some below the legal age of 19, mostly after dark or in private. Arguments, also disallowed, were not uncommon, as was theft, the sale of drugs and alcohol, and loud music and voices late into the night; for some, the Mission was a chance to get away from the house and to have a week-long party. With the exception of verbally expressed disapprobation, the only control over behavior was of the type that I saw in the following trouble case.

DISPUTE CASE 5

Disputants: Two Micmac men.
Date: 1983.
Location: Chapel Island.

Facts: Two men started a fistfight, in the middle of a crowd at the Mission, in broad daylight.

Outcome: Several bystanders told them to leave the island, and they did so.

Normally, Micmac who do not hold an office will not do what these people did, because the one with the responsibility for maintaining order should be the one to come forward to punish rule-breakers. Grand Council officeholders were expected to ferret out wrongdoing and correct it in the best manner. However, nobody in authority undertook the task.

The standards of behavior at the Mission had fallen to their lowest ebb at the time that I witnessed the following case:

LEGAL CASE 17

Defendant: A young Micmac man attending the Mission.
Authority: A captain from Eskasoni.
Date: 1981.
Location: Chapel Island.

Facts: A young man was sitting outside of his tent on Chapel Island in the middle of the day drinking wine from a bottle. One of the captains came by and the drinker greeted him by saying, "Hello [captain's name]." Then he took another gulp of wine and said, "How's the man?"

Outcome: The Captain told the young man that drinking was not allowed at the Mission. The young man put his bottle away for a while, but later retrieved it and began to drink once more.

Comment: Later that day another fellow who had also been drinking came by the drinking man and soon began to insult the first man's family, obviously trying to provoke a fight and thereby embarrass the first man. The first man later told me that he had felt like beating the other man, but did not want to show his disrespect for the Mission. He vowed to take revenge in the future, however.

Another example of the erosion of leadership and authority of the Grand Council over Mission matters concerns the use of land on the island. Before the 1960s, people attending the Mission stayed in tents and wigwams on the southwest end of the island. Later, people began to build small camps (cabins) on the southeast end of the island, on the other side of the church from the tents. Since that time, virtually all available space on that side of the island has been taken up with camps. In the 1980s, some people began to build their camps on the western side of the island, on the shore where the tenting area is located. The Grand Council issued a rule that no more were to be built there, because the building of camps reduced the amount of space available to the people who use tents. Still, a few more people erected camps. The Grand Council spoke out against the practice of building camps in the prohibited area, but to no avail. At about the time of the 1988 Mission, the following notice appeared in the *Micmac News* (Marshall 1988a):

Notice
We the Grand Council are asking people that are building cabins along the tenting area on the Island not to build any more cabins along that area. If you want to build a cabin you have to ask one of the Captains. John D. Johnson would be the proper person to ask.

Thank You
Grand Council Chief

Because no sanctions were set forth, and because there is no more space available for camps in the area that had been set aside for building camps, I predicted in 1987 that the erection of camps in the tent area would continue. When I returned in 1995, I saw that my prediction had been correct.

The Grand Council maintains its role as administrator of the Mission. It undertook to renovate the old church, built in the late 19th century, and not long thereafter to rebuild it when it was destroyed by fire in December 1976. It handled the financial transactions with lending institutions and provided labor as well. The Grand Council also decides the Sunday on which St. Anne's Day (July 26) will be celebrated. It invites the priests and regulates the business enterprises on the island during the Mission, as in the following case.

LEGAL CASE 18

Defendants: Several operators of gambling concerns.
Authority: Grand Council.
Date: 1982.
Location: Chapel Island.

Facts: For several years entrepreneurs attending the Mission have operated gambling enterprises, mostly the "wheel of fortune" game, as it is popularly known, a game that resembles roulette. They plied their trade on the island itself on the understanding that they would pay a fee for that right; the businessmen on *qa'me:k* ("the other side") are not required to pay any fees. These fees support the building of the new church and expenses incidental to the operation of the Mission. In 1981 they failed to pay those fees.

Outcome: In 1982 the Grand Council prohibited operation of the games on the island. In later years, the fees were paid and the games once again appeared on the island.

For a time the Grand Council abjured its responsibility to police behavior at the Mission. This was because efforts on the part of the Grand Council to control behavior directly would bring about considerable antipathy from the people and the Grand Council rules very democratically, on the basis that the people like and find agreeable its members and their decisions. Since behavioral standards have changed over the years, the Grand Council today no longer wishes to enforce old standards. To do so would be to undermine their popularity and, ultimately, their authority. One member of the Grand Council told me how, in his youth in the 1930s, the Grand Council would patrol the campgrounds looking for troublemakers and any sort of misbehavior. I asked why he himself did not perform that function now. He replied that nobody would ever pay attention either to him or to his commands. The democratic Grand Council holds values that are no longer psychologically internal to many of the younger generation and will not enforce those values among people who do not share them.

Nevertheless, the Grand Council accepts the responsibility of administering the Mission. So, as a supreme authority, it has allowed other agencies to do its police work instead (see, for example, Legal Case 14). The *'Saqmaw* in 1984 experimented by asking the Royal Canadian Mounted Police to police the parking lot at *qa'me:k* and the waterway between the *qa'me:k* and Chapel Island. The experiment failed because Micmac people resented the presence of the RCMP.

The Priest Takes Control of Behavior at the Mission and the Grand Council Again Takes the Reins

The Eskasoni parish priest had heard complaints for years about how bad the behavior at the Mission had become. In 1986, the Grand Council selected him to host the Mission, to say Mass, hear confessions, and perform funerals.

That year, the priest decided to take action to improve the social conditions at the Mission. He selected some young men to work as event policemen, to help him enforce the following rules:

1. No drinking or drug abuse is allowed on Chapel Island. Those who are inebriated will be prevented from entering the island.

2. There is to be no loud music late at night.

3. The boat service to the island will cease at 11:00 p.m., with no one allowed to enter the Island after that time.

4. There is to be no fighting.

The following case shows how one of these rules was applied.

LEGAL CASE 19

Defendant: A young Micmac woman of about 20 years of age.
Authority: A Micmac event policeman under the authority of the priest.
Date: July, 1987.
Location: Chapel Island.

Facts: The woman was caught with a can of beer in her hand after dark on the Chapel Island.

Outcome: The policeman removed her from the island and told her not to return until the next day.

During his speech at the close of the 1986 Mission, the priest asked the crowd whether or not they liked the new rules. Nearly everyone there signified by clapping their hands or shouting that they did like them. Of course, those listening to the priest were mostly older people who supported the traditional norms. Those younger people who wished for relaxed behavioral standards were not in attendance. The priest vowed to continue the application of the rules and the "police" system. The new rules led many of the older people who had avoided the mayhem of the Mission for years to return. By the 1990s, the Grand Council had acquired control of this new "police" system and once again established its authority over behavior there. Moreover, Grand Captain Alex Denny has long sought to improve the moral fiber of the people by using his annual St. Anne's Day speech to exhort the Micmac to abstain from drugs and alcohol, to retain the use of the Micmac language, and to bring up their children properly and responsibly.

Overview

The Grand Council has its roots in military conflict, the so-called French and Indian wars. When the wars ended and the Catholic priests had left the Micmac, the members of the Grand Council became religious leaders and functionaries, governing their communities largely through sermons and lectures.

The Grand Council maintained its authority by earning and keeping the respect of the other members of the group. They earned respect partly by deciding only those legal cases that involved crimes. Any attempt by a Grand Council member to involve himself in a civil matter would have been seen as unacceptable personal bias. However, disputes that got out of hand and became socially disruptive to more than a few people were treated as criminal offenses. People who caused harm were handled by the Grand Council or by the reserve's constable, an RCMP employee, if at least one was a resident on the reserve. Two small reserves had no constables and so captains would act as policemen and take the troublemakers, whose guilt they had already ascertained, to the police department of the nearest town. They would then let the courts handle the individual's punishment. In cases in which the reserves had Micmac constables, those constables acted under the direction of a Grand Council member (see Legal Case 5).

We may abstract the following legal principles from Grand Council decisions:

GRAND COUNCIL LEGAL PRINCIPLE 1

Anyone who causes significant damage, loss, or injury to another party is guilty of a criminal offense, unless such damage, loss, or injury is due to accident or insanity (abstracted from Legal Cases 5, 6, 8, and 9).

GRAND COUNCIL LEGAL PRINCIPLE 2

Activities and behavior that promote a positive image of the Micmac people to the outside world must flourish and failure to promote these activities constitutes a criminal offense (abstracted from Legal Cases 10, 13, and 15, and Dispute Case 8).

GRAND COUNCIL LEGAL PRINCIPLE 3

Civil disputes that cause social disruption to more than a few people constitute criminal offenses (abstracted from Legal Case 13).

The case of the *'Saqmaw*'s approval of Centralization (Dispute Case 4) shows several other important qualities of Micmac leadership and legal authority. By throwing down the medal, the *'Saqmaw* showed that he did not wish to lead without popular support. Many other Micmac leaders in Nova Scotia and in New Brunswick bands have also left office when they did not receive the support of the band (Hamilton 1984). On Cape Breton Island, even *Indian Act* chiefs have resigned their offices when they felt that the members of the band failed to support them.

Second, Dispute Case 4 shows just how it happens that leadership can lose potency in the face of popular social pressure. Rather than agreeing to abide by the wishes of the majority and fight Centralization, the *'Saqmaw* simply abdicated his role in intergovernmental affairs for the rest of his long term.

Finally, this case shows the susceptibility of the *'Saqmaw*, and indeed all Micmac leaders and authorities, to political pressure from subordinates. The *'Saqmaw* has the authority to remove his subordinates from their offices in the Grand Council, yet in some cases he prefers to allow them to dictate conditions to his actions and to reverse his rulings than to dismiss them.

When the priests returned to serve the Micmac in the 1940s after an absence of more than 150 years, the preaching careers of the Grand Council members ended, and with them an important means of social control. There was also a tremendous increase in vigilance by the Indian Agent and a resultant crackdown on a variety of crimes, especially alcohol consumption. Whereas the members of the Grand Council had punished only the socially disruptive consumption of alcohol, with lectures and public humiliation, the Indian Agent and the reserve constable punished all alcohol consumption and possession with jail and fines. Naturally enough, Micmac soon learned to fear not the Grand Council, but rather the Indian Agent. The effectiveness of the Grand Council's psychological sanctions diminished.

By the 1960s, the legal authority of the Grand Council outside of the Mission itself had virtually ended. The Micmac people, in that decade, were being exposed in large numbers to the urban outside world as never before. Much of this occurred through employment in Boston, Toronto, Halifax, and Maine. Acculturation accelerated, and many saw the way of life that the Grand Council represented as an anachronism. As fits the general pattern of Micmac culture, when these leaders and authorities began to see support for their policies fade they then gradually ceased to lead or to enforce the traditional rules. Moreover, the strongest Grand Council legal authority died, and with him the determination to uphold the aboriginal Micmac legal system, at least outside of the Mission. Although no longer an important legal force on the reserve, the Grand Council has since greatly increased its political power vis-à-vis external powers by fighting for treaty rights.

Government under the Indian Agent, 1942–1971

Since Confederation in 1867, the Canadian federal government assumed responsibility from the provinces for the welfare of Indians, administering government services and programs from Ottawa. From that time until 1942, the Indian Agents on Cape Breton were paid a small sum of money to work part-time on reserves administering relief payments, helping to run the school (if any), and seeing to whatever problems cropped up on behalf of Indian Affairs. In actuality, the Indian Agent was usually all but a stranger on most reserves. But with the creation of the Centralization Program in 1942, the Indian Agent lived and worked on the Eskasoni reserve 24 hours a day. In overseeing the Centralization Program, he made rules and principles designed to achieve the goals of Centralization. The Indian Agent became a forceful political and legal presence on the Eskasoni reserve and from 1942 to 1971 acted as an administrator and legal authority. His purposes and functions were:

1. To move the Indian population of Cape Breton to Eskasoni (until 1949).
2. To use the housing and the space available for the efficient building of houses.
3. To create additional housing.
4. To compel the Micmac to adopt agriculture and animal husbandry.
5. To enforce the provisions of the Canadian *Criminal Code* and of the *Indian Act*.
6. To operate the reserve's school.

7. To administer employment and welfare programs.

8. To operate a cooperative store on the reserve (until about 1960).

The Indian Agent of the era was virtually an autocratic dictator. Both Micmac and past and present Indian Affairs staff members have described the Indian agent of the period as "God on the reserve." He derived his power from his official position in Indian Affairs, his control over the reserve's special constable, his willingness to prosecute offenders of Canadian federal law, and especially his discretionary control over relief payments to, and employment of, Micmac people by Indian Affairs. For a time, the Indian Agent at Eskasoni also had magisterial powers, given to him because of the distance between the reserve and the provincial courthouse. His actions were limited only by Canadian law and by the choice of some to refuse to move to Eskasoni during Centralization, where the Indian Agent lived. For example, the following Political Case (the term refers to trouble cases that political authorities resolve using political means and for political reasons, rather than by legal means according to a legal principle; political decisions lack the legal attribute of intention of universal application).

POLITICAL CASE 1

Party: Eskasoni residents who both owned automobiles and received relief payments.
Authority: Indian Agent.
Date: 1950s.

Facts: After the house building projects wound down at the end of the Centralization Program and many of the men lost employment, an increasing number of families resorted to accepting relief payments. The Indian Agent sought to reduce the attractiveness of welfare by decreeing that all welfare recipients must turn in their automobile license plates to receive welfare payments. Some were prepared to do this when a Micmac man protested the order, saying that only the province could command the return of license plates.

Outcome: In the face of this political opposition, the Indian Agent abandoned this order.

The Indian Agent also applied himself to halting truancy and damage to government property, and especially to ending alcohol use and possession. The Micmac of Eskasoni regarded his inflexible measures enforcement as draconian, and they served only to increase Eskasonians' dislike of both Indian Affairs and the Indian Agent.

The Indian Agent actively involved himself in the settlement of some of the newcomers. In one instance he commanded a Micmac man, then working in the United States, to return to Eskasoni to work at a job offering one-third the pay. After the man had settled into his new house on the reserve, the Indian Agent decided that he wanted the man to live closer to his office (located in the former band office building), so that it would be easier for the Indian Agent to call on him when needed (see Legal Case 24). The man complied, although he had to ask the permission of a third man to build his house on his land. The Indian Agent's legal control over the band largely ended in 1971, when a popular protest led by the band's chief forced Indian Affairs to remove its personnel from the reserve. Since then, Indian Affairs bureaucrats have administered Indian Affairs programs from offices at a distance, and have little influence over day-to-day life on the reserves.

Law under the Indian Agent

This section presents a brief overview of law under the Indian Agent. The subject of Indian Agent land tenure law is treated below.

The Indian Agent primarily applied criminal law; the society whose interests he protected was, of course, Canada as a whole and not Eskasoni in particular. He also applied civil law, on occasion, to resolve disputes between band members, although he usually expected Eskasonians to solve their own civil problems. He enforced both the *Indian Act* and the *Criminal Code* in their entirety, but the majority of his cases involved alcohol use (illegal for most Canadian Indians without special permits, until about 1960) and truancy. In the first years after the start of the Centralization Program, the Indian Agent had been granted magisterial authority because of the difficulties in transporting those involved in legal cases back and forth to the nearest courthouse and jail. In addition, the Indian Agent would often direct the reserve's constables in policies toward the enforcement of federal laws. Those he found guilty of offenses to the *Indian Act* and the *Criminal Code* often served jail terms. He directed the constables to take truants to school, by force if necessary, and sometimes deprived the parents of truants of their right to receive relief payments. The Indian Agent was also concerned that federal property be protected from damage. Federal property at that time comprised everything on the reserve except the personal belongings of the reserve's inhabitants. Those who damaged housing, for example, were punished under the provisions of the *Criminal Code*, and sanctions included incarceration (see Legal Cases 26, 27, and 28).

Many Eskasoni Micmac considered the Indian Agent's law highly unjust. Accustomed to owning their own housing, they wanted to be able to do with it as they wished. The Grand Council had never punished those who had used alcohol responsibly. Children were accustomed to attending school as they wished, and even forgoing formal education altogether, because in many respects Micmac children enjoy the same freedom of behavior as do adults.

More especially, the Micmac considered the Indian Agent's physical and economic sanctions unjustly harsh. Used to the psychological sanctions of the Grand Council, which consisted largely of verbal admonitions, the Micmac felt that incarceration for actions that harmed no one else (drinking or damaging one's own house) made no sense at all. Equally unjust, they believed, was to take relief payments from the parents of truant children, which they viewed as immoral because it punished all of the family's children with hunger in response the actions of one child.

Government under the Band Council

Presently, the leadership of, and much of the authority over, the band reside with the chief and council, known collectively as the Band Council. Provision for the creation of Indian bands and for the election of Band Councils was made by the federal *Indian Act* in the 19th century, but the federal government did not impose it in most parts of Nova Scotia until the 1950s and 1960s. In 1956, Indian Affairs apparently decided that Eskasoni's time had come. By Indian Affairs policy, the Indian Agent then gradually relinquished much of his authority to the Band Council. A 1969 protest by the Band Council and some Eskasoni band members against the presence of the Indian Agent on the reserve was one important factor that led Indian Affairs in 1971 to remove non-Indian Indian Affairs personnel from the reserve to nearby Sydney, leaving the Band Council with more control over band affairs.

Though the *Indian Act* and Indian Affairs determine its structure, declare official functions, and provide remuneration, the Band Council is a thoroughly Micmac body of political leaders and legal authority. Its members are Micmac chosen for office by other Micmac, even though popular election is not a traditionally Micmac method of selection. The Band Council has been able to manipulate its performance of its official functions to serve the interests of the band as well as its own political interests. Moreover, as shown below, the Band Council has exercised legal authority in making laws that conform to Micmac ideals and needs, and that often conflict with the provisions of the *Indian Act* and the policies of Indian Affairs.

Leadership Qualities

The following attributes bring candidates for chief success at the polls:

1. What the Micmac call *es'pe:k* ("he [she] is high up"). In other words, he has shown his superiority to others by having accomplished something important, and is well respected for it.

2. A good command of English, for the purpose of communicating with Indian Affairs. For this reason, older people are rarely elected.

3. The support of well-respected members of the community, especially elders.

4. Being fairly large and strong, able physically to intimidate adversaries or, more importantly, resist intimidation by others. Other than the tradition of male leadership, this is why no women have been elected chief in this band. A few other Nova Scotia Indian bands have elected women chiefs.

5. Intelligence.

6. Ability to give the impression, at least, of fairness and evenhandedness with all band members. Conversely, loyalty to those who provide political support in the

election in terms of the "spoils" the chief awards. People view these awards as a measure of generosity that reflects on a chief personally.

7. Acquires increased federal aid for the band.

8. Incumbency. Incumbents enjoy a great advantage, unless they greatly offend their constituents.

9. Many loyal consanguineal and affinal kin who provide political support.

10. The ability to speak eloquently and persuasively, and convince followers to do as you wish.

These qualities (except 2 and 7) are desirable in candidates for the office of councillor as well. Since councillors have no official reasons to interact directly with Indian Affairs, they do not need to speak English well to perform their duties, nor can they reasonably promise to acquire more federal aid for the band.

Thus, the modern chief in some important ways resembles the non-Grand Council *'Saqmaw* of old, who also rose to prominence on the basis of qualities of generosity (qualities 6 and 7 are frequently understood as the modern equivalent), as well as qualities 2, 4, 5, 9, and 10.

Structure

The Band Council's structure is modeled on that of the mayor and council of an ordinary municipal government. The chief and councillors are elected on the same date for coincident two-year terms. The voters, male and female band members at least 18 years of age residing on the band's reserve, elect one chief and a variable number of councillors, depending on the band's population; the *Indian Act* was changed in 2000 to allow band members living off the reserve to vote. Because of its large size, Eskasoni has 12 councillors, the maximum number that the *Indian Act* permits. From 1966 until 2004, the Eskasoni band had 10 councillors and was organized geopolitically by electoral sections, popularly known by the people of Eskasoni as wards; there were five wards and the band members of each ward elected two councillors from among the adults who lived within that same ward. Indian Affairs pays the chief and councillors for their services. Since their positions do not constitute full-time employment, the chief and councillors may also collect full relief (welfare) benefits if they do not otherwise work full-time.

THE WARD SYSTEM

The *Indian Act* (R.S.C. 1985, c. I-5, s. 74(4)) provides that, for voting purposes, a reserve may be divided "into not more than six electoral sections containing as nearly as may be an equal number of Indians eligible to vote." The reserve was undivided when the first Band Council was elected in 1956.

The reserve, because of the results of the Centralization Program, was polarized by residence. Those living on the eastern portion of the reserve (*'Qamsipu:k* or "located on the other side of the river [or stream or brook]") are predominantly original settlers of the reserve. *'Qamsipu:k* is to the east of Gregwa Brook (Figure 3). Those who live in the central portion (known variously as Eskasoni, *Apamuek*, or Middletown) are a mix of original residents and those newly arrived as a result of the Centralization Program, while those who lived in the Castle Bay region at the far western end consist of newcomers entirely. Castle Bay is that portion of the reserve added during the Centralization Program of the 1940s and lies to the west of the pre-Centralization reserve boundary (see Figures 1 and 3).

The original residents were able to elect people to the Band Council from among their own ranks more easily than the newcomers could. Some maintain today that this was because of their greater abilities, hard work, and intelligence. It seems more likely that they enjoyed greater solidarity and were able to coordinate their efforts better than the others, who, originating from more than five separate reserves, were politically divided and slow to become accustomed to each other.

In any event, when a Castle Bay man was elected chief, he decided to have the band vote on a referendum to adopt the ward system, to ensure the people of Castle Bay political representation; the measure passed in 1966. The ward boundaries are decided by the band's electoral officer who, aided by data on the population of each household, uses a ruler and pen to divide a map of the reserve into five equally populated portions. Since the reserve is laid out around a single highway running roughly east to west, it was decided to divide the reserve using lines perpendicular to this road. This method originally preserved, as well, the distinctions the reserve residents recognize in their social geography, especially the three major sections of Castle Bay, *'Qamsipu:k*, and Eskasoni–*Apamuek*–Middletown.

There are exceptions to this last statement. For years, wards 2 and 4 straddled recognized divisions, and many people disliked this. Especially upset were those who live in *'Qamsipu:k*. They were divided among wards 1 and 2, with ward 2 also including another part of the reserve (*Apamuek*), with which the residents of *'Qamsipu:k* feel no especial affinity, and who wanted to see this changed.

The placement of the ward boundaries, adjusted by population before the biennial elections, also affects the election of political candidates. Just as gerrymandering in New York City can keep a candidate from being elected to office in his own district, so too do the ward boundaries divide candidates from their base of power, namely, their kin. In the 1986 election one man running for office from his own ward lost the support of his patrilineage because they lived in the next ward, even though their houses were only a few hundred feet away. In such a small community, one or two votes sometimes spell the difference between victory and defeat.

Competition for votes can become quite keen and a councillor in office will sometime even move supporters from their own wards for a few weeks so that they can be considered residents in the incumbent's ward. One councillor promised a single woman in another ward a brand new house if she would move into her aunt's house three weeks before the election and vote for him.

The system of representation by ward did much to redress the problem of geographically uneven expenditures of government assistance money. However, some of the people in the western portion of the reserve complained that no physical development to which they could point with pride had come to them. Beginning around 1980, some of the people of the Castle Bay region felt so strongly about the question that they began to talk about separating to form a separate band and reserve. At one point several meetings were held to discuss the matter more formally. As a result, the chief agreed to build the new band office and other administrative buildings in Castle Bay rather than in central Eskasoni, as had originally been planned. While it is true that all but one of the band's development projects have been built in the central and eastern wards, these have often been so located because of factors relating to the nature of the development needs (an oyster bed needed a quiet saline bay, a furniture factory needed an available building) or the proximity to the geographic or demographic center of the reserve (the school, the old band office).

The ward system ended in 2004, abolished by the Band Council to allow people to vote for the councillors they really wanted. The chief at the time is the son of the chief who initiated the ward system on this reserve.

Functions

Functions as Indian Affairs Employees

The chief alone carries the authority to represent the band's interests to federal, provincial, and municipal governments. The federal and provincial governments designed it thus (they like to deal with as few people as possible); the chiefs prefer it (they like to have as much power as possible); the people allow it (they had previously allowed the *'Saqmaw* of the Grand Council the same authority); and the councillors tolerate it (though some would like to know more about what the chief and Indian Affairs decide together in their meetings).

The *Indian Act* charges Band Councils with the authority to create by-laws to regulate many band and reserve affairs. The Eskasoni Band Council has made negligible use of this authority, since it enjoys considerable political and legal power over the people of the reserve, and because Canadian courts, which decide cases of violations of band by-laws, are not required to take judicial notice of these statutes. This political power gives the Band Council the ability to institute its own laws and operate its own legal system, irrespective of Indian Affairs, the *Indian Act,* or the statutes it may or may not create.

In point of fact, it is the function of Eskasoni Band Council members as Indian Affairs employees that receives virtually all of their attention: Indian Affairs has given the Band Council the responsibility for most of the duties once performed by the departed Indian Agent. As salaried employees of Indian Affairs, the central responsibility of members of the Band Council is to administer Indian Affairs public assistance funds. These include, but are not limited to, new housing and housing repair funds, relief, "special needs" monies for emergencies and for occasional purchases of clothing and durable goods, education funds, various special grants for different development projects, and the budgets of the police and fire departments, most of which originate solely from Indian Affairs. The Band Council has also served as the contractor for the houses built on the reserve since the 1990s.

The Band Council selects and pays the members of the school board, which disburses the education funds (in 2001 the chief dissolved the school board for the rest of his term in office and the Band Council administered education directly). Since the Eskasoni band took control of the reserve's school system from Indian Affairs in 1981, the school board has been responsible for hiring and firing teachers, administrators, and other school employees, most of whom are band members.

The chief, with the cooperation of the councillors, hires the staff of the band office, the secretaries, the band manager, the welfare officers, building supervisors and construction workers, the firemen, the police officers, and a utilities worker, as well as snowplow operators, furnace repairmen, washer and dryer mechanics, carpenters, masons, electricians, plumbers, firewood cutters, and the other people who supply goods and services to the band community.

The chief and council also select the administrator of the housing program and, until the 1990s when the band began to perform nearly all construction on the reserve, the contractors who built the houses and who installed water and sewer pipes. The chief and every pair of councillors from each ward controlled separate and equal funds for the construction and repair of houses. Normally, the chief has no control over the award of welfare, housing, and repair monies supplied by Indian Affairs, but at Eskasoni band councillors have allowed the chief to have control over one-sixth of the band's housing funds, so as to stand a better chance of reelection. Some chiefs have also managed to acquire funding sources outside the control of the councillors. Thus, the chief and members of the council decide independently on the allocation of this money. Councillors decide on the distribution of several types of monies. To reduce the effects of politics on the distribution, from 1966 to 2004 both councillors for each ward were supposed to approve grants of money for several purposes, notably new housing.

The above stand as the official duties of the chief and council. However, elected band officials' greatest goal is reelection, since the salaries and other benefits paid them are among the best available on the reserve. To achieve this, they perform their official functions in such a way as to build a system of political patronage, as described below.

The Chief's Functions as Band Leader

In addition to the official functions already mentioned, the members of the band as a whole expect the chief to advance the political interests of the band and the reserve, a responsibility the chief inherited from his aboriginal predecessors, the Grand Council chief and captain. In addition to the general goals discussed below, the chief also responds to complaints directly from band members. The band demands that the chief perform six types of duties on its behalf:

1. *To mediate between band members and external individuals and organizations, and to protect the band and reserve from unwanted outside intrusions.*

Though band members may take legal action in Canadian courts against a non-Indian trespassing on the reserve, the Eskasoni band has allowed the chief authority to decide what should be done with non-band members on the reserve. One councillor running for re-election in 1986 circulated a petition asking that all non-Indians be evicted from the reserve; this, however, turned out to be nothing more than a ploy intended to win votes.

The chief may also restrict the behavior of occasional visitors to the reserve. In one instance the chief prevented a creditor from repossessing a band member's car, even though the creditor had every legal right to repossess the car under the *Indian Act* (the creditor ultimately did repossess; see Legal Case 79). Non-band members also require the chief's permission to speak at band meetings. In one case on another reserve, a Micmac woman received permission from the chief of another band to address a meeting of band members on the chief's reserve. When she began to speak, however, some women present asked her who had given her permission to speak, but before she could answer the women shouted her down. At Eskasoni, a Micmac woman who lived on the reserve spoke, even though she belonged to another band. The chief had not given her permission to speak, but he did not prevent her from making her oration, even though some members of the audience were angry with her for having spoken at their band meeting.

2. *To regulate the use of the reserve and its natural resources.*

Most Micmac dislike the use of any significant amount of reserve resources for the disproportionate benefit of one or a few individuals; for instance, some tell the chief to limit the harvesting of wood, especially when it spoils the natural beauty of the reserve (see Legal Case 64). Conversely, the chief who served from 2000 to 2006 belongs to the lineage that has cut more wood on the reserve by far than any other. Micmac in general have an understandably strong and historical hatred for non-Micmac individuals who make money at their expense. Those band members who wish to cut timber on reserve land are supposed to obtain the chief's permission, though few bother. One man had the chief draw up a letter giving him permission to clear land, written on Band Council stationery and signed by the chief, in case the chief later decided to oppose his logging activities for personal political reasons.

Until the late 1980s, few on the reserve had the equipment necessary to cut much timber. One man, for example, deforested an entire hillside, even though it took him years to do so, carrying one log at the time by hand. Further, until the early 1990s nearly all the timber on the reserve was considered either too young or too inaccessible to be harvested economically. Those who wanted to cut large amounts bought stumpage off of the reserve. In 1986 and 1987 only two individuals cut large amounts of wood off the reserve. Fewer than a dozen cut small amounts of wood on the reserve; two or three cut firewood for sale, mostly to the band and band members, and the rest selectively cut pulpwood for sale to a pulpmill. In the early 1990s lumberjacks cut the entire northeastern part of the reserve after one outfit pushed a road through (see Dispute Case 56).

3. *To acquire economic aid from outside of the reserve.*

As sole representative of the band to the federal government, this is the chief's primary duty. It includes increasing the budgets for welfare grants, employment, education, and for the improvement of the reserve's physical plant, such as roads, buildings, and utilities, among others. The incumbent chief used the following list of aid given to the band in 1984 through 1986 as an advertisement in his 1986 bid for reelection. Some of what the band received, however, had more to do with previously established Indian Affairs programs than with the chief's efforts. Moreover, some of these forms of assistance, although promised, have not yet been delivered by Indian Affairs. The list includes: a new water supply system, completion of the sewer main, paving of roads, 34 new houses, housing repairs, an alcohol and drug rehabilitation center, a new welfare office, a new band office (planned), a water line for two streets, and street lights.

Also on this list is money for welfare, special needs (unusual expenses), adult care (care of the elderly), and the payment of fuel and electricity for senior citizens during the winter months. It also mentions an education budget of Can$6.7 million, which pays for the operation of the reserve school, for students to attend maritime colleges and universities, and for students to attend local high schools. Further, it includes the creation of an economic development corporation that has invested in one band enterprise, a planned industrial park, and a plan for development of a tourist park, as well as programs for 20 people trained in computer use, 20 people trained to rehabilitate older houses for more efficient heating fuel use, four people trained to understand economic development, four people trained in research and survey techniques, three people trained to manage housing, and 28 people trained in silvicultural techniques.

The chief makes most of the decisions as to what new programs and goals the band will pursue, such as the construction of a day care center or new water supply system.

4. *To ensure that the band administration functions as it should.*

The chief hires competent workers and fires those who do not do their jobs properly. The chief who hires on the basis of a combination of competence and political patronage generally acquires the most popular support.

5. *To take responsibility for handling complaints about how the Band Council performs its functions and especially how the Band Council spends its money on its populace.*

The chief has the unenviable job of fielding numerous requests from band members for new houses, house repairs, monies to start businesses, and jobs. These requests arrive frequently and constitute perhaps the most time-consuming aspect of the position. A good chief or, at least, one who wishes to earn reelection, must balance the amount of money available to him, the genuine needs of the people, and the political repercussions of denying aid to powerful political supporters.

6. *To receive requests from band members to help adjudicate or resolve civil disputes between band members, as discussed below.*

The chief tries to remain uninvolved in such matters, but does decide some of these cases.

Strategies in Electoral Politics

THE CHIEF'S AND COUNCILLORS' CONTROL OVER VOTERS

The rewards of office for chiefs and councillors consist not only of high salary and prestige, but also the opportunity to put their own names, and those of relatives and friends, at the head of lists for employment and for public aid such as housing, special needs, business grants, and loans.

The chief and councillors have used their authority from the performance of official duties to build a powerful, yet vincible, system of political patronage. They reward their political supporters with employment, new houses, and financial benefits, while those who do not support them at the polls usually receive only that assistance to which Indian Affairs guidelines specifically entitle them. In short, the members of the Band Council make political contracts with band members, exchanging goods and services for votes. Virtually all Micmac rely exclusively on the Band Council for such things as housing, housing repairs, and additions, as well as for major appliances and children's clothing. After one election, a woman who supported the re-elected chief and councillors nevertheless bemoaned the fate of those who had voted against them, saying, "A lot of people are going to get nothing." Therefore, candidates for office use political patronage in particular to win election. As members of the boards of directors of several public agencies that benefit the Micmac, chiefs also receive generous per diem payments to attend directors' meetings.

Some of the Nova Scotia Micmac chiefs have direct financial and political control of several public agencies, each of which serves the entire Nova Scotia Micmac population. These include an agency that grants loans for economic development, one that protects abused children, a provincial Micmac newspaper (now defunct), a drug and alcohol rehabilitation program, an education program, and others. The chiefs of Nova Scotia, until recently united as the board of directors of the (now essentially defunct) Union of Nova Scotia Indians (UNSI), operate several smaller subagencies as well. The chiefs of each and every Nova Scotia band constitute the boards of directors for these agencies, most of which are funded exclusively by Indian Affairs. Together these agencies employ more than 100 people. Any one chief's control over an agency derives not only from his voting seat on the board, but through his band's control over a portion of the agency's funds. Indian Affairs allocates funds for the agencies to the individual bands on a proportionate, per capita basis, and gives control over those funds to the individual Band Councils. Eskasoni, whose population approaches one-third that of the total Nova Scotia Micmac population, thus controls nearly one-third of the funds allocated by Indian Affairs for each agency's budget. This gives the chief of Eskasoni, again with the compliance of his councillors, great financial leverage in compelling an agency's administrators to accede to his wishes in hiring and firing practices.

On the other hand, the chief also rewards talented and capable individuals with employment, no matter their political history. This he does to make his administration run efficiently and to attempt to enlist the political loyalties of talented opponents, especially those widely respected in the community.

One key aspect of the Eskasoni chief's political strategy is to make the Band Council an indispensable source of income for band members. For most people, this means relief (welfare) checks for various things, including basic support, or a job financed or otherwise controlled by the Band Council. He especially strives to control large economic development projects, because it is through his control of these that he can reward his supporters with jobs.

Because the chief has a finite amount of aid to give, he tends to reward the larger, more solidary lineages. Individuals who do not have many kin typically receive little or nothing, whatever their political preference; whichever way they vote, they will not likely change the outcome of an election. As one Micmac woman who had been repeatedly passed over for housing assistance told me, "the big families get everything." Micmac often refer to these large solidary lineages in English as "the big families"; the Micmac terms for family, kin, or lineage are *nikmaq* ("my family [kin or lineage]"), *kikmaq* ("your family [kin or lineage]"), and so on. Thus, the modern imposed political system has strengthened the importance of the lineage. Perhaps as a result of this, bilateral kinship relations have become less important, seen in the fact that Micmac language terms for various kin are rapidly falling into disuse, even though other parts of the Micmac vocabulary survive.

Each major lineage has a leader who is a political leader, the legal authority over disputes within the lineage, and the spokesperson for the lineage. Generally speaking, the patriarch (or occasionally the matriarch in cases of dominant women and widows) of the extended family or descent group makes sure that the other members of the family vote for the family's benefactor. This represents a concrete example of one aspect of Micmac loyalty: if the politician grants material favors, the entire lineage or extended family is expected to reciprocate with its votes. In a few cases, a parent has been known to expel an offspring from the house, temporarily at least, for voting against his or her wishes (see Legal Case 44).

Politicians call those individuals who promise a candidate their votes, usually to receive some promise of material aid, but do not deliver them, "backstabbers." Likewise, many individuals will not vote for a candidate unless he gives or promises them aid before the election. One man who belongs to a tiny lineage that cannot deliver many votes, and therefore who never received aid from the long-time incumbent chief, always voted against him because "he never gave me so much as a nail."

As time has gone on, the politically privileged and powerful have gained more and more power at the expense of the politically unprivileged (see especially Chapter 6, Legal Change 9). While political privilege can wax or wane and any number of political circumstances can benefit the unprivileged, the only good hope for most of the unprivileged to acquire housing is a close election for the office of chief. In such as case, the incumbent chief may borrow money to build many new houses, in hopes of acquiring every possible vote.

The political contest itself can be extremely contentious. If one decides not to vote for the chief, or an incumbent councillor, one had better vote for an opponent and hope that he or she is elected, to have any chance of receiving discretionary assistance from the Band Council over the next two years. For this reason, virtually everyone eligible to vote does; those very few who abstain almost always do so because they are equally friendly with two or more of the candidates, rather than because of apathy. Because the chief in the past controlled less of the wealth directly available to the individual band members than the councillors, some people disenchanted with the political process did not vote for the chief, but did vote for the councillors, who could more effectively render assistance. Presently, the chief has acquired, through various means, control of his own funds, with which he can reward supporters.

The Chief's Control Over Councillors

A particularly important part of the chief's patronage scheme involves control over the councillors, which may be great. Chiefs derive their power from the control they have over the band's financial affairs and from their unique position as the middleman between the band and Indian Affairs. Generally speaking, councillors stand a better chance of achieving re-election and personal profit by cooperating with a popular chief than by opposing him. The chief sometimes makes a political alliance with a councillor by using his considerable popularity to help a councillor to obtain re-election, in return for the councillor's cooperation in other political matters. Of course, should public opinion turn against the chief, those with whom he is allied generally face political difficulties as well, as occurs from time to time.

The chief also has final say over much of the aid that councillors may give to recipients, as seen in the following case.

POLITICAL CASE 2

Defendant: A lame-duck councillor.
Authority: The chief.
Date: 1986.

Facts: After the 1986 election, one lame-duck councillor used his remaining days in office to write purchase orders for building supplies for himself and for his relatives and friends.

Outcome: So that the councillor did not put the band into debt for a long time, and thus limit the band's ability to help people in need, the chief ended the councillor's spending spree by telling the building supply store to reject that particular councillor's purchase orders.

The most important means that the chief has to restrict the actions of councillors is his control of most of the employment on the reserve. Bands receive public assistance programs of many types from federal agencies. Most federal agencies communicate with the chief alone on such matters, rather than with the Band Council as a whole, probably for reasons of convenience. The chief thus acquires sole control of many employment positions, which he may use to reward his political supporters, or which he gives to councillors to give to their own relatives or supporters in turn. In this way councillors become politically indebted to the chief. The following example shows how the chief takes control of employment opportunities.

POLITICAL CASE 3

Party: N, a young, unemployed man.
Authority: The chief.
Date: 1987.

Facts: A new training program had been set up for some of the young men of several bands. The trainees were to be paid a wage during the course of the program that was far more than the relief payment that they would otherwise receive. The director of the program, a man belonging to another band, chose N for inclusion in the program.

Outcome: A short while later, the director told N that he would no longer be included. The chief had taken control of all positions available to his band and had handed them out to supporters.

Why Political Patronage Survives

This system of political patronage survives largely because Nova Scotia, and particularly its Indian reserves, suffers from economic depression. There are few job opportunities for reserve residents; most Micmac lack extensive formal education, and some off-reserve employers hold biases favoring white job applicants. Furthermore, many Micmac have little interest in employment off the reserve and dislike working amidst non-Micmac people. Most of the business concerns created as a result of economic development projects on the reserve have not succeeded, with the notable exception of a band-operated fishing business established in the late 1990s. The few private enterprises that Micmac individuals have created and run successfully are small and cannot hire many workers. This leaves most people dependent on federal aid programs, which the Band Council administers. So far as the voters are concerned, money and jobs constitute the single most important electoral issue facing the band. In short, the chief and council have little reason to change the basic contractual arrangement of giving aid or employment in exchange for votes. Thus, this situation will likely remain until widespread prosperity arrives in the Maritimes.

Band Council Law at Eskasoni

Introduction: Politics and the Application of Law

Before discussing Eskasoni Band Council law itself, it is important to describe the general attitude of the Micmac to those legal authorities who also have political authority. Political influence may be found in many of the legal decisions of authorities, as seen in the following.

LEGAL CASE 20

Party: An Eskasoni softball team.
Authority: A Micmac board regulating the summer games.
Date: Nova Scotia Indian Summer Games, 1987.
Location: A mainland Nova Scotia reserve.

Facts: This Eskasoni team, one of several at the tournament, had been doing well in the competition. One evening, the supervisory board administering the tournament decided to move up the time of the Eskasoni team's next game to early the next morning. Though the new time was posted, the team was having a party at the time and nobody informed them of the change. The members of the team arrived at the field the next day at the originally scheduled time, only to find that they had lost the game by default due to tardiness. The team appealed the decision to the board.

Outcome: Those board members who are members of and represented mainland Nova Scotia bands, and who thus were already rivals of the Cape Bretoners, predictably voted against the Eskasoni team's appeal. The board member from Eskasoni also voted against the Eskasoni team and this angered the members of the team, who believed that he should have voted in their favor in support of the band. But the Eskasoni band member on the board sat on the other side of the Eskasoni political fence from the members of the Eskasoni team, and thus the team should not have been too surprised at the vote.

In short, in cases in which Micmac authorities decide disputes among Micmac people, it is often not a case of whether a decision is political or legal, but rather of which political interest it will reflect.

However, a great many cases show that the Micmac often attempt to avoid political influence in legal decisions. Leaders sometimes avoid political influence by choosing socially external, non-Micmac authorities, as in the following examples. In the 1980s, the Micmac frequently held softball tournaments in the summer and hockey tournaments in the winter. The larger tournaments feature competition among many teams representing several bands. For these tournaments, the Micmac Band Councils hire non-Indian referees. Few of the players would trust a Micmac referee to render fair decisions. Even if the referee were a member of a band uninvolved in the competition, he would not be trusted because his band may be friendly towards several of the competing bands, and less friendly towards others.

During the biannual Micmac Princess Pageants, one of which is held at the Nova Scotia Indian Summer Games and another at each of the winter carnivals that take place on most reserves, girls of about 16 years of age compete on their abilities, talents, and appearance. Those running the event choose the judges; in some years, community members act as judges, but in other years pageant administrators recruit people from outside the community specifically to avoid personal biases.

The Eskasoni Band Council's Legal Authority

When the first bona fide *Indian Act* Band Council took office in Eskasoni in 1957, it acquired control over monies given them by the Canadian federal government. With their status as the only political body in Eskasoni to enjoy federal recognition, the Band Council usurped the leadership and authority roles that had once belonged to the Grand Council.

Although the police and Royal Canadian Mounted Police enforce the Canadian *Criminal Code* and the province's traffic statutes, and the Canadian courts try the cases, the chief and council have made a considerable amount of law at Eskasoni in the decades since 1957, some of it beyond the scope provided by the *Indian Act*. Most of this law pertains to real property (see Part IV, Real Property Law under the Modern Band Council).

All groups experience civil disputes, and the Eskasoni Micmac are no exception. The Eskasoni Band Council avoids dealing with such disputes for two reasons. First is the tradition, inherited from the Grand Council, of leaving the resolution of civil disputes to the parties themselves. Second, the Band Council is chosen politically and functions politically, and all members of the community acknowledge this. Most people in the reserve regard the Band Council members as politically biased, and therefore undesirable as a legal authority. Furthermore, band members commonly assume modern Micmac authorities will render their decisions on the grounds of political interest and personal self-interest, rather than as disinterested third parties acting on the basis of just legal principles. Whether or not this understanding always accurately reflects reality is debatable. Certainly it is true at times, and just as certainly authorities make unbiased judgments. As one band councillor told me concerning civil disputes: "No matter how I decide, someone is going to accuse me of favoritism." Another band member said that "everything on the reserve is political." On the other hand, many voters desire and even rely on bias in their leaders, so long as that bias favors them above others.

Despite the political bias, some parties to disputes either feel that they have nowhere else to turn to resolve the dispute, or are willing to take a chance that the case will be decided in their favor, and so ask the Band Council to adjudicate. For its part, the Band Council sees any role as adjudicator as a political liability. The chief and many of the councillors spend some of their time away from the reserve, and are incommunicado much of the time that they are on the reserve. One councillor rented a camping trailer and left her house. Another had his wife answer the door and tell visiting constituents that he was asleep, even in the middle of the day. This behavior is an attempt to avoid having to make legal decisions, as well as a way to avoid having to refuse the many requests for the limited amount of aid that the councillors have to give away. Making legal decisions in civil cases and denying requests for aid can cost future political support by offending present and potential supporters. A general Micmac ideal of behavior (see Table 1), not to become involved in others' disputes, also applies to modern Band Council legal authorities. The chief and council only hear real property cases involving disputes between individual band members reluctantly, and then always decide in favor of the resident, thereby almost always preserving the status quo (see Part IV).

Efforts to regulate civil social problems on the reserve often bring the chief and council more ingratitude and political opposition than appreciation. In 1972, for example, a great many feral, semi-feral and semi-domesticated dogs ran in packs around the reserve, frightening people, upending trash cans, and chasing deer. Many of these dogs suffered from malnutrition and disease. The Band Council decided to act after receiving many complaints. It ruled that on the day of the round up that all dogs not confined or licensed would be destroyed. After the round up, several people protested vehemently that their pets had been killed. Some owners had neglected to confine their animals, some had claimed ownership of dogs that habitually ran freely, and some others did not wish to pay the small licensing fee. In any case, the killing caused a great public outcry against the Band Council. Since then little effort has been made to curb the population of feral and semi-feral dogs, and their number has again grown. As late as the late 1990s, the Band Council continued to experience strong opposition to dog control, but at the same time also received many complaints about the feral animals. The Band Council has for some years now selectively killed individual problem animals, using humane and very unobtrusive methods.

When they do concede to adjudicate civil cases, the Band Council often creates toothless sanctions, as seen in the following case.

LEGAL CASE 21

First party: A Micmac woman.
Second party: Her female neighbor.
Authority: The Band Council.
Date: 1967.

Facts: The two parties had a disagreement. The second party, as a result, would hurl insults and physical objects at the first party whenever she walked by. The first party asked the Band Council to stop the harassment.

Outcome: The Band Council wrote the second party a letter that instructed her to cease her harassment. It was to no avail. The first party later reported to the Band Council that the second party continued to harass her. The Band Council replied that they could do no more and that they would take no further action.

In all instances, the Band Council seeks to minimize its own involvement in civil disputes between band members, and indeed all who are present on the reserve. In Legal Case 75, for example, though the chief made a decision that limited the activities of a white missionary on the reserve, he had a man who was a councillor and a policeman deliver the decision to the missionary, thus reducing his own involvement. In Legal Case 85, one party to a civil dispute telephoned Indian Affairs for help, at which an Indian Affairs administrator became angry with the Band Council for failing to take authority in the dispute. Again, the Band Council limited its own authority so as to avoid political backlash. The Band Council's avoidance of civil disputes between band members (and others) is part of its political strategy; deciding a case can result in at least one of the parties angry with the decision and who may vote against the authority in the next election. This stance by the Band Council also accords with Behavioral Postulate 3 and Behavioral Corollaries C, D, and E (see Table 1).

Summary

Within a relatively short time the modern Micmac have experienced two massive and wrenching changes in their political leadership and authority. When the Grand Council's authority and leadership gave way to that of the Indian Agent, and in turn to the Band Council, the Eskasoni government changed its goals, its means of achieving its goals, and the type of people in charge.

The thread common to almost all Micmac leaders has been the bestowing of material benefits on their followers. The Grand Council was an exception to this pattern; it gave its followers no material wealth, but did provide leadership of a very high moral caliber, one sincerely aimed at maintaining or improving the moral and physical well being of the Micmac people of Cape Breton. The Grand Council consisted of men of probity who governed with law and justice foremost in mind. Because of this justness, people emulated them, followed their examples, and accepted their judgments and advice. Further, because their members normally occupied their offices for life, they could make decisions insulated from personal political concerns.

The Indian Agent, by contrast, ruled through the use of naked federal authority (described below). His superiors charged him with changing many of the physical conditions of Eskasoni life. Of course, the Indian Agent had only to satisfy his superiors in Indian Affairs, who had appointed him. His failure to pay heed to Micmac concepts of justice earned him the enmity of many band members. However, different Indian Agents had different relationships with the Micmac people collectively and individually, and some have enjoyed long personal friendships with Micmac.

The Band Council, like the Grand Council, also cares about the moral standards of the band (see Legal Cases 56, 114, 115, 117, 119, and 120), but its members' overriding concern is re-election. To achieve this, they use political patronage. Those candidates for re-election who best use their economic power, gained from the federal government, to reward political supporters are usually re-elected. Though many band members wish that the Band Council would govern with the ideals of justice that the Grand Council espoused, such a system is incompatible with the practice of voting for the candidates who provide economic benefit. In short, band politics is often a one-issue affair, and that issue is money. The Grand Council governed primarily with legal authority and persuasion, while the Band Council governs primarily through the use of political authority.

Analysis and Summary of Legal Systems

Analysis

One useful analysis of the various government systems described above is to examine the differences between them in their observance of Micmac behavioral ideals (see Table 1), as a means of assessing their relative degrees of justness. This analysis does not include an examination of the Indian Agent as a legal authority, because the Indian Agent never held an interest in conforming to these ideals, nor did he have any great reason to want to do so. At the family/descent group level, authorities differ widely in their observance of these ideals. The ability at this level to exercise authority contrary to behavioral ideals depends largely on the economic dependence of offspring and other descendants. If the descendants rely on the patriarch or matriarch for economic subsistence, then they are more or less forced to accept the authority of their parents, grandparents, and other relatives. Welfare assistance often undermines this authority by allowing young people to have their own houses. Many escape parental and grandparental authority by living away from the rest of the family. In some instances, because of a housing shortage, the welfare office will pay for young parents to live in apartments off the reserve, thereby further eroding parental control.

Unlike law at the family level, law at the Grand Council level rarely operated by coercion. The Grand Council enjoyed a popular mandate to disregard Behavioral Postulate 3 and Corollaries C, D, and E (see Table 1) concerning the adjudication of offenses, because people saw it as acting in favor of the interests of the entire Cape Breton Micmac population, and because it was important that someone stop crime. On the other hand, its own followers forbade the Grand Council from interfering in civil cases. The Micmac of Cape Breton willingly allowed themselves to be led by the Grand Council, so long as the Grand Council made popular and just decisions. If it did not, its authority declined (see Legal Case 10 and Dispute Case 4).

The Band Council, on the other hand, may not disregard Micmac behavioral ideals with impunity, since it is regarded as a partisan political group whose interests coincide with those of many band members most of the time, but not of all and not all of the time. Further, the federal police (RCMP) and the tribal police control much of the violent criminal activity, and so the Band Council avoids taking part in this function. As a result, in civil cases between private parties the Band Council either avoids adjudication, takes no action (see Legal Cases 66, 67, and 71), hands out very weak sanctions (see Legal Cases 21 and 54), or depends on the willingness of the parties to accept the decision (see Legal Cases 40, 55, 68, and 69). The Band Council actively seeks to prosecute and adjudicate only those cases involving disputes between the Band Council and private individuals and groups. These are the only cases for which the Band Council supplies coercive sanctions, and which band members can effectively oppose only during elections (see, for example, Legal Cases 57, 60, 61, 76, 94, 101, and 103, and Political Cases 7 and 8).

Summary

The legal systems at the four legal levels described above differ greatly in their laws, in their goals, and in their sanctions. The legal systems at the family/descent group level make criminal and civil rules designed to encourage offspring to behave properly. Their sanctions include verbal admonishment, corporal punishment (such as spanking) for younger children, and denial of real property rights (discussed later). There is considerable variation in legal systems at this level.

The Grand Council used law to reduce strife that threatened social integrity and to maintain a high moral standard of behavior. The Grand Council made and enforced only criminal laws and avoided civil disputes. Some cases that our legal system might treat as civil disputes were handled as criminal ones by the Grand Council (see Legal Cases 6 and 13). It used primarily psychological sanctions, and even apparently physical sanctions were intended to provide more of a psychological than physical effect (see Legal Cases 5, 6, 7, 11, and 12).

Like the Grand Council, the Indian Agent took far less interest in civil offenses than criminal ones, though this was largely because he felt that civil disputes between band members rarely warranted his attention. Many of the rules he applied on the reserve conformed to those applied to Canada as a whole, even though the Eskasoni band members felt many of these to be unjust, usually because the Canadian laws prohibited actions that the Micmac felt hurt no one but the party involved, and should therefore not be prohibited (Legal Cases 26, 27, 28, and 38).

In addition to the principles that they applied in their decisions, the Grand Council differed from the Indian Agent in that the former used almost entirely psychological sanctions, and its economic sanctions were restitutive (see Legal Cases 6 and 10), while the Indian Agent relied on coercive physical sanctions and used punitive economic sanctions rather than restitutive ones (see Legal Cases 26, 27, 28, and 29).

The law that the Band Council creates contrasts enormously with that of its predecessors. The Band Council concerns itself primarily with disputes between itself and band members. The Band Council uses economic sanctions in cases in which a band member reneges on a political contract (see Legal Cases 57, 61, and 80). The Band Council takes little interest in offenses to the Canadian *Criminal Code* (except when committed by non-band members, as discussed in Part IV); these are handled by the Royal Canadian Mounted Police, the band's constabulary (by the 1990s, full-fledged members of the RCMP), the Canadian court system, and especially through extralegal social control, primarily ostracism, revenge, social withdrawal, and territorial defense (see below). However, like the Grand Council, the Band Council is reluctant to involve itself in civil disputes between private parties, so as to maintain its political power. It is asked to adjudicate many such disputes, and often does, but hands out such weak sanctions that it frequently depends on the willingness of the parties to accept its decisions voluntarily (Legal Cases 21, 40, 55, 58, 66, 67, 69, 71, 89, 94, 97, and 98).

Because the Micmac find it financially difficult to leave their own reserves, those who live on reserves cannot easily escape the jurisdiction of their Band Councils, as they had traditionally been able to escape the control of those legal authorities with whom they disagreed, including the Grand Council (Legal Case 10).

The Grand Council and the Band Council represent two greatly different types of authority. Their purposes differed enormously as well: the Grand Council tried to control social friction internal to the society and ignored disputes over land, whereas the Band Council has largely ignored internal social disputes and has, from a legal standpoint at least, concentrated almost solely on the control of real property ownership and use (see Part IV), so as to manipulate them for both the common good and political self-interest. The bodies of law the two authorities developed bear this difference out. Further, the laws developed by the Grand Council dealt only with criminal matters; those developed by the Band Council deal primarily with the legal relationship between private individuals and the Band Council itself. Even more important than the scope or application of the laws developed by the two authorities are the functions of the laws of the two systems, as will be seen.

Part III:

Real Property Law Before the Band Council System

CHAPTER FOUR

Land Tenure at the Band Level: Hunting Territories

The next four chapters describe and analyze the Micmac land tenure systems that exist or have existed at three separate legal levels. In addition, I describe and analyze the changes that have occurred in these systems over time. These preceded the Band Council land tenure system, and provide the context from which, and in which, the Band Council system developed. The Grand Council does not appear here because its legal system did not deal with real property rights; the Grand Council did not decide civil cases and the Micmac consider land tenure cases to be civil cases (with the exception of trespass by non-band members, as discussed below). The three legal levels I present are those of the family/descent group, the Canadian courts, and the Indian Agent. In addition, I evaluate the evidence for an early system of hunting territories and discuss the significance of real property disputes left unadjudicated.

Evidence suggests the possibility of an early land tenure system, that of individual hunting territories. Although well known among other Northern Algonkians, early historical records provide but one description of a hunting territory system among the Micmac, in the Gaspé:

> It is the right of the head of the nation, according to the customs of the country, which serve as laws and regulations to the Gaspesians, to distribute the places of hunting to each individual. It is not permitted to any Indian to overstep the bounds and limits of the region which shall have been assigned him in the assemblies of the elders. (Le Clercq 1910:238)

We do not know how many *'Saqmaq* may have used such a system or where else it may have existed. Nor do we know whether the *'Saqmaw* mentioned above demarcated the territories with an eye to reducing friction among band members, whether he rewarded favored followers with good territories or punished obstreperous others with poor ones, whether he used the territories to establish or enlarge the geographical limits of his authority, or whether he simply attempted to make the effort of hunting among his followers more efficient. Le Clercq also noted that many Micmac did not follow any *'Saqmaw* because they did not want his help or authority. Did these people participate in a hunting territory system? Did they have any reason to do so?

Further, we know nothing of the way the system worked. How was the territorial system adapted to the need to migrate, or was it ever so adapted? Did parents pass rights in territories to their offspring? Did those who had territories have the right of alienation or were they always assigned by the *'Saqmaw*? How were transgressions of territorial boundaries resolved? These questions will forever go unanswered.

Frank Speck (1922) gave a description of Micmac hunting territories that still elicits scholarly interest today (Chute 1999). Speck claimed to have found a system of hunting territories among the Micmac of mainland Nova Scotia and Cape Breton. Two aspects of the data he presents bring his findings immediately into question, however. First, Speck found a total of 46 hunting territories in mainland Nova Scotia (1922:105) and a further 15 in Cape Breton (1922:110–112). This is an impossibly low number, considering that the Canadian census records the Micmac population of Nova Scotia in 1891 at well over 1,000 people (Appendix A). Prins (1988:261–264) noted a similar discrepancy. He also examined census records, and found many more Micmac who listed their occupation as "hunter" in the census than could be consistent with the number of territories. Moreover, Prins may not have realized that, until World War II and the Centralization Program of the 1940s provided the bulk of the Nova Scotia Micmac population with wage labor jobs for the first time, nearly every Micmac man and adolescent male in Cape Breton hunted for at least a part of his family's food, and not merely the ones listed as hunters by the census. Second, the rigidly geometric boundaries of the territories on Speck's map follow no natural geographic features, as would be expected for actual hunting territories.

Wallis and Wallis (1955:172) also claimed to have found evidence of Micmac hunting territories in 1911, though they relied entirely on hearsay evidence from their informants. One informant said that the chief allotted territories annually; another that he did so every seven years.

The claim that the turn-of-the-century Micmac used hunting territories has three other major deficiencies. One of these is the linguistic evidence. Neither of Silas Rand's Micmac dictionaries (Rand 1888, 1902) mentions any Micmac terms even vaguely synonymous with "hunting territory." Had territories existed, this would have to be considered an unlikely omission considering the great scope and depth of these works.

A second problem concerns migration. Why would people have hunting territories if they migrated? Conversely, why would they migrate if they had hunting territories? Data taken from census returns show that Micmac migrated a great deal at the end of the 19th century (Appendix H). Informants tell me that some of the sites to which people moved were well known as good hunting sites. While this is not proof of an absence of hunting territories, it does suggest that the use of hunting territories would be, to a degree at least, incompatible with the way in which most Micmac people lived at turn of the century.

The third problem derives from data I collected from older Micmac. Cape Breton Micmac old enough to have either used hunting territories when Speck or Wallis and Wallis did their fieldwork, or to have heard about them, all maintained that no such territories did in fact exist. They said that no such thing was necessary, and could think of no reasons why there ever might have been any. The amount of land available to them to hunt was great in comparison to their own numbers and, moreover, game is mobile. What the elders did give me was a good bit of information on specific places where good hunting could be found, and which consequently drew a lot of hunters regularly. The idea that there were places that had a lot of game and that regularly attracted many hunters makes much sense and further argues against the notion of a hunting territory system.

Moreover, the situation commonly found among hunters and gatherers, that in which the best hunters acquire political power through his hunting ability, was absent among the Cape Breton Micmac by the 20th century. By that time, the combination of Micmac traditional hunting skills, European firearms, and European encroachment made the average Micmac hunter capable of wiping out all the big game in his region.

Finally, because the *'Saqmaw* of Cape Breton did not decide civil disputes, and because the Micmac treat all real property disputes as civil disputes, it is difficult to envision how such a system of territories could have been made to work as a legal system among the Cape Breton Micmac.

In sum, there is little concrete evidence available that favors the existence of Nova Scotia Micmac hunting territories since at least the middle of the 19th century, and considerable evidence argues against it.

CHAPTER FIVE

Indian Land Tenure at the National Legal Level: The Imposition of the *Indian Act*

The law that the Canadian courts apply to Indians consists of a set of federal statutes (contained in the *Indian Act*), treaties, special agreements between the federal and provincial governments, general federal and provincial statutes, and common law principles passed down from Great Britain.

This chapter discusses and analyzes those federal statutes that apply to land tenure on Indian reserves, and which are contained within the *Indian Act*.

The *Indian Act*

Before 1867 each colony regulated Indian peoples separately and independently. This regulation consisted primarily of setting aside reserve lands for Indian use and little else; few colonies had much money to spend on Indians, and once the Indians were pacified there was little political will to expend much time or effort on them.

On July 1, 1867, the *British North America Act, 1867* (also known as the *Constitution Act, 1867*) created the Dominion of Canada and gave the Canadian Parliament complete legislative authority over the nation's Indians. Further, it created three major types of statutes that apply to Indians. Since 1868, these statutes have been included in a separate *Indian Act*:

1. Statutes that determine who is and who is not eligible for legal status as an Indian and as a member of an Indian band. Until 1985, the simple rule was that anyone whose natural father was legally Indian was also Indian by law.

2. Statutes that maintain the existence of lands reserved for the exclusive use of Indian bands (Indian reserves) and that regulate the use of those lands.

3. Statutes that regulate the governance of Indians living on reserves.

Analysis of Provisions on Real Property Rights on Indian Reserves: Legal Correlates

The *Indian Act* was originally intended to provide Indians land on which they could live unmolested by non-Indians. To prevent Indians from alienating reserve lands, and to give the Crown a measure of control over their lives, title of ownership remained with the Crown. The *Indian Act* allows Indians rights of residence, and *ususfructus*, on the reserve. Additionally, it grants band members, groups of band members, or the band as a whole the right to lawfully possess surveyed lots on the reserve. However, the rights of lawful possessors of reserve land are less than those normally enjoyed by possessors of off-reserve land under British, Canadian, and U.S. common law.

The *Indian Act* provisions on rights any party may have with respect to reserve lands can be presented simply as an analysis of legal correlates, an analysis developed by Pospisil (1971:315; Figure 2). There are six dimensions of contrastive features that differentiate each type of rightsholder under the *Indian Act* real property statutes. These dimensions are as follows:

Right to expropriate interests in reserve land (yes for eminent domain or yes for Indian welfare). The Crown may take reserve land in an eminent domain procedure. The Minister of Indian Affairs may take reserve land, or any portion of a reserve, if doing so is for the benefit of the Indians of the band, as the Minister may see fit (*Indian Act*, R.S.C. 1985, c. I-5, s. 18(2)).

Right to create zones and to regulate the use of reserve land (yes or no). The Band Council holds sole authority to create special zones within the reserve for regulatory purposes and to otherwise regulate the use of reserve land (*Indian Act*, R.S.C. 1985, c. I-5, s. 81).

Right to remove resources from a reserve (yes or no). Only those with a license from the Minister of Indian Affairs may remove resources from an Indian reserve. Even Indian band members lawfully possessing land on a reserve may not legally remove a stick of wood from their own reserve without this license. (*Indian Act*, R.S.C. 1985, c. I-5, s. 93).

Right to reside on the reserve (yes or no). Only members of an Indian band to whom the reserve has been assigned may legally reside on that reserve (*Indian Act*, R.S.C. 1985, c. I-5, s. 2). People who are not members of a particular band may reside on the reserve assigned to that band only with a license from the Minister of Indian Affairs (*Indian Act*, R.S.C. 1985, c. I-5, s. 28). Though Indians who are not members of that band may not legally reside on that reserve, the *Indian Act* specifically grants Indians the right to allege trespass to authorities on the reserve only in cases involving non-Indians (*Indian Act*, R.S.C. 1985, c. I-5, ss. 30, 31).

*Right of use and benefit (*ususfructus*)* (on allotted land or unallotted land). Only the allottee or lawful possessor may use and benefit from allotted land (*Indian Act*, R.S.C. 1985, c. I-5, ss. 2, 20, 81).

Right to surrender interests in reserve land to Her Majesty (yes or no). Only the band assigned to a reserve may, by a majority vote of those eligible to vote, surrender reserve lands to the Crown (*Indian Act*, R.S.C. 1985, c. I-5, s. 37). The Crown can then sell or lease the land for the band's benefit. This is the only way in which a band can sell or lease reserve land to another party. The band may surrender any of its various interests in reserve lands unconditionally or conditionally, for whatever period of time it wishes (*Indian Act*, R.S.C. 1985, c. I-5, s. 38).

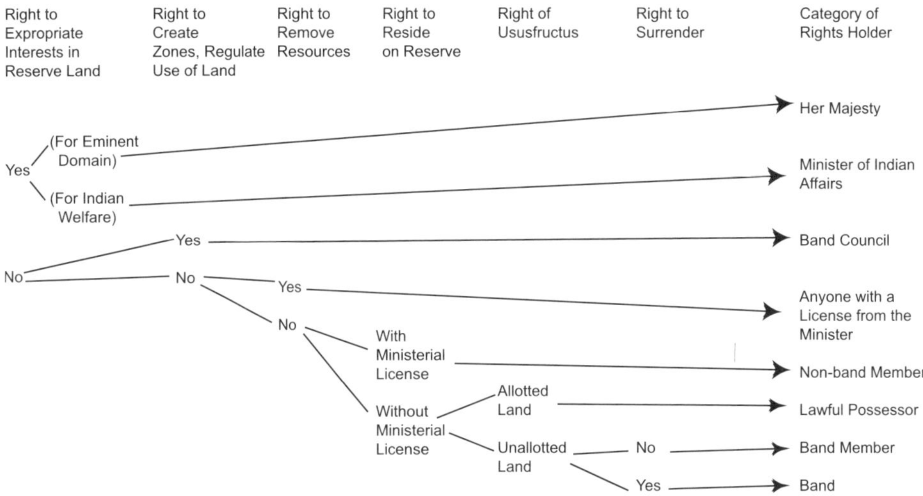

FIGURE 2. Analysis of *Indian Act* real property rule legal correlates. The Canadian government's system of Indian land tenure is represented here diagrammatically in terms of contrastive legal correlates.

Summary

The foregoing shows that the *Indian Act*'s land tenure provisions protect the rights of the band members to reside on and use the reserve. Members of the band may use the natural resources found on the reserve, but may not (except with a license from the Minister) take them from the reserve (and thereby benefit someone other than the band or a band member). The band as a whole must agree to the surrender of interests in reserve land. And, with the exception of people with licenses from the Minister, only band members may occupy a reserve.

Lawful Possession

For band members, the most significant difference in rights in reserve lands under the *Indian Act* lies in the difference between having a right to the lawful possession of a lot (also known as allotment) and merely having the right to reside on reserve land that is not lawfully possessed. Lawful possession refers to the possession by individuals of private land on a reserve. Here, possession is the same as possession under common law, and may be defined as the entitlement to physically hold land and fixtures such as dwellings.

Unless a band member or group of band members lawfully possesses reserve land, the band as a whole possesses it (*Brick Cartage Ltd. v. The Queen*, [1965] 1 Ex.C.R. 102; *Mathias et al. v. Findlay*, [1978] 4 W.W.R. 653, 87 D.L.R. (3d) 239). Indian Affairs and the Canadian courts make a great distinction in the rights a band member may have in lawfully possessed land and in those a band member has in land that is not lawfully possessed, which therefore remains the possession of the band. A later chapter will show that the Eskasoni band's own legal system reduced the rights of lawful possession that the *Indian Act* granted.

History of Lawful Possession

Authorities have set aside lands for Indians in Nova Scotia since 1792, and elsewhere in Canada perhaps earlier. In 1869, the Parliament passed *An Act for the gradual enfranchisement of Indians, the better management of Indian Affairs, and to extend the provisions of the Act 31st Victoria*, Chapter 42 (S.C. 1869, c. 6; 32–33 Victoria). This act amended the previous year's *An Act providing for the organisation of the Department of the Secretary of State of Canada, and for the management of Indian and Ordnance Lands* S.C. 1868, c. 42 (31 Victoria), the first in what has become a long line of acts, each popularly known as the "*Indian Act*."

For the first time, this act (S.C. 1869, c. 6) provided for the lawful possession, and conversely criminal possession, of lands set aside for Indians. Specifically, the act states that:

> In Townships or other tracts of land set apart or reserved for Indians in Canada, and subdivided by survey into lots, no Indian or person claiming to be of Indian blood, or intermarried with an Indian family, shall be deemed to be lawfully in possession of any land in such Townships or Tracts, unless he or she has been or shall be located for the same by the order of the Superintendent General of Indian Affairs; and any such person or persons, assuming possession of lands of that description, shall be dealt with as illegally in possession, and be liable to be summarily ejected therefrom, unless that within six months from the passing of this Act, a location title be granted to such person or persons by the said Superintendent General of Indian Affairs or such officer or person as he may thereunto depute and authorize; but the conferring of any such location title shall not have the effect of rendering the land covered thereby transferable or subject to seizure under legal process. (*An Act for the gradual enfranchisement of Indians,...* S.C. 1869, c. 6, s. 1)

The same act provided that on the death of the lawful possessor, the offspring would have life estates in the lot, and that on their deaths, or in the case of the possessor's not leaving issue, the parcel of land shall vest again in the Crown for the benefit of the band (S.C. 1869, c. 6, s. 9).

The purpose of creating a distinction between lawful and criminal possession on a reserve (though these lands were not so named until later) was obvious: to grant individual Indians private interests in land, and so to settle them as a way of moving them closer to assimilation. Since the first section of the act stipulates that, when the reserve is surveyed into lots, the occupants must have a location title to possess land lawfully, and because Indians, unless owning land personally, would be liable to trespass charges on land other than a reserve, the *Indian Act* created a powerful reason to settle: either the Indian did so, or he faced ejectment.

Many Indians, if not most, did not face this possibility, because their reserves were not surveyed into lots until much later. On the Cape Breton reserves, Indian Affairs did not begin the lengthy and as yet unfinished process of drawing lots until the 1960s.

If the early *Indian Act* attempted to punish those who fought assimilation, then it rewarded those who enfranchised. Enfranchisement here refers to the exchange of legal status as an Indian for that of an ordinary Canadian citizen. For the individual, it meant that the *Indian Act* would no longer apply to him or her, that he or she would no longer be able to reside on lands set aside for Indians, would no longer be exempt from the payment of taxes, and would no longer be able to take advantage of the special material and financial aid given to Indians by the government. But by enfranchising, the individual would acquire rights prohibited to Indians (until about 1960), notably the rights to purchase or consume alcoholic beverages and for men (and later women) to vote in Canadian elections.

Those men who enfranchised acquired as a reward rights in land. A man who wanted to be enfranchised (and who had reached a certain "level of civilization") would be issued a Letters Patent for the land to which he had already been allotted or would be allotted (S.C. 1869, c. 6, ss. 13, 14, 16, 17). By authority of these sections, the enfranchisee would acquire a life estate in the lot described by the Letters Patent.

The enfranchisee was able to pass his life estate to any of his children by will, and to all of his children according to provincial laws in cases of intestacy; the child or children receiving their father's interest in this way would have a fee simple interest in the lot.

In brief, then, the creation of the distinction of lawful possession of lands among lands set aside for the use of Indians was to settle the Indians of Canada, most of whom were highly migratory, and to hasten the process of assimilation. And whereas today lawful possession gives an Indian greater rights in the land he occupies, in 1869 the new distinction deprived some Indians of the use of lands that had been set aside for the exclusive use of Indians. The penalty applied to Indians for residing on a reserve without having lawful possession of a lot, ejectment, later disappeared from the statutes.

In *An Act to Amend and consolidate the laws respecting Indians* (S.C. 1876, c. 18; 39 Victoria), an early *Indian Act*, the legislation concerning lawful possession changed substantially. Most importantly, the band (with the approval of the Superintendent General of Indian Affairs) gained the right to determine who may or may not receive a location ticket. In other words, the band could now control, for any reason, those Indians who were allowed to reside on the lands where they had settled, and those who were not.

Also, the lawful possessor could now transfer his location ticket, with the permission of an elected Band Council and the Superintendent General, to another member of the band (S.C. 1876, c. 18, s. 8). The 1876 *Act* further specified new inheritance rules: the interest of the deceased devolved one third to the widow and two thirds to the children equally; should there be no nuclear family members living, the ticket would devolve to the nearest living relative.

Finally, the 1876 *Act* provided that an Indian without lawful possession of a lot who is removed from the lands set aside for the use of Indians must be compensated for improvements by the Indian assuming possession of the lot, or from band funds, as the Superintendent General may decide.

An Act to Amend and consolidate the laws respecting Indians (S.C. 1880, c. 28) altered the wording regarding who has and does not have lawful possession on a reserve. It removed the stipulation that the reserve must be surveyed into lots before any one resident can be deemed either to have lawful possession or not. It states simply that:

> No one shall be deemed to be lawfully in possession of any land in a reserve, unless he or she has been or shall be located for the same by the band or council of the band, with the approval of the Superintendent General. (S.C. 1880, c. 28, s. 17)

The reason behind this change is unclear. It left many Indians living on reserves without lawful possession of the lands they occupied, because their reserves had not been surveyed into subdivisions. Certainly, the Canadian government did not remove those who were now not in lawful possession in undivided reserves. Perhaps they intended lawful possession, and its attendant rights, as a reward for more assimilated Indians with commercial or agricultural realty. Or perhaps legislators reasoned that because the reserves had been set aside for Indians, and no Indians on the undivided reserves could have lawful possession, there could not be both lawful and unlawful possession of the same land, and thus no criminal possession. These are only speculations. In any event, the legislators retained provision for the dispossession of those without lawful possession.

In 1951, the Canadian Parliament again altered the rules concerning lawful possession on an Indian reserve, to a form essentially the same as that applied today; the document that accomplished this, *An Act respecting Indians* (*Indian Act,* S.C. 1951, c. 29), also changed the name of the physical evidence of lawful possession from "location ticket" to "Certificate of Possession," or simply "CP," as it is popularly known.

One of the new features of the 1951 *Indian Act* is temporary lawful possession.

> Where possession of land in a reserve has been allotted to an Indian by the council of the band, the Minister may, in his discretion, withhold his approval and may authorize the Indian to occupy the land temporarily and may prescribe the conditions as to use and settlement that are to be fulfilled by the Indian before the Minister approves of the allotment. (*Indian Act,* S.C. 1951, c. 29, s. 20(4))

> Whenever a Certificate of Possession or Occupation was, in the opinion of the Minister, issued to or in the name of the wrong person, through mistake, or contains any clerical error or misnomer, or wrong description of any material fact therein the Minister may cancel the Certificate and issue a corrected Certificate in lieu thereof. (*Indian Act,* S.C. 1951, c. 29, s. 26)

The new provisions gave the Minister greater power to grant, transfer, or cancel Certificates of Possession. This meant that the Minister could guide the use of the lot and the industry of the possessor by exerting control over the status of the Certificate of Possession. Section 20(4) shows that the Parliament regarded allotment as a privilege, which it intended to motivate industriousness. I have not, however, seen any evidence that the Minister has ever made any use of these powers with respect to Eskasoni.

An Indian living on a reserve acquired a means to redress any erroneously assigned lawful possession causing injury (*Indian Act,* S.C. 1951, c. 29, s. 26). Errors can occur when a Band Council inadvertently gives lawful possession to person A, who occupies lot A, but the legal description on the Certificate of Possession is for lot B, occupied by individual B. Unless corrected by the Minister, this situation would give person A the right to take possession of realty occupied by individual B or even force him to leave. In fact, however, the Department of Indian Affairs and Northern Development has given the elected Band Councils as a whole determinative power over who has, and who does not have, lawful possessory interests in reserve lands (see Legal Case 73).

The 1951 *Indian Act* stipulated that those Indians who enfranchised no longer received Letters Patent for their lawfully possessed lots; instead, it forced them to transfer those lots to another member of the band or to the band itself if they left the reserve, because as non-Indians they no longer had the right as band members to live on a reserve. This preserved the boundaries of the reserve, but must have made the option of enfranchisement much less attractive.

The last alteration in the rules on lawful possession came in 1985 (*Indian Act,* R.S.C. 1970, c. I-6, as amended by R.S.C. 1985, c. 27), when all sections pertaining to enfranchisement were found by the courts to offend the 1981 Canadian Bill of Rights and were repealed (Hawley 1986:75). This is significant only in that the procedures for releasing interests as a lawful possessor on enfranchisement no longer apply.

Allotment and the Housing Program

After the end of the Centralization Program in 1949, and through the foreseeable future, Indian Affairs has given the superintendents of each agency, and later each band, a sum of money based on the population of each band, so that annually houses could be built for destitute band members. A per capita formula determined that *x* number of houses would be built for every *y* number of band members each year (the proportion has changed over the years).

Until 1985, many band members complained that the money supplied for each house was insufficient to complete construction; there might not be any plasterboard on the wall studs, for example, or linoleum on the floors, and there was never a floor in the basement.

In 1985, the Eskasoni Band Council decided to take advantage of an option presented by Indian Affairs to allow the Canada Mortgage and Housing Corporation (CMHC) to finance the band's housing projects. This made most of the people living on the reserve very happy, because the CMHC provided more money for the construction of each new house than did Indian Affairs, and it required that the houses be built to code, meaning that they must be more or less completed and constructed in accordance with the latest construction regulations. Further, because complete housing packages were purchased from national building supply chains, the houses were completed down to the lighting fixtures, living room carpet, and vinyl siding.

Under the current arrangement, the money that previously had gone to building the house shell and foundation now applies to the down payment for the house. The mortgages run for 25 years, and payments differ according to the cost of the particular model of house, falling in the range of Can$250 to Can$300 or more per month. Over the past few years, moreover, Indian Affairs has given additional funds to those bands who make the most efficient use of their housing funds. By 1996, the Band Council and Indian Affairs had built more than 200 of these new houses at Eskasoni.

Indian Affairs provides funding for on-reserve housing. The CMHC, in turn, provides loans to individuals for housing. Indian Affairs and CMHC administer on-reserve housing programs under the *National Housing Act* (R.S., c. N-10, s. 98) and under the Indian On Reserve Housing Regulation. CMHC makes loans to individual Indians, and Indian Affairs guarantees to CMHC the repayment of the loans. It also requires the band's permission to take band funds if an individual borrower defaults on a loan. The band requires, in turn, that the borrower agree to cancellation of his or her Certificate of Possession for the period of the mortgage and to vacate the house on default. Otherwise, if a lawful possessor built a CMHC house on his property, the band, Indian Affairs, and the CMHC would have no way to force mortgage payments, because none of these parties could foreclose on the mortgage and take possession of the house. If the borrower has no Certificate of Possession, a 1988 amendment to Section 89 of the *Indian Act* allows the band to sue the borrower for compensation. In 1999, Indian Affairs was at work on a way to allow lawful possessors to keep both their Certificates of Possession and their mortgages, on the principle that possessors take better care of the houses than those who have less of a legal interest in them. Now, Certificates of Possession are suspended until the mortgage is paid.

This legislation allows lending institutions to recoup their losses. In Nova Scotia, where most Indians rely on relief, such a lending policy makes little sense. Instead, in that province Indian Affairs and the Band Councils made a different arrangement. For those collecting relief, a band's housing subsidies from Indian Affairs (in 1987 approximately $30,000 per house, which has grown considerably since then) are paid to relief recipients in their biweekly checks in the amount to be paid to CMHC and then deducted from the checks before recipients receive them. The band then pays the amount due the CMHC. This guarantees that housing recipients can keep possession of their houses. For people with full-time employment, who are supposed to pay their own mortgages, payments are made in this way should they lose their jobs and accept relief. In practice, the Eskasoni Band Council makes the mortgage payments for these people as well, as a gesture of political goodwill, in recognition of the principal of social equality among all band members, and as an incentive to keep band employment levels as high as possible.

One aspect of this scheme may at some point prove inequitable to some. For example, if an employed individual who never had lawful possession is awarded a CMHC house by the band (or rather the down payment for it) and makes the CMHC loan payments for 35 years, there is no federal legal statute or law that prohibits a Band Council from expropriating the house for, let us say, political reasons, once the mortgage is paid in full. In Eskasoni, however, the Band Council's own law protects the interests of ownership of all individual possessors against the Band Council.

Allotment and Commerce

Over the years, Indian Affairs has acted to make allotment a flexible tool to accomplish tasks that can advance policy, but for which the *Indian Act* does not provide. One of its aims is to foster economic development.

Economic development faces many obstacles, including the danger that the band will expropriate the land and buildings of an entrepreneur. It is, however, unlikely that the federal courts would allow the Band Council to do so without making just compensation and, certainly, the Eskasoni Band Council has never made or threatened to make such an expropriation. Another danger is that a band member may, if enough of a bully, build his house on lands that another may be using, for example, for agricultural or silvicultural purposes.

Only allotment provides protection for commercial enterprises under federal statute. If an Indian has allotment, the Band Council cannot expropriate his property, except by recommending that the Crown do so with a compensated federal expropriation; any trespasser can be removed by the Royal Canadian Mounted Police or provincial police, just as on privately owned property outside of the reserve.

Allotment may also help secure credit. The *Indian Act*, which provides the band and its members with integrity of the reserve and band finances, states simply: "Reserve lands are not subject to seizure" (R.S.C. 1985, c. I-5, s. 29). Therefore, lending agencies rarely grant loans to entrepreneurs on the reserve, or to anybody else on the reserve for that matter, since they cannot secure them with real property. Over the years, Indian Affairs has initiated several loan and loan–grant programs to stimulate economic development, and some have enjoyed modest success. In many cases the loans were never repaid, and the revolving credit funds of several programs were exhausted. So, Indian Affairs began to use the Certificate of Possession itself to entice the debtors to repay their loans. For certain kinds of loans, Indian Affairs will ask the lawful possessor to relinquish his lawful possession to the band until the individual repays the loan in full; Indian Affairs guarantees the loan should the promisor fail to repay. Loans made by the CMHC are among the more common examples of this.

Used in this way, a lawful possessory interest cannot be a security, because a security requires an investment of money. Technically speaking, it could possibly play a role as collateral. But since lawful possession is generally given for the asking at no cost, and since lawful possession generally confers no special rights under the Eskasoni band's land tenure system, it has no market value in nearly all instances and therefore no one uses it as collateral in this community.

Rather, the loss of lawful possession constitutes a penalty the promisor must bear until such time as the loan is fully repaid. But since the debtor is as a member of the band, entitled to the same housing privileges as every other member, he or she may occupy the house and its lot after lawful possession is revoked, and his or her material situation does not usually change. In other words, the possibility of losing lawful possession represents a negligible penalty.

Lawful possession may also be encumbered by a judgment lien (not a true lien, but rather a hypothecary right), though the circumstances required for this are rare. An Indian that lends to another Indian but receives no repayment can complain to the courts or to Indian Affairs, which may bring the case to court on his or her behalf. If the court directs, a judgment lien could be placed on the debtor's Certificate of Possession. But again, because realty is not subject to seizure under legal process, the lien usually has no significant bearing on the lawful possessor, except that the lien remains on the certificate when the lot is transferred and any new possessor acquires liability for the debt.

Summary

Lawful possession originated as part of a package of rewards intended to induce migratory Indians to settle and to assimilate into white Canadian society, with the final goal to be a change in legal status from Indian to non-Indian, known as enfranchisement.

By the 1960s the federal government had removed all legal disadvantages to having Indian status and enfranchisement lost whatever attraction it had once had for Indians. The right to acquire and hold lawful possession of reserve lands remains on the books, however. It became a useful protection for possessors of property against the vagaries of an erratic Band Council or greedy neighbor. For this reason, lawful possession finds wide use on some reserves.

At Eskasoni, however, lawful possession has not enjoyed much popularity. As will be discussed later, principles of acceptable behavior and a powerful indigenous legal system have made lawful possession unnecessary and, in some cases, undesirable.

Summary of *Indian Act* Land Tenure Rules

Before discussing the tenurial system under the Indian Agent and Indian Affairs, I will summarize the *Indian Act* (R.S.C. 1985, c. I-5) land tenure rules that apply to Indian reserves. Both the Indian Agent and Indian Affairs were expected to obey and to apply these rules to the Indians of Eskasoni. The rules on ownership are followed by those applying to possession.

Ownership

Reserve ownership is vested in the federal Crown.

Rights of Acquisition, Holding, and Disposition

The Crown may set aside lands for the use of Indians, and hold those lands (R.S.C. 1985, c. I-5, s. 2). It may sell, lease, or dispose of reserve lands as it wishes, but only if those lands have been surrendered by a majority of the band members eligible to vote who vote on the question of surrender (R.S.C. 1985, c. I-5, s. 53). Adverse possession does not run against reserve lands (R.S.C. 1985, c. I-5, s. 31). The Parliament of Canada or the province (with the consent of the Governor in Council) may take reserve lands for public purposes through eminent domain expropriation (R.S.C. 1985, c. I-5, s. 35). Reserve lands may not be seized under legal process (R.S.C. 1985, c. I-5, s. 29).

Ususfructus

By stipulation of the *Indian Act*, only Indians of the band to which a particular reserve has been assigned may reside on that reserve and use its resources, whether mineral, floral, or faunal (R.S.C. 1985, c. I-5, ss. 2, 18). However, no one may remove from the reserve most floral or mineral resources without written permission of the Minister of Indian Affairs (R.S.C. 1985, c. I-5, s. 93). Unused or uncultivated land may be improved or cultivated at band expense, with the consent of the Band Council, and proceeds resulting from the improvement go to the band and to pay rent to the allottee, if applicable (R.S.C. 1985, c. I-5, s. 58). A band may relinquish its rights of *ususfructus* to a part or whole of a reserve by way of a surrender (R.S.C. 1985, c. I-5, s. 2), usually so that the land may be leased or sold for the band's financial gain.

Possession

Right of Acquisition

Possession of unallotted land is in the band (R.S.C. 1985, c. I-5, s. 20). Any band member may lawfully possess land in a reserve that is assigned to his or her band if the Band Council allots that land to that individual, and if the Minister of Indian Affairs approves (R.S.C. 1985, c. I-5, s. 20).

Right of Holding

If the federal or provincial government should expropriate land that is lawfully possessed, the Minister of Indian Affairs may direct that the possessor be compensated for any permanent improvements, to be paid by the new possessor or by the band (R.S.C. 1985, c. I-5, s. 23). Lawful possessors have the exclusive right of possession (including rights of *ususfructus*) to the land that they possess (R.S.C. 1985, c. I-5, s. 20).

Right of Disposition

A lawful possessor may transfer his or her right of possession to the band or to another band member or members, if so approved by the Minister of Indian Affairs (R.S.C. 1985, c. I-5, s. 24). This right to transfer includes transfer by contract, sale, or gift. If a lawful possessor ceases to be a member of a band, he or she must transfer the right of possession to either the band or to another band member within six months. Otherwise, possession reverts to the band and, if the Minister of Indian Affairs directs, the band must pay compensation for permanent improvements on that land (R.S.C. 1985, c. I-5, s. 25).

Testamentary Succession

An Indian may bequeath his or her lawfully possessed realty to any other band member or to the band through a will, which may take any form (R.S.C. 1985, c. I-5, ss. 42, 43, 44, 45).

Intestamentary Succession

In cases in which the deceased leaves issue, then the lawfully possessed property is divided *per stirpes*. If no living issue exists, the property is divided among the parents in equal shares or to the survivor if one is dead. If no living issue or parents survive, then the property goes to the deceased's siblings, in equal shares. If there are no living issue, parents, or siblings, then the property goes to the next of kin and is distributed equally among those related to an equal degree. Though dower and curtesy are disallowed, the surviving spouse has a right to occupy any lands in which the deceased spouse had lawful possession for as long as he or she lives (R.S.C. 1985, c. I-5, ss. 48, 49, 50).

This provision conflicts with Micmac ideals of justice. The Micmac believe that the marital property should always go to the surviving spouse first, and to issue second, and I am aware of no cases in which issue were given priority over spouses under principles of actual practice on the reserve.

Ususfructus

Ususfructus of allotted lands belongs to the possessor, though the possessor may lease or alienate these rights to the band or to other band members as he or she wishes (R.S.C. 1985, c. I-5, ss. 20, 28). The Band Council may also regulate the raising of domestic animals, bees, and poultry on reserve lands with by-laws (R.S.C. 1985, c. I-5, s. 81).

Rights Limited by *Servitus*

Statute or law does not prohibit limitations of rights by *servitus*, such as rights of way, covenants, and trusts, among others.

Hypothecary Rights

Mortgages and judgment liens on allotted Indian reserve lands are valid only if held by the band or by another band member, because only they may claim a right of possession to reserve land (R.S.C. 1985, c. I-5, s. 31). Mortgage holders and judgment lien holders, however, hold lesser rights in reserve lands than those available to mortgage and judgment lien holders generally, because reserve lands cannot be seized under the law (R.S.C. 1985, c. I-5, s. 29).

CHAPTER SIX

Changes in Canadian Indian Land Tenure

When the *Indian Act* first appeared in 1867, it complicated the law by creating a separate class of people, Indians, to whom separate statutes applied. It also created a separate category of land, Indian reserves, to which some long-accepted common law principles fail to apply.

The courts have made many decisions modifying statutes pertaining to Indian interests in real property. Many, if not most, of the reported Canadian court decisions involving Indians are on issues of land and land use. This is not surprising considering that many Indians live on reserves, which are federal lands regulated by the *Indian Act*, that many provinces want rights in reserve and Crown lands, that many Indians often obtain much of their food by hunting and fishing (or did so until recently), that a considerable number of Indians believe that Indians in truth hold "aboriginal title" (of ownership) to virtually all the lands of Canada, and because land claims and the interpretation of Indian treaties leave ample room for disagreement between Indian and Canadian leaders. I searched through the legal principles found in all reported Canadian court decisions from 1867 through 1989 that apply to Indian interests in real property, as well as similar legal principles made by the Canadian Supreme Court from 1989 through 2001. From this collection of legal principles I have selected those that brought about changes in Canadian Indian land tenure, and present these here. In addition to a description and analysis of the law, this examination also provides an account of the dimensions and directions of these legal changes and of the social and political forces responsible for producing them.

Changes in Canadian Indian Land Tenure

Since the first *Indian Act*, Indians have acquired greater rights in land. Most of these gains came in the 1960s and later, largely because funds were available to provincial Indian political associations from the federal government through the offices of Indian Affairs, in particular the Test Case Funding Program. This program has paid for the services of attorneys, and legal and historical research, particularly pertaining to treaties and anthropological evidence. The effects of these funds may be seen in the increase in reported decisions since the 1960s, especially in the number of actions obviously brought for the purpose of establishing precedents, and in the many brought on poor legal foundations, perhaps on the chance that favorable verdicts would be rendered. The following are the changes in Canadian Indian land tenure law.

Legal Changes in Reserve Land, Right of Possession, and Right of Acquisition

Legal Change 1

Early legal principle. Indians may gain lawful possession of reserve lands only by allotment by the Superintendent of Indian Affairs and not by adverse possession. *Delorimer v. Cross* (1937), [1937] 62 Que.K.B. 98.

Present legal principle. Band possession of unallotted reserve land confers on the band the same possessory rights as those granted a fee simple estate owner in his or her lands. *Brick Cartage Ltd. v. The Queen* (1964), [1965] 1 Ex.C.R. 102; *Mathias et al. v. Findlay*, [1978] 4 W.W.R. 653, 87 D.L.R. (3d) 239.

Legal Change 2

Early legal principles. A mortgage deed to reserve land is void and reserve land is immune to seizure. *Black v. Kennedy* (1877), [1875–1883] Man.R.temp.Wood 144. With the exception of security taken on articles for which the entire purchase price has not been paid, no Indian real or personal property on a reserve may be seized by the court in a judgment against an Indian, even on behalf of another Indian. *Atkins v. Davis* (1917), [1917] 38 O.L.R. 548.

Present rule. Section 89 of the *Indian Act* now permits courts to seize the property of an Indian on a reserve in judgments favoring another Indian (no decisions reported).

Legal Changes in Reserve Land, Right of Possession, and Right of Holding

Legal Change 3

Early legal principles. Since the Crown holds title of ownership to reserve lands, only it, and not Indians, may bring legal action with regard to reserves. *Bastien v. Hoffman* (1867), [1867] 17 L.C.R. 238.

A band does not have standing to maintain an action of trespass against a band member for trespass on reserve land that is not lawfully possessed. *D'Ailleboust v. Bellefleur* (1918), [1918] 25 R.L.N.S. 50.

Only band members with lawful possession of reserve land may bring an action of trespass, and for lawfully possessed lands only. *Point v. Dibblee Construction Co.* (1934), [1934] 2 D.L.R. 785.

All actions concerning reserve land must involve the Crown as a party, since the Crown holds title of ownership to reserve lands. *Wallace v. Fraser Companies* (1973), [1973] 8 N.B.R. (2d) 455.

Present legal principles. The band, represented by its Band Council, has a possessory interest in the reserve. *Brick Cartage Ltd. v. The Queen*, [1965] 1 Ex.C.R. 102 [1964].

The band has a possessory interest in reserve land and thus may maintain an action of trespass against a band member. *Joe et al. v. Findlay et al.*, [1980] 109 D.L.R. (3d) 747.

Indians may bring legal action for trespass on reserve land. *Johnson v. British Columbia Hydro and Power Authority* (1981), 27 B.C.L.R. 50; *Custer and Morin v. Hudson's Bay Company Developments Ltd. et al.*, [1982] 4 W.W.R. 139, appeal [1983] 1 C.N.L.R. 1 (1983).

The band may prohibit non-band members from trespassing on a reserve. *Manitoba Teacher's Society et al. v. Chief and Council of the Fort Alexander Indian Band et al.*, [1985] 1 C.N.L.R. 163 (1984); *Dunstan v. Hell's Gate Enterprises Ltd. et al.*, [1986] 3 C.N.L.R. 47, appeal [1989] 2 C.N.L.R. 36 (1985).

Members of an Indian band may physically restrain non-band members from trespassing on the band's reserve. *R. v. Morin* (1989), [1990] 1 C.N.L.R. 127. Reserve lands taken by the province that do not clearly extinguish band interest remain reserve lands for the purpose of taxation by the band. *Osoyoos Indian Band v. Oliver (Town)*, [2001] 3 S.C.R. 746.

Legal Changes in Reserve Land, Right of Possession, and Right of Disposition

Legal Change 4

Early legal principle. The Department of Indian Affairs and Northern Development (Indian Affairs) may grant licenses to non-Indians to use reserve lands without the consent of a band or Band Council. *Point v. Dibblee Construction Co.* (1934), [1934] 2 D.L.R. 785.

Present legal principle. The band must grant an easement for large electrical power transmission lines to be installed on a reserve. *Johnson v. British Columbia Hydro and Power Authority* (1981), 27 B.C.L.R. 50.

Legal Change 5

Early legal principle. Reserve land may be leased only after it has been lawfully surrendered. *Point v. Dibblee Construction Co.* (1934), [1934] 2 D.L.R. 785.

Present rule. The Minister may lease for the benefit of any Indian on his application for that purpose the land of which he is lawfully in possession without the land being surrendered.

This legal change was effected by Section 58(3) of the *Indian Act* and affirmed by *Regina v. Devereux* (1965), [1965] 51 D.L.R. (2d) 546.

Legal Change in Reserve Land, Right of Possession, and Right of Ususfructus

LEGAL CHANGE 6

Early legal principle. The *British North America Act, 1867* gives Parliament the exclusive right to legislate concerning Indians, and since Parliament used this right to create unequal rights for male and female Indians, an inequality that allowed Indian women who married non-Indian men to be prohibited from residing on reserve lands, the inferior Canadian Bill of Rights cannot be used to alter or amend that inequality. *Attorney-General of Canada v. Lavell; Isaac v. Bédard* (1973), [1973] 38 D.L.R. (3d) 481.

Present rule. By a 1985 amendment to the *Indian Act*, Indian women who marry non-Indian men no longer lose their Indian status and, therefore, their right to reside on a reserve.

Legal Changes in Non-reserve Lands, Rights of Ownership, and Rights Limited by Servitus

LEGAL CHANGE 7

Early legal principle. Only the Governor in Council may direct the lease, management, and sale of surrendered reserve lands. *Rex v. Cowichan Agricultural Society* (1950), [1951] 1 D.L.R. 96.

Present legal principle. The Governor in Council's duty to determine the use of surrendered reserve lands is a trust and the band must agree that the use of the surrendered lands intended by the Governor in Council is the best use in the band's interest. *Guerin et al. v. The Queen and National Indian Brotherhood* (1984), [1985] 1 C.N.L.R. 120.

LEGAL CHANGE 8

Early legal principles. The Crown has a paramount estate in Indian lands, on which the Indian (aboriginal) title of ownership is a mere burden. *St. Catherines Milling and Lumber Company v. The Queen,* [1887] 13 S.C.R. 577, appeal (1888), [1888] H.A.C. 46.

Aboriginal rights are not recognized in Canada. *Regina v. Discon and Baker* (1968), [1968] 67 D.L.R. (2d) 619.

For an Indian group to obtain an injunction to prevent construction on non-reserve land, it must clearly establish Indian (aboriginal) rights to the land. *La Société de Développment de la Baie James et al. v. Kanatewat et al.* (1974), [1975] Que. C.A. 166.

A claim of aboriginal title of ownership is insufficient to maintain a real action in court. *Uukw et al. v. The Queen in Right of the Province of British Columbia and the Attorney General for Canada,* [1986] 4 C.N.L.R. 111, appeal (1987), [1988] 1 C.N.L.R. 173.

Present legal principles. A claim of aboriginal title is sufficient for the granting of an interlocutory injunction. *Jules v. Harper Ranch Ltd.* (1989), [1989] 3 C.N.L.R. 67.

Aboriginal title is *sui generis* and confers exclusive rights to the occupation and use of land so held. *Delgamuukw v. British Columbia,* [1997] 3 S.C.R. 1010. The Crown must consult with Indian peoples on the use of lands to which the Indian peoples concerned claim ownership rights, even when such ownership has not been established. *Haida Nation v. British Columbia (Minister of Forests),* [2004] 3 S.C.R. 511; *Taku River Tlingit First Nation v. British Columbia (Project Assessment Director,* [2004] 3 S.C.R. 550.

LEGAL CHANGE 9
Early legal principle. An aboriginal right to hunt does not exist. *Regina v. Discon and Baker* (1968), [1968] 67 D.L.R. (2d) 619.

Present legal principles. The aboriginal right to hunt exists where it has not been extinguished by treaty and is guaranteed by the *Constitution Act, 1982. Sparrow v. The Queen et al.* (1986), [1987] 1 C.N.L.R. 145.

The federal *Migratory Birds Convention Act* has no effect on the aboriginal rights of Indians to hunt migratory game birds. *R. v. Flett,* [1987] 3 C.N.L.R. 70, appeal (1989), [1989] 4 C.N.L.R.128.

Indians with an aboriginal right to fish for food may fish for food during closed season if this fishing does not obstruct conservation schemes. *R. v. Archie* (1989), [1989] 4 C.N.L.R. 114.

An aboriginal right to fish can exist independently of aboriginal title. *R. v. Cote,* [1996] 3 S.C.R. 139.

LEGAL CHANGE 10
Early legal principle. The Migratory Birds Convention Act applies to restrict Indian hunting of migratory birds in the prairie provinces. *Daniels v. The Queen* (1968), [1968] 2 D.L.R. (3d) 1.

Present legal principle. The Migratory Birds Convention Act does not apply to Indians of the provinces of Alberta, Saskatchewan, and Manitoba, because these people have a right to hunt in any season, guaranteed by the Natural Resources Transfer Agreements. *R. v. Flett,* [1987] 3 C.N.L.R. 70, appeal (1989), [1989] 4 C.N.L.R. 128.

Analysis of Canadian Indian Land Tenure Changes

Of all changes in the law, Legal Change 1 easily stands as the most important, especially since it allowed Legal Changes 3 and 4 to occur. It transformed the band's interest in reserve land from one of rights of *ususfructus* to rights of possession. The decision by the Exchequer Court of Canada (*Brick Cartage Ltd. v. The Queen,* [1965] 1 Ex.C.R. 102), which plainly recognized Indian band possession of reserves, received little official notice by political and legal authorities. It was not until the

1978 British Columbia Supreme Court decision of *Mathias et al. v. Findlay*, [1978] 4 W.W.R. 653, 87 D.L.R. (3d) 239, reinterpreted the *Indian Act* to give bands possession of unallotted reserve lands that Indian Affairs and the other courts recognized band possession of unallotted portions of reserves. Thus, before 1964 or 1978 (depending on the court decision cited), no legal entity had rights of possession to unallotted portions of Indian reserves.

Legal Change 2 gave Indian creditors the right to assume possession of debtors' realty. This change, made by the *Indian Act*, creates an improved commercial climate on the reserves. By hiring Indians as bank officers, lending institutions have a way to acquire a financial stake in allotted lands. The Indian bank officers may acquire possession of the lots that another Indian has put up as collateral for a bank loan. This legal change also helps to reduce fraudulent transactions by Indians with allotments.

Legal Change 3 gives Indians the right to take legal action to protect their interests in reserve land. The *Indian Act* forbids trespass on reserves by persons other than members of the band to which the reserve is assigned. Section 31 of the *Indian Act* provides that the Attorney General of Canada, on behalf of an Indian or band, may bring action against a non-Indian trespasser.

The *Mathias v. Findlay* decision, however, paved the way for two important legal changes. These changes involve the rights of bands as possessors to have legal standing to initiate legal actions concerning reserve lands (Legal Change 3), and to grant easements (Legal Change 4). In 20th-century Canada and the United States, possessors of real property generally have gradually gained legal rights, often at the expense of the rights of owners. Legal Change 3, moreover, gave the Band Council the right to prevent band members from occupying band land; lands allotted to individuals or subgroups fall outside the Band Council's jurisdiction, however.

Legal Change 3 constitutes a broad change. It gave Indians the right to initiate legal action against non-Indian trespassers on reserves, a right that applies not only to the possessors of the reserve (the band as a whole) but also to individual band members. However, it may be exercised with non-Indians, and not with respect to Indians who belong to another band with no right to occupy the reserve in question. Clearly, the court in this instance took an interest in granting relief to Indians from the actions of non-Indians, above and beyond the rights guaranteed by the *Indian Act*.

Legal Change 4 allows the possessor of reserve land (the band or bands) to block the construction of high tension power lines across reserve land by refusing to grant the electric utility an easement, even when the owner of the reserve land (the Crown) approves such construction. Here the court created a truly novel principle, although one that conflicts with established common law, which provides that only the owner of real property, and not merely its possessor, can agree to an easement. This legal change came about, obviously, to grant Indians protection of their use and enjoyment of reserve lands. It also gives bands a potential additional source of income: should a band grant an easement, it would likely ask the power company to pay handsomely for it.

Legal Change 5 grants the band and individual band members additional rights concerning reserves. By alteration of the *Indian Act*, a lawful possessor of a lot on a reserve may lease that land to anyone without surrendering the land. This change benefits the individual lawful possessor, who can lease the land to another party without the band approving it, with a surrender. It also benefits the band in that part of the reserve need not be surrendered, probably to be lost forever as a part of the reserve, allowing the band to derive economic benefit from it. The primary function of the change was to facilitate entrepreneurial activity in reserve communities. Although, generally speaking, the *Indian Act* and the Canadian courts have made the rights of the band paramount over the rights of the individual band members, this change is an exception.

Before Legal Change 6, Indian women who married non-Indians lost their Indian status, and with it the most important rights associated with that status, rights of *ususfructus* to reserve lands (by provision of the *Indian Act*). The prohibition against living on reserves posed a major problem for those women who married non-Indian men and then divorced them. Forbidden to return to the reserves, and even to live with their own families, they sometimes experienced great economic hardship as a result. The provisions of the *Indian Act* that caused Indian women to lose their Indian status on marriage to non-Indians were repealed after a public outcry in the news media for the equal treatment under the law for men and women.

Turning now to legal changes affecting Indian rights in lands outside of reserves, we see that here, too, Indians have gained rights. Legal Change 7 represents an attempt by the courts to allow Indians to derive greater economic benefit from the lands they surrender. By establishing that the federal government's control over the use of surrendered lands constitutes a trust, the courts have given Indians a voice in determining how the surrendered lands are to be used and thus, perhaps, to realize greater profits from the sale or leasing of such land. This change, probably intended to prevent Indian Affairs complacency in dealing with surrendered lands, instead prompted Indian Affairs to refuse to approve future surrenders of Indian reserve lands.

Legal Change 8 indicates that the legal doctrine of aboriginal title of ownership is gaining credibility with the courts. Just what kind of rights those Indians found to have valid aboriginal title will ultimately have is yet to be fully determined.

Legal Change 9 is a potent change, in which the courts essentially declared that aboriginal hunting and fishing rights shall continue wherever they remain unextinguished by treaty. A significant gain, it means that many of Canada's Indians have rights to hunt and to fish when and as they wish (subject only to hunting and fishing safety laws).

Legal Change 10 signifies an especially obvious attempt to advance Indian rights of *ususfructus*, in that it contravenes the normally accepted sequence of legal pre-emption. The provinces of Alberta, Saskatchewan, and Manitoba received ownership of the natural resources within their borders through a gift from the federal government. As a conditional stipulation to the gift, Indians living in those provinces would have the right to hunt at any time of the year.

These terms conflict with those of the *Migratory Birds Convention Act*, which limits hunting of certain migratory birds to ensure Canadian cooperation with the terms of a treaty with the United States to protect these birds. Normally, federal statutes enacted to create compliance with international treaty pre-empt those with which they conflict. In this case, however, the rights of Indians within Canadian borders were deemed more important than a statute that provides for compliance with an international treaty.

Conclusion

The *Indian Act* intended to give Indians special privileges to help them prosper in the face of challenges posed by non-Indian society. When the *Indian Act* provisions came into being in 1867, Indians were dying off rapidly (see, for example, Brown 1869:459). At that time, too, provincial governments allowed settlers and land speculators to buy up large parcels of lands that had been reserved for Indian use. Further, non-Indians were permitted to take natural resources from those lands (*Vanvleck et al. v. Stewart et al.*, [1860] 19 U.C.Q.B. 489). Perhaps for this reason Parliament gave itself exclusive legislative authority over Indians and Indian lands in the *British North America Act of 1867* and used the *Indian Act* to protect Indian use of reserve lands.

This federal protection, of course, has been paternalistic, and not always competently applied. As times have changed, paternalism has become less and less seemly. Certainly, it has become all the more obvious as Indian leaders have become more sophisticated in their understanding of non-Indian Canada, and assertive in their use of the Canadian political and legal systems. Legal Changes 1, 2, 3, 4, 5, and 7 have increased Indian autonomy and reduced paternalism significantly.

Now that the danger posed to the very survival of Indian peoples has passed, attention has focused on their economic status, which generally lags behind that of non-Indians. Legal Changes 4, 5, 7, 8, 9, and 10 attempt to improve Indian economic conditions by allowing Indians greater access to resources located outside of reserves.

For lands off of the reserve, courts have recently granted to Indians rights to hunt and to fish that were unimaginable 30 years ago, especially those arising from treaty provisions.

In sum then, the Canada's courts (and Parliament) have changed Canadian Indian land tenure, increasing Indian rights to control the use of reserve land and making it easier to use it profitably without losing control of it (Legal Change 5), while also making it more difficult for Indians to alienate their rights to reserve land (Legal Change 7). Sexual inequality under the law has also ended (Legal Change 6).

Indians have gained tremendous rights of *servitus* for non-reserve lands. They have gained rights of *ususfructus* on these lands, thereby limiting the rights of owners and of other holders of similar rights (Legal Changes 8, 9, and 10). The political questions raised by these legal changes ensure that legal wrangling will continue for some time to come, especially since the development of a vocal non-Indian movement in response to the changes involving non-reserve lands. This movement protests the diminution of non-Indian rights in proportion to the creation of greater rights for Indians (Smith 1995).

CHAPTER SEVEN

The Eskasoni Real Property Legal System under Indian Affairs, 1942–1978

We now move on to a unique period in the history of Eskasoni land tenure, when at first the Indian Agent alone, and later the Indian Affairs bureaucracy, became the dominant legal authorities of the community. From 1942 to 1978, the Indian Agent and Indian Affairs managed real property on the reserve with an eye to economic and administrative efficiency and, in large measure, conformity with the *Indian Act*. This was also the first universal reserve-wide real property legal system. Initially, the Indian Agent and Indian Affairs were authoritarian in imposing this legal system, often with little regard for Micmac behavioral, political, or legal ideals. However, as time went on, Indian Affairs has governed more and more with Indian wants in mind.

Domination of reserve life by Indian Affairs began with the start of the Centralization Program in 1942. This turbulent period saw many political and legal changes. The various Indian agents who governed the reserve from 1942 to 1972 frequently used idiosyncratic rules and legal principles, so of course the law applied to the reserve changed each time a new agent took office.

In 1956, the Eskasoni band officially came into being, and in 1957 the Eskasoni Band Council took office for the first time. The Band Council acquired control of privately occupied housing, while the Indian Agent retained control over the public buildings. In 1972, the Indian Agent left the reserve at the Band Council's request. Since then Indian Affairs bureaucrats have administered Cape Breton's Indians from offices off the Eskasoni reserve. In 1978, *Mathias et al. v. Findlay*, [1978] 4 W.W.R. 653, 87 D.L.R. (3d) 239, established that the band had possession of all unallotted reserve lands, essentially ending most Indian Affairs control over Eskasoni land tenure and beginning an era of true indigenous control.

An Early Indian Affairs Rule on Rights of *Ususfructus*

Sometime after the federal government took control over Indian administration and welfare in the 19th century, Indian Affairs instituted the following rule under the authority of Section 2 of the *Indian Act*, which states that the use of the reserve is held by the Crown for the members of the band.

INDIAN AFFAIRS RULE 1

All natural resources harvested or mined on a reserve are the property of the Crown and must be purchased to be used. The proceeds from the sale of these are credited to the band, for use by the Band Council.

Neither Indian Affairs nor the Indian Agent enforced this rule at Eskasoni, for two reasons. Because of the poverty on the reserve, the Indian Affairs staff believed that enforcement would pose too great a financial burden on those who depended on natural resources, such as wood. Second, there was no legally bona fide band to whom the proceeds could be given. By 1978 *Mathias v. Findlay* made the rule unenforceable.

House, Yard and Field Siting under the Indian Agent

During Centralization and afterward, the Indian Agent busily engaged himself in building new houses and public buildings (an administration building and store, a livestock barn, a sawmill, and school buildings, among others). In this he enjoyed complete control over the siting of these buildings and in the selection of woodlots to be cut to supply lumber for construction.

The established behavioral rule for rights in land before Centralization was that people did not build houses on, or otherwise occupy or use land, that others owned without the owner's permission (see Chapter 8, Eskasoni Real Property Behavioral Rule 2). Obviously, this conflicted with the aims of the Indian Agent as he tried to settle several hundred immigrants during Centralization. Therefore, the Indian Agent promulgated a new rule for the rights to land among Eskasoni residents.

INDIAN AGENT RULE 1

Families and individuals may claim exclusive rights only to land that they themselves have cleared of forest.

But the Indian Agent seemed to place no importance on the fact that with this rule he allowed strangers to settle virtually in the dooryards of people who did not want their new neighbors. He based his decision in the following case on this rule.

LEGAL CASE 22

First party: CZ, a man from mainland Nova Scotia.
Second party: The T lineage of Eskasoni.
Authority: Indian Agent.
Date: 1940s.

Facts: CZ moved his family to Eskasoni during Centralization. He chose as the site of his new home a spot in an uncleared area that the T lineage regarded as its own. Members of the large and powerful T lineage protested that the new arrival planned to build on land that they had claimed. Normally, under traditional behavioral principles, a first claim to land adjoining one's dwelling, whether cleared or forested, establishes the claimant as owner (see Chapter 8, Eskasoni Real Property Behavioral Rule 1).

Outcome: The Indian Agent decided in favor of CZ and found the T lineage's claim to the disputed land defective, because they had not cleared it. CZ built his house on the lot.

Comment: The decision only mattered as far as the Indian Agent was concerned because it did not end the civil dispute, which was based on Eskasoni Real Property Behavioral Rule 1, as was the following case.

DISPUTE CASE 6

First party: A Micmac man, CZ.
Second party: The members of the T lineage.
Date: 1940s.

Facts: Eventually the confrontation between the two parties came to threats of violence by members of the T lineage against CZ.

Outcome: CZ stood his ground and carved out of the T lineage's territory a territory of his own for himself and his lineage. Many members of the Eskasoni community admired CZ's ability to defend himself and his interests. In the 1960s they elected him chief, and after he left this office he served for many years as a band councillor.

From Legal Cases 22 and 39 we may abstract the following legal principle:

INDIAN AGENT LEGAL PRINCIPLE 1
All, and only, uncleared reserve land is open to settlement and to the building of private housing.

Perhaps to quell the disharmony between the new arrivals and the original residents, the Indian Agent also attempted to regulate, to a small degree at least, the land rights among individual Eskasoni residents. He gave householders hand-drawn plats that showed the boundaries of their lots and their names written inside them. None of this was authorized by the *Indian Act*. He further instituted a system whereby landowners could sell their interests in land to other Micmac. This too the *Indian Act* did not authorize, since no one on the reserve had lawful possession of any land on the reserve. These led much later to civil disputes (see Legal Cases 71 and 72). The Indian Agent rule can be expressed as follows.

INDIAN AGENT RULE 2
Indians living on the Eskasoni reserve may alienate their individual interests in real property to one another, without the need for lawful possession.

In the following case, the Indian Agent's decision to create bounded lots on the reserve initiated conflict.

LEGAL CASE 23

First party: PE.
Second party: PC.
Authority: Indian Agent.
Date: About 1950.

Facts: PE, an early arrival to Eskasoni under the Centralization Program, lived across the reserve's main road from Bras D'Or Lake. The main road was separated from Bras D'Or Lake by a narrow strip of land. To get to the lake, PE crossed this strip using a pathway perpendicular to the main road. It was not until the Indian Agent gave PC, who lived next to the path on that narrow strip of land, a plat of his lot that the dispute began. PC, relying on the plat, erected a fence around the border of his lot, a fence that encompassed the path to the lake. PE objected to PC that he had removed his access to the lake. PC showed PE his plat, which plainly indicated that the pathway fell inside his lot. PE said to PC that he should not take his right of access, which he had been using for years. PC stood firm in his refusal to allow PE to cross his land. PE went to the Indian Agent and asked him to make it so that he could once again use his path to the lake.

Outcome: The Indian Agent re-drew the boundaries on the plat so that PC's lot no longer included the pathway, which has from that time forward stood outside of the boundaries of any lot. It may still be seen in Indian Affairs' own surveys of Eskasoni (see Figure 5, Map 8).

The following two cases indicate the strength of the authority that the Indian Agent held over the siting of people and housing on the reserve.

LEGAL CASE 24

Defendant: AG.
Authority: Indian Agent.
Date: Late 1940s.

Facts: AG worked for the Indian Agent, assisting him with construction projects. He became so valuable to the Indian Agent that the latter decided that AG should live near the administration building so he could be easily summoned (most of the reserve had no telephone service at the time). AG protested that he liked his situation as it was and did not want to move.

Outcome: AG moved to the house to which the Indian Agent directed him, several miles from his former residence.

LEGAL CASE 25

Defendant: BF.
Authority: Indian Agent.
Date: Late 1940s.

Facts: BF wanted the house that was to be built for him to be close to the main road. The Indian Agent had ordered that, for the sake of appearance, all new houses were to be constructed at some distance from the road, which according to informant recollections was at least 45 meters (50 yards).

Outcome: The house was built at a distance from the road.

Comment: The Micmac regarded this order as demeaning. They felt that it implied that both they and their houses were unpresentable.

From Legal Cases 22 through 25 we may abstract the following legal principle.

INDIAN AGENT LEGAL PRINCIPLE 2

Subject to Indian Agent Legal Principles 1 and 4, and the *Indian Act* provision that only Indians may occupy reserve lands, the Indian Agent may direct the use of reserve lands and the siting of all occupancy and houses as he wished.

The Indian Agent's authority to implement this principle was apparently limited only by his desire to achieve his overall goal of moving the Micmac population to Eskasoni, as seen in the following dispute case.

POLITICAL CASE 4

First party: Indian Agent.
Second party: PE.
Date: 1940s.

Facts: At the beginning of the Centralization Program, Indian Affairs' first challenge was to encourage the Micmac living on outlying reserves to move to the two more central locations in Nova Scotia. Enticements took the form of material advantages, most importantly promises of employment and new houses. PE was one of the first whom the superintendent asked to move to Eskasoni, perhaps because he was hard working and was interested in acquiring personal wealth. The superintendent promised him a job, a new house, and his choice of location. When PE made his site choice, the superintendent vetoed it and told PE that he would have to live elsewhere, because that parcel had been earmarked for a different purpose. PE replied that he would not move to Eskasoni if he could not have the lot he wanted.

Outcome: The superintendent gave in to the demand and later gave PE a plat of the immediate area showing PE's newly drawn lot with his name on it. This shows that, even though the Indian Agent had a great deal of autocratic authority, he was sometimes vulnerable to the political pressures of certain individuals. PE cleared the lot and raised potatoes, carrots, and other vegetables in a field he created behind his house.

The Indian Agent's Management of Reserve Housing

Control of Damage to Property

Every Micmac nuclear family immigrating to Eskasoni was given a house or, if one were not immediately available, a tent. Many believed, at least at first, that they had been given ownership of these houses and tents outright. This was not the case, as they soon found out. In some instances the Indian Agent had individuals who broke windows or otherwise damaged the houses charged under the Canadian *Criminal Code* with destruction of government property.

The following are examples of the Indian Agent's policy of bringing charges for this type of offense.

LEGAL CASE 26

Defendant: A Micmac man.
Authority: The Indian Agent and the Canadian Federal Court (I consider the Indian Agent in this case a legal authority because he used his authority to bring charges, which otherwise would not have been brought, and therefore to determine whether or not the destruction of Indian Affairs property on a reserve constituted a legal offense).
Date: 1940s.

Facts: The defendant lived in a shack with a leaky roof. His newborn child needed protection from the rain, and so he took a government-issue tent, cut it up, and constructed with it a shelter for the baby inside the shack.

Outcome: The Indian Agent discovered this and had the man prosecuted for destruction of public property. The defendant received a jail term of three months.

LEGAL CASE 27

Defendant: A Micmac man, K.
Authority: The Indian Agent and the Canadian Federal Court.
Date: Late 1940s.
Facts: K broke a window of the house in which he lived.

Outcome: The Indian Agent had him prosecuted by the Canadian court system and he received a fine for breaking the window.

LEGAL CASE 28

Defendant: A trio of teenage boys.
Authority: The Indian Agent and the Canadian Federal Court.
Date: Late 1940s.

Facts: The three boys broke a window of a house on the reserve.

Outcome: The Indian Agent had the three boys prosecuted in court and they were placed on probation.

From Legal Cases 26 through 28, we may abstract the following legal principle.

INDIAN AGENT LEGAL PRINCIPLE 3

An individual who damages a building or any other federal government property on the reserve is liable to federal prosecution for that damage.

Evictions

Indian Affairs also regulated itself and its employees in one very important respect, using a rule that Indian Affairs had created and enforced ever since it began to administer housing, as follows.

INDIAN AFFAIRS RULE 2

The Indian Agent may not evict a resident of a house unless there is another house waiting for the evictee to occupy immediately.

Indian Affairs administration ensured that each Indian Agent obeyed this rule by approving only those evictions in which the Indian Agent attested that another house was available. The operation of the rule in an atypical situation can be seen in the following case.

LEGAL CASE 29

Defendant: RN, a Micmac man.
Authority: Indian Agent.
Date: 1940s.

Facts: Because of the influx of immigrants to the reserve in the 1940s, many families new to Eskasoni found themselves with no houses in which to live. When one family notified the Indian Agent that they would be in the United States for some months, RN, a man without a house, asked the Indian Agent whether his family could use the house while the first family was away. The Indian Agent promised that RN could use the house, but only until the family to whom the house had been given returned. When the family was about to return, the Indian Agent visited RN and asked him to vacate the house. The defendant claimed that the house was now his because he was now living there, and in the argument that followed he beat the Indian Agent rather severely.

Outcome: The Indian Agent managed, finally, to evict RN and his family from the house. He also laid assault charges against RN in a Canadian court. Had the Indian Agent acceded to RN's demands, he would have effectively evicted the original inhabitants of the house without providing a place for them to live.

We may abstract the following legal principle from this decision.

INDIAN AGENT LEGAL PRINCIPLE 4

No person may be evicted from a house unless there is another house waiting for the evictee to occupy immediately.

The Micmac found this legal principle to be fair and accepted it as just.

Real Property Law under Indian Affairs, 1957–1978

After Eskasoni's first Band Council took office in 1957, the Indian Agent began to reduce his role in administration of reserve affairs. He stayed on the reserve to advise the new Band Council, to act as Indian Affairs' supervisor of day-to-day Band Council business, and to administer some categories of federal monies. But even though he no longer made decisions as to who received new housing (over the protests of some Micmac who felt that Band Council decisions had shortchanged them), he did assert some authority over land and housing. In fact, he retained a preponderance of control over real property use and established and enforced rules for the Micmac use of real property. Indian Affairs, as a representative of the Crown, considered the Crown's ownership interest in reserve land superior to the rights of residence and *ususfructus* that the *Indian Act* granted to Indians. This official position continued until 1978, when the Canadian court system handed down *Mathias et al. v. Findlay*, [1978] 4 W.W.R. 653, 87 D.L.R. (3d) 239.

In the following example of this dominance, the Indian Agent told a Band Council to prevent band members from selling and trading houses among themselves. In a 1958 letter from the Indian Agent to the chief of a Cape Breton band, the Indian Agent wrote:

> Dear Mr. Phillips:
>
> It has come to our attention that there has been a number of housing transfers among the residents of the Reserve. This practice must cease immediately and I would ask that you and the councillors ensure that Andrew Bernard vacate Michael J. Googoo's house, and return to his own house. This is to Andrew Bernard's benefit since we intend to have his own house repaired. (Public Archives of Canada, RG 10, vol. 8493, file 50/3-1, part 1)

If this letter had any effect, it was temporary. Only a few years later, for example, a man traded his house at Eskasoni for one in Whycocomagh. The man told me that, unlike some cases today, that "there were no papers to sign or anything else, just a trade."

Indian Affairs sometimes also exercised its authority over the placement of new housing. Many Micmac in the 1960s chose relatively inaccessible sites, to ensure personal peace and privacy. This practice cost Indian Affairs a great deal of money in the construction of extensive water, sewer, electrical, and telephone lines. To reduce this cost, Indian Affairs decided to construct new housing in densely built subdivisions. The location of the only such subdivision built before 1978 (see Figure 5, Map 9) caused a dispute over land rights.

LEGAL CASE 30

First party: The M family.
Second party: The people of Eskasoni.
Third party: Indian Affairs.
Authority: Indian Affairs.
Date: 1960s.

Facts: In the 1960s, Indian Affairs decided to situate in one small subdivision all of the new housing to be built at Eskasoni during a period of several years. Indian Affairs placed the subdivision in an area that the M family claimed as its own and had partially cleared. The M family objected strenuously to Indian Affairs' choice of location.

Outcome: Indian Affairs located the subdivision (known as 74 Street) on land to which the M family had laid claim, over the M family's objections. The people of Eskasoni also strenuously objected to the new scheme, because it placed members of many different and sometimes incompatible nuclear families and lineages in close proximity. Those who predicted that the new plan would lead to strife were unfortunately proved correct. Ever since, 74 Street has been synonymous with conflict. As recently as 2007, a woman complaining of her inability to get the band office to pay for some housing repairs remarked "I live on 74 Street, so all my windows have been broken." Much of this conflict has centered around a single lineage's attempt to control the subdivision (see Chapter 16, Dispute Case 74).

Legal Change

The decision in Legal Case 30 was a change in the law that the Indian Agent and Indian Affairs together had administered on the Eskasoni reserve. Until this point, Indian Agents had recognized pre-existing claims to land based on residence (see Legal Case 39). Instead, Indian Affairs decided that real property law on the reserve was to conform closely to *Indian Act* rules. No longer did Indian Affairs allow the Indian Agent leeway in making decisions to permit Indians to use the reserve lands as they wanted, or as the Indian Agent had previously allowed on an ad hoc basis. Indians were to have only the rights guaranteed by the *Indian Act*. This meant, essentially, that only lawful possession could limit Indian Affairs actions. For example, Indian Affairs forbade the sale of unallotted lands from one band member to another, which had been previously allowed by an earlier Indian Agent, extinguishing Indian Agent Rule 1 (see above). Unlike in Legal Case 30, the Indian Agent could no longer allow people to claim cleared land as their own; only allotted land was to be safe from settlement by others or from use by Indian Affairs for the settlement of band members. Thus, Indian Affairs extinguished Indian Agent Legal Principle 1.

Lawful Possession and Expropriation

Indian Affairs' greatest attempt to assimilate and acculturate the people of the reserve, and also to curry political favor with superiors, was to try to interest them in using the statutory provisions for lawful possession. The people of this community have, as a whole, never seen much advantage in acquiring lawful possession, having been able to manage their affairs well without it.

The Indian Act specifies rules for two types of expropriation, those by the Canadian Parliament or provincial legislature, and those by the Minister of Indian Affairs (*Indian Act*, R.S.C. 1970, c. I-6, ss. 35, 18). I will deal here with the latter only, because there have occurred no cases of the former at Eskasoni. Section 18(2) states:

> The Minister may authorize the use of lands in a reserve. But where an individual Indian, immediately prior to such taking, was entitled to the possession of such lands, compensation for such use shall be paid to the Indian.

Indian Affairs has in years past initiated on reserves various public projects, or acted on Band Council requests for public projects, that require the removal of Micmac housing or the use of allotted or occupied land. These public projects have included band offices, schools, fire stations, sewage treatment plants, and other installations for the benefit of the band as a whole.

By authority of the *Indian Act,* the Minister, and not the Band Council, makes all decisions to expropriate realty, accepts most of the administrative burden involved in expropriations, and pays the entirety of the costs involved in compensating individuals for interests in lands expropriated. Under the *Indian Act,* the Band Councils have no authority to make decisions on expropriations, though they may recommend to the Minister building projects that they wish to see completed, and the location of those projects, by way of Band Council resolutions.

When Indian Affairs created Band Councils in Nova Scotia, it asked them to award allotment to people whose lots were to be expropriated by the federal government. The band would then purchase the lawful possessory interest from the individual, and Indian Affairs would pay compensation to the possessor through the Band Councils. Indian Affairs compensates those with lawful possession not for the improvements that the possessor has made, but rather for the value of the property, by authority of Section 18(2) (see above). Hence, if the Band Council had built for an individual a new house, and then given him or her lawful possession of the lot on which it was built, the Band Council would have to pay the possessor the market value of the entire property to expropriate it, even though the possessor had paid nothing for the property and may have expended no labor or money to improve it. Thus, a lawful possessor receives far more money in an expropriation than does someone who simply resides on land that the government wants to use. Indian Affairs allows the band to select its own appraiser to determine the value of the properties being expropriated, a policy that has won it some degree of approval on the reserve.

Quitclaim Deeds, Allotment, and a Disparity in Compensation for Expropriations

In an attempt to build political support among Indian people, Indian Affairs has for many years paid compensation to those whom it displaced in building projects. To ensure that those displaced by federal projects received compensation, they had to have a legal interest in the property to which they moved, namely, lawful possession.

However, by the 1960s, Indian Affairs' program to award a Certificate of Possession beforehand to those whose lands were to be expropriated for federal projects became mired in paperwork. If the lot intended for allotment was unsurveyed, the backlog in requests for surveys meant a three-year wait before Indian Affairs could even begin to process the paperwork for the Certificate of Possession, which itself took another two years. To avoid a logjam in the construction of new projects, Indian Affairs turned to the use of the quitclaim deed.

From the first, Indian Affairs has compensated Nova Scotia Micmac for their expropriated interests in improved realty, whether the individuals had an allotment or not, even though Section 23 of the *Indian Act* merely provides that Indians who have made improvements on lands to which they had no allotment may be paid compensation for these improvements if removed from those lands, at the discretion of the Minister; such payments are made from band funds. For example, if an individual had built his house using his own capital, and had improved the land around it, Indian Affairs compensated him for the full value of his investment of money and labor if it expropriated the land, even though he was not in lawful possession of it.

An individual who did not have allotment of his or her own lot could simply sign a quitclaim to whatever interest there was in the house and surrounding land. Probably to stimulate an interest in acculturation, Indian Affairs did not compensate those who signed quitclaims as well as those who transferred lawful possession back to the band in an expropriation. When Eskasoni built a large new school in the late 1970s, compensation for interests taken from those who lived on the building site varied considerably.

LEGAL CASE 31

Party: BG.
Authority: Minister of Indian Affairs.
Date: Mid-1970s.

Facts: BG lawfully possessed a lot that was needed by Indian Affairs for the construction of a school.

Outcome: The Minister expropriated the lot and granted BG $16,570 for her lot and house.

LEGAL CASE 32

Party: DD.
Authority: Minister of Indian Affairs.
Date: Mid-1970s.

Facts: DD lawfully possessed a lot that Indian Affairs wanted for the construction of a school.

Outcome: The Minister expropriated the lot and gave DD $15,232 for his interest in his lot and house.

LEGAL CASE 33

Party: KL.
Authority: Minister of Indian Affairs.
Date: Mid-1970s.

Facts: KL was the lawful possessor of a lot that Indian Affairs wanted for the construction of a school.

Outcome: The Minister expropriated the lot and gave KL a Certificate of Possession to another lot in compensation, as he had requested.

LEGAL CASE 34

Party: DF.
Authority: Minister of Indian Affairs.
Date: Mid-1970s.

Facts: DF was the lawful possessor of a lot that Indian Affairs wanted for the construction of a school.

Outcome: The Minister expropriated the lot and gave DF $3,574 and a Certificate of Possession to a portion of another lot in compensation.

LEGAL CASE 35

Party: GT.
Authority: Minister of Indian Affairs.
Date: Mid-1970s.

Facts: GT resided on a lot to which he had no lawful possession, and which was needed by Indian Affairs for the construction of a school.

Outcome: GT signed a quitclaim deed to his lot and received less than $300 compensation for his interest in the lot.

LEGAL CASE 36

Defendant: GT.
Authority: Band Council and Indian Affairs.
Date: Mid-1970s.

Facts: When construction of the school got under way, GT (see Legal Case 35) refused to honor the terms of the quitclaim and declined to vacate his house. The Band Council sought the assistance of the federal government in evicting GT and he received the following letter from the director of the Atlantic Region in the Department of Justice:

> Dear Sir:
>
> We have been advised by the Eskasoni Band Council that you are illegally trespassing on lands you have transferred to the Band. Unless you remove yourself and your family, along with any items to which you are entitled, within seven (7) days of this letter, action will be commenced in the Federal Court of Canada in order to have you removed, physically if necessary, from the land. There will be no further notice.

Outcome: GT abandoned the lot.

Comment: In this case, the Band Council relied on the federal government for enforcement of a contract with the band member. In years to come, the Band Council abandoned the federal government as an enforcer and relied on itself as its power grew.

After this, some individuals realized that they could profit simply by lawfully possessing any lands needed in an expropriation. And, of course, all that is needed for allotment is a properly executed Band Council resolution, after which Indian Affairs nearly always grants allotments to individuals. A moneymaking scheme using these elements led to the case presented below.

LEGAL CASE 37

Defendant: TV, a former Band Council member.
Authority: Indian Affairs.
Date: 1981.

Facts: The Band Council requested and received Indian Affairs approval for the construction of a public utilities project on the reserve. An earlier Band Council, of which TV had been a member, located the project on lots to which TV had lawful possession. TV asked Indian Affairs for compensation for the expropriation of his land for the project.

Outcome: Indian Affairs did not grant compensation, nor did the band expropriate possession of the lots. Indian Affairs ruled that because TV had received his Certificate of Possession while a councillor his actions constituted a conflict of interest. Therefore, Indian Affairs had TV sign a release of right of way to the property where the project was constructed and TV retained his allotment.

Comment: This is, by common law standards, an odd use of the right of way, which is normally for access and not for fixtures such as a utility plant.

The Band Council Attacks Indian Affairs Law

Even before taking predominant control over band real property law in 1978, the Band Council did what it could to dismantle Indian Affairs and Indian Agent law. When the Eskasoni Band Council first took office in 1957, Indian Affairs gave it discretion over many of the matters relating to private housing, while it held on to control over most of the reserve's land and public buildings (until the 1978 *Mathias v. Findlay* decision). On taking office, the Band Council immediately halted the enforcement of Indian Agent Legal Principles 1, 2, and 3 (see above). However, inasmuch as the federal government owns the reserve, and still possessed most of it, federal law and Crown prosecutors continued to protect its interests. The disposition of Legal Case 30 exposes some of the conflict between the Micmac and Indian Affairs over land tenure. The early Band Council had little genuine control over land tenure matters, even though its members had been elected to accept that responsibility. Another example of this conflict can be found in the following case, in which, although the Band Council did not wish to punish a man for destroying an old house where he had once lived, the Crown prosecutor decided that federal interests needed to be protected.

LEGAL CASE 38

Defendant: PS.
Authority: The reserve's Special Constable, Nova Scotia Provincial Court.
Date: About 1970.

Facts: Around 1970, PS, a man with a mild developmental disability who spoke only Micmac, moved out of his old, deteriorated house into a new one next door, which he had received from the Band Council. After he moved into the new house, he decided that the old house was decrepit, could never be repaired for the use of another family, and, standing empty, presented a hazard to the children in the neighborhood. For these reasons he burned it down. The reserve's constable, a Micmac man seeking to curry favor with his superiors in the Royal Canadian Mounted Police, arrested him for arson. The Crown prosecutor decided to prosecute the case, despite opposition from the Band Council.

Outcome: The hapless man lost the case and received a jail sentence.

The Micmac of Eskasoni opposed PS's prosecution. Until a major change in policy in 2008 (see Chapter 17), no one at Eskasoni has been prosecuted in a Canadian court for arson or for the destruction of any housing, band property or not. But it was not until 1978 that the Band Council could fully eradicate *Indian Agency Legal Principles 2* and *3* as operative legal principles on the reserve.

Summary

At this point it would be well to summarize Eskasoni real property law as it existed until 1978, the date when the Micmac regained primary control of land tenure on the Eskasoni reserve. In the era of early colonial influence, and possibly even later, there is rather scant evidence that some Micmac bands, in some periods, had some system of individual or group territories, or both. What the impetus for creating these territories may have been, the possible functions of the territories, and the reasons for their demise, are all unknown.

Moving forward to the early 20th century, we come to a period of Grand Council rule. The Grand Council did not decide civil cases and, because all disputes over land were considered civil matters, land tenure as such did not exist at the band level. Traditionally, whoever resided on a piece of land had the customary, but not legally protected, rights of possession and ownership as long as residence was maintained (see Chapter 8, Eskasoni Real Property Behavioral Rules 1, 2, and 3). Individually owned pieces of land were separated from each other by uncleared free land, and real property law existed solely at the family/descent group legal level. Later, the construction of permanent housing caused the genesis of a rule that provided that one owns a house until alienating it, thus protecting rights to housing while the owners were away (see Chapter 8, Eskasoni Real Property Behavioral Rule 4).

With the Centralization Program, the Indian Agent became the most powerful legal authority on the Eskasoni reserve and based his legal decisions on his own rules as well as those of the *Indian Act*. The Indian Agent's legal principles (and, where applicable, rules) on land tenure on the Eskasoni reserve from 1942 to 1978 are summarized here.

Ownership

Under Section 2 of the *Indian Act*, the Crown owns all reserve lands and all real property situated thereon. This gives the federal government the right to site housing as it wishes and to prosecute those who damage housing (Legal Cases 26, 27, 28, 29, and 38). The Micmac rights of possession are secondary to the rights of the owner and are therefore subject to the right of the Indian Agent to expropriate possession from one Micmac person to give it to another (Legal Cases 23, 29, and 30). Further, the Indian Act could not dispossess a Micmac of his or her interests in housing, except through eviction by the Indian Agent or Indian Affairs, in which case it was required that another house be given immediately (Legal Case 29).

Possession

The Eskasoni Micmac held possessory interests in the lands they occupied. A Micmac may take possession of land that he has cleared, and may retain possession of the cleared land and the buildings on it (Legal Case 22). However, the *Indian Act* does not recognize this interest as lawful possession. Further, during the Centralization Program and even later, the Indian Agent allowed possessors to sell their possessory interests to other Micmac living on the reserve (Indian Agent Legal Principle 2) and to prevent use of cleared land they claimed as their own by other parties (Indian Agent Legal Principle 1). This even though these practices conflicted with the *Indian Act*, which provides that only lawfully possessed lands may be transferred and then only from one band member to another or to the band (Legal Cases 71 and 72). At that time there were no bona fide *Indian Act* bands in Nova Scotia, and thus there could be no lawful possession; the *Indian Act* makes no provision for one resident to give the mere right of residence to another party. Later Indian Agents conformed more closely to the stipulations of the *Indian Act* and extinguished the right of Eskasoni residents to transfer possessory rights to unallotted lands. No Indian Agent exercised the limitation of rights by *servitus*, probably to keep legal principles and rules concerning land use simple.

When the Centralization Program began in 1942 the Eskasoni Micmac suddenly confronted an imposed alien land tenure system for the first time, some principles of which they found unjust (Indian Agent Legal Principles 1, 2, and 3). The Band Council extinguished these principles when it first took office in 1957, although, because it did not control the police force until years later, it was unable to protect the man who burned his house in 1970 from arson charges (Legal Case 38).

The period 1957 to 1978 saw both political and legal confusion. The Band Council ostensibly controlled band affairs, but since the federal government owns the reserve and, at the time, possessed all but those parts of it allotted to individuals and groups of individuals, it governed most real property rights. When the federal government decided to make expropriations, it compensated those with lawful possession at a much higher rate than others (Legal Cases 31, 32, 33, 34, and 35). This, at the time, constituted the only meaningful distinction created by lawful possession so far as the people of Eskasoni were concerned.

Part IV:

Real Property Law under the Modern Band Council

CHAPTER EIGHT

Extralegal Factors in the Eskasoni Land Tenure System

The rest of this book treats this study's principal focus, the creation after 1978 of a novel land tenure system by a recently settled band of Micmac. However, a full appreciation of the significance of the new system requires a background knowledge of several other formative factors. Two of the most important of these are ideas on categories of real property rights and ideas about the just acquisition and exercise of those rights. Although the Eskasoni Band Council developed this novel land tenure system after 1978 and made structural changes to it in following years, these new laws did not arise out of thin air; historical social and political factors played an enormous role in their creation.

Communalism

Although the Algonkian Indian people of this region are well known in the literature as examples of communal societies (Leacock 1954; Lee 1988), there is no evidence within living memory of communalism in Eskasoni Micmac society, in which nearly everything is individually owned (that is, until the very recent changes in the law described below). Almost all houses, in fact, are owned by a single person, the exceptions being cases in which Indian Affairs persuades some newlyweds to acquire joint tenancy in lawfully possessed marital homes (only four in Eskasoni). All private businesses are owned by a single person; and all businesses that begin as partnerships rather quickly end up as single-owner enterprises.

Moreover, all the Micmac with whom I have spoken on the issue have all identified Indian Affairs and Ottawa as the sources of any ideas of communalism in the band. On the idea that the band owns the reserve communally, or indeed anything communally, one Micmac elder told me: "We *never* had that idea. They [Indian Affairs] were the ones who brought that." As we shall see, this cultural value has had a powerful influence on the land tenure system.

As elsewhere, people will sometimes use arguments involving communal rights to secure more rights for themselves, as in the following case.

DISPUTE CASE 7

Party: EH, a man approximately 35 years of age.
Party: UI and DS, two other men about the same age.
Date: Late 1950s.

Facts: The Indian Agent had earlier designated a certain woodlot to be used to supply firewood for the elderly. EH decided that he wanted to cut some wood there for himself. UI and DS argued with EH that the woodlot and the road leading to it were to supply wood only for the elderly. EH argued that "Eskasoni is for everybody."

Outcome: EH went on to cut wood for himself. He thought that UI and DS might try to fight him over the disagreement, but they did not.

Comment: EH was clearly making opportunistic use of an argument in favor of communalism. See Dispute Cases 21 and 59 for examples in which he became distraught over loss of his own private interests.

Extralegal Behavioral Rules of Land Ownership Rights

Although, and with the exception of the alien federal and Indian Agent systems, the Eskasoni people had no band-wide land tenure system until 1978, they nevertheless relied on a set of customary rules to establish just rights in real property, rules that the people of the community commonly understand as operative and value positively. However, as will become clear, an individual must be prepared to defend personally whatever rights are acquired by these traditional rules against those who would seek to limit them, because these rights traditionally were not upheld or enforced by any legal system.

Traditional Rules

ESKASONI REAL PROPERTY BEHAVIORAL RULE 1
An individual acquires ownership of free (unoccupied or unused) land by being the first to reside on that land or the first to use it. Free land consists of land that was never occupied or that was abandoned by a previous owner. Micmac usually describe free land as "land that no one owns." This rule applies to all forms of land, including residential sites, wooded areas, logging roads, waterfront and beach land, and natural meadows.

ESKASONI REAL PROPERTY BEHAVIORAL RULE 2
Ownership rights over land include rights of alienation, possession, and usufruct, as well as the right to prevent its occupation, possession, or use by others.

ESKASONI REAL PROPERTY BEHAVIORAL RULE 3
Ownership rights terminate on the abandonment of the land, as when one's wigwam is moved to a different location and residence established there or, in the case of woodlots, cessation of both use and intent of continued use.

While most people behave justly and properly with respect to the rights of others to real property, not everyone does. In contemporary conflicts involving these rules, claims of ownership are strengthened by frequent use of the land, and by clearing or fencing of the land.

Eskasoni Real Property Rights, 1800s–1940s: Absence of a Reserve-wide Land Tenure System

Two important features characterize the pre-Centralization Cape Breton Micmac real property rights system. The first is that disputes over realty were rare. The second is that disputes were settled by the parties involved, rather than by legal authorities, except in cases of intrafamilial or intradescent group disputes, which the lineage patriarch or matriarch adjudicated.

Migration and Real Property Rights

By examining data from the Canadian censuses of 1871, 1881, and 1891, it is possible to draw a useful picture of the mobility of the Cape Breton Micmac during the latter part of the 19th century. Because the Micmac by tradition do not maintain any claim of individual ownership or possessory rights to land that they abandon, a high migration rate would suggest that permanent settlement is uncommon and that, therefore, interests in particular pieces of real property and a system of legal rights to protect these interests would be undeveloped. The data indicate, in fact, that the migration rate was high during the period of 1871 to 1891 (see Appendices A and H).

The Evidence Supplied by Census Data

Migration rates here are expressed as the sum of the percentage of the population that emigrates and the percentage of the population that immigrates during the measured period. Thus, if all of the people living in one location at the start of the measured period emigrated, and all of the people living there at the end of the measured period had immigrated, the migration rate for that location would be 200%. The average Micmac migration rate for all Cape Breton locations, including non-reserve lands, was at least 104.8% from 1871 to 1881, and at least 87% from 1881 to 1891. These migration figures are calculated very conservatively and are likely much higher (see Appendices A and H).

Elderly Micmac in the 1980s stated that the first substantial settlement took place in the early part of the 20th century. This implies that Micmac in earlier times had little stake in the particular lands that they occupied at any given moment, economic or otherwise. Though migration figures alone cannot stand as proof for such a claim, they do help to corroborate evidence, described earlier, that real property law did not exist.

The census data also support the proposition that the Micmac of the time had few, if any, laws for real property, by providing information on domiciles, recorded overwhelmingly as wigwams. Wigwams cannot, by any stretch of the imagination, be considered fixtures or real property. They are temporary structures that, because of the impermanence of the materials with which they are constructed, only survive a short time. Furthermore, the covering of a wigwam is by design easily transportable, as are its poles if one has a wagon or boat. One census taker indicated that some Indians had recently left his census district "taking their houses with them."

Leaving a wigwam behind when traveling did not pose an undue hardship on a migrating family; material for poles was readily available, and large birch trees, which supplied bark for the coverings, were at that time plentiful, even though they do not grow everywhere on Cape Breton Island. Moreover, the substitute for birch bark, tarpaper, could be had at any local store for the price of a basket or two.

Farming of Little Importance. The census evidence shows that few Micmac of the late 19th century farmed. This suggests that only a few Micmac had a concern for or attachment to the land that they occupied, a characteristic that farmers acquire. Moreover, the Micmac were horticulturalists who planted only small plots of potatoes primarily for their own use, as opposed to agriculturalists who grow field crops for sale. Further, potatoes can be left alone without cultivation for months at a time, freeing the farmer to travel during the warm months, as many older Micmac told me they did in the early part of the century.

Summary of Census Data Evidence. The census data provide evidence that corroborates the accounts of older informants that a Cape Breton Micmac real property legal system above the level of the family/descent group did not develop until well into the 20th century.

A second reason for the rarity of disputes over land can be seen in a map of Eskasoni in 1927 (see Figure 3). Noticeable is the abundance of land relative to the small number of people and houses. Competition for land did not exist, because land was not scarce. There was more than enough land for houses and potato gardens, for firewood, for ashwood, and for pulpwood, at least until the imposition of the Centralization Program in the 1940s. Also important is that houses were separated from one another by wooded land (not shown in the map). Thus, there was no encroachment on the private land of others by yards, gardens, houses, or other human uses.

An understanding of most of the salient aspects of the pre-Centralization real property rights system can be had from an examination of the following dispute case:

DISPUTE CASE 8

First party: A Micmac man, F.
Second party: A second Micmac man, S.
Third party: Indian Agent (parish priest).
Date: 1930s.
Location: Whycocomagh reserve (Cape Breton Island).

Facts: The Whycocomagh reserve includes a salt marsh of at least 30 acres. A portion of that marsh had been cleared of brush to serve as a hayfield to produce salt hay, an excellent food for horses and cattle. Those who kept horses and cattle each had established rights to a strip of the cleared area. Wooden posts separated the strips from one another. At one point, F, one of the men with rights to a strip of this hayfield, moved the post between his strip and the next strip to have more hay. The man with rights to the next strip, S, moved that stake back in the opposite direction. F became outraged,

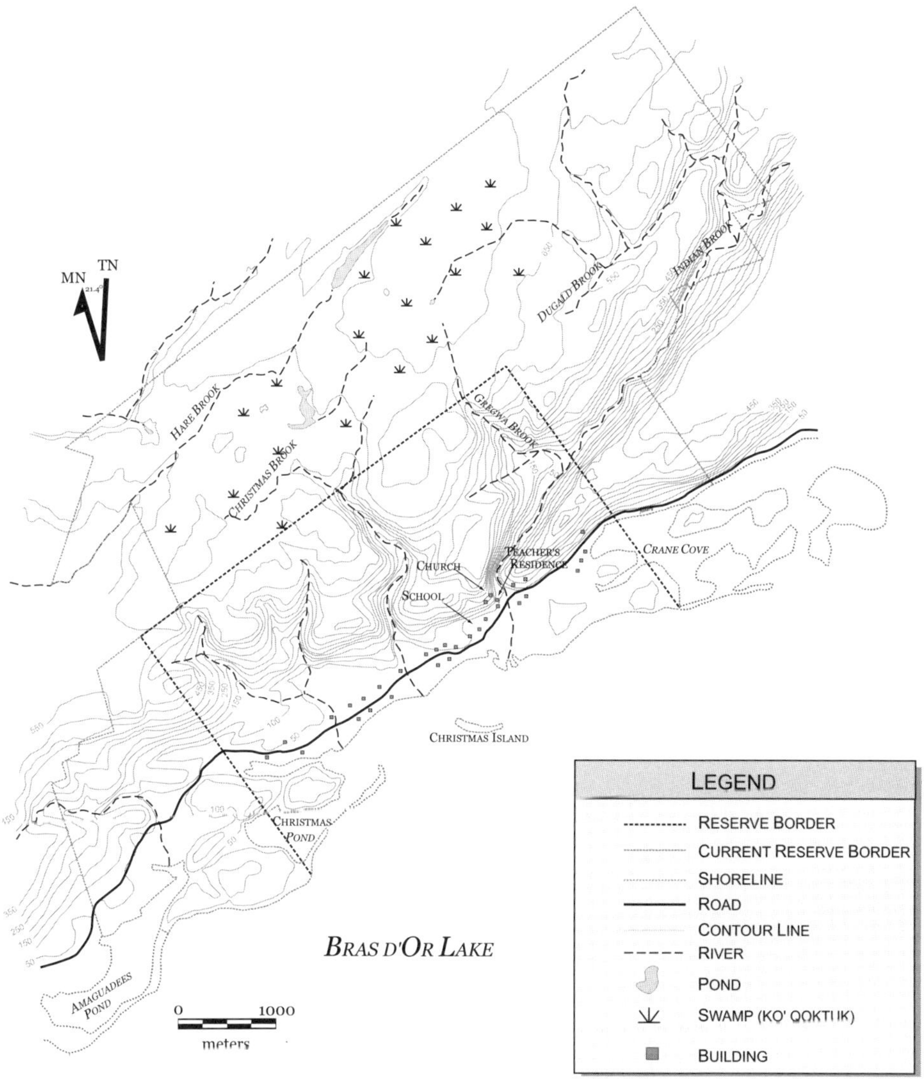

FIGURE 3. Map B: Settlement map of Eskasoni in 1927.

claiming that S had attempted to defraud him, and again moved the stake to have more of the hayfield as his own. Subsequently, the stake moved back and forth several times, until one of the parties made a public declaration that he would shoot the next person who moved the stake. Up until this point the dispute was not distinguishable from other disputes over property; though such disputes were fairly rare, they were settled by the parties to the disputes themselves.

Outcome: The shooting threat alarmed some of the other band members. Several of them went to the reserve's Indian Agent, who was also the priest of the band's parish. They apprised him of the conflict. The Indian Agent resolved the dispute by drawing new lines for users of the hayfield, granting each family who owned horses and cattle a strip of hayfield for its own use.

At the same time, the Indian Agent settled another perennial source of dispute. In the northern portion of the reserve there is a forested hillside that band members used to supply their firewood needs and as a source of pulpwood cut for sale. As soon as a lumberjack cut a road to a woodlot, it would usually happen that others would rush in to cut wood for themselves. The Indian Agent resolved this problem by promulgating a new set of rules for woodcutting. He drew lines up the side of the hill, north to south, which separated sections of woodland one from another, and assigned one section to each descent group.

This case illustrates several important points. The first is that the Grand Council did not intervene, even though the chief himself lived on the same reserve and knew of the dispute. In any event, a stern lecture, the Grand Council's sanction of choice, would likely not deter men whose passions had grown so great.

Second, the dispute was not brought to the attention of the Indian Agent until the possibility of homicide became apparent. Before this, no one but the disputants themselves were involved in the dispute. This laissez-faire social attitude towards the disputes of others agrees with the reports of other informants on the pre-Centralization real property rights system: individuals were left to handle their own disputes without outside interference (see Table 1, Behavioral Corollary E). In this case a truly extraordinary condition, the shooting threat, caused some to abandon that practice.

Third, the decision lacked two attributes of a legal decision. There was no sanction for wrongdoing, and the attribute of *obligatio* was ignored (no legal principle was enunciated): the Indian Agent made no attempt to affix blame, or to discuss the rights and duties of the parties to the dispute. He instead suggested a plan that was to reduce the potential of future conflict. This solution had two advantages. It won the approval of the members of the band, because it was equitable and because the Indian Agent had not imposed it on them. They were free to accept or reject it. Perhaps because the original parties to the dispute were not blamed as wrongdoers, they too accepted the solution. It also maintained the status quo. It set up a rule, the interpretation of which was left to individual band members, as before. Thus, the Indian Agent's settlement obviated the need for a legal system which would have undoubtedly involved him in time-consuming future legal actions had he invoked one.

Though the Indian Agent had no authority under the *Indian Act* to impose a legal system, or even to decree new rules, other Indian Agent personnel in the Centralization period made such impositions frequently, as discussed previously. This Indian Agent's choice to make a new rule, rather than to make a legal decision, undoubtedly was a reason for the parties to the dispute to accept the solution, and shows that this Indian Agent had an acute understanding of Micmac culture.

Why did the Micmac accept the pronouncements of the Indian Agent on the rights of band members to reserve land? The first reason is that this Indian Agent was an external authority. As such, he had no strong personal or political ties to any party or disputes, generally speaking, and thus had no prejudicial bias favoring one party over another. Second, despite frequently proffered statements to the contrary, some Micmac correctly regard reserves as Crown (federal) property. In the past they at least sometimes deferred to the owner of the property where they lived. Third, the Indian Agent distributed relief payments and thus had a status as something of a big man in Micmac society. Fourth, as the parish priest, he was respected as a holy man. Fifth, he obviously understood Micmac culture well and succeeded in designing a solution that conforms to Micmac ideas of justice and honor. Sixth, he rarely involved himself in Micmac disputes and normally left all disputes to the parties involved, as the Micmac prefer.

Micmac occasionally also found themselves forced to defend the boundaries of their reserves against encroachment by non-Indians. Until the 1970s, Indian Affairs rarely defended reserve boundaries, perhaps for political reasons. When the various bands began to take legal action against those non-Indians who had encroached on reserve lands, Indian Affairs was forced to fulfill its assigned role as protector of reserve lands. In the 1930s, though, the Micmac were on their own, as seen in the following case.

DISPUTE CASE 9

First party: Several Micmac men living on the Whycocomagh reserve.
Second party: A non-Indian man who claimed reserve land as his own.
Location: Whycocomagh reserve, Cape Breton.
Date: 1930s.

Facts: The Whycocomagh Micmac had long believed that the eastern border of their reserve extended much farther east than was generally accepted at the time, and that the non-Indian people living on the immediate far side of the recognized border were in fact living on reserve land. They had no physical proof to support this, however. Rather, they had an agreement with the landowner of a parcel immediately to the east of the reserve that a river separating the reserve from his land would be the boundary between the reserve and his private lot. The agreement was that whenever the river's course changed, the boundary would change with it. One day a group of Micmac men walked some distance up the river and artificially diverted it in a more easterly direction, thereby enlarging the reserve. The landowner accused the Micmac of behaving unfairly.

Outcome: When the landowner went to complain to the Micmac of Whycocomagh, several armed men who refused to accede to his demands to restore the river's previous course met him. He threatened to bring the matter before the courts, but never did so. The Micmac of Whycocomagh believe that he never brought legal action because he knew that the courts would find out that non-Indians occupied a large portion of the reserve.

Comment: It was not until the 1970s that the people of Whycocomagh discovered evidence that the reserve was actually considerably larger than any of them had thought, and they initiated a land claims suit in federal court to recover the lost land.

Newer Rules

House Ownership

The three traditional rules worked quite well when the Micmac lived in wigwams and when there was more than enough land to satisfy everyone's needs. However, around the turn of the 20th century (and in the case of a few people, even earlier), some Micmac began to build and live in frame houses. Of course, no one wanted their houses to be considered abandoned property while they were away hunting, fishing, or selling baskets, so they created and abided by the following rule:

ESKASONI REAL PROPERTY BEHAVIORAL RULE 4

The builder of a house has ownership of the house until alienating it, and each subsequent owner has the right of ownership until alienating it.

Testamentary Succession of Real Property

For decades it has been the practice for many older people, before their own death, to inform the intended recipients of their property, both real and personal, what each was to receive. An elderly individual would frequently give away or sell many worldly possessions while still alive, or would sometimes declare in written instructions to the family the disposition of the property. However, few could read and write, and so few made written wills. Many made oral bequests. In any event, the wills were only rarely seen or handled by any authority outside of the immediate family. In the absence of any instructions by the deceased, commonly the deceased's spouse or a family matriarch or patriarch would decide on the disposition of the deceased's property, usually according to the following rule.

ESKASONI REAL PROPERTY BEHAVIORAL RULE 5

In the case of intestacy, the real property of the deceased is to go to the surviving spouse. If there is no surviving spouse, it is to go to the eldest surviving offspring, regardless of sex, so that the recipient can use it to care for younger offspring.

Sometimes relatives and friends quarreled over the property of the deceased, with victory going to the quickest, the strongest, or the most cunning. This situation pertains today. The only law involved in the disposition of a decedent's property was and is administered within the family by a respected male or female elder (if there is one), according to that family's own legal principles. Thus Eskasoni Real Property Behavioral Rule 5 still applies in these decisions.

In recent years, in many cases, the elderly leave their property to lineal descendants who have little. This means that offspring of the second descending generation, rather than the first (who have often already established themselves), usually receive the deceased's automobiles, houses, and other property (see, for example, Dispute Case 38).

Property Ownership: Concepts and Questions

Confusion Over the Ownership of Housing Today

The Eskasoni Band Council land tenure system did not develop in a historical vacuum. Not only did it depend on traditional ideas of justice, but it had to contend with embedded ideas and principles in the culture introduced by the federal government and the Indian Agent. These principles caused confusion among the members of the band, some of whom continued to rely on them years after the Band Council had set up its own land tenure system, one which made no use of the federal principles (see Legal Case 57).

As discussed below, an analysis of the law reveals that the modern Eskasoni Band Council considers primary residents the outright owners of the houses where they live (Band Council Legal Principle 2), yet the Band Council has, under certain circumstances, threatened to revoke this ownership (see Legal Cases 55, 56, and 94, and Political Cases 7 and 8), confusing people. I use the term "primary residence" to refer to first residence, a status which the holder, the primary resident, may alienate to any subsequent individual. I call the interest that the primary resident has "ownership," because it includes the rights of possession, *ususfructus*, and alienation (although by operation of the *Indian Act*, the owner may not alienate to any party but a band member or members or the band).

An even greater source of confusion was the introduction of welfare housing: housing built at public expense rather than at the occupant's expense. The confusion began with Centralization and continues to this day. Before the Centralization Program of the 1940s determining the ownership of a house was simple. According to Eskasoni Real Property Behavioral Rule 4, the builder or financier of a house maintained ownership until alienating it. The only impediment to the owner's exercise of the rights of ownership was the *Indian Act* prohibition against non-band members' residence on Indian reserves. Even this did not pose an insurmountable obstacle to the right to alienate. Indian house owners could sell their houses to non-Indians, who simply moved the structures to their own land over the ice and snow in winter, and at least two people did this when they abandoned the *'Potlotek* reserve to move to Eskasoni during Centralization.

During this early period, a house was conceived of as a chattel for which there is no chattel paper. It thus belonged to the same legal class of property as a shirt; once payment is transferred to the seller, the purchaser takes possession and becomes the sole interested party.

The confusion over which party or parties ultimately owns a house on the reserve began with the Centralization Program. For the first time, houses in which the Eskasoni Micmac lived were built at the expense of Indian Affairs rather than of the individual resident. Since the beginning of the Centralization Program nearly all of the more than 600 houses built on the Eskasoni reserve have been built solely or primarily at Indian Affairs' expense; only three remain that date to before the 1940s, perhaps 20 or so were built by Indians at their own expense from the 1950s through the 1980s, and a few dozen houses have been structurally extended or improved at the expense of those residing in them. Most, if not all, people prefer to have houses built by Indian Affairs and the Band Council, because these agencies can afford to build much larger and better equipped houses than individuals usually can. Indian Affairs also began to pay for maintenance, renovation, and additions to reserve houses. Used to thinking of houses as belonging to the party that paid for them or their construction, this change caused many Eskasoni Micmac to rethink the ownership rights in the houses where they lived. Doubts about Micmac ownership of reserve housing deepened when Micmac were prosecuted for damaging houses built by Indian Affairs, which, under the *Indian Act,* were Crown property (see Legal Cases 26, 27, and 28).

When the Eskasoni Band Council came into being it acquired administrative authority over the disposition of new private housing to band members and the granting of allotments. Some Micmac took this to mean that the Band Council had some sort of ownership rights over their houses, perhaps the same as previously exercised by Indian Affairs. The federal arson prosecution of a man for burning down his own house, over Band Council objections, cast doubt on this idea as well (see Legal Case 38).

Those families who have not depended on relief payments (welfare) and have maintained, repaired, or extended their houses at their own expense usually regard the entirety of the structures they occupy as their own property. It is, for many of them, a matter of pride that they have received no aid in the form of either relief payments or financial assistance for house repair or modification. This understanding of individual ownership rights persists, despite the provisions of the *Indian Act,* because no authority has in recent decades challenged these beliefs through any action.

Needless to say, because nearly all band members receive both welfare housing and relief payments for subsistence, these beliefs are those of a tiny minority, perhaps a few dozen nuclear families or fewer. A much larger class of people, maybe one-half of the band's population, believe themselves to hold undivided interests in their house and lot, but accept housing repairs and modifications from the Band Council. This situation is analogous to, let us say, a case in which an indigent non-Indian individual, owner in fee simple of his own house, accepts free winterization repairs from a state agency. The understanding that monetary aid bears no connection to legal interests in realty accords with the *Indian Act.*

Because their own houses were built at band expense, many of the people on the reserve regard the houses where they live as belonging to the band. However, as they conceive of the situation, the residents hold greater rights to the houses they occupy than do any other members of the band. The fact that they regard a house as the property of the Band Council leads many to the logical correlate that the Band Council bears sole responsibility to maintain the house. For these people, the relationship of resident to house is analogous to that of tenant to tenement, with an important distinction. Under Canadian, British and U.S. common law, the tenant is liable for whatever damages he or she causes, and indeed has a duty to mitigate damages; the resident of the house on the reserve bears no such responsibility. A Band Council may, if it wishes, bring a lawsuit in a Canadian court against an individual causing damage, though to maintain a good political reputation the Eskasoni Band Council refrains from this.

Additional evidence for the idea that a house does not belong to the occupant comes in the form of the well-known inability of an occupant to acquire an ordinary mortgage from a bank; because the houses sit on federal land that cannot be seized, no bank will provide mortgages.

Many of those who regard the houses as band property refuse to spend any of their own funds on the house that they occupy. They say that because the Band Council gives assistance to fix houses that the Band Council should provide repairs in every case in which they are needed. Some display an extreme reluctance to spend any of their own money on housing repair or construction costs, as seen in the following example.

A man to whom the Band Council had given all the supplies for a building project for his house picked up purchase orders from the band office as he needed them. One day he needed only a pound of nails, but rather than go directly to the store and spend his own money, he went the extra mile or so to the band office and waited for many minutes for a Band Council purchase order to be written out before returning in the direction of the store.

A conflict of expectations arises because the Band Council, for political reasons, usually regards occupants as owners of their houses. The Band Council expects, or at least prefers, that band members attend to the maintenance of the houses they occupy, and often rewards those who do by giving them whatever housing improvements they request. Most band members, however, expect the Band Council to maintain the houses they live in.

In the wet Cape Breton climate, the lack of proper maintenance can destroy a house quickly, often in fewer than 10 years. Thus the Band Council faces the problem of motivating people to take better care of their houses so that they last longer. Such motivation is difficult to achieve among those people who believe that the houses where they live are not their own property, or who are accustomed to decades of social assistance programs that have repaired their houses at no cost to them. Many houses are inadequately painted or in other ways unprotected from the weather, and since the early 1980s the Band Council and Indian Affairs have built houses that are as maintenance free as possible.

How is it that those who believe that the Band Council owns their houses also know that they can alienate their houses to others? They answer that they can only do so on the chief's sufferance, which he could revoke at any time.

Because of these factors the Eskasoni Micmac have very unclear ideas about the ultimate ownership of their houses. As the first bona fide *Indian Act* chief of Eskasoni described the Eskasoni people in the 1980s, "deep down they know that they don't own their own houses."

On the other hand, there has been no urgent or great need to establish a definite answer to the question of who truly owns the houses on the reserve because, with rare exceptions, no one faces the prospect of being forced from their houses. Moreover, people on the reserve still maintain their extralegal rights under Eskasoni Real Property Behavioral Rule 2 to remove trespassers from their houses and lands, to alienate their real property (at least, to the Band Council or to other band members), and to otherwise use the real property over which they have control in whatever way they desire, including razing it.

The M Descent Group Lands

A second and quite different source of confusion over real property ownership rights on the Eskasoni reserve arose from popular beliefs about the supposedly legally anomalous M descent group lands. Driving west through the central part of the Eskasoni reserve on the main road, the casual observer sees densely constructed housing and then an area next to the creek where nobody lives. After passing a cemetery and church and traveling approximately 1,200 meters (or about three-quarters of a mile), there are large beautifully kept lawns surrounding but eight houses, and behind them, on the hill, sits a long line of houses a mere three meters (about 10 feet) or so apart. Why, one wonders, do some people live so closely together, while others nearby enjoy such great amounts of space?

In this large part of the reserve lies a parcel of land of more than two dozen acres that a prominent family has claimed as its own property for longer than members of the band can remember. The M descent group members claim that the Crown granted them the fee simple ownership of the land in the 19th century, in the same way as other lands in the region were granted to immigrant settlers and others who wanted land. This type of grant is popularly known as a "Crown grant."

A 19th-century cadastral sheet of the reserve and its environs seems to lend some credibility to the claim. Within the solid-line boundary of the reserve is a smaller area bound with dashed lines, inside of which is written "D. M. and sons." Unlike all the other lots marked on the cadastral sheet, and the reserve itself, this quasi-lot did not include a reference to a listing in the Book of Registered Grants, the authority for Crown (original) grants of land by the British government.

The question is how the provincial Crown could give ownership of the same piece of land to two parties, if the family's claim to fee simple ownership is true. This is in fact a problem that faced the Indian Agent when the Centralization Program first began at Eskasoni in the early 1940s. Before this, Indian Agents had very little to do with most aspects of reserve life, and had little reason to involve themselves with real property matters internal to the interests of the band community.

When the Indian Agency was placed on the reserve itself during Centralization, Indian Affairs chose a central location, on M descent group lands, to construct a building intended to house the reserve's administrative center and a cooperative store. This choice prompted a dispute with the M descent group and, on inquiry, the superintendent found that other members of the band supported the descent group's claim. The case is as follows.

LEGAL CASE 39

First party: PM.
Second party: The superintendent of the Eskasoni Indian Agency.
Authority: Indian Affairs.
Date: 1940s.

Facts: The Indian Agent had decided to build an administrative building and store in the center of the Eskasoni reserve. The M descent group claimed ownership of the land that the Indian Agent selected for the building. When the superintendent spoke with PM, PM said that he would sell the land that Indian Affairs wanted. Indian Affairs made further inquiry to the Department of Lands and Forests in Halifax, which could not find any proof that any member of any family had ever received any grant of any kind in that area. Their records showed only the setting aside of land for the entire reserve.

Outcome: Whether or not Indian Affairs purchased the land or compensated the M descent group for the loss of its use is not independently verifiable; Indian Affairs records omit the decision and the Indian Agent involved is deceased. There is evidence that Indian Affairs probably recognized the M descent group claim to some degree. For one thing, the M descent group, and many other people on the reserve, say that the payment was made. Second, Indian Affairs did not build any new housing on the land that the M descent group claimed, even during the Centralization period when the Indian Agent directed some workers to move close to the center of the reserve to be nearer their work and more easily within reach. Third, Indian Affairs has, from the beginning of Centralization in 1942 until the late 1970s, nearly always compensated individual Indians for their interests in realty, if Indian Affairs or its employees damaged such interest. Whether this was out of a sense of fairness, or in the interest of good relations with the Micmac people, or for some other reason is unclear. Another Indian Agent of the Eskasoni agency said that he had always respected the M descent group's claim to the land simply because it was the fair thing to do. However, by the late 1960s Indian Affairs had terminated this policy and now usually recognizes only loss of lawful possession and improvements as compensable (see Legal Case 30).

In sum, members of the band universally agree that the Indian Agent provided compensation, and this is taken as further proof supporting the popular belief in M descent group ownership of the land.

This puzzles many band members; they wonder how it is that an individual can own land in fee simple that is also reserve land. The true legal status of the land is not widely known to band members, and members of the M descent group prefer this. Nevertheless, people accepted this "ownership" and did not encroach on the land. To complicate the question, the M descent group in the 1960s received allotment to some, but not all, of the lands to which they lay claim of ownership, yet they still claim the same larger area as their own. Once, when a man was looking for a place to build a house for his family, he decided that a beautiful spot overlooking Bras D'Or Lake was what he wanted. The M descent group sold him a part of the land to which they lay claim of ownership, but it was not land to which they themselves had lawful possession.

The purchaser paid $1,000 for a parcel of this land, and received a handwritten paper that the M descent group seller purported to be a conveying instrument for that land. When the purchaser showed the defective deed to Indian Affairs and asked for a Certificate of Possession to the land, Indian Affairs informed him that he had paid his money for nothing, that no one had lawful possession of the lot, and that if he wanted a Certificate of Possession he would have to ask the Band Council for one. Some years later, another person bought some land from the same man. The M family seller told him that "this land is yours now, and nobody can take it from you." This land is part of the same lot from which the first purchaser acquired his land.

The Band Council has not encroached on or expropriated M descent group lands, because it allows families and individuals to own the real property that they reside on versus the Band Council.

Yet another source of confusion over land ownership rights originated in a federal program to give World War II veterans land as a reward for their service to the country. Since the federal government could not give ownership of reserve land to Indian veterans, it instead paid the bands a sum of money to build houses for the veterans. Many of the veterans, however, claimed ownership of the land on which the houses were built, as veterans who were fee simple owners of land off of the reserve did. Some on the reserve today accept these erroneous claims as valid and call the land involved "veteran land." Some people also conflate "veteran land" and lawfully possessed land, labeling the latter category of land with the former term.

Band Possession of Land

The federal legal decision that gave possession of unallotted land to the band created still more confusion. As mentioned earlier, the Micmac conceive of land as falling into one of two ownership categories, owned or free, in agreement with Eskasoni Real Property Behavioral Rule 1. The belief in two ownership categories still applies to lands within the reserve. However, sometime later, perhaps after the 1978 *Mathias v. Findlay* decision that established that bands, and not the Crown, possess unallotted reserve lands, some Micmac at Eskasoni began to think of land unowned by individuals as belonging to the band as a whole and found themselves in harmony with federal law. This belief is expressed in the following rule.

ESKASONI REAL PROPERTY BEHAVIORAL RULE 6

The band as a whole owns reserve land that is unowned by individuals.

It must be stated, however, that most band members do not consider this rule valid, in force, or in any other way applicable, and many who see the reserve divided into owned and free lands oppose it politically (according to Eskasoni Real Property Behavioral Rule 1). Unlike Eskasoni Real Property Behavioral Rules 1 through 5, Eskasoni Real Property Behavioral Rule 6 is therefore not universally considered just.

Furthermore, because the Eskasoni legal system divides land into free and owned, and individuals come to own land simply by using or occupying it, this rule has little if any applicability in actual legal cases. Rather, some cite it as justification for the Band Council to regulate use of reserve lands (Legal Cases 64, 100, and 104).

Summary

Today more than half the members of the Eskasoni band believe themselves to have the greatest share of ownership rights in the houses in which they reside. The other half or so regard the band as the owners of the houses where they live, but believe themselves to have a greater interest in those houses than do any other band members. Overall, however, the issue causes confusion. The question of the M descent group lands, which seems to many to involve fee simple ownership of a parcel of reserve land, also perplexes the many band members ignorant of the true legal status of those lands. The same applies to "veteran land." Thus, we may conclude that some use whatever claims they can to establish whatever rights they can to land on the reserve (see, for example, Legal Cases 97, 98, 99, and 110).

Despite the confusion over the ultimate ownership of houses, the Eskasoni Micmac behave in many respects as if they do own their houses. They control occupancy, chase away trespassers, and sell whatever interests they have in them to other band members or to the band. Their behavior regarding real property use ideally follows a handful of customary rules, all but one universally considered just (Eskasoni Real Property Behavioral Rule 6). These rules, some quite old, in essence give the owner of land (who acquires ownership by being the first to reside on it) the right to use it and the house on it as he or she wishes, until alienating it.

As we shall see, ideas on just property rights often differ considerably from the legal principles actually applied on the reserve.

A System of Extralegal Social Control

A final, yet central, influence on the modern land tenure system consists of an intricate system of extralegal social control, aspects of which are completely novel. To preserve the ability of this system to function, in 1987 the Band Council made a fundamental change to its land tenure system.

The Micmac prefer extralegal means of social control, both today and in the past. Part of this preference results from a general dislike and distrust of authority. An authority, by definition, is in some way superior to others. The Micmac disdain anyone who makes himself or herself superior to others, and have no respect for those who obey any authority's commands too readily. This attitude, I am convinced, survives from the earlier period of hunting and gathering mobility, when survival required social flexibility and individual freedom of action, and any overly centralized authority would cause severe logistical difficulties. Legal authorities, in performing their duties as authorities, in addition violate the following Micmac behavioral ideals: Behavioral Postulate 3, Behavioral Corollary C, Behavioral

Corollary D, and Behavioral Corollary E (see Table 1). Further, legal authorities frequently have personal biases of their own against one party or another, especially if they are, as is usually the case, also political authorities.

Ostracism

The Micmac use ostracism as a means of social control far more often than any other method. It is the basic way of dealing with improper behavior, on which all other forms of dealing with improper behavior are built. When one individual offends another, the offended individual ceases or greatly reduces social contact with the offender, and the offender sometimes loses the goodwill of those others who learn of the offense as well. Former friends avoid those who have offended them by refusing to pay them visits, by ignoring them if they visit, and by ignoring them in public. Accustomed to frequent and generous positive social reinforcement in daily life, Micmac individuals typically feel ostracism's effects very strongly.

Commonly, someone who offends another loses social contact only with that individual and perhaps some of his or her family and lineage. However, some people manage to offend the entire community. Those who commit serious crimes belong to this group, as do those who change their religious affiliation away from Catholicism.

A good example of this latter instance concerns the few band members who in recent decades have converted to the Baha'i faith. Until this time, all Micmac on the reserve were firm adherents of the Catholic faith, and the rest of the band reacted strongly against the Baha'is. Few people would talk to them or visit them. Those who did were frequently ostracized themselves. Baha'is find it difficult to get jobs in the band government and malicious stories are sometimes spread about them (for example, that they worship the Devil and hold their prayer services in the nude).

The extent of this ostracism can be seen in the following example. A Micmac man had befriended a Protestant man who had come to the reserve to try to convert Micmac people to his denomination (see Legal Cases 74 and 75). The missionary tried to interest his Micmac friend in converting. The Micmac man refused, primarily because he did "not want to be 'cut-off' like '*Sosep*,'" who was ostracized for his conversion to the Baha'i faith. In other words, to have converted would have meant ostracism by the community, and this he would not countenance.

Revenge and Self-help

"Revenge is very important to Micmac people," a Micmac man once told me. The Band Council does not regulate revenge; in fact, Band Council members themselves often engage in political revenge to punish "backstabbers." Micmac do make use of the Canadian court system in criminal cases, even though a criminal conviction leaves the civil dispute between the criminal and the victim unresolved. Take, for example, the following dispute cases, which make use of the Family Home Territory (defined as the immediate environs of an extended family or patrilineal descent group living together; see Physical Structure, below).

DISPUTE CASE 10

First party: GS, a young man.
Second party: A small family living a few kilometers (about two miles) away.
Date: Late 1970s.

Facts: GS killed a young male member of the second party (see Dispute Case 11). He served several years in prison after receiving a manslaughter conviction in a Canadian court.

Outcome: The prison term diminished neither the right nor the duty of the second party to beat or to kill the first party in revenge. As one member of the family said to me, referring to her neighborhood, "He'd better not come around here, or we'll take care of him." The dispute will apparently last as long as both parties remain alive.

DISPUTE CASE 11

First party: GS, a young man of the S lineage who killed another man in a fight.
Second party: PV, a friend of the deceased.
Date: Late 1970s.

Facts: GS had killed another man in a fight. Before he was sentenced to prison by the courts, PV met GS at the band's community hall at a late-night dance.

Outcome: PV beat GS severely, and was later arrested and punished by the provincial court for this attack. However, for years afterward, PV was very fearful every time he walked on the reserve's main road where it entered GS's Family Home Territory (described more fully below). The S lineage is, to quote a member of the band, "the most feared family on the reserve."

Generally speaking, an injured party's use of the Canadian court system to punish offenders is considered an attempt to shift the aggrieved party's responsibility for personal revenge to the courts, as well as to punish the offender with an often unjustly harsh punishment. Ideally, the injured party should be able to redress any wrongs without having to resort to the assistance of a third party, such as a court. Reliance on either police or the courts brands a man as weak (although women frequently use these means).

Social Withdrawal

Micmac usually use ostracism to control the behavior of other community members. But those unusual individuals who commit serious crimes, or who otherwise seriously offend community sensibilities, escape retribution only at the sufferance of all the individual members of the group. In these instances, revenge is accomplished in one of three ways: by a complaint to the police, if the offense is prohibited by Nova Scotia or Canadian law; with a beating with fists; or by group vigilante action against the offender. Group vigilante action typically involves beatings, though in one case it involved arson (see Dispute Case 15).

DISPUTE CASE 12

Offender: CC.
Offended: Friends of OT, the woman killed by CC.
Date: 1986.

Facts: CC was driving late one night and failed to see his friend OT, a young lady, who was standing in the road attempting to get his attention to get a ride. He ran into OT and killed her. Although the Royal Canadian Mounted Police investigation into the accident cleared CC of all culpability, some of the women's friends blamed him for OT's death.

Outcome: One night several OT's women friends saw CC and beat him severely. CC, it was said, did little to defend himself.

Comment: This is a rare case. Other than domestic quarrels, Micmac men and women almost never fight each other.

The offender can in many situations avoid recrimination by withdrawing from public contact or by leaving the group altogether. Public exposure, on the other hand, invites members of the group to take action against the offender, as in the following cases.

DISPUTE CASE 13

Offender: FG, a middle-aged man.
Offended: The Eskasoni band.
Offense: Incest, sex with minors.
Date: About 1979.

Facts: The offender outraged public sensibilities by having sexual relations with his daughter and other young people. An informant told me privately that he had reported the alleged offense to the police, because, he said, he "saw him around too much."

Outcome: The police investigation ultimately led to a lengthy prison sentence for the man. Whether or not the informant's account is accurate is unclear. The important point is that the offender did not seclude himself after his transgressions became public knowledge. Someone reported him, though the identity of that person is not public knowledge.

Compare the behavior of the offender in the previous case with the behavior of the offenders in the following two cases.

DISPUTE CASE 14

Offender: AB, a man approximately 35 years of age.
Offended: The Eskasoni band.
Offense: Incest.
Date: Early 1980s.

Facts: AB had had sex with minors and had served a prison sentence for his crime. Sometime after he returned from prison he began to have sex with his daughter.

Outcome: As soon as the new offense became public knowledge, AB secluded himself in his house. He left the house only rarely in future years; his parents brought him food and other necessities. In this way he escaped further punishment. This offense apparently went unreported to the police, since no further legal action was taken against AB.

DISPUTE CASE 15

Offender: RA, a 40-year-old man (the boyfriend).
Offended: The Eskasoni band.
Third party: The reserve priest.
Offense: Making threats to harm the priest and to burn down the church.
Date: Mid-1980s.

Facts: RA began a romantic and sexual relationship with a woman (mentioned in Dispute Case 14) while they lived with her father, AB. After the relationship continued for a while, AB moved into his own small shack. Later the woman told her boyfriend, RA, that the reserve's priest had forced her to have sex with him. This enraged RA, the only person on the reserve to believe her accusation. RA went to the bishop's house on mainland Nova Scotia and woke him in the middle of the night. When the bishop arrived at the door, RA repeated what his girlfriend had told him, threatened the priest with bodily harm, and also said that he would set fire to the reserve's church unless the Catholic Church removed the priest from the reserve.

Outcome: As punishment for making this threat, the Catholic Church excommunicated RA. The band was also enraged by RA's actions. RA made no attempt to leave the reserve, and sometime later some young men broke the windows of his shack. Not long after this, when RA remained at large on the reserve, some men set fire to the shack while RA slept; the fire department arrived soon after, and there was little damage. RA also had to fight several of the people who most disliked him. RA decided that his best course of action was to leave the reserve. He dismantled his shack and had it moved to Malagawatch (*'Malakawe:j*), a nearby and nearly uninhabited reserve. RA himself never moved there, but remained on the reserve for a few months longer, staying with friends. He later moved to Boston, where he lived for more than two years before returning to his reserve. Though still an unpopular figure (more than one person told me "no one wants him around"), he was thereafter able to walk around the reserve largely unimpeded.

One Micmac man earned popular displeasure another way and reacted as others have to unpopularity. This man had spent much of his adult life working and traveling in the United States and returned to the reserve as a mature man. What happened after his return is the subject of the following dispute case.

DISPUTE CASE 16

Offender: Q, a man approximately 35 years of age.
Offended: Many people on the Eskasoni reserve.
Date: Early to mid-1980s.

Facts: Q is a likeable, highly intelligent person. His only fault, in the eyes of others, is that he drinks too much and then pesters people for money to buy liquor. After he had gotten as much money from his neighbors and acquaintances as he could through polite requests, he began to annoy people so that they would pay him just to leave them alone. He rarely paid his debts. He traveled all over the reserve to keep from asking money of the same people every time he wanted it.

Outcome: Gradually Q began to offend people to the degree that there were houses where he was not welcome, and then entire parts of the reserve where he dared not to go for fear of being verbally harassed or even beaten. He later spent almost all of his time in his house or in a handful of places where he was still welcome. According to his brother, he remains in the house because "that's how he stays out of trouble." He also avoided repaying his debts by remaining inside his house.

Comment: By the 1990s, Q had controlled his drinking, acquired a good job, and ceased asking for money. His reputation in the community soared as a result.

In sum, the offenders in these dispute cases had become so offensive that they became unwelcome in all homes, and therefore the reserve as a whole. They mitigated their exposure to retribution and punishment by withdrawing from public contact.

Mobility, Settlement, and Territorial Defense

The Eskasoni Micmac use a fourth type of extralegal social control, a novel type of territorial defense. Like the other forms of extralegal social control, it involves creating distance between the disputants.

Traditionally, the Micmac used, in addition to revenge, ostracism, and social withdrawal, the option of mobility to achieve social control extralegally. When disputes erupted, one party (or both) would find proximity to the other intolerable, and would pack up and leave. Of course, this did not mean that the dispute had ended, but it was at least arrested, and if and when the parties again met, months or years afterward, tempers had usually cooled.

As the Micmac gradually settled and adopted permanent housing, and especially as welfare rules and band politics made it difficult to change residence, the popular option of moving away from trouble became prohibitively expensive for most. Few have been willing to leave the reserve to avoid confrontation, because this would mean leaving family, a permanent and valuable house, most welfare payments, and other financial benefits, especially employment. Having almost completely lost the option of mobility as a way to arrest the progress of disputes, the Eskasoni Micmac have turned instead to the use of the land they occupy to stop disputes. When a dispute occurs, each party (and, often, some or all of the young men of the family/descent group of each party as well) will defend his or her territory from intrusion by the other party. This provides a deterrence to actual physical confrontation between the parties and halts the dispute.

Physical Structure

Micmac territories at Eskasoni have a telescoping or nesting structure. Some of the smallest territories fit into a larger territory, and several of these make up a yet larger type of territory, and so on. The smallest territory is that of a nuclear family, or even a single individual living alone in a house and apart from any kin. The next larger territory, which I call the Family Home Territory, comprises the immediate environs of an extended family or patrilineal descent group living together. This territory has no specific term of reference in the Micmac language; in fact, the Micmac language has no term that translates as "territory." Instead, each Family Home Territory is known by the name of the family patriarch, usually, or the matriarch, or sometimes by the name of an individual owner. For example, if the individual concerned is named *San* ("John"), his Family Home Territory will be known as *'Sanek* ("John's place," "John's land," or "John's territory"). Some others are known by the name of the lineage group whose members reside on the territory. Otherwise, the land itself is discussed in terms of ownership, with people saying, for example, "this land is mine" (*ni:n ma'qamikewm 'ula*) or "your land" (*ki:l ma'qamikewm*).

The Family Home Territory is closely identified with the prestige of the family living there. It is ideally a place where disreputable acts do not occur, because these would reflect badly on the people living there. A member of the family or lineage who engages in disreputable behavior, such as fighting, drinking heavily, or committing adultery, usually does it elsewhere. Non-lineage members who enter a house and behave badly are asked to "respect this house" by altering their behavior. The Family Home Territory is crucial to the building of solidary lineages for the purpose of gaining power in band politics.

The next larger territory I call the reserve subsection, which includes one or more Family Home Territory. Subsections coincide with particular streets or neighborhoods and are known by the names of those streets or neighborhoods, such as 74 Street or George Street. Again, this has no corresponding Micmac term.

The reserve as a whole also contains three sections, each made up of subsections. These three sections are *'Qamsipu:k*, *Apamuek*–Eskasoni–Middletown, and Castle Bay. For handling disputes, the level of the reserve forms the largest exclusive territory.

Territorial Systems of Defense Against Individuals

This territorial system has several functions. The first, the territorial system of defense against individuals, uses territorial boundaries to ensure the safety of individuals and groups.

When an individual initiates a serious dispute, he or she typically wishes to avoid contact with the enemy or the antagonized public, and stays home. There it is usually safe, because public opinion regards entering a home or territory itself as an attack on the individual, a major breach of acceptable behavior considered an aggressive, offensive, and highly inflammatory act. The victim may, according to community norms, justifiably beat the intruder, as well as enlist sympathetic brothers and other patrikin to accomplish this. This right formed the principle underlying the threat made in Dispute Case 10.

This system of defense by threat of violence applies almost exclusively to people in their late teens through their late thirties; older people simply avoid each other and each other's homes (Family Home Territory) and rarely engage in violence. Further, it is unseemly and rare for men and women to fight each other; women fight women and men fight men. Finally, the territorial system's telescoping structure makes defense of central importance. To enter the most exclusive level of territory, which includes the rival's home, is to invite violence, as in the following cases.

DISPUTE CASE 17

First party: FM.
Second party: KF.
Date: 1985.

Facts: FM and KF had had a long-running dispute that involved several points of disagreement; in short, they simply disliked each other very much. Both lived in the same reserve section, but in different subsections. One day, FM decided to have it out with KF, and after drinking considerable alcohol left his house and walked over to KF's reserve subsection, entering his territory.

Outcome: KF obliged FM's desire to fight and promptly gave FM a bloody nose, ending the matter for the time being.

DISPUTE CASE 18

Party: VS, a male member of the S lineage.
Party: Several male members of the Y lineage.
Date: 1993.

Facts: Some members of both the S and Y lineages do not like each other and have a history of mutual hostility. They occupied separate reserve sections and individuals members of the two lineages generally avoided entering each other's sections. One night, VS attended a drinking party in the Y lineage's reserve section. After VS taunted some members of the Y lineage, a fight broke out.

Outcome: Several members of the Y lineage beat VS so badly that he died.

This dispute continued:

DISPUTE CASE 19

Party: Male members of the S lineage.
Party: GY, a male member of the Y lineage.
Date: 1997.

Facts: GY, who had been involved in the beating of VS, was one day riding his all-terrain vehicle and strayed into the S lineage's reserve section. Some of the S lineage's members were riding in the same area, saw GY, and gave chase, intending to beat him.

Outcome: GY managed to escape.

DISPUTE CASE 20

Party: Male members of the G lineage.
Party: Male members of the Y lineage.
Date: Early 1980s.

Facts: Many members of the Y and G lineages had a long history of mutual dislike. One night several armed members of the Y lineage entered the Family Home Territory of the G lineage, obviously hoping to provoke a fight.

Outcome: The members of the G lineage remained in their homes and did not fight the Y lineage members. Though the G lineage thereby lost some face as a result of this weakness, and the Y lineage strengthened its reputation as toughs, the latter also reinforced their image as dangerous, improperly behaved, and uncontrolled. The two remain rivals.

Dispute Case 11 provides another example of this phenomenon. PV did not experience physical violence, but certainly knew from the rules of the system that he had reason to be afraid when in GS's Family Home Territory (see also Dispute Case 31).

This system bears a superficial resemblance to the kind of "turf battles" found among some urban gangs, in which any member of one gang can act violently toward any member of another, even if no personal wrongs have occurred. Further, all members are expected to support and defend all other members. The gang turf system usually forces young men traveling through a particular turf to display some sign of respect toward the gang associated with that turf. The Micmac territorial system has none of these features. In marked contrast to gang behavior, the Micmac system of defense against individuals allows anyone to travel anywhere, except when a particular single individual is excluded from a particular territory because of an ongoing dispute. This system does not generalize to other individuals, such as members of the disputant's family, lineage, household, Family Home Territory, or reserve section.

Typically, if a dispute erupts, each party will avoid the other's territory. In many cases, the immediate kin of the two parties themselves will also become embroiled. For example, if a disputant enters his enemy's territory, not just his enemy may fight him, but the enemy's brother, father, son, or even cousins and nephews. In some cases, if a man who is a brother to a party to a dispute enters the brother's enemy's territory, he may be beaten as well. On the other hand, friendship can also fully trump kinship considerations. A brother of a party to a dispute may be good friends with the brother of his brother's enemy. In such cases, the two friends would be able to visit each other without impediment. While members of one Micmac lineage often share dislike of the members of another, it is quite often true that the brother of a disputant may enjoy a close friendship with his brother's enemy and would remain completely uninvolved in a fight between the two. Micmac value friendship and idealize individualism too greatly to form permanent alliances based on kinship that function in every instance. Friendship often takes precedence over kinship.

In contrast to this system of territorial defense stand the actual Eskasoni gangs. The reserve had a few youth gangs from the late 1940s until the early 1970s, with a few more emerging recently, and sometimes the members of these gangs used the territorial system specifically to provoke a fight. During the 1950s and 1960s especially there was considerable gang activity among teenage boys and young men (it took the band's tribal police force until the 1970s to disband the gangs, according to one tribal officer). Each reserve section had one or more gangs associated with it; for a member of one gang living in one section to enter another section was an invitation to fight. As one man from *Qamsipu:k* related, going to Castle Bay "was like running the gauntlet."

The Reduction of Violence

Whereas the infamous gang turf territorial system binds the integrity of territorial boundaries directly to group vanity and invites violence, the Micmac telescoping territorial defense system reduces violence and the likelihood of future violence.

THE PHYSICAL SEPARATION OF DISPUTANTS

In cases of mild disputes, in which violence will not occur, disputants simply do not visit each other's houses. When a serious dispute occurs, the party in the right expects the party in the wrong to avoid the former's territory. For the wrongful party in a serious dispute to enter the territory of the other party is to issue a challenge to the injured party, who has the right to call his sympathetic male kin to his aid to fight off the intruder (subject to consideration of friendship, as mentioned above). Of course, in most dispute cases, both parties feel justified in their actions in the dispute. In such instances, the territorial avoidance and defense is mutual. Both disputants are expected each to avoid the other's territory and, when the system works, as it usually does, the dispute is arrested. This system works identically for women and girls, although such disputes are far less common; men and boys never fight against women and girls.

Territorial avoidance procedure makes use of the telescoping structure of the territories. As mentioned earlier, the general rule is that a disputant avoids entering the largest exclusive territory of which the other disputant is a resident. Thus, two disputants living adjacent to each other would avoid only each other's house lots. Someone living in Eskasoni who had a dispute with someone living on the *Waqamatkuk* reserve would not enter any part of the *Waqamatkuk* reserve. I once asked an acquaintance who lived in a part of the reserve section of *Apamuek* to accompany me to 74 Street, also in *Apamuek*. "No, no," he said, "I don't go there, that's *'Sosepek*," explaining that he had had a strong disagreement with a man named *'Sosep* ("Joseph") who lived on that street; the entire area of the street, a recognized reserve subsection, and not simply *'Sosep*'s Family Home Territory, was off limits to him. This same individual also had a dispute with a person living on the Whycocomagh reserve, and would not enter that reserve at all. The geographical reference made in Dispute Case 10 referred to the entirety of Castle Bay, where the second party lived; the first party, the killer, lived in *Apamuek*. Another man, living in Castle Bay, could not enter *'Qamsipu:k*, because he had allegedly impregnated a young woman there and had abjured his responsibility to the child and the woman (see Dispute Case 31). In actuality, he did sometimes enter *'Qamsipu:k* to visit a brother who lived there, but when he went he quickly entered his brother's house and never left it while in that reserve section.

The use of territories in the conduct of disputes also ties closely to matters of prestige. Those who have done wrong and cannot travel freely on the reserve lose face as a result of this inability to get about. The injured party can use this fact to further reduce a foe's honor by issuing statements intended to be circulated back to the foe: [named area] *'ni:newey* (the named area "is mine") or, even more forcefully, [named area] *'ni:newey pasik* (the named area "is mine exclusively"). When spoken publicly these are strong warnings to avoid the territory or, conversely, may be intended and understood as invitations to come to fight. If the adversary does not go to the territory of the antagonizer, people say *jipalatl* ("he [she] fears him [her]"), meaning that still more honor has been lost.

On the whole, and despite the fact that some violence occurs, this system of territories functions extremely well to maintain the physical separation of disputants, and therefore to keep violence to a low level.

Finally, the territorial system of threatened violence in defense against individuals does not assume great importance to all patrilineages or individuals. A great many lineages and their members eschew violence; they either publicly bawl out intruders or use this system only as a potential tool of last resort. Moreover, even in the case of "the most feared family in Eskasoni," some members have nothing to do with the physical intimidation or the defense mechanisms involved, seeing this means of attaining political power as unworthy of them and, at the least, as unnecessary to their goals.

Territoriality and the Reduction of Potential Future Disputes

The Micmac of Eskasoni believe, as a general rule with exceptions, that outsiders cause trouble, and therefore act warily in their presence. Outsiders living in one's Family Home Territory, for example, can be troublesome primarily because they do not fall under the jurisdiction of their family/descent group's patriarch or matriarch while there, and thus cannot be controlled by legal means. The legal authority of the patriarch or matriarch extends only to members of the family or lineage, because at this legal level the law operates on the personality principal. Those who immigrate into another large territory, such as a section or reserve, may also potentially cause trouble in their new locations because they live away from their own patrilineal families, whose opinions they value, and who can thus control them legally. In other words, people who move into a region where all are strangers are less likely to care whether they offend their neighbors, simply because these neighbors' opinions do not matter as much as those of their kin and friends. Moreover, some people reason, if the immigrant were a good person, why would he or she leave his or her own family and neighborhood? Or, even, wish to leave it?

Simply reducing the number of one's neighbors, particularly non-patrilineally related neighbors, inevitably reduces conflict, and Micmac verbalize this belief frequently. The fewer social contacts one has, the less the likelihood that friction will come about. The same attitude is seen in the Eskasonians' sentiment that there are simply too many people in the band. In some instances, the Family Home Territory provides a home for an entire phratry of two to four patrilineages, who form political alliances, live together with few disputes among them, and who frequently work together to keep unwanted individuals or families from settling in their midst (see Dispute Cases 23 and 75). In such cases, no one has legal authority over the phratry, but rather each lineage's head provides the legal authority and political leadership for his own lineage. Within the phratry, lineages achieve cooperation politically, as seen in this next case.

DISPUTE CASE 21

First party: LS.
Second party: EH.
Date: 1960s.

Facts: LS and EH were the patriarchs of their respective lineages. They formed a phratry in the 1940s when they built their houses near each other on the Eskasoni reserve, which was undergoing Centralization. This phratry is united by common origin (both are from the same community), intermarriage (LS married EH's sister), common values (both value hard work and self-sufficiency), and common political leanings. Both had several children, and when one of LS's children became an adult LS gave him a piece of land for his house, which is between his house and EH's. EH, however, considered that land his own and had earmarked it for his own offspring.

Outcome: EH and LS argued, but EH ultimately gave in just to keep the peace. This is not a legal decision, because neither had authority over the other, but a political one.

The Eskasoni Micmac reduce the frequency of future disputes by using territorial boundaries to restrict or prevent immigration of potentially troublesome individuals and families. This restriction applies to the Family Home Territory, reserve section, and reserve territory levels; band members can even prevent non-band member Micmac from becoming band members, thus denying them Band Council housing assistance and other financial support, and therefore making it difficult to settle on the reserve.

A Family Home Territory is normally open to settlement only by members of the patrilineal family that occupies it, their spouses and offspring and, in a few cases, members of related or allied lineages. No individual may build a house on the Family Home Territory of another patrilineage without the permission of the patrilineage patriarch or matriarch; if he or she tried to do so, the members of that patrilineage would use any means of self-redress available to stop the intrusion, including violence (see Dispute Cases 23, 70, and 73) .

Some of the reasons for this have already been given. However, there is another critical factor, reputation. Reputation in Eskasoni is of central importance, as it is generally in small face-to-face societies. But in Eskasoni, in addition to personal behavior, individuals and families are also judged on the behavior that takes place in their Family Home Territories. In a sense, behavior in the Family Home Territory may be even more important than that associated with an individual or family more generally. Hence, people behave very differently on their Family Home Territories than elsewhere. The worst behaviors are public drinking or public intoxication, adultery or fornication, and fighting. People who engage in these behaviors usually attempt, with considerable effort, to do so elsewhere. The annual trip to the blueberry fields in July and August has considerable appeal for this reason alone.

One time a man pointed out his daughter's very young illegitimate son and said "that's the blueberry fields."

Therefore, it makes sense that people will try to exclude others from the Family Home Territory, because they cannot be controlled legally but yet have the potential to damage the reputation of the Family Home Territory and those who live there.

Violence was the response to unwelcome intruders in the following cases.

DISPUTE CASE 22

First party: MV.
Second party: The X lineage.
Date: 1986.

Facts: After the incarceration of NF (see Legal Case 41), and before their divorce, VF, his wife, began seeing other men. These she brought to the house she had shared with her husband, which was on the Family Home Territory of the X family, to whom NF was half-brother and stepson, and son (to his mother). Soon VF settled on one man, MV, a non-Indian, as her lover, and he stayed with VF in the house.

Outcome: RC's stepfather and half brothers, the men of the X family, feared that MV would claim ownership of RC's house and make it his permanent home. After telling him repeatedly to leave, to no effect, they beat him and sent him away from the Family Home Territory.

Comment: According to those disinterested observers with whom I spoke on the reserve, this was a justifiable case of the men of the X lineage, as one woman put it, "protecting their territory." VF should not have brought her lovers to her husband's Family Home Territory. She finally moved out of the house to live in a nearby city, where she met another boyfriend.

DISPUTE CASE 23

First party: HJ, a woman.
Second party: YP, a member of the P lineage.
Third party: FX, a member of the X lineage.
Date: 1997.

Facts: The members of the P and X lineages had lived amicably near each other for decades, since the initial settlement of Castle Bay during Centralization. In 1997, HJ, looking for a place to locate her mobile home, asked the Band Council whether she could live on a site that happened to be between YP's P lineage nuclear family and FX's X lineage nuclear family. The Band Council approved, but with the stipulation that the site not be too far from the road, so that the Band Council would bear less expense servicing the site.

Outcome: When HJ began to ready the site for her mobile home, YP and FX came out brandishing tools and threatened HJ with them. HJ dropped her interest in living on that lot.

The most obvious instance of the desire to keep outsiders from settling in one's Family Home Territory may be seen in Legal Cases 97, 98, and 99. In these cases, the Band Council sought to build a new housing subdivision in a lineage's Family Home

Territory, only to meet great resistance that greatly delayed and altered the project. Just a few years later that same lineage donated the use of some of this very land for the construction of public powwow grounds. Because it was used once per year, it did not provide an opportunity for permanent settlement. Moreover, it somewhat assuaged public hostility for the refusal to allow the construction of the subdivision.

Territorial Defense for Peace and Quiet

Yet another form of territorial behavior derives from the need for peace and quiet, as in the following cases, in which legal control cannot be exercised.

DISPUTE CASE 24

First party: Several groups of teenagers.
Second party: The FX family.
Date: 1998.

Facts: FX (one of the families involved in Dispute Case 23) also had trouble with groups of teenagers who roamed through the area, often late at night and in the early morning hours. They often made so much noise that they woke all who lived within earshot. In an attempt to prevent the teenagers from using the backyard as a travel route, the FX family built a fence around it.

Outcome: The teenagers tore the fence down 10 times during the period of March through July.

DISPUTE CASE 25

First party: Unknown.
Second party: Young neighborhood children.
Date: 1997.

Facts: Adjacent to some apartment buildings and behind two private residences lay some uncleared land. A walking trail in these woods is used by the neighborhood children. Someone placed barbed wire through the grass and bushes on and beside the trail to prevent children from using it.

Outcome: Unknown.

Comment: The mother of one child who played in the area remarked that for someone to do such a thing is "really bad."

All-terrain vehicles pose a new problem. In the past, off-road vehicles such as motorcycles and snowmobiles were so expensive that they were rare and only driven by adults. Today children drive ATVs every day of the year and can turn lawns into mud bogs in the spring. The children and young adults often cross privately owned land without permission, leading to some disputes.

DISPUTE CASE 26

First party: TR, a young man riding an ATV.
Second party: EH, an older woman with grown children.
Date: About 1995.

Facts: EH had grown tired of ATV riders driving through her property at all hours of the night, keeping her awake. The police could not stop the ATV riders from creating a public nuisance, so EH put up a sign prohibiting ATV riders from crossing her property. She knew that this measure alone would be insufficient to stop the ATV riders, so she put nails through some roofing shingles and placed the shingles on the ground with the nails protruding upward. TR did not heed the sign and ran over the nails, flattening all four of his tires.

Outcome: TR became very angry (a full set of new tires costs $700) and wanted to fight with EH. However, once he learned that EH's son is JH, one of the best fighters on the reserve, he declined to pursue the matter.

DISPUTE CASE 27

First party: Various ATV riders.
Second party: RT, a man living uxorilocally with his wife's lineage.
Date: 1997.

Facts: Shortly after a couple built their house they decided to fix their lawn, but realized that they could not have a lawn with all the ATVs that crossed it nearly every day. So RT put large rocks in the path that the ATVs took across his lawn.

Outcome: The riders drove over the rocks.

DISPUTE CASE 28

First party: Various ATV riders.
Second party: ZB.
Date: 1997.

Facts: The ATV riders constantly crossing his lawn meant ruination of ZB's lawn as well as a danger to his young children. ZB erected a fence in the path of the riders.

Outcome: The riders tore down the fence every time ZB erected it.

Not all people defend their territorial interests. Some adhere to traditional mores (see Table 1, Behavioral Corollary C) and tolerate neighbors who behave badly, as in the next case.

DISPUTE CASE 29

First party: The TO family.
Second party: DS and his family.
Date: About 1990.

Facts: The DS family moved to a secluded and remote part of the reserve, some distance from all but one other family, members of DS's wife's lineage. Some years after they moved to this idyllic spot, another family had a house built directly across the road. DS knew the family and predicted, correctly, that they would bring disturbance. Now, several times a month, the young TO family hosts a loud party. The situation is not so objectionable in the winter, but in the summer when DS and his family sleep with their windows open, DS frequently is kept awake until 3:00 a.m. or later.

Outcome: DS took no action to prevent his neighbor's arrival. When I asked him why he did not do anything to thwart his neighbor's initial ingress into the Family Home Territory, he replied, "There's nothing you can do to stop them." More than a decade later, he was awarded a new house and had it constructed in another part of the reserve.

The Generalization of Animosity and a Preference for the Natal Reserve Section

Micmac often generalize animosity, justly or not, to other lineages or bands. Just as the tourist mugged in New York City may hate or fear all New Yorkers, so too have many Eskasoni people come to dislike, for example, many members of the Shubenacadie band on the mainland. The following are two examples of how this generalization of animosity occurs.

DISPUTE CASE 30

First party: F, a man from Eskasoni.
Second party: Hockey players from the Shubenacadie band.
Date: 1986.
Location: A hockey arena in Sydney, Nova Scotia.

Facts: F was a member of an Eskasoni hockey team that competed in the annual Nova Scotia Micmac hockey tournament. His son played for an Eskasoni juvenile team in the same tournament. During his game against a Shubenacadie juvenile team, a Shubenacadie player struck and injured the son with the butt of a hockey stick seriously enough to require hospitalization.

Outcome: The day after his son's injury, F's team faced a Shubenacadie team in the tournament. During this game, F struck a Shubenacadie player with his hockey stick in retaliation for his son's injury.

DISPUTE CASE 31

First party: D and G, brothers.
Second party: Many of the people of *'Qamsipu:k*.
Date: 1980s.

Facts: D and G are brothers who grew up in Castle Bay. It is widely accepted that D once had a girlfriend in *'Qamsipu:k* whom he impregnated and subsequently abandoned, abdicating all responsibility for the child. As a result, many of the people living in *'Qamsipu:k* disliked D. One *'Qamsipu:k* resident remarked: "We don't like people who come to our neighborhood, get a girl pregnant, and take off." G lives in *'Qamsipu:k* because his wife, who was raised there, was able to find them a house and land in that part of the reserve. People in *'Qamsipu:k* dislike G because he is D's brother. G must bear the brunt of the consequences of his brother's impropriety, which consist largely of avoidance and verbal harassment, but no violence. G therefore spends most of his time in Castle Bay and *Apamuek*, and when he is in *'Qamsipu:k* stays inside his house much of the time.

Outcome: Both D and G remain unwelcome in *'Qamsipu:k* years after the impropriety.

In Dispute Cases 30 and 31, animosity was generalized in three directions. In the first case, the anger of the man whose son was injured was generalized to all who belong to the group of which his son's attacker was a member. In

Dispute Case 31, D offended not only the family of his former girlfriend, but virtually all the people who live in her reserve section. Those who were offended in turn generalized their resentment over the offense to the entire family of the offender.

Overall, people tend to blame other people from another band, another reserve section, or another lineage for all the improper behavior of all people from each of these groups. This does not necessarily translate into conflict, but it often results in arguments and wary and reserved social interaction. Thus someone who moves from *'Qamsipu:k* to Castle Bay may never become an accepted member of the neighborhood. Given this means of social control, it is no wonder that the Centralization Program caused so much social upheaval.

Of course, not every Micmac generalizes his or her opinions of and behavior toward other groups. In fact, many take pride in treating others solely on their individual merits; one may have an adversarial relationship, for example, with one man, but be the best of friends with his siblings. Generalization of antipathy often occurs between members of groups who do not have long-term familiarity with each other.

Moreover, in some few cases people who have immigrated from other groups have ultimately become some of the most beloved members of their new neighborhoods. Although unusual, some have even been invited to build houses in the Family Home Territories of unrelated families.

And to be sure, troublemakers do cause problems within their own reserve sections. But there the troublemakers and their proclivities are well known, and their behavior can be controlled by ostracism, revenge, vigilantism, and especially by the legal authority of their own patrilineages, which work toward their eventual withdrawal from the area (see, for example, Dispute Case 15). This general wariness toward outsiders does not seem on the face of it to square with the well-known pattern of hunter–gatherers, including Micmac, to readily share food and other necessities with others, strangers included. However, generosity does not automatically imply friendliness. Many observers of Micmac and related cultures mistake the two, which may in fact share nothing in common. Rather, I believe that the general wariness towards strangers serves a vital function, that of reducing conflict in cases in which no effective legal control applies.

The barriers placed against immigration into reserve sections and Family Home Territories have increased social division and inhibited social intercourse. The degree to which social disunity has developed can be seen in that many adults cannot identify some other members of the band on sight, despite having grown up in the same community of approximately 3,000 people (as of 2000). I believe, finally, that this strategy has survived into the present from the Micmac's relatively recent hunter–gatherer past. This generalized animosity leads to a preference for living in one's own natal reserve section.

Couples usually live virilocally in the sense that they almost always live in the husband's natal reserve section, even if not near his parents. Although a patrilineage will usually prevent an outsider from settling in the midst of its Family Home Territory, even settling in a reserve section where one did not grow up is difficult, if not impossible, for other reasons. The preference is for one's own reserve section or subsection, and there is a fear of the possibility of life-long status as an outsider, a status that the outsider's children often inherit. The effect of this status is clear and common for married women. Because the Micmac reside virilocally for the most part, many women end up living in a foreign reserve section. Often treated as outsiders for the rest of their lives, these women usually spend a great deal of time visiting with their own families, and typically develop friendships with women who, like themselves, moved from other reserve sections to live with their husbands' families. The same is true for those few men who live with their wives' families, though they of course have fewer chances to make friends locally.

Therefore, most Micmac prefer to remain in their own natal reserve sections, and sometimes even subsections. Although Eskasoni is a small community, although many of its descent groups' members are spread throughout the reserve, and although people originally from different bands are settled in all parts of the reserve, there is usually a strong affinity for, and identification with, one's own natal reserve section or subsection. This affinity sometimes manifests itself in rivalries. Some people, teenagers and young adults mostly, for example, disparagingly refer to Castle Bay as "Cowshit Bay," an allusion to the importance of animal husbandry there in past decades, and one that characterizes its inhabitants as unsophisticated. In response, some Castle Bay residents have characterized those living in other parts of the reserve as drunks or as violent and dangerous. In the late 1970s and early 1980s there was a popular movement in Castle Bay to secede from Eskasoni and form both a separate reserve and band. A Castle Bay resident discussing the movement with a *'Qamsipu:k* man was told that Castle Bay could not secede because, he said jokingly, "every town has to have its ghetto." A housing subdivision was built in the 1960s and 1970s along a single road in *Apamuek* (see Legal Case 30); a cheap fortified wine known as "74" was popular there and the reserve's priest dubbed the road "74 Street." The name stuck, and the residents now use the name with a certain left-handed dignity.

Territorial Behavior to Strengthen Lineage Solidarity

Many larger, politically ambitious lineages find a third function of territoriality even more important. In the quest for political power on the reserve, and for the ability to acquire the material benefits that accompany this power, no method comes close to that of creating solidarity in a large lineage as a way of inducing its members to vote for the patriarch's choice of candidates. When the members of a lineage achieve solidarity, then employment, housing, and many other benefits flow to them from elected politicians, who hope to gain the large block of votes that the lineage can deliver. This obviously represents a relatively new function for lineage solidarity, developing since 1957.

Lineal solidarity depends on a strong leader or authority who has the ability to enforce political discipline among the members of lineage (see Legal Case 44). This he cannot accomplish if significant numbers of members live outside of the Family Home Territory (see Dispute Case 72 for an example of the enormous power that solidarity can give a lineage).

Some of the smaller lineages also make extensive use of the Family Home Territory to increase solidarity and political power as do the larger lineages, but many others do not or feel that efforts to increase their own political power in this way would be largely in vain because of their small size. In such cases, the members of the smaller lineages have limited political aspirations, do not quarrel with their neighbors, and seem content to live peaceably under the protection of the reserve's police force. Often members of such lineages live dispersed among other families and settle neolocally or, in a few cases, even uxorilocally. This characterization also applies to those individuals in the larger lineages who fail to see the advantage of lineage solidarity.

Of course, the patriarch of the lineage group living within the Family Home Territory must maintain order within the group by adjudicating disputes between members, otherwise the group might fly apart and lose its political advantage. Some members of the lineal group, especially in more recent times, believe the negative effects of living under a powerful lineage or family patriarch outweigh the benefits of living in the Family Home Territory with most of the rest of one's lineage, as we see in the following case.

DISPUTE CASE 32

Party: AG.
Party: FG and RG, AG's father and mother.
Date: About 1990.

Facts: FG and RG frequently sought to end AG's pursuit of his lifestyle, which they found unhealthful and disreputable. When AG married and had children, the Band Council awarded him and his family a house. AG wanted to have his house built at some distance from FG and RG to escape his parents' authority. His parents wanted AG nearby so they could continue to try to control his behavior. This dynamic also characterizes individual members of the larger lineages who fail to see the political advantage of lineage solidarity.

Outcome: AG had his house built in a subdivision in the same reserve subsection as his parents, but outside of the lineage's Family Home Territory.

Comment: Many of the other young families in the same subdivision also had their houses built there to escape lineage and parental authority.

CHAPTER NINE

Civil Disputes: Unadjudicated Contemporary Real Property Cases

Civil disputes between private parties make up by far most of the disputes in the community, both for real property and generally. The contemporary treatment of civil real property disputes between private parties differs little from the traditional treatment: in the past, civil disputes received no legal adjudication whatsoever. Presently, although the Band Council will adjudicate civil disputes between private parties, it only infrequently and reluctantly does so, as discussed earlier. On the other hand, the Band Council always decides disputes between the Band Council and private band members.

Real Property Cases Without Legal Adjudication

There are three reasons why the Micmac give little legal attention to civil disputes between private band members, outside of the jurisdiction of family/descent group legal authorities; two of these have already been introduced:

1. The Band Council avoids making legal decisions in civil cases between private band members to avoid political retaliation at the polls.

2. Micmac generally dislike authority in any form and always distrust legal authorities, whom they suspect of political bias. This accords with a traditional preference for self-redress, in which the individual shows ability and strength of character by handling disputes personally.

The third reason for the inactivity of the legal system concerning private civil real property cases is that when the Band Council does consent to decide such a case, it always gives greater rights to the primary resident at the time of the decision. Some Micmac perceive this practice to be a mark of unprincipled injustice that makes the Band Council undesirable as a legal authority. On the other hand, this strategy forces private parties to work out their own differences, which agrees with traditional values, and which most Micmac therefore see as just.

The Band Council members know that many of the people of Eskasoni regard the Band Council as politically biased. Realizing this limitation, they attempt to create a system of assigning legal rights in housing and land that will reduce the likelihood of such future disputes.

The Micmac therefore rely on self-redress in handling real property disputes in most instances. The use of self-redress conforms to Behavioral Postulate 3 and

Behavioral Corollary E (see Table 1), and constitutes the preferred method even when the danger of serious violence is great, as seen in some of the cases below. The following dispute cases are beyond the scope of effective legal resolution on the reserve. The Band Council does not regulate contracts between band members, even those involving real property. The Band Council also usually avoids taking part in disputes that occur within the Family Home Territory, regarding them as more properly the purview of the lineage patriarch or matriarch (see Legal Cases 42 through 50). The Band Council played no part in the following cases.

DISPUTE CASE 33

First party: OQ, a man in his fifties.
Second party: IK, a businessman in his forties.
Date: 1970s.

Facts: OQ acquired a house and lot from his brother, who had earlier given a small portion of that lot to the businessman IK. IK built a store on that small portion, which was re-surveyed as a separate lot and to which he acquired allotment. IK later decided that he wanted the entire original lot for himself, a lot to which OQ did not have lawful possession. IK and his brothers went to OQ's house one evening with guns and threatened him and his family with physical harm if OQ did not vacate and give him the lot. OQ, a former paratrooper, ignored IK's demands. When the Band Council awarded OQ a new house, he decided to have it built behind his old house. IK again went with his brothers and demanded that he build the new house in another location, outside the bounds of his lot.

Outcome: OQ again defied IK and built his house on the same lot. IK eventually ceased his efforts to force OQ from the lot, where OQ's family still resides. The two men remained hostile to each other until OQ's death.

DISPUTE CASE 34

First party: RR.
Second party: QK.
Date: 1985.

Facts: RR received a new house from the Band Council and sold his old house to QK with a quitclaim deed. Because QK had little money, the two parties agreed that QK was to pay installments as his welfare checks arrived, and QK took up residence in the old house.

Outcome: As time went by, QK never paid the money he owed, despite RR's demands. RR had no way to force QK to pay for the house in which he lived. Since buyers who establish primary residence face no threat to their ownership by any legal authority, those who promise to pay after the sale cannot be forced to pay; in such cases, the seller has no recourse to recover the money promised as the price of the sale. RR knew that it would be futile even to approach the Band Council for assistance. The dispute remains unresolved and largely forgotten.

DISPUTE CASE 35

Party: KC, a young woman.
Authority: SU.
Date: 2000s.

Facts: KC is a police officer. She rented a house to live in from SU. After a while she claimed ownership of the house, using her residence and authority as a police officer to help secure that ownership. SU protested.

Outcome: KC has ownership of the house.

DISPUTE CASE 36

First party: CV.
Second party: JH.
Date: 1987.

Facts: CV began construction of a house for one of his offspring, on what he believed was his own land. When the machinery to dig the hole for the foundation arrived, JH, who lived next door, emerged brandishing a shotgun. JH claimed that the land that CV intended for the use of his family was hers.

Outcome: After a discussion, the two parties reached an understanding on the location of their mutual property boundary and the dispute ended peacefully.

Comment: JH used the shotgun to indicate that she took the matter seriously; violence was extremely unlikely.

Testamentary and Intestamentary Succession of Property

Property Succession

It may seem odd to discuss the subject of inheritance in a section dealing with extralegal means of regulating real property, since inheritance holds such an important place in many legal systems. However, the Micmac of Eskasoni have never legally controlled the inheritance of real property, with the partial exception of those systems of law at the family/descent group level that include such a feature. Traditionally, Eskasoni Real Property Behavioral Rules 1, 2, and 3 covered all contingencies after the death of a landowner. People were so mobile, and land so freely available, that any dispute over land could find its resolution in mobility, with no loss of value to any party.

But settlement and the adoption of more permanent frame housing in the 20th century raised the question of what to do with the dwellings and lots of those who died. Property succession was a new problem because people had until then lived in wigwams on abundant land. Mitigating the importance of rights in housing in the period shortly after settlement was the poverty of the time; very few people had much of an estate to leave their heirs. Housing, as valuable as it is today, was not so then. One could build a house for 10 dollars' worth of materials in the 1920s and 1930s, and so houses were often worth less than the price of a horse or cow. Further, early houses degraded very quickly in the damp climate. The use of vapor barriers was unknown and walls and timbers often began to rot soon after houses were erected. Paint was generally considered an expensive extravagance, as it is by some even today, and this markedly hastened the deterioration of housing. For example, only three of the more than 440 houses standing in Eskasoni in 1987 existed before the Centralization building program. In short, there often was not much of a house to leave to one's heirs, and offspring frequently desired newer housing. The disposition of land, again, was not an object of competition, because land was in great abundance.

Some real property owners made use of wills, but in cases of intestate death, with no Indian Affairs involvement, the ideal behavior rule was as follows (see Chapter 8):

ESKASONI REAL PROPERTY BEHAVIORAL RULE 5
In the case of intestacy, the real property of the deceased is to go to the surviving spouse. If there is no spouse, it is to go to the eldest surviving offspring, regardless of sex, so that the recipient can use it to care for younger offspring.

If the owner and one other co-habiting individual occupy the house, that individual, who is usually related to the owner by kinship, acquires ownership (generally this is by earlier agreement between owner and co-habitant and shows congruence with Eskasoni Real Property Behavioral Rule 1). Should there be no surviving offspring or co-habitant, there is no accepted rule as to who receives the property. In such circumstances, either relatives get together to make a decision or a dispute over the disposition of the property arises.

Eskasoni Real Property Behavioral Rule 5 provides legal protection only when a spouse survives to adjudicate, because such cases are decided at the family/descent group legal level. In all cases I am aware of, the surviving spouse has always received the property of the deceased without dispute. If there were a dispute, the remaining spouse would exercise his or her legal authority as head of household. On the other hand, when the last remaining parent dies, disputes over the disposition of the realty frequently occur, because no individual with legal authority over the property remains (see Dispute Cases 37, 38, and 39).

This rule applies to all cases except those very few in which property is lawfully possessed, and then Indian Affairs administers the disposition of the property in accord with *Indian Act* provisions. In essence, provisions of the two legal systems conflict and, in fact, there may be a dispute over who actually owns or possesses the property, even after an Indian Affairs ruling. However, to my knowledge only one dispute (Dispute Case 67) over the disposition of the few allotted lots that belonged to deceased persons has to this point occurred, and in this case lawful possession played no part in the outcome.

Disputes over property succession still go without legal resolution today. In fact, property succession cases are one of the largest classes of real property disputes and, because they are civil disputes, receive no adjudication. The following are several such disputes.

DISPUTE CASE 37

First party: TB, a young woman.
Second party: CB, her younger sister.
Date: 1985.

Facts: The parents of TB and CB died before the new house that the Band Council had given them could be completed. According to Eskasoni Real Property Behavioral Rule 5, and by the wishes of the parents, TB, as the oldest offspring, was to receive ownership of the house. Instead, CB moved herself and her children into the house. TB continued to live in the old house with her offspring and her siblings.

Outcome: With the parents dead, there was no legal authority with jurisdiction over the dispute. Because TB disliked confrontations, she did not try to force CB from the new house. The dispute ended when TB died.

Comment: People regarded CB's actions as unjust.

DISPUTE CASE 38

First party: PT, a man in his twenties.
Second party: FH, chief of the band.
Date: Early 1990s.

Facts: TH was father to FH and mother's father to PT. PT and his grandfather had enjoyed an unusually close relationship. When TH died, his will left his house and its contents to PT, who was just beginning a family of his own and needed a house. FH also enjoyed a close relationship with his father, TH, and had a strong sentimental attachment to his father's house. Both men, in short, wanted ownership of the house on grounds of consanguineal relationship to the owner and sentimental attachment. PT also wished to raise his family there. When TH died, a conflict arose over the disposition of the house. PT relied on the will. FH argued that the will was invalid on several grounds, and that therefore he, as his son, should inherit the house. Tempers flared.

Outcome: It was suggested that FH offer to use his influence with the Band Council to have it award PT one of the new houses to be built by the band that year, that PT be allowed to take some mementos from TH's house, and that TH's house and the rest of the contents of the house go to FH. PT and FH both found these terms agreeable and the dispute ended, although some animosity remains.

DISPUTE CASE 39

Party: DFG, a daughter of RTG.
Party: FSG, a daughter of RTG.
Party: JKG, a teen-aged grandson of RTG.
Date: Early 1990s.

Facts: RTG lived alone with her grandson, JKG. She intended that JKG receive the house they shared when she died. However, after RTG's death DFG took possession of the house.

Outcome: FSG responded by forcibly taking possession from DFG and returning it to JKG.

Comment: People spoke very highly of FSG and her actions following this dispute.

The Division of Marital Realty on Divorce and Separation

A news story in September 1998 quoted then Minister of Indian Affairs Jane Stewart, who was studying the issue of matrimonial property on Indian reserves (the *Indian Act*, which pre-empts provincial statute, is silent on this), as saying that "because of a legislative gap First Nations members [Canadian Indians] do not have the real property rights of other Canadians when their marriages dissolve" (New Factfinder to Advise . . . 1998:5).

A Micmac elder was more forthright when she told me, also in 1998, that, "the law on the reserve is crooked as hell," referring to the fact that on divorce men often manage to acquire sole ownership of the house in which the couple lived, even in cases in which the wife has custody of the couple's children. This to many constitutes an injustice.

Most cases of property division in divorce receive no legal attention. The *Indian Act* includes no provision for such cases, and because the cases frequently involve Family Home Territories, and because lineages frequently defend these territories very resolutely, the Band Council rarely tries to involve itself as an authority. Micmac divorce cases are handled by the provincial court system in the same way as non-Indian cases, since the *Indian Act* does not regulate divorce specifically.

However, when a couple contests the division of matrimonial assets, particularly the house, the provincial courts frequently decide these cases as well, often ignoring the rules of the *Indian Act*. The *Indian Act* makes only one clear distinction in realty on the reserve, between that which is individually lawfully possessed and that which is possessed by the band. The court may thus not award property possessed by the band, which includes nearly all the houses on the reserve, to either spouse. The ability of the provincial court to make these decisions arises from these factors:

1. Indian Affairs does not involve itself in many of the day-to-day legal affairs of individual band members.

2. Many of the provincial judges are ignorant of the *Indian Act* and its various provisions, and even of the fact that many of the legal questions concerning reserves are to be decided on the basis of federal rather than provincial law. For example, one Micmac man on a New Brunswick reserve escaped conviction of a crime because a judge issued a provincial search warrant for his house rather than the necessary federal one.

3. The Band Council regards the houses on the reserve as property owned by the families residing in them, which they may alienate to any band resident. The Band Council effectively gives residents rights in their houses similar to those enjoyed by

people who live off the reserve who hold fee simple title of ownership. In brief, it does not interfere with the provincial courts by informing them that the *Indian Act* governs reserve realty.

4. Those individual band members who do know that the provincial courts cannot rule on questions of reserve realty do not tell the provincial judges. This is, I believe, because they usually regard the principle of matrimonial property settlement that provincial courts use as just; the principle (apparently from such decisions) is that the spouse who wins custody of the children receives ownership of the house.

Interestingly enough, it was during Eskasoni's very first divorce case that the Band Council attempted to define a legal solution for the control of marital property after divorce. While I would ordinarily place the following case in a chapter on law, this is actually the only legal case on the disposition of marital property in the band's history and does not reflect the later treatment of the issue. I was unable to find other instances in which the Band Council involved itself in marital property disputes.

LEGAL CASE 40

First party: RB, the wife.
Second party: FB, her husband.
Authority: Band Council.
Date: About 1979.

Facts: RB and FB, a married couple, had been awarded a new house by the Band Council for their family. Because of FB's physical abuse, RB filed for divorce before the new house could be completed. FB did not strongly desire custody of the children, so RB took custody. The court made no ruling on the question of housing because it had not been asked to do so. After the divorce, FB tried to retain possession of both old and new houses, and kept his children and former wife from occupying them.

Outcome: The Band Council, which apparently shares the same idea of justice with Canadian courts on this issue, denied FB possession of the new house, took possession itself, and then awarded the house to RB for her use and for that of the children. FB retained ownership of the old house.

Comment: This decision was politically a very easy one for the Band Council to make because it was possible for the two parties to each have one house. This situation has since been rare. Before this case, there was no divorce in this society of staunch and observant Roman Catholics. Unhappy couples would simply separate rather than take the actual step of divorcing.

The people of the community saw the Band Council decision as just. The legal principle abstracted from this case is:

BAND COUNCIL LEGAL PRINCIPLE 1

In the event of divorce, the parent who is awarded custody of the couple's children by the provincial courts will be allowed possession and ownership of the matrimonial house.

The Band Council later made this principle the basis of a formal band by-law (statute). However, in actual practice political factors made it unenforceable and effectively extinguished it. The Band Council does not have the political power to impose similar decisions on band members with marital property in a Family Home Territory. Whereas the Band Council had intended for this principle to stand forever to protect the interests of women and children, the political realities of the reserve community have not allowed this. The Family Home Territory stands so decisively as a political factor that the concept of marital property can be said not to operate within established Family Home Territories. Essentially, ownership of the house remains with the spouse who is a member of the lineage with the Family Home Territory in which the couple lived. Since the Micmac are patrilineal and usually virilocal, this means that the house usually remains with the husband, as seen in the following cases.

Where there is no Family Home Territory, ownership of the house can fall to either party. And, in both cases, the question of which party has custody of the children seems to have little, if any, bearing on the outcome, which is usually a private decision.

DISPUTE CASE 40

First party: RA, the wife.
Second party: SA, her husband.
Date: 1986.

Facts: RA and SA had been married for nearly two decades when RA decided that she had had enough of the poor way SA treated her. The marital home was located in A family territory. RA left her husband and went to live with another man.

Outcome: RA left both the house and her children behind to live with another man. SA never moved from the house and raised the children by himself.

DISPUTE CASE 41

First party: CU, the husband.
Second party: RU, his wife.
Date: About 1990.

Facts: CU and RU were in conflict over lifestyle matters and, after a decade of marriage, divorced. Both parents share care of the children. The marital house was located in the U Family Home Territory.

Outcome: The marital house, because it was in the U Family Home Territory, remained in CU's hands. RU moved to an apartment in the nearby city.

DISPUTE CASE 42

First party: LV, the husband.
Second party: PV, his wife.
Date: 1985.

Facts: LV and PV had a stormy marriage that came to an end. The couple lived in a new house in the V Family Home Territory. LV used a technique to achieve possession of his house that has now become fairly famous and imitated, because it gives the husband's behavior the outward appearance of moral probity. LV moved out of the marital house to live with his parents next door, and left his wife and children in the marital house. Although to all appearances this seemed magnanimous, he in fact had no intention of giving up the house. While PV lived there, LV and his lineage covertly harassed her by forbidding her the use of the yard, and by giving her the cold shoulder.

Outcome: Unable to withstand this emotional pressure, PV left the house and her children behind and eventually left the reserve permanently.

Comment: Several men told me that they admired LV's cleverness in keeping ownership of the marital house, but still making the situation seem as if he did whatever he could to assist his former wife. Whether or not this was the first use of this strategy I cannot say, but several other men used it later. Although several men have praised the cleverness of the artifice, the tactic is quite transparent to many I have heard discuss it. Two similar cases follow.

DISPUTE CASE 43

First party: PC, the wife.
Second party: TC, her husband.
Date: 1995.

Facts: The couple had been married nearly a decade when they decided to divorce. TC gave PC the marital house, located in the midst of C Family Home Territory, and she cared for the children there. However, TC harassed PC every two weeks or so. After PC began to see another man, TC began to threaten the new boyfriend.

Outcome: For PC, these new threats were the last straw. She abandoned the house, took her kids, and left the C family territory. TC regained possession of the house and lives there alone. PC later acquired a house of her own.

DISPUTE CASE 44

First party: AE, the wife.
Second party: DE, her husband.
Date: Early 1990s.

Facts: When AE and DE divorced, DE allowed AE to live in the marital house. This house was in E family territory and the E family acted to make AE uncomfortable.

Outcome: After spending some time enduring the E family's harassment, AE wanted to leave. However, DE's intention that AE go and leave the house behind for the E family to use backfired. AE had the house moved to another part of the reserve, near her own patrilineage.

Comment: The house would ordinarily have remained where it was constructed and, because it lay in E territory, would have remained in E family possession. AE was fortunate to be able to have the Band Council move the house, which is unusual because of the expense involved. It is all the more unusual, because the house was on land lawfully possessed by DE's father and thus, under the *Indian Act,* the house belonged to him.

DISPUTE CASE 45

First party: CD, the wife.
Second party: TD, her husband.
Date: About 1990.

Facts: After several years of co-habitation and then marriage, CD and TD acquired a new house from the Band Council. The house was built in CD's (Z lineage) Family Home Territory in *Qamsipu:k* over TD's objections. TD wanted the house built in the D Family Home Territory, or at least in his own reserve section of Castle Bay. The members of the Z lineage dislike the members of the D lineage, and TD found living in Z Family Home Territory unpleasant. Later, the couple divorced.

Outcome: After the divorce, CD kept custody of the children and ownership of the house. An outsider in the Z Family Home Territory, TD wanted nothing to do with the house.

DISPUTE CASE 46

First party: PG, the husband.
Second party: SG, his wife.
Date: 1987.

Facts: PG and SG had been married well over a decade. Their marriage was rocky, often because SG frequently saw other men. The marital house sat in the middle of G Family Home Territory. Finally, SG decided to leave PG for another man.

Outcome: PG kept the house, where he lives with and raises the couple's children. SG continues to live with another man.

DISPUTE CASE 47

First party: BG, the wife.
Second party: TG, her husband.
Date: Early 1980s.

Facts: TG and BG married and, after a few years and several children, decided that they were incompatible. TG is the brother of PG (see Dispute Case 46). The marital house of TG and BG, like that of PG, is in G Family Home Territory.

Outcome: BG left the marital house and went to live with her own patrilineage. The house and the couple's children remained with TG.

The following two cases show with particular clarity the importance of the influence of the Family Home Territory even when opposed by provincial court decision.

LEGAL CASE 41

First Party : NF, the husband.
Second party: BF, his wife.
Authority: Provincial court judge.
Date: 1986.

Facts: NF was in jail. He and his wife had a great many differences and she wanted a divorce, to which he agreed. He also allowed her custody of the children, which she wanted. Both, however, wanted ownership of the house, which is in the F family territory.

Outcome: The judge awarded BF ownership of the house because she had custody of the children.

Comment: NF, his mother, and his siblings were unhappy about the outcome of the case. They did not fully appreciate that the Eskasoni Band Council and the Canadian courts act independently.

They felt that the applicable legal principle here should have been:

BAND COUNCIL LEGAL PRINCIPLE 2

Primary residence in a house confers on the primary resident a right of ownership to the house against the Band Council that the Band Council will not normally alter.

NF and BF did abide by the decision, however. As it turned out, they reconciled some months after the husband left prison. The dispute continued in the next case.

DISPUTE CASE 48

First party: BF, the wife.
Second party: NF, the husband.
Date: About 1990.

Facts: After the provincial court awarded BF the marital house, the F lineage made BF's stay in the house uncomfortable. Later, BF attempted to trade houses with a kinsman of her former husband's family, so that he could be with his relatives and she could be rid of her former affines, but this was to no avail because the kinsman did not wish to displace NF, whom the members of the lineage considered the rightful owner of the house.

Outcome: When NF returned from jail, BF abandoned the house, at least in part because of F lineage pressure. NF now lives in the house with BF's children, a second wife, and their children. BF lives off the reserve.

Comment: This case shows that the provincial court's decision (which was erroneous under Canadian law in any event, since it contravenes the *Indian Act*) could overcome the otherwise critical importance of the Family Home Territory.

The following cases indicate what can happen to the disposition of marital property in cases in which no Family Home Territory is involved.

DISPUTE CASE 49

First party: PM, the husband.
Second party: RM, his wife.
Date: 1985.

Facts: PM and RM had been married several years and had several children when RM, who lived with her husband in the M Family Home Territory, found another site for the couple's new house. This house was built outside of the M Family Home Territory and therefore outside of the influence of the affines, who sometimes make things difficult for new brides. This move did not save the marriage, however, and the couple separated and divorced within two years of the construction of the new house.

Outcome: PM returned to live in his Family Home Territory and RM kept the new house. The couple shared custody of the children.

DISPUTE CASE 50

First party: LP, the wife.
Second party: UP, her husband.
Date: 1987.

Facts: LP and UP had been married about two decades when UP decided that he would be happier with someone else and separated from his wife. The marital house was not in a Family Home Territory.

Outcome: UP decided to give LP the marital house, although he liked the house's location. He had the marital house moved to LP's choice of location (in her lineage's Family Home Territory) and had a new house built on the old foundation for his own use. The parents share custody of the couple's one child.

DISPUTE CASE 51

First party: CR, the wife.
Second party: RR, her husband.
Date: About 1990.

Facts: After nearly a decade of marriage and several children, CR and RR decided that they would be better off apart. They agreed that CR would raise the children and that she should do so in the marital house, which was not in a Family Home Territory.

Outcome: RR left the custody of the children to CR. Because she had the children, RR felt that she should have the marital house for the benefit of the children. RR now lives alone in a small dwelling.

DISPUTE CASE 52

First party: UT, the husband.
Second party: CT, his wife.
Date: 1998.

Facts: UT and CT had a stormy decade-long relationship, living together in a new house in a housing subdivision that was not part of a Family Home Territory. UT often found himself in minor trouble with the law, sometimes because of his behavior toward his wife. Because of his sometimes violent threats against her, the provincial court barred him from entering his marital house and he lived next door with his brother. Both UT and CT each claimed the marital house. After repeated attempts to salvage the marriage and their family (the courts finally placed all of their children in foster homes), they concluded that the marriage would not work.

Outcome: CT, originally from another reserve, left the house to live on her home reserve with her parents. UT now lives in the marital house alone.

DISPUTE CASE 53

First party: JY, the wife.
Second party: FY, her husband.
Date: About 1990.

Facts: After more than a decade of marriage, JY and FY decided to divorce. FY wanted to keep the house, at least in part because it was on property that had belonged to his father. There was no Family Home Territory, however, because FY's only close living relative, his sister, had married a man from another part of the reserve and had gone to live with him. Both JY and FY wanted the house, and it was agreed that JY would have primary custody of the children.

Outcome: While the long divorce process continued, both JY and FY found other mates, with whom they lived, leaving the marital house empty. Because the house was empty, FY feared that JY would somehow acquire it through court order, Band Council pressure, or her private action. FY sold the house and its lot before JY could take any action.

From these cases we may abstract the following rule:

ESKASONI REAL PROPERTY BEHAVIORAL RULE 7

In cases in which the marital house is built on a Family Home Territory, it will be owned by the spouse whose lineage owns the Family Home Territory where the house is built, after a divorce or separation.

Disputes over Usufructary Rights

In addition to the disputes over the ownership or possession of land, conflicts over usufructary rights also sometimes arise. As expected in an area as heavily forested and sparsely populated as Cape Breton, rights in woodlots constitute the most important usufructary rights on the reserve. Despite their great economic value, no legal authorities protect these rights on the reserve. In this, however, the Eskasoni band seems to differ from at least two other Cape Breton bands, *Potlotek* (Chapel Island) and Whycocomagh.

Lumberjacks in Whycocomagh sometimes contested the rights to woodlots, until the reserve's Indian Agent proposed the novel and acceptable solution to the problem (see Dispute Case 8). Other Cape Breton reserves likewise had no legal system to control land use. At the *Potlotek* reserve, woodlot roads have long been the subject of disputes. The construction of roads to woodlots presents the most daunting portion of the timber cutting business, requiring a great deal of time, effort, and expense. A 1968 Indian Affairs report prepared by Forester A.N. Anderson included the following on timber cutting on the *Potlotek* reserve.

> Past cutting policy has been to locate a short road at random into a wooded area, then remove only top quality spruce and fir for export pulpwood 3 ½ feet in length.

> The residual stand is left to blow down and rot. Under this system, a road services very few areas as the wood is removed only a few hundred feet from either side of the road. It is understood that once a road is constructed, all Indians have equal rights to cut wood in the above manner. (Public Archives of Canada, RG 10, vol. 8511, file 50/20-7, part 2)

In short, the fact that every member of the *Potlotek* band had equal rights to a woodlot once the road to the woodlot was built meant that few wished to invest the time and effort to make more than the most rudimentary, short road, thus hampering the profitable and manageable production of wood on the reserve.

The people of Eskasoni, on the other hand, have long abided by customary rules that regulated the use of woodlots and logging roads, making the exploitation of wood resources efficient and orderly; those who constructed woodlots and logging roads owned them, but were also responsible for defending their rights against trespassers. In addition to Eskasoni Real Property Behavioral Rules 1, 2, and 3, several other corollary rules pertain specifically to rights in woodlots:

1. An individual may cut wood in any and all areas not owned by others or subject to the woodcutting rights of others. One may therefore cut on free land situated at some distance from the settled areas of the reserve. Further, one may cut on forest land located directly in the vicinity of, or directly behind, one's own house, and which is not also directly behind someone else's house, unless the second individual has released his or her claim to that wood. In any event, land directly behind one's house is normally considered to belong to the owner of the house (see, for example, Legal Cases 96 and 97). Some hold the opinion, ignored by others, that lumberjacks should not cut outside of the reserve sections where they themselves live.

2. By building a road to a woodlot, from which one plans to remove wood, one acquires ownership of the woodlot and the road to that woodlot. The builder has all rights of ownership.

3. Once cut, all wood belongs to the one who cut it, until alienated.

The last rule applied to the following two cases.

DISPUTE CASE 54

First party: RV, a Micmac woodcutter.
Second party: LA, a Micmac man.
Date: 1986.

Facts: RV had been cutting some firewood for sale. One day some pieces of wood fell off his overloaded truck and remained by the side of the steep logging road for several days.

LA decided to take the wood for himself, in broad daylight. Another man caught him in the act and informed RV of LA's actions.

Outcome: Unknown. RV had responsibility to take any action in the matter; no legal authority would have intervened. All I asked acknowledged that RV owned the wood and that LA had acted improperly.

DISPUTE CASE 55

First party: EB.
Second party: Unknown actors.
Date: 1986.

Facts: EB had cut several cords of tree-length birch and maple to sell later as firewood. He left the wood near where he had cut it to season over the summer months. As the weeks went by, a party or parties unknown began to take some of the wood bit by bit.

Outcome: EB hid near the wood several times to try to catch the thieves, but never succeeded.

Because of the expense and time involved in building logging roads, many pulp cutters try to acquire usufructary interests in woodlots to which others have built logging roads, and therefore own. The owners give, but to my knowledge never sell, limited usufructary rights to friends and relatives, as gestures of friendship or to gain political support. Normally, those who do not own woodlots of their own have interest only in acquiring usufructary rights in woodlots and not ownership. Woodlands are never sold (the one exception being some partially logged land sold to another party who intended to use it as powwow grounds). These cases conform to Eskasoni Real Property Behavioral Rule 2.

In the 1980s, I saw several instances in which people built roads to woodlots. In all cases, others acknowledged the ownership rights of those who built the roads. People either acquired from the owner usage rights of their own, refrained from using the roads, or used the roads and woodlots secretly, often at night. However, by the 1990s, in at least one important instance, the popular recognition of the rights of the road builder and first user of the woodlot had deteriorated, as seen in the following case.

DISPUTE CASE 56

Parties: Several lumbering enterprises.
Date: Early 1990s.

Facts: Because of its inaccessibility, a large section of the northeast corner of the reserve remained virgin timberland until the 1990s. By then, one party managed to build a road into the area. Other lumberjacks quickly followed. Each cutting operation sought to gain as much advantage in the richly wooded area as possible before others could obtain the available wood. Several of the parties argued that fair dividing lines should be created, so that each party could get a share.

Outcome: Various parties disregarded the attempt at dividing the woodlands, and went ahead and cut as much as they possibly could, until all the economically harvestable wood was exhausted.

One type of usufructary rights case involves children taking apples growing in others' yards, as seen in the cases below.

DISPUTE CASE 57

First party: Two children.
Second party: RS, a middle-aged woman.
Date: 1970s.

Facts: The children, two sisters, snuck into the yard of a neighbor and began picking her apples to eat.

Outcome: RS caught them and told them to leave, and they did.

Comment: The sisters went to pick apples in the yard of another neighbor, who did not mind. RS later gave the apples she grew to Halloween trick-or-treaters.

DISPUTE CASE 58

First party: Several neighborhood children.
Second party: S, a man in his thirties.
Date: 1985.

Facts: The children were one day climbing the apple trees belonging to S, and eating the green fruit. S saw them.

Outcome: S chased the children away, but they returned again and again, until S built a fence around his yard.

The problem of reducing or eliminating unwanted intrusion onto one's land is a thorny one, because to do so is considered a sign of unwelcomeness, and thus rudeness, by community standards. Some have attempted to solve the problem by erecting fences. Interestingly, people on the reserve nearly always construct fences that do not actually prevent people from walking wherever they wish, either by excluding footpaths, or by incorporating ungated openings wherever footpaths enter the lot. The fences function rather to communicate to pedestrians that their use of the land to get from one point to another is unwanted, as if the builder were to say, "I will allow you to cross my land here if you really want to, because to prevent you would be rude, but I would rather that you did not." Most fences are wooden. In Dispute Case 58, however, S used barbed wire and completely enclosed the yard. This was widely remarked on as a truly rude and unjustified gesture, and S later dismantled his fence (see also Dispute Cases 24 through 29).

Finally, there is simple trespass. For this analysis, I define trespass as the entrance or remaining on a property by a party against the owner's wishes. The following dispute involves rights to a lake floor oyster bed.

DISPUTE CASE 59

First party: EH, a man.
Second party: Two or three older men.
Date: About 1970.

Facts: EH, unhappy as a welfare recipient, was always looking for ways to support his family through his own efforts. He decided to try raising oysters. He put tree branches in the water to attract spat and registered his oyster farm with the province, which guaranteed a right to exclusive use of that portion of the Bras d'Or lake bed. Some years later, as the oysters neared maturity, several older men happened on them and, perhaps thinking they were wild oysters free for the taking, took and ate them.

Outcome: When EH learned of the loss of his oysters, he consider telling the older men that they had eaten his oysters, and that he had exclusive rights to that oyster bed. However, since Micmac etiquette discourages dispute, especially with elders, EH said nothing (see Table 1, Behavioral Corollary C). He abandoned the idea of raising oysters.

The Eskasoni Micmac universally recognize the right of the property owner to prevent anyone from being present on his or her property (Eskasoni Real Property Behavioral Rule 2). Recognition of this customary rule usually causes the trespasser to readily exit the property of another on being asked by the owner. In all trespass cases involving band members, self-redress constitutes the only remedy available to the owner. The following cases show the widespread recognition of the rule against trespass.

DISPUTE CASE 60

First party: JC, a young woman.
Second party: The reserve's police.
Date: 1985.

Facts: JC was an avid motorcyclist. Although illegal, she often rode her unregistered, off-road motorcycle on the shoulder of the main road, because this was the only way for her to get from one part of the reserve to another. One day the reserve's police saw her and gave chase. JC darted into her own driveway and disappeared into her house. The policeman parked his cruiser at the end of the driveway and waited. After some time had passed, JC's father's brother, who was at JC's house for a visit, came out and told the policeman to leave the property, because he had no permission to remain.

Outcome: The policeman left.

DISPUTE CASE 61

First party: GB, a man.
Second party: W, a neighbor of GB's brothers.
Date: 1986.

Facts: W, in order that his children not be exposed to the evils of alcohol consumption, forbade people from walking in front of his house carrying uncovered containers of alcoholic beverages. One day, GB walked across his front yard carrying an uncovered wine bottle. W emerged from his house and told GB not to go in front of his house with uncovered wine bottles.

Outcome: G apologized somewhat insincerely for his actions, and made preparations to leave W's property. However, he began to argue with W about W's possession of B family property, which the B family regarded as improper, and which was the source of a long-standing dispute (see Dispute Case 65 and Legal Case 66).

DISPUTE CASE 62

First party: V, a young man.
Second party: KO, a woman in her sixties.
Date: 1986.

Facts: V, a man from the neighborhood, walked over KO's front lawn. KO did not like people to trample her lawn.

Outcome: KO became angry and yelled at V to get off her lawn, which he did.

DISPUTE CASE 63

First party: Several young adults.
Second party: X, a man in his late twenties.
Date: 1987.

Facts: X had just become a house owner for the first time. He had been happy to get the house because he and his wife had a young child. However, it was near the community hall, which hosts dances on many weekends where there are many young adults and a fair amount of alcohol consumption. Some of these young adults had long been accustomed to walking home along a footpath that went by X's house. Often they did so at midnight or later, talking loudly and laughing, waking X, his wife, or their child. X told the young adults that they could not come onto his land to go home.

Outcome: The trespassing young adults reacted angrily, and continued to trespass. X considered building a fence, but rejected it as a futile effort, knowing that the trespassers would simply tear it down. The dispute remains unresolved.

DISPUTE CASE 64

First party: VA, a man.
Second party: XU, another man.
Date: Late 1990s.

Facts: VA decided to build his house in an uninhabited part of the reserve that is both inaccessible and has a wonderful view. At his own expense he constructed a very long driveway from a public road to the house site. Others, including XU, also wanted to build in that neighborhood once the new driveway had been built.

Outcome: VA told XU that, because he does not own the land surrounding his house, he cannot stop any building there. However, he informed XU that he would not give permission to XU to use his driveway, thereby effectively preventing XU from building a house in the neighborhood.

Summary

Parties to civil real property disputes usually have no effective legal recourse for settling grievances. Only when a family patriarch or matriarch is present to render a decision within the family/descent group can effective legal resolution take place (see Chapter 10). The Band Council typically avoids hearing these disputes, and when it does it usually preserves the status quo (see below). The Micmac people themselves, further, often prefer that no authority, especially a biased or potentially biased one, hold their fates in its hands. This is true even in cases of potentially violent disputes. Rather, they rely on self-help, Eskasoni Real Property Behavioral Rules 1 through 6, and Indian Affairs plats of surveyed reserve lots. Of course, there are always those who behave unscrupulously and who sometimes meet resistance from the other party (see Dispute Case 33) or not (see Dispute Case 37).

One could easily come to the conclusion that Dispute Case 64 indicates a weak legal system that cannot effectively protect individuals and groups from each other under certain circumstances. This assessment would not be false. It would, however, constitute a virtually complete misunderstanding of why the system is yet attractive to the Micmac people.

The Micmac hold dear dispute resolution mechanisms that provide individuals, heads of nuclear families, authorities, and others maximum individual freedom of action, responsibility, and autonomy, a taste for which the Micmac have probably retained from before European arrival. By contrast, the Micmac view many aspects of the European American legal system as restrictive, authoritarian, illogical, and even dictatorial. To be sure, there are times when the residents of the reserve are glad to have the power of the federal legal system available to aid them. Women, especially, like the ability to rely on the federal legal system when men threaten violence in a dispute.

Handling one's own problems earns individuals a great deal of respect and builds status within the community. Requesting help from an authority is considered demeaning and a sign of weakness. The importance of a demonstrated ability to handle one's own problems cannot be overstated. Finally, the Band Council realizes that the people prefer self-redress and regard the Band Council as politically biased, and thus prefer not to have legal or quasi-legal solutions forced on them. The Band Council has accommodated this preference within its responsibility to administer the band's needs by creating a system of rights in housing and land that reduces the likelihood of disputes, as will be seen below.

CHAPTER TEN

Family/Descent Group Land Tenure

We leave now the subject of disputes handled without legal authority or decision and move on to discuss the various land tenure systems that the people of the reserve use today.

The earliest Micmac land tenure law undoubtedly appeared at the family/descent group legal level, although modern law at this level differs from that of earlier times, if only because of the advent of permanent housing. The head of the family/descent group, usually the eldest capable male or, if he is dead, his widow, has legal control over the other members of the family/descent group within the Family Home Territory. The patriarch's or matriarch's authority extends only so far as his or her familial parental or grandparental authority. This authority operates on the personality principal and applies as a political force rather than as a legal authority to non-lineage members (see Dispute Case 22). When the legal authority of the family/descent group dies, legal authority no longer applies to the family/descent group or the Family Home Territory as a whole. Rather, the family/descent group splits socially and geographically into as many legal jurisdictions as there are offspring of the next generation who are heads of households. However, the members of the original family/descent group still cooperate to defend the original, larger Family Home Territory from unwanted intrusion (as discussed in Dispute Cases 19, 22, 23, 24, 65, 71, 73, 74, and 75) because of a commonality of interest. Though I was unable to record any legal cases decided at this level from earlier periods, informants tell me that disputes were settled largely according to the rules represented by Eskasoni Real Property Behavioral Rules 1, 2, and 3.

The actual laws regulating the use of a Family Home Territory may differ significantly from one family/descent group to another, as might be expected. Therefore, my concern in this chapter is with the laws on to the rights of authority that the family/descent group matriarch or patriarch commands. These laws pertain uniformly from one end of the reserve to the other, subject only to the authority's personal ability to exercise authority.

Family/Descent Group Authority

In contemporary times, as the following cases show, authorities control house ownership to control the behavior of economically dependent family members.

LEGAL CASE 42

Defendant: CD, TD's son.
Authority: TD, his father.
Date: 1997.

Facts: CD lived at home with his parents. One day CD was taking care of his son, who lived with his mother in another part of the reserve. CD's son did something that caused CD to slap him rather hard. CD's mother scolded him for hitting his son so hard and CD became angry. He then swore at his mother and told her "he's my son."

Outcome: TD told CD not to speak to his mother that way, and evicted him from the house.

LEGAL CASE 43

Defendant: FD, a man in his thirties.
Authority: TD, his father.
Date: 2000.

Facts: FD, unmarried and childless, lived with his parents. When his mother became ill and TD had to spend time and effort to attend to his wife's needs, FD began to assert authority over his younger siblings in a way contrary to TD's wishes.

Outcome: TD evicted FD from his house.

LEGAL CASE 44

Defendant: FI, a young man.
Authority: DI, FI's father.
Date: 1986.

Facts: During the 1986 band elections, DI promised his lineage's votes to certain candidates. After the voting concluded, he discovered that FI had voted against his instructions.

Outcome: DI evicted FI from the house as punishment.

LEGAL CASE 45

Defendant: WD, a young man of about 20 years of age.
Authority: HD, his father.
Date: 1987.

Facts: HD had been awarded a new house by the Band Council and decided to allow his son to live in the old house. WD was told that he could live there as long as he did not have parties with his friends there, nor drink or use drugs. Within a short time WD began to engage in the prohibited activities.

Outcome: HD evicted WD from the old house, forcing him to live in his parents' new house and under their direct supervision.

LEGAL CASE 46

Defendant: DX, a young single mother.
Authority: GX, her father.
Date: 1986.

Facts: DX was in her early twenties, had three children, one of whom was but a few months old. She had lived with her parents all of her life. DX, her mother, had had to do much of the work of caring for her grandchildren, because DX was sometimes an irresponsible mother. GX had recently received a new house from the Band Council and his family had moved into it, leaving the old house empty. DX's brothers wanted to live in the house, but GX felt that they were too irresponsible to live on their own. He allowed DX to live in the old house, on the condition that she take proper care of her children; he and his wife believed that living on her own might induce her to be more mature.

Outcome: After several months, it became clear that DX was not taking proper care of her children. GX evicted her from the house and forced her to live with his family and under his supervision. GX had his sons dismantle the house and sold the lumber.

Comment: DX later received from the Band Council an older house of her own at some distance from her father's Family Home Territory. She thus ultimately escaped her father's authority.

From these cases, and also Legal Case 81, we may abstract the following legal principles.

FAMILY/DESCENT GROUP LEGAL PRINCIPLE 1

Owners of houses may license their use by others, without compromising their ownership rights. Behavioral conditions attached to these licenses may be used to control the behavior of younger members of the family/descent group.

FAMILY/DESCENT GROUP LEGAL PRINCIPLE 2

Owners may control the interests of other members of the family/descent group in real property within the Family Home Territory.

Married couples, and other mature people, typically refuse to accept the kind of parental control used in the above cases. They demand to own their own houses, and often acquire them from the Band Council. However, the patriarch or matriarch of the descent group has legal authority to decide who may and who may not build their new houses on the Family Home Territory and can decide where these houses will be situated, as in the following case.

LEGAL CASE 47

First party: FD, a middle-aged married man.
Second party: SX.
Authority: GX, FD's wife's father.
Date: 1986.

Facts: FD, who broke with the normal Micmac pattern of virilocality by living with his wife's descent group (because he is from another band), owned a house given him by the Band Council. He had had the house built on GX's Family Home Territory, with GX's permission. After building the house very close to SX, GX's married stepson, FD, and SX began to display a strong mutual dislike for each other. SX, who owned a tiny, run-down house, later received a new house from the Band

Council. GX decided that SX would have his new house built on the other side of FD's house, also very close to it. FD protested, and asked that SX's house be built elsewhere on GX's Family Home Territory.

Outcome: GX did not alter his decision and SX's new house was built just a few feet from FD's.

Comment: FD later tried to persuade the Band Council to move his house to another part of the reserve, but the Band Council refused on economic grounds. The next year, however, FD and SX became more amicable in their relationship.

From the decisions rendered in Legal Cases 47 and 52 (see below), we may abstract the following legal principle.

FAMILY/DESCENT GROUP LEGAL PRINCIPLE 3
The lineage patriarch or matriarch may control the settlement of people and building siting on his or her Family Home Territory.

While the death of the patriarch or matriarch often spells the end of intra-lineage cohesion and unity of purpose, there is frequently a member of the lineage that takes control when Family Home Territory integrity is threatened, as in the following case and in Legal Case 96.

LEGAL CASE 48
Party: XB.
Authority: GB, her oldest sibling.
Date: 2008.

Facts: XB had spent much of her life living off the reserve. She decided to return to the reserve to live with her husband and children in a mobile home on her lineage's Family Home Territory. However, after some years there she decided that she liked life better off the reserve. Strapped for cash, she decided to try to persuade the Band Council to build her a house, so that she could sell it and use the proceeds to buy a house off the reserve. She intended to sell the house to the highest bidder, essentially, and this meant that the house would go to someone who is not a lineage member, since none of the members of her lineage had much money or needed a house.

Outcome: When GB, who had been given control over the Family Home Territory by his father before the latter's death, heard about this plan, he vetoed it, in the interest of keeping the Family Home Territory intact. XB has respected his decision.

Change in Real Property Law at the Family/Descent Group Level

The advent of permanent housing and crowding have together brought about change in the real property law at the family/descent group level. We may conceive of the question in terms of an emergent conflict between Eskasoni Real Property Behavioral Rule 2 (ownership rights over land; see Chapter 8) and the more recently developed Eskasoni Real Property Behavioral Rule 4 (which allows a house owner rights of ownership until alienating them; see below). In earlier times, of course, the wigwam owner simply folded up his wigwam after a dispute with the landowner, and moved on. As Eskasoni became more and more densely populated, and as defense of patrilineal Family Home Territories became increasingly important, permanent virilocal residence on the patriarch's Family Home Territory became the norm. The questions for the Eskasoni Micmac became whether the landowner or the house owner has the greater rights to the house, and who may govern its occupancy and use.

The Eskasoni Micmac regard house owners' rights as superior to those of the landowner. Once someone other than the patriarch or matriarch comes to legitimately own a house on a patriarch or matriarch's Family Home Territory, the patriarch or matriarch's legal authority over who resides in that house, and the ability to evict them for improper behavior, both largely end, as in the following cases.

LEGAL CASE 49

First party: CX.
Second party: SX.
Authority: GX, CX's father and SX's stepfather.
Date: 1987.

Facts: When SX received his new house from the Band Council, his old house was left empty. SX's younger brother, CX (about 19 years of age), had a girlfriend and a child by her. SX felt that he would be better off if CX could live with his girlfriend and child in their own house, and so allowed them to live in the old house. Previously, CX had lived with his parents, and GX considered CX immature for his age. GX was angry with SX for allowing CX to live in his old house; he wanted SX to evict CX, to force him to live with him until he could responsibly live on his own.

Outcome: SX remained adamant and disobeyed GX's order. CX continued to reside in SX's old house, and his frequently improper behavior did not sway SX in the least to change his mind.

SX may not have been able to alienate the house to CX had CX not been a member of the same lineage. This particular lineage has a great interest in maintaining solidarity and in keeping outsiders at a distance, which would likely have prevented SX from alienating the house to a non-lineage member. Further, SX himself would not wish to bring in an outsider, nor would most outsiders wish to live surrounded by members of a potentially unfriendly lineage. I know of no cases in which a member of the lineage who was not the lineage's authority alienated real property within the lineage's Family Home Territory to a non-lineage member (but see Legal Case 50). There is, however, at least one case in which a non-lineage member did so.

DISPUTE CASE 65

First party: W, a man.
Second party: ARG, a man.
Third party: Two B brothers.
Date: 1985.

Facts: After W had left the house he sold to the Band Council (see Legal Case 56), he moved himself and his family into a house that was between the houses of the two B brothers. The B brothers inhabited a Family Home Territory together and, although they no longer had a family patriarch or matriarch since their parents died, they decided together to allow non-lineage member ARG to use an uninhabited lineage-owned house on their Family Home Territory. When ARG left, he gave the house to W, against the wishes of the B brothers. The B brothers considered the houses B family property, because they had given only a license for ARG to possess the house temporarily, and not ownership or the right to alienate possession. ARG relied on his primary residence to establish his ownership and therefore believed that he had a right to alienate ownership of the property to W. The B brothers tried to convince W to move, but to no avail. Fighting with W was out of the question: W was the reserve's strongest man and the B brothers, who already suffered a poor reputation in the community, did not wish to damage it further by fighting.

Outcome: W refused to move. The B brothers later brought the case to the Band Council for adjudication (see Legal Case 66), but lost their case to have W evicted. W later left voluntarily when the Band Council gave him a new house.

LEGAL CASE 50

First party: FL, a man.
Second party: BT, a mother.
Authority: GL, FL's father.
Date: 1993 and later.

Facts: FL gave BT his house shortly after he moved to another reserve. After BT took up residence in FL's house, GL began to ask BT to vacate the house on the grounds that it belonged to him and his family, because it was given to FL, and because the house sits on the L Family Home Territory, of which he is the patriarch. BT, needing a house for herself and her children, and unable to find another because of the shortage of housing on the reserve generally, politely fended off GL's entreaties and remained in the house.

This case is a bit odd in one respect. Normally, a member of a lineage who is not the patriarch or matriarch of the lineage and Family Home Territory would not dare offend the other members of the lineage by alienating ownership of his house to a nonlineage member. However, in this case BT is GL's natural niece, although not by law. By the kinship reckoning used on the reserve, however, BT has rights as a lineage member and GL should not object to her possession of the house, even though as the authority of his Family Home Territory he has the right to accept or expel anyone on the Family Home Territory. BT relies on these rights, as well as the right of the owner (PL), to alienate his property as he wishes. On the other hand, the patriarch always has the right to control ingress into his Family Home Territory. GL's requests come about twice each year. I asked BT why she did not ask the Band Council to send a letter to GL telling him to cease his harassment. BT replied, "He'd never listen to them."

Outcome: The case remains unresolved, but GL does not exercise force sufficient to drive BT from the house, and seems more and more resigned to BT's presence with every year that passes.

Comment: This case may be considered either a dispute case or a legal case in which

GL attempts, weakly, to assert the territorial principle of law to drive BT out. As in all other cases of family and lineage law in this society, the personality principle is by far stronger than territorial.

We may contrast the previous case with the following, in which a man living away from his own Family Home Territory found it easier to disobey his family authority.

LEGAL CASE 51

First party: FT, a young man.
Second party: ST, FT's mother.
Authority: CT, FT's brother and ST's oldest son.
Date: 1985.

Facts: FT lived with ST on another reserve. One day FT had an argument with ST, walked out of the house, and went to live in CT's house in Eskasoni. ST ordered CT to evict FT from his house, so that he would have to return to ST's house and live under her authority.

Outcome: CT refused ST's entreaty. Instead, he proclaimed that, as his brother, FT was welcome in his house as long as he lived.

Comment: After a few weeks, FT and ST concluded their disagreement and FT went home to live with his mother once again.

As discussed previously, while a cohesive lineage and Family Home Territory generally improves the political prospects of the lineage, attempting to achieve this solidarity with lineage members who want a great deal of independence from lineage authorities can mean, for some individuals, that unity becomes more trouble than it is worth (see Dispute Case 32).

Those who live on the Family Home Territory of a particular lineage place themselves to different degrees under the control of the lineage's authority. However, some people are ungovernable. For this reason only rarely do lineage authorities allow people other than their own lineage members to settle on their Family Home Territories. In a few cases, though, even members of one's own lineage are uncontrollable, as in the following case.

LEGAL CASE 52

Defendant: VK, a man in his thirties.
Authority: JK, his mother.
Date: 1986.

Facts: VK was mentally disturbed and unable to function fully in society. He lived in his mother's house, where he became more and more troublesome and uncontrollable in his actions. JK feared that he might injure his younger siblings and her, because he is very large and strong. JK ordered VK to leave the house as soon as he could find another place to live. VK then declared that he wished to build a house on JK's land.

Outcome: JK forbade him to build a house on her Family Home Territory, where he would have been an irremovable source of trouble.

Comment: VK later received permission from another man to build a house on the latter's Family Home Territory, though at a distance from where he himself resided. Normally the eldest male holds authority over the entire family/descent group. In this case, however, JK has a much stronger personality than her husband and acts as legal authority and political leader of the family.

Few disagreements over house occupancy and use between a patriarch or matriarch and offspring living in their own houses on the same Family Home Territory become open disputes. The patriarch or matriarch of the Family Home Territory lacks sufficient authority to alter an owner's occupancy, use, or rights of alienation to his or her house in most cases, and therefore will rarely attempt to impose such a decision. However, from Legal Cases 47, 49, 52, 68, and 70 and Dispute Case 65 we may abstract the following legal principle, which shows that Eskasoni Real Property Behavioral Rule 2 no longer applies in its original form.

FAMILY/DESCENT GROUP LEGAL PRINCIPLE 4
The patriarch or matriarch may control the initial settlement of people and building construction on his or her Family Home Territory, but may have limited authority over the ownership, possession, and alienation of houses on the Family Home Territory once other parties have acquired ownership.

Summary

The real property law at the family/descent group level was altered as a result of permanent housing and settlement (sedentarization). Before this, the landowner could always easily evict someone who lived in a wigwam or shanty (see Chapter 8, Eskasoni Real Property Behavioral Rule 2). With the new technology of permanent housing, however, a new type of real property ownership was created: the ownership of permanent structures. The new right of ownership of houses conflicts with rights of ownership to the land. Houses may be owned by anyone, but the land (the Family Home Territory) is owned by the patriarch or matriarch of the family/descent group by virtue of primary residence. Ownership of a house pre-empts land ownership rights; the landowner cannot evict an owner of a house, nor can he or she expropriate ownership of the house. The patriarch or matriarch may order that the house owner leave along with the house, but this depends on the willingness of the house owner to comply, as well as a willingness of the Band Council to pay the moving costs involved (see Legal Case 70). Of course, political action, in the form of violence or, more commonly, harassment, can be used, but this is considered unjust and would expose the initiating party to public ostracism in disputes between members of the same lineage. The harassment of intrusive aliens is considered just, however (see Dispute Case 22 and Legal Case 94). Thus the change of law may be expressed by the resolution of the conflict between Eskasoni Real Property Behavioral Rule 2 and Family/Descent Group Legal Principle 1 (the latter corresponding to Eskasoni Real Property Behavioral Rule 4), as this resolution is expressed in Family/Descent Group Legal Principle 4. The change represents a diminution of the original landowner's rights of ownership.

CHAPTER ELEVEN

Relations between the Band Council and Band Members, 1985–1987

We arrive now at a description and analysis of the principles of the modern reserve-wide real property legal system. In a very real sense, the modern system began in 1978, when the band acquired possession of the unallotted portions of the reserve (nearly all of the reserve) by federal law. Since then the Eskasoni Band Council has controlled real property law at the reserve legal level. Until that time, the permission of Indian Affairs was required even for something as small as the allocation of house repair money, and the Band Council could not prevent the prosecution of a man who burned down his old house (see Legal Case 38). Indian Affairs essentially relinquished all its control as a legal authority over band real property, with the exception that it now makes contracts offering incentives to motivate Band Councils to do as it wishes. This chapter describes real property law that was in place when I first observed it in detail, from 1985 to 1987, and I use these data as a basis for the comparison and analysis of later changes (see Chapter 16).

The Eskasoni land tenure system can be divided into three categories of laws distinguished by the types of parties involved in legal disputes. The largest and most politically significant category consists of law that the Band Council applies to legal relations between the Band Council and private band members. The second category is criminal law, applied by the chief to non-band members, and the third category is that of the law that the Band Council applies to civil disputes between private band members. Each category of law is treated in a separate chapter.

This tripartite body of Band Council law represents a land tenure system that is novel in nearly all respects. The land tenure system of the Eskasoni Band Council differs from that of the Grand Council (the traditional legal authorities) and from those of the Canadian courts, Indian Affairs, and the Indian Agent. Finally, it does not represent any sort of amalgamation of these systems. The Band Council also continues to make legal innovations to satisfy the needs of the members of the band in a changing world.

The Band Council has made its primary role as a legal authority the balancing of the real property interests of the Band Council against the real property interests of individual band members and lineages. Though most disputes over real property consist of civil disputes between private band members, the Band Council is not often approached to hear such cases and attempts to avoid deciding them. It does, however, make decisions in some of these cases when asked, and many parties adhere to these decisions. Overall, however, the land tenure system continues to respect and protect the age-old emphasis on individual rights and the responsibility of the individual to defend those rights.

The first portion of this chapter concerns the law regulating the relationship between the Band Council and the ordinary members of the band with respect to real property rights. The second section discusses real property contracts between the Band Council and politically privileged band members.

Regulation of Competing Real Property Interests

This section deals with the basic rights in land of an occupant of housing, which the Band Council guarantees to all band members. It also treats the special contractual rights and duties that the Band Council has created for certain individuals.

General Laws

Sections 81, 83, and 85(1) of the *Indian Act* (R.S.C. 1985, c. I-5) empower the Band Council to legislate by-laws (statutes) that regulate activities on health, the observance of law and order, and disorderly conduct; control domestic animals; create zones for the regulation of building construction and use; regulate the construction of utilities and roads; give allotments of reserve lands; control weeds; regulate beekeeping and the raising of poultry; regulate the water supply and the holding of games; control the activities of traveling salespersons on the reserve; regulate hunting, fishing and trapping; control trespassing; regulate the residence of band members on the reserve; grant rights to the spouses and children of band members; levy taxes on band members; regulate the sale, possession, manufacture, and use of alcohol; and provide sanctions for the violations of a band by-law.

Under the *Indian Act*, Canadian courts have the power to adjudicate alleged violations of these by-laws, although they are not required to take judicial notice of band by-laws (*R. v. Bear*, [1982] 35 N.B.R. (2d) 181). The Eskasoni Band Council has enacted several formal band by-laws, but has made no discernable use of them. Rather, the Band Council acts as an independent legal authority and it makes decisions that control a variety of behaviors.

Basic Rights

In contrast to the provisions of the *Indian Act*, the Band Council has granted band members a host of rights that do not appear in the federal statute.

Right of Residence

The Eskasoni Band Council grants to all members of the Eskasoni band, their spouses, children, and guests the right to reside anywhere on the reserve, as can be seen in the practice that people do in fact place their houses in many parts of the reserve, apparent in the following case, and in Legal Case 89.

LEGAL CASE 53

Party: A woman seeking a place for her mobile home.
Authority: Band Council.
Date: 1997.

Facts: A woman who had just acquired a mobile home sought a place to site it. A place that she liked was between two other homes, and she wondered whether she would be allowed to place her home there. She asked the Band Council for a declaratory decision.

Outcome: The Band Council approved her choice, but asked that she locate her house close to the road so that the Band Council could inexpensively provide it with utility services.

Comment: The Band Council allows band members to place their houses more or less wherever they wish. Although in this case the Band Council did not pose a problem for the woman, her neighbors did (see Dispute Case 23).

Not all Band Councils provide this freedom; some prohibit certain band members and all non-band members from residing on the reserve.

Rights of Ownership

A band member who lives on the reserve can acquire ownership of land or a single-family dwelling against the Band Council by fact of primary residence in the dwelling or on the land. Primary residence and ownership usually inheres in the male head of the household; the only exception is when the Band Council gives a house to a wife, rather than to a husband, and this circumstance may cause friction between the husband and wife. Even in cases in which the Band Council has strong political reasons to take action against a particular group or individual, it has never (until 2006) denied any band members the right of ownership to the houses that they occupy (with the exception of special contractual agreements, as discussed below). A clear illustration of this principle may be seen in the following case.

LEGAL CASE 54

Defendant: BT, a Micmac mother.
Authority: The Band Council.
Date: 1993–1997.

Facts: BT had been living for many months with a boyfriend while looking for permanent housing for herself and her children. She heard that a recently married young man who had been awarded a new house had left this house to live with his bride on his bride's home reserve. BT telephoned FL and asked him whether she could borrow his house, to which he agreed. After she had lived there for some months, she decided that it would make a nice permanent home for her family and asked FL whether he would give her the house, to which he agreed again.
Members of the Band Council expressed unhappiness with this conveyance. They considered the house Band Council property because they had

given it to FL such a short time previously, and that for this reason FL had no right to alienate it. Of course, the real issue here was one of political patronage. Band Council members who give a band member a new house normally expect political support from the recipient for years to come. By giving up the house and moving away so shortly after receiving it, FL had cost the Band Council a good deal of money and given little or no political support in return. Because new houses cost more and more each year, the members of the Band Council must plan their patronage strategies very carefully and generally cannot afford to give houses to people who will not support them in the polls.

The Band Council tried several political measures to reduce BT's desire to stay in the house. First, they stated that they recognized FL as the legitimate owner of the house, and not BT. Then the Band Council claimed that the house belonged to the band, and that therefore BT should pay rent to the Band Council to occupy the house, at a rate of $200 per month. BT paid the rent for several months, until a band councillor from another ward told her privately that she should stop paying rent because she was the only person on the reserve paying to live in a dwelling on the reserve. BT ceased paying the rent, and the Band Council took no action in return. Otherwise, the Band Council ignored her.

Outcome: After years of ignoring her occupation of a house to which the Band Council claimed ownership, the Band Council in 1997 informed BT that it recognized her as the owner of the house.

Comment: The significance of this case is that BT's primary residence, and therefore her rights of ownership, never met serious challenge, although some members of the Band Council wished very much to reacquire possession of the house.

The right of people to acquire the right of house ownership against the Band Council by simple primary residence is so well entrenched that band members take it for granted. However, we can abstract a useful principle from Legal Cases 54, 55, 56, and 95, a principle that has its historical and philosophical roots in Eskasoni Real Property Behavioral Rule 4.

BAND COUNCIL LEGAL PRINCIPLE 2

Primary residence in a house confers on the primary resident a right of ownership to the house against the Band Council that the Band Council will not normally alter.

In the following two cases, the Band Council used its political and legal powers to attempt to promote justice. The first case concerns the allocation of housing on the reserve by need, the second the personal behavior of a young man. In both cases, the Band Council attempted to use its power over real property to bring about changes in behavior. In neither case did it seem that the Band Council ever intended to act on its threats.

LEGAL CASE 55

Defendant: QF, a Micmac man.
Authority: Band Council.
Date: 1987.

Facts: QF and his four brothers lived together in one house after their parents died. The house burned down and the Band Council gave them a new one. QF, the oldest, also acquired status in the band's welfare records as "head of household," a designation intended solely for welfare purposes. And although the Band Council made it clear that all five brothers each had a right to live in the house, QF forced all his brothers from it even before the construction of the house was completed. He argued that because he was "head of household," the Band Council had given him sole ownership of the house. As the years went by, people in the community became angry with the Band Council for having given QF the house. They objected to QF living alone in a new house while many families with children had no houses of their own. They also noted to councillors that QF was often away from the reserve and that a needed house stood empty much of the time.

Most of the people who brought these accusations to the Band Council wanted the house for themselves. The Band Council had QF attend one of their meetings, at which it threatened to evict him from the house. The chief and councillors were concerned that he had broken the contractual agreement to allow all five brothers to share the house. QF lied to the Band Council, saying that the house was open to all his brothers, although all but one had by that time found permanent housing of their own. The Band Council knew that this was a lie, but ignored it in their effort to get the remaining homeless brother sheltered. In the opinion of some members of the family, although not QF, all five brothers, as well as two sisters, continue to hold undivided ownership interest in the land on which the house sits and that they inherited from their father.

Outcome: The Band Council allowed QF to retain ownership of his house pending the successful fulfillment of his contract to provide housing for his brothers. QF brought his one remaining homeless brother to his house for several months, but later evicted him.

In fact, the Band Council, bound by Band Council Legal Principle 2, would never have evicted QF from his house, but only brought suit to try to force him to assist his siblings. A band councillor expressed his dismay over QF, his treatment of his brothers, his ownership of the house, and the outcome of the case: "There is nothing we can do about it."

The Band Council also decided the following inheritance case on the basis of Band Council Legal Principle 2, rather than the ostensible reasons for the outcome.

LEGAL CASE 56

Party: GR, a man in his early 20s.
Authority: Band Council.
Date: 1996.

Facts: When his father died in 1996, GR was the last remaining member of his nuclear family. As the only person living in the house, he established primary residence and the right of ownership to it.

The Band Council had received reports that GR's lifestyle after the death of his father had become increasingly unclean. The Band Council decided to inform GR that ownership of the house would not go to him if his behavior did not improve, and that a final decision would be made in 60 days. GR became angered at this and publicly stated that "if I do not get the house, no one will get the house," a threat to burn it down. He did, however, improve his behavior for the 60-day period.

Outcome: Claiming to see an improvement, the Band Council awarded GR ownership of the house. The Band Council could not decide against GR, a decision that would contravene Band Council Legal Principle 2, which the Band Council has never done.

Comment: This case represents an attempt by the Band Council to use what limited means it has at its disposal to improve GR's behavior for his own good and that of the community.

Contractual Agreements

Band members' rights to real property can be limited by their own contracts. The second central feature of the modern real property legal system consists of the contractual agreements between the Band Council and individual band members, usually involving political patronage, and the right of an occupant of a house to ownership of the house against the Band Council. The following legal case shows how contractual obligations between the Band Council and band members may abridge the resident's right of ownership.

LEGAL CASE 57

Defendant: W, a man.
Authority: Band Council.
Date: 1980.

Facts: W lived in a new house that the Band Council had given him. He decided to sell his house back to the Band Council for cash, even though he had no other housing for himself, his wife, and children. The chief approved the sale and had a check made out to W. One of the councillors of the ward gave the house to one of his constituents. When the new owner went to take possession, W refused to relinquish possession, greeting her at the door and denying her entry. The new owner telephoned her councillor, who in turn telephoned the chief. The councillor and the chief, at the time two of the best fighters in the band, went to confront W, who was then possibly the reserve's strongest man. The chief and councillor told W to vacate the house. W protested, citing the Band Council's rule that house occupants cannot be evicted, especially if they have no other house in which to live. This supposed Band Council rule is actually the old Indian Agent Legal Principle 4, which the Band Council has never upheld as a legal principle. W was attempting to both keep the house and defraud the Band Council of the sale price. The chief and councillor also told W that Band Council Legal Principle 2 did not apply in his case, because his agreement to sell his house nullified his right of ownership. W then showed the chief and councillor a letter from a psychiatrist, which stated that W was not responsible for his actions. This argument the chief and councillor also held to be immaterial.

Outcome: W finally desisted in his claim and vacated the house.

Comment: W was to acquire over the next few years, on the basis of his family's needs (they were now homeless, of course), another two houses, each of which he sold back to the Band Council. The negative publicity surrounding these sales became so great that W eventually was unable to sell his house back to the band. W has acquired a derogatory nickname because of his irrational behavior in this case and in other matters (see also Legal Case 85).

From Legal Cases 57 and 61 we may abstract the following legal principle:

BAND COUNCIL LEGAL PRINCIPLE 3
House and land ownership is subject to any contractual agreements made between an individual and the Band Council.

Allotment and the Leasing of Real Property

Indian Act regulations on residence, lawful possession, and reserve lands influenced the way in which Indian Affairs allocated housing resources. Under Indian Affairs rules, an individual must have lawful possession of a house on a reserve to lease it to another person or to the band. Without lawful possession, the intended lessor has no greater right to the house under Canadian Indian law than does the intended lessee. And because the band owns any real property not allotted to individuals, it makes no sense for it to pay another party rent for its own property. As a result, Indian Affairs would not approve expenditures of money for rents for properties that were not lawfully possessed by some party other than the band; that is, until about 1990, when the Band Council acquired nearly full control over its government funds, thereby allowing it to enter leasing agreements with whomever it wished under whatever terms it negotiated.

And because Indian Affairs and the Canadian courts do not control real property law on the reserve, leases between private parties also take place. However, the success of such leases depends entirely on the goodwill of the parties to the lease, because no legal authority recognizes them. Most people lease their houses when they expect to be away for long periods. In instances in which no large family or descent group on the same Family Home Territory defends the owner's interests, it is possible that another band member would take residence in the house, and as a resident be considered an owner by the Band Council (see Band Council Legal Principle 2). Although I am unaware of this occurring at Eskasoni, it has happened at other Nova Scotia reserves. Probably for this reason people have told me that they fear leaving their houses empty for more than a few days or weeks. There is a well-founded fear of vandalism; when some few teens see an uninhabited house, they appropriate it for parties where, often, drug and alcohol use takes place. And, of course, people lease their houses to make money. An owner who plans to be away for an extended period usually rents or lends the house to people who can be trusted to return it. For example, one couple leased a house from another for a year and paid rent in the form of repairs to the house. Another man rented a house from a friend for a monthly cash payment. And while the Band Council does not recognize these leases as legally valid or grant them legal protection, it does nothing to oppose them. The Band Council does not guarantee the lessor the right to collect rent from the lessee, nor to regain possession from the lessee (see Band Council Legal Principle 2). In fact, the Band Council does not act as a legal authority in any financial contract between private parties.

However, when an owner of unallotted property approached the Band Council to ask it to lease that property on behalf of an indigent tenant, the Band Council, which has limited funds available for housing, would until sometime in the 1990s use the Indian Affairs rule as a pretext to deny the request. One solution to providing housing to those without can be seen in the following case.

LEGAL CASE 58

First party: KR.
Second party: C.
Authority: GR, one of the ward's band councillors.
Date: 1986.

Facts: KR had been living in a small house when he was given access for one year to a house that he liked much better. He approached C and asked her whether she wished to rent the small house for the year. C asked her councillor whether the Band Council would pay for her rent. The councillor told C that the Band Council would not pay rent on her behalf, because the property was not lawfully possessed, and then told her to move into the house, thereby allowing her to acquire ownership through residency. KR, on discovering that he would not receive any rent for the house, asked C to vacate it. The councillor advised C to throw out any of KR's personal property that remained in the house, telling her that this would extinguish KR's interest in the house, giving her complete ownership (Band Council Legal Principle 2, but in violation of Eskasoni Real Property Behavioral Rule 4). The only remaining property belonging to KR was a stove. The councillor told C to throw it out and he would give her a new stove of her own. Initially, C did not wish to destroy the stove by exposing it to the elements, and told KR to take it from the house. KR did not and eventually C threw it out into her yard.

Outcome: C acquired ownership of the house as far as the Band Council was concerned.

Comment: As discussed below, the principle stating that the Band Council will not pay rent for realty not lawfully possessed was frequently violated in 1986 and 1987, and its enforcement depended more on political patronage than allotment. In fact, the Band Council pays rent to those political supporters it wishes to favor, regardless of whether they have lawful possession or not. Moreover, the councillor who rendered this decision had, by 1993, become one of the biggest landlords of nonlawfully possessed realty on the reserve. People have long considered the acquisition of interests in real property by adverse possession, as in this case, unjust. Even C, who stood to benefit, resisted acquiring ownership by this means.

From this case, we may abstract the following principle:

BAND COUNCIL LEGAL PRINCIPLE 4

The Band Council will rent a house or apartment on behalf of an indigent Indian tenant only in cases in which the rental property is lawfully possessed.

This principle essentially duplicates Indian Affairs rules to the same effect and is notorious to band members, although it is modified by contracts available to the politically privileged, as discussed below.

Limitations to Ownership Rights

In addition to the general limitations to ownership of housing on the reserve, the Band Council has made some very specific restrictions to band members' ownership rights.

Access during Housing Construction

The following two cases show that the Band Council attempted to improve construction practices in the face of popular opposition. Some people, through ignorance, promote poor maintenance and construction practices, as in the following case.

LEGAL CASE 59

First party: PB.
Second party: Workers building PB's house.
Authority: Construction supervisor.
Date: 1970s.

Facts: During the construction of his house, PB found out that the workmen intended to place vapor barriers in the walls. He objected, saying that the plastic sheets would prevent the house from breathing.

Outcome: The construction supervisor allowed PB to have his way and did not install the vapor barriers. Several years later, the rot caused by the omission of the plastic sheeting required $2,800 to repair.

The Band Council instituted a new rule to prevent such occurrences:

BAND COUNCIL REAL PROPERTY RULE 1

No one awarded a new house by the Band Council may enter that house until construction is completed.

This rule was applied in the following case.

LEGAL CASE 60

Defendant: VB.
Authority: The construction supervisor, a Band Council employee.
Date: 1986.

Facts: VB and his family had been awarded a new house. VB went to the new house while it was still under construction, wanting to walk around inside it and inspect it.

Outcome: The construction supervisor denied him entry because it was not completed, as directed by the Band Council.

From this decision, we may abstract the following legal principle:

BAND COUNCIL LEGAL PRINCIPLE 5
No one awarded a new house by the Band Council may enter that house until construction is completed.

Contractual Opportunities for the Politically Privileged

Individuals and families with political privilege, a special class of people, have access to another type of contractual right. The politically privileged are those band members who belong to families of Band Council members or who have benefited the members of the Band Council with loyalty, friendship, and many votes and other political favors, as well as leaders of those lineages whose size and solidarity make them powerful. (Of course, an individual who is politically privileged with respect to one politician may not be so privileged with another.) As a result, they have the ability to make profitable contracts with the Band Council which other band members cannot do. These include the sale and rental of housing to the Band Council and other band members, and ownership of housing occupied by others. As seen in Legal Cases 57, 61, 63, 80, 105, 106, 107, and 108, contracts between the Band Council and politically privileged band members override the operation of Band Council Legal Principle 2.

Alienation

From 1985 through 1987, the Band Council did not regulate sales or gifts of property by one band member to another. Indian Affairs rules do not recognize sales of unallotted property, nor does the Band Council, yet both authorities allow them to take place. However, the Band Council made the following rule concerning house sales:

BAND COUNCIL REAL PROPERTY RULE 2
The Band Council prohibits the use of the band's funds to purchase housing from individuals (with the exception of expropriations ordered and paid for by Indian Affairs).

This rule is meant to conserve limited housing funds. These sales compromise the achievement of the common goal of Indian Affairs and the band to build more houses to accommodate the growing population. According to some informants, the issue has been discussed at several band meetings and the band members have always agreed that there should be no sale of houses to the band. Further, Indian Affairs did not approve such expenditures, and it had authority over all Band Council expenditures until about 1990 (apparently some disbursements could be hidden from Indian Affairs). Of course, when some (usually politically privileged individuals) wanted to sell their houses, they were able to do so.

One reason for this is that Band Council members benefit politically by buying houses, transgressing this rule. By paying the owner for his house, the chief or a councillor gives a favor to a political supporter and expects support in future elections in return. The house is acquired at a cost substantially less than that of building a new one, and is given away as a political favor to yet another family or couple. Although some councillors do buy housing from individuals, others find it politically more advantageous to refuse to buy housing at all, thereby keeping the rule against housing purchases uncorrupted.

Quitclaim Sales of Housing

For a time in the 1980s (discussed in detail below) all band members awarded new housing were required to give their old houses to the Band Council. However, even then the Band Council allowed some political supporters with new houses to give or sell their old houses to other individuals, by way of a quitclaim deed. In at least one case, though, the Band Council allowed the transfer of a house from one band member to another, because the house was so old that the Band Council had no interest in acquiring it to award to another family. Sometimes a seller gave the house away for a token fee, but in other instances there was a profit through the sale (see Dispute Case 34). Other than allowing the sale and providing the quitclaim deed forms, the Band Council took no part.

Leasing of Real Property to the Band Council

As noted above, the *Indian Act* requires that an individual must have lawful possession of a house to lease it to another person or to the band. However, in the 1980s those without lawful possession might, if they enjoyed political favor, own houses and rent them to the band. The question of lawful possession may in fact play no role whatsoever in a party's ability to lease property to the Band Council. A band office worker, for example, owned at least two houses without lawfully possessing them and rented them to the band to use in the housing of indigent band members. Others did likewise. The political nature of this kind of contract can be seen in the following case.

LEGAL CASE 61

First party: R, a man.
Second party: The chief.
Authority: The chief.
Date: 1986.

Facts: R for many years strongly supported the incumbent chief politically. As the patriarch of a large lineage, his support gave the chief many votes at each election. Some years before R had built a small house at his own expense on a part of the reserve far from his own dwelling. He and the chief contracted for the band to lease the house from him, for the use of a welfare recipient, and the chief gave him a signed statement, written on Band Council stationery, acknowledging his ownership of the house. The political contract, thus, was that the band would allow R ownership of the house and pay him rent in return for his pledge of support for the chief. Before the 1986 election, R had a disagreement with the chief over an unrelated matter and R supported a challenger for the office of chief. R thus broke his contract with the chief.

Outcome: Within two weeks after the chief's reelection, the Band Council informed R that he no longer owned the house that the band leased from him and would receive no more rental payments for it. The Band Council attempted to make Band Council Legal Principle 2 effective for that house. R pointed out the letter that gave him ownership, a letter that would prove embarrassing to the chief should it become known either to Indian Affairs or to the other members of the band. The chief then demanded that R sell the house to the band, which he did after they haggled over the price.

Comment: R was one of many who own houses rented to the Band Council, but the only one, at the time, who had a dispute with the Band Council over ownership rights.

From Legal Case 61, we may abstract the following legal principle:

BAND COUNCIL LEGAL PRINCIPLE 6

The politically privileged may own houses in which other people reside, so long as they remain politically privileged.

One of the more important conclusions to be drawn from Legal Case 61 is that, for the politically privileged, Band Council Legal Principle 2 is not enforced when it conflicts with political patronage needs. In fact, the data suggest that this rule is nothing more than support for an excuse that Band Council members use when they wish to withhold aid (rent payments) from those who do not support them politically.

The Band Council initially kept the program feasible by keeping it secret; most people did not know to ask to take advantage of it. The politically privileged felt especially favored by their secret status, especially because its secrecy made them seem all the more distinguished. Those living next door to rented units usually did not even know that these were rented. In some cases, even tenants in rented units did not know that the housing was rented.

Those not politically privileged are treated as was the woman in the next case.

LEGAL CASE 62

Party: ZF, an elderly woman.
Authority: The Band Council.
Date: 1980s and 1990s.

Facts: ZF owned two houses on her lawfully possessed lot. She lived in one with her family and attempted to lease the other to the Band Council on behalf of an indigent tenant. She made repeated requests to this effect over a period of decades.

Outcome: The Band Council refused her request with the excuse that the building was in substandard condition. ZF pointed out that another individual on another part of the reserve was renting to the Band Council a building in much worse condition, but the Band Council refused to change its decision.

Another way to deny benefit to nonpolitically privileged people is by condemnation of the property. When the band member a acquires new house to replace an older one, the older one is condemned. The logic here is that if the old house was suitable for habitation, the band member would not need a new one. And, once condemned, a non-politically privileged band member cannot lease the old house to the band to house an indigent person (see Legal Case 107). Of course, the politically privileged usually do not face this possibility. As one member of the band said, referring to condemned housing: "There's nothing wrong with those houses. They just don't want to pay for them."

LEGAL CASE 63

Party: NF, a man.
Authority: The Band Council.
Date: 2002.

Facts: When ZF (see Legal Case 61) died, she left her Certificate of Possession to the lot and one of the houses on the lot to RF, her son. To another son, NF, she left the house she had been trying to rent to the Band Council. NF lived off the reserve. By 2002, with a new chief in office, NF became politically privileged and sought to rent his house to the Band Council, even though he did not live on the reserve and the house sat on a lot lawfully possessed by another.

Outcome: The Band Council agreed to the request. When NF asked for assistance in repairing the structure, the Band Council agreed to make the repairs in exchange for two months' rent.

By 1993 some councillors (including several who lost their seats in the 1992 election) had become landlords of many houses. They bought the houses from owners and would then rent them to the Band Council, which pays rent on behalf of the tenants, the sellers. In this way the original owner benefits from the deal (by gaining the price of the sale and losing no rights to reside in the house), as does the landlord (by receiving rents).

Real Property Speculation

Speculation in real property is an extremely rare practice; I was able to find only one instance of it, and this involved the purchase of a house by an appointed member of the band administration. The band employee later sold this house to the band, so that it could be given to another family, for a far higher sum. Four factors prevent the practice from becoming widespread. First, most people have insufficient money to invest. Second, speculation is a major violation of proper Micmac etiquette, because one Micmac makes money at the expense of another. (Those who benefit at the expense of the Band Council or band believe, on the other hand, or at least claim, that the money involved is "just government money" and not really property of the band members.) Third, most investors wish to own property for the long term, so as to rent it to the Band Council. Fourth, and most importantly, speculation in real property would be politically disadvantageous for the Band Council, one of very few parties on the reserve financially capable of purchasing realty at its fair market value. It would imply tremendous favoritism for a single person, far above that given to other supporters of the chief and councillors (in which the Band Council allows a speculator to buy a house, with the intention that the Band Council would subsequently buy it for a higher price).

Rights of Ususfructus: *Natural Resources*

As noted earlier, popular sentiment charges the chief with a responsibility to control the use of the reserve's natural resources by members of the band. He does so in response to political pressure from some members; namely, those who support Eskasoni Real Property Behavioral Rule 6. With the occasional temporary exception of gravel, the only important resource in significant demand is wood. Those who cut small amounts of wood, for firewood or for sale as pulpwood, in their own Family Home Territories do not require the chief's permission. Those who wish to cut large amounts for sale should ask the chief for an oral or written license. In fact, the rule is frequently violated, and some, even those who cut pulp nowadays, have never heard of it. Indeed, in the early 1990s there was considerable dispute over several band members cutting large amounts of wood in the northern portion of the reserve (see Dispute Case 56). Yet the Band Council did nothing to control this dispute, suggesting that the Band Council does not in fact control disputes between band members over usufructary rights on the reserve. The following case clarifies the situation.

LEGAL CASE 64

Party: BB.
Authority: The Band Council.
Date: 1987.

Facts: BB started a business cutting firewood for sale. He constructed his own logging road and cut virgin timber. However, he cut trees along the crest of a hill visible to those living on much of the reserve, disfiguring the skyline. People in the band complained to the Band Council.

Outcome: The Band Council ordered BB to cease cutting firewood, and he complied. "There were too many complaints," he said.

From this case and the non-prosecution of all other woodcutting operations we can abstract the following legal principle:

BAND COUNCIL LEGAL PRINCIPLE 7

The Band Council may halt woodcutting operations that deface the natural beauty of those parts of the reserve easily visible from settled areas and roadways, to the point that band members complain publicly.

Land Tenure in Other Bands

Not every Micmac band makes use of a legal principle that gives occupants of housing the right of ownership against the band. This section provides an inkling of the comparative absence of band member rights on other Micmac reserves. Take, for example, the following case.

POLITICAL CASE 5

Defendants: Several Micmac families.
Authority: The chief of the band.
Date: Early 1980s.
Location: A reserve near Eskasoni.

Facts: Several families politically opposed the sitting chief. Only those who ordinarily reside on a reserve may vote for either chief or councillor of the band (*Indian Act*, R.S.C. 1985, c. I-5, s. 77). The chief provided the defendants with housing outside of reserve boundaries at band expense.

Outcome: Once off the reserve, the families posed less threat to the chief's political career.

At various times at some other Nova Scotia Micmac reserves, such as at Shubenacadie in the 1980s, an occupant had to maintain occupancy of a house more or less continuously, or the Band Council would award occupancy to another family.

In the following case, which occurred at the Horton reserve in the western part of mainland Nova Scotia, a couple were evicted from a house that they had acquired from a band member there (Gloade 1989; Halliday 1989).

LEGAL CASE 65

Defendant: Harold Gloade and his wife.
Authority: Chief Rita Smith.
Date: 1989.
Location: Horton reserve.

Facts: Gloade was given the use of a house on the reserve by a member of the band. After a time the chief notified him that he would have to vacate the house. According to Gloade, the house's owner gave his permission for Gloade to remain as long as he wished. Gloade also claimed that the chief wanted to give possession of the house to a third party. According to the chief and a councillor of the band, on the other hand, the original possessor of the house wished to regain possession and the Band Council had a duty to deliver it to him.

Outcome: Gloade left the house as the Band Council ordered. He had asked to remain and had appealed his case to Indian Affairs. Indian Affairs, however, only decides cases of lawful possession and leaves all other judgments involving possession of land by band members to the Band Councils. Hence, it refused jurisdiction over this case, which did not involve lawful possession.

Summary

The Band Council guarantees band members with primary residence in their houses ownership of the houses, but against the Band Council only. This guarantee does not grant rights against other band members (discussed below). No matter who the occupant believes owns the house—whether the occupant, the band, or the Crown—the Band Council regards houses as the property of the primary resident (see Legal Case 95). The right of ownership includes the rights of possession and alienation to another band member. This guarantee, however, is subject to the terms of contractual agreements between the owner and the Band Council, to matrimonial property law, and to ownership by politically privileged individuals.

The Band Council does not regulate the usufructary rights of band members to reserve land, with the exception of those who damage the natural beauty of the forest (see Legal Case 64). Residence in, and ownership of, a new house cannot begin until the builders have completed that house. This legal principle allows the builders to construct the house properly (see Legal Case 59).

The Band Council had once desired to control the disposition of marital housing after divorce in a way that the members of the band considered just (see Legal Case 40). However, political pressure from some band members caused the Band Council to stop regulating ownership of marital property.

Finally, the data show that the politically privileged are able to avoid a law that applies to other band members, by owning houses occupied by others for renting to the band or for speculation (see Legal Cases 61 and 63).

CHAPTER TWELVE

Real Property Civil Law for Private Parties

The previous chapter discussed types of law that deal with real property disputes between individuals and the Band Council, and which the latter adjudicates firmly and resolutely.

As we saw earlier, on the other hand, the Band Council does not often adjudicate civil disputes. Most disputes on the reserve involve two or more individual band members, with no involvement of the Band Council as a party to the cases. The Band Council only with reluctance takes part in civil cases. When I asked a band member once why he did not take his civil dispute to the chief, he replied: "The less his phone rings, the better he likes it." Band councillors also involve themselves in private disputes only reluctantly because doing so can cost political support, since someone always takes offense to a decision.

Furthermore, it is unusual for private parties, that is, parties not members of the Band Council administration, to seek legal resolution of disputes over realty. Three factors militate against the use of legal authority in such instances. The first of these is the belief that families and individuals are responsible for avenging an injury by retaliating against the injuring party (see Chapter 8). To request that an authority decide the outcome of a dispute simultaneously leaves the civil dispute unresolved and demeans oneself as weak.

A second factor is the Micmac ideal of social egalitarianism. To the Micmac, all people are basically equal in worth and should therefore be treated uniformly. This ethic makes it difficult for Micmac to allow a third party to adjudicate a dispute, because it implies that the third party is somehow superior (see Behavioral Postulate 3, Table 1). The final and most important factor preventing legal settlement of most real property disputes is that many Micmac believe that their leaders and authorities decide civil disputes on the basis of their own personal or political interests, rather than the merits of each case.

Band Council Legal Decisions in Private Civil Cases

Interestingly, when the Band Council does consent to hear a case, usually after repeated insistence from a party that believes itself injured, it usually makes no changes in the situation as it is when first brought before it, as seen in the following cases (in accord with Band Council Legal Principle 2).

LEGAL CASE 66

First party: W.
Second party: Two B brothers.
Authority: Band Council.
Date: 1985.

Facts: After W left the house he sold to the Band Council (see Legal Case 56), he moved himself and his family into a house that was between the houses of the two B brothers. The house originally belonged to a member of the B family and had been lent to another individual for as long as he wished to use it. The man who had had the loan of the house gave the house to W when he moved to a newly built house. The B brothers and W dislike each other, and the B brothers complained to the Band Council, asking it to take possession of the house from W and then to return it to them. They claimed that the man who had given W the house was himself only a guest of the B family and thus had no right to give ownership of the house to W. The house was B family property, they said, it was in the middle of their Family Home Territory, and furthermore it was needed for a brother who had no home of his own. W responded by arguing that if the Band Council was to evict people from their houses, that it should begin with the B brothers, because each was single and living alone in his own house, allowed to do so even in the midst of a housing shortage. He argued that he had a wife and children to shelter. He also claimed that there was a Band Council rule against single persons living alone having their own housing.

Outcome: The Band Council allowed W to retain ownership of the house in which he lived; because he had established primary residence in the house, he was entitled to ownership. Whatever agreements the B family had made with earlier possessors of the house were immaterial. W's claim that there exists a Band Council rule that single persons living alone cannot own their own housing is incorrect. Rather, the Band Council pursues a policy of not awarding new housing to single individuals, because of the great housing shortage.

Comment: W voluntarily left the disputed house some months later after receiving a new house. The Band Council later razed the empty building due to its poor condition.

LEGAL CASE 67

First party: PB.
Second party: RO.
Authority: The Band Council.
Date: Early 1990s.

Facts: PB had acquired a mobile home from the Band Council, but needed a place to put it. He approached FC, who gave him some of his own land for the trailer. RO, a neighbor, objected to the Band Council that he did not want PB living near him, because he sometimes behaved oddly. He asked the Band Council to remove PB's trailer from the area.

Outcome: The Band Council declined to alter the situation.

The Band Council does not use strong measures to give teeth to its civil decisions, and this is why people do not often go to the Band Council for adjudication of disputes over real property. The *Indian Act* contains no provisions giving a Band Council power to remedy such situations through by-laws. I was present in 1986 when a councillor, discussing a civil case, said that "all we can do is send them a letter," referring to a letter in which the Band Council politely and with no mention of sanctions asks the party in the wrong to cease occupation of the other party's property. Only those rare people intimidated by such a letter would alter their behavior as a result. One example of this is a case related to Legal Case 53 (see also Legal Case 49).

From the decisions of Legal Cases 66, 67, 68, 69, and 71 we may abstract the following legal principle:

BAND COUNCIL LEGAL PRINCIPLE 8
The Band Council decides civil cases between private parties to preserve the ownership rights of the primary resident and maintain the status quo.

From Legal Cases 66 and 71 we may abstract the following legal principle:

BAND COUNCIL LEGAL PRINCIPLE 9
No contracts made between private individuals have any bearing on Band Council decisions.

Band Council Legal Principles 8 and 9 accord with Band Council Legal Principle 2.

Houses as Personal Property and the Question of Land Ownership

Legal decisions affirming the ownership rights of the primary resident make the civil law for private individuals similar to the law on the relationship between the Band Council and the private individual.

First or primary residence alone accords an individual a right of ownership of a house and of the land surrounding a dwelling. Once residence has ceased, as it often did in the days when most people lived in wigwams and migrated, the land is open to residence and ownership by another individual (see Eskasoni Real Property Behavioral Rule 3). This traditional distinction between free and occupied or owned land obviously has great antiquity, and many hunting and gathering cultures share it.

The tenet still applies even though people no longer live in wigwams and migrate very little. Micmac frequently consider houses as personal property, just as they did wigwams, rather than as real property affixed to the ground. They do not share the great theoretical and practical distinction between personalty and realty in British, American, and Canadian common law. Band Council law also treats houses as personal property rather than as fixtures, as do the parties to several cases (see Legal Cases 68, 69, 70, 73, and 95, and Dispute Cases 44, 50, and 73).

Any band member can build a house anywhere on the reserve (subject to the site's successfully passing a percolation test) either with the permission of another person whose land it is, by building on a piece of land to which no one else has laid claim of ownership, or, in a few cases, by overpowering an owner's opposition to use of his or her land. Most of the reserve, therefore, according to the Micmac, consists of free land that "belongs to no one," as several Micmac people have described it. This provides another major contrast with western common law tradition, in which some legal entity always has ownership of a piece of land. If a house is destroyed or is in ruins and the resident has moved away, then the land where the house sat becomes once again free land, no longer owned by any individual or group.

Likewise, an individual who moves his or her house retains no interest in the land where it sat. When the house arrives at its new location, the occupant acquires an ownership interest in the land surrounding the new site, unless another owns it.

It is primary residence in a house that establishes ownership interests in real property, and not the reverse, as in the British, Canadian, and U.S. common law systems.

One of the potential problems Band Council Legal Principle 2 engendered concerns houses newly built on land owned by someone other than the primary resident of the new house, a situation that has only recently emerged, a result of a fast growing population and crowding (see Figure 4).

For the Band Council, the legal questions are as follows: Does the owner of the land acquire ownership of the newly built structure, by virtue of its placement on his or her land, or would it belong to the resident? Further, would the owner of the new house acquire ownership of the land on which it sits through residency, despite the earlier established ownership right of the landowner? The Band Council answered these new questions in the following decisions.

LEGAL CASE 68

First party: JB.
Second party: VB, his brother.
Authority: The Band Council.
Date: 1986.

Facts: VB lived in a house on his own lot. JB later moved his house to VB's lot at VB's invitation, to be closer to his brothers. Sometime after this, VB's behavior became erratic and he frequently spent time in jail. During his periods of freedom he harassed JB and attempted to gain ownership of JB's house, on the legal ground that it sat on his lot. JB asked the Band Council to decide who had ownership of the house that he occupied and of the land where it was.

Outcome: The Band Council decided that JB owned the house, while the land on which it sat belonged to VB. This decision accords with popular Micmac ideas about property.

Comment: JB, though happy to be declared the owner of the house, felt that the Band Council's judgment was somewhat ridiculous. "Is my house hanging in the air?" he asked one day. Despite the judgment, when not in jail VB continued to harass JB.

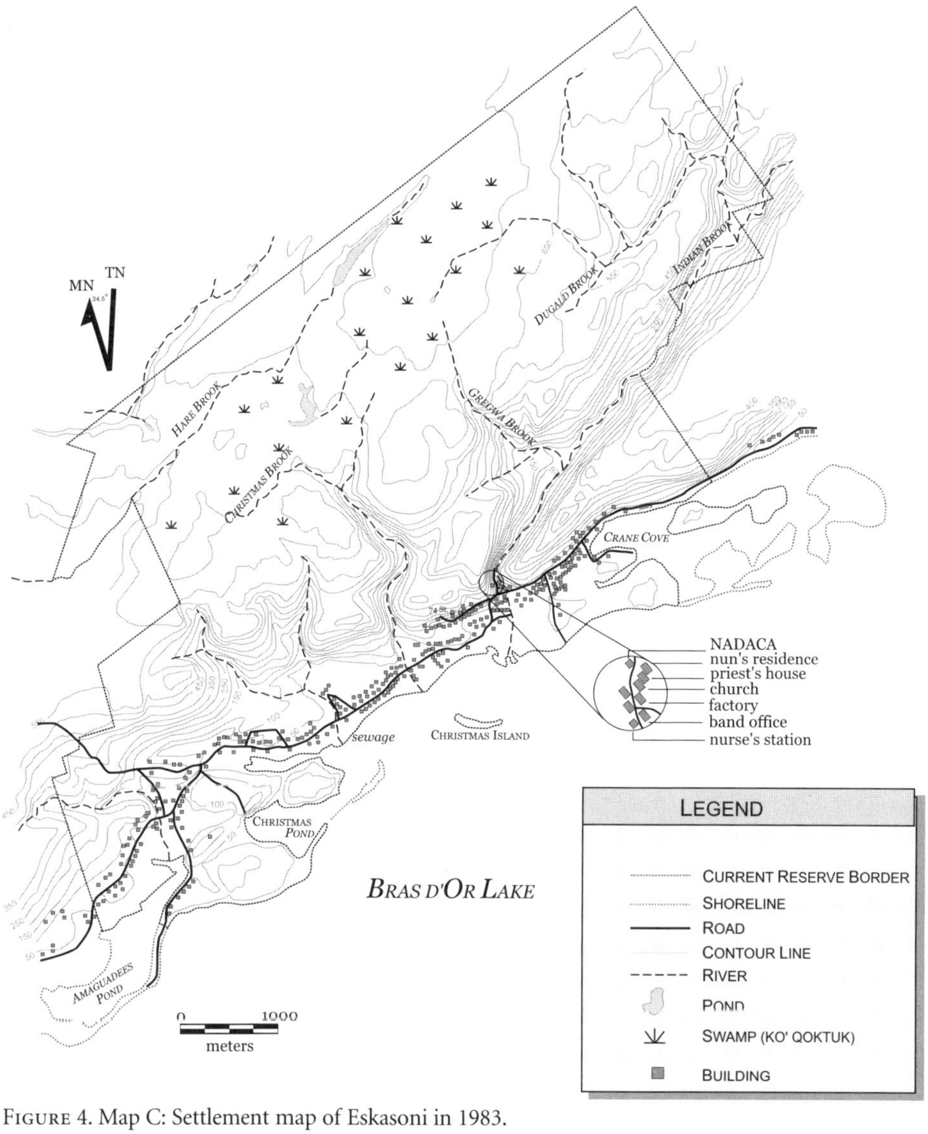

FIGURE 4. Map C: Settlement map of Eskasoni in 1983.

LEGAL CASE 69

First party: JB.
Second party: ZB, another brother.
Authority: The Band Council.
Date: 1986.

Facts: To escape VB's harassment, JB had the Band Council move his house to a lot that ZB owned, at ZB's invitation. Shortly after the move, ZB attempted to assert rights of ownership to JB's house, on the basis that it was on his lot. He asked the Band Council to take possession of the house and award ownership to him.

Outcome: The Band Council maintained the rights of JB to ownership of his house. The fact that ZB first resided on and owned the lot on which JB's house sat was held to be of no consequence.

From Legal Cases 66, 67, 68, and 69 (and also from Legal–Political Case 1; see Chapter 14) we may abstract the following legal principle:

BAND COUNCIL LEGAL PRINCIPLE 10

Only the fact of primary residence gives the right of ownership to a house; ownership of land by itself gives no right to own or possess housing on it. Housing may thus be legally personal property in situations in which the land on which it is located belongs to another individual.

From Legal Cases 68 and 69 we may abstract the following legal principle:

BAND COUNCIL LEGAL PRINCIPLE 11

The primary resident on a plot of land owns it, no matter who later builds on it, so long as residence is maintained. Ownership of a house and the land on which it is situated are thus divisible.

These legal principles conform both to traditional ideals of justice and to customary rules of behavior (Eskasoni Real Property Behavioral Rules 1 through 5). In the six other cases that I collected in which people moved their houses, it was always the later settlers rather than the original residents of the land who moved, a general pattern that all Micmac I consulted confirmed. One of these follows.

LEGAL CASE 70

Party: U, a young man.
Authority: K, U's older female relative.
Date: 1985.

Facts: U had recently built a house on K's Family Home Territory, with K's permission. Not long thereafter U and K began to quarrel and K asked U to leave.

Outcome: U complied and had the Band Council move his house from K's Family Home Territory to another part of the reserve (see also Dispute Case 44 and Legal Case 69).

Comment: I first inquired about this case when I saw the house moving down the road, something that seemed incongruous for such a sparsely populated, and not particularly wealthy, community (since then I have seen quite a number of houses moved). When I asked whether the owner of the moved house was there first, or was a later settler on the plot, I was told, "It's *always* the one who came later who moves." All cases of which I am aware of agree with this statement.

Band Council legal principles here agree with Family/Descent Group Legal Principles 2, 3, and 4.

An examination of Legal Cases 66, 68, and 69, and Legal–Political Case 1 (see

Chapter 14) reveals a critical feature of Band Council decisions concerning civil cases between band members: because the Band Council does not force parties to accept its decisions in such cases, the success of all such decisions rests on the willingness of the parties to accept them voluntarily. This feature distinguishes Band Council law for civil cases between private parties from law for cases involving the Band Council as a party; in the latter category, the Band Council will force compliance on the other party if it resists. Why should a private party seeking to acquire rights from another private party adhere to the Band Council's decision, if it could take those rights by force? Having the Band Council approve one's actions helps to maintain or improve one's reputation. It also provides support for a position that may be otherwise widely or strongly opposed by band members.

Appeals to External Authorities

Though the Band Council attempts to prevent legal cases from reaching external authorities, such as Indian Affairs and the Canadian court system, to maintain legal jurisdiction and political control, some cases eventually reach these authorities when an individual believes it is to his or her benefit to appeal a Band Council decision. This is particularly true when a party believes that the Band Council has made, or would make, an adverse decision on the basis of political or personal self-interest; in such circumstances, the party to the case may seek an external authority (see also Legal Case 81). Individuals turn to Indian Affairs to adjudicate such disputes, especially if they seek to dislodge the interests held by a party by virtue of primary residence, as evidenced by the following dispute. Threats to appeal lawful possession cases to outside authorities have caused lawful possession to be given weight in some Band Council decisions.

LEGAL CASE 71

First party: The P brothers.
Second party: Members of the AP family (patrilateral kin of the P brothers).
Authority: The Band Council.
Date: 1986.

Facts: In 1948, the P brothers' father purchased some land from another band member. This transaction was carried out under the authority of the Indian Agent, because at that time there were no lawfully possessed (allotted) lands on the reserve and therefore no statutory right for one band member to sell land to another. Furthermore, the Indian Agent had no authority under the *Indian Act* to sanction the sale. The following letter by the seller, dated October 23, 1948, was written on a piece of Indian Affairs stationery:

> To [*name of purchaser*],
>
> This will acknowledge the receipt of seventy five dollars ($75.00) as payment in full for that piece of land purchased from the late [*name given*] of Eskasoni, situate between the lot occupied by [*name given*] and the lot at present being

> occupied by myself. This lot has an approximate road frontage of 175 feet and a depth of 275 feet approximately. It is bounded on the East by [*name given*] lot, the west by [*name given*], the South by Indian Reserve lands and the north by the Provincial Department of Highways.
>
> All title, rights, etc. is relinquished by me in favor of [*name of purchaser*] by virtue of this receipt.
>
> [*Signed by seller, and witnessed by the Indian Agent*]

The purchaser later died and his young sons (the P brothers) were raised by different families. In subsequent decades kin of the buyer (the AP family) moved onto the lot, which was vacant, and built their homes on it. The lot has never been allotted. In the 1980s one of the brothers, using the above letter as proof of his right to ownership of the lot as an heir to his father's estate, asked the Band Council to give him and his brothers ownership of the lot. Weighing against the P brothers was the fact that the fairly large AP family steadfastly supported the incumbent chief at the polls.

Outcome: The Band Council denied the P brothers' request, thereby maintaining the rights of the primary residents, the members of the AP family.

Comment: Certainly, it is doubtful that the Band Council felt itself under obligation to give weight to arrangements made by the Indian Agent.

LEGAL CASE 72

First party: The P brothers.
Second party: The AP family.
Authority: Indian Affairs.
Date: 1986.

Facts: One of the P brothers took his argument (see Legal Case 71) to Indian Affairs.

Outcome: Indian Affairs ruled that unless allotment was involved, Indian Affairs could do nothing to alter the situation.

LEGAL CASE 73

First party: FC.
Second party: DE.
Authority: Indian Affairs.
Date: 1980s.

Facts: FC had built his house near that of his parents in the 1970s, on a lot that was lawfully possessed by DE, who lived across the street. When FC discovered the allotment, he asked Indian Affairs to correct what he felt was an unjust situation (that he lived on land to which another man held rights of possession) by awarding him lawful possession to the lot. Whether or not he approached the Band Council for assistance I do not know, but in any event the Band Council did nothing to alter the situation as it stood.

Outcome: Indian Affairs replied that it could not revoke a person's right to lawful possession and that FC should ask DE to transfer lawful possession of the lot to him.

Comment: The fact that DE had lawful possession did not alter FC's ownership, use, and enjoyment of the lot, as Band Council law recognizes and protects. He also leased to the Band Council another structure on the same lot, for the benefit of the resident. That lawful possession of his lot by another made no difference to his rights in the land points out the insignificance that the Eskasoni authorities give lawful possession.

Summary

The Band Council tends to shy away from civil cases. When it does make a decision, it decides in favor of the status quo at the time of the decision. This means that it gives the primary resident at the time of the decision ownership rather than the other party. Further, the parties follow the Band Council decision voluntarily, because there are no strong sanctions for failure to obey the Band Council in civil cases.

This principle owes its existence, obviously, to traditional ideas on just rights in property, although it did not acquire status as a legal principle until recently, when legal authorities supported it.

However, the Band Council, in attempting to uphold traditional ideas concerning ownership rights, has faced genuine difficulty, due to the new technology of permanent structures: Who owns the new permanent structures, the primary resident and owner of the house or the primary resident and owner of the land where the house sits? The Band Council decided to make ownership of the two kinds of property divisible, even though this new law ultimately costs the band a great deal of money in house-moving expenses, and even though it contravenes the *Indian Act* and established western common law.

Finally, because they perceive the Band Council as politically biased, band members occasionally will try to appeal Band Council decisions to Indian Affairs and the Canadian courts. However, because most cases do not involve allotment, this is usually to no avail.

CHAPTER THIRTEEN

Access to Reserve Lands by Non-band Members

In Canada, under the *Indian Act*, access to, and residence on, reserve lands is limited to the band(s) to which the lands are assigned; one band may have assigned to it two or more reserves, and one reserve may be assigned to two or more bands. Only members of that band to which a reserve is assigned have rights to possession of land on that reserve. Others, even other Indians, may not (*Indian Act*, R.S.C. 1985, c. I-5, s. 30).

In the case of non-Indians, the *Indian Act* provides that an Indian, or band, or the Crown can bring a legal action in the Federal Court of Canada if a non-Indian unlawfully occupies or possesses, claims adversely the right to occupation or possession of, or trespasses on a reserve or part of a reserve (*Indian Act*, R.S.C. 1985, c. I-5, s. 31).

The prohibition against non-Indian occupation of a reserve does not apply to cases in which the Minister has granted permission (*Indian Act*, R.S.C. 1985, c. I-5, s. 28[2]), in the case of a minister of religion who is invited into a lawfully possessed home on a reserve (see *Regina v. Gingrich*, [1958] 31 C.R. 306), or when someone leases allotted land with the permission of the allottee.

Practical Realities

In actuality, though, non-Indians use reserve land often. Schoolteachers go to the school daily, without ministerial permits, to teach the children. One white teacher lives on the reserve with an Indian family, the parish (reserve) priest and several nuns live next to the church, and several non-Indian men and women live with their Indian wives and husbands or girlfriends and boyfriends. Many construction projects use non-Indian workers. In addition, outsiders carry out business on the reserve: delivery people, sales people, and repair workers, among others. And while it might seem, because the *Indian Act* defines who is and who is not a band member, or who has the right to reside on the reserve, that this is an intrusion of federal law into band law, the question for bands depends rather on economics. The Band Council receives various public assistance monies from the Department of Indian Affairs and Northern Development on a per capita band member basis. The Eskasoni Band Council steadfastly refuses to use any of these monies to support non-band members. Not only does it not give relief payments or special needs money to non-band members, it will not usually provide funding for housing for women married to or living with male non-band members (although it does provide housing assistance to men married to or living with female non-band members; this carries on the old distinction in the *Indian Act* in which non-Indian women married to Indian men were considered Indians, but Indian women married to non-Indian men lost their Indian status). On a related note, the Band Council also refused to accept and administer provincial welfare monies for non-Indian welfare recipients living on the reserve, until a Canadian court case forced them to do so in 2003 (CHRT 2003). In this way, the Band Council discourages male non-band members from living on the reserve, although it allows them the right to do so if they wish.

According to all informants I asked, the Band Council limits the operation of Band Council Legal Principle 2 for non-band members with the following Band Council rule:

BAND COUNCIL REAL PROPERTY RULE 3
Non-band members may reside on the reserve, subject to the conditions set forth in Band Council Legal Principle 12, but may own neither houses nor land on the reserve (no recorded cases).

Under the Eskasoni Band Council legal system, all of these people occupy or otherwise use reserve land at the sufferance of the chief.

The Chief's Control

While any individual band member can initiate a complaint of trespass to the chief, Eskasoni Micmac accord the chief the responsibility to ascertain the wishes of the members of the band (usually by hearing complaints from band members about the behavior of the non-Indians) concerning non-band members and to apply controls to their behavior. The chief has at his disposal the following sanctions: (1) legal action in the Canadian courts under authority of the *Indian Act*; (2) the use of the reserve's police to remove the offender from the reserve; (3) the threat of bodily harm (see Legal Case 76, which took place on another reserve); and, the most commonly used in Eskasoni, (4) the option to ask the offender to leave the reserve, to restrict access to the reserve, or to modify his or her behavior while on the reserve. The following cases show the chief's central position in this matter well.

LEGAL CASE 74
First party: IN, a missionary.
Second party: The band's Church Committee and several individuals.
Authority: The chief.
Date: 1986.

Facts: Sometime in the mid-1980s IN began to visit the Cape Breton reserves to proselytize on behalf of a Protestant church, an organization that works specifically with Indians in Canada. He was friendly, and people on the reserve seemed unopposed to his presence. However, with few exceptions, the Micmac of Eskasoni are all Catholics;

they disliked his efforts to proselytize and to attempt to induce them to leave the Catholic Church. IN asked the chief for the use of a band building for religious services and religious instruction.

Outcome: The chief, acting out of concern for the wishes of the majority of the members of the band, denied IN the use of any band building for religious services.

LEGAL CASE 75

First party: The band's Church Committee.
Second party: IN.
Authority: The chief.
Date: 1986.

Facts: After the chief's decision (see Legal Case 74), IN continued to preach, although he had made no lasting converts and though resentment toward his activities mounted. The Church Committee, which works with the priest on church matters, and which frequently says publicly what the priest says privately, came out strongly against IN and his actions. The members of the Committee complained to the chief.

Outcome: The chief rather reluctantly decided that IN may visit the reserve whenever he wishes, but may not proselytize. IN has respected this decision.

Comment: The chief's decision in this case conflicts with the principle in *Regina v. Gingrich* ([1958] 31 C.R. 306), which allows clergy to minister to residents of an Indian reserve.

In the following similar cases, the chief of a nearby reserve expelled two non-Indians, but his decision was reviewed by Indian Affairs, which criticized him on procedural grounds and because his decision clearly did not reflect the wishes of the members of the band. Here federal law conflicted with band law on that reserve.

LEGAL CASE 76

Defendant: The non-Indian boyfriend of a band member.
Authority: The band's chief.
Date: About 1970.
Location: A reserve near Eskasoni.

Facts: The chief disliked the presence of any white people on his reserve. One evening, some Micmac were finishing work at their basket shop. A couple and their adult children were among those present, including a daughter and her white boyfriend.

Outcome: The chief later arrived with his brother, brandishing a tire iron, threatening the white man with physical harm, and telling him to leave. He and his girlfriend left.

LEGAL CASE 77

Defendant: The parish priest.
Authority: The chief.
Date: About 1970.
Location: A reserve near Eskasoni.

Facts: The chief (see Legal Case 76) opposed the presence of any white people on his reserve, even to the point of opposing the ministrations of the band's priest.

Outcome: The chief told the priest that he could only come onto the reserve once a week to hear confessions and to say Mass. The priest obeyed the chief's decision.

The chief's decisions in these last two cases prompted the following decision by Indian Affairs.

LEGAL CASE 78

Defendant: The chief.
Authority: Indian Affairs.
Date: About 1970.
Location: A reserve near Eskasoni.

Facts: Indian Affairs discovered that the chief (see Legal Case 76) had forcibly expelled a person from the reserve and greatly reduced the access of another.

Outcome: Indian Affairs told the chief that he could not continue in this way. It said that he could, rather, have non-Indians arrested by the police and charged with an offense to the Criminal Code, but that threatening them with bodily harm was unacceptable. Indian Affairs also verbally chastised him for acting contrary to the desires of the members of his band, who had wanted the presence on the reserve of those whom the chief had excluded. Apparently, Indian Affairs only takes notice of claims of trespass when the trespasser causes some sort of nuisance or harm to the reserve or band, and acts only at the request of a band member. At least, this was the case at the time.

Comment: While the *Indian Act* forbids non-band members from trespassing on reserves, it does not compel legal action against those who do.

The Eskasoni Band Council specifically forbids non-band members from appropriating real or personal property possessed or owned by an Indian individual without the owner's or possessor's consent, as in the following case.

LEGAL CASE 79

Defendant: A non-Indian automobile repossessor.
Authority: The chief.
Date: About 1980.

Facts: VT had not made the payments on a car he had purchased. One day a repossessor showed up on the reserve to take possession of the vehicle. VT did not want his car taken and summoned the chief.

Outcome: The chief forbade the repossessor entry onto the reserve (according to Band Council Legal Principle 12). Some months later, VT relinquished possession of the car to the lender.

Comment: The chief's decision contradicted Canadian Indian law (*Indian Act*, R.S.C. 1985, c. I-5, s. 89[2]), which permits a seller with the right of possession the right to repossess the chattel sold, even if it is located on a reserve.

On this reserve, on the other hand, it was not unusual in the period from 1985 to 1987 to see a car that was to be repossessed remain on the reserve for a year or more until the purchaser agreed to relinquish it.

The general rule repeated to me concerning the presence of non-Indians on the reserve is essentially that no non-Indian is allowed to be on the reserve unless invited by someone on the reserve, and that person may be on the reserve after nightfall only if inside someone's house by invitation. By examining the actual legal decisions made at Eskasoni (see Legal Cases 74, 75, and 79), however, we may abstract the following legal principle:

BAND COUNCIL LEGAL PRINCIPLE 12

The chief allows non-Indians on the reserve at his sufferance and may use this sufferance to control offensive behavior, which includes proselytizing and repossession of property.

CHAPTER FOURTEEN

Lawful Possession under the Band Council

We now arrive at the most important contradiction between the Canadian and Eskasoni Band Council legal systems. This chapter discusses the feature of the federal legal system that most powerfully intrudes into the Eskasoni Band Council land tenure system, lawful possession (allotment), and how the Eskasoni Band Council manages to operate its legal system according to its own principles despite this intrusion.

The Administration of Allotment at Eskasoni

For Indian Affairs to award an allotment, the Band Council must first recommend such allotment on behalf of the individual or group. The majority of a quorum of Band Council members does so by signing a Band Council Resolution to that effect. The resolution must also contain a precise and accurate description of the lot, which is usually by reference to a plat drawn by surveyors supplied by Indian Affairs.

After its signing, the Band Council Resolution is sent to Indian Affairs regional headquarters, where it is checked and then sent on to Ottawa for approval. I have neither seen nor heard evidence that a Band Council Resolution for a Certificate of Possession was rejected for other than reason of clerical error, in which case it is corrected and resubmitted.

A Profile of Allotment at Eskasoni

To arrive at a better understanding of the use of allotment on the reserve, it is important to know how many and what kind of people make use of it (Table 2, Figure 5).

There are correlations between allotment and several other factors. It does not seem unreasonable to find that people who have lived and worked outside of the reserve community for long periods, and so been exposed to the wider North American culture, have developed an appreciation of the benefits of land ownership under federal law. There are 21 such people with Certificates of Possession.

Others who appear with some frequency in the ranks of the lawful possessors

TABLE 2. Profile of lawful possessors at the Eskasoni reserve in 1987 holding a Certificate of Possession (CP).

Total lots allotted (total number of CPs)	80
Total CP holders	67
Total households with CPs	61
Individuals holding one CP alone	42
Individuals holding two CPs alone	5
Individuals holding three CPs alone	3
Individuals holding five CPs alone	2
Married couples holding one CP jointly	4
Individuals holding one CP jointly with spouse and child, and one CP alone	1
Percentage of all (440) households with CPs	13.9
Percentage of individuals holding CPs	3.3

are those whose families lived in Eskasoni before the Centralization Program. These have vigorously defended as their own the land they live on, and usually other lands as well, especially from the "newcomers" brought in by the Centralization Program. There are 18 such people with Certificates of Possession. There are also people who have become leaders in the community through their involvement in the band government, or by success in business. There are eight such people with Certificates of Possession. There are a further 16 lawful possessors who either did not fit the above categories, or whom I did not know well enough to place in any of the other three categories. Allottees have been counted only once, though several fit into more than one category.

I do not suggest any sort of causative effect by the use of these categories. Rather, I feel that a correlation exists, although it is far from perfect. Many who have been heavily exposed to non-Indian culture have long experience in band politics or have tried to keep the "new" people out of the reserve, but do not have Certificates of Possession, nor do they care to acquire them.

The profile that I present here describes the situation as it existed in 1987, the year after the Band Council ban on the awarding of new Certificates of Possession. Since 1987, little has changed. Most important among the changes has been the passing of interests in lawfully possessed lots to the multiple offspring of possessors through intestate succession *per stirpes*. Several lots have changed hands, and a few lawful possessory interests have been traded, given, or sold back to the band.

Lots, Housing, and Lawful Possession in Eskasoni in 1987

The use of surveyed lots on the Eskasoni reserve (see Figure 5) is not universal; lots, after all, were imposed by Indian Affairs and are not required by the Band

Council for its own purposes. In fact, the Band Council frequently regards them as a pernicious source of disputes over land rights and use. But because disputes over land use are occasionally settled by using lot boundaries (see Dispute Cases 36 and 66), people see them as significant for this purpose alone; otherwise, they pay them little attention. Houses sometimes straddle lot boundaries (see Figure 5, maps 2, 5, 6, 7, 8, 9, and 11), indicating that, to the people involved, the boundaries ordinarily hold no significance. For example, one man noted that part of his new house strayed over the line dividing his lot from his neighbor's and joked that he hoped that his neighbor would not one night appear in his bedroom, because that room is in the portion of the house on the other man's lot. The implication is that the idea of determining real property rights with lot boundaries is ridiculous. Even more indicative of Micmac indifference to Indian Affairs and its intentions is that some houses straddle the boundaries between allotted and unallotted lots (see Figure 5, maps 6, 8, and 11), thereby indicating that allotment itself holds little or no significance to some Eskasoni Micmac.

No correlation exists between allotment and geographic location. Housing density is greater and lot size smaller in the eastern portion of the reserve than in the western (initial settlement occurred earlier in the east), and there are many vacant lots, both allotted and not. Also important is that nearly all private buildings devoted to commercial use are on allotted lots (see Figure 5, maps 8 and 9). As will be seen below, the most important consequence of allotment is that it protects ownership rights in cases in which the owner threatens to bring a dispute before a federal legal authority.

Conflict between the Two Legal Systems

Under the federal system, an individual acquires possession only if the Band Council and Indian Affairs award lawful possession. Under the Eskasoni Band Council system, ownership is acquired through primary residence. It is therefore possible that two or more parties will acquire interests in the same piece of real property under the provisions of the two different legal systems.

In most cases, the two systems do not conflict, simply because people rarely exercise their rights under the federal system. The rights granted under the indigenous system strike most people as more just. As we saw in Dispute Case 44, for example, the possessor of a house by lawful possession of the lot on which the house sits did not exercise possessory rights to the house, but allowed his former daughter-in-law to keep it and move it off the lot.

In other instances as well all parties concerned behave as if lawful possession did not exist. As we have already seen, the Band Council gave lawful possession little or no weight in decisions to lease private property for the benefit of indigent tenants, despite the efforts of Indian Affairs to the contrary. Take as further examples the following two cases involving rental of housing to the Band Council.

In Legal Case 73 (see Chapter 12), a man (the primary resident) lived on a lot

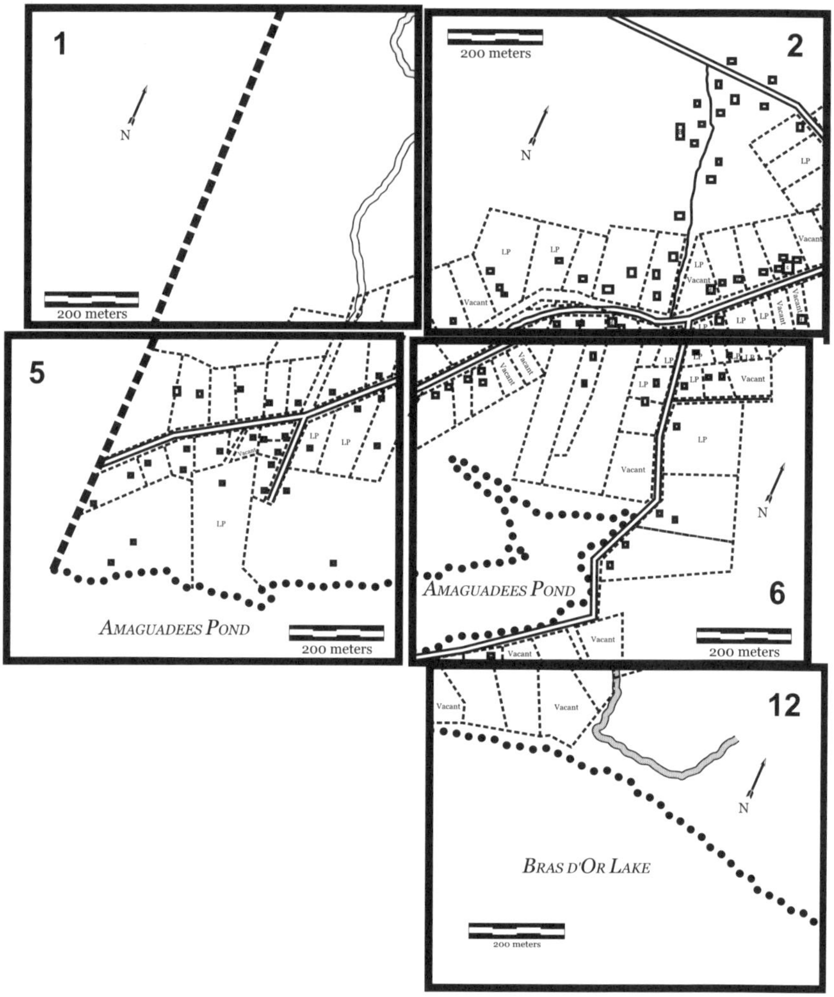

FIGURE 5. Map D: Settlement maps of Eskasoni in 1987, indicating lots and lawful possession. These 14 numbered maps, and one key map, are constructed from information presented in original Indian Affairs maps of the reserve. These maps show the spatial relationships between house and lot location, and between allotted lots and those not allotted. Buildings are not drawn to scale, however, locations relative to each other and to lot boundaries are accurate. Source: Eskasoni Band Council.

to which lawful possession belonged to a second party. The owner under the Band Council system (the primary resident) erected other housing on the lot that he rented to the Band Council for the use of the tenants. Lawful possession therefore seems to be of no importance to the owner, the lawful possessor, the Band Council, or the tenants.

In another instance, a man inherited by testamentary succession his mother's mother's house, but the lot on which it is located is lawfully possessed. This went as

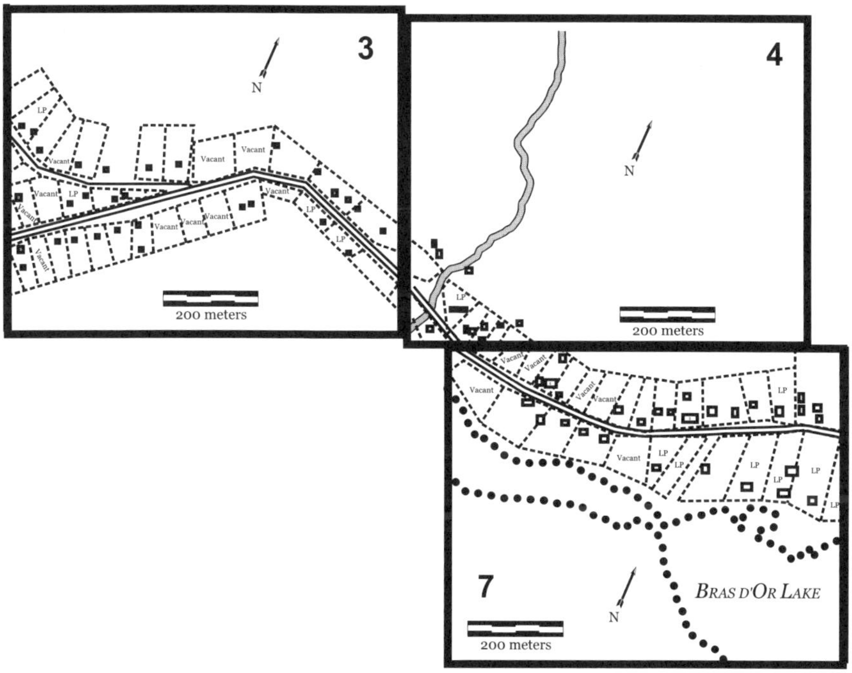

Figure 5 continued.

an undivided interest to all of the mother's mother's children. The man later rented the house to the Band Council for the benefit of a tenant.

The Eskasoni chief also took no judicial notice of allotment in this next case.

Legal Case 80

First party: RM.
Second party: PM, his brother.
Authority: The chief.
Date: 1985.

Facts: RM, his wife and children lived in a house on the same lot where his two brothers had their houses. The three brothers, along with a brother and sister living elsewhere, each have a one-fifth interest in the lawful possession of the lot through the intestate death of their father, who had lawfully possessed the lot at the time of his death. These interests have not been consolidated or altered. RM's wife had grown up in another part of the reserve and did not like living as an outsider in her husband's reserve section. RM, on the other hand, wanted to remain where he was, in his Family Home Territory.

One day RM's wife set fire to the house. She anticipated, at the time, that if the house burned down her family would be without housing and the Band Council would be obliged to provide them with a new house that she could have built in her favorite location. However, the fire did not cause much damage, so she set fire to the house

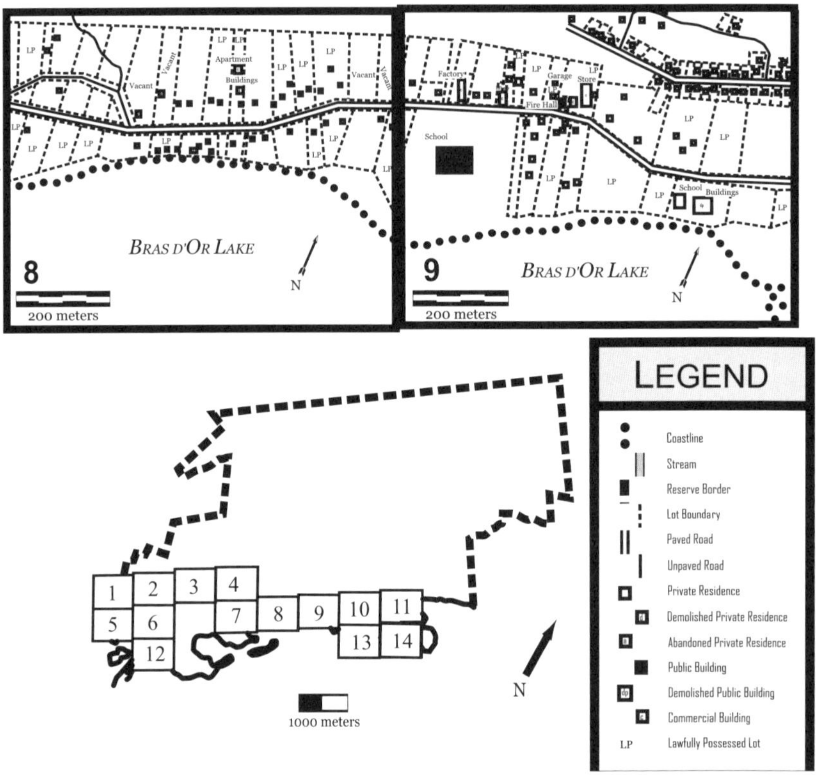

FIGURE 5 CONTINUED.

again twice the next day. Each time the reserve's firemen extinguished the blaze before the house could sustain any serious damage. Later, RM and his wife had an argument and abandoned their house, taking their children with them. After the house had stood empty for a few weeks, PM, RM's brother who lived next door with several children in an old house that was in poor condition, decided to take ownership of RM's house and asked the Band Council to fix the house for him.

Outcome: The chief gave PM the materials needed for repair, thereby approving PM's acquisition of ownership of the house, but stipulated that PM must supply the labor for the repairs himself, to which PM agreed. According to rumor, the chief allowed PM to take ownership of RM's house because RM did not fulfill a political contract (see Band Council Legal Principle 3). Several months later RM returned to live in the house that PM had once possessed.

This case is significant because the land on which the two houses sat was lawfully possessed. The houses involved, though purchased at Indian Affairs and band expense, were in fact lawfully possessed by RM, PM, and their three siblings. The chief therefore has no authority over the possession of the buildings under the *Indian Act.* The Band Council as a whole may pass by-laws that regulate the construction, repair, or use of buildings, whether possessed by the band or by

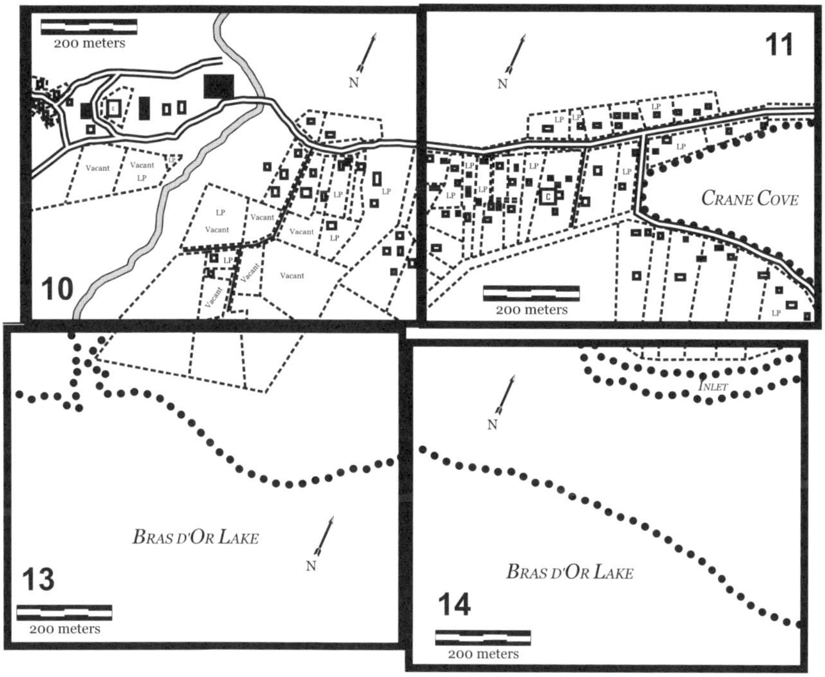

FIGURE 5 CONTINUED.

individuals (*Indian Act*, R.S.C. 1970, c. I-6, s. 81[h]), but not by-laws that control possessory rights to lawfully possessed lands. The chief has obviously extended his legal authority well beyond the power granted him under the *Indian Act*. He has done so through his control of the political patronage system; those who want the material rewards that he has to give must obey his decisions and vote for him. In this case, allotment carried no weight. It is also important to note that RM's and PM's three siblings, all at the time strong supporters and beneficiaries of the chief, did not oppose either PM's expropriation or the chief's decision.

The Band Council also ignores lawful possession when deciding to raze dilapidated housing (see Legal Case 103 and Dispute Case 66). The cases below show that family/descent group authorities may likewise pay no attention to a lawful possessory interest.

LEGAL CASE 81

Defendant: ML.
Authority: OL, his mother.
Date: 1986.

Facts: ML is the son of OL and YL, and has a sister BL. YL had lawful possession of a large lot. When ML and BL each married, YL, their father, gave ML the east and BL the west portions of the lot, and kept the central portion for himself. The lot was re-surveyed and three smaller lots were created. Each of the three, the two offspring and their father, thereby had lawful possession separately. Years later YL died and lawful possession of his lot passed to his wife, OL. Some years after that, ML put up a 20-foot by 20-foot (6 by 6 meter) building on what he believed was the western edge of his lot, next to his mother's lot. Shortly thereafter, OL began to complain to ML that her lot ran further east, that the building was on her lot, and that she did not like it. ML believed differently, according to what he remembered his father telling him about the boundaries at the time YL gave him his lot.

Outcome: ML deferred to his mother and moved the building.

Comment: Interestingly, neither ML nor his mother consulted the official records, which would have helped them settle the dispute in accordance with the survey. ML instead accepted his mother's decision as to where the boundary line lay. My own research into the official records show that OL was indeed correct, but again, the question of lawful possession and survey were not considered. The sanction that ML feared was maternal displeasure, and not the Band Council, police, or the Canadian courts.

Parties engaged in private disputes may also fail to give lawful possession determinative weight, as in the following cases.

DISPUTE CASE 66

First party: ZB, a man in his thirties.
Second party: TI, a man in his thirties.
Date: 1985 to the early 1990s.

Facts: ZB and TI owned adjacent lots. ZB lived on his lot, while TI lived in a house elsewhere on the reserve. ZB built a fence around his yard, or what previous inhabitants of the house had always considered its yard. TI drove by, saw the fence, and removed that part of the fence that encroached onto his lot. He relied on the Indian Affairs surveyor's plat of the reserve, which used lot boundaries that did not reflect the previously accepted boundaries. He later showed the plat to ZB. He also showed ZB evidence that he had a Certificate of Possession for the lot. ZB, though angry, did not seek to rebuild the fence. He accepted the Indian Affairs lot boundary lines as determinative of the geographical extent of his interest in his lot and the dispute ended temporarily. The Band Council later removed the ramshackle building on TI's lot because it posed a safety hazard.

Outcome: ZB years later extended his lawn to cover nearly all of TI's lot, including the site of the shack, and now he and his family use the lawn as their own. TI has turned his attention to other affairs and the dispute is forgotten.

Comment: A significant feature of this dispute is that the legal authority (the chief and council) does not recognize Indian Affairs lot boundary lines, which TI used to support his argument, as having any bearing on any of its decisions, whether legal or not. As the band manager at the time told me, "those are Indian Affairs' lines, not ours."

DISPUTE CASE 67

First party: MC, a man in his forties.
Second party: FC, his brother.
Date: 1986.

Facts: FC occupies a lot that DE, who lives on another lot, lawfully possesses. The parents of MC and FC died within a few weeks of each other. MC had been living in the United States and went to Eskasoni for the funerals. The father's will, about which MC knew very little, stipulated that the house that the parents had occupied was to go to MC on the death of both. FC, on the other hand, wanted possession of the house for his offspring and did not mention the will or its provisions to MC. Some weeks after the funerals MC went to his brother's house and asked whether their parents had left a will. FC became angry and chased MC from his yard.

Outcome: Wishing to avoid conflict, MC decided that he would not pursue his claim to ownership of the house; he did not complain to the Band Council, to Indian Affairs, or to the Canadian courts. FC later gave the house to one of his offspring. The dispute between MC and FC remains unresolved. MC later left the reserve permanently. That the lot is lawfully possessed played no part in the outcome of the case. This case resembles instead other disputes over property succession that do not involve lawful possession (see Dispute Cases 37, 38, and 39).

In cases in which a party insists on his or her rights under lawful possession, the Band Council will grant those rights material effect.

LEGAL CASE 82

Party: HG.
Authority: The Band Council.
Date: Mid-1980s.

Facts: The Band Council wished to acquire some land that HG owned and possessed lawfully, for a road construction project. HG wished to sell, but asked a price that the Band Council did not want to pay.

Outcome: After many months of negotiation, the Band Council and HG arrived at an agreement and the Band Council purchased the land that HG lawfully possessed.

LEGAL CASE 83

First party: GX.
Second party: TD, a neighbor.
Date: 1991 or 1992.

Facts: Shortly after GX became a widow, TD erected a fence on her property to make it seem that the boundary between the two lots was much farther to the west, thus favoring TD with more land. GX's lot is lawfully possessed. GX asked the chief to adjudicate her dispute with TD. The Band Council investigated her claim, consulted their maps showing lot locations, and found that GX's claim was valid. The Band Council told TD that he could not put up a fence where he did.

Outcome: TD dismantled the fence.

Usually, the owner by primary residence and the possessor by lawful possession are one and the same. But what happens if a party acquires lawful possessory rights under the federal system to property that a second party owns under the Eskasoni Band Council system by primary residence and the first party wishes to exercise his or her rights under the federal system? Such a circumstance occurred twice and both times caused major uproars within the community.

LEGAL—POLITICAL CASE 1

First party: TE.
Second party: The U brothers.
Third party: The Band Council.
Authority: The Band Council and the regional Indian Affairs office.
Date: 1986.

Facts: Around 1975 TE returned to Eskasoni after having lived in Boston for several years. Not long thereafter he acquired a Certificate of Possession for his lot. Some years later, two of the U brothers received new houses from the band and decided to have them built on a point of land near TE's house. They did not know that the spot they had selected was within the boundaries of TE's lot and nobody at the band office caught the error. TE waited until the houses were completed and then attempted to take possession of them. The houses had not yet been delivered, so the Band Council still possessed them. Because it had not yet delivered on its promise to supply the houses to the U brothers, the Band Council became an active party to the dispute. The U brothers told TE that if the dispute could not be solved peacefully and in their favor, then they would settle it with their fists. As one member of the band administration expressed it to me at the time, the dispute was "ready to explode." Under federal statute, any lawful possessor has the right of possession, including the right to eject trespassers, the right to have the federal police (the Royal Canadian Mounted Police) remove the trespassers if the local constables will not do so, and the right to possess fixtures (such as houses) on the possessed land. The local Canadian police and courts usually defer to Indian Affairs on matters pertaining to the *Indian Act* because of their relative inexperience with that legislation.

Outcome: The Band Council took no action on behalf of TE's claim for months, thereby rendering his claim based on lawful possession invalid. It continued to recognize the U brothers as owners of the houses. At some point, the regional office of Indian Affairs joined the Band Council as authority to this dispute. It agreed with the Band Council and the U brothers that to allow TE to take possession or ownership of the new houses would be an injustice. Indian Affairs likewise refused to allow TE to take possession of the two new houses; it had invested a great deal of money in them and had an obligation to provide housing for the people of the reserve. Indian Affairs and the Band Council offered to resurvey the lot so as to exclude the U brothers' houses and create a new lot for TE with the same surface area. TE accepted this solution.

Comment: There were many reasons why TE finally accepted the decision and did not attempt to take the dispute to federal court. The first was that he would have suffered even more ostracism by the community had he not; the standards of justice on the reserve dictate that once an individual receives a house, that house is his until he relinquishes it (see Eskasoni Real Property Behavioral Rule 4). To take ownership of a house simply because it is on one's lot struck people there as absurd and unjust.

As one member of the band told me concerning this case, it was immoral for "one man to be able to take another man's house just because he has a piece of paper." Those I spoke to about the case said that TE should not be allowed to do what he had been planning to do, and one band councillor said that "CPs [Certificates of Possession] mean nothing on the reserve." Further, the political problems that TE could have faced had he not accepted the ruling would have been severe; not only was the U brothers' father a councillor for the ward, but their brother's wife is the chief's sister. Third, it was also likely that he would have to beat the U brothers in a fistfight to hang on to the houses and the U brothers were renowned fighters. Finally, TE was given a good job on the reserve at about the same time as he accepted this solution.

For many Micmac, the possibility of using lawful possession to gain ownership of someone else's property indicates that the Euro–Canadian law promotes immorality. The following dispute, played out over three interrelated cases, shows another solution to the conflict between the two legal systems.

LEGAL CASE 84

First party: AS.
Second party: HS, his son.
Authority: AS.
Date: 1986.

Facts: AS moved to Eskasoni from another Cape Breton reserve during the 1940s Centralization Program. After he had built his house and cleared some land, the Indian Agent gave him a plat of a small section of the reserve that showed his lot, and which had AS's name on the lot; the lot boundaries had been hand drawn on paper by the Indian Agent. In 1956, Indian Affairs created bands and held the election of chiefs and councillors as the *Indian Act* provided. One of the responsibilities of the new Band Councils was to allot lands within the reserve, and this meant that Indian Affairs had to have the lots professionally surveyed. Apparently, the surveyors knew nothing about any of the old plats and simply drew lots around the houses and gardens as they existed at the time. In 1969, AS's wife's mother, who lived on a nearby lot, requested and received allotment. Accidentally, however, the Band Council and Indian Affairs granted her a Certificate of Possession for AS's lot, not her own lot, and no one caught the error.

Several years later, AS's wife's mother died and left in her will the Certificate of Possession for AS's land to her grandson, TM. About a decade later, AS's son HS returned to live in his parents' house, after spending several years away from the reserve. Afterward, AS's wife died and the Band Council hired HS as an office worker. HS then made a discreet inquiry to Indian Affairs to attempt to acquire a Certificate of Possession to his father's lot and was informed that TM had it. TM readily agreed to transfer his Certificate of Possession to HS in return for HS's help in getting a Certificate of Possession from the Band Council for the lot where he had his own house. HS thereby acquired lawful possession of his father's lot.

Sometime thereafter, AS and HS argued and AS attempted to correct his son's behavior by reminding him that he was living in his father's house and could not do as he pleased. HS informed his father that the situation was just the opposite, that it was he who owned the house and the land, and that AS owned nothing. After this, HS made it clear to his father that he was not welcome in the house. AS was, of course, heartbroken by this turn of events and for a while made plans to leave the house and live elsewhere.

Outcome: AS changed his mind and decided to reassert his authority over his household. When AS was out of the house HS would bring his girlfriend and other friends home. AS did not mind this very much, except that they often left the house a mess. On one such occasion AS and HS argued over the issue and AS evicted the both of them.

Comment: As the outcome shows, AS retained his authority over his household, even though the federal court system and Indian Affairs would have considered him a guest in his son's house. HS feared AS's possible paternal sanctions more than any sanctions that the court system could impose. Most in the community took a very dim view of HS over his actions.

This decision did not conclude the dispute.

LEGAL—POLITICAL CASE 2

First party: AS.
Second party: HS.
Authority: The band's chief.
Date: 1986.

Facts: AS asked the chief for a ruling on his rights to the house and lot against those of HS.

Outcome: The chief ruled publicly that AS owned the house, but that HS owned the land. This decision resulted from the direct collision between the ownership rights that AS had through his original occupation and primary residence under the traditional system and the lawful possessory rights that HS held under the federal system. The chief could not deny either one, especially since HS was determined to gain by his acquisition of lawful possession, hence the political nature of this part of the decision. Therefore, the chief privately allowed HS to have actual ownership of the land and the house, but told AS and other members of the band that AS owned the house. AS on the other hand maintained possession; no party wished to deprive AS of his right to possess the house. The public would have opposed a Band Council decision to give HS possession, because to do so would have breached basic standards of morality.

Nevertheless, HS's action in attempting to gain ownership of his father's house drew widespread condemnation from members of the community. In fact, although it told AS that he owned the house, the Band Council had only awarded him possession of the house. Because HS enjoyed political privilege (he worked for the chief and supported him), and because the courts give lawful possession decisive weight, the Band Council subsequently awarded HS ownership of the house and quietly paid him rent for it on behalf of AS. The Band Council, most importantly, protected AS's right of possession as primary resident. This decision did conform to the reserve's law to the degree that it preserved the possessory rights of the primary resident, even though it contradicts federal law.

Comment: Although AS disliked the stated decision, he apparently felt that he had little real choice but to accept it. He was not to discover for several years that the Band Council in fact regarded both the house and land as HS's property. The Band Council, at least, preserved as much as it could of AS's rights under Band Council law.

It could not grant him ownership, because of HS's lawful possession. It did, however, manage to keep his right of possession, in effect creating, for the first time in Band Council law, a life interest. The Band Council managed to acquire AS's possession for life through political means.

Realizing that the chief had made a politically biased decision, AS appealed to Indian Affairs for a ruling.

LEGAL CASE 85

First party: AS.
Second party: HS.
Authority: Indian Affairs.
Date: 1986.

Facts: AS complained to Indian Affairs about the chief's decision (see Legal–Political Case 2) and asked for information on the rights of a lawful possessor.

Outcome: An Indian Affairs staff member told AS that whoever held the Certificate of Possession for the lot also possessed the house, and became angry that the Band Council was not performing its duty to make proper decisions in such matters.

Although the final solution benefited AS, in that he had a house to live in until he died, AS wished for more. He had wanted to be able to give a grandson his house and land when he died, and very late in life found that he could not. He became very unhappy at this, but in the end saw some humor in the situation: "Let them fight over it," he once told me with a smile. After AS died, HS sold the property to a relative.

Thus, there are three levels of legal and political power in this dispute, as follows:

1. The household legal level, in which the father maintains authority no matter what federal statute allows.

2. The band level, at which the case was decided on the basis of the laws of two legal systems, laws that conflict enormously. In this instance, the Band Council made a political decision designed to reach a peaceful settlement and maintained the possessory rights, if not the ownership rights, of the party who acquired them by primary residence.

3. The federal legal level. Had it been asked to do so, Indian Affairs might have revoked the Certificate of Possession under Section 26 of the *Indian Act*, namely, that it was issued in error. Or, alternatively, it could have ruled that HS had all the rights to the house and lot to which lawful position entitled him.

From Legal Cases 80, 82, 91, and 103, and Legal–Political Cases 1 and 2, we can abstract the following legal principle:

BAND COUNCIL LEGAL PRINCIPLE 13

The Band Council ignores lawful possession when no party insists on rights under the provisions of lawful possession; it will give the lawful possessor possession of property owned by another party by primary residence in cases in which the primary resident will not lose possession of a dwelling; and it will preserve by political means either possessory or ownership rights to dwellings acquired by primary residence against the lawful possessor of the same property.

Years after the ban on new Certificates of Possession took effect (see below) lawful possession continues to cause problems in a society used to thinking in terms of the principles of the indigenous system of acquiring rights by primary residence. Some of the difficulty lies in the federal system's reliance on permanent boundary lines and use of these as reference points for the establishment of ownership. The Eskasoni system depends on use and residence to establish ownership. Even in cases in which both parties to a land dispute have lawful possession, this difference in establishing ownership can still wreak havoc.

DISPUTE CASE 68

Party: HS.
Party: MS, his brother.
Date: 1997–1998.

Facts: Some years before the dispute, MS had built an apartment building on his lawfully possessed lot, which adjoined his father's (AS's) lawfully possessed lot. Knowing the Eskasoni system of law, under which a party establishes ownership by use, MS built his building so that part of it lay a few feet over the line onto his father's lot, although nobody paid any attention to this at the time. After HS acquired AS's lot (see Legal–Political Case 2), and after AS died, HS sought to profit by his brother's action. He made a commotion over the violation of his lot boundary.

Outcome: MS reluctantly purchased the small section of HS's lot under the apartment building. Neither the Band Council nor Indian Affairs imposed a settlement on the parties. Again, HS was popularly condemned for his behavior.

The ruckus that Legal–Political Cases 1 and 2 created caused the Band Council to take action to further reduce the influence of allotment.

The End of the Awarding of Allotments

Restricting Allotment

Even before the Band Council took the final step of refusing to approve any further allotments, many people in the band opposed the use of lawful possession and the Band Council made acquiring allotment difficult, as seen in the following cases.

LEGAL CASE 86

Party: W.
Authority: The Band Council.
Date: Early 1980s.

Facts: W felt that he could somehow benefit by having lawful possession of a parcel of woodland and asked the Band Council for allotment. The Band Council responded that it might grant allotment if W fenced the lot or in some other way indicated exclusive use of the lot. Not long thereafter, W showed a representative of the Band Council that he had fenced off the lot. By nailing poles to trees, he had "fenced" more than one acre.

Outcome: Determining that W had no genuine or even logical reason to have lawful possession, the Band Council denied his application. W was widely regarded as less than fully sane as a result of this case.

LEGAL CASE 87

Party: FT and IO.
Authority: The Band Council.
Date: Early 1980s.

Facts: FT and IO, two of the band's politically and economically shrewdest men, formed a partnership. They applied to the Band Council for allotment of a lot where they planned to build a tavern, which would have been the only establishment serving alcohol on the reserve. They argued that the Certificate of Possession would provide the business venture with needed security.

Outcome: The Band Council acknowledged that having a business constituted a legitimate need for allotment and approved the application. However, there were some discussions before the approval. Some members felt that alcohol posed a significant threat to the band and a tavern would bring further harm. Others felt that the proposed business would never materialize or succeed, and that FT and IO simply wanted a Certificate of Possession to the land. One band councillor would have approved the application more readily had there been a provision for the Certificate of Possession to return to the band should the business fail.

Comment: The tavern was never built, least in part because of community opposition.

Ending New Allotments

The disputes that Legal–Political Cases 1 and 2 resolved caused both the band and the Band Council considerable headaches, including scolds from Indian Affairs. These cases convinced the Band Council that Certificates of Possession caused enormous trouble and returned no discernable gain.

Many members of the band and Band Council also foresaw another problem, a conflict between lawful possession and the band's housing needs. In recent decades, the Band Council has worked hard to meet the band's rapidly growing need for housing and space for housing, increasingly difficult in part because of the shortages of suitable and desirable land. Despite the reserve's size of 8,800 acres, it has little relatively flat land available for building houses (see Figures 4 and 7).

While it is possible to build on the sides of hills, the higher costs would result in the construction of fewer houses. Also, most of the reserve remains unserviced by roads or water, sewer, and electrical lines. A recipient of a new house who wants it built far from existing service lines must pay for the construction of these lines, an expense that very few are willing or able to bear.

Finally, and perhaps most importantly, is the great degree to which individuals and families defend their own interests in land against other private parties and against the Band Council. As a general rule of behavior, according to a long-time band manager, a member of the band staff responsible for implementing the Band Council's policies, "whenever anyone gets any kind of a claim" on any land they tend to defend that claim vigorously. Such private claims, obviously, impede the Band Council's ability to find places to site houses. The lawful possessory interest bolsters these claims and therefore works against the Band Council's ability to find land for house siting and for the other needs of the band and the people. It can also lead to family disputes, such as that of Legal–Political Case 2, which the Band Council assiduously seeks to avoid.

Because of these factors, the Band Council issued its last Certificates of Possession for unpossessed lands on the reserve in 1986, a mere eight years after the band gained possession of the reserve. The Band Council had decided to stop granting new Certificates of Possession and has actually bought a few existing ones back from their owners. The chief voluntarily transferred lawful possession of his personal house and lot to the band. In one instance the Band Council approved a business loan on the condition that lawful possession of a lot be transferred back to the band. Before Legal–Political Cases 1 and 2, the Band Council often granted lawful possessory interests to people who asked for them, particularly before 1978, when Indian Affairs had great control over the reserve and strongly advocated that band members acquire lawful possessory interests to encourage acculturation and assimilation.

The band and the Band Council continue to try to minimize the effects of lawful possession, even while acknowledging its existence, as in the following cases.

LEGAL CASE 88

Party: DJ, a man.
Authority: The Chief.
Date: 2005.

Facts: The band was in the process of constructing sidewalks throughout the reserve. The chief, knowing that DJ has lawful possession of his lot, asked DJ for permission to use some of DJ's lot for the construction of the sidewalk. DJ agreed to this, on the condition that he be compensated monetarily for the loss of a portion of his lot. The chief was noncommittal. The band later built the sidewalk, and DJ pressed his demand for compensation, to no avail.

Outcome: The chief resigned his office not long thereafter, and thus DJ lost a portion of his lot without compensation. In effect, this meant that lawful possession counted for naught in this case.

Comment: DJ ran for the office of chief in 2008. One of the points of his platform was to call for greater legal weight to be given to lawful possession on the reserve.

It is interesting to compare this case with Legal Case 83 and Dispute Case 71. In all three cases, territorial defense is involved. However, in Legal Case 83 and Dispute Case 71, the parties opposing the administration were supported by large solidary lineages. DJ, whose lineage is large although anything but solidary, was safely ignored. As the final outcome of the land expropriations in Legal Cases 96 and 97 show, a powerful and privileged private party can nullify the effect of an unfavorable Band Council decision. Lawful possession remains less important than political privilege. The pattern of large solidary lineages producing political privilege also holds true in awards of housing and employment.

DISPUTE CASE 69

First Party: DJ.
Second Party: VJ , DJ's younger brother.
Third Party: AU.
Date: 2008.

Facts: DJ had lawful possession of his lot, which he had inherited from his mother. VJ's brother's house also sat on this lot, making it, under federal law, DJ's property as well. VJ later sold his house to AU, an unrelated third party. DJ did not like AU, especially living so close to him. In 2006, DJ managed to get AU to sign an agreement to leave or to remove the house within two years, by July 2008, and this agreement was witnessed by two band councillors. AU had hoped to get the Band Council to move his house at band expense, but this request was rejected as too expensive. Instead, the band's CEO and lawyer asked DJ to sign a quitclaim to the house. This request DJ rejected, and continued to rely on his lawful possession to attempt to gain control of the house.

As time went on, it became obvious that AU had no intention of leaving, despite his agreement to do so. AU once told DJ that "the house is not yours." AU was also accustomed to driving across DJ's lawn to get to his house. DJ responded by putting large rocks around his lawn. Once AU had some gravel delivered to level out his driveway. DJ told the deliveryman not to spread the gravel, which remained in a single large pile blocking the driveway.

Outcome: This apparently was enough for AU, who vacated the house in June 2008. DJ had to resort to physical and mental pressure to remove AU. The law would not assist him.

The Certificate of Possession has always meant relatively little to most people on the Eskasoni reserve, as these cases show; the authority on the reserve would like to ignore it and even Indian Affairs in Legal–Political Case 1 did not give it determinative weight. Also, Certificates of Possession do not assist in the exploitation of resources. Again, on-reserve authorities avoid giving them weight in a dispute and virtually all individuals still rely on self-redress. Perhaps most importantly, lawful possession conflicts with the highly valued Eskasoni Real Property Behavioral Rules 1 through 5 (see Chapter 1), and therefore many consider it unjust.

Many also disliked the Certificate of Possession as a symbol of elitism, a tool of assimilation, and a way to lose face. Because it creates a sense of inequality, people rarely talk about lawful possession, and many who have it do not admit it readily. In contrast, on another Cape Breton reserve where band members are much more acculturated allotment is commonly used.

Two band councillors each told me individually that they were personally responsible for leading the Band Council to the decision to end the awarding of Certificates of Possession on the reserve. Another person who works for the Band Council told me that it was the councillors from his ward, a ward that these two councillors did not represent, who had first refused to accept any more requests for Certificates of Possession. All the leaders, it seemed, wished to take credit for the new policy. They all gave rather vague answers as to why they had ended the practice, however, saying that "no one needs them" and "they don't do anybody any good."

Despite a history of promoting the use of lawful possession on reserves, some at Indian Affairs also dislike it. Several staff members told me that Indian Affairs had suggested to the Band Councils that they halt the practice to acquire more control over housing and, therefore, the voters. It makes good political and economic sense, in short. They even suggested that the Band Councils buy back Certificates of Possession by making whatever discretionary aid an individual is to be awarded contingent on the transfer of the certificate back to the band. Indian Affairs could have the most to gain by ending the practice, given the substantial amount of paperwork necessary to award allotment, which includes searching records and verifying statements for new and replacement certificates. Indian Affairs uses its own funds for private surveyors and has to pay a significant amount each time lawfully possessed lands are expropriated. Other Indian Affairs staffers, on the other hand, continue to advocate lawful possessory interests for individuals and families on reserves because those with a sense of ownership of their houses would take better care of them, resulting in economic savings for Indian Affairs. Eskasoni stands alone in not awarding lawful possessory interests, according to an Indian Affairs staff member.

Since 1986, the Eskasoni Band Council has approved 94 lawful possessory interests for private parties, although these consist entirely of either transferals of previously existing lawful possessory interests from one party to another or the division of lots already lawfully possessed.

The Band Council policy reduces the number of private land interests, preserves available free land, gives the Band Council some leeway to economically meet the housing needs of the band, and, most importantly, helps preserve the viability of the indigenous land tenure system, which grants ownership rights on the basis of primary residence.

Avoiding Conflicting Interests in Real Property

The contradiction between the two legal systems has led the Eskasoni Band Council to vigilantly prohibit the creation of conflicting interests to the same piece of land.

Specifically, it attempts to prevent the construction of housing on lawfully possessed land by parties other than the lawful possessor, and band members as well try to avoid this problem. For example, when a woman sought in 1996 to move a mobile home onto her parents' land, she inquired about the boundary with the next lot, saying she had heard that it was lawfully possessed and did not want to put her trailer on her neighbor's lot.

In the following case, the Band Council did, significantly, raise the question of whether or not lawful possession interests came into play.

LEGAL CASE 89

Party: TZ (wife) and AZ (husband), a married couple.
Party: FC.
Authority: The Band Council.
Date: 1999 to 2004.

Facts: TZ and AZ are both from other reserves, although TZ has many kin living in Eskasoni. They decided that they would like to live in Eskasoni on land adjacent to that occupied by one of TZ's kin, FC. FC did not want TZ and AZ living so close to him. He agreed to allow them there in return for a fee of $1,000, which he said was to defray his own expenses in clearing the land and constructing a driveway, but was intended as a polite request to TZ and AZ to build elsewhere. TZ and AZ asked the Band Council whether or not FC could impose any conditions on their plans to move to the spot they chose.

Outcome: The Band Council ruled that FC "has no papers" (that is, no Certificate of Possession) for the lot where his house is situated, and so could not ask for any money for the lot that AZ and TZ wanted, nor do anything to prevent AZ and TZ from moving there. TZ and AZ ultimately built a house nearby, but outside the bounds of FC's territory.

Comment: This case is unusual in that most people in the community abide by the traditional system of gaining ownership rights by first use or residence. Most people would have paid the $1,000 or looked elsewhere for a lot. Most people also would not settle where they are not wanted.

Summary

Lawful possession creates interests that obstruct a Band Council's and family/descent group's ability to meet the needs of their respective groups. Lawful possession also creates interests in land that are considered by the people of the reserve to be immoral. Real property interests under the federal system originate from the Band Council and Indian Affairs and not from primary residence or use, as is commonly believed. The immorality of the system becomes especially clear when people attempt to use lawful possession to wrest possession from those who have acquired it legitimately by primary residence or use.

Lawful possession impedes the operation of the indigenous legal system, which operates on the principle that parties acquire ownership rights by primary residence or use, and which the people of the band consider just. The indigenous legal authorities attempt to preserve legitimately acquired rights whenever they can, even to the point of using extralegal means (political measures).

As the data indicate, only when parties to a dispute insist on giving lawful possession weight, and when they have the political willingness and strength to do so, do interests granted by lawful possession alter the outcome of a dispute. Through both legal and political means the Band Council manages to eviscerate the effect of the *Indian Act*'s and Canadian courts' strongest tool in the regulation of land use on the reserve.

CHAPTER FIFTEEN

Band Council Real Property Laws: Legal Correlates, 1986–1987

To provide as deep an analysis as is possible of land tenure in this community, this chapter presents the Band Council real property laws in force on the Eskasoni reserve in the years 1986 and 1987 examined in terms of their legal correlates and distinguishing the various types of entitled parties according to their rights. The most obvious features of this system pertain to the acquisition of rights of access to land and ownership, which band members acquire simply by being band members, and by primary residence, respectively.

Right to use reserve land (with or without the sufferance of the chief). The first dimension distinguishes those people who have a right of access to the reserve without needing the permission of the chief (band members) from those who require his permission to live on the reserve with a host (non-band members). See Legal Cases 73, 74, and 78.

Right to own real property (yes or no). Only someone who establishes primary residency has the right of ownership. In accordance with the high value that Micmac place on individuality, each parcel of real property or domicile has but one owner by residence, although any number of people may live at one residence. Non-band members may only reside in or on real property on the reserve, but may not own it (Figure 6; see Legal Cases 54, 68, 69, and 95).

Right to control owners' disposition of real property (yes or no). This dimension distinguishes Band Council members from all others. Band Council members (until the changes described in Chapter 16) forbade the sale or razing of old houses (see Political Case 6). Band Council members are also not required to be band members, although Eskasoni voters have elected only band members (see Figure 6).

Right to own houses in which others reside (yes or no). Only members of the class of band members who enjoy political privilege may own houses in which other people reside. Normally, according to Band Council Legal Principle 2, only residents have the right of ownership. This right applies even to the politically privileged who do not have lawful possession of the realty, in contravention of the *Indian Act* (see Legal Cases 61 and 62).

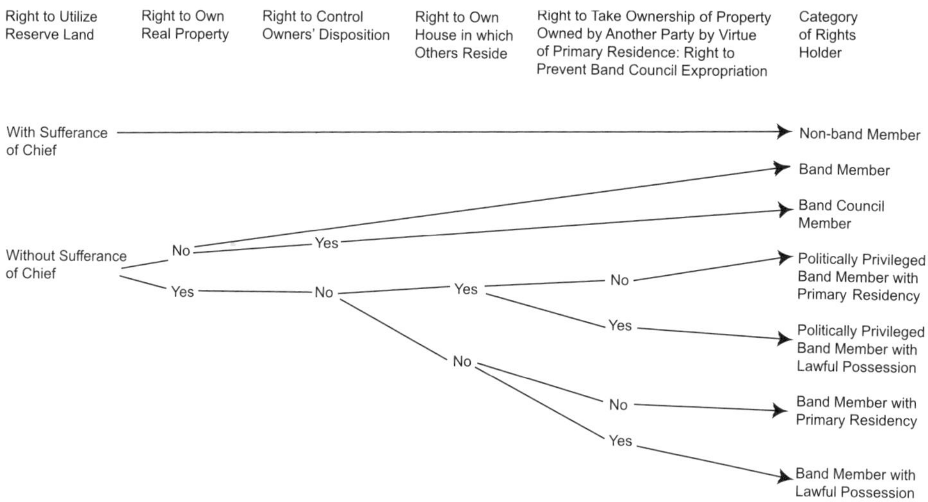

FIGURE 6. Analysis of modern Band Council real property law legal correlates. The Eskasoni Band Council land tenure system, administered by the chief and council, is represented diagrammatically in terms of contrastive legal correlates.

Right to ownership of property owned by another party through primary residence; right to prevent Band Council expropriation (yes or no). This dimension distinguishes band members with lawful possession from those without it (see Legal Cases 82, 83, and 91, and Legal–Political Case 2).

Summary of the Eskasoni Land Tenure System

The following is a summary of those portions of the Eskasoni land tenure system that did not change from 1980 to 1987, as described above. It includes law at the Band Council and family/descent group legal levels.

Ownership

RIGHT OF ACQUISITION

According to law at both Eskasoni Band Council and family/descent group legal levels, anyone may acquire ownership of land and housing simply by being the first to reside on or in it, or by using it, acquiring primary residence. One may also acquire ownership of any adjacent land simply by claiming it, unless it belongs to another (see Legal Cases 68, 69, and 95). And, of course, one may also acquire primary residence, and therefore ownership, from someone who as owner has the right to alienate. At the family/descent group level, the owner of land controls the initial location of housing on the land (see Legal Cases 47 and 52). One may acquire ownership of forest or waterfront lands by being the first to make discernible use of these lands (see Dispute Case 59). Non-band members may not acquire ownership of real property on the reserve, according to Band Council Real Property Rule 3 (no legal cases collected). The politically privileged may acquire ownership of property in which others reside.

Right of Holding

At the Band Council level, the primary resident and owner has ownership against the Band Council only (see Legal Cases 54, 55, 58, and 95). In civil disputes, Band Council law protects the ownership rights of the primary resident reluctantly and weakly; ownership under the law only applies in such cases in which the parties to the dispute obey the Band Council's pronouncements (see Legal Cases 66, 68, 69, 71, 89, and 94). Only the politically privileged may own houses in which others reside (see Legal Cases 61 and 62).

The lawful possessor under the federal legal system has rights under the Band Council system that outweigh the ownership rights that other parties establish by primary residence. However, the Band Council uses political means to prevent the lawful possessor from taking possession or ownership rights in dwellings from those who establish such rights by primary residence (see Legal–Political Cases 1 and 2).

At the family/descent group level a legal authority with ownership may control initial possession of land and housing (see Legal Cases 47 and 52), but the individual house owners have control over the subsequent ownership, possession and use of their housing (see Legal Cases 49 and 50).

Rights of Disposition

Disposal rights. At both the Band Council and family/descent group levels, there are no legal restrictions on the Micmac to give or sell the land or housing that they own to any other band member, with the exception that lineage authorities oppose non-lineage members owning property within their territories (see Dispute Case 71 and Legal Cases 47, 49, 50, 63, and 94).

Testamentary rights. Neither Band Council or family/descent group levels provide legal regulation of testamentary rights. An owner of realty may leave his real property to anyone, but must depend on the goodwill of the rest of the extended family to respect the terms of the will. The Eskasoni Micmac usually use oral wills, if any at all, although use of written wills is becoming more common. The execution of written wills may be turned over to Indian Affairs, or sometimes the band's priest, though Indian Affairs only administers real property conveyances in cases in which the property is lawfully possessed.

Intestate succession. There is no legal regulation of intestamentary succession. If there is no will, real property typically goes by customary rule to the surviving spouse or, if there is none, then to the eldest offspring (see Dispute Case 37).

In cases in which a spouse survives, to my knowledge this principle has never been violated; the surviving spouse is a respected legal authority. However, when there is no surviving spouse, not infrequently disputes end with the most determined or combative offspring owning the parents' real property, or at least the largest or most desirable part of it (see Dispute Cases 37 and 67).

Possession

Legal control of possession under indigenous law normally occurs only at the family/descent group level, in cases in which the patriarch or matriarch, as legal authority, revokes a possessory interest of a family/descent group member (see Legal Cases 42, 43, 44, 45, and 46; but see also Legal–Political Case 2). Otherwise, the law leaves possessory interests unregulated despite politically motivated claims to the contrary (see Legal Cases 55 and 56). By customary rule, any owner may grant any possessory interest to another, including *ususfructus*, under any conditions (see Chapter 1, Eskasoni Real Property Behavioral Rule 2). Most owners, though, only grant licenses to possess property that they own, since primary residence or first use by customary rule is the sole requirement for ownership. These licenses typically remain valid only so long as the licensee does not violate the conditions attached to the license (see Legal Cases 45 and 46). The owner has no legal protection in such cases, however, and must rely on good relations with the licensee, which in turn depend largely on the judicious selection of trustworthy licensees. Disputes over leases of lawfully possessed real property may of course be adjudicated in Canadian courts, though I know of no such occurrences within this band.

Trespass

Trespass is legally regulated only at the Band Council level and as a legal offense applies only to non-band members. Non-band members may be present on the reserve only at the chief's sufferance, which he may withdraw, wholly or partially, at any time (see Legal Cases 74, 75, and 79). By customary rule, real property owners can remove anyone on or in their real property without their permission (see Chapter 1, Eskasoni Real Property Behavioral Rule 2, and Dispute Cases 60, 61, 62, 63, and 64).

Comparison of the Regulation of Eskasoni Real Property Use

At this point it would be well to provide a summary comparison of the modern Eskasoni Band Council real property legal system with those of its predecessors, the legal systems of the Grand Council and the Indian Agent. There is of course no comparison to be made with the legal system of the Grand Council: the Grand Council did not regulate real property matters, although there has been continuity between the customary real property behavioral ideals of the past and the laws of the Eskasoni Band Council legal system. (When the Band Council does agree to hear a case, it decides in favor of the ownership rights of the primary resident [see Legal Cases 66, 67, 68, 69, 71, and 94 and Band Council Legal Principle 8], thus rendering decisions that agree with traditional principles of justice.)

Comparison with the Indian Agent Legal System

The Band Council land tenure system may be contrasted with that of the Indian Agent. The first difference between the two systems is that the Band Council, unlike the Indian Agent, does not force residents to accept the construction of new houses, along with their unwelcome owners, in their Family Home Territories (see Legal Case 30), although the Band Council attempted unsuccessfully to do just this in 1987 (see Legal Cases 96, 97, and 98). The Band Council leaves the question of house siting up to the recipients of the new houses (however, this was limited for some beginning in 1998, with the new rule that first-time house owners must have their houses built in a subdivision). The house recipient, under Band Council law, is responsible for acquiring ownership of his or her own site for a house. Under the Indian Agent's system, the Indian Agent could and did change possessory interests so as to site houses as he pleased, often over the objections of the occupants and their neighbors (see Legal Cases 25 and 30).

Second, the Band Council regards the primary resident or first user of a piece of real property as the owner, rather than the Crown. The owner may alienate the house, or destroy it by fire or by razing (see Legal Case 80 and Political Case 6), and may also enjoy freedom from expropriation of a dwelling and eviction by legal authorities, unless there is a failure to perform a contract of sale involving delivery of possession. None of these rights were available under the Indian Agent (see Legal Cases 29 and 38).

Third, the Band Council, to secure political support, engages in contractual relationships with band members involving realty. These include the exchange of housing for votes, the purchase of band members' housing, and political privilege, also in return for votes (see Legal Cases 61, 63, 80, 105, and 107). The Indian Agent was not elected by Micmac voters and so had no need to please individuals by engaging in these practices.

Fourth, Indian Affairs and the Indian Agent pursued a policy of giving fair compensation for expropriated real property interests (see Legal Cases 31, 32, 33, 34, and 35), a policy that the Band Council has not continued (see Legal Cases 96, 102, and 103), with the exception of the one case in which someone insisted on exercising rights conferred by lawful possession (see Legal Case 81).

Fifth, both systems recognize a politically privileged class. In the Indian Agent's system, the *'Saqmaw* of the Grand Council received a prize farm. Under the Band Council, several politically privileged people were able to acquire ownership of houses in which others reside.

CHAPTER SIXTEEN

Change in Eskasoni Band Council Real Property Law

This chapter takes up those features of the Band Council real property law that changed from approximately 1980 through 2009 and the reasons why. Many of the changes to date involve the concept of property ownership. Other than the cessation in the creation of new lawful possessory interests, the most important of these changes resulted indirectly from settlement. Settlement first destroyed the prime means of Micmac social control, mobility. With the members of the band now more numerous and living in valuable permanent housing in a relatively confined area, people can no longer easily move to arrest disputes and now rely on three other traditional methods of social control: ostracism, social withdrawal, and revenge. In addition, they have relied greatly on a system of defense against individual disputants, a recent invention. This system of territories functions to maintain a physical and social distance between actual and potential disputants. With the exceptions of Legal Changes 5, 9, and 10 (see below), all the changes in the land tenure have come about to protect that system of territories, and thereby achieve more effective social control, as well as to secure the other three forms of extralegal social control. As will be seen, all four forms of social control are interrelated and function in a coherent and predictable way under any particular set of circumstances.

Before addressing the real property law changes themselves, however, I describe the increasing importance of the Family Home Territory, which plays a great role in most changes in the land tenure system.

A Social Change in the Importance of the Family Home Territory

The reserve's population continues to climb rapidly, at an annual rate of 3.09% during the period from 1949 to 2000. This has caused a proportionate decrease in land readily available for housing. Crowding, combined with settlement, has made the Family Home Territory more important. These territories have grown to accommodate the lineages' new generations, to provide for future generations, and to maintain space between lineage members in adjoining territories. As Family Home Territories have grown in size and in number, the amount of space available for new house construction has fallen, to the point that people all over the reserve now experience difficulty in finding space for new houses, especially in *'Qamsipu:k*. Compounding the problem is that some young adults wish to live away from their own lineage's Family Home Territory to escape parental and lineal authority, meaning that they want to live on free land outside of any Family Home Territory. At the same time, most prefer to live in their natal reserve sections to avoid being outsiders in other sections.

As we have already seen, people have long attempted to keep outsiders out of their Family Home Territories by opposing their entry. See, for example, Legal Case 66 and Dispute Cases 22 through 28, as well as the following case.

DISPUTE CASE 70

First party: PO.
Second party: GYU.
Date: 1987.

Facts: PO had heard rumors that GYU was planning to build a house next door to him on some uncleared land. PO did not want this neighbor so close to him and so cleared the land and built a large circular driveway there to establish a claim of ownership to it, thereby protecting it from being used by GYU as a house lot. However, this action could reduce the likelihood that GYU would build a house on the cleared land, but not prevent it.

Outcome: GYU never proceeded with his plans to locate his house on the disputed land.

People have also tried ingenious methods to prevent the Band Council from locating other families or nuisances near them, as in the following case.

LEGAL CASE 90

Party: XO.
Authority: The Band Council.
Date: 1987.

Facts: The Band Council had just awarded XO a new house, which XO wished to have built on some land in crowded *'Qamsipu:k*. The house was to be located immediately adjoining a spot that the Band Council had chosen for a road to a new subdivision, which the Band Council intended to build in *'Qamsipu:k* (see Legal Case 94). XO did not want to endure the nuisance that this road would soon pose and so, during the night before the basement to his house was to be excavated, he moved the stakes directing the construction crew to a location that would block the planned road. By the time the Band Council realized what had happened, the foundation had been poured directly in the path of the planned road.

Outcome: Because the house construction had already begun, the Band Council gave up the idea of locating a road there and looked for another location.

In 1997 in a similar case, a man built his new house directly in the path of a road intended to link up and extend two existing subdivisions. In this he was aided by a band councillor, who told the man of the Band Council's plans.

The increased encroachment has led people to rely on all available means to protect the Family Home Territories, including reliance on lawful possession. Although the Band Council ceased awarding new lawful possessory interests in 1986, since then the Certificate of Possession has achieved legal importance. By the middle to late 1990s, the Band Council had become much less apt to ignore individuals who persisted in pressing claims for rights in land on the basis of their Certificates of Possession. One reason, certainly, is the political turmoil created by some cases (such as Legal Cases 84 and 96 and Legal–Political Cases 1 and 2). During the course of these cases every adult member of the band heard details of just how much weight a Certificate of Possession carries under federal law. And at the same time the reserve's increasing population resulted in a greater need for private parties to defend their property interests against both the Band Council (as a result of Legal Change 3; see below) and other band members, as in the following case.

LEGAL CASE 91

Party: GB, a recently widowed woman in her sixties.
Authority: The Band Council.
Date: Early 1990s.

Facts: GB's recently deceased husband had been during his life exceptionally politically powerful, perhaps as a result of his great strength of character. GB's husband had owned a large lot for which he had a Certificate of Possession, and on which he and most of his many offspring and their children had built houses. He defended his family's political, financial, and property interests fiercely. After he died, the Certificate of Possession for the lot went to his widow. It was shortly afterward, also, that the Band Council told her that it wanted to build a road through her property to a subdivision that the Band Council had plans to construct.

Outcome: GB told the Band Council that she had lawful possession of her lot and that she would fight in front of federal authorities the Band Council or any other party who sought to encroach on her lot. The Band Council withdrew its request as a result.

The 1990s saw other individuals become more cognizant of lawful possession as a special kind of property interest. As mentioned previously (see Chapter 14), in 1996 a woman planning to move a mobile home to just inside the very edge of her parents' lot inquired of both her band councillor and the band's housing manager and construction supervisor about the location of the boundary to the lot, because she had heard that the adjacent lot was lawfully possessed. She explicitly wished to avoid the kind of dispute seen in Legal–Political Case 1.

In short, because of political pressure from Indian Affairs and from individual band members knowledgeable about federal law (who are demanding more rights with respect to land), the Band Council finds itself forced to make decisions concerning real property on the basis of lawful possession in cases in which people with lawful possession insist on relying on their rights.

While it may seem that the Certificate of Possession has determinative weight here, as GB and her deceased husband had always hoped and relied on, nothing could be further from the truth. What does matter is that the landowner belongs to a solidary lineage, as seen in the following case.

DISPUTE CASE 71

Party: AS.
Authority: The Band Council.
Date: Early 1990s.

Facts: AS is the patriarch of one of the largest, most politically united, and powerful lineages on the reserve and also owns one of the largest, flattest, and most centrally located parcels on the reserve. The Band Council wanted to use this land for a large building development, but knew that they could not simply take it from AS, even though the land is not lawfully possessed. The size, unity, and power of the lineage make it a political obstacle impossible to overcome. So the Band Council asked AS for the land it wanted.

Outcome: AS considered his lineage and its future needs and refused the request. The Band Council shelved plans to develop the parcel for housing.

Comment: This case is a concrete example of the power available to the large solidary lineages and not available to smaller and/or less solidary lineages and families (in contrast, see Legal Cases 88, 100, 101, and 102).

DISPUTE CASE 72

Party: PB.
Authority: The Band Council.
Date: Late-1990s.

Facts: PB owned an old 1940s-style Centralization house and acquired a new one around 1990. He had his new house built directly in front of his old house and for a while used the old house for storage. The Band Council felt that the old house was an eyesore and a danger, and so wanted to tear it down. The Band Council asked PB for permission to tear the house down.

Outcome: PB wanted the house out of the way as well and so granted permission. As PB's wife said, "they have to ask permission if they want to tear down your house."

By far the most common means of creating living space for new families is not to rely on lawful possession, but rather to enlarge the Family Home Territory by building on free land, usually behind existing buildings. Some have enlarged or solidified their Family Home Territory by driving non-kin living on or adjacent to the Family Home Territory off their land, as in the following cases.

DISPUTE CASE 73

First party: BQ.
Second party: TW.
Date: 1990s.

Facts: TW lived in a house near BQ's house. BQ, a person who often gets his way, told TW that if he sold the house that he lived in, that the house would have to be moved, implying that the land where the house was would thereby belong to BQ and the Q lineage's Family Home Territory.

Outcome: TW complied. When he sold the house he had the purchaser move the house.

Comment: Other people in the band generally consider this sort of behavior reprehensible, even though they understand and sympathize with BQ's rationale.

DISPUTE CASE 74

First party: The L lineal descent group.
Second party: FG and her children.
Date: 1980s to 1997.

Facts: When the 74 Street housing development was built in the 1960s, it became home to people from a great many descent groups, because for a time all new houses were built there (by Indian Affairs order) and all those who received new houses during its construction were forced to live there. This resulted in a certain amount of social friction. The L descent group has been attempting to get substantial control of the subdivision, thereby making it not so much their Family Home Territory as simply a haven where they can live among neighbors with whom they feel comfortable. They have been using a variety of means to remove individuals and members of descent groups with whom they do not get along. FG and her family is one such group. FG's parents had been given a house on 74 Street in the 1960s, but left when they received another new house in the 1980s, which they had built in a more desirable location. They gave their daughter, FG, and her children their old 74 Street house. The L descent group did not like FG and her children living on 74 Street and began a campaign of harassment toward them, including verbal harassment of the children and even damaging the siding of the house with rocks and air guns. FG sought for more than a decade to trade houses with anyone who could provide her a living space outside of 74 Street, but the L group's fierce reputation meant that nobody chose to take advantage of FG's offer.

Outcome: Finally, in 1997, someone traded an old mobile home for FG's frame house.

Comment: Other members of the band rank the L descent group the lowest among all descent groups in the community, in part because of behavior such as this, which strongly contravenes Micmac ethical standards, especially because FG and her family are so innocuous. However, all understand the L group's goal and several people on the reserve have also used airguns as harassment tools. The family that acquired FG's house has good relations with the L descent group.

In the following case, a man enlarged his Family Home Territory by causing his neighbor to move.

DISPUTE CASE 75

First party: The S descent group.
Second party: OI.
Third party: DS, a member of the S descent group.
Date: 1970s to 1996.

Facts: The S descent group shares its Family Home Territory with two other lineages in a larger phratry. All three lineages individually hold prestige and collectively wield enormous political power. In the 1970s, OI had his house built on the western portion of the Family Home Territory, even though the S descent group considered that land a natural extension of its own Family Home Territory and asked OI not to build his house on it. During the 1980s, OI leased the house to a tenant whose behavior was deemed inappropriate by members of the S lineage. The S lineage members made the tenant feel unwelcome by shouting at her whenever they saw her. It was during that period that the house caught fire and sustained major damage. This damage has never been repaired, nor the house reinhabited, but OI maintained his claim to ownership of the house and the disputed land for some years. In 1996, a member of the S descent group, DS, who had been living elsewhere on the reserve received a new house and had it built almost directly behind OI's house, but with a separate driveway to the side. OI complained that DS had built his house on his property. The members of the S group have made it clear to OI that his presence is not welcome on the S Family Home Territory.

Outcome: The Band Council eventually tore down the uninhabited house. Members of the S descent group regard the dispute as concluded, and OI seems to have no further intention of maintaining possession of either the house or land.

Comment: As one member of the S descent group said to me after this, "we just got control of our territory."

The interesting aspect of Dispute Cases 73, 74, and 75 is that the goal of the territorial behavior is simply to have neighbors with whom the inhabitants could feel comfortable. As seen in Dispute Cases 22 through 28, and Legal Cases 95, 96, and 97, many people are now willing to fight harder to get access to land and to keep others out. The traditional Micmac ideal has always been for the individual or group to strive for self-sufficiency, to accept or take as little from one's neighbor as possible, and to generously give to others one's personal and real property as needed. In the past, however, there was sufficient land for anyone to give some away and still keep a distance from one's neighbors.

Ten Changes in Real Property Law

The efforts to protect the system of social control through territorial defense described above caused or otherwise influenced some of the changes in real property law I discuss below. These changes occurred entirely because of the desire of families to keep troublesome or potentially troublesome individuals away. The most important way that the Micmac of Eskasoni have attempted in recent years to accomplish this has been to control the ownership and possession of real property. All the following legal changes occurred under a single legal authority, the incumbent chief of the reserve and the rest of his Band Council, and result from settlement, crowding, the growing importance of territorial control, and fiscal issues.

Legal Change 1: Ownership Rights to Old Houses

I consider this early modification to the basic law a change because its genesis can be readily identified as an idea introduced by Indian Affairs.

In the 1970s, Indian Affairs attempted to end a then growing practice in which some recipients of new housing gave their old housing to single people, usually young adult kin. Indian Affairs believed, because nearly all reserves had nuclear families who were without housing of their own, that the Band Council should be able to give the replaced housing to the families with the greatest need. To return ownership of the replaced houses to the Band Councils, Indian Affairs directed Band Councils to have families scheduled to receive new houses sign quitclaims to their replaced houses before taking possession of the new houses. In other words, band members were offered a contract: in return for new houses, they had to give up ownership of their old ones.

Though Indian Affairs could not coerce the bands into implementing the new policy, many, if not most or all, Micmac bands and Band Councils initially accepted the idea of the new regulations. Band members liked the idea in the abstract because it made more housing available. The Band Councils liked it because it gave their members a chance to give two houses to political supporters for each new house built. Thus, as a matter of course, people signed quitclaim deeds to their old houses before occupying their new houses. In the following case, however, this did not happen.

LEGAL CASE 92

Defendant: KC.
Authority: The Band Council.
Date: About 1980.

Facts: KC requested and received a new house, but when the house was awarded, nobody at the band office remembered to have her sign a quitclaim to the old house. KC moved into the new house and wanted her brother, a single man without a house of his own, to move into the old house.

Outcome: The Band Council told her that she could not do that and ordered her to return the old house to the band. The Band Council later assigned it to another family.

Of course, general legal policies are always subject to modification by individual contractual arrangements as in the following case.

LEGAL CASE 93

Defendant: QF.
Authority: The Band Council.
Date: 1980.

Facts: In 1969, the father of QF and his brothers, a widower, died and, according to Micmac tradition, left his house to his oldest child, QF. In 1980 the house was destroyed by fire. The Band Council approved the building of a new house for QF and his brothers. The band manager, according to the Band Council rule, asked QF to sign a quitclaim to the old house and to the land. QF refused, saying that the Band Council had given them the house with no strings attached. One of the band councillors who had been there at the time supported QF.

Outcome: The band manager ripped up the quitclaim form.

We may abstract the following legal principle from these cases:

BAND COUNCIL LEGAL PRINCIPLE 14

A person who receives a new house supplied by the Band Council must return ownership of the old house to the Band Council, subject to individual contractual conditions.

Although the new law was popular in the abstract, the actual implementation frequently caused problems. This is because existing housing is not a homogeneous commodity, but rather a valuable item often located in well-defended Family Home Territories.

When the Band Council awards a new house to a family, the recipient can have the house built more or less anywhere. Usually the owner builds the new house on the same lot or adjacent to it, to stay in the Family Home Territory and remain close to patrikin. A secondary reason is the scarcity of free land.

The head of the household controls his social environment, his Family Home Territory, by preventing occupancy by undesirable non-kin in the house in which he formerly resided in one of two ways: either by giving ownership of the house to a desirable person, usually a member of one's own nuclear family, or by destroying the house. When another member of the family acquires the property, it is generally an offspring who is raising his or her own family. If the house is destroyed, it is usually because the house is too old or decrepit to warrant repair. In some cases, however, the razed houses would have been easily repairable or were adequate as they stood.

Not only do families with new houses want to retain control over their old houses, but these older houses, frequently in a Family Home Territory, are unattractive to members of other lineages, even those with a strong need for housing. People rarely want to risk living in an unpleasant social environment by occupying such a house. The Band Council literally could not give some of these older houses away. In the following case, a family desperately needing housing accepted an older house from the Band Council, even though it was in another lineage's Family Home Territory.

LEGAL CASE 94

First party: SK.
Second party: BN.
Authority: The Band Council.
Date: 1986.

Facts: SK received a new house, which he had built adjacent to his old house. He had intended to keep the old house for the future use of some of his offspring, but a ward councillor gave it to BN's family instead. SK asked the Band Council to evict BN and to return to him possession and ownership of his old house.

Outcome: The Band Council declined to alter the situation as it stood, and BN retained ownership by virtue of residency.

Comment: Some months later, SK and his family managed, through frequent, loud verbal harassment, to drive BN from the house and to retake occupancy and ownership. Interestingly, the Band Council apparently did nothing to uphold BN's rights of residence and ownership against SK. SK was popularly considered just in his actions.

The following case revolves around some of the same issues, but involves a mobile home.

LEGAL CASE 95

First party: Several Eskasoni families.
Second party: LE.
Authority: The Band Council.
Date: 1985.

Facts: LE lived for many years with his wife and children in a mobile home given to him by the Band Council, one of the very few on the reserve at the time. When he received a new house, which he had built adjacent to the mobile home, several families who wanted housing for themselves approached members of the Band Council asking for possession of the mobile home. In contrast to most older housing, which remains in the possession of the original owners because it cannot be economically removed, a mobile home can be easily moved. LE wished to retain ownership of the mobile home so that he could either sell it or later give it to one of his children. The Band Council wanted to take the house to give it to another family who needed it immediately. LE argued that other people had been allowed to keep their houses when awarded a new one.

Outcome: When it seemed that the Band Council was about to take his mobile home, LE had a friend of his take up residence in it, with the understanding that the friend would return ownership to LE when he wished to leave. This prevented the Band Council from awarding it to another family, because the Band Council does not expropriate housing that is owned by reason of residence (see Band Council Legal Principle 2).

Comment: Mobile homes were rare on the reserve in 1985. They have since become more numerous, particularly as a means to provide inexpensive and quickly available rental housing.

The Band Council reacted to this defense of Family Home Territory boundaries by eventually ceasing to ask for quitclaims in return for new housing in instances in which the replaced house sits in a Family Home Territory.

By the time that the Band Council heard these cases, it had already allowed many families to retain ownership of replaced housing because of the problem posed by Family Home Territories. In these other instances, political favoritism or the mediocre condition of the older houses could also have been factors in the decision by council members to allow new house recipients to retain ownership of replaced housing.

Only two years after Legal Case 92 another similar set of circumstances occurred. A woman and her family had been living in an old 1940s (Centralization-era) structure. She married for a second time, and later her family was awarded a new house. She gave the old house, in her Family Home Territory, through a quitclaim deed to her brother, also a single man. The Band Council tacitly approved this by supplying the quitclaim deed form used in the transfer.

In any event, as LE (see Legal Case 95) noted in his defense, the Band Council had by 1985 allowed several people to retain ownership of their old houses on receiving new ones. And, since the Micmac theory of justice rests on the legalistic premise that all individuals must be treated uniformly under the law, the Band Council had difficulty justifying its decisions to retake ownership of any older houses. The Band Council, elected democratically, derives its legal authority from a popular mandate. The growing popular dissatisfaction with the unequal treatment by the Band Council resulted in the chief's decision in 1987 to cease to require that new house recipients sign quitclaim deeds to their replaced houses. This resulted in the extinguishment of Band Council Legal Principle 14.

Legal Change 2: Weakening of the Rule against House Razing

In another effort to increase the amount of housing available, the Band Council forbade the destruction of housing, except in cases in which a house could not be made fit for human habitation. The rule on the destruction of houses is as follows:

BAND COUNCIL REAL PROPERTY RULE 4

A house may not be destroyed or dismantled except when decrepit and then only under the special permission of the Band Council.

The role of political interest in the weakening of this rule can be seen in the following dispute.

> POLITICAL CASE 6
>
> *First party:* NA.
> *Second party:* BC, a councillor.
> *Date:* 1987.
>
> *Facts:* NA, a young man with very few kin on the reserve, wanted to move away to the nearby largely uninhabited reserve of Malagawatch. He had no money to buy lumber to build a small house there and so decided to take lumber from his house on the reserve, an older building where he had lived alone for some time. BC, a councillor of the ward, arrived and told NA to cease the destruction of the house so that it could be used to house a needy family. Shortly after this exchange began, a benefactor of NA arrived who, because of his large family and aggressive style of negotiating with members of the Band Council, was powerful in ward politics. He defended NA's actions on the grounds that other people had not been prevented from taking their houses apart for their lumber.
>
> *Outcome:* The councillor relented, and NA continued to dismantle the house until he had the lumber he needed.

In the same year a politically powerful individual razed his band-built house, which was in excellent condition, to provide space for a larger house in the same place. Many people on the reserve became angry with him and with the Band Council for allowing the destruction of valuable housing.

Therefore, the second legal change in the Eskasoni land tenure system weakened the rule against the destruction of sound houses; some people, at least, are now able to dismantle their old houses and keep the lumber.

I do not know whether the inability to enforce the rule against the destruction of usable housing is what eventually caused the rule to be entirely extinguished. Destruction of housing in good condition remains uncommon because of its scarcity and the widespread belief that housing destruction is improper and wasteful. Nevertheless, most Micmac also believe strongly that, as a basic right of ownership, individual owners should have complete control over the ultimate disposition of any of their property, including housing.

Legal Change 3: Band Council Rights to Expropriate Land in Family Home Territories

Until 1987, the Band Council expropriated neither occupied nor unbuilt land that private individuals claimed as part of their own Family Home Territories. There is still enough land in many parts of the reserve for the Band Council to use without having to resort to incurring the disfavor of potential political supporters; federal expropriations are quite another matter, as discussed elsewhere. This rule may be expressed as follows:

BAND COUNCIL REAL PROPERTY RULE 5

The Band Council will not expropriate real property owned by band members.

This is the legal case that extinguished this rule.

LEGAL CASE 96

Defendants: The Q lineage.
Authority: The Band Council.
Date: 1987.

Facts: The Q lineage denied others the opportunity to build houses in a large territory in *'Qamsipu:k* to which it had put forth a claim of ownership, based on proximity and long historical claim of ownership. But *'Qamsipu:k* is very crowded by Micmac standards and many people could find no place there to build a house (see Figure 4). Quite a few young families there wanted to live outside of their Family Home Territories to escape lineal authority, but remain within their own reserve sections. Several people asked the chief and councillors to find them places for their houses in the reserve section of *'Qamsipu:k*. The chief realized that the only place where a new subdivision could be built was a large uninhabited piece of land that the Q lineage had claimed as its own, preventing others from settling there. None of the land involved was lawfully possessed, nor was it occupied. Previously, when the Band Council and Indian Affairs decided to build a new subdivision, it had always been outside of *'Qamsipu:k*, in places where the land was either free or that the owners had freely given or sold to the band for building houses. The exception to this is the 74 Street subdivision in *Apamuek* (see Figure 4), which was built before the decision in *Mathias v. Findlay* ([1978] 4 W.W.R. 653, 87 D.L.R. (3d) 239), under the control of Indian Affairs, without Band Council support, and against the wishes of Eskasoni band members (see Legal Case 30). But in *'Qamsipu:k* the only large parcel of unbuilt land available belongs to the

Q lineage, and they do not wish to part with it. The Q lineage denied the Band Council permission to use that land.

Outcome: After a deliberation of many months, the chief decided to place a new subdivision in an unbuilt portion of the disputed area.

Comment: This decision brought a great change to the law on the reserve. While band members had long taken private interests in land from their neighbors, the Band Council had never previously expropriated interests in real property from individuals.

From this decision we can abstract a new legal principle that effectively extinguishes Band Council Real Property Rule 5:

BAND COUNCIL LEGAL PRINCIPLE 15

Any unbuilt reserve land owned by individual private band members may be expropriated by the Band Council for the construction of development projects ordered by the Band Council.

Legal Change 4: The Right of the Band Council to Expropriate Land

Within days of the decision rendered in Legal Case 96, an event occurred that caused the Band Council to amend its new legal principle.

LEGAL CASE 97

Party: BQ, a member of the Q lineage.
Authority: The Band Council.
Date: 1987.

Facts: After the Band Council decided to expropriate the piece of land that the Q lineage claimed as its own and refused to relinquish, heavy machinery moved in to begin preparing the land for the construction of the new subdivision. At this point, BQ became angry and threatened the operators of the machinery with violence should they proceed.

Outcome: The Band Council dropped its plans to build a subdivision on land that the Q lineage claimed as its own.

Comment: Although this dispute took place in 1987, as of 1999 the parties still considered the case technically open, according to a news report (CBC News 1999). In proposing violence, BQ exceeded community standards of acceptable behavior by a wide margin. However, others, seeing that this tactic succeeded, have copied it. This case initiated a new type of defense of Family Home Territories across the reserve, as seen in the next cases.

By 2006 the subdivision had been built and occupied, but its only inhabitants are members of the Q lineage.

LEGAL CASE 98

Party: RF.
Authority: The Band Council.
Date: Early 1990s.

Facts: RF and his girlfriend lived in a new house in one of the new *Apamuek* subdivisions. When the Band Council decided to enlarge the subdivision by constructing new housing and a road behind RF's girlfriend's house, RF became upset at losing his large backyard. When the heavy machinery moved in, RF threatened the operators with violence.

Outcome: The Band Council dropped its plans to construct the housing and the road.

Comment: In this case as well, RF earned himself a lowered popular reputation through his actions, which exceeded standards of acceptability. RF subsequently broke up with his girlfriend and left the area. The Band Council went on to continue building housing in the region, but one block away from the house owned by RF's ex-girlfriend.

LEGAL CASE 99

First party: QF (RF's brother).
Second party: TF, a third brother.
Authority: The Band Council.
Date: 2000.

Facts: TF, brother to QF, approached the Band Council to supply extensive repairs to his house. The Band Council, eyeing some land behind TF's house for housing construction, offered to pay for the repairs to TF's house in return for the land. TF agreed. QF believed that the rest of his family had undivided ownership interests in the land, which TF could not alienate by himself. QF informed the Band Council that he had not alienated his interest in the land and told it to cease its efforts to prepare the land for building construction. QF threatened to publicly disclose information about Band Council members that would prove embarrassing to them if the plans continued.

Outcome: The Band Council discontinued plans to use the area.

Interestingly, QF in this case used the indivisibility of Family Home Territory land as the basis for his argument. Previously (see Legal Case 55) he had argued that the land he himself possessed belonged to him, and that therefore the family land he and his siblings inherited is divisible. Plainly, the issue of the divisibility of inherited Family Home Territory land has yet to be established both by custom and under the law.

Legal Cases 97, 98, and 99 show individuals within the lineage emerging as leaders to defend individual and group interests in land. This process preserves first of all the individual's own interests, but also those of the extended family or lineage.

This case is also notable because the Band Council rather cleverly offered a deal to TF in return for the repairs. It supplied the repairs, which it has an obligation to eventually provide in any case, in return for TF giving up whatever interest he has in the land. The Band Council thereby reduced, but obviously did not eliminate, political opposition from the F patrilineage.

Not all expropriations meet with an effective defense of ownership interests.

LEGAL CASE 100

Party: XB.
Authority: The Band Council.
Date: Early 1990s.

Facts: XB, a member of a tiny and dispersed lineage, built his house in a secluded area away from his own kin and was unhappy when the Band Council later took the land around him to build a housing subdivision that almost entirely surrounds him.

Outcome: XB's complaints fell on deaf ears and the subdivision was built.

Comment: Band Council members said that XB knew when he built his house that the Band Council wanted the use of adjoining lands.

LEGAL CASE 101

Party: Several members of dispersed patrilineages.
Authority: The Band Council.
Date: Late 1980s to early 1990s.

Facts: The Band Council decided to build its new, large band office complex in an unbuilt part of Castle Bay. However, members of several nearby patrilineages claimed ownership of pieces of the parcel that the Band Council intended to use. Several patrilineages protested that they owned the land where the new band office was to be built.

Outcome: The Band Council ignored these protests and built the band office on the disputed land, giving the patrilineages' claims no weight.

Band Council expropriations differ from those of Indian Affairs in that the Band Council does not compensate those whose interests it expropriates. The following case is an example of this.

LEGAL CASE 102

Party: UB.
Party: WU.
Authority: The Band Council.
Date: About 1990 to late 1990s.

Facts: UB had been living in a house belonging to his father across the road from that of his parents when his father sold the house UB was living in to another party. To compensate UB for his loss, his father gave him a parcel of land behind his house. UB began clearing the land for a house of his own. As he cleared the land slowly over months, WU, who owned a construction company and contracted with the Band Council, approached UB and asked for some of the land to build houses. UB, believing that the Band Council would compensate him for the land (as Indian Affairs had once done), agreed. UB's lineage is tiny and dispersed. WU built several houses on the property. After a while, UB asked the Band Council for payment for the land it used for the housing.

Outcome: The Band Council considered that the houses belong to the people living in them, and therefore refused to stand as a party to the case. It also therefore declined to pay UB any money or other form of compensation.

Comment: One who knew the parties involved and the case remarked that UB "only did that for the money."

The Band Council defends its policy of not paying compensation for land it expropriates by stating that it does not recognize private claims of ownership to unoccupied land. However, before Legal Case 96 in 1987, the Band Council did recognize such rights of ownership in that it never expropriated such lands. The new policy clearly reflects the political necessity of the Band Council's having to provide housing for people in their natal reserve sections, as well as a budget barely adequate (and many say inadequate) to provide for the needs of the growing population.

From Legal Cases 96 through 102 we may abstract the following legal principle, which amends Band Council Legal Principle 15:

BAND COUNCIL LEGAL PRINCIPLE 16
The Band Council may expropriate any unbuilt reserve land for construction projects ordered by the Band Council, except in those cases in which owners present powerful political opposition to expropriation.

Legal Change 5: The Right of Band Members to Reside Where They Wish

In 1998, the Band Council, in an attempt to make housing more available for young families, embarked on a radical new change in the band's real property law by requiring all people acquiring new houses for the first time to live in one of the new subdivisions in *Apamuek* and Castle Bay (Figure 7). We may express this rule as:

BAND COUNCIL REAL PROPERTY RULE 6
All individuals receiving a new house in their own name from the Band Council for the first time must have their houses built in one of the new subdivisions (no disputes recorded).

Building on free land often causes economic problems for the band. First, the process expands existing and creates new Family Home Territories, reducing the amount of free land available to others. People in the band have complained about the shortage of available land for building houses since the early 1990s, and in *'Qumsipu:k* at least since the 1980s. Second, when people decide to build in an area without electrical, water, and sewer services, it costs the Band Council more to bring those services in than if electrical, water, and sewer lines already exist (in some cases, the Band Council forces those who want to live in distant, unserviced places to pay the cost of new electrical lines, but in many others, for political reasons, the Band Council underwrites the expense). Wells and septic tanks also ultimately result in higher costs. This has meant that fewer houses in total can be built. In most cases, those who choose isolated locations are young people building their houses away from their own Family Home Territories to escape the lineage legal authority. As a way of accommodating this desire to live away from the Family Home Territory, the Band Council has turned to building subdivisions.

Indian Affairs has in recent years rewarded those Band Councils that efficiently use their housing money with yet more money, hence the Band Council's new rule. The new housing policy also dictates that much of the new housing consist of duplexes. This means that this housing cannot come wholly under the

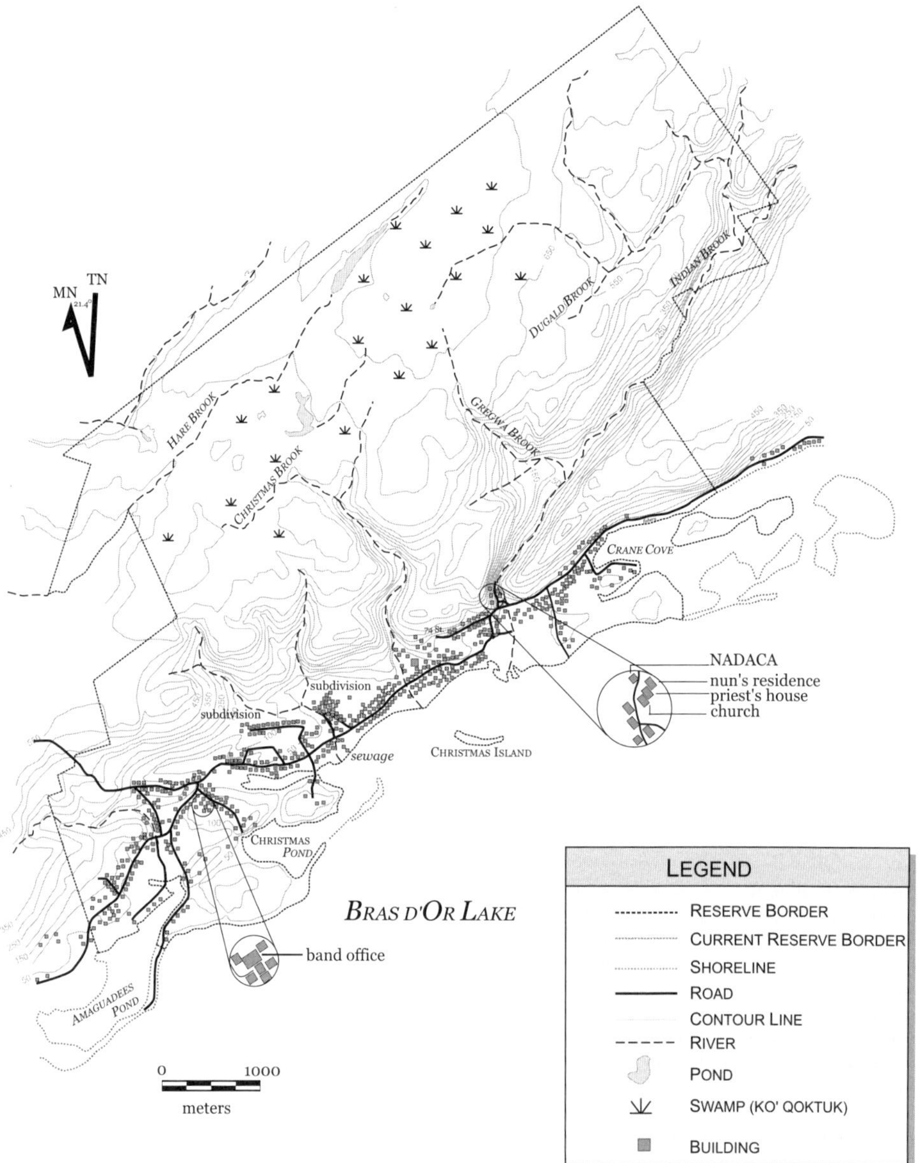

FIGURE 7. Map E: Settlement map of Eskasoni in 1998.

control any one primary resident, and thus the Band Council has a good chance of retaining control of most of it.

This new rule effectively limits the traditional and undisputed customary right of those who already have housing to freely site houses (for which there were no dispute cases). In other words, the cherished traditional right to live anywhere on the reserve no longer exists for some first-time house owners.

By allowing people who have already owned housing to locate new housing where they wish, the Band Council only in usual circumstances must bear the cost of constructing housing in remote locations. Settled families do not usually want to move from their own Family Home Territories, and those building or maintaining large solidary lineages would of course not consider leaving their own Family Home Territories, which are already serviced. It is the young who normally want to strike out on their own, who wish to leave the strictures of lineal and family authority, and who tend to go looking for free land on which to build.

Legal Change 6: Rights to Old Housing

Settlement and permanent housing has created another problem that Micmac ancestors did not have: what to do with nuisance buildings. The Band Council assumes responsibility for the safety of the members of the band, and sometimes this responsibility extends to real property matters that involve questions of safe housing. The Band Council repairs older houses and, in cases in which houses are beyond repair, it ensures that the houses are razed so that they cannot pose a hazard to the band's population, as seen in the following case.

LEGAL CASE 103

Defendant: FW, a man in his thirties.
Authority: The Band Council.
Date: About 1990.

Facts: FW inherited a house on lawfully possessed property in the mid-1980s. He lived there for a few years before moving back to live with his parents, leaving the house unoccupied. Area teenagers began to use the house as a hangout and set it afire several times. Each time the reserve's fire department extinguished the fires. The Band Council notified FW that the house was a safety and fire hazard that FW should remedy. FW ignored the notice.

Outcome: The Band Council had the house torn down.

Comment: This case shows that concerns of both the band and the Band Council can override even lawful possessory interests.

LEGAL CASE 104

Party: Owner of a trailer.
Authority: The Band Council.
Date: 1998.

Facts: By 1998, the Eskasoni powwow had become a focal point of community pride. A dilapidated trailer near the powwow grounds was considered, because of its placement, to detract from the annual celebration.

Outcome: The Band Council ruled the trailer an eyesore and removed it.

Comment: This case was unusual only because of the proximity of the trailer to the powwow grounds. There are many other unattractive buildings in the community.

From these cases we may abstract the following legal principle:

BAND COUNCIL LEGAL PRINCIPLE 17

The rights of ownership of structures is subject to public safety and community appearance concerns, and the Band Council may order the razing or removal of housing that it deems poses a hazard to public safety or is an eyesore.

Legal Change 7: Right to Own Property Where Others Reside

In the 1980s, nearly everybody on the reserve believed that the only the primary resident could own a house; people took the Band Council at its word that only the Band Council could lease only lawfully possessed housing. However, a few politically privileged people were allowed to own housing where others lived, so long as they remained politically privileged. The entire point of this new form of ownership was to be able to rent those houses, and later apartments, to the Band Council. The political status that allowed individuals to own property in which others resided was very secret. Someone could be living next to a rented house and not know that it was owned by someone other than the person living there. In some cases, even those living in houses owned by others did not know that the houses were owned by somebody else.

Of course, this did not remain secret for very long; by the 1990s, renting to the Band Council suddenly became very popular. In one of the reserve's five wards alone there were more than 20 houses rented at band expense. One councillor bought a nearly new house, which had cost the band between $30,000 and $40,000 to construct, for a mere $500. A great many people demanded the right to be able to own property where others lived. The Band Council apparently did not oppose this widespread political demand; I was unable to find any cases in which the Band Council forbade such ownership after the 1980s.

BAND COUNCIL LEGAL PRINCIPLE 18

Band members may own housing in which others reside.

A common attitude on the reserve about the Band Council's funds is that "it's just government money," and so does not matter. Needless to say, the financial burden on the Band Council quickly grew to be quite heavy, to the point that the number of new houses that it could build was drastically reduced.

Legal Change 8: Creation of a Third Category of Political Privilege

With the law now permitting ownership of housing in which others reside, the Band Council faced a big problem: how to control, for both political and financial reasons, the number of people renting to the Band Council.

The Band Council responded by creating three classes of political privilege for the right to rent property to the Band Council. Those with no political privileges have no right to rent property to the Band Council (see Legal Case 61). Those with full political privileges have undiminished rights to rent to the Band Council, regardless of where the owner lives and regardless of who has the Certificate of

Possession to the land (see Legal Case 63). The change here involves the creation of a third class of people, those with moderate political privileges, who are liable to reductions in the rents they are paid, on a variety of grounds.

One tactic that the Band Council tries to use is to argue that, because the owner of the house has previously received so much assistance from the Band Council in the form of house repairs and household furnishings, it is only fair that the owner receive a reduced rent.

LEGAL CASE 105

Party: OS, a young man.
Authority: The Band Council.
Date: 1997.

Facts: OS inherited a house from his grandmother and, because he already had a place to live elsewhere, decided to rent the house to a relative. The Band Council initially paid the rent at the going rate of $400 per month. Later the Band Council attempted to reduce the rent to $200, on the grounds that it paid for many of the repairs, improvements, furnishings and appliances in the house. The Band Council's premise is that because his family had already benefited greatly from the Band Council over the years, it was not fair to the rest of the band that he continue to receive benefits at such a disproportionate rate. But OS's grandmother was an unusual woman. She prided herself on her independence and had accepted no assistance from the Band Council. Also, she saved everything, including all receipts for everything she ever purchased. OS showed these receipts to the Band Council as proof that the Band Council had paid for nothing in the house.

Outcome: The Band Council therefore did not lower the rent payment.

Another tactic used on some is the argument that they cannot own the property on the reserve if they are not living on the reserve themselves. This originates in the *Indian Act*, which states that those living off the reserve may not have lawful possession of property on the reserve. This rule has little meaning, because it only deals with Band Council against owner relations; when someone leaves the reserve, someone else living at the house is, by absence of the owner, the primary resident and thus owner, so far as the Band Council is concerned. In civil matters, since the Band Council rarely takes part, the rule is therefore unimportant. When property owners move away from the reserve, they have no further use for the real property on the reserve and usually alienate it by selling it or giving it away. However, with the recent possibility of renting the property to the Band Council on behalf of a tenant, there is good reason to retain ownership of property on the reserve. However, many of the people living on the reserve believe that the reserve's and band's resources should benefit only those who live on the reserve. Leaving the reserve to live elsewhere is often equated with disloyalty. Therefore, the Band Council made the following rule.

BAND COUNCIL REAL PROPERTY RULE 7
Band members living off the reserve may not own property on the reserve.

As will be seen below, this rule really only comes into play when the property is rented. It otherwise has no meaning because it applies only to Band Council and property owner relations as the Band Council does not regulate civil disputes.

LEGAL CASE 106

Party: OS, a young man.
Authority: The Band Council.
Date: 2004.

Facts: OS had inherited his grandmother's house. Not long thereafter, he left the reserve to live with and later marry a woman on another reserve. Since he had no use for the house, he rented it to the band to house a relative of his. He had been told by the Band Council that he could not live off the reserve and rent this house to the Band Council. He pretended that he still lived on the reserve by going to the band office to collect his rent check every month in person. The people at the band office knew what he was doing, however, and told him that this situation could not continue.

Outcome: OS eventually sold the house to his sister, with the Band Council paying the purchase price on her behalf. In this way, everyone benefited, not least the Band Council, which was freed of having to pay rent in perpetuity.

LEGAL CASE 107

Party: FS, a man.
Authority: The Band Council
Date: 2004.

Facts: Until a few years ago, FS had lived on the reserve all his life and owned a house there. He decided he would be happier living off the reserve in a city. When he left, he leased his house to the Band Council on behalf of a tenant. For several years, he maintained the fiction that he was still living on the reserve by occasionally picking up his rent checks in person, though he did not do this regularly. The Band Council told him that he could not continue to receive rent while living off the reserve.

Outcome: FS and the Band Council came to a mutually agreeable solution to this dispute, one suggested by the Band Council. FS agreed to a lower monthly rent payment, $300 rather than the $400 that he had been getting, in lieu of either returning to the reserve or giving up ownership of the property.

Comment: This same arrangement was also applied to another absentee landlord in a very similar set of circumstances.

Compare these cases with Legal Case 63 (see Chapter 11), in which the owner enjoyed full political privilege and therefore was not threatened with a rent reduction, although he lives off the reserve. We can conclude that these threats apply only to the moderately privileged.

Some of the moderately privileged were threatened with a simple rent reduction.

LEGAL CASE 108

Party: GR.
Authority: The Band Council.
Date: 1998.

Facts: With the monthly fees being paid out reaching new heights, in 1998 the Band Council decided that it would try to save money by simply cutting the per unit rent payment for some landlords in half, from $400 to $200. The assumption was that landlords would have little choice but to go along, because few if any could make any other use of the properties they owned, nor could they afford to give up any rental income. One large landlord, who had other considerable sources of income, balked. He said that he would rather turn out his renters and turn his largest multi-unit dwelling into a mansion for himself and his family, leaving the Band Council with the headache of housing the tenants.

Outcome: Faced with this possibility, the Band Council dropped its plan to slash rental fees.

The 1990s also saw the Band Council try to stem rental activity by using condemnation, applying it to older housing that the Band Council was replacing with new housing on behalf of the owners, as in the following case from 2005.

LEGAL CASE 109

Party: PT.
Authority: The Band Council.
Date: 2005.

Facts: PT had lived for several years in an old house with his young and growing family. He requested and was lucky enough to receive one of the few houses being built by the Band Council. Construction began in 2005 at the rear of his old house. He applied to rent the old house to the Band Council to be used to house indigent people.

Outcome: The Band Council denied the application, saying that it had condemned the old house as a precondition to receiving his new house and it was therefore ineligible for use as a rental unit.

Comment: As one man said: "There's nothing wrong with those houses. The Band Council just doesn't want to pay for them."

This set of circumstances is indicative of a pattern in this community. The Band Council makes stringent rules, knowing that many will obey them out of fear of losing rights and other benefits. On the other hand, this is a political ploy, in which some receive "exceptions" and, grateful to their benefactors in the Band Council, vote for them in the elections.

Therefore we can draw only one conclusion from these cases:

BAND COUNCIL LEGAL PRINCIPLE 19

The ability to rent real property to the Band Council depends on one's level of political privilege.

An interesting and important feature of those with moderate political privilege is that they all lack a solidary lineage with an intact and functioning Family Home Territory.

Legal Change 9: The Arrival of Communalism—Housing Expropriation and the "New Rules"

In 2004, the Band Council found itself in the undesirable position of having far too few funds to come even close to meeting the housing needs of the rapidly growing Eskasoni population.

This financial situation resulted partly from a combination of three practices which began years earlier. The first is the commitment to pay the monthly mortgage bill for all the houses built using Canadian Mortgage and Housing Corporation mortgages—essentially all single-family houses constructed since 1985. The second is the practice of paying private landlords the rental fees incurred in housing band members in privately owned houses and apartments. The Band Council has compounded this problem for years by readily agreeing to pay the rental fees for many people all over the reserve. As a political measure, this practice pleases both the tenant and the owner, as well as the councillors who approve the rent payments and garner political support as a result. The practice became so widespread that property owners came to see it almost as a right to be able to rent property, in almost any condition, to the Band Council, simply because the Band Council had made so many such contracts that to refuse a request would be seen as political bias. The third is a decades-long policy of borrowing money to build housing, a policy designed to increase support for incumbents during campaigns.

The political dynamic between the Band Council and property owners so favored property owners by the mid-1990s that even then the Band Council began to think of ways to give itself the ability to turn down requests to rent property in a way that would cause it a minimum amount of political damage.

Many of the buildings rented at band expense were initially also built at band expense and given to people to live in. The recipients of these houses in some cases sold the houses to landlords, many at the customary rate of $5,000, a fraction of the cost of building. Others found new housing, often again built at band expense, and rented their old houses out to the Band Council on behalf of tenants they found. Furthermore, the Band Council frequently also bears the cost of maintaining and repairing these rental units; this deal for the landlord is one of simple political patronage.

In 2004, feeling that the money could be better used to create new housing, several band councillors sought a way to reduce the enormous sums the band was spending on the rents. The Band Council made legislation, popularly known as "the new rules," which it distributed in leaflet form to the community the following year, 2005 (Appendix J). One important rule, applied with verbal modifications to those in the leaflet, is the following, which for the first time creates communal property in the community.

BAND COUNCIL REAL PROPERTY RULE 8

The band owns all the houses on the reserve that were built at band expense; only those who built or extend their houses at their own expense or have lawful possession have ownership of those houses.

The new policy clearly contravenes the most basic right extended by the Eskasoni Band Council for decades, the right of primary residents to ownership of the structures in which they live. One intention of the new policy was to immediately end the payment of rents for most rental properties on the reserve. As such, it brought immediate comments of dissatisfaction from people in the community, particularly those who owned rental property built at band expense.

To make the new policy abundantly clear, and to guard against dispute, the Band Council once again began to require that all people occupying a house and receiving a new one sign a quitclaim deed to the old house before taking possession of the new one. The old houses were ideally to be distributed by the welfare department, often in conjunction with the occupant's and occupant's family's wishes.

These "new rules" came about during a period in which band members generally became more and more conscious of competition for land, a realization of the growing value of real property, and unsureness over the question of proper behavior with respect to other band members over questions pertaining to real property, as seen in the following case.

LEGAL CASE 110

Party: SQ, a member of the Q lineage.
Authority: The Band Council.
Date: 2004.

Facts: As a result of an unrelated dispute with the Band Council, SQ demanded the Band Council pay the sum of $2,500 to use the powwow grounds. The Q lineage considers itself the owner of those grounds and has long occupied the surrounding area. In the past, it donated use of those powwow grounds to the band at no cost.

Outcome: The band paid the money requested.

Comment: One of the people who told me of this case used it as an example of how ridiculous he thinks the state of regulation of reserve land usage is today. He said that the members of the Q lineage "don't own that land." He also commented, indicating the mountain across the road, "as things stand now, I could claim that whole mountain." In 2006, when the Q lineage again asked for payment, the Band Council moved the powwow to another site.

The Band Council decided that it would try to control its costs and the disposition of housing not specifically by changing rental policy, but comprehensively by changing the rules pertaining to ownership. Later verbal modifications included a provision for a house owner to bequeath ownership to a family member, and a warning that because the band owns the houses, it would expropriate housing from those single people behaving disreputably (the "party house" rule; see below). As one young adult put it, "the new rules are real strict."

The new policy became a major source of dispute between the majority of councillors and the chief.

DISPUTE CASE 76

First party: The Chief.
Second party: The majority of the members of the Band Council.
Date: 2004–2006.

Facts: The chief had been at odds with the majority of the band councillors, especially since the 2004 election. One of the major points of contention was with the provision in "the new rules" that states that the band owns most houses on the reserve, which therefore cannot be rented to the band on behalf of the tenants. The band ceased to pay rent for most of the rental properties on the reserve. "The new rules" also gave control over the assignment of new housing, and the reassignment of older housing, to band members and to the welfare officers, as opposed to the chief and councillors, who had been using control over housing gifts to acquire votes. These and other issues angered the chief, who used political patronage as a major campaign strategy.

Outcome: The chief began to pay the rent to the landlords on the reserve out of revenue streams he had developed and controlled. He also co-opted one of his opponents on the Band Council by providing him with an apartment building to lease to the band on behalf of the tenants. Still, arguments between the chief and councillors increased until the chief, fed up, resigned his office in May 2006. He ran again for the office of chief in 2006 and 2008, but lost each time.

What effect have these drastic changes in the rules had on the law or on behavior? With the exception of the "party house" rule, very little. A major reason is that, after the great drop in new housing construction beginning around 2000, people began to regard housing as a scarce commodity—which indeed it is—and therefore began to hold on tightly to what they had. It was the ready availability of new, modern housing, coupled with the desire to leave old 1940s housing stock, that led to the exchanging of houses in the 1980s and 1990s. Established families got the modern housing and younger families moved out of their parents' houses into the old housing. The younger families then established themselves and eventually acquired modern housing. But with few houses being built, people clung to what they had, unsure whether they could acquire another house of any kind.

For a time, the Band Council made an effort to enforce the new rules every regard, as seen here.

LEGAL CASE 111

Party: PT.
Authority: The Band Council.
Date: 2005.

Facts: As a result of Legal Case 107, the Band Council realized that it had failed to secure ownership of the old house with a quitclaim deed, as the new regulations stipulated. It asked PT to transfer ownership to the Band Council. PT refused, on the grounds that he had himself paid for the original structure and all extensions.

Outcome: The Band Council ceased its attempts to acquire ownership of the house.

LEGAL CASE 112

Party: XZ, a woman who acquired a new house.
Authority: The Band Council.
Date: 2004.

Facts: Several years before, XZ acquired a new house and gave her old one to a relative, with Band Council approval. At the time no one asked her to sign a quitclaim deed to her old house. One of her councillors, a leader for the creation and implementation of the "new rules" policy, went to her and asked her to sign the quitclaim, which she did. After the thinking the matter over, and consulting with friends, XZ realized that (under the old law) the Band Council should at least compensate her monetarily. So she asked the Band Council for compensation in the amount of $7,000. When making this request, she also claimed that she never signed a quitclaim deed.

Outcome: The Band Council refused the request. It cited both "the new rules" and the fact that she had previously signed a quitclaim deed to the property, which it produced.

Comment: Because this rule requires that the owners sign a quitclaim, it actually seems to reinforce the concept behind the old law that the primary resident has ownership, which must be released. In fact, all the quitclaim does is to put additional political pressure on house owners to give up old houses as part of a contractual arrangement to acquire new ones, which is in fact what had been going on for many years. It helps to tilt the balance of control in favor of the Band Council a bit more.

When the band councillor involved in this case related it to me, he indicated with pride that he was one of the architects of the new rules, and went on to say how he thought the new policy was much better and more intelligent. He mentioned that the old policy, especially the Band Council practice of paying landlords for the items necessary to repair their rental properties, was "stupid."

"The New Rules" Meet Their End

In Legal Case 112, occupation of the old house ended up going to the owner's relative. When I mentioned to this band councillor that housing allocation is not purely an economic problem, that the Band Council cannot simply put a family in the house merely on the basis of need or other eligibility, and that certain people cannot live side by side, it seemed from his reaction that the question had never come up for discussion in the Band Council. This is exactly the problem that doomed the Band Council reappropriation of used housing the first time that it was tried, in the 1980s (see Legal Cases 92, 93, 94, and 95). He thought for a while and then said, "let them worry about it." When I asked how it could be that the Band Council had that same year ostensibly transferred control over the disposition of new and used band housing to the welfare officers, to reduce political factors, when councillors have no other real means beside gifts of housing to try to get themselves reelected, he had no answer, except to say "maybe they don't." Some members of the Band Council sometimes do things that other Band Council members do not know about. Shortly thereafter, the rule was changed to give the welfare officers control over older housing, while the Band Council continued to control awards of new housing, so as to increase incumbents' chances of reelection.

Most importantly, the politically privileged have retained their powers to rent housing to the band, throughout this change in the law, as seen in the following case, which took place at the same time as the expropriations (discussed below). The band would have no place to put all of the tenants who could conceivably have been evicted, had the rent payments actually stopped.

DISPUTE CASE 77

First party: ON.
Second party: YX, a wealthy and politically privileged woman.
Third party: The Band Council.
Date: Late March 2006 to 2009.

Facts: ON has lived for more than 20 years in rental housing, first in a trailer and then in a small house owned by YX. She contemplated making substantial improvements to the house in 2006, but did not wish to spend her own money to improve a house she does not own. She asked the Band Council to buy it from YX, so that it would be hers and she could improve it. When she told two council members that the Band Council had paid over $96,000 in rent on her behalf over the years, more than twice the cost to build the house, they were shocked and immediately went to the landlord to try to purchase the building.

Outcome: YX refused to sell.

Comment: In this case, YX owns the house by having lawful possession of the lot on which it sits. However, she and other landlords do own property built at band expense, located on land that is not lawfully possessed and that they rent to the Band Council (no disputes recorded). No band members truly consider the band as having ownership rights in housing, despite the expropriations that occurred during the same period as this case. This dispute continues as of this writing (2009) without resolution.

But the new rules proved most vulnerable to long-standing political forces in the community. Those with power continue to use it for profit. Two acts in particular killed "the new rules," by revealing to band members at large that the leaders and the privileged do not obey them. First, one of the Band Council members sold a house. At about the same time, a prominent supporter of some of the Band Council members bought a house from another band member, as seen in the following case.

LEGAL CASE 113

First party: DW, a man.
Second party: KO, a man.
Third party: HO, KO's brother.
Authority: The Band Council.
Date: 2005.

Facts: A woman with a seven-year-old house died and left ownership of the house to a son, KO, who happened to be in the hospital at the time. Another son, HO, who was living at the house, sold the house to DW, an unrelated man, for $5,000. This deprived HO, KO, and their siblings of a place to live. KO, the owner, challenged the sale, as did a councillor, on the fact that it violated the new Band Council rules. Further, the mortgage, which the band pays, is many years from being paid in full.

Outcome: The Band Council allowed the sale to stand, probably because of the political power DW wields. The house was thereafter occupied by DW's daughter.

Comment: An observer of the case remarked in disgust, "imagine that, taking advantage of a drunk," referring to HO.

These events, the need of elected officials for the support of the politically powerful, along with considerable public opposition to band ownership of private homes, killed the effectiveness and observance of the "new rules" within one year. As one opponent of the new rules said of the Band Council, "They have to learn. It's a shame people have to defend their own houses. A man's home is his castle." Another band member said emphatically, "the band doesn't own any houses!" The band councillor who authored and most prominently championed the "new rules" lost his seat in the 2006 election. After the statement of the new rules in 2004, one of its architects and most vocal proponents lost his bid for reelection to the Band Council. Another long-time Band Council member lost in 2006.

The overall pattern of recent political change is to announce a strict new rule as a means of increasing political control. The great many who are timid and fear the loss of benefits will obey, as even today some still will not work for fear of losing their Band Council paid mortgage subsidies, even though the 1980s rule that people who work will not receive these subsidies has never really been enforced (see Legal Case 54). The politically powerful and the aggressive receive special exemptions from the rules (for example, to keep their houses, or to rent property to the Band Council), and so will be obliged to return the favor in the form of support polls. This method of acquiring political supporters is financially less expensive than giving houses or employment. But behind it all is a legal authority too weak to do much, as was revealed when the Band Council first attempted to expropriate property in the 1980s (see Legal Case 95).

By 2006, the "new rules" were essentially forgotten, the victims of widespread opposition, as well as corruption of the rules by Band Council members and other politically powerful people.

EXPROPRIATIONS AND COMMUNAL OWNERSHIP

Communal ownership has succeeded on another front, however. The year 2006 saw yet another development related to the housing shortage. Powerful and politically privileged band members have been putting pressure on the Band Council to supply housing, arguing that some single people do not deserve housing because of their behavior (they have long used exactly the same argument to acquire employment for members of their own lineages by pointing out that person X or person Y is not doing his or her job properly, and that a member of their own lineage deserves the job more). Finally bowing to years of this sort of pressure, especially from people who hope to get some of these houses for their own use, the Band Council began to dispossess people of their houses under the authority of their new "party house" rule (see below). In every case of which I am aware, the houses so expropriated were given to members of large, solidary lineages with intact Family Home Territories or band officer families.

ESKASONI REAL PROPERTY BEHAVIORAL RULE 9

Unmarried house owners who frequently have drunken, unruly parties in their houses lose possession of the houses.

LEGAL CASE 114

Defendant: PG, a woman.
Authority: The Band Council.
Date: 2006.

Facts: PG's sister, who has children, was given a house by the Band Council. Later she and her children moved to another reserve and she gave her house to PG, who had children of her own. Later, PG behaved so badly that Mi'kmaq Family and Children's Services took her children from her. Her alcohol and drug parties were frequently a nuisance to the community.

Outcome: The Band Council evicted her from the house.

LEGAL CASE 115

Defendant: WJ, a woman and a member of the J lineage.
Authority: The Band Council.
Date: 2006.

Facts: WJ's house was what was popularly known as a "party house." Her children had been removed by Mi'kmaq Family and Children's Services and the house itself was in shambles. When she asked the Band Council to repair her house, they agreed, and she moved out to let them do the work.

Outcome: When the repairs were completed, the Band Council instead approved the transfer of the house to another party, a kinsperson of a band office employee who administers housing matters for the band, thereby expropriating it from WJ. This transfer of possession occurred shortly before WJ was due to have custody of her children returned to her, which would have entitled her once more to possession of the house.

Comment: The J lineage is itself politically powerful and privileged, which is why WJ had a house in the first place.

LEGAL CASE 116

Defendant: AT, a woman.
Authority: The Band Council.
Date: 2006.

Facts: AT owned a house on the reserve. She left this house to live with a man on another reserve and installed her brother in the house to hold it for her.

Outcome: Because she abandoned the house, AT lost ownership, and the Band Council expropriated the house.

Comment: One of the most interesting features of this expropriation is how it was carried out. The Band Council waited until the occupant left the house and then, with police present, had the furniture loaded into a truck that took it to be stored in an old building once used as a community hall. Then, it told the family chosen to use the house that it must move in immediately.

This indicates that the Band Council and everyone concerned acknowledges the importance of residence in establishing ownership. The Band Council appears to be seeking a measure of legitimacy in its behavior by stretching the concept of abandonment to include someone who leaves the house, and the concept of establishing ownership by primary residence to the families moved into the house. It seems to indicate that the principle that the band owns all publicly-financed housing is a weak one which even the Band Council seems not to want to lean too heavily on.

The same thing occurred in the following case.

LEGAL CASE 117

Defendant: FK, a woman.
Authority: The Band Council.
Date: 2006.

Facts: FK knew that the Band Council was planning to take her house for her alleged improprieties. To prevent them from doing so, she did not leave her house for two weeks. Finally, she had to leave her house to get some food.

Outcome: As soon as she left, the Band Council truck was there to remove her belongings, which were also taken to the former community hall. Another family was moved in immediately.

Comment on Legal Cases 116 and 117: This method of eviction indicates that the Band Council and everyone concerned acknowledges the importance of residence in establishing ownership. The Band Council seems to be seeking a measure of legitimacy in its evictions by stretching the concept of abandonment to include someone who leaves the house even for a few hours, and the concept of establishing ownership by primary residence to the families moved into the house. This indicates that the principle that the band owns all publicly financed housing is a weak one that even the Band Council seems not to want to lean too heavily on. Nevertheless, in all, six people lost their houses in 2006.

LEGAL CASE 118

Defendant: TS, a widow.
Authority: The Band Council.
Date: 2006.

Facts: TS, a widow, learned that both her son VS and granddaughter RS were scheduled to be dispossessed of their housing under the new "party house" rule. She asked the Band Council not to do this, because she did not want the responsibility of housing two such badly misbehaving people.

Outcome: The Band Council deferred to her wishes and did not expropriate the houses of these two people, at least for the time being.

Comment: Two years later, one had lost ownership of her house and the other had lost his house to fire.

Interestingly, the Band Council does not automatically become the owner of old houses once the occupants receive a new one; rather it requires that the owners sign a quitclaim deed to the old house. This is further proof of the Band Council's impotence, as well as recognition that the old principle of establishing ownership by primary residence remains important. The preponderance of political power lies in the hands of those who hold individual rights.

The years 2007 to 2009 saw even more expropriations as public support for them increased even in the face of opposition from kin of those who lost housing. The terrific scarcity of housing has driven the process of change, and many expropriations have occurred at the behest of the politically privileged, who desire the houses for their own use. Whatever the circumstances of the expropriations, the politically privileged seem more often than not to be the beneficiaries, as in the following case.

LEGAL CASE 119

First party: QN, a young woman.
Second party: AP another woman.
Third party: FP, the band welfare director.
Authority: The Band Council.
Date: 2007.

Facts: QN owned a house that she used to hold frequent drug and alcohol parties. As a result of these parties, QN lost custody of her children and the interior of the house was largely destroyed. FP expropriated her house under Band Council Real Property Rule 9 and awarded it to AP, his close relative. QN's family protested the expropriation on two grounds. First, they argued that the award constituted a conflict of interest. Second, they argued that QN was on the verge of regaining custody of her children from Micmac Family and Children's Services. Therefore, the loss of her house meant that she could not regain custody, because she no longer had a dwelling to house them.

Outcome: The Band Council ultimately declined to alter AP's ownership of the house.

Comment: The political climate in the community clearly disfavors the owners of "party houses."

LEGAL CASE 120

First party: TS, a widow.
Second party: RS, her granddaughter.
Authority: The Band Council.
Date: 2008.

Facts: Although TS had previously saved RS's house, she could not do it a second time. RS had been convicted of selling illegal drugs and was imprisoned. The Band Council announced that it would take her house to give it to someone else. TS argued against this and even made plans to live in her granddaughter RS's house to prevent it from being taken. She claimed that it is a "rule" that the Band Council could not take a house if someone sleeps there and has a bed in it (she obviously was unaware of the details of Legal Cases 116 and 117). TS's children dissuaded her from pursuing the fight, telling her *elmie* ("go home").

Outcome: The Band Council expropriated RS's house.

Comment: TS was very angry at the expropriation. She complained that the Band Council expropriated RS's house "just because she sold drugs," by way of saying that it seemed to her a pretty thin justification for such a serious act as expropriation. The S lineage, although somewhat disunified by the death of their patriarch, remains "the most feared family" in Eskasoni. However, the immoral behavior of RS was so clear cut and indefensible, that the S lineage did nothing to defend her. This case and Legal Case 115 show that this legal change provides the powerful with a weapon against which even other powerful lineages are defenseless.

From these cases we may abstract the following legal principle:

BAND COUNCIL LEGAL PRINCIPLE 20
Unmarried house owners who frequently have drunken, unruly parties in their houses will lose possession of their houses.

The law thus appears in conflict with itself. Band members consider their own right of ownership by primary residence solidly established. The Band Council, on the other hand, bases its right to expropriate "party houses" on band ownership of housing. The vast majority of band members support the expropriations, and nearly all band members view the expropriations as simple forfeitures for improper conduct that do not otherwise affect ownership rights (comparable to the property forfeitures allowable in the United States in some drug cases). The right of owners by primary residence to the rights of possession, use and alienation remains, but so does the new law allowing Band Council expropriation of "party houses." Many of the very same people who applaud the expropriations also vow to defend their own ownership of their houses with whatever means at their disposal, including violence. Excepting "party house" expropriations, basic ownership rights do seem unaffected.

All expropriated houses sit outside of Family Home Territories. This is for two reasons. The Band Council could not, and would not attempt to, expropriate a house in a Family Home Territory that had any sort of functioning defense mechanism. This represents a concrete example of an advantage of having a Family Home Territory: the family or lineage can prevent loss of valuable housing even in cases in which the Band Council and the politically privileged are determined to acquire it. Second, if the misbehaving person lived in a Family Home Territory, the patriarch or matriarch would usually attempt to stop such misbehavior, even if it meant removing the person from the house and dismantling it (see Legal Case 46; not all misbehaving people can be controlled even on their Family Home Territories, and there are many such people).

This series of events is illuminating in several respects. First, the fact that the Band Council has chosen to partially address the shortage of housing by expropriating houses to benefit the politically privileged indicates a government dependent on the politically powerful and a growing gulf between the material benefits available to the politically privileged and everyone else. In the long run, ceasing the payment of rental fees to landlords would do more to ameliorate the housing shortage than this policy of expropriation, as the Band Council of 2004–2006 realized. Obviously, political concerns prevent this.

Second, the expropriation of the houses of those who misbehave enjoys wide support, although obviously not by the immediate families of those losing their housing. Yet these very same people who stand behind the expropriations vigorously defend private ownership of their own houses, making statements like "They [the Band Council] don't own these houses," as well as that earlier quote expressing the view that a man's home is his castle. The question of expropriation is entirely a moral one and the logical coherence of ownership rights or of the law in general is not considered. And, with the exception of the politicians who initiated the idea of expropriations, they consider neither the legal basis for expropriations, nor the obvious conflict between the idea of band ownership of expropriated housing and their own private ownership of their own housing. They do trust the Band Council to make fair decisions in the expropriations and do not fear the loss of their own housing to expropriation.

What makes these expropriations of housing different from the expropriations of unbuilt land, which began two decades earlier (see Legal Case 96), is that in the case of unbuilt land there is always the argument made by some that unbuilt land is really free and unowned land. This of course depends on the perspectives of those involved, and even the time period and relative scarcity of land. When there were relatively few people around, there were no difficulties in claiming large parcels of land as one's own. As land has become increasingly scarce, maintaining those claims of ownership against the claims of people who wished to use the land for housing and other needs became more difficult. In the case of occupied housing, there is no room for discussion. The primary occupant owns the house. Therefore, the band's expropriation of occupied housing marks a true revolution in ownership rights.

To reiterate, as far as most band members are concerned, this legal change represents merely a more rigorous application of moral principle, rather than a change in the underlying law. Moreover, Band Council Legal Principle 20 has been applied to fewer than 3% of the house owners in Eskasoni. On the basis of this evidence, and despite the fact that Band Council Legal Principle 2 stands in direct opposition to Band Council Legal Principle 20, we must conclude that Band Council Legal Principle 20 amends rather than extinguishes Band Council Legal Principle 2.

Legal Change 10: Pursuing Prosecution in Federal Criminal Court

The other way that the Band Council used the concept of group ownership viably is in the prosecution of arson. In an effort to make more housing available to the band, the Band Council has begun having arson cases prosecuted, cooperating with the RCMP to do so, as in the following cases.

LEGAL CASE 121

First party: BP, a father.
Second party: TP, his daughter.
Authority: The Band Council, RCMP and the Canadian Federal Court.
Date: 2008.

Facts: BP and TP had an explosive argument. To punish her father, TP burned his house down.

Outcome: TP was prosecuted for arson under the Canadian Criminal Code and imprisoned.

LEGAL CASE 122

First party: DC, a husband.
Second party: GC, his wife.
Authority: The Band Council, RCMP and the Canadian Federal Court.
Date: 2009.

Facts: The marriage of DC and GC became increasingly troubled over the years. At about the same time that their new house was completed, the two separated. To prevent his wife from gaining possession of the house, DC burned it down.

Outcome: The Band Council and RCMP had DC prosecuted for arson. This represents a complete change from earlier policy (see Legal Case 38).

From these cases we may abstract the following:

BAND COUNCIL LEGAL PRINCIPLE 21
Those who commit arson will be prosecuted for the crime in federal criminal court.

The contradiction between the ownership rights established by primary residence on the one hand, and the expropriations of "party houses" and punishment of arson cases, will doubtlessly resolve itself one day. In the meantime, it persists because the vast majority of people in the community believe that they will themselves experience no repercussions from the new laws, and because they wish those who abuse housing to be stopped.

The Consequences of Change in the Land Tenure System

Let us recapitulate the changes in land tenure described above.

Summary of Legal Changes

LEGAL CHANGE 1
Former legal principle. Band Council Legal Principle 14 states that a person who receives a new house supplied by the Band Council must return ownership of the old house to the Band Council, subject to individual contractual condition (see Legal Case 90).

Change. The chief and Band Council stopped enforcing this principle in 1987, thereby extinguishing it, because of political pressure and the weight of their own earlier failures to take old housing in all cases (including Legal Case 93).

Legal Change 2
Former rule. Band Council Real Property Rule 4 states that a house may not be destroyed or dismantled except when decrepit and then only under the special permission of the Band Council.

Change. The chief and Band Council stopped applying this rule uniformly for reasons of political patronage, and thus as a legal rule it is seriously weakened and probably unenforceable (see Political Case 6).

Legal Change 3
Former rule. Band Council Real Property Rule 5 states that the Band Council will not expropriate real property owned by band members.

Change. Band Council Legal Principle 16 states that any unbuilt reserve land owned by individual private band members may be expropriated by the Band Council for the construction of development projects ordered by the Band Council.

Legal Change 4
Former principle. Band Council Legal Principle 16 states that any unbuilt reserve land owned by individual private band members may be expropriated by the Band Council for the construction of development projects ordered by the Band Council.

Change. Band Council Legal Principle 16 states that the Band Council may expropriate any unbuilt reserve land for construction projects ordered by the Band Council, except in those cases in which owners present powerful political opposition to expropriation.

Legal Change 5
New rule. In 1998, the Band Council promulgated a new rule that we may express as Band Council Real Property Rule 6, which states that all individuals receiving a new house in their own name from the Band Council for the first time must have their houses built in one of the new subdivisions (no disputes recorded).

This new rule effectively limits the traditional customary right of freedom of house siting for those who do not already have housing.

Legal Change 6
Former legal principle. Band Council Legal Principle 2 states that primary residence in a house confers on the primary resident a right of ownership to the house against the Band Council that the Band Council will not normally alter.

Amending legal principle. Band Council Legal Principal 17 states that the rights of ownership of structures is subject to public safety and community appearance concerns, and the Band Council may order the razing or removal of housing that it deems poses a hazard to public safety or is an eyesore.

LEGAL CHANGE 7
Former legal principle. Band Council Legal Principle 2 states that primary residence in a house confers on the primary resident a right of ownership to the house against the Band Council that the Band Council will not normally alter.

New legal principle. Band Council Legal Principle 18 states that band members may own housing in which others reside.

LEGAL CHANGE 8
New legal principle. Band Council Legal Principle 19 states that the ability to rent real property to the Band Council depends on one's level of political privilege.

LEGAL CHANGE 9
Former legal principle. Band Council Legal Principle 2 states that primary residence in a house confers on the primary resident a right of ownership to the house against the Band Council that the Band Council will not normally alter.

Amending legal principle. Band Council Legal Principle 20 states that unmarried house owners who frequently have drunken, unruly parties in their houses will lose possession of their houses.

This new legal principle amends Band Council Legal Principle 2.

LEGAL CHANGE 10
Former legal principle. Band Council Legal Principle 2 states that primary residence in a house confers on the primary resident a right of ownership to the house against the Band Council that the Band Council will not normally alter.

Amending legal principle. Band Council Legal Principle 21 states that those who commit arson will be prosecuted for the crime in federal criminal court.

Analysis

Remarkably, these many changes all occurred in the short period from 1985 to 2008. An analysis of these legal changes reveals that two patterns of territorial behavior. Most of the changes (Legal Changes 1, 2, 4, 5, 8, and 9) touch on the Family Home Territory and lineal solidarity. Legal Change 3 pertains to the telescoping territorial system used to arrest disputes. The first change, the repeal of the Band Council Legal Principle 14, which had earlier forced recipients of new housing to transfer ownership of old housing to the band, allowed families to maintain the integrity of their Family Home Territories. The change in the law means that owners can now maintain ownership of the old houses; this removes the threat of the Band Council placing or allowing unwanted, unrelated families into Family Home Territories (see Legal Case 94). The intrusion of a foreign family into the Family Home Territory can lead to great social friction.

The second change, the weakening of the legal rule against the razing of old houses, achieves the same purpose. With owners now able to destroy their old housing, they can keep all housing in the Family Home Territory from possible use by unrelated and possibly unfriendly families.

The third change, which allows the Band Council to expropriate land unoccupied by buildings owned by individuals for the construction of housing development projects, protects the integrity of reserve section boundaries against immigration by allowing young people to find housing within their natal reserve sections. The Band Council's right to expropriate land that belongs to a private individual for housing in a crowded reserve section gives those living in that section the ability to remain there rather than to be forced to live outside of it. By being able to live in their natal reserve section, people are exposed to fewer hostilities, and so fewer disputes, violent and non-violent, result. Further, it protects the interest of those living in other reserve sections to be free of immigrants.

The fourth legal change reflects the influences of increased crowding. The territorial interests of those protecting the integrity of the Family Home Territory boundaries conflict with the territorial interests of those looking for living space in their own natal reserve sections, but outside of their patrilineal home territories.

The effect of territorial defense, increased by these legal changes, creates or increases social disunity. This process occurs in three ways. In the first place, civil disputes rarely resolve themselves fully. Wrongs committed decades earlier remain a sore point between disputants and there is the potential for violence to flare up, as sometimes occurs. This is especially true when, often, both disputants feel that they have acted justifiably. There is no legal authority to make statements on the just rights of one party and the just duties of the other. Thus, there are many instances of people who, even though physically separated, harbor strong ill will toward others also living on the reserve.

In the second place, territorial defense prevents the otherwise normal movement of people within the community. Those engaged in a dispute may have difficulty performing their jobs, or even visiting friends and relatives (see, for example, Dispute Cases 10, 11, 18, 19, and 31). And this system affects virtually everyone, although the most affected by far are young men. I once heard a band councillor remark to his wife that there was only one person on the reserve "who can go anywhere in Eskasoni." One result of this system of social control is that many ordinary activities become difficult or impossible for some members of Eskasoni society. For example, a band office worker having a dispute with someone in *'Qamsipu:k* is unable to go to *'Qamsipu:k* to perform his official duties there. An individual who lives in Castle Bay, but who has a dispute with someone in *Apamuek*, does not shop at stores in *Apamuek*. A carpenter living in *Apamuek* who has a dispute with someone in Castle Bay can only build houses in *Apamuek* and *'Qamsipu:k*. These are but a few actual examples of what happens when disputes limit the geographic and social mobility of disputants. The true daily functioning of this process is much more complex and involves many people. The system of territorial defense prevents intersettlement, and each reserve section or subsection becomes established as the domain of a few families. Women, of course, often settle in new reserve sections, but then pay the price of living as strangers in their husbands' reserve sections for the rest of their lives. This problem has strained many marriages (see Legal Case 79).

Third, territorial defense causes many to identify themselves first as members of reserve sections, rather than of the band or reserve as a whole, and repeatedly reinforces that identification. This practice constantly revives old rivalries (such as that between the original residents of Eskasoni living in *Apamuek* and *'Qamsipu:k* and newcomers, who live primarily in *Apamuek* and Castle Bay). This was a major factor leading, in the late 1970s, to a very nearly successful movement by Castle Bay residents to secede from the Eskasoni band. Although Indian Affairs may not have officially permitted this (see the example of another band: CBC News 2000), politicians in Castle Bay say that Indian Affairs would have had no choice but to allow the secession. It would in any case have been a de facto sociopolitical schism.

In short, the recent changes in the land tenure system have reduced social friction, including violence, by promoting territorial defense and social disunity. To put it another way, the system of territorial defense became important as an extralegal means of social control; so important, in fact, that the land tenure system changed to accommodate and strengthen it. There were also changes to societal organization. Social schism is the traditional Micmac response to dispute (see Legal Case 10), creating two or more groups where there previously had been one. This process is now all but impossible, because of financial considerations (very few would give up the relief payments and free housing available with band membership on the reserve), political considerations (it is difficult to join another band and live on its reserve, because members of other bands have few financial resources and so share them reluctantly), and the reluctance of Indian Affairs to create additional bands and reserves (to avoid the additional administrative burden). The legal changes strengthen the territorial defense system and create quasi-schisms in the Eskasoni band, physically separating subgroups and individuals but not moving them apart geographically.

The idea that the Eskasoni band is less, rather than more, of an actual cohesive and solidary group finds support in several facts.

1. The band was created by federal statute in Ottawa. It consists of a class of people who share a culture and who are entitled to live on a reserve, rather than a group.
2. The band members have no common function; the band is an administrative unit.
3. Although the Eskasoni people have selected a leader, who does in fact lead on some issues, he is easily disobeyed. Further, his primary job is not to lead, but to acquire material benefits for the people of the reserve (as may be seen in the campaign literature that the chief used for reelection, which cites only these benefits and no leadership

achievements). In fact, character and material benefits are the primary issues that decide elections and never the direction of the band, with the exception that decisions likely to lead to assimilation are considered very negatively.

The fifth change plainly works towards opposite ends. It integrates rather than divides, although the Band Council ordered the change for economic reasons and not to improve social unity. People from all parts of the reserve end up as neighbors and, according to all reports I have heard, get along quite well, even watching each other's houses when away. This change, according to several politicians I spoke to, represents an attempt to strike directly at the heart of the solidary lineages by breaking down the integrity of the Family Home Territories. It attempts to deprive the solidary lineages of political power by eroding the number of lineage members loyal to the lineage leaders.

On the other hand, and most importantly, the new rule poses no genuine threat to the overall system of territoriality. Those who live in the subdivisions may not particularly relish their living situations, but most have little interest in preserving the Family Home Territories of their own lineages in any event; many want to escape the home territories and their sometimes overbearing authorities. But, this new rule does not prevent any family who wishes to keep its children living in the group's Family Home Territory from doing so, thereby maintaining both lineage solidarity and the integrity of the Family Home Territory. Lineage leaders accomplish this by asking for new houses for the older members of the group, which are built in the Family Home Territory, and by giving the younger members of the lineage the old houses. Many of the lineage authorities will not consider allowing their young adults to live anywhere else than the Family Home Territory. Those solidary lineages who continue to defend their Family Home Territories continue to prosper at the expense of families and lineages who do not, and who are not, solidary. The Band Council itself makes a slight concession to the principle of lineal solidarity. It tells an individual who is receiving a new house in a subdivision to take two lots, one for himself and one for a brother.

Finally, the new rule does not affect the telescoping system of territorial defense against individual disputants. People still make use of the system, with the exception that the dimension of the Family Home Territory is largely absent from the calculation of defense behavior in the subdivisions. People simply rely solely on reserve sections and subsections instead.

In 1999, there were mixed feelings about the new rule. Many proclaimed they would never live in a subdivision. Young people found the matter rather more difficult. Some welcomed the opportunity to escape their parents' control; but even among those opposed to the new subdivisions, few can afford to pass up the opportunity to acquire new housing of their own, even if its location leaves something to be desired. Moreover, many of those who live in the new subdivisions still spend a great deal of their time in their parents' Family Home Territories, and over the past five years many have returned to these Family Home Territories when able to get a house there. The years 2004 to 2009 have seen a flood of now older offspring, many with older children of their own, trying to return to their Family Home Territories. The exchange of freedom from family authority for geosocial separation from family seems to hold an often temporary attraction primarily for people in their twenties and early thirties.

The integrative effect of Legal Change 5 has limited scope. And most importantly, the integrative pressure it represents has no effect at all on those segments of the population who most wish to remain politically, socially, and geographically separate and distinct from the general population, the solidary patrilineages.

Legal Change 6 represents a small common sense change to rid the community of nuisance buildings whose owners have no further interest in using. This change makes even more sense if one remembers that in this community most individuals lack the money to properly demolish buildings on their own. This change is neutral with respect to the integrity of the Family Home Territory, since it only applies to old housing, not to rights in land.

Legal Changes 7 and 8

One of the most recent changes in law creates three classes of people according to level of political privilege. The system works by the imposition of rules. These rules cow most people on the reserve into compliance, because they fear the loss of benefits. So suggestible are the majority of the people that some still obey the rule that only people who collect relief will have their mortgage payments made by the Band Council. These people will not take employment for fear of losing these mortgage payments, despite the fact that in many hundreds of cases dating back to the 1980s no one on the reserve has paid the mortgage payment for his or her house.

Some others, however, want greater benefits and see their political power as a bargaining chip to obtain them. Some of these people are politically valuable enough to receive full or partial immunity from the rules from politicians. The fully privileged have complete immunity from the rules, the moderately privileged, a much larger class, have only partial immunity. The development of the personality principle within the legal system reflects the exceptional political importance of certain key individuals and families within the political system.

Legal Change 8 indicates that the size and solidarity of lineages and the existence of functioning Family Home Territories plays a large role in determining the degree of political privilege that an individual is able to acquire.

Legal Changes 9 and 10

Legal Changes 9 and 10 represent a political reaction to a housing shortage. People are using whatever means they can to acquire and retain housing. The politically privileged use their influence to prompt Band Council expropriations. Those with Family Home Territories use them to block expropriations. The weak, those single people with drug or alcohol dependency issues who live outside of the protection of Family Home Territories, lose their housing. The vast majority, those who are married and live largely sober lives, continue to rely on rights of ownership by primary residence. Political pressure for housing access has overwhelmed traditional legal principle. I predict that if available housing remains rare, Legal Changes 9 and 10 will remain. If, on the other hand, the housing shortage eases considerably, Legal Changes 9 and 10 should vanish. In either case, I expect that the Family Home Territory will continue to grow in importance for the foreseeable future.

These changes resulted from the actions of a coalition of the politically privileged (who demand housing be made available to them in return for the support they have given elected Band Council members), the majority of Band Council members (who wish to be able to show voters that they are working to supply housing), and the moral and pragmatic band members who argue for the responsible use of housing so as to make it more generally available. They therefore slightly weaken the traditional right to maintain ownership by primary residence.

When the Band Council promulgated these changes, it relied on the concept of band ownership of nearly all housing as a legal basis, an idea that has its roots in Canadian Indian law, and which Indian Affairs has long prompted band councils to accept and use. The people of Eskasoni have steadfastly rejected this idea at every turn (see for example the discussion of the "new rules" above). However, once the people began to conceptualize the expropriations as forfeitures for misbehavior, and prosecutions for arson as simple crimes, they accepted them. The Band Council itself no longer characterizes these takings as expropriations based on band ownership. Thus we see that legal ideas that originate even partly from external legal systems must be transformed into an entirely different legal concept before they can be successfully applied.

The Band Council made Legal Changes 9 and 10 without any immediately apparent intended effects on the Family Home Territories. Legal Change 9, however, has made the value and importance of the Family Home Territories rise significantly. The Family Home Territories provide the only widely available protection from Band Council housing expropriations in the community (lawful possession also provides protection, but is available only to a very few). Furthermore, by the time Legal Change 9 came about, the Family Home Territories had become so strong that the inability of the Band Council to expropriate housing from within them was taken for granted. And while Legal Change 5 came about to allow the Band Council to challenge the power of the solidary lineages, Legal Change 9, by expropriating housing, thereby forces the inhabitants of those houses to return to their lineages' Family Home Territories. In this manner it increases the power of the resident solidary lineages and partially rolls back the effects of Legal Change 5.

Legal Change 9, although it disperses lineage members of the solidary lineages to the subdivisions (they take the houses after they have been forfeited), and thus promises to weaken the very lineages who benefit from it, is ironically a direct result of the power of the solidary lineages who pushed for its imposition.

An analysis of Legal Change 9 points out the key position of territorial behavior, the Family Home Territory, and especially of its effect on the solidarity of some lineages, to an understanding politics and land tenure in this community. Land tenure and changes to it must be understood in terms of these dynamics.

CHAPTER SEVENTEEN

Pertinent Theoretical Topics

Some of the data presented here warrant further reflection. The theoretical topics of multiple legal systems, globalization and modernity, resistance and identity, territoriality, settlement, legal change in small societies, and the function of law are analyzed and discussed below in light of these data.

Multiple Legal Systems

Pospisil (1958a:272–278) broached the theory of multiple legal levels, stating that there is one legal system for each functioning subgroup of a society. The Micmac data presented here support the validity of this theory, especially the idea that small societies within larger state societies can and do operate their own effective legal systems, despite conflict with the national system.

These three levels of law certainly are among the most salient features of the Eskasoni land tenure system: the Canadian federal legal level, the Band Council level, and the family/descent group level. From 1957 through 1964 these also coexisted with the Grand Council and Indian Agent legal levels.

The family/descent group level of law comprises several independent legal systems. Each family/descent group has a patriarch or a matriarch who acts as a legal authority for the rest of the group. This legal level represents the most important legal control over improper behavior on the reserve, adjudicating far more legal cases than either of the others. However, it is impossible to adequately describe this level here, because there are in fact as many systems as there are legal authorities, and each system often differs significantly from the next in its laws, sanctions, and enforcement.

However, there is one legal principle common to all family/descent group land tenure systems, and it differs from those used by the Band Council land tenure system. Under Family/Descent Group Legal Principle 1, the owner of a house may allow residence by others in the house without losing ownership (Legal Cases 45 and 46). Under Band Council law, only the politically privileged may own a house in which others reside, according to Band Council Legal Principle 6 (see Legal Cases 61, 62, and 63). Under the *Indian Act*, however, a single individual may have possession of multiple houses, so long as they are situated on lawfully possessed land, a consideration irrelevant at the other two levels.

A great difference exists between land tenure at the family/descent group and Band Council levels, on the one hand, and Canadian Indian land tenure on the other; the family/descent group and Band Council authorities emphasize contracts (see Legal Cases 44, 45, 46, 54, 55, 56, 57, 61, 63, 65, 71, 75, 82, 93, 95, 99, 105, 106, 107, 108, 110, 113, and 115), whereas the Canadian Indian land tenure system primarily emphasizes the status of rightsholders and land: the Indian has different rights from those of a non-Indian, the lawful possessor's rights differ from those who do not have lawful possession. The law treats reserve land differently from non-reserve land, and allotted land differently from unallotted land.

Sanctions also differ among the three levels. As far as legal authorities at the family/descent group and Band Council levels are concerned, three of the most important sanctions are the enforced fulfillment of contracts, their cancellation, and the institution of conditions on behavior (Legal Cases 44, 45, 46, 54, 55, 56, 57, 61, 65, 75, 95, 99, 105, 106, 107, 108, 110, 113, and 115,). The *Indian Act* provides for punitive sanctions, such as incarceration and fines.

However, it is under the Canadian Indian and Eskasoni Band Council land tenure systems that the band members' most basic rights are established. Without these rights, those granted by the family/descent group authorities probably could not exist, or at least exist as they do.

Before discussing the enormous differences between the land tenure legal systems of the Canadian government (see Figure 2) and the Eskasoni Band Council (see Figure 6), it is important to describe how two systems that in some ways contradict each other might co-exist. Part of the answer lies in the Canadian government's official *laissez-faire* attitudes toward the enforcement of Canadian Indian land tenure law. Cases that might be brought before a federal court or before the Minister of the Department of Indian Affairs and Northern Development (Indian Affairs) simply remain untried. A good example of this is *Re Attorney-General of Nova Scotia and Millbrook Indian Band et al.*, [1978] 93 D.L.R. (3d) 230, in which the court took notice that many non-Indians were living in a trailer park on a Micmac reserve, in violation of the *Indian Act*. By 1987, a decade later, no official action had been taken to change the situation to satisfy the terms of the *Indian Act*. The Indians of the reserve did not want a change, because they profited by the rents that the trailer owners paid. The approach Indian Affairs took at the time was to try to exempt the portion of the reserve occupied by the trailer park from those sections of the *Indian Act* that prohibited non-Indians from occupying reserve lands.

In nearly all instances, Indian Affairs brings land tenure cases to court only when they are of benefit to the Indians, and even then usually only at the request of Indian parties. This is because many Canadians hold liberal positions on questions of Indian concerns, and favor circumstances in which Indians have a large measure of self-determination. Further, Indian Affairs wants to avoid criticism by Indians in the press that it is not doing its job, to help Indians, or that it is hindering them in the pursuit of their legitimate goals. In short, the federal government finds it politically untenable to intercede in internal band affairs in most cases.

Of course, another very important reason for coexistence of two very different legal systems is secrecy; Indian Affairs and the courts simply never come to know of many of the infractions of the *Indian Act*, at least officially, and the Micmac typically keep knowledge of such infractions from the ears of non-Indians. For example, it is legal under Eskasoni law to sell natural resources (notably wood) from reserve lands without a license from the Minister, but illegal under the *Indian Act*.

This is not to say that Indians in Canada do not use the Canadian courts in land tenure cases. There are more than 200 reported decisions in such cases, and probably several times that number of unreported decisions. Even Eskasoni residents have used the Canadian courts on occasion. Rather, the only conclusion we can draw is that the Eskasoni Band Council leadership provides on the whole a legal system for dealing with land tenure matters on the reserve that most of the Eskasoni people, most of the time, believe to be just.

Ownership and Possession

Before addressing the specific differences between the two legal systems, there is the matter of a certain similarity. The most complex feature of both Canadian Indian and Eskasoni land tenure systems concerns the classes of entitled parties, although these classes are for the most part incongruent (see Figures 2 and 6). In both systems, the many classes of entitled parties arose primarily from a desire by authorities to allow Indians use of reserve lands and to tightly restrict non-Indian use. In addition, the Band Council recognized two classes of parties with greater rights than others: allottees and the politically privileged.

The complexity both systems share with respect to classes of entitled parties is balanced by a simplicity in the number of legal categories of real property, also shared by both systems, although again the classes do not correspond.

In the case of the Canadian Indian system, this simplicity resulted from the Canadian government's idea that all land on a reserve should be used to benefit all the Indians who have a right to live on the reserve. For example, proceeds from the leasing of reserve lands for agriculture or grazing must be paid to the band as a whole (*Indian Act*, R.S.C. 1985, c. I-5, s. 58). On the other hand, the opportunity for Indians to become lawful possessors of reserve land was added, initially, to induce assimilation. Thus there are essentially two categories of reserve land in the Canadian Indian legal system: unallotted reserve land and allotted reserve land. The *Indian Act* does, however, provide for the possibility of more categories by allowing Band Councils to create zoning regulations, although none of the Cape Breton bands have made discernable use of this provision.

The Eskasoni Band Council land tenure system superficially resembles the Canadian Indian system in that it divides land into only two types. These types, however, differ greatly from those of the Canadian system. Under the Eskasoni system, one of these is free land, which is not owned, occupied, or in use, and is available for ownership by any band member. Once land is in use as a home site, logging site, or any other use (such as "tree tipping," to get boughs for wreath manufacturing), it becomes owned land and is no longer free. The primary resident or first user becomes the owner. Customary behavioral rules (see Eskasoni Real Property Behavioral Rules 1, 2, and 3) dictate that owned land may not be used by a non-owner without the permission of the owner, and the Band Council and individual parties usually observe these rules. Under the Canadian system, authorities assign lawful possessory interests by reference to specified, surveyed lot boundaries, irrespective of use or residence. Otherwise, the band as a whole possesses the land.

The collision between these two systems can most clearly be seen in the handling of lawful possession cases. As much as possible, the Band Council ignores the interests established by lawful possession, as when it pays rent to the owners of buildings that sit on lots lawfully possessed by third parties. It also ignores lawful possessory interests when the parties to a dispute do not seek to have rights arising from these interests come into play.

However, in cases in which a party demands the exercise of his or her lawful possessory rights under statute, the Band Council has no choice but to enforce them, because it would be forced to do so by federal courts in any event (see Legal Cases 83 and 91). However, it always protects the ownership or possessory rights in dwellings established by primary residence under the indigenous system, even if it has to resort to political means (see Legal–Political Cases 1 and 2).

Two things leap out here. One is the relative paucity of instances in which the Band Council does make decisions that give lawful possession weight. Another is that the Band Council will give lawful possession weight even in civil cases between private parties, which it otherwise decides in favor of the primary resident, because of the great pressure the federal government could potentially exert.

Real and Personal Property

One of the more interesting differences between Canadian Indian law and Eskasoni Band Council law is the division between real and personal property. Under Canadian Indian law (and indeed all law in the British common law tradition), fixtures (such as houses) are real property, except in some rare cases. Certainly, the *Indian Act* does not provide for houses to be considered personal property.

Under Eskasoni Band Council law, the ownership rights of the house owner are not infrequently separate and distinct from the ownership rights of the land owner of the land beneath the house (see Legal Cases 47, 66, 68, 69, 70, 80, and 94, and Dispute Case 44). This concept of houses as personal property survives from the earlier days of wigwams.

The two systems also differ in rights of *ususfructus* and expropriation. Below is a discussion of these specific differences, followed by a discussion of how the people on the reserve treat the *Indian Act* provisions on possession and surrender.

Rights of Ususfructus

RIGHT OF RESIDENCE

Under both the Canadian Indian and Eskasoni legal systems, Eskasoni band members have a right to live on the reserve assigned to the Eskasoni band (see *Indian Act*, R.S.C. 1985, c. I-5, s. 2). One difference between the two legal systems is that, under the Canadian Indian system, a Band Council may revoke the right of a band member to build a house on his or her reserve (see *Joe et al. v. Findlay et. al.*, [1980] 109 D.L.R. (3d) 747), while the Eskasoni system makes no such provision.

In the case of those who are not band members, there is a substantial difference in right of occupation. Under the Canadian Indian system, the Minister may grant any person a license to occupy reserve land for a fixed term of up to one year, or longer with the approval of the Band Council (*Indian Act*, R.S.C. 1985, c. I-5, s. 28). Under the Eskasoni system, a non-band member may reside on reserve land only at the chief's sufferance. Such sufferance may last forever, but may also end at any time.

The license granted by the Minister and the sufferance granted by the chief function in very different ways. Under the Canadian system, the Minister grants a license so that the recipient may accomplish some worthwhile, legitimate task. Under the Eskasoni system, the chief takes less interest in the worth of non-band member's goals than in his or her behavior while in the community. The withdrawal of sufferance is the chief's major means of controlling offensive behavior by outsiders; he may even withdraw his sufferance only partially, still with an eye to controlling behavior (see Legal Cases 74 and 75).

OTHER RIGHTS OF *USUSFRUCTUS*

The Canadian Indian legal principle for other rights of *ususfructus* is that band members may use unallotted reserve land only in common, and not individually (*Joe et al. v. Findlay et. al.*, [1980] 109 D.L.R. (3d) 747); that is, an individual band member should compensate the band for his or her use of resources from unallotted sections of the reserve. The *Indian Act* stipulates that a non-band member may lease reserve land with a license from the Minister. The *Indian Act* rule pertaining to lawfully possessed land states that only the lawful possessor may use such land (*Indian Act*, R.S.C. 1985, c. I-5, ss. 20, 58). Natural resources from the reserve may not be taken from the reserve without a license from the Minister (*Indian Act*, R.S.C. 1985, c. I-5, s. 93).

Under the Eskasoni system, the fundamental distinction is between owned land and free land. The only legal principles and rule that apply are Band Council Legal Principle 2 (giving right of ownership against the Band Council), Band Council Legal Principle 7 (prohibiting woodcutting that defaces easily observed parts of the reserve), and Band Council Real Property Rule 5 (preventing the Band Council from expropriating interests in real property from band members). Otherwise, individuals and groups face no legal impediments to the unencumbered use of free land. Most Eskasoni people regard as absurd the notion that an individual should compensate the band as a whole for the use of the reserve's resources. Land that is owned, however, may be only used by permission of the owner; on the other hand, the owner has only the option of self-help to prevent another from using his or her land or the natural resources on it. Theft is corrected by self-help and ostracism. Under Eskasoni law, only those who have the right to own land on the reserve also have the right to remove resources from the reserve.

Expropriation

Under Canadian Indian law, the Crown may expropriate any interest that Indians have in reserve land, if the Indians are compensated (*Indian Act*, R.S.C. 1985, c. I-5, s. 35). If an individual or group lawfully possesses the land, then the lawful possessors receive the compensation; if not, then the band as a whole receives the compensation. Further, by authorization of Section 23 of the *Indian Act*, the Minister may compensate any Indian for improvements he or she may have made on land from which he or she has been removed.

The Band Council, of course, has no control over the Crown's actions. It may not expropriate interests in lawfully possessed land, a right reserved for the Crown; however, the Band Council may recommend that the Crown expropriate certain lawfully possessed lands. For unpossessed land (possessed by the band as a whole), the Band Council, within certain limitations, may do as it pleases under Canadian Indian law.

Eskasoni law, on the other hand, relies on the distinction between land that is owned by an individual and free land. Until 1987, the Band Council never expropriated any land in which a private party held an interest. However, this legal principle changed with Legal Case 96, in which the Band Council established its right to expropriate *unbuilt* land for the development of housing. In 2006, the Band Council began to expropriate "party houses" from their owners. In no cases does the Band Council pay compensation for the interests it expropriates. It will, however, purchase lawfully possessed interests.

The Band Council for several years upholds interests in land that the Canadian Indian law does not; namely, the right of ownership free from the threat of expropriation. Subject to Band Council Legal Principle 19, the vast majority of houses remain free from the threat of possibility of expropriation. Subject to Band Council Legal Principle 19, the vast majority of houses remain free from the threat of possibility of expropriation.

Legal Change

Most significant is that the two legal systems both changed during the same period, though in radically different ways. The Canadian Indian system has changed to allow Indians, both individually and together in bands, more and greater rights in land, both on and off reserves. This has resulted mainly from changes in the national political climate. The Eskasoni system, in contrast, has changed primarily to allow the residents of the reserve greater ability to improve territorial integrity, territorial defense, and social segmentation.

The tremendous difference in the ways that the legal systems have changed points out the extent of their independence and difference in function.

Conclusion

The Canadian Indian and Eskasoni Band Council land tenure systems both apply to the people of Eskasoni, although their legal principles and rules differ radically. The two systems contrast most fundamentally in the scope of powers held by their respective legal authorities. Under the Canadian Indian system, derived essentially from British common law, alienable rights are created according to legal principles and rules, and disputes over these rights are regulated by an authority.

The Eskasoni system of land use, including the land tenure system, shares some philosophical precepts with the traditional land use system. The traditional land use system was not in the least a legal system, but rather one that depended on self-help resolution of disputes and the observation of behavioral ideals. The system of land use first relied partially on legal means when the Band Council was instituted. The Band Council is a legal authority that has political interests in the use of land. It regulates its own use of land legally, and in a way that generally conforms to band members' standards of just behavior, both out of political self-interest. It generally avoids deciding disputes between two or more private band members, allowing them the opportunity to settle their own grievances. The Canadian Indian land tenure system does not often accord with Micmac ideals of justice, and it is simply a matter of fortunate happenstance when it does. Moreover, the Canadian Indian land tenure system has neither anticipated nor responded to the needs of the Micmac as they settled, as have the Eskasoni Band Council and family/descent group land tenure systems.

Globalization and Modernity Theory

A current fashion in anthropology, and the biggest bugbear, is a study of globalization and modernity. This theory examines various sorts of transnational forces and their effects on "local" societies throughout the world. The field consists, by and large, of studies describing a gloomy future of increasingly uniform global culture and decreasingly unique "local" cultures. So devastating is this process that globalization and modernity are usually reified, as many have argued because of the danger they present to smaller "local" and, particularly, non-Western cultures (Tsing 2000:353). In sum, this theory is another version of the old "social forces" theory (although, to his credit, Appadurai [1996a, 1996b, 2001] represents something of an exception to this generalization). It is generally the "modern" Western cultures that are portrayed as dominating non-Western cultures, leading them to become more like Western cultures. As Appadurai (2001:199) put it, "in such a theory, it is unlikely that there will be anything mere about the local." Mbembe (2001:43) sees the future as one of a "destruction of social entities or their forced incorporation into larger configurations."

Although this book treats as its central subject the effect of the world economy, society, and their political and legal influences on a Canadian Indian people, it does not reach the same conclusions as do the popular modernization and globalization studies. The problem is that the data on the Micmac land tenure system conflict with the idea that all culture is everywhere becoming global. In fact, the Eskasoni data indicate just the opposite—that the only time that Western land tenure prevailed was during the short period (from 1942 to 1978) that the Canadian federal government imposed an authority (the Indian Agent) who could be physically present seven days a week on the reserve. Although the Indian Agent applied federal law exclusively throughout that period, as soon as he left the law became completely different. Moreover, the Canadian federal government continues to apply Canadian federal law on the reserve, which the Eskasoni people vigorously resist. Certainly, federal law bears the stamp of "modernity." The question is why the Micmac persist not only in keeping their own legal system, but improving on it with innovation after innovation.

The answer, I think, has to do with the kinds of globalization and modernity studies done so far. Most of these have looked primarily at superficial parts of culture, in an attempt to describe how and where they have moved. By and large, these studies have been quite successful and well done.

What has been largely missing is a scientific, that is to say systematic, treatment of culture as a whole. Culture is not an indivisible monolith, and different parts react differently to different influences. Looking only at the superficial aspects of Micmac culture, such as housing, clothing, music, and the arts, we can see that everywhere these have become remarkably Western. This is why the study by Inglehart and Baker (2000), which looks at basic values, has come to such a different conclusion. In this study the authors found that basic values are everywhere persisting very nicely, despite the assault by Western culture. The authors, unfortunately, have little to say that is convincing about why values survive while other parts of the culture change.

I submit that the same is true for law. While increasingly law at the national level is in fact looking everywhere the same, law in the small towns and villages is not. The anthropological and legal studies presented in the *Journal of Legal Pluralism and Unofficial Law* show this quite nicely. Moore (1998) provides an excellent study describing in detail just how the decision made by a local *panchayat* in India had legal and social effect, despite its great difference from principles upheld by national law. And even writers at *Time* magazine see regions of "locality" in the world system today; writer Michael Elliott (2003:29) began a story on the war in Iraq with: "In Southern Iraq, local tribal leaders have sorted out property disputes and murder cases for centuries without the help of police and courts."

Values and laws resist the attacks of fashion, globalization, and modernity, because they both frame understanding of, and help to solve, important problems. Simply put, Western, or indeed any foreign solution, does not always resolve the important problems. Take for example the federal introduction of lawful possession;

this was an attempt to solve any and all real property disputes. Instead, the Eskasoni Micmac find that it promotes immorality and resist it. And they resist it not out of any self-conscious desire to resist the forces of globalization, but simply because it creates problems rather than solves them.

The problem-solving nature of law brings up yet another criticism of globalization and modernity theory, that they are nothing more than diffusionism in another guise in many, though not all, respects. And diffusionism, whether in its original form, or in its current guise as theories of modernity and globalization, rests on the premise that humanity is essentially uninventive (Ember and Ember 1996:36). Having seen over 29 years the tremendous ingenuity of the Eskasoni Micmac in using their legal system to solve problems, I can only characterize them as essentially creative.

Resistance and Identity Theory

A current trend in anthropological and popular writings on the aboriginal peoples of North America deals with the topics of "ethnicity," "identity," "resistance," "cultural survival," and similar terms. While there is much of explanatory value to these works, to my mind the overall approach has serious shortcomings.

Works of this class usually claim that the aboriginal peoples, by retaining their "ethnicity" and "cultural identity," are still manifestly Indian, and therefore remain culturally and socially distinct from the greater North American mainstream. Those using the "resistance" model of Indian against non-Indian relations generally oppose assimilation and acculturation both as desirable goal and as an understanding of what actually occurs in modern Indian societies. They substitute instead the "resistance" model of Indian–non-Indian interaction. This model portrays the Indian reaction to non-Indian behavior as one of resistance to cultural assimilation and political interests. What is interesting about this is that resistance to cultural assimilation is bound up with political resistance, as if the two were part of the same phenomenon. They are in fact decidedly different. North American Indians have become tremendously more successful in the pursuit of their political goals in the past few decades, while at the same time losing traditional culture.

But by focusing on this issue, the studies stressing Indian ethnicity, identity, cultural survival, and cultural resistance tend to portray Indian cultural change as occurring along a bipolar axis, with traditional culture at one end and European American culture at the other.

This approach carries with it some built-in limitations, all of which derive from the narrow focus of the studies. To my mind they lack an understanding of the various problems that the subjects of the study feel are important. The problems of resistance, ethnicity, and identity are important, to be sure, but hardly the kinds of concerns that occupy the day-to-day attentions of the people, despite what the popular media may say.

It is on these daily problems, moreover, that people expend their greatest efforts and intelligence. And it is concerning this that I express my second reservation about some recent studies. These many studies, with their emphasis on a bipolar theory of culture change, do not take into account the remarkable innovations North American Indians use to solve the mundane problems they face. This is more than a simply academic matter in understanding another people, or society and culture generally. By ignoring innovation, we ignore a large part of a people's humanity, for what is ultimately more human than the ability to create novel ideas and solutions?

The Scale of Legal Change in Small Societies (and Otherwise)

It has long been uncritically accepted that the law of small non-Western societies is traditional and largely unchanging, especially as compared with Western law, which is supposedly dynamic in comparison (see, for example, Renteln and Dundes 1995). On the other hand Pospisil (1971:230) has noted that legal innovation in small societies may be more common than previously realized. Rodman (1985:620, 622) concurs and adds that such innovations may be substantial, according to data he collected in Vanuatu. My data on the Micmac support the contentions of Pospisil and Rodman; the chapter on legal change is the longest chapter on the subject of law in this volume.

I suggest further that legal innovation may be even more common and extensive in small societies than in large state societies. In large state societies, decades or centuries of accumulated customary law and precedent, on which authorities rely in making decisions, inhibit significant legal innovation. While it is true that modern state societies may use hundreds and even thousands of people whose only job it is to write new statutes and decide laws, major changes in the law take place rarely. Certainly, changes as great as the changing of the government's right to acquire ownership of used housing (see Legal Case 95) and creation of the right of the government to expropriate private property for non-contractual reasons (see Legal Case 96) come along but rarely. Yet, both of these changes occurred within two years in a society of only 2,000 people. Likewise, the transition from a wholly individualistic ownership system to one that incorporates communal and group ownership represents a tremendous change in the philosophical underpinnings of the legal system.

Most impressive here has been the constant effort to change ownership rights rather than deal with expenditure issues directly. This indicates nothing more than the willingness of the leadership to use land tenure to further their own political careers. With the Band Council owner of all houses, everyone now can be thankful to the Band Council for the roof over their heads. The procedure is to draft ever stricter rules and then give supporters special, secret exemptions in return for political support. The close relationship between law and politics is clear here. This results in a three class system of land tenure that depends on political privilege. The personality principal of law has become more important over the years. Certainly this example of legal evolution does not fit any classical theories of which I am aware.

Not only do small societies not often bear the burden of a large accumulation of recorded precedents spanning long periods on which legal authorities may rely, but they also do not have a judiciary well insulated from purely political personal motivations. For example, the Eskasoni Band Council has repeatedly attempted to gain control over old housing stock, each time forgetting that this cannot be done, because Family Home Territories control housing and social environments (see Legal Case 110 and the following cases). In many small societies, as with the Micmac, the political authorities and the legal authorities are the same people. When this combination of power in the hands of one person or a few people occurs in large societies, legal change may also occur rapidly, as it did in Germany under Hitler, in the Soviet Union under Lenin and Stalin, in Singapore under Lee Kwan Yew, in China under Mao, and in Cambodia under Pol Pot (I certainly do not intend to indicate any likeness between Micmac leaders and these historical figures beyond the rapidity of the legal change they oversaw). In these instances, the leaders had grand personal political goals and the ability to achieve them because of nearly complete political and legal authority and the subordination of the legal system to their personal political goals.

As important to legal dynamism as few precedents and powerful authority are, a willingness to experiment is crucial. In this regard, the Eskasoni Band Council has shown a terrific willingness to cast aside policies that have not succeeded in favor of trying new ones. The specific conditions promoting this rapid legal change can be seen in the example of the "new rules." The judiciary is relatively weak and beholden to political interests, and thus dependent on popular support to help formulate and carry out its policies. It therefore rather easily adopts new policies that group members request — all the changes that the Band Council makes are in response to popular requests, usually from people who feel that they themselves can personally benefit from the new laws, particularly laws that deprive some of ownership rights in favor of others. On the other hand, there are a great many people who favor the status quo and do not want to lose their previous rights. The result is that laws frequently change, and sometimes change again back to their original state because of this seesaw political battle. In a changing environment, such a program cannot help but favor adaptability, even if the cost is short-term social and political turmoil. The Eskasoni legal system very efficiently adjusts to changes in conditions and the desires and needs of the people. Unlike Western state societies, there are no statutes or laws whose origins people cannot remember.

Territoriality

Dyson-Hudson and others (especially Cashdan 1983) have cast the question of territorial behavior in terms of defense of resources, because of the desire to retain possession of the resources to be found on such territories (Bishop [in Cashdan

1983:57], on the other hand, argues that aggressive behavior in defense of territory really defends ritual knowledge and wives, rather than subsistence resources). Dyson-Hudson and Smith (1978:36) wrote: "In our view, territoriality is a subset of resource-defense strategies, and resource defense is in turn an aspect of subsistence strategies." This seems to be the prevailing idea within anthropology today.

Plainly, Dyson-Hudson and Smith (1978) write of mobile foragers, pastoralists, and horticulturalists still engaged in acquiring food using traditional technologies. They discuss territorial behavior that results from disputes over usufructary rights to resources in different places.

The Micmac data suggest that once people settle and largely divorce themselves from the traditional food quest, other territorial issues not directly related to material needs can come to the fore. First among these is the system of territorial defense against individual disputants, in which individuals and groups defend territorial boundaries against enemies. Thus, unlike the traditional systems Dyson-Hudson and Smith treat, it is not land itself that the disputants defend nor, with the exception of living space, the disposition of marital houses following divorce/separation, and the "party houses" of single people, all of which are unusual, the resources on them, but rather the boundaries of the territory and thus the safety of the people who live there. Second, the Micmac system also preserves the peace by keeping individuals and groups involved in disputes at a distance from each other, thereby arresting the dispute. Third, this system keeps out foreign individuals who can be troublesome. The family/descent group legal authorities' power rests largely on the personality principal. They can legally only control members of their own families and lineages. Therefore, it makes sense to use the Family Home Territory's boundaries to exclude foreigners, who are less likely to obey their authority, even when in their Family Home Territory. Additionally, people defend reserve section boundaries by making those who were not born there feel like outsiders.

Fourth, the territorial system has become valuable in building the kind of lineage solidarity necessary to acquire significant political power in elections and, therefore most importantly, to acquire material benefits provided by members of the Band Council. For the family/descent group authority to maintain control of family or descent group votes, the latter must usually remain close by; those who live at a distance tend to become independent. The Family Home Territory provides a place for lineage solidarity to emerge and to grow, because it requires three physical dimensions. And, given the permanent nature of modern housing, not just any land will do. Once housing is first established, that place becomes the locus of the Family Home Territory. Other superior, larger sites can and do exist, but these cannot be used because of the permanence of existing housing and the cost of building new housing.

Of course, territorial behavior in defense of usufructary rights to resources remains (see Dispute Case 55), although this is no longer a significant feature of the culture. In short, territoriality was developed and is maintained for other than material reasons. The anthropological discussion of territoriality thus far has focused on the defense of the territory itself. Territoriality as a concept seems to me to include all behavior that has a territorial component; that is, which takes place with reference to some established territorial boundary, as with the territorial principle of law. By discussing only cases in which people defend interests in actual parcels of land, we unnecessarily restrict investigation of human territorial behavior, and therefore our understanding of it.

Most recent work on territory and territoriality has been done in conjunction with globalization and modernity studies. Appadurai (1996a, 1996b, 2001) has made the strongest claims, but he and many others, including Applbaum (2000), Bestor (2001), Collins (2002), Kosansky (2002), and Stoller (2003) repeatedly stress the decreasing importance of territory now and in the future, even to the point of declaring the nation-state form of sociopolitical organization moribund (Appadurai 1996b:158–177). A well-known recent trend in anthropology concerns the idea of cultural globalization, one aspect of which some have called "deterritorialization." Essentially, this simply means that, because of changes in communication and transportation, culture features, capital, and goods now cross international boundaries far more easily than they did in the past. This has given rise to a fear that territorial boundaries no longer mean very much. In fact, Appadurai has gone so far as to claim that the forces of globalization will indeed weaken and perhaps destroy the nation-state (Appadurai 1996a, 1996b:19), a prediction that, thus far at least, seems less and less likely all the time. In my view, what Appadurai and a few others call "deterritorialization" is really nothing more than acculturation with a new face. What they discuss is actually how modern technology has shrunk physical distances even more in terms of cultural change. The forces they describe also affect regions within territories and, further, not all parts of culture are moving to other places (Inglehart and Baker 2000; Esmer 2006; Friedman 2006:457–504).

Appadurai's idea is that with globalization, culture (as well as money and information) spreads across boundaries, meaning that it is difficult to point to any one area of the globe as having a particular culture. He errs in inferring from this that culture is spreading out, forming something of a "global culture," and that sociopolitical territories are weakening or have ceased to exist. The fallacy here is the failure to realize that cultural differences and similarities frequently play no part in forming territorial polities or boundaries. For instance, the United States and Canada, which share very similar cultures, are independent nation-states, whereas within the United States there are many American Indian peoples whose cultures are about as different from those of white or black Americans as can possibly be imagined. Further, boundaries by themselves often mean very little. Not only can one group place boundaries inside the territories of other groups (such as the Distant Early Warning system, or D.E.W. Line), boundaries by themselves do not imply social control of all people within the boundary. To repeat an earlier point, parts of the Middle East and Africa are essentially out of the control of their central governments (Elliott 2003:28). Likewise, parts of the U.S. state of Alaska and the Northwest Territories and the Yukon Territory in Canada remained outside of effective national control until the 1940s or even later. In short, the question of cultural globalization has nothing inherently to do with territories or boundaries.

One of the most important patterns I discovered in Micmac society is that those lineal groups that achieve solidarity using the territorial principle of law succeed politically far more often than those who do not. The principal effect of this application of the law seems to be in creating a geographically homogeneous group, by excluding those people deemed detrimental to group solidarity, and creating a place for the group's members to reside. This territorial group cannot be infiltrated by those who may injure the chain of command within the group.

Furthermore, territoriality creates a solidary group that because of its geographic boundaries maintains status as a group in the eyes of others even after its leaders, the matriarchs and the patriarchs, die. This allows the group to come together around a particular issue under a temporary leader; the group stays together cohesively, and can act as a group from time to time even in the absence of an established leader. Its members are also accorded group status by others in the larger community. With this illusory status as a group, even when its members are greatly divided, individual members of this group are treated as if they are members of a powerful group. Thus, each individual, as a representative of such a territorial group, carries with him or her the political weight of that assumed group. The political advantages of this behavior are obvious. Some such lineages have no legal or other dispute cases rendered in these pages simply because no one would dare challenge them.

This principle can be easily seen in some of the cases already cited. In Dispute Cases 71 and 75 we see the powerful and highly territorial S lineage prevailing over the Band Council. In Political Case 6 the benefactor, who belongs to a powerful and highly territorial lineage, prevails over the band councillor. In Legal Cases 96 and 97 another large and highly territorial lineage prevailed. "Party house" expropriations cannot take place within Family Home Territories. In contrast, we have in Legal Case 99, one case in a series of attempts by the Band Council to take the land of a man who belongs to a dispersed lineage; meanwhile his neighbors, who have access to the same land, are highly territorial and have not been bothered by the Band Council. In Legal Case 100, a man living with his wife and children but with no kin nearby could not stop the Band Council from expropriating land he felt was his. Similarly, in Legal Case 101 several lineages that are dispersed, including one very large one, could not stop the Band Council from expropriating their land. Finally, in Legal Case 102 another dispersed lineage could not stop its land from being taken. Moreover, in cases that pertain to non-land tenure matters outside of the scope of this work in general the pattern is the same. The territorially unified groups succeed far more often than those not territorially unified.

Settlement

Studies of settlement have generally neglected to look at the resulting changes in real property law in favor of studying examining changes to technology and economy and the effects of those changes on political systems. Anthropologists have generally neglected the study of hunter-gatherer settlement in favor of that of pastoralists. They have also expended far greater effort to understand Old World settlement rather than New World settlement.

Most studies of settlement (often called "sedentarization") make two common conclusions. One is that migratory peoples are always forced to settle against their will. The second is that settlement causes social disintegration and cultural decay (or, rarely, benefit).

On the latter, Goldschmidt (1980:58–59) noted that settlement of the Sebei caused an increase in the practice of witchcraft and hostilities between co-wives. Fahim (1980) found that settlement was socially unhealthy for the Nubians. Salzman (1980a, 1980b) discovered that Shah Nawazi settlement caused the "decline of lineage corporateness and solidarity," and the decline of the family authority structure. Draper (1975) learned that settlement caused !Kung women to lose economic power and, thus, political power. Emanuel Marx (1980) and Frantz (1980) did similar studies. Lee (1979) and Kent (1989) show that sedentarization increases violent behavior. Dinero (1997) argues, on the other hand, that settlement has provided women and girls with opportunities unavailable to them in a nomadic lifestyle, and therefore settlement has had some positive effects. Yet other studies stress the process by which settlement provides for further acculturation (for example, Meir and Ben-David 1995). Kent (1995a, 1995b) has argued that a Kalahari Basarwa group has not become less egalitarian as a result of settlement alone, but rather that the accompanying exposure to Western values and economic development programs have led to increased inequalities. Fratkin, Roth, and Nathan (1999) have argued that settlement has negatively affected children's nutritional well-being, and that what benefits settlement has brought have not been equally shared. Other more unusual studies have been Black-Michaud (1986), who found that settlement represented an impermanent state of affairs for a pastoral group, and Ellen (1978), who discovered that Nualu settlement patterns were determined by ecological constraints, as well as cultural concepts and preferences.

No doubt the findings made by these studies bear much truth, but in my view these and others lack accounts of the positive and clever means whereby settling societies adapt to new conditions through innovation. I find this omission somewhat odd, given the human ability to adapt and frequently to prosper in the face of change. These studies treat the subject populations as passive acceptors or rejecters of external influences and not as creative actors with some control over their own fates. Among the Micmac, the development of a territorial system of social control, and change in real property law to accommodate it, represents, to my mind, inspired genius. The system of defense against individuals, the changes in real property law made to protect it, and indeed the entire land tenure system, are novel; they are not traditional, they are certainly not adopted from the Canadian culture, and they did not arise as some combination of the two. The changes in the Micmac land tenure system due to settlement have helped both to keep the society functioning and to preserve extralegal measures as the preferred means of social control. The preference for extralegal means of social control is a traditional part of Micmac culture (see Table 1, Behavioral Corollary E). Yet, as far as I know, other studies of settlement have produced nothing similar, and instead have preferred to focus on social and cultural disruption.

The Introduction of Communalism

It is of some value, I think, to look at the factors accompanying the transition from an economic system that is purely individualistic to one that has, for the first time in living memory, a measure of communalism, that is, group ownership of property. I have identified the following factors in the Eskasoni transition:

1. A scarcity of some important good; in this case, housing.

2. A society in which private parties lack the power to take what they want from other private parties.

3. A government weak enough to be reliant on powerful elements of the larger society; not an autocratic society.

4. A government powerful enough to expropriate property from members of society.

5. A society whose philosophy supports, on moral grounds, the dispossession of the property of the undeserving and its acquisition by the deserving, however these categories are framed. In this case, the undeserving of property are single people who use drugs and alcohol excessively and the deserving are families who do not so misbehave.

The Function of Law

However, in one respect at least, the Micmac have created a legal change more profound than those experienced by the people of Vanuatu, the Kapauku, the Soviets, the communist Chinese, the Khmer Rouge, and the Nazis. Among these political authorities achieved, or attempted to achieve, a new social order, or at least a significant change in the social order. Among the Micmac there have been significant changes in the laws but, more importantly, the function of law itself changed to encourage social disunity and divergence. This change in function has occurred not as an accidental or unintended effect, but as a deliberate measure.

Most of the aforementioned data and analysis pertain to territorial behavior associated with lineage solidarity and Family Home Territories. But the law and legal change made to support the territorial behavior associated with dispute arrest (see Legal Change 3 above) are of great importance as well because they exist to increase social peace by increasing social disunity.

This conclusion contradicts received wisdom about the ultimate function of law. According to several eminent legal theorists, law functions to provide social peace to ultimately achieve social unity and cohesion. Quotations from four of these scholars, Grotius, Pufendorf, Llewellyn, and Hoebel, follow.

According to Hugo Grotius:

> And this tendency to the conservation of society, which we have now expressed in a rude manner, and which tendency is in agreement with the nature of the human intellect, is the source of *jus*, or Natural Law, properly so called. (Whewell 1853:xliv)
>
> In the next place, since it is conformable to Natural Law to observe compacts, (for some mode of obliging themselves was necessary among men, and no other natural mode could be imagined) Civil rights were derived from this source, mutual compact. For those who had joined any community, or put themselves in subjection to any man or men, those either expressly promised, or from the nature of the case must have been understood to promise tacitly, that there would conform to that which either the majority of the community, or those to whom the power was assigned, should determine. (Whewell 1853:xlviii–xlix)
>
> For all the Mother of Right, that is, of Natural Law, is Human Nature; for this would lead us to desire mutual society, even if it were not required for the supply of other wants; and the Mother of Civil Laws, is Obligation by mutual compact; and since mutual compact derives its force from Natural Law, Nature may be said to be the Grandmother of Civil Laws. [The genealogy is, Human Nature: Natural law: Civil Laws.] But Natural Law [which impels us to society] is *reinforced* by Utility, for the author of Nature ordained that we should, as individuals, be weak, and in need of many things to make life comfortable, in order that we might be the more impelled to cling to society. But Utility is the *occasion* of Civil Laws; for the association or subjection by mutual compact, of which we have just spoken (15) was at the first instituted for the sake of some utility. And accordingly, they who prescribe laws for others, in doing this aim, or ought to aim, at some Utility, to be produced to them for whom they legislate. (Whewell 1853:xlix–l).
>
> For as a citizen who violates the Civil Law for the sake of present utility, destroys that institution in which the perpetual utility of himself and his posterity is bound up; so too a people which violates the Laws of Nature and Nations, beats down the bulwark of his own tranquility for future time. And even if no utility were to arise from the observation of Law, it would be a point, not of folly, but of wisdom, to which we feel ourselves drawn by nature. (Whewell 1853:li).

From Samuel von Pufendorf we read the following.

> 7. Thus then man is indeed an animal most bent upon self-preservation, helpless in himself, unable to save himself without the aid of his fellows, highly adapted to promote mutual interests; but on the other hand no less malicious, insolent, and easily provoked, also as able as he is to inflict injury upon another. Whence it follows that, in order to be safe, he must be sociable, that is, must be united with men like himself, and so conduct himself toward them that they may have no good cause to injure him, but rather may be ready to maintain and promote his interests.
>
> 8. The laws then of this sociability, or those which teach how a man should conduct himself, to become a good member of human society, are called natural laws.
>
> 9. So much settled, it is clear that the fundamental natural law is this: that every man must cherish and maintain sociability, so far as in him lies. From this it follows that,

> as he who wishes an end, wishes also the means, without which the end cannot be obtained, all things which necessarily and universally make for that sociability are understood to be ordained by natural law, and all that confuse or destroy it forbidden. The remaining precepts are mere corollaries, so to speak, under this general law, and the natural light given to mankind declares that they are evident. (Pufendorf 1927(2):19)

To restate what Grotius and Pufendorf have said, then, both natural and "civil" laws (actual laws, as opposed to the essentially philosophical and religious natural law) function ultimately to create or maintain societal unity and to prevent societal fragmentation. Karl Llewellyn and E. Adamson Hoebel agree.

> Enough unhealed breaches between members break the group, and tensions, left alone, can build up potential toward explosion.
>
> The bare-bones aspect of this law-job is plain enough: get enough of it done to leave the group still in being as a group. One or another member or faction can be cut down or cut off, and the group be still "the" group; bitterness can seethe; the line of adjustment may prove to be merely that what Big Fist wants, he gets. But if the group stays a group, and neither explodes nor dibbles away into disintegration, the bare-bones survival need is met. (Llewellyn and Hoebel 1941:294)

Thus, we here have several noted legal scholars who assert that law functions ultimately not to safeguard the lives, health, and property of individuals, as may be popularly believed, but to maintain the life, health, and unity of the society.

The Micmac data suggest to me that the changes in real property law represent something unique, or at least not widely reported. It is the only case I know of in which laws have been made to intentionally encourage social disunity. There are in our own culture, of course, laws that neither promote nor reduce social unity. Laws that require the payment of fines for failing to pay a parking meter, for example, fall into this category. There are even laws that encourage disunity unintentionally, whose functions differ from their purposes. The legal repression of independence movements in the colonies of imperial powers seeks to prevent the dissolution of empires, for example, but often ends up encouraging the success of those very independence movements.

But if what Grotius, Pufendorf, Llewellyn, and Hoebel say is true, then we should be able to find no laws that directly and intentionally promote further social disunity. Some might argue that the U.S. Jim Crow laws and the laws to banish Jews and Gypsies from Nazi Germany promoted disunity. This is not the case. Jim Crow laws attempted to prevent the initial unification of two separate and distinct societies. The removal of the Jews and Gypsies was an attempt to increase social unity by removing elements of social heterogeneity. But the Eskasoni Micmac are extremely homogeneous. They are racially and ethnically homogeneous. They speak the same language, hold the same values, worship at the same church, elect the same leaders, intermarry, and so forth. Thus, the Eskasoni example is one of a homogeneous society gravitating toward social disjunction.

What is it that presents such a danger to society that Natural Law—supposedly universal by virtue of having been created by God and knowable by all simply through rational intuitive thought—came about? With the exception of the elements and disease (which law can do little to control), the main danger to people is the depredations of others. Pufendorf discussed this danger at some length in another work (Seidler 1990).

Well-organized groups pose the greatest threat, of course, whether external to the society or an internal subgroup, especially if well armed. The best defense against such a challenge, obviously, lies in a large, well-organized and armed society united in pursuit of the common goal of defense. If a people is plagued by enemies with military might, then a large and well-ordered society that provides its own defense is a means to self-preservation, and in such case a system of laws would have to be created and enforced to achieve an organized society capable of providing for its own defense. Without these laws, of course, squabbles would eventually lead to major social schisms that would destroy the integrity of the society, leaving its members prey to external dangers, to say nothing of civil war. Such is the case for nation-states, as well as for the Cheyenne, who coalesced into a tribe as a result of their proximity to large, powerful enemies, and whose legal system Llewellyn and Hoebel (1941) described.

On the other hand, if a society faces few or no external threats, or faces them only rarely, if its nuclear families and even individuals are technologically and economically self-sufficient, and if the society can fragment or dissolve with no detriment to its members, then there may be no advantage to those in that society to live in dense cooperative groups. In such a social, economic, and military situation, the members of the society might find it more desirable (whether consciously or not) to disperse, and so achieve a degree of social peace with very little litigation, equal to the social peace found in a densely settled society with an effective civil legal system. Once the physical and social conditions for a peaceful life have been met, why are additional laws necessary? Certainly, there are personal freedoms to be had in such a society that those in a society with many laws do not share. This situation of relatively few laws, few legal actions, and relatively great social dispersal and disunity was the Micmac situation until recent decades (although it must be remembered that the Micmac did unite to a degree to oppose external foes in the French and Indian War and the Revolutionary War).

The changes in the Micmac land tenure system disprove the suppositions made by Grotius, Pufendorf, Llewellyn, and Hoebel (and others as well) as universal truths. Their idea that law renders social peace that preserves large groups intact, and so increases the chances of individual human survival, does not hold true for the Eskasoni Micmac. In Eskasoni, law is intended maintain a system of territorial defense that works to disunify society so that social peace may be preserved. For the Eskasoni Micmac, then, social peace assumes the ultimate function of law, standing above that of social unity. The value of a unified and cohesive society varies from one society to another.

Census Data, 1871–1891

The following annotated list of Indians was assembled from the Nova Scotia censuses of 1871, 1881, and 1891 (Public Archives of Canada, Ottawa). A total of 10 data elements are presented and described here: (1) census year; (2) individual identification number; (3) first name; (4) last name; (5) location (town, village, city, or reserve where Indians were found); (6) age (in years unless otherwise noted); (7) education level; (8) housing; (9) occupation; and (10) marital status. Data that were either illegible, unclear, or deemed inaccurate are marked with a question mark. Names of Cape Breton Micmac that could have been reversed (that is, family name switched with personal name) and could not be corrected are noted as "reversed?"

Identification of Indians in the Nova Scotia Census

In these censuses, Indians were distinguished from non-Indians in different ways. In 1871, census takers entered the "origin" (racial and ethnic identification) of each person in a separate column on the census sheet, and all three censuses listed a category of "religion" for religious affiliation (all Micmac, with the exception of one family converted to the Baptist faith, were Roman Catholics at the time). Most of the population of Nova Scotia emigrated to Canada from Scotland and England, and most of these were Anglican and Protestant, though a minority of Scottish descent are Roman Catholics. The only other uniformly Roman Catholic group is of French descent, easily separated from all others by their last names, and because they lived then, as many still do, in small, isolated, and homogeneously French towns and villages, many of which are located in western Cape Breton Island.

A great many Micmac people were easily identified because they almost always lived in groups of several families or more. Furthermore, these groups usually lived in places where they were accustomed to travel, many of which are, and were at that time as well, Indian reserves. Housing type also proved to be an important way to determine Indian identification. Most Micmac at the time lived in wigwams, usually identified in the census as shanties. Nearly all non-Indians of the time, by contrast, lived in houses.

The categories of "trade" and "occupation" in the censuses provided another dependable clue to Indian status. Most of the Indian families of that period earned money by making and selling ash splint baskets. Some Micmac, mostly women, were noted as "basketmakers," and others, mostly men, as "coopers." Indian coopers made barrels for fishermen, who used them to ship their product. Other Indians were labeled "hunters." No non-Indians in the census were described by any of these three terms.

Questions about education and literacy were also helpful. Most Indians were illiterate in the English language, while many, if not most, in the non-Indian population were literate in either English or French. Further, few Indian children attended school (a question asked in 1881), while many non-Indian children did.

Finally, family names provided a good way to identify Indians. Certain names are associated with the Micmac population, though many non-Indians share some of these (see Appendix G).

With all this information used to distinguish Indians from non-Indians in the censuses, it is probable that this appendix is an accurate record of all Micmac Indians found in the Nova Scotia censuses of 1871, 1881, and 1891.

Inaccuracies in the Data

There are many inaccuracies in the census data as collected, most of which cannot now be corrected. The greatest problem is omission of many of the Micmac in Nova Scotia, undoubtedly because the Micmac of the time lived in inaccessible areas where the census takers did not go. Another issue for the census takers was the language barrier. It is doubtful that any census takers knew the Micmac language, and it is likely that few Micmac of the period spoke English fluently. Many Micmac first names were faithfully copied by some census takers ("Sulian" instead of the English William, or "Sutick" instead of Judith). However, others were not quite so careful and apparently put down whatever they thought they heard. Thus, we have "Mickle" instead of "Michael" and "Coko" instead of "Googoo." Sometimes the census takers simply could not spell. A particularly difficult problem is that of reversed first and last names, or the garbling of both. Since many Micmac names can be used as either a first or last name, these issues are not immediately resolvable.

Nevertheless, it was possible to correct some errors. If and when the people whose names were erroneously listed in one census appeared in the next, the earlier censuses could be amended (for example, people in nuclear and extended families could be identified in the later census by first name, age, and by the gender and number of children). Because of the great amount of time that this procedure required, the searching and correction was limited to Cape Breton people; the mainland Nova Scotia data are supplied here essentially as found in the original records. In at least one case, a Micmac family name had come into existence not long before the 1871 census. A man of Scottish origin had been living with a group of Micmac on Cape Breton Island. In the 1871 census, some of his offspring referred to themselves as "Scotchmen," and thus "Scotchman" was recorded as their family name. In fact, these people were known by the family name "Alex," which was the Scotsman's first name (corrected in the 1871 census figures supplied). His descendants today keep this appellation as their legal family name. Several men were identified as "Belonic" in the data, although "Pelonik" is a woman's name.

Ages are also frequently distorted. One would expect a person's age to be recorded as 10 years older in the 1881 census than in the 1871 census, but this was often not the case. It seems either that many Micmac did not pay much attention to chronological age or that the census takers were content to judge ages with their own eyes. (This is still true of many older Nova Scotians today. Most visitors to the Eachdriadh Archives in Sydney, Nova Scotia, seek old church records to determine their own ages, to be able to apply for pensions, and not a few have found, to their regret, that they had been eligible for some years. Since pensioners may only collect from the date of application, money that would have been received by filing earlier cannot be claimed.)

Education and literacy is another category dependent on census methodologies. Many Micmac of the period were literate in the Micmac language, though not so in English.

Only one census taker mentioned this, and it is quite possible that many literate Micmac were described as illiterate. Conversely, those literate in Micmac may have been described as literate, leading the reader of census data to conclude that they were literate in English. On the other hand, the housing data are probably largely valid, with one obvious inconsistency: the residents of the Sydney reserve were shown as having houses in 1881, and shanties (wigwams) in 1891, which seems unlikely.

ID no.	First name	Last name	Age in years	Location
CENSUS DATA FOR 1871				
1	John	Adley	8	Waqamatkuk (Middle River, Cape Breton reserve)
2	Mary	Adley	1	Waqamatkuk (Middle River, Cape Breton reserve)
3	Noel	Adley	42	Waqamatkuk (Middle River, Cape Breton reserve)
4	Peronoel	Adley	8	Waqamatkuk (Middle River, Cape Breton reserve)
5	Sarah	Adley	58	Waqamatkuk (Middle River, Cape Breton reserve)
6	Simon	Adley	12	Waqamatkuk (Middle River, Cape Breton reserve)
7	Susan	Adley	31	Waqamatkuk (Middle River, Cape Breton reserve)
8	Allison	Alex	68	Potlotek
9	Andrew	Alex	16	River Inhabitants (Cape Breton Island)
10	James	Alex	15	River Inhabitants (Cape Breton Island)
11	John	Alex	30	Potlotek
12	Madeline	Alex	13	River Inhabitants (Cape Breton Island)
13	Margret	Alex	16	Potlotek
14	Mary	Alex	38	River Inhabitants (Cape Breton Island)
15	Mary	Alex	59	Potlotek
16	Mary	Alex	16	Potlotek
17	Michaelw	Alex	40	River Inhabitants (Cape Breton Island)
18	Noeljoe	Alex	19	River Inhabitants (Cape Breton Island)
19	Thomas	Alex	41	River Inhabitants (Cape Breton Island)
20	Thomas	Alex	10	River Inhabitants (Cape Breton Island)
21	Andrew	Basque	15	Plaister Cove ('Malakawe:j reserve)
22	Ann	Basque	43	Plaister Cove ('Malakawe:j reserve)
23	Ann	Basque	50	Guysborough Co., Subdistrict: Melford
24	Caroline	Basque	4	Guysborough Co., Subdistrict: Melford
25	Jeff?	Basque	27	Guysborough Co., Subdistrict: Melford
26	Joe	Basque	9	Guysborough Co., Subdistrict: Melford
27	John	Basque	21	Guysborough Co., Subdistrict: Melford
28	Larry	Basque	50	Guysborough Co., Subdistrict: Melford
29	Mary	Basque	18	Guysborough Co., Subdistrict: Melford
30	Mary	Basque	22	Guysborough Co., Subdistrict: Melford
31	Michael	Basque	12	Plaister Cove ('Malakawe:j reserve)
32	Mike	Basque	14	Guysborough Co., Subdistrict: Melford
33	Noel	Basque	?	Guysborough Co., Subdistrict: Melford
34	Noel	Basque	2	Guysborough Co., Subdistrict: Melford
35	Andrew	Battiste	68	Paqtnkek Reserve area
36	Joe	Battiste	57	Antigonish Co., Subdistrict G, Division 2, St. Andrews
37	John	Battiste	21	Paqtnkek Reserve area
38	Noel	Battiste	11	Paqtnkek Reserve area
39	Abraham	Beetle	58	New Glasgow, Division 3, Part 2
40	Jenny	Beetle	33	Pictou Co., Merigomish, Pictou Landing Reserve area
41	Louis	Beetle	2	Pictou Co., Merigomish, Pictou Landing Reserve area
42	Mary	Beetle	8	New Glasgow, Division 3, Part 2
43	Maryann	Beetle	52	New Glasgow, Division 3, Part 2
44	Maryann	Beetle	14	New Glasgow, Division 3, Part 2
46	Sally	Beetle	11	New Glasgow, Division 3, Part 2
47	Andrew	Bernard	21	North Sydney
48	Annmary	Bernard	71	Eskasoni (Cape Breton reserve)
49	Bella	Bernard	7	North Sydney
50	Bridget	Bernard	?	North Sydney
51	C	Bernard	80	Waqamatkuk (Middle River, Cape Breton reserve)
52	Charlot	Bernard	4	Eskasoni (Cape Breton reserve)
53	Christy	Bernard	32	Eskasoni (Cape Breton reserve)
54	Elizabeth	Bernard	4	North Sydney

Education	Housing	Occupation	Marital status	Notes
School	House	?	Single	
?	House	?	Single	
Can read	House	Cooper, fisherman	Married	
?	House	?	Single	
Can read	House	?	Widowed	
School	House	?	Single	
Can read	House	?	Married	
Literate	Shanty or wigwam	Farmer	Married	
?	Shanty or wigwam	Cooper	Single	
?	Shanty or wigwam	?	Single	
Literate	Shanty or wigwam	?	Married	
?	Shanty or wigwam	?	Single	
?	Shanty or wigwam	?	Single	
Illiterate	Shanty or wigwam	?	Married	
Illiterate	Shanty or wigwam	?	Married	
?	Shanty or wigwam	?	Married	
Illiterate	Shanty or wigwam	Cooper	Single	
?	Shanty or wigwam	Cooper	Single	
Illiterate	Shanty or wigwam	Cooper	Married	
?	Shanty or wigwam	?	Single	
?	Shanty or wigwam	Cooper	Single	
Illiterate	Shanty or wigwam	?	Widowed	
Illiterate	Shanty or wigwam	Basketmaker	Married	
?	Shanty or wigwam	?	Single	
Illiterate	Shanty or wigwam	Cooper, fisherman	Married	
?	Shanty or wigwam	?	Single	
Illiterate	Shanty or wigwam	Cooper, fisherman	Married	
Illiterate	Shanty or wigwam	Cooper, fisherman	Married	
Illiterate	Shanty or wigwam	Basketmaker	Married	
Illiterate	Shanty or wigwam	Basketmaker	Married	
?	Shanty or wigwam	?	Single	
?	Shanty or wigwam	?	Single	
?	Shanty or wigwam	?	Single	
?	Shanty or wigwam	?	Single	
Literate	Shanty or wigwam	Cooper	Widowed	
Illiterate	Shanty or wigwam	Cooper, fisherman	Married	
Literate	Shanty or wigwam	?	Single	
?	Shanty or wigwam	?	Single	
Illiterate	Shanty or wigwam	Chief	Married	
Illiterate	Shanty or wigwam	?	Widowed	
?	Shanty or wigwam	?	Single	
?	Shanty or wigwam	?	Single	
Illiterate	Shanty or wigwam	?	Married	
?	Shanty or wigwam	?	Single	
?	Shanty or wigwam	?	Single	
Illiterate	Wigwam	Basketmaker	Married	
Literate	House	?	Single	
?	Wigwam	Basketmaker	Single	
?	Wigwam	?	Single	
Literate	Shanty or wigwam	Cooper, fisherman	Married	Male
?	House	?	Single	
Literate	House	?	Single	
?	Wigwam	Basketmaker	Single	

1871 Census Data • Continued

ID no.	First name	Last name	Age in years	Location
55	Francis	Bernard	70	North Sydney
56	Francis	Bernard	6	North Sydney
57	Gabriel	Bernard	70	Eskasoni (Cape Breton reserve)
58	Harriet	Bernard	22	North Sydney
59	Helen	Bernard	60	North Sydney
60	Helen	Bernard	3	North Sydney
61	Jerome	Bernard	23	North Sydney
62	John	Bernard	9	North Sydney
63	Louisa	Bernard	80	Waqamatkuk (Middle River, Cape Breton reserve)
64	Louisa	Bernard	25	North Sydney
65	Mabel	Bernard	19	North Sydney
66	Mary	Bernard	29	Eskasoni (Cape Breton reserve)
67	Mary	Bernard	28	North Sydney
68	Mary	Bernard	30	North Sydney
69	Mary	Bernard	24	North Sydney
70	Mary	Bernard	19	North Sydney
71	Marya	Bernard	9	North Sydney
72	Michael	Bernard	9	North Sydney
73	Noel	Bernard	27	North Sydney
74	Noel	Bernard	23	North Sydney
75	Noel	Bernard	5	North Sydney
76	Peter	Bernard	12	Waqamatkuk (Middle River, Cape Breton reserve)
77	Stephen	Bernard	26	North Sydney
78	Stephen	Bernard	5	North Sydney
79	Susan	Bernard	8	Waqamatkuk (Middle River, Cape Breton reserve)
80	William	Bernard	39	North Sydney
81	Francis	Chaumabl	28	Cheticam
82	Benjamin	Christmas	7	Eskasoni (Cape Breton reserve)
83	Cecily	Christmas	27	Eskasoni (Cape Breton reserve)
84	Elizabeth	Christmas	2	Eskasoni (Cape Breton reserve)
85	Flora	Christmas	5	Eskasoni (Cape Breton reserve)
86	Hubert	Christmas	12	Eskasoni (Cape Breton reserve)
87	Jane	Christmas	20	Eskasoni (Cape Breton reserve)
88	Joanna	Christmas	3	Eskasoni (Cape Breton reserve)
89	John	Christmas	30	Eskasoni (Cape Breton reserve)
90	Joseph	Christmas	27	Eskasoni (Cape Breton reserve)
91	Joseph	Christmas	14	Eskasoni (Cape Breton reserve)
92	Judith	Christmas	64	Eskasoni (Cape Breton reserve)
93	Mary	Christmas	17	Eskasoni (Cape Breton reserve)
95	Maryann	Christmas	16	Eskasoni (Cape Breton reserve)
96	Michael	Christmas	38	Eskasoni (Cape Breton reserve)
97	NuelL	Christmas	2	Eskasoni (Cape Breton reserve)
98	Pall	Christmas	24	Eskasoni (Cape Breton reserve)
99	Pall	Christmas	10	Eskasoni (Cape Breton reserve)
100	Pall	Christmas	67	Eskasoni (Cape Breton reserve)
101	Peter	Christmas	?	Eskasoni (Cape Breton reserve)
102	Stephen	Christmas	?	Eskasoni (Cape Breton reserve)
103	Susan	Christmas	1	Eskasoni (Cape Breton reserve)
104	Suttie	Christmas	34	Eskasoni (Cape Breton reserve)
105	Theresa	Christmas	27	Eskasoni (Cape Breton reserve)
106	Alvin	Cremo	1	Potlotek
107	Andrew	Cremo	16	Potlotek
108	Bella	Cremo	3	Waqamatkuk (Middle River, Cape Breton reserve)
109	Betsy	Cremo	11	Waqamatkuk (Middle River, Cape Breton reserve)

Education	Housing	Occupation	Marital status	Notes
Illiterate	Wigwam	Basketmaker	Married	
?	Wigwam	Basketmaker	Single	
Literate	House	Farmer, cooper	Married	
Illiterate	Wigwam	Basketmaker	Married	
Illiterate	Wigwam	Basketmaker	Married	
?	Wigwam	Basketmaker	Single	
Illiterate	Wigwam	Basketmaker	Married	
?	Wigwam	?	Single	
Literate	Shanty or wigwam	?	Married	
Illiterate	Wigwam	Basketmaker	Married	
?	Wigwam	Basketmaker	Married	
Literate	House	?	Single	
Illiterate	Wigwam	Basketmaker	Widowed	
Literate	Wigwam	Basketmaker	Married	
Illiterate	Wigwam	Basketmaker	Married	
?	Wigwam	Basketmaker	Single	
?	Wigwam	Basketmaker	Single	
?	Wigwam	Basketmaker	Single	
Illiterate	Wigwam	Basketmaker	Married	
Illiterate	Wigwam	Basketmaker	Married	
?	Wigwam	Basketmaker	Single	
Illiterate	Shanty or wigwam	?	Single	
Literate	Wigwam	Basketmaker	Single	
?	Wigwam	Basketmaker	Single	
?	House	?	Single	
Illiterate	Wigwam	Basketmaker	Married	
Illiterate	House	Pecheur	?	Born Nova Scotia
?	Shanty or wigwam	?	Single	
Illiterate	House	?	Married	
?	Shanty or wigwam	?	Single	
?	Shanty or wigwam	?	Single	
?	Shanty or wigwam	?	Single	
?	House	?	Married	
?	House	?	Single	
Illiterate	House	Farmer, cooper	Married	
Can read	House	Farmer, cooper	Married	
?	Shanty or wigwam	?	Single	
Can read	House	?	Married	
?	Shanty or wigwam	?	Single	
?	Shanty or wigwam	?	Single	
Can read	Shanty or wigwam	Farmer, cooper	Married	
?	Shanty or wigwam	?	Single	
Literate	Shanty or wigwam	Farmer, cooper	Married	
?	Shanty or wigwam	?	Single	
Literate	House	Farmer	Married	Born New Brunswick
?	Shanty or wigwam	?	Single	
?	House	?	Single	
?	House	?	Single	
Can read	Shanty or wigwam	?	Single	Born Prince Edward Island
Literate	Shanty or wigwam	Farmer, cooper	Married	
?	Shanty or wigwam	?	Single	
?	Shanty or wigwam	?	Single	
?	Shanty or wigwam	?	Single	
?	Shanty or wigwam	?	Single	

1871 Census Data • Continued

ID no.	First name	Last name	Age in years	Location
110	Cathy	Cremo	6	Waqamatkuk (Middle River, Cape Breton reserve)
111	Elizabeth	Cremo	9	Potlotek
112	Francis	Cremo	?	Waqamatkuk (Middle River, Cape Breton reserve)
113	Hanna	Cremo	40	Potlotek
114	Hanna	Cremo	4	Potlotek
115	Harriet	Cremo	6	Potlotek
116	Isidor	Cremo	5	Waqamatkuk (Middle River, Cape Breton reserve)
117	Moses	Cremo	4	Waqamatkuk (Middle River, Cape Breton reserve)
118	Nancy	Cremo	7	Waqamatkuk (Middle River, Cape Breton reserve)
119	Noel	Cremo	34	Waqamatkuk (Middle River, Cape Breton reserve)
120	Peter	Cremo	40	Potlotek
121	Pierro	Cremo	32	Waqamatkuk (Middle River, Cape Breton reserve)
122	Steven	Cremo	?	Waqamatkuk (Middle River, Cape Breton reserve)
123	Susan	Cremo	26	Waqamatkuk (Middle River, Cape Breton reserve)
124	Theresa	Cremo	30	Waqamatkuk (Middle River, Cape Breton reserve)
125	Ann	Dennis	24	North Mountain (Cape Breton, 'Malakawe:j reserve)
126	Belonic	Dennis	53	North Mountain (Cape Breton, 'Malakawe:j reserve)
127	Mary	Dennis	19	North Mountain (Cape Breton, 'Malakawe:j reserve)
128	Mike	Dennis	22	North Mountain (Cape Breton, 'Malakawe:j reserve)
129	Andrew	Denny	48	Whycocomagh (Cape Breton reserve)
130	Angelick	Denny	5	Eskasoni (Cape Breton reserve)
131	Ann	Denny	19	Mabou Division 1
132	Eliza	Denny	16	Eskasoni (Cape Breton reserve)
133	Elizabeth	Denny	23	Eskasoni (Cape Breton reserve)
134	Elizabeth	Denny	51	Whycocomagh (Cape Breton reserve)
135	Fanny	Denny	18	Waqamatkuk (Middle River, Cape Breton reserve)
136	Flora	Denny	9	Eskasoni (Cape Breton reserve)
137	Jane	Denny	3	Eskasoni (Cape Breton reserve)
138	Jessie	Denny	19	Whycocomagh (Cape Breton reserve)
139	John	Denny	54	Eskasoni (Cape Breton reserve)
140	John	Denny	29	Eskasoni (Cape Breton reserve)
141	John	Denny	22	Whycocomagh (Cape Breton reserve)
142	John	Denny	24	Mabou Division 1
143	Mary	Denny	1	Eskasoni (Cape Breton reserve)
144	Matthew	Denny	3	Eskasoni (Cape Breton reserve)
146	Msusan	Denny	21	Whycocomagh (Cape Breton reserve)
147	Noel	Denny	31	Eskasoni (Cape Breton reserve)
148	Noel	Denny	32	Whycocomagh (Cape Breton reserve)
149	Pall	Denny	35	Eskasoni (Cape Breton reserve)
150	Peter	Denny	21	Eskasoni (Cape Breton reserve)
151	Peter	Denny	1	Whycocomagh (Cape Breton reserve)
152	Simon	Denny	19	Eskasoni (Cape Breton reserve)
153	Susan	Denny	30	Eskasoni (Cape Breton reserve)
154	Susan	Denny	30	Eskasoni (Cape Breton reserve)
155	Susan	Denny	26	Eskasoni (Cape Breton reserve)
156	Alice	Duce	8	Eskasoni (Cape Breton reserve)
157	Bridget	Duce	45	Eskasoni (Cape Breton reserve)
158	Catharine	Duce	14	Eskasoni (Cape Breton reserve)
159	Lewis	Duce	60	Eskasoni (Cape Breton reserve)
160	Mary	Duce	48	Eskasoni (Cape Breton reserve)
161	Maryann	Duce	5	Eskasoni (Cape Breton reserve)
162	Noel	Duce	50	Eskasoni (Cape Breton reserve)
163	Susan	Duce	16	Eskasoni (Cape Breton reserve)
164	Susan	Duce	66	Eskasoni (Cape Breton reserve)

Education	Housing	Occupation	Marital status	Notes
?	Shanty or wigwam	?	Single	
?	Shanty or wigwam	?	Single	
?	Shanty or wigwam	?	Single	
Literate	Shanty or wigwam	?	Married	
?	Shanty or wigwam	?	Single	
?	Shanty or wigwam	?	Single	
?	Shanty or wigwam	?	Single	Male
?	Shanty or wigwam	?	Single	
?	Shanty or wigwam	?	Single	
Can read	Shanty or wigwam	Cooper, fisherman	Married	
Literate	Shanty or wigwam	Cooper	Married	
Can read	Shanty or wigwam	Cooper, fisherman	Married	Male
?	Shanty or wigwam	?	Single	
Can read	Shanty or wigwam	?	Married	
Can read	Shanty or wigwam	?	Married	
Illiterate	Shanty or wigwam	?	Single	
Illiterate	Shanty or wigwam	Cooper	Widowed	
?	Shanty or wigwam	?	Single	
Illiterate	Shanty or wigwam	Cooper	Single	
Illiterate	Shanty or wigwam	Farmer, cooper	Married	
?	House	?	Single	
?	Shanty or wigwam	?	Married	
School	House	?	Single	
Illiterate	House	?	Married	
Illiterate	Shanty or wigwam	?	Married	
?	House	?	Single	
School	House	?	Single	
?	House	?	Single	
?	Shanty or wigwam	?	Single	
Literate	House	Farmer	Married	
Literate	House	Cooper	Married	
Illiterate	Shanty or wigwam	Farmer, cooper	Single	
Illiterate	Shanty or wigwam	Fisherman, cooper	Married	
?	House	?	Single	
?	House	?	Single	
Illiterate	Shanty or wigwam	?	Single	
Literate	House	Cooper	Married	
Illiterate	Shanty or wigwam	Farmer, cooper	Married	
Can read	House	Cooper	Married	
School	House	Cooper	Single	
?	Shanty or wigwam	?	Single	
?	House	Cooper	Single	
Illiterate	House	?	Married	
Illiterate	House	?	Married	
Can read	House	?	Married	
?	House	?	Single	
Illiterate	House	?	Married	
?	House	?	Single	
Can read	House	Farmer, cooper	Married	
Literate	House	?	Married	
?	House	?	Single	
Can read	House	Cooper	Married	
?	House	?	Single	
Illiterate	House	?	Single	

1871 Census Data • Continued

ID no.	First name	Last name	Age in years	Location
165	Francis	Ducee	60	Eskasoni (Cape Breton reserve)
166	Ann	Ducie	25	Potlotek
167	Esther	Ducie	5	Potlotek
168	Fanny	Ducie	19	Potlotek
169	Joseph	Ducie	31	Potlotek
170	Madlin	Ducie	11	Potlotek
171	Mary	Ducie	3	Potlotek
172	Anne	Francis	44	Waqamatkuk (Middle River, Cape Breton reserve)
173	Betty	Francis	8	New Glasgow, Division 3, Part 1
174	Bridget	Francis	13	Mabou Division 3
175	Christy	Francis	53	Mabou Division 3
176	Duncan	Francis	30	Mabou Division 1
177	Jenny	Francis	57	Pictou Co., District 3
178	Jessy	Francis	66	Waqamatkuk (Middle River, Cape Breton reserve)
179	Joe	Francis	12	New Glasgow, Division 3, Part 1
180	Joe	Francis	69	Waqamatkuk (Middle River, Cape Breton reserve)
181	Joseph	Francis	18	Mabou Division 3
182	Michael	Francis	58	Pictou Co., District 3
183	Paul	Francis	4	New Glasgow, Division 3, Part 1
184	Sally	Franncis	35	Mabou Division 1
185	Ann	Fraser	8	Paqtnkek Reserve area
186	Catharine	Fraser	30	Paqtnkek Reserve area
187	Esther	Fraser	4	Paqtnkek Reserve area
188	Mary	Fraser	2	Paqtnkek Reserve area
189	Mary	Fraser	80	New Glasgow, Division 3, Part 1
190	Michael	Fraser	?	Paqtnkek Reserve area
191	William	Fraser	33	Paqtnkek Reserve area
192	Bridget	Gabriel	28	Eskasoni (Cape Breton reserve)
193	Caroline	Gabriel	2	Pictou Co., West River and Greenhill
194	Grizzi	Gabriel	34	Pictou Co., West River and Greenhill
195	Isabella	Gabriel	30	Sydney District 2 (King's Road reserve 1881/1891)
197	Lewis	Gabriel	40	Eskasoni (Cape Breton reserve)
198	Maryjoe	Gabriel	?	Eskasoni (Cape Breton reserve)
199	Nicholas	Gabriel	36	Sydney District 2 (King's Road reserve 1881/1891)
200	Richard	Gabriel	5	Pictou Co., West River and Greenhill
201	Sally	Gabriel	12	Pictou Co., West River and Greenhill
202	William	Gabriel	38	Pictou Co., West River and Greenhill
203	Andrew	Googoo	15	Whycocomagh (Cape Breton reserve)
204	Ann	Googoo	23	Whycocomagh (Cape Breton reserve)
205	Catharine	Googoo	23	Whycocomagh (Cape Breton reserve)
206	Francis	Googoo	58	Plaister Cove ('Malakawe:j reserve)
207	Francis	Googoo	35	Whycocomagh (Cape Breton reserve)
208	James	Googoo	2	Whycocomagh (Cape Breton reserve)
209	Joe	Googoo	60	Waqamatkuk (Middle River, Cape Breton reserve)
210	Joe	Googoo	?	Waqamatkuk (Middle River, Cape Breton reserve)
211	John	Googoo	26	Waqamatkuk (Middle River, Cape Breton reserve)
212	Joseph	Googoo	58	North Sydney
213	June	Googoo	2	Plaister Cove ('Malakawe:j reserve)
214	Margaret	Googoo	28	Waqamatkuk (Middle River, Cape Breton reserve)
215	Margaret	Googoo	1	Whycocomagh (Cape Breton reserve)
216	Mary	Googoo	18	Plaister Cove ('Malakawe:j reserve)
217	Mary	Googoo	4	Waqamatkuk (Middle River, Cape Breton reserve)
218	Mary	Googoo	9	Whycocomagh (Cape Breton reserve)
219	Maryan	Googoo	26	Waqamatkuk (Middle River, Cape Breton reserve)

Education	Housing	Occupation	Marital status	Notes
Illiterate	House	Fisherman	Widowed	Born Newfoundland
Illiterate	Shanty or wigwam	?	Married	
?	Shanty or wigwam	?	Single	
?	Shanty or wigwam	?	Single	
Literate	Shanty or wigwam	Cooper	Married	
?	Shanty or wigwam	?	Single	
?	Shanty or wigwam	?	Single	
Can read	House	?	Single	
?	Shanty or wigwam	?	Single	
?	Shanty or wigwam	?	Single	
Illiterate	Shanty or wigwam	?	Widowed	Born Prince Edward Island
Illiterate	Shanty or wigwam	Cooper	Married	
Illiterate	Shanty or wigwam	?	Married	
Can read	House	?	Married	
?	Shanty or wigwam	?	Single	
Can read	House	Cooper, fisherman	Married	
?	Shanty or wigwam	Cooper	Single	
Illiterate	Shanty or wigwam	?	Married	
?	Shanty or wigwam	?	Single	
Illiterate	Shanty or wigwam	?	Married	
?	?	?	Single	
Literate	?	?	Married	
?	?	?	Single	
?	?	?	Single	
Illiterate	Shanty or wigwam	?	Widowed	
?	?	?	Single	
Literate	?	Cooper	Married	
Can read	House	?	Married	
?	Shanty or wigwam	?	Single	
Illiterate	Shanty or wigwam	?	Married	Female
Illiterate	Shanty or wigwam	?	Married	
Literate	House	Farmer, cooper	Married	
?	House	?	Single	
Illiterate	Shanty or wigwam	Cooper	Married	
?	Shanty or wigwam	?	Single	
?	Shanty or wigwam	?	Single	
Can read	Shanty or wigwam	Cooper	Married	
?	Shanty or wigwam	?	Single	
Literate	Shanty or wigwam	?	Married	
Illiterate	Shanty or wigwam	?	Married	
Illiterate	Shanty or wigwam	Cooper	Widowed	
Illiterate	Shanty or wigwam	Farmer, cooper	Married	
?	Shanty or wigwam	?	Single	
Can read	Shanty or wigwam	?	Widowed	
?	Shanty or wigwam	?	Single	
Illiterate	Shanty or wigwam	Cooper, fisherman	Married	
Illiterate	Wigwam	Basketmaker	Single	
?	Shanty or wigwam	?	Single	
Can read	Shanty or wigwam	?	Married	
?	Shanty or wigwam	?	Single	
?	Shanty or wigwam	?	Married	
?	Shanty or wigwam	?	Single	
?	Shanty or wigwam	?	Single	
Can read	Shanty or wigwam	?	Married	

1871 Census Data • Continued

ID no.	First name	Last name	Age in years	Location
220	Maryann	Googoo	1	Whycocomagh (Cape Breton reserve)
221	Mclara	Googoo	6	Whycocomagh (Cape Breton reserve)
222	Melizab	Googoo	25	Whycocomagh (Cape Breton reserve)
223	Msusan	Googoo	18	Whycocomagh (Cape Breton reserve)
224	Noel	Googoo	26	Plaister Cove ('Malakawe:j reserve)
225	Noel	Googoo	8	Waqamatkuk (Middle River, Cape Breton reserve)
226	Noname	Googoo	2	Waqamatkuk (Middle River, Cape Breton reserve)
227	Peter	Googoo	27	Waqamatkuk (Middle River, Cape Breton reserve)
228	Peter	Googoo	25	Whycocomagh (Cape Breton reserve)
229	Peter	Googoo	7	Whycocomagh (Cape Breton reserve)
230	Samuel	Googoo	3	Whycocomagh (Cape Breton reserve)
231	Sarah	Googoo	66	Whycocomagh (Cape Breton reserve)
232	Simon	Googoo	42	Whycocomagh (Cape Breton reserve)
233	Steven	Googoo	3	Waqamatkuk (Middle River, Cape Breton reserve)
234	Thomas	Googoo	66	Eskasoni (Cape Breton reserve)
235	Andrew	Gould	12	Eskasoni (Cape Breton reserve)
236	Christy	Gould	40	North Sydney
237	Colchia?	Gould	8	Eskasoni (Cape Breton reserve)
238	Elizabeth	Gould	9	North Sydney
239	Francis	Gould	10	Eskasoni (Cape Breton reserve)
240	Helen	Gould	18	North Sydney
241	John	Gould	34	Eskasoni (Cape Breton reserve)
242	John	Gould	14	North Sydney
243	John	Gould	52	North Sydney
244	Joseph	Gould	6	Eskasoni (Cape Breton reserve)
245	Madaline	Gould	32	Eskasoni (Cape Breton reserve)
246	Maryann	Gould	65	North Sydney
248	Thomas	Gould	10	North Sydney
249	Joseph	Gregui?	60	Eskasoni (Cape Breton reserve)
250	Mary	Gregui?	60	Eskasoni (Cape Breton reserve)
251	Maryan	Gregui?	20	Eskasoni (Cape Breton reserve)
252	Ann	Grigman?	70	Potlotek
253	Noel	Grigman?	34	Potlotek
254	Bell	Gunwa	22	North Mountain (Cape Breton, 'Malakawe:j reserve)
255	Joe	Gunwa	36	North Mountain (Cape Breton, 'Malakawe:j reserve)
256	Marya	Gunwa	19	North Mountain (Cape Breton, 'Malakawe:j reserve)
257	Noel	Gunwa	47	North Mountain (Cape Breton, 'Malakawe:j reserve)
258	Noel	Gunwa	16	North Mountain (Cape Breton, 'Malakawe:j reserve)
259	Francis	Herney	43	Eskasoni (Cape Breton reserve)
260	John	Herney	1	Eskasoni (Cape Breton reserve)
261	John	Herney	42	Eskasoni (Cape Breton reserve)
262	Joseph	Herney	12	Eskasoni (Cape Breton reserve)
263	Madelin	Herney	9	Eskasoni (Cape Breton reserve)
264	Mary	Herney	31	Eskasoni (Cape Breton reserve)
265	Maryann	Herney	11	Eskasoni (Cape Breton reserve)
266	Noel	Herney	18	Eskasoni (Cape Breton reserve)
267	Peter	Herney	36	Eskasoni (Cape Breton reserve)
268	Susan	Herney	35	Eskasoni (Cape Breton reserve)
269	Thomas	Herney	4	Eskasoni (Cape Breton reserve)
270	Madalin	Huddly	22	Pictou Co., District 3
271	Maggie	Huddly	9	Pictou Co., District 3
272	Mary	Huddly	14	Pictou Co., District 3
273	Maryann	Huddly	20	Pictou Co., District 3
274	Nancy	Huddly	24	Pictou Co., District 3

Education	Housing	Occupation	Marital status	Notes
?	Shanty or wigwam	?	Single	
?	Shanty or wigwam	?	Single	
Illiterate	Shanty or wigwam	?	Married	
?	Shanty or wigwam	?	Single	
Illiterate	Shanty or wigwam	Cooper	Married	
?	House	?	Single	
?	Shanty or wigwam	?	Single	Female
Can read	Shanty or wigwam	Cooper, fisherman	Married	
Illiterate	Shanty or wigwam	Farmer, cooper	Married	
?	Shanty or wigwam	?	Single	
?	Shanty or wigwam	?	Single	
Illiterate	Shanty or wigwam	?	Widowed	
Illiterate	Shanty or wigwam	Farmer, cooper	Married	
?	Shanty or wigwam	?	Single	
Can read	Shanty or wigwam	Cooper	Widowed	Born Newfoundland
?	House	?	Single	
Illiterate	Wigwam	Basketmaker	Married	
?	House	?	Single	
?	Wigwam	Basketmaker	Single	
?	House	?	Single	
?	Wigwam	Basketmaker	Single	
Literate	House	Cooper	Married	
?	Wigwam	Basketmaker	Single	
Illiterate	Wigwam	Basketmaker	Married	
?	House	?	Single	
Literate	House	?	Married	
Illiterate	Wigwam	Basketmaker	Widowed	
?	Wigwam	Basketmaker	Single	
Literate	House	Farmer, cooper	Married	
Literate	House	?	Married	
?	House	?	Single	
Illiterate	Shanty or wigwam	?	Widowed	
Literate	Shanty or wigwam	Cooper	Widowed	
Illiterate	Shanty or wigwam	?	Single	
Illiterate	Shanty or wigwam	?	Single	
Illiterate	Shanty or wigwam	?	Single	
Illiterate	Shanty or wigwam	Cooper	Widowed	
Illiterate	Shanty or wigwam	?	Single	
Can read	Shanty or wigwam	Farmer, cooper	Married	
?	Shanty or wigwam	?	Single	
Literate	Shanty or wigwam	Cooper	Widowed	
?	Shanty or wigwam	?	Single	
?	Shanty or wigwam	?	Single	
Literate	Shanty or wigwam	?	Married	Born Newfoundland
?	Shanty or wigwam	?	Single	
?	Shanty or wigwam	Cooper	Single	
Illiterate	Shanty or wigwam	Cooper	Married	
Can read	Shanty or wigwam	?	Married	
?	Shanty or wigwam	?	Single	
Illiterate	Shanty or wigwam	?	Single	
?	Shanty or wigwam	?	Single	
Illiterate	Shanty or wigwam	?	Single	
Illiterate	Shanty or wigwam	?	Single	
Illiterate	Shanty or wigwam	?	Single	

1871 Census Data • Continued

ID no.	First name	Last name	Age in years	Location
275	Peter	Huddly	7	Pictou Co., District 3
276	Sally	Huddly	34	Pictou Co., District 3
277	Ann	James	16	Plaister Cove ('Malakawe:j reserve)
278	Jane	James	23	Waqamatkuk (Middle River, Cape Breton reserve)
279	John	James	22	Waqamatkuk (Middle River, Cape Breton reserve)
280	Mary	James	2	Waqamatkuk (Middle River, Cape Breton reserve)
281	Mary	James	11	Waqamatkuk (Middle River, Cape Breton reserve)
282	Michael	James	24	Plaister Cove ('Malakawe:j reserve)
283	Michael	James	6	Waqamatkuk (Middle River, Cape Breton reserve)
284	Susan	James	20	Plaister Cove ('Malakawe:j reserve)
285	Susan	James	13	Waqamatkuk (Middle River, Cape Breton reserve)
286	Annmary	Joe	25	Division 4, River Inhabitants (Cape Breton reserve)
287	Benjamin	Joe	37	Antigonish Co., Subdistrict G, Division 2, St. Andrews
288	Charles	Joe	4	Antigonish Co., Subdistrict G, Division 2, St. Andrews
289	John	Joe	?	Antigonish Co., Subdistrict G, Division 2, St. Andrews
290	Madeline	Joe	25	Division 4, River Inhabitants (Cape Breton reserve)
291	Mary	Joe	50	Division 4, River Inhabitants (Cape Breton reserve)
292	Maryann	Joe	30	Antigonish Co., Subdistrict G, Division 2, St. Andrews
293	Noel	Joe	29	Division 4, River Inhabitants (Cape Breton reserve)
294	Paul	Joe	55	Division 4, River Inhabitants (Cape Breton reserve)
295	Peter	Joe	15	Antigonish Co., Subdistrict G, Division 2, St. Andrews
296	Sarah	John	6	New Glasgow, Division 3, Part 1
297	Bellin	Julian	10	Plaister Cove ('Malakawe:j reserve)
299	Ciles	Julian	50	Plaister Cove ('Malakawe:j reserve)
300	Elizabeth	Julian	17	Plaister Cove ('Malakawe:j reserve)
301	Mary	Julian	4	Plaister Cove ('Malakawe:j reserve)
302	Maryann	Julian	19	Plaister Cove ('Malakawe:j reserve)
303	Peter	Julian	62	Plaister Cove ('Malakawe:j reserve)
304	William	Julian	8	Plaister Cove ('Malakawe:j reserve)
305	Joe	Lafford	34	Antigonish Co., Antigonish
306	Samuel	Lafford	30	Antigonish Co., Subdistrict G, Division 1, St. Andrews
307	Sarah	Lafford	28	Antigonish Co., Subdistrict G, Division 1, St. Andrews
308	William	Lafford	4	Antigonish Co., Subdistrict G, Division 1, St. Andrews
309	Cicily?	Lewis	17	Potlotek
310	Isabel	Lewis	44	Antigonish Co., Subdistrict G, Division 2, St. Andrews
311	Janet	Lewis	43	Eskasoni (Cape Breton reserve)
312	Michael	Lewis	60	Eskasoni (Cape Breton reserve)
313	Molly	Lewis	8	Eskasoni (Cape Breton reserve)
314	Nancy	Lewis	59	Potlotek
315	Nancy	Lewis	18	Eskasoni (Cape Breton reserve)
316	Noel	Lewis	34	Potlotek
317	Noel	Lewis	?	Eskasoni (Cape Breton reserve)
318	Peter	Lewis	45	Antigonish Co., Subdistrict G, Division 2, St. Andrews
319	Susan	Lewis	26	Potlotek
320	Joseph	Louis	25	North Sydney
321	Annie	Marble	5	New Glasgow, Division 3, Part 2
322	Ellen	Marble	2	Antigonish Co., Subdistrict G, Division 2, St. Andrews
323	Mary	Marble	28	Antigonish Co., Subdistrict G, Division 2, St. Andrews
324	Noel	Marble	3	New Glasgow, Division 3, Part 2
325	Peter	Marble	6	Antigonish Co., Subdistrict G, Division 2, St. Andrews
326	Charles	Marshall	38	Potlotek
327	Charlotte	Marshall	54	Potlotek
328	John	Marshall	19	Potlotek
329	Joseph	Marshall	69	Potlotek

Education	Housing	Occupation	Marital status	Notes
?	Shanty or wigwam	?	Single	
Illiterate	Shanty or wigwam	?	Widowed	
?	Shanty or wigwam	?	Single	
Can read	Shanty or wigwam	?	Married	
Illiterate	Shanty or wigwam	Cooper, fisherman	Married	
?	Shanty or wigwam	?	Single	
?	Shanty or wigwam	?	Single	
Illiterate	Shanty or wigwam	Cooper	Married	
?	Shanty or wigwam	?	Single	
Illiterate	Shanty or wigwam	?	Married	
?	Shanty or wigwam	?	Single	
Illiterate	Wigwam	Basketmaker	Married	
Illiterate	Shanty or wigwam	Cooper	Married	
?	Shanty or wigwam	?	Single	
?	Shanty or wigwam	?	Single	
Illiterate	Wigwam	?	Single	
Illiterate	Wigwam	Basketmaker	Married	
Illiterate	Shanty or wigwam	?	Married	
Illiterate	Wigwam	Cooper	Married	
Illiterate	Wigwam	Cooper	Married	
?	Shanty or wigwam	?	Single	
?	Shanty or wigwam	?	Single	
?	Shanty or wigwam	?	Single	Female
Illiterate	Shanty or wigwam	?	Married	Female
?	Shanty or wigwam	?	Single	
?	Shanty or wigwam	?	Single	
?	Shanty or wigwam	?	Single	
Literate	Shanty or wigwam	Seaman	Married	
?	Shanty or wigwam	?	Single	
Illiterate	Shanty or wigwam	Cooper	Single	
Illiterate	Shanty or wigwam	Cooper	Married	
Illiterate	Shanty or wigwam	?	Married	
?	Shanty or wigwam	?	Single	
?	Shanty or wigwam	?	Single	
Illiterate	Shanty or wigwam	?	Married	
Illiterate	Shanty or wigwam	?	Married	
Illiterate	Shanty or wigwam	boat builder	Married	
?	Shanty or wigwam	?	Single	
Literate	Shanty or wigwam	?	Single	
?	Shanty or wigwam	?	Single	
Literate	Shanty or wigwam	Fisherman	Married	
?	Shanty or wigwam	?	Single	
Illiterate	Shanty or wigwam	Cooper	Married	
Literate	Shanty or wigwam	?	Married	
Illiterate	Wigwam	Basketmaker	Single	
?	Shanty or wigwam	?	Single	
?	Shanty or wigwam	?	Single	
Illiterate	Shanty or wigwam	?	Widowed	
?	Shanty or wigwam	?	Single	
?	Shanty or wigwam	?	Single	
Literate	Shanty or wigwam	Cooper, fisherman	Married	
Literate	Shanty or wigwam	?	Married	
?	Shanty or wigwam	?	Single	
Literate	Shanty or wigwam	Cooper	Married	

1871 Census Data • Continued

ID no.	First name	Last name	Age in years	Location
330	Mary	Marshall	11	Potlotek
331	Maryann	Marshall	26	Potlotek
332	Susan	Marshall	2	Potlotek
333	Thomas	Marshall	?	Potlotek
334	Isabel	Martin	11	Eskasoni (Cape Breton reserve)
335	Mary	Martin	39	Eskasoni (Cape Breton reserve)
336	Nancy	Martin	13	Eskasoni (Cape Breton reserve)
337	Andrew	Michael	28	Eskasoni (Cape Breton reserve)
338	Ann	Michael	67	Eskasoni (Cape Breton reserve)
339	Ann	Michael	23	Eskasoni (Cape Breton reserve)
340	James	Michael	25	Eskasoni (Cape Breton reserve)
341	Joe	Michael	1	Waqamatkuk (Middle River, Cape Breton reserve)
342	John	Michael	85	Eskasoni (Cape Breton reserve)
343	Peter	Michael	2	Eskasoni (Cape Breton reserve)
344	Joe	Molly	38	Waqamatkuk (Middle River, Cape Breton reserve)
345	Julieann	Molly	32	Waqamatkuk (Middle River, Cape Breton reserve)
346	Madelin	Molly	2	Waqamatkuk (Middle River, Cape Breton reserve)
347	Mary	Molly	1	Waqamatkuk (Middle River, Cape Breton reserve)
348	Maryann	Molly	22	Waqamatkuk (Middle River, Cape Breton reserve)
349	Matty	Molly	?	Waqamatkuk (Middle River, Cape Breton reserve)
350	Simon	Molly	26	Waqamatkuk (Middle River, Cape Breton reserve)
351	Christopher	Morris	5	Eskasoni (Cape Breton reserve)
352	Joe	Morris	14	Eskasoni (Cape Breton reserve)
353	Solomon	Morris	12	Eskasoni (Cape Breton reserve)
354	Stephen	Morris	10	Eskasoni (Cape Breton reserve)
355	Andrew	Muse	20	Pictou Co., Mclennan's Mountain
356	Francis	Muse	13	Potlotek
357	Francis	Muse	23	Pictou Co., Mclennan's Mountain
358	Joseph	Muse	61	Potlotek
359	Mary	Muse	2	Potlotek
360	Mary	Muse	25	Pictou Co., Mclennan's Mountain
361	Stephen	Nevin	25	North Sydney
362	Ann	Nicholas	29	Potlotek
363	Ann	Nicholas	28	Eskasoni (Cape Breton reserve)
364	Anthony	Nicholas	17	Big Pond (Cape Breton)
365	Caroline	Nicholas	11	Big Pond (Cape Breton)
366	Esther	Nicholas	44	Big Pond (Cape Breton)
367	Isabell	Nicholas	8	Big Pond (Cape Breton)
368	John	Nicholas	?	Eskasoni (Cape Breton reserve)
369	John	Nicholas	18	New Glasgow, Division 3, Part 1
370	John	Nicholas	30	Pictou Co., Mclennan's Mountain
371	John	Nicholas	89	Eskasoni (Cape Breton reserve)
372	Jonoel	Nicholas	36	Eskasoni (Cape Breton reserve)
373	Joseph	Nicholas	45	Big Pond (Cape Breton)
374	Maryann	Nicholas	?	Potlotek
375	Maryann	Nicholas	14	Big Pond (Cape Breton)
376	Paul	Nicholas	28	Pictou Co., Mclennan's Mountain
377	Peter	Nicholas	31	Potlotek
378	Santana?	Nicholas	78	Eskasoni (Cape Breton reserve)
379	Steven	Nicholas	2	Eskasoni (Cape Breton reserve)
380	Thomas	Nicholas	14	Pictou Co., Mclennan's Mountain
381	Tom	Nicholas	15	New Glasgow, Division 3, Part 1
382	Ann	Noel	30	Pictou Co., District 3
383	Annasl	Noel	2	Pictou Co., District 3

Education	Housing	Occupation	Marital status	Notes
?	Shanty or wigwam	?	Single	
Literate	Shanty or wigwam	?	Married	
?	Shanty or wigwam	?	Single	
?	Shanty or wigwam	?	Single	
?	House	?	Single	
Illiterate	House	Quiltworker	Widowed	
?	House	?	Single	
Can read	House	Cooper	Single	
Can read	House	?	Married	
Can read	House	?	Single	
Can read	House	Cooper	Single	
?	Shanty or wigwam	?	Single	
Can read	House	Farmer, cooper	Married	
?	House	?	Single	
Can read	Shanty or wigwam	Cooper, fisherman	Married	
Can read	Shanty or wigwam	?	Married	
?	Shanty or wigwam	?	Single	
?	Shanty or wigwam	?	Single	
Illiterate	Shanty or wigwam	?	Married	
?	Shanty or wigwam	?	Single	
Can read	Shanty or wigwam	Cooper, fisherman	Married	
?	Shanty or wigwam	?	Single	
?	Shanty or wigwam	Cooper	Single	
?	Shanty or wigwam	?	Single	
?	Shanty or wigwam	?	Single	
Illiterate	Shanty or wigwam	?	Single	
?	Shanty or wigwam	?	Single	
Illiterate	Shanty or wigwam	Cooper	Married	Born Cape Breton
Illiterate	Shanty or wigwam	Cooper	Widowed	
?	Shanty or wigwam	?	Single	
Illiterate	Shanty or wigwam	?	Married	Born Cape Breton
?	Wigwam	Basketmaker	Single	
Literate	Shanty or wigwam	?	Married	
Illiterate	House	?	Single	
?	Shanty or wigwam	?	Single	
?	Shanty or wigwam	?	Single	
Illiterate	Shanty or wigwam	?	Married	
?	Shanty or wigwam	?	Single	
?	House	?	Single	
?	Shanty or wigwam	Cooper	Single	
Illiterate	Shanty or wigwam	Cooper	Single	
Illiterate	House	Cooper	Married	Born New Brunswick
Illiterate	House	Cooper	Married	
Illiterate	Shanty or wigwam	Cooper, fisherman	Married	
?	Shanty or wigwam	?	Single	
?	Shanty or wigwam	?	Single	
Illiterate	Shanty or wigwam	?	Single	
Literate	Shanty or wigwam	Cooper	Married	
Illiterate	House	?	Married	
?	House	?	Single	
?	Shanty or wigwam	?	Single	
?	Shanty or wigwam	?	Single	
Illiterate	Shanty or wigwam	?	Married	
?	Shanty or wigwam	?	Single	

1871 Census Data • Continued

ID no.	First name	Last name	Age in years	Location
384	Catharine	Noel	21	Whycocomagh (Cape Breton reserve)
385	Dennis	Noel	44	North Mountain (Cape Breton, 'Malakawe:j reserve)
386	Edward	Noel	10	Division 4, River Inhabitants (Cape Breton reserve)
387	Ester	Noel	26	Whycocomagh (Cape Breton reserve)
388	Gabriel	Noel	19	Potlotek
389	Hugh	Noel	20	Waqamatkuk (Middle River, Cape Breton reserve)
390	Jacob	Noel	18	Whycocomagh (Cape Breton reserve)
391	James	Noel	26	Plaister Cove ('Malakawe:j reserve)
392	James	Noel	12	Plaister Cove ('Malakawe:j reserve)
393	James	Noel	5	Whycocomagh (Cape Breton reserve)
394	Jessie	Noel	3	Whycocomagh (Cape Breton reserve)
395	Joe	Noel	16	Whycocomagh (Cape Breton reserve)
396	John	Noel	73	Plaister Cove ('Malakawe:j reserve)
397	Julie	Noel	9	Whycocomagh (Cape Breton reserve)
398	Lara	Noel	22	Plaister Cove ('Malakawe:j reserve)
399	Lewis	Noel	70	Potlotek
400	Lewis	Noel	19	Plaister Cove ('Malakawe:j reserve)
401	Madalin	Noel	20	Plaister Cove ('Malakawe:j reserve)
402	Madlin	Noel	?	Whycocomagh (Cape Breton reserve)
403	Madlin	Noel	24	Whycocomagh (Cape Breton reserve)
404	Mary	Noel	35	Division 4, River Inhabitants (Cape Breton reserve)
405	Mary	Noel	9	Division 4, River Inhabitants (Cape Breton reserve)
406	Mary	Noel	7	Whycocomagh (Cape Breton reserve)
407	Mary	Noel	55	Whycocomagh (Cape Breton reserve)
408	Mary	Noel	?	North Sydney
409	Mary	Noel	42	North Mountain (Cape Breton, 'Malakawe:j reserve)
410	Mary	Noel	76	Mabou Division 3
411	Maryann	Noel	50	Potlotek
412	Maryann	Noel	28	North Sydney
413	Maryann	Noel	9	Pictou Co., District 3
414	Merrin	Noel	15	Plaister Cove ('Malakawe:j reserve)
415	Michael	Noel	27	Waqamatkuk (Middle River, Cape Breton reserve)
416	Michael	Noel	36	Whycocomagh (Cape Breton reserve)
417	Michael	Noel	36	Pictou Co., District 3
418	Mitchel	Noel	12	Waqamatkuk (Middle River, Cape Breton reserve)
419	Noel	Noel	16	Potlotek
420	Noel	Noel	33	Plaister Cove ('Malakawe:j reserve)
421	Noel	Noel	6	Whycocomagh (Cape Breton reserve)
422	Noel	Noel	11	Whycocomagh (Cape Breton reserve)
423	Noel	Noel	3	Whycocomagh (Cape Breton reserve)
424	Noname	Noel	8	Plaister Cove ('Malakawe:j reserve)
425	Peter	Noel	1	Plaister Cove ('Malakawe:j reserve)
426	Peter	Noel	4	Division 4, River Inhabitants (Cape Breton reserve)
427	Peter	Noel	66	Whycocomagh (Cape Breton reserve)
428	Peter	Noel	3	North Sydney
429	Peter	Noel	7	Pictou Co., District 3
430	Rose	Noel	50	Plaister Cove ('Malakawe:j reserve)
431	Rose	Noel	76	Plaister Cove ('Malakawe:j reserve)
432	Sarah	Noel	5	Potlotek
433	Sophie	Noel	21	Waqamatkuk (Middle River, Cape Breton reserve)
434	Steven	Noel	24	Plaister Cove ('Malakawe:j reserve)
435	Steven	Noel	?	Plaister Cove ('Malakawe:j reserve)
436	Steven	Noel	4	Pictou Co., District 3
437	Suasn	Noel	5	Waqamatkuk (Middle River, Cape Breton reserve)

Education	Housing	Occupation	Marital status	Notes
Illiterate	Shanty or wigwam	?	Married	
Illiterate	Shanty or wigwam	Cooper	Married	
?	Wigwam	?	Single	
Illiterate	Shanty or wigwam	?	Married	
?	Shanty or wigwam	?	Single	
?	Shanty or wigwam	Cooper	Single	
?	Shanty or wigwam	Cooper	Single	
Illiterate	Shanty or wigwam	Cooper	Single	
?	Shanty or wigwam	?	Single	
?	Shanty or wigwam	?	Single	
?	Shanty or wigwam	?	Single	
?	Shanty or wigwam	?	Single	
Illiterate	Shanty or wigwam	Cooper	Married	
?	Shanty or wigwam	?	Single	
Illiterate	Shanty or wigwam	?	Married	
Literate	Shanty or wigwam	Cooper	Married	
?	Shanty or wigwam	Cooper	Married	
Illiterate	Shanty or wigwam	?	Married	
?	Shanty or wigwam	?	Single	
Illiterate	Shanty or wigwam	?	Single	
Illiterate	Wigwam	Basketmaker	Married	
?	Wigwam	?	Single	
?	Shanty or wigwam	?	Single	
Illiterate	Shanty or wigwam	?	Married	
?	Wigwam	?	Single	
Illiterate	Shanty or wigwam	?	Married	
Illiterate	Shanty or wigwam	?	Widowed	
Literate	Shanty or wigwam	?	Married	
Literate	Wigwam	Basketmaker	Married	
?	Shanty or wigwam	?	Single	
?	Shanty or wigwam	Cooper	Single	Male
Can read	Shanty or wigwam	Cooper, fisherman	Married	
Illiterate	Shanty or wigwam	Farmer, cooper	Married	
Illiterate	Shanty or wigwam	?	Married	
?	Shanty or wigwam	?	Single	
?	Shanty or wigwam	?	Single	
Illiterate	Shanty or wigwam	Cooper	Married	
?	Shanty or wigwam	?	Single	
?	Shanty or wigwam	?	Single	
?	Shanty or wigwam	?	Single	
?	Shanty or wigwam	?	Single	
?	Shanty or wigwam	?	Single	
?	Wigwam	?	Single	
Illiterate	Shanty or wigwam	Farmer, cooper	Married	
?	Wigwam	?	Single	
?	Shanty or wigwam	?	Single	
Illiterate	Shanty or wigwam	?	Married	
Illiterate	Shanty or wigwam	?	Married	
?	Shanty or wigwam	?	Single	
Illiterate	Shanty or wigwam	?	Married	
Illiterate	Shanty or wigwam	Cooper	Single	
?	Shanty or wigwam	?	Single	
?	Shanty or wigwam	?	Single	
?	House	?	Single	

1871 Census Data • Continued

ID no.	First name	Last name	Age in years	Location
438	Susan	Noel	5	Whycocomagh (Cape Breton reserve)
439	Thomas	Noel	48	Division 4, River Inhabitants (Cape Breton reserve)
440	Thomas	Noel	5	Division 4, River Inhabitants (Cape Breton reserve)
441	Victor	Noel	13	Whycocomagh (Cape Breton reserve)
442	William	Noel	76	Plaister Cove ('Malakawe:j reserve)
443	William	Noel	41	Whycocomagh (Cape Breton reserve)
444	William	Noel	27	North Sydney
445	Nancy	Oliver?	20	Potlotek
446	Peter	Oliver?	26	Potlotek
447	Andrew	Paul	48	Potlotek
448	Andrew	Paul	70	Eskasoni (Cape Breton reserve)
449	Ann	Paul	44	Potlotek
450	Annie	Paul	7	New Glasgow, Division 3, Part 1
451	Annie	Paul	17	Pictou Co., Merigomish, Pictou Landing Reserve area
452	Annmary	Paul	7	Pictou Co., District 3
453	Ashley	Paul	4	Pictou Co., District 3
454	Ben	Paul	3	Mabou Division 3
455	Betsy	Paul	36	Mabou Division 3
456	Christie	Paul	25	New Glasgow, Division 3, Part 1
457	Christie	Paul	13	Pictou Co., Merigomish, Pictou Landing Reserve area
458	Dada	Paul	?	Mabou Division 3
459	Elizann	Paul	9	Pictou Co., District 3
460	Ellen	Paul	9	Mabou Division 3
461	Francis	Paul	18	Potlotek
462	Francis	Paul	16	Eskasoni (Cape Breton reserve)
463	Francis	Paul	10	New Glasgow, Division 3, Part 1
464	Francis	Paul	48	Pictou Co., Merigomish, Pictou Landing Reserve area
465	Janet	Paul	7	Pictou Co., Merigomish, Pictou Landing Reserve area
466	Jenny	Paul	28	Pictou Co., District 3
467	John	Paul	30	New Glasgow, Division 3, Part 1
468	Joseph	Paul	82	Potlotek
469	Joseph	Paul	50	Colchester Co., Upper Stewiacke
470	Joseph	Paul	40	Eskasoni (Cape Breton reserve)
471	Labrador	Paul	40	Colchester Co., Upper Stewiacke
472	Louis	Paul	24	New Glasgow, Division 3, Part 1
473	Louis	Paul	17	Mabou Division 3
474	Louisa	Paul	9	New Glasgow, Division 3, Part 1
475	Lusally	Paul	22	Eskasoni (Cape Breton reserve)
476	Madaline	Paul	22	New Glasgow, Division 3, Part 1
477	Madlin	Paul	30	Eskasoni (Cape Breton reserve)
478	Mary	Paul	17	Potlotek
479	Mary	Paul	16	Colchester Co., Upper Stewiacke
480	Mary	Paul	11	New Glasgow, Division 3, Part 1
481	Mary	Paul	16	Pictou Co., District 3
482	Mary	Paul	35	Pictou Co., Merigomish, Pictou Landing Reserve area
483	Maryann	Paul	34	Pictou Co., District 3
484	Maryann	Paul	18	Pictou Co., Merigomish, Pictou Landing Reserve area
485	Mathew	Paul	39	Pictou Co., District 3
486	Michael	Paul	1	Potlotek
487	Michael	Paul	37	Pictou Co., District 3
488	Nancy	Paul	8	Potlotek
489	Noel	Paul	?	Pictou Co., District 3
490	Noel	Paul	22	Pictou Co., Merigomish, Pictou Landing Reserve area
491	Noel	Paul	17	Pictou Co., Merigomish, Pictou Landing Reserve area

Education	Housing	Occupation	Marital status	Notes
?	Shanty or wigwam	?	Single	
Illiterate	Wigwam	Cooper	Married	
?	Wigwam	?	Single	
?	Shanty or wigwam	?	Single	
Illiterate	Shanty or wigwam	Cooper	Married	
Illiterate	Shanty or wigwam	Farmer, cooper	Married	
Illiterate	Wigwam	Basketmaker	Married	
Illiterate	Shanty or wigwam	?	Single	
Illiterate	Shanty or wigwam	Cooper	Married	
Illiterate	Shanty or wigwam	Fisherman	Married	
Can read	House	Farmer, cooper	Widowed	
Illiterate	Shanty or wigwam	?	Married	
?	Shanty or wigwam	?	Single	
?	Shanty or wigwam	?	Single	
?	House	?	Single	
?	House	?	Single	
?	Shanty or wigwam	?	Single	
Illiterate	Shanty or wigwam	?	Married	
Illiterate	Shanty or wigwam	?	Married	
?	Shanty or wigwam	?	Single	
?	Shanty or wigwam	?	Single	
?	House	?	Single	
?	Shanty or wigwam	?	Single	
?	Shanty or wigwam	Fisherman	Married	
?	House	Cooper	Single	
?	Shanty or wigwam	?	Single	
Illiterate	Shanty or wigwam	Cooper, fisherman	Married	
?	Shanty or wigwam	?	Single	
Illiterate	Shanty or wigwam	?	Married	
Illiterate	Shanty or wigwam	Cooper	Married	
Literate	Shanty or wigwam	?	Married	
Illiterate	Shanty or wigwam	Cooper	Married	
Literate	House	Cooper	Married	
Illiterate	Shanty or wigwam	?	Married	
Illiterate	Shanty or wigwam	Cooper	Married	
?	Shanty or wigwam	Cooper	Single	
?	Shanty or wigwam	?	Single	
Literate	House	?	Married	
Illiterate	Shanty or wigwam	?	Married	
Literate	House	?	Married	
?	Shanty or wigwam	?	Married	
?	Shanty or wigwam	?	Single	
?	Shanty or wigwam	?	Single	
?	House	?	Single	
Illiterate	Shanty or wigwam	?	Married	
Illiterate	House	?	Married	
?	Shanty or wigwam	?	Married	
Illiterate	House	Boat builder	Married	
?	Shanty or wigwam	?	Single	
Illiterate	Shanty or wigwam	Laborer	Married	
?	Shanty or wigwam	?	Single	
?	Shanty or wigwam	?	Single	
Illiterate	Shanty or wigwam	Cooper	Married	
?	Shanty or wigwam	?	Single	

1871 Census Data • Continued

ID no.	First name	Last name	Age in years	Location
492	Noel	Paul	2	Pictou Co., Merigomish, Pictou Landing Reserve area
493	Noel	Paul	40	Mabou Division 3
494	Noname	Paul	2	New Glasgow, Division 3, Part 1
495	Noname	Paul	9	Pictou Co., District 3
496	Peter	Paul	60	New Glasgow, Division 3, Part 1
497	Peter	Paul	15	Pictou Co., Merigomish, Pictou Landing Reserve area
498	Richard	Paul	3	Mabou Division 3
499	Sally	Paul	2	Pictou Co., District 3
500	Sally	Paul	51	Pictou Co., Merigomish, Pictou Landing Reserve area
501	Sarah	Paul	10	Potlotek
502	Stephen	Paul	36	Eskasoni (Cape Breton reserve)
503	Sulian	Paul	5	Eskasoni (Cape Breton reserve)
504	Susan	Paul	15	Potlotek
505	William	Paul	12	Mabou Division 3
506	Angelic	Peters	14	Antigonish Co., Subdistrict G, Division 2, St. Andrews
507	Hanah	Peters	?	Antigonish Co., Subdistrict G, Division 2, St. Andrews
508	Joe	Peters	4	New Glasgow, Division 3, Part 1
509	Joseph	Peters	44	Antigonish Co., Subdistrict G, Division 2, St. Andrews
510	Mary	Peters	40	Antigonish Co., Subdistrict G, Division 2, St. Andrews
511	Stephen	Peters	11	Antigonish Co., Subdistrict G, Division 2, St. Andrews
512	Donald	Philip	4	New Glasgow, Division 3, Part 1
513	James	Philip	20	New Glasgow, Division 3, Part 1
514	Joe	Philip	7	New Glasgow, Division 3, Part 1
515	John	Philip	19	New Glasgow, Division 3, Part 1
516	Michael	Philip	60	New Glasgow, Division 3, Part 1
517	Michael	Philip	4	New Glasgow, Division 3, Part 1
518	Sally	Philip	52	New Glasgow, Division 3, Part 1
519	Anne	Philips	27	Cape Breton Co., Howley's Ferry
520	Harriet	Philips	24	Cape Breton Co., Howley's Ferry
521	Joseph	Philips	50	Cape Breton Co., Howley's Ferry
522	Mary	Philips	40	Cape Breton Co., Howley's Ferry
523	Mary	Philips	17	Cape Breton Co., Howley's Ferry
524	Noel	Philips	6	Cape Breton Co., Howley's Ferry
525	Susan	Philips	20	Cape Breton Co., Howley's Ferry
526	Will?	Philips	15	Cape Breton Co., Howley's Ferry
527	Ann	Pictou	8	Paqtnkek Reserve area
528	James	Pictou	16	Paqtnkek Reserve area
529	Mary	Pictou	50	Paqtnkek Reserve area
530	Mary	Pictou	21	Paqtnkek Reserve area
531	Noel	Pictou	28	Paqtnkek Reserve area
532	Sarah	Pictou	24	Paqtnkek Reserve area
533	Alice	Poulette	11	Mabou Division 1
534	Catharine	Poulette	97	Plaister Cove ('Malakawe:j reserve)
535	Catharine	Poulette	9	Waqamatkuk (Middle River, Cape Breton reserve)
536	Christopher	Poulette	19	Waqamatkuk (Middle River, Cape Breton reserve)
537	Cmary	Poulette	76	Waqamatkuk (Middle River, Cape Breton reserve)
538	Edward	Poulette	33	Mabou Division 1
539	Isabel	Poulette	30	Mabou Division 1
540	Jfrancis	Poulette	12	Waqamatkuk (Middle River, Cape Breton reserve)
541	Lisa	Poulette	5	Mabou Division 1
542	Maryann	Poulette	53	Waqamatkuk (Middle River, Cape Breton reserve)
543	Alex	Prosper	3	Paqtnkek Reserve area
544	Angelic	Prosper	36	Mabou Division 3
545	Ann	Prosper	11	Paqtnkek Reserve area

Education	Housing	Occupation	Marital status	Notes
?	Shanty or wigwam	?	Single	
Illiterate	Shanty or wigwam	Cooper	Married	
?	Shanty or wigwam	?	Single	Female
?	Shanty or wigwam	?	Single	Female
Illiterate	Shanty or wigwam	Cooper	Widowed	
?	Shanty or wigwam	?	Single	
?	Shanty or wigwam	?	Single	
?	House	?	Single	
Illiterate	Shanty or wigwam	?	Widowed	
?	Shanty or wigwam	?	Single	
Literate	House	Cooper	Married	
?	House	?	Single	
?	Shanty or wigwam	?	Single	
?	Shanty or wigwam	?	Single	
?	Shanty or wigwam	?	Single	
?	Shanty or wigwam	?	Single	
?	Shanty or wigwam	?	Single	
Illiterate	Shanty or wigwam	Cooper, fisherman	Married	
Illiterate	Shanty or wigwam	?	Married	
?	Shanty or wigwam	?	Single	
?	Shanty or wigwam	?	Single	
Illiterate	Shanty or wigwam	Cooper	Single	
?	Shanty or wigwam	?	Single	
?	Shanty or wigwam	Cooper	Single	
Illiterate	Shanty or wigwam	Cooper	Married	
?	Shanty or wigwam	?	Single	
Illiterate	Shanty or wigwam	?	Married	
Illiterate	House	?	Single	
Illiterate	House	?	Single	
Illiterate	House	?	Married	
Illiterate	House	?	Married	
Illiterate	House	?	Single	
?	House	?	Single	
Illiterate	House	?	Single	
?	House	?	Single	
?	Shanty or wigwam	?	Single	
?	Shanty or wigwam	?	Single	
Literate	Shanty or wigwam	?	Widowed	
Literate	Shanty or wigwam	?	Married	
Literate	Shanty or wigwam	Cooper	Single	
Literate	Shanty or wigwam	?	Single	
?	Shanty or wigwam	?	Single	
Illiterate	Shanty or wigwam	?	Single	
?	Shanty or wigwam	?	Single	
?	Shanty or wigwam	Cooper	Single	
Can read	Shanty or wigwam	?	Single	
Illiterate	Shanty or wigwam	Cooper, fisherman	Married	
Illiterate	Shanty or wigwam	?	Married	Born Newfoundland
?	Shanty or wigwam	?	Single	
?	Shanty or wigwam	?	Single	
Illiterate	Shanty or wigwam	Basketmaker	Widowed	
?	Shanty or wigwam	?	Single	
Illiterate	Shanty or wigwam	?	Widowed	
?	Shanty or wigwam	?	Single	

1871 Census Data • Continued

ID no.	First name	Last name	Age in years	Location
546	Betsie	Prosper	19	Mabou Division 3
547	Bridget	Prosper	9	Paqtnkek Reserve area
548	Catharine	Prosper	11	Paqtnkek Reserve area
549	Charley	Prosper	14	Mabou Division 3
550	Charlot	Prosper	30	Paqtnkek Reserve area
551	Chris	Prosper	12	North Sydney
552	Christie	Prosper	9	Mabou Division 3
553	Christopher	Prosper	53	Paqtnkek Reserve area
554	Elizabeth	Prosper	?	North Sydney
555	Elizabeth	Prosper	21	Mabou Division 3
556	Ellen	Prosper	33	Eskasoni (Cape Breton reserve)
557	Eunice	Prosper	23	Paqtnkek Reserve area
558	Flo	Prosper	23	Paqtnkek Reserve area
559	Gabriel	Prosper	?	Paqtnkek Reserve area
560	Hannah	Prosper	24	Antigonish Co., Antigonish
561	Isabel	Prosper	17	Paqtnkek Reserve area
562	James	Prosper	36	Paqtnkek Reserve area
563	James	Prosper	1	Paqtnkek Reserve area
564	James	Prosper	15	Antigonish Co., Antigonish
565	Jane	Prosper	29	Paqtnkek Reserve area
566	Joanna	Prosper	10	Paqtnkek Reserve area
567	John	Prosper	58	Paqtnkek Reserve area
568	Joseph	Prosper	28	Paqtnkek Reserve area
569	Joseph	Prosper	36	Paqtnkek Reserve area
570	Levi	Prosper	13	Paqtnkek Reserve area
571	Louis	Prosper	9	Mabou Division 3
572	Madelin	Prosper	30	North Sydney
573	Martin	Prosper	27	Paqtnkek Reserve area
574	Mary	Prosper	15	Paqtnkek Reserve area
575	Mary	Prosper	40	Paqtnkek Reserve area
576	Mary	Prosper	8	Paqtnkek Reserve area
577	Mary	Prosper	60	Paqtnkek Reserve area
578	Mary	Prosper	6	North Sydney
579	Mary	Prosper	54	Antigonish Co., Antigonish
580	Mary	Prosper	18	Antigonish Co., Antigonish
581	Maryrose	Prosper	6	Paqtnkek Reserve area
582	Michael	Prosper	20	Paqtnkek Reserve area
583	Nancy	Prosper	18	Paqtnkek Reserve area
584	Noel	Prosper	4	Paqtnkek Reserve area
585	Noel	Prosper	1	Paqtnkek Reserve area
586	Paul	Prosper	44	Eskasoni (Cape Breton reserve)
587	Peter	Prosper	24	Paqtnkek Reserve area
588	Peter	Prosper	12	Eskasoni (Cape Breton reserve)
589	Peter	Prosper	8	Antigonish Co., Antigonish
590	Sarah	Prosper	21	Paqtnkek Reserve area
591	Stephen	Prosper	15	Paqtnkek Reserve area
592	Susan	Prosper	35	Paqtnkek Reserve area
593	Susan	Prosper	24	Mabou Division 3
594	William	Prosper	34	North Sydney
595	Ann	Richard	5	Potlotek
596	Betsy	Richard	19	Waqamatkuk (Middle River, Cape Breton reserve)
597	Catharine	Richard	29	Potlotek
598	John	Richard	48	Waqamatkuk (Middle River, Cape Breton reserve)
599	Julie	Richard	12	Waqamatkuk (Middle River, Cape Breton reserve)

Education	Housing	Occupation	Marital status	Notes
?	Shanty or wigwam	?	Single	
?	Shanty or wigwam	?	Single	
?	Shanty or wigwam	?	Single	
?	Shanty or wigwam	?	Single	
Literate	Shanty or wigwam	?	Single	
?	Wigwam	Basketmaker	Single	Male
?	Shanty or wigwam	?	Single	
Literate	Shanty or wigwam	Cooper	Married	
?	Wigwam	?	Single	
Illiterate	Shanty or wigwam	?	Single	
Illiterate	Shanty or wigwam	?	Married	
Literate	Shanty or wigwam	?	Married	
Literate	Shanty or wigwam	?	Married	Female
?	Shanty or wigwam	?	Single	
Illiterate	Shanty or wigwam	?	Single	
?	Shanty or wigwam	?	Single	
Literate	Shanty or wigwam	Cooper	Married	
?	Shanty or wigwam	?	Single	
?	Shanty or wigwam	?	Single	
Literate	Shanty or wigwam	?	Married	Female
?	Shanty or wigwam	?	Single	
Literate	Shanty or wigwam	Cooper	Widowed	
Literate	Shanty or wigwam	Cooper	Married	
Literate	Shanty or wigwam	Cooper	Married	
?	Shanty or wigwam	?	Single	
?	Shanty or wigwam	?	Single	
Illiterate	Wigwam	Basketmaker	Married	
Literate	Shanty or wigwam	Cooper	Single	
?	Shanty or wigwam	?	Single	
Literate	Shanty or wigwam	?	Widowed	
?	Shanty or wigwam	?	Single	
Literate	Shanty or wigwam	?	Widowed	
?	Wigwam	Basketmaker	Single	
Illiterate	Shanty or wigwam	?	Widowed	
?	Shanty or wigwam	?	Single	
?	Shanty or wigwam	?	Single	
Literate	Shanty or wigwam	?	Single	
?	Shanty or wigwam	?	Single	
?	Shanty or wigwam	?	Single	
?	Shanty or wigwam	?	Single	
Illiterate	Shanty or wigwam	Cooper	Married	
Literate	Shanty or wigwam	Cooper	Single	
?	Shanty or wigwam	?	Single	
?	Shanty or wigwam	?	Single	
Literate	Shanty or wigwam	?	Widowed	
?	Shanty or wigwam	?	Single	
Literate	Shanty or wigwam	?	Married	
Illiterate	Shanty or wigwam	?	Single	
Illiterate	Wigwam	Basketmaker	Married	
?	Shanty or wigwam	?	Single	
?	House	?	Single	
Literate	Shanty or wigwam	?	Married	
Can read	House	Cooper, fisherman	Married	
?	House	?	Single	

1871 Census Data • Continued

ID no.	First name	Last name	Age in years	Location
600	Madlin	Richard	15	Waqamatkuk (Middle River, Cape Breton reserve)
601	Maryann	Richard	27	Waqamatkuk (Middle River, Cape Breton reserve)
602	Peter	Richard	30	Potlotek
603	Sarah	Richard	9	Potlotek
604	Paul	Sappier	60	Pictou Co., District 3
605	Mabel	Selome	22	New Glasgow, Division 3, Part 1
606	Madeline	Selome	43	New Glasgow, Division 3, Part 1
607	Margaret	Selome	12	New Glasgow, Division 3, Part 1
608	Mathew	Selome	51	New Glasgow, Division 3, Part 1
609	Noel	Selome	12	Paqtnkek Reserve area
610	Charlot	Selome?	85	Paqtnkek Reserve area
611	Charlot	Selome?	15	Paqtnkek Reserve area
612	Isabel	Selome?	7	Paqtnkek Reserve area
613	Isabel	Selome?	38	Paqtnkek Reserve area
614	John	Selome?	49	Paqtnkek Reserve area
615	Joseph	Selome?	52	Paqtnkek Reserve area
616	Mary	Selome?	19	Paqtnkek Reserve area
617	Michael	Selome?	8	Paqtnkek Reserve area
618	Noel	Selome?	20	Paqtnkek Reserve area
619	Peter	Sipu	20	Pictou Co., Mclennan's Mountain
620	John	Solomon	64	Sydney District 2 (King's Road reserve 1881/1891)
621	Christopher	Steven	25	Antigonish Co., Subdistrict G, Division 1, St. Andrews
622	Ellen	Steven	17	Antigonish Co., Subdistrict G, Division 1, St. Andrews
623	Ann	Stevens	7	Eskasoni (Cape Breton reserve)
624	Betsy	Stevens	20	Waqamatkuk (Middle River, Cape Breton reserve)
625	John	Stevens	50	Eskasoni (Cape Breton reserve)
626	Joseph	Stevens	1	Eskasoni (Cape Breton reserve)
627	Mary	Stevens	32	Waqamatkuk (Middle River, Cape Breton reserve)
628	Maryann	Stevens	?	Eskasoni (Cape Breton reserve)
629	Pall	Stevens	16	Eskasoni (Cape Breton reserve)
630	Sarah	Stevens	7	Eskasoni (Cape Breton reserve)
631	Tom	Stevens	68	Waqamatkuk (Middle River, Cape Breton reserve)
632	Christopher	Sylliboy	2	Whycocomagh (Cape Breton reserve)
633	Isabell	Sylliboy	24	Whycocomagh (Cape Breton reserve)
634	John	Sylliboy	28	Whycocomagh (Cape Breton reserve)
635	Mary	Sylliboy	28	Whycocomagh (Cape Breton reserve)
636	Maryann	Sylliboy	24	Whycocomagh (Cape Breton reserve)
637	Msusan	Sylliboy	65	Whycocomagh (Cape Breton reserve)
638	Noel	Sylliboy	70	Whycocomagh (Cape Breton reserve)
639	Sophia	Sylliboy	27	Whycocomagh (Cape Breton reserve)
640	Steven	Sylliboy	26	Whycocomagh (Cape Breton reserve)
641	Charlot	Thomas	17	Paqtnkek Reserve area
642	Joanna	Thomas	4	Paqtnkek Reserve area
643	Madelin	Thomas	43	Paqtnkek Reserve area
644	Maryann	Thomas	10	Paqtnkek Reserve area
645	Mattie	Thomas	6	Paqtnkek Reserve area
646	Michael	Thomas	14	Paqtnkek Reserve area
647	Peter	Thomas	50	Paqtnkek Reserve area
648	Francis	Tom	18	New Glasgow, Division 3, Part 1
649	Hanah	Tom	46	New Glasgow, Division 3, Part 1
650	James	Tom	15	New Glasgow, Division 3, Part 1
651	Louis	Tom	4	New Glasgow, Division 3, Part 1
652	Louis	Tom	48	New Glasgow, Division 3, Part 1
653	Maryann	Tom	9	New Glasgow, Division 3, Part 1

Education	Housing	Occupation	Marital status	Notes
?	House	?	Single	
Can read	House	?	Married	
Literate	Shanty or wigwam	Carpenter, fisherman	Married	
?	Shanty or wigwam	?	Single	
Illiterate	Shanty or wigwam	Laborer	Single	
Can read	Shanty or wigwam	?	Single	
Illiterate	Shanty or wigwam	?	Married	
?	Shanty or wigwam	?	Single	
Illiterate	Shanty or wigwam	Hunter	Married	
?	Shanty or wigwam	?	Single	
Literate	Shanty or wigwam	?	Widowed	
?	Shanty or wigwam	?	Single	
?	Shanty or wigwam	?	Single	
Literate	Shanty or wigwam	?	Married	
Literate	Shanty or wigwam	Cooper	Married	
Literate	Shanty or wigwam	Hunter	Widowed	
?	Shanty or wigwam	?	Single	
?	Shanty or wigwam	?	Single	
?	Shanty or wigwam	Cooper	Single	
Illiterate	Shanty or wigwam	Cooper	Single	
Illiterate	Shanty or wigwam	?	Widowed	
Illiterate	Shanty or wigwam	Cooper	Married	reversed?
?	Shanty or wigwam	?	Married	reversed?
?	House	?	Single	
Can read	House	?	Single	
Illiterate	House	Farmer, cooper	Widowed	
?	House	?	Single	
Illiterate	House	?	Single	
?	House	?	Single	
?	House	Farmer	Single	
?	House	?	?	
Illiterate	House	Cooper, fisherman	Widowed	
?	House	?	Single	
Illiterate	House	?	Single	
Illiterate	House	Farmer, cooper	Married	
Illiterate	House	?	Married	
Illiterate	House	?	Single	
Illiterate	House	?	Married	
Illiterate	House	Farmer, cooper	Married	
Illiterate	House	?	Married	
Illiterate	House	Cooper	Married	
?	Shanty or wigwam	?	Single	
?	Shanty or wigwam	?	Single	
Can read	Shanty or wigwam	?	Married	
?	Shanty or wigwam	?	Single	
?	Shanty or wigwam	?	Single	
?	Shanty or wigwam	?	Single	
Can read	Shanty or wigwam	Cooper	Married	
?	Shanty or wigwam	Cooper	Single	
Illiterate	Shanty or wigwam	?	Married	
?	Shanty or wigwam	?	Single	
?	Shanty or wigwam	?	Single	
Illiterate	Shanty or wigwam	Cooper	Married	Born Prince Edward Island
?	Shanty or wigwam	?	Single	

1871 Census Data • Continued

ID no.	First name	Last name	Age in years	Location
654	Michael	Tom	26	New Glasgow, Division 3, Part 1
655	Michael	Tom	24	Pictou Co., District 3
656	Sarah	Tom	18	Pictou Co., District 3
657	Colcite?	Tomah	32	Eskasoni (Cape Breton reserve)
658	Joe	Tomah	28	Eskasoni (Cape Breton reserve)
659	Joe	Tomah	12	Eskasoni (Cape Breton reserve)
660	John	Tomah	70	Eskasoni (Cape Breton reserve)
661	Marie	Tomah	5	Eskasoni (Cape Breton reserve)
662	Mary	Tomah	65	Eskasoni (Cape Breton reserve)
663	Nancy	Tomah	16	Eskasoni (Cape Breton reserve)
664	ABE	Toney	4	Pictou Co., District 3, Cape John
665	Ann	Toney	18	Pictou Co., West River and Greenhill
666	Ann	Toney	3	Pictou Co., District 3, Cape John
667	Bella	Toney	45	Pictou Co., District 3, Cape John
668	James	Toney	47	Pictou Co., West River and Greenhill
669	Joseph	Toney	50	Pictou Co., District 3, Cape John
670	Michael	Toney	19	Pictou Co., District 3, Cape John
671	Nancy	Toney	?	Pictou Co., District 3, Cape John
672	Noel	Toney	25	Pictou Co., District 3, Cape John
673	Peter	Toney	23	Pictou Co., West River and Greenhill
674	Peter	Toney	12	Pictou Co., District 3, Cape John
675	Sally	Toney	15	Pictou Co., District 3, Cape John
676	Sarah	Toney	23	Pictou Co., District 3, Cape John
677	Susan	Toney	24	Pictou Co., West River and Greenhill
678	Elizabeth	Welsh	8	Plaister Cove ('Malakawe:j reserve)
679	Mary	Welsh	27	Plaister Cove ('Malakawe:j reserve)
680	Maryann	Welsh	10	Plaister Cove ('Malakawe:j reserve)
681	Michael	Welsh	41	Plaister Cove ('Malakawe:j reserve)
682	Thomas	Welsh	1	Plaister Cove ('Malakawe:j reserve)
683	Ann	Wilmot	47	Potlotek
684	Francis	Wilmot	56	Potlotek
685	Francis	Wilmot	13	Pictou Co., District 3
686	Hannah	Wilmot	17	Pictou Co., District 3
687	Hannah	Wilmot	10	Pictou Co., District 3
688	Madlin	Wilmot	9	Potlotek
689	Madlin	Wilmot	1	Potlotek
690	Mary	Wilmot	6	Potlotek
691	Maryann	Wilmot	20	Potlotek
692	Maryann	Wilmot	30	New Glasgow, Division 3, Part 1
693	Maryann	Wilmot	28	Pictou Co., District 3
694	Michael	Wilmot	27	Potlotek
695	Napoli	Wilmot	13	Pictou Co., District 3
696	Sally	Wilmot	8	Pictou Co., District 3
697	Stephen	Wilmot	3	Potlotek
698	Thomas	Wilmot	60	New Glasgow, Division 3, Part 1
699	Thomas	Wilmot	55	Pictou Co., District 3

Education	Housing	Occupation	Marital status	Notes
Illiterate	Shanty or wigwam	Cooper	Married	
Illiterate	Shanty or wigwam	Laborer	Married	
Illiterate	Shanty or wigwam	?	Married	
Illiterate	House	?	Widowed	
Illiterate	House	?	Single	
?	House	Quiltworker	Single	
Illiterate	House	Farmer, cooper	Widowed	
?	House	?	Single	
Illiterate	House	Quiltworker	Widowed	
?	House	Quiltworker	Single	
?	Shanty or wigwam	?	Single	
?	Shanty or wigwam	?	Single	
?	Shanty or wigwam	?	Single	
Literate	Shanty or wigwam	?	Married	
Illiterate	Shanty or wigwam	Cooper	Married	
Literate	Shanty or wigwam	Cooper	Married	
?	Shanty or wigwam	Cooper	Single	
?	Shanty or wigwam	?	Single	
Literate	Shanty or wigwam	Cooper	Married	
Illiterate	Shanty or wigwam	Cooper	Single	
?	Shanty or wigwam	?	Single	
?	Shanty or wigwam	?	Single	
Literate	Shanty or wigwam	?	Married	
Illiterate	Shanty or wigwam	?	Married	
?	Shanty or wigwam	?	Single	
Illiterate	Shanty or wigwam	?	Married	
?	Shanty or wigwam	?	Single	
Illiterate	Shanty or wigwam	Cooper	Married	
?	Shanty or wigwam	?	Single	
Illiterate	Shanty or wigwam	?	Married	
Literate	Shanty or wigwam	Farmer	Married	
?	Shanty or wigwam	?	Single	
?	Shanty or wigwam	?	Single	
?	Shanty or wigwam	?	Single	
?	Shanty or wigwam	?	Single	
?	Shanty or wigwam	?	Single	
?	Shanty or wigwam	?	Single	
Literate	Shanty or wigwam	?	Single	
Illiterate	Shanty or wigwam	?	Married	
Illiterate	Shanty or wigwam	?	Married	
Literate	Shanty or wigwam	Farmer	Single	
?	Shanty or wigwam	?	Single	Male
?	Shanty or wigwam	?	Single	
?	Shanty or wigwam	?	Single	
Illiterate	Shanty or wigwam	Cooper	Married	
Illiterate	Shanty or wigwam	?	Married	

1871 Census Data • Continued

ID no.	First name	Last name	Age in years	Location
CENSUS DATA FOR 1881				
1	Andrew	Abram	60	Truro, Millbrook Reserve area
2	Charlot	Abram	9	Truro, Millbrook Reserve area
3	John	Abram	1	Truro, Millbrook Reserve area
4	Joseph	Abram	12	Truro, Millbrook Reserve area
5	Louis	Abram	15	Truro, Millbrook Reserve area
6	Madeline	Abram	44	Truro, Millbrook Reserve area
7	Moses	Abram	18	Truro, Millbrook Reserve area
8	Noel	Abram	25	Truro, Millbrook Reserve area
9	Sarah	Abram	20	Truro, Millbrook Reserve area
10	Benjamin	Adley	8	Waqamatkuk (Middle River, Cape Breton reserve)
11	Jane	Adley	76	Waqamatkuk (Middle River, Cape Breton reserve)
12	John	Adley	11	Pictou Co., Pictou Landing (reserve)
13	Mary	Adley	12	Waqamatkuk (Middle River, Cape Breton reserve)
14	Noel	Adley	56	Waqamatkuk (Middle River, Cape Breton reserve)
15	Peter	Adley	17	Pictou Co., Pictou Landing (reserve)
16	Sally	Adley	65	Pictou Co., Pictou Landing (reserve)
17	Simon	Adley	22	Waqamatkuk (Middle River, Cape Breton reserve)
18	Andrew	Alex	27	Potlotek, Chapel Island (Cape Breton reserve)
19	John	Alex	40	Potlotek, Chapel Island (Cape Breton reserve)
20	Maggie	Alex	9	Potlotek, Chapel Island (Cape Breton reserve)
21	Mary	Alex	49	Potlotek, Chapel Island (Cape Breton reserve)
22	Mary	Alex	26	Potlotek, Chapel Island (Cape Breton reserve)
23	Mary	Alex	7	Potlotek, Chapel Island (Cape Breton reserve)
24	Maryann	Alex	25	Potlotek, Chapel Island (Cape Breton reserve)
25	Maryann	Alex	6	Potlotek, Chapel Island (Cape Breton reserve)
26	Nancy	Alex	1	Potlotek, Chapel Island (Cape Breton reserve)
27	Peter	Alex	3	Potlotek, Chapel Island (Cape Breton reserve)
28	Thomas	Alex	52	Potlotek, Chapel Island (Cape Breton reserve)
29	Agnes	Andrew	8	Eskasoni (Cape Breton reserve)
30	Ann	Andrew	7	Eskasoni (Cape Breton reserve)
31	Flora	Andrew	20	Eskasoni (Cape Breton reserve)
32	Frank	Andrew	22	Eskasoni (Cape Breton reserve)
33	Frank	Andrew	10	Eskasoni (Cape Breton reserve)
34	Joe	Andrew	44	Eskasoni (Cape Breton reserve)
35	Louis	Andrew	52	Eskasoni (Cape Breton reserve)
36	Magdelin	Andrew	50	Eskasoni (Cape Breton reserve)
37	Margaret	Andrew	17	Eskasoni (Cape Breton reserve)
38	Mary	Andrew	44	Eskasoni (Cape Breton reserve)
39	Maryjane	Andrew	4	Eskasoni (Cape Breton reserve)
40	Sarah	Andrew	19	Eskasoni (Cape Breton reserve)
41	Sarah	Andrew	33	Eskasoni (Cape Breton reserve)
42	Stephen	Andrew	42	Eskasoni (Cape Breton reserve)
43	Steven	Andrew	3	Eskasoni (Cape Breton reserve)
44	William	Andrew	16	Eskasoni (Cape Breton reserve)
45	Gabriel	Andrrew	12	Eskasoni (Cape Breton reserve)
46	Andrew	Basque	26	Waqamatkuk (Middle River, Cape Breton reserve)
47	Jessie	Basque	13	Whycocomagh (Cape Breton reserve)
48	Mary	Basque	1 mo	Waqamatkuk (Middle River, Cape Breton reserve)
49	Mary	Basque	42	Waqamatkuk (Middle River, Cape Breton reserve)
50	Michael	Basque	23	Waqamatkuk (Middle River, Cape Breton reserve)
51	Simon	Basque	17	Whycocomagh (Cape Breton reserve)
52	Stevenjo	Basque	28	Waqamatkuk (Middle River, Cape Breton reserve)

Education	Housing	Occupation	Marital status	Notes
?	Shanty or wigwam	Cooper	Married	
?	Shanty or wigwam	?	Single	
?	Shanty or wigwam	?	Single	
?	Shanty or wigwam	?	Single	
?	Shanty or wigwam	?	Single	
?	Shanty or wigwam	?	Married	
?	Shanty or wigwam	Cooper	Single	
?	Shanty or wigwam	Cooper	Married	
?	Shanty or wigwam	?	Married	
?	House	?	Single	
?	House	?	Widowed	
?	Shanty or wigwam	?	Single	
?	House	?	Single	
?	House	Cooper	Widowed	
?	Shanty or wigwam	?	Single	
?	Shanty or wigwam	?	Widowed	
?	House	Cooper	Single	
?	Shanty or wigwam	Cooper	Married	
?	Shanty or wigwam	Farmer, cooper	Married	
?	Shanty or wigwam	?	Single	
?	Shanty or wigwam	?	Married	
?	Shanty or wigwam	?	Married	
?	Shanty or wigwam	?	Single	
?	Shanty or wigwam	?	Married	
?	Shanty or wigwam	?	Single	
?	Shanty or wigwam	?	Single	
?	Shanty or wigwam	?	Single	
?	Shanty or wigwam	Farmer, cooper	Married	
?	Wigwam	?	Single	
?	House	?	Single	
?	Wigwam	?	Married	
?	Wigwam	Cooper	Married	
?	Wigwam	Cooper	Single	
?	Wigwam	Cooper	Married	
?	Wigwam	Cooper	Married	
?	Wigwam	?	Married	
?	Wigwam	?	Single	
?	House	?	Married	
?	House	?	Single	
?	House	?	Single	
?	Wigwam	?	Married	
?	House	Farmer	Married	
?	Wigwam	?	Single	
?	Wigwam	Cooper	Single	
?	Wigwam	Cooper	Single	
?	Shanty or wigwam	Cooper	Married	
?	House	?	Single	
?	Shanty or wigwam	?	Single	
?	Shanty or wigwam	?	Single	
?	Shanty or wigwam	?	Single	
?	House	?	Single	
?	Shanty or wigwam	?	Single	

1881 Census Data • Continued

ID no.	First name	Last name	Age in years	Location
53	Susan	Basque	18	Waqamatkuk (Middle River, Cape Breton reserve)
54	Andrew	Battiste	25	Potlotek, Chapel Island (Cape Breton reserve)
55	Elizabeth	Battiste	19	Potlotek, Chapel Island (Cape Breton reserve)
56	Joseph	Battiste	70	Heatherton (Paqtnkek Reserve Area)
57	Mary	Battiste	61	Heatherton (Paqtnkek Reserve Area)
58	Steven	Battiste	1	Potlotek, Chapel Island (Cape Breton reserve)
59	Janet	Beadle	44	Pictou Co., Pictou Landing (reserve)
60	Louis	Beadle	10	Pictou Co., Pictou Landing (reserve)
61	Moses	Beadle	3	Pictou Co., Pictou Landing (reserve)
62	Paul	Beadle	14	Pictou Co., Pictou Landing (reserve)
63	Peter	Beadle	19	Pictou Co., Pictou Landing (reserve)
64	Annie	Bem?	19	Tracadie (Paqtnkek Reserve Area)
65	Mary	Bem?	43	Tracadie (Paqtnkek Reserve Area)
66	Peter	Bem	22	Tracadie (Paqtnkek Reserve Area)
67	John	Bem?	10	Tracadie (Paqtnkek Reserve Area)
68	Joseph	Bem?	18	Tracadie (Paqtnkek Reserve Area)
69	Mary	Bent	3	Truro, Millbrook Reserve area
70	?	Bernard	1	North Sydney
71	?	Bernard	10	North Sydney
72	Andrew	Bernard	25	Eskasoni (Cape Breton reserve)
73	Andrew	Bernard	36	North Sydney
74	Annmary	Bernard	78	Eskasoni (Cape Breton reserve)
75	Ben	Bernard	1	North Sydney
76	Bridget	Bernard	25	Sydney (King's Road reserve 1881/1891)
77	Bridget	Bernard	11	North Sydney
78	Christy	Bernard	40	Eskasoni (Cape Breton reserve)
79	Christy	Bernard	33	Sydney (King's Road reserve 1881/1891)
80	Ellen	Bernard	16	North Sydney
81	Ellen	Bernard	79	North Sydney
82	Fanny	Bernard	13	Amherst
83	Francis	Bernard	6	Sydney (King's Road reserve 1881/1891)
84	Francis	Bernard	19	North Sydney
85	Francis	Bernard	22	North Sydney
86	Francis	Bernard	8	North Sydney
87	Francis	Bernard	79	North Sydney
88	Gabriel	Bernard	65	Eskasoni (Cape Breton reserve)
89	Gabriel	Bernard	80	Sydney (King's Road reserve 1881/1891)
90	Harriet	Bernard	8	North Sydney
91	Harriet	Bernard	34	North Sydney
92	Helen	Bernard	2 mo	North Sydney
93	Henry	Bernard	36	Sydney (King's Road reserve 1881/1891)
94	Jane	Bernard	3	North Sydney
95	Jane	Bernard	10	North Sydney
96	Jessie	Bernard	3	North Sydney
97	John	Bernard	58	North Sydney
98	Lawrence	Bernard	39	North Sydney
99	Louis	Bernard	40	Sydney (King's Road reserve 1881/1891)
100	Madelin	Bernard	11	North Sydney
101	Madeline	Bernard	1	Eskasoni (Cape Breton reserve)
102	Madeline	Bernard	50	North Sydney
103	Madeline	Bernard	20	North Sydney
104	Magdelin	Bernard	30	Sydney (King's Road reserve 1881/1891)
105	Mary	Bernard	38	Eskasoni (Cape Breton reserve)

Education	Housing	Occupation	Marital status	Notes
?	Shanty or wigwam	?	Married	
?	Shanty or wigwam	Farmer, cooper	Married	
?	Shanty or wigwam	?	Married	
?	House	Cooper, farmer	Married	
?	House	?	Married	
?	Shanty or wigwam	?	Single	
?	Shanty or wigwam	?	Widowed	
?	Shanty or wigwam	?	Single	
?	Shanty or wigwam	?	Single	
?	Shanty or wigwam	?	Single	
?	Shanty or wigwam	?	Single	
?	House	?	Married	
?	House	?	Widowed	
?	House	Hunter	Married	reversed?
?	House	?	Single	
?	House	Hunter	Single	
?	Shanty or wigwam	?	Single	
?	Shanty or wigwam	?	Single	Female
?	Shanty or wigwam	?	Single	Male
?	Shanty or wigwam	Cooper	Married	
?	Shanty or wigwam	Coal trimmer	Married	
?	Shanty or wigwam	?	Married	
?	Shanty or wigwam	?	Single	
?	House	?	Married	
?	Shanty or wigwam	?	Single	
?	Shanty or wigwam	?	Single	
?	House	?	Single	
?	Shanty or wigwam	?	Single	
?	Shanty or wigwam	?	Married	
?	Shanty or wigwam	?	Single	Born New Brunswick
?	House	?	Single	
?	Shanty or wigwam	Coal trimmer	Single	
?	Shanty or wigwam	Cooper	Married	
?	Shanty or wigwam	?	Single	
?	Shanty or wigwam	?	Married	
?	Shanty or wigwam	Cooper	Married	
?	House	Cooper	Married	
?	Shanty or wigwam	?	Single	
?	Shanty or wigwam	?	Married	
?	Shanty or wigwam	?	Single	
?	House	?	Single	
?	Shanty or wigwam	?	Single	
?	Shanty or wigwam	?	Single	
?	Shanty or wigwam	?	Single	
?	Shanty or wigwam	?	Married	
?	Shanty or wigwam	Coal trimmer	Married	
?	House	Cooper	Married	
?	Shanty or wigwam	?	Single	
?	Shanty or wigwam	?	Single	
?	Shanty or wigwam	?	Single	
?	Shanty or wigwam	?	Married	
?	House	?	Married	
?	Shanty or wigwam	?	Single	

1881 Census Data • Continued

ID no.	First name	Last name	Age in years	Location
106	Mary	Bernard	18	Eskasoni (Cape Breton reserve)
107	Mary	Bernard	90	Sydney (King's Road reserve 1881/1891)
108	Mary	Bernard	32	Sydney (King's Road reserve 1881/1891)
109	Mary	Bernard	4	North Sydney
110	Mary	Bernard	6	North Sydney
111	Mary	Bernard	6	North Sydney
112	Mary	Bernard	34	North Sydney
113	Mary	Bernard	37	North Sydney
114	Mary	Bernard	45	Amherst
115	Mary	Bernard	19	Amherst
116	Maryann	Bernard	21	North Sydney
117	Maryann	Bernard	2	North Sydney
118	Michael	Bernard	2	North Sydney
119	Nicholas	Bernard	34	Sydney (King's Road reserve 1881/1891)
120	Noel	Bernard	6	North Sydney
121	Noel	Bernard	3	North Sydney
122	Noel	Bernard	36	North Sydney
123	Noel	Bernard	40	Amherst
124	Peter	Bernard	2	Amherst
125	Ronald?	Bernard	6	North Sydney
126	Samuel	Bernard	6	North Sydney
127	Stephen	Bernard	57	Amherst
128	Susan	Bernard	8	Sydney (King's Road reserve 1881/1891)
129	Susan	Bernard	8	North Sydney
130	William	Bernard	45	North Sydney
131	Louisa	Cakum?	46	Colchester Co., Salmon River (reserve)
132	Benjamin	Charlie?	46	Heatherton (Paqtnkek Reserve Area)
133	Elizabeth	Charlie?	12	Heatherton (Paqtnkek Reserve Area)
134	Ellen	Charlie?	14	Heatherton (Paqtnkek Reserve Area)
135	Sarah	Charlie?	44	Heatherton (Paqtnkek Reserve Area)
136	Ben	Christmas	52	Truro, Millbrook Reserve area
137	Ben	Christmas	16	Sydney (King's Road reserve 1881/1891)
138	Bridget	Christmas	7	Eskasoni (Cape Breton reserve)
139	Cecily	Christmas	37	Eskasoni (Cape Breton reserve)
140	Christy	Christmas	18	Antigonish Co., Antigonish
141	Ellen	Christmas	2	Eskasoni (Cape Breton reserve)
142	Flora	Christmas	14	Sydney (King's Road reserve 1881/1891)
143	George	Christmas	9	Truro, Millbrook Reserve area
144	Herbert	Christmas	22	Sydney (King's Road reserve 1881/1891)
145	Isabella	Christmas	3	Sydney (King's Road reserve 1881/1891)
146	Isabella	Christmas	2	Sydney (King's Road reserve 1881/1891)
147	Isabella	Christmas	21	Sydney (King's Road reserve 1881/1891)
148	Jerry	Christmas	9 mo	Sydney (King's Road reserve 1881/1891)
149	John	Christmas	44	Eskasoni (Cape Breton reserve)
150	John	Christmas	2 mo	Sydney (King's Road reserve 1881/1891)
151	Joseph	Christmas	26	Sydney (King's Road reserve 1881/1891)
152	Magdelin	Christmas	24	Sydney (King's Road reserve 1881/1891)
153	Margaret	Christmas	3	Eskasoni (Cape Breton reserve)
154	Mary	Christmas	24	Sydney (King's Road reserve 1881/1891)
155	MaryanGE	Christmas	14	Eskasoni (Cape Breton reserve)
156	Michael	Christmas	52	Sydney (King's Road reserve 1881/1891)
157	Michael	Christmas	4	Sydney (King's Road reserve 1881/1891)
158	Noel	Christmas	13	Eskasoni (Cape Breton reserve)

Education	Housing	Occupation	Marital status	Notes
?	Shanty or wigwam	?	Married	
?	House	?	Married	
?	House	?	Single	
?	Shanty or wigwam	?	Single	
?	Shanty or wigwam	?	Single	
?	Shanty or wigwam	?	Single	
?	Shanty or wigwam	?	Married	
?	Shanty or wigwam	?	Married	Born Newfoundland
?	Shanty or wigwam	?	Married	Born New Brunswick
?	Shanty or wigwam	?	Married	Born Prince Edward Island
?	Shanty or wigwam	?	Single	
?	Shanty or wigwam	?	Single	
?	Shanty or wigwam	?	Single	
?	House	?	Single	
?	Shanty or wigwam	?	Single	
?	Shanty or wigwam	?	Single	
?	Shanty or wigwam	?	Married	
?	Shanty or wigwam	?	Married	Born New Brunswick
?	Shanty or wigwam	?	Single	Born New Brunswick
?	Shanty or wigwam	?	Single	
?	Shanty or wigwam	?	Single	
?	Shanty or wigwam	Cooper	Married	Born New Brunswick
?	House	?	Single	
?	Shanty or wigwam	?	Single	
?	Shanty or wigwam	Coal trimmer	Widowed	
?	Shanty or wigwam	?	Single	
?	House	Cooper	Married	
?	House	?	Single	
?	House	?	Single	
?	House	Basketmaker	Married	
?	Shanty or wigwam	Cooper	Married	not Roman Catholic
?	House	Cooper	Single	
School	House	?	Single	
?	House	?	Married	
?	Shanty or wigwam	?	Single	
?	House	?	Single	
?	House	?	Single	
School	Shanty or wigwam	?	Single	not Roman Catholic
?	House	Cooper	Married	
?	House	?	Single	
?	House	?	Single	
?	House	?	Married	
?	House	?	Single	
?	House	Cooper, farmer	Married	
?	House	?	Single	
?	House	Cooper	Married	
?	House	?	Married	
?	Wigwam	?	Single	
?	House	?	Single	
School	House	?	Single	
?	House	Cooper	Married	
?	House	?	Single	
School	Wigwam	?	Single	

1881 Census Data • Continued

ID no.	First name	Last name	Age in years	Location
159	Noel	Christmas	10	Eskasoni (Cape Breton reserve)
160	Noel	Christmas	5	Sydney (King's Road reserve 1881/1891)
161	Paul	Christmas	23	Antigonish Co., Antigonish
162	Paul	Christmas	76	Eskasoni (Cape Breton reserve)
163	Paul	Christmas	36	Eskasoni (Cape Breton reserve)
164	Sarah	Christmas	11	Truro, Millbrook Reserve area
165	Susan	Christmas	49	Truro, Millbrook Reserve area
166	Susan	Christmas	11	Eskasoni (Cape Breton reserve)
167	Susan	Christmas	24	Sydney (King's Road reserve 1881/1891)
168	Theresa	Christmas	40	Eskasoni (Cape Breton reserve)
169	Thomas	Christmas	4	Eskasoni (Cape Breton reserve)
170	Victor	Christmas	9	Eskasoni (Cape Breton reserve)
171	Christy	Christopher	11 mo	Town of Guysborough (Subdistrict F)
172	Ellen	Christopher	29	Town of Guysborough (Subdistrict F)
173	John	Christopher	3	Town of Guysborough (Subdistrict F)
174	Maryann	Christopher	7	Town of Guysborough (Subdistrict F)
175	Michael	Christopher	8	Town of Guysborough (Subdistrict F)
176	Steven	Christopher	35	Town of Guysborough (Subdistrict F)
177	Elizabeth	Cope	12	Antigonish Co., Antigonish
178	Freeman	Cope	17	Antigonish Co., Antigonish
179	Alvin	Cremo	11	Potlotek, Chapel Island (Cape Breton reserve)
180	Angelic	Cremo	2	Waqamatkuk (Middle River, Cape Breton reserve)
181	Ann	Cremo	52	Potlotek, Chapel Island (Cape Breton reserve)
182	Ann	Cremo	14	Potlotek, Chapel Island (Cape Breton reserve)
183	Anncath	Cremo	16	Waqamatkuk (Middle River, Cape Breton reserve)
184	Betsy	Cremo	22	Waqamatkuk (Middle River, Cape Breton reserve)
185	Elizabeth	Cremo	17	Potlotek, Chapel Island (Cape Breton reserve)
186	Harriet	Cremo	16	Potlotek, Chapel Island (Cape Breton reserve)
187	Isadore	Cremo	15	Waqamatkuk (Middle River, Cape Breton reserve)
188	John	Cremo	7	Waqamatkuk (Middle River, Cape Breton reserve)
189	John	Cremo	3	Waqamatkuk (Middle River, Cape Breton reserve)
190	Margaret	Cremo	4	Waqamatkuk (Middle River, Cape Breton reserve)
191	Moses	Cremo	10	Waqamatkuk (Middle River, Cape Breton reserve)
192	Nancy	Cremo	19	Waqamatkuk (Middle River, Cape Breton reserve)
193	Noel	Cremo	47	Waqamatkuk (Middle River, Cape Breton reserve)
194	Noel	Cremo	87	Whycocomagh (Cape Breton reserve)
195	Peter	Cremo	53	Potlotek, Chapel Island (Cape Breton reserve)
196	Peter	Cremo	22	Potlotek, Chapel Island (Cape Breton reserve)
197	Peter	Cremo	44	Waqamatkuk (Middle River, Cape Breton reserve)
198	Susan	Cremo	39	Waqamatkuk (Middle River, Cape Breton reserve)
199	Theresa	Cremo	43	Waqamatkuk (Middle River, Cape Breton reserve)
200	Annie	Dennies	30	North Mountain (Cape Breton, 'Malakawe:j reserve)
201	Beloni	Dennies	81	North Mountain (Cape Breton, 'Malakawe:j reserve)
202	Bella	Dennis	24	Whycocomagh (Cape Breton reserve)
203	Esther	Dennis	15	Cape Breton Co., North Side Mira
204	Francis	Dennis	39	Cape Breton Co., North Side Mira
205	Joe	Dennis	25	Whycocomagh (Cape Breton reserve)
206	Lucy	Dennis	10	Cape Breton Co., North Side Mira
207	Maggie	Dennis	2	Whycocomagh (Cape Breton reserve)
208	Mary	Dennis	1 mo	Cape Breton Co., North Side Mira
209	P	Dennis	3	Cape Breton Co., North Side Mira
210	Susan	Dennis	22	Cape Breton Co., North Side Mira
211	Susan	Dennis	17	Cape Breton Co., North Side Mira

Education	Housing	Occupation	Marital status	Notes
School	House	?	Single	
?	House	?	Single	
?	Shanty or wigwam	Cooper	Single	
?	House	Cooper, farmer	Widowed	
?	Wigwam	Cooper, farmer	Married	
School	Shanty or wigwam	?	Single	not Roman Catholic
?	Shanty or wigwam	?	Married	not Roman Catholic
School	House	?	Single	
?	House	?	Married	
?	Wigwam	?	Married	
?	House	?	Single	
School	Wigwam	?	Single	
?	Shanty or wigwam	Cooper	Single	
?	Shanty or wigwam	Cooper	Single	
?	Shanty or wigwam	Cooper	Single	
?	Shanty or wigwam	Cooper	Single	
?	Shanty or wigwam	Cooper	Single	
?	Shanty or wigwam	Cooper	Single	
?	Shanty or wigwam	?	Single	
?	Shanty or wigwam	Cooper	Single	
?	Shanty or wigwam	?	Single	
?	Shanty or wigwam	?	Single	
?	Shanty or wigwam	?	Married	
?	Shanty or wigwam	?	Single	
?	Shanty or wigwam	?	Single	
?	Shanty or wigwam	?	Single	
?	Shanty or wigwam	?	Single	
?	Shanty or wigwam	?	Single	
?	Shanty or wigwam	?	Single	
?	Shanty or wigwam	?	Single	
?	Shanty or wigwam	?	Single	
?	Shanty or wigwam	?	Single	
?	Shanty or wigwam	?	Single	
?	Shanty or wigwam	?	Single	
?	Shanty or wigwam	Cooper	Married	
?	House	?	Widowed	
?	Shanty or wigwam	Farmer, cooper	Married	
?	Shanty or wigwam	Farrier	Single	
?	Shanty or wigwam	Cooper	Married	
?	Shanty or wigwam	?	Married	
?	Shanty or wigwam	?	Married	
?	Shanty or wigwam	?	Single	
?	Shanty or wigwam	Hunter, fisherman	Widowed	Male
?	Shanty or wigwam	?	Married	
?	Shanty or wigwam	?	Single	
?	Shanty or wigwam	?	Married	
?	Shanty or wigwam	Farmer	Married	
?	Shanty or wigwam	?	Single	
?	Shanty or wigwam	?	Single	
?	Shanty or wigwam	?	Single	
?	Shanty or wigwam	?	Single	
?	Shanty or wigwam	?	Married	
?	Shanty or wigwam	?	Single	

1881 Census Data • Continued

ID no.	First name	Last name	Age in years	Location
212	Albert	Denny	2	Antigonish Co., St. Joseph's
213	Almira	Denny	2	Pictou Co., Pictou Landing (reserve)
214	Angelic	Denny	25	Pictou Co., Pictou Landing (reserve)
215	Angelic	Denny	16	Eskasoni (Cape Breton reserve)
216	Bridget	Denny	3	Eskasoni (Cape Breton reserve)
217	Eliza	Denny	2	Eskasoni (Cape Breton reserve)
218	Elizabeth	Denny	30	Eskasoni (Cape Breton reserve)
219	Fanny	Denny	5	Eskasoni (Cape Breton reserve)
220	James	Denny	26	Eskasoni (Cape Breton reserve)
221	Jane	Denny	7 mo	Eskasoni (Cape Breton reserve)
222	Jane	Denny	13	Eskasoni (Cape Breton reserve)
223	Janet	Denny	11	Pictou Co., Pictou Landing (reserve)
224	John	Denny	37	Antigonish Co., St. Joseph's
225	John	Denny	33	Pictou Co., Pictou Landing (reserve)
226	John	Denny	64	Eskasoni (Cape Breton reserve)
227	John	Denny	39	Eskasoni (Cape Breton reserve)
228	Joseph	Denny	9	Eskasoni (Cape Breton reserve)
229	Julie	Denny	20	Eskasoni (Cape Breton reserve)
230	Lewis	Denny	7	Antigonish Co., St. Joseph's
231	Mary	Denny	13	Eskasoni (Cape Breton reserve)
232	Maryann	Denny	3	Eskasoni (Cape Breton reserve)
233	Mathew	Denny	14	Eskasoni (Cape Breton reserve)
234	Michael	Denny	8	Eskasoni (Cape Breton reserve)
235	Noel	Denny	9	Eskasoni (Cape Breton reserve)
236	Noel	Denny	41	Eskasoni (Cape Breton reserve)
237	Paul	Denny	45	Eskasoni (Cape Breton reserve)
238	Peter	Denny	12	Eskasoni (Cape Breton reserve)
239	Sarah	Denny	28	Antigonish Co., St. Joseph's
240	Susan	Denny	34	Eskasoni (Cape Breton reserve)
241	Susan	Denny	40	Eskasoni (Cape Breton reserve)
242	Susan	Denny	5	Eskasoni (Cape Breton reserve)
243	Ann	Doucette	34	Potlotek, Chapel Island (Cape Breton reserve)
244	Catharine	Doucette	25	Eskasoni (Cape Breton reserve)
245	Esther	Doucette	15	Potlotek, Chapel Island (Cape Breton reserve)
246	Fanny	Doucette	3	Potlotek, Chapel Island (Cape Breton reserve)
247	Flora	Doucette	34	Eskasoni (Cape Breton reserve)
248	Francis	Doucette	3	Potlotek, Chapel Island (Cape Breton reserve)
249	Joe	Doucette	40	Potlotek, Chapel Island (Cape Breton reserve)
250	Louis	Doucette	70	Eskasoni (Cape Breton reserve)
251	Mary	Doucette	13	Potlotek, Chapel Island (Cape Breton reserve)
252	Maryann	Doucette	14	Eskasoni (Cape Breton reserve)
253	Maryann	Doucette	10	Potlotek, Chapel Island (Cape Breton reserve)
254	Noel	Doucette	38	Eskasoni (Cape Breton reserve)
255	Noel	Doucette	7	Potlotek, Chapel Island (Cape Breton reserve)
256	Elizabeth	Duncan	35	Guysborough Co., Larry's River
257	Francis	Duncan	36	Guysborough Co., Larry's River
258	Francis	Duzzy	86	Eskasoni (Cape Breton reserve)
259	John	Edwards	84	River Inhabitants (Cape Breton Island)
260	Charlot	Francis	11	Truro, Millbrook Reserve area
261	Elisabeth	Francis	25	Town of Guysborough (Subdistrict F)
262	Ellen	Francis	2	Town of Guysborough (Subdistrict F)
263	JIPY	Francis	53	Eskasoni (Cape Breton reserve)
264	John	Francis	0	Potlotek, Chapel Island (Cape Breton reserve)

Education	Housing	Occupation	Marital status	Notes
?	Shanty or wigwam	?	Single	
?	Shanty or wigwam	?	Single	Female
?	Shanty or wigwam	?	Married	
School	Wigwam	?	Single	
?	House	?	Single	
?	Wigwam	?	Single	
?	Wigwam	?	Married	
?	House	?	Single	
?	Wigwam	Cooper	Married	
?	House	?	Single	
School	Wigwam	?	Single	
?	Shanty or wigwam	?	Single	
?	Shanty or wigwam	Cooper	Married	
?	Shanty or wigwam	Cooper	Married	
?	House	Chief, cooper	Widowed	
?	Wigwam	Cooper	Married	
School	Wigwam	?	Single	
?	Wigwam	?	Married	
?	Shanty or wigwam	?	Single	
School	House	?	Single	
?	Wigwam	?	Single	
School	Wigwam	?	Single	
School	Wigwam	?	Single	
School	House	?	Single	
?	Wigwam	Cooper	Married	
?	House	Cooper, hunter	Married	
School	House	Cooper	Single	
?	Shanty or wigwam	?	Married	
?	House	?	Married	
?	Wigwam	?	Married	
?	Wigwam	?	Single	
?	Shanty or wigwam	?	Married	
?	House	?	Single	
?	Shanty or wigwam	?	Single	
?	Shanty or wigwam	?	Single	
?	Shanty or wigwam	?	Married	
?	Shanty or wigwam	?	Single	
?	Shanty or wigwam	Farmer, cooper	Married	
?	House	Cooper, farmer	Widowed	
?	Shanty or wigwam	?	Single	
?	House	?	Single	
?	Shanty or wigwam	?	Single	
?	Shanty or wigwam	Cooper	Married	
?	Shanty or wigwam	?	Single	
?	Shanty or wigwam	?	Married	
?	Shanty or wigwam	Boat builder	Married	
?	Wigwam	Cooper	Single	
?	House	Farmer	Married	Born United States
?	Shanty or wigwam	?	Single	
?	Shanty or wigwam	Cooper	Married	
?	Shanty or wigwam	Cooper	Single	
?	Shanty or wigwam	?	Married	Female
?	House	?	Single	

1881 Census Data • Continued

ID no.	First name	Last name	Age in years	Location
265	Joseph	Francis	5	Potlotek, Chapel Island (Cape Breton reserve)
266	Julieann	Francis	7	Potlotek, Chapel Island (Cape Breton reserve)
267	Kate	Francis	18	Potlotek, Chapel Island (Cape Breton reserve)
268	Louisa	Francis	3 mo	Truro, Millbrook Reserve area
269	Madeline	Francis	11	Potlotek, Chapel Island (Cape Breton reserve)
270	Mary	Francis	20	New Glasgow
271	Mary	Francis	89	Pictou Co., Pictou Landing (reserve)
272	Mary	Francis	26	Truro, Millbrook Reserve area
273	Mary	Francis	18	Eskasoni (Cape Breton reserve)
274	Mary	Francis	2	Potlotek, Chapel Island (Cape Breton reserve)
275	Mary	Francis	1 mo	Town of Guysborough (Subdistrict F)
276	Maryann	Francis	43	Truro, Millbrook Reserve area
277	Maryann	Francis	30	Potlotek, Chapel Island (Cape Breton reserve)
278	Maryann	Francis	66	Potlotek, Chapel Island (Cape Breton reserve)
279	Maryjane	Francis	12	Truro, Millbrook Reserve area
280	Maurice	Francis	26	New Glasgow
281	Michael	Francis	73	Eskasoni (Cape Breton reserve)
282	Michael	Francis	35	Potlotek, Chapel Island (Cape Breton reserve)
283	Nancy	Francis	9	Truro, Millbrook Reserve area
284	Noel	Francis	38	Truro, Millbrook Reserve area
285	Noel	Francis	25	Town of Guysborough (Subdistrict F)
286	Peter	Francis	8	Truro, Millbrook Reserve area
287	Peter	Francis	9	Potlotek, Chapel Island (Cape Breton reserve)
288	Sarah	Francis	15	Truro, Millbrook Reserve area
289	Susan	Francis	18	Truro, Millbrook Reserve area
290	Catharine	Fraser	38	Tracadie (Paqtnkek Reserve Area)
291	Esther	Fraser	14	Tracadie (Paqtnkek Reserve Area)
292	Joanna	Fraser	8	Tracadie (Paqtnkek Reserve Area)
293	John	Fraser	6	Tracadie (Paqtnkek Reserve Area)
294	Mary	Fraser	12	Tracadie (Paqtnkek Reserve Area)
295	Mary	Fraser	3	Tracadie (Paqtnkek Reserve Area)
296	Michael	Fraser	10	Tracadie (Paqtnkek Reserve Area)
297	William	Fraser	45	Tracadie (Paqtnkek Reserve Area)
298	Ann	Gabriel	15	Antigonish Co., Antigonish
299	Bella	Gabriel	17	Antigonish Co., Antigonish
300	Bernard	Gabriel	76	Antigonish Co., Antigonish
301	Bridget	Gabriel	37	Eskasoni (Cape Breton reserve)
302	Charlot	Gabriel	14	Eskasoni (Cape Breton reserve)
303	Cristy	Gabriel	48	Antigonish Co., Antigonish
304	Eliza	Gabriel	16	Antigonish Co., Antigonish
305	Elizabeth	Gabriel	0	Antigonish Co., Antigonish
306	Ellen	Gabriel	4	Antigonish Co., Antigonish
307	Francis	Gabriel	5	Eskasoni (Cape Breton reserve)
308	Gabriel	Gabriel	6	Antigonish Co., Antigonish
309	Isabell	Gabriel	27	Antigonish Co., Antigonish
310	Janet	Gabriel	13	Antigonish Co., Antigonish
311	Janet	Gabriel	2	Antigonish Co., Antigonish
312	John	Gabriel	18	Antigonish Co., Antigonish, District 8
313	Joseph	Gabriel	18	Antigonish Co., Antigonish
314	Lewis	Gabriel	31	Antigonish Co., Antigonish
315	Louis	Gabriel	49	Eskasoni (Cape Breton reserve)
316	Magdalin	Gabriel	1 mo	Eskasoni (Cape Breton reserve)
317	Mary	Gabriel	22	Antigonish Co., Antigonish

Education	Housing	Occupation	Marital status	Notes
?	House	?	Single	
?	House	?	Single	
?	Shanty or wigwam	?	Single	
?	Shanty or wigwam	?	Single	
?	House	?	Single	
?	Shanty or wigwam	?	Married	
?	Shanty or wigwam	?	Widowed	
?	Shanty or wigwam	?	Married	
?	Shanty or wigwam	?	Single	
?	House	?	Single	
?	Shanty or wigwam	Cooper	Single	
?	Shanty or wigwam	Basketmaker	Widowed	
?	House	?	Married	
?	Shanty or wigwam	?	Widowed	
?	Shanty or wigwam	?	Single	
?	Shanty or wigwam	?	Married	
?	Shanty or wigwam	Cooper	Married	
?	House	Farmer, cooper	Married	
?	Shanty or wigwam	?	Single	
?	Shanty or wigwam	Cooper	Married	
?	Shanty or wigwam	Cooper	Married	
?	Shanty or wigwam	?	Single	
?	House	?	Single	
?	Shanty or wigwam	?	Single	
?	Shanty or wigwam	?	Single	
?	Shanty or wigwam	?	Married	
?	Shanty or wigwam	?	Single	
?	Shanty or wigwam	?	Single	
?	Shanty or wigwam	?	Single	
?	Shanty or wigwam	?	Single	
?	Shanty or wigwam	?	Single	
?	Shanty or wigwam	?	Single	
?	Shanty or wigwam	hunter	Married	
?	Shanty or wigwam	?	Single	
?	Shanty or wigwam	?	Single	
?	Shanty or wigwam	Cooper	Married	
?	House	?	Married	
School	Shanty or wigwam	?	Single	
?	Shanty or wigwam	?	Married	
?	Shanty or wigwam	?	Single	
?	Shanty or wigwam	?	Single	
?	Shanty or wigwam	?	Single	
?	House	?	Single	
?	Shanty or wigwam	?	Single	
?	Shanty or wigwam	?	Single	
?	Shanty or wigwam	?	Single	
?	Shanty or wigwam	?	Single	
?	Shanty or wigwam	?	Single	
?	Shanty or wigwam	?	Single	
?	Shanty or wigwam	Cooper	Married	
?	House	Cooper	Married	
?	House	?	Single	
?	Shanty or wigwam	?	Single	

1881 Census Data • Continued

ID no.	First name	Last name	Age in years	Location
318	Maryann	Gabriel	9	Antigonish Co., Antigonish
319	Maryann	Gabriel	7	Antigonish Co., Antigonish
320	Michael	Gabriel	6 mo	Antigonish Co., Antigonish
321	Moses	Gabriel	58	Antigonish Co., Antigonish
322	Nancy	Gabriel	32	Antigonish Co., Antigonish
323	Nancy	Gabriel	41	Antigonish Co., Antigonish
324	Nancy	Gabriel	51	Antigonish Co., Antigonish, District 9
325	Noel	Gabriel	8	Antigonish Co., Antigonish
326	Noel	Gabriel	10	Eskasoni (Cape Breton reserve)
327	Richard	Gabriel	14	Antigonish Co., Antigonish, District 7
328	Sarah	Gabriel	22	Antigonish Co., Antigonish
329	Sarah	Gabriel	3	Eskasoni (Cape Breton reserve)
330	Susan	Gabriel	10	Eskasoni (Cape Breton reserve)
331	Vincent	Gabriel	56	Antigonish Co., Antigonish, District 13
332	Agnes	Googoo	32	Whycocomagh (Cape Breton reserve)
333	Amary	Googoo	11	Whycocomagh (Cape Breton reserve)
334	Amary	Googoo	9 mo	Whycocomagh (Cape Breton reserve)
335	Andrew	Googoo	4	Antigonish Co., Antigonish
336	Andrew	Googoo	24	Whycocomagh (Cape Breton reserve)
337	Bella	Googoo	26	Antigonish Co., Antigonish
338	Benjamin	Googoo	27	Antigonish Co., Antigonish
339	Betty	Googoo	14	Waqamatkuk (Middle River, Cape Breton reserve)
340	Betty	Googoo	7	Waqamatkuk (Middle River, Cape Breton reserve)
341	Catharine	Googoo	31	Whycocomagh (Cape Breton reserve)
342	Charles	Googoo	11	Antigonish Co., Antigonish
343	Charles	Googoo	16	Antigonish Co., Antigonish
344	Elizabeth	Googoo	29	Antigonish Co., Antigonish
345	Ellen	Googoo	20	North Sydney
346	Flora	Googoo	12	Waqamatkuk (Middle River, Cape Breton reserve)
347	Frances	Googoo	2 mo	Waqamatkuk (Middle River, Cape Breton reserve)
348	Francis	Googoo	44	Antigonish Co., Antigonish
349	Francis	Googoo	9	Whycocomagh (Cape Breton reserve)
350	Francis	Googoo	38	Whycocomagh (Cape Breton reserve)
351	Gabriel	Googoo	4	Whycocomagh (Cape Breton reserve)
352	Isabell	Googoo	28	Antigonish Co., Antigonish
353	James	Googoo	13	Whycocomagh (Cape Breton reserve)
354	Jmary	Googoo	3 mo	Whycocomagh (Cape Breton reserve)
355	Joe	Googoo	45	Antigonish Co., St. Joseph's
356	John	Googoo	26	North Sydney
357	John	Googoo	32	Waqamatkuk (Middle River, Cape Breton reserve)
358	John	Googoo	2	Whycocomagh (Cape Breton reserve)
359	Maggie	Googoo	2	Antigonish Co., Antigonish
360	Maggie	Googoo	10	Whycocomagh (Cape Breton reserve)
361	Margaret	Googoo	30	Waqamatkuk (Middle River, Cape Breton reserve)
362	Mary	Googoo	36	North Sydney
363	Mary	Googoo	6	Whycocomagh (Cape Breton reserve)
364	Maryann	Googoo	13	Antigonish Co., Antigonish
365	Michael	Googoo	1	Whycocomagh (Cape Breton reserve)
366	Moses	Googoo	3 mo	Antigonish Co., Antigonish
367	Msusan	Googoo	2	Whycocomagh (Cape Breton reserve)
368	Nancy	Googoo	32	Whycocomagh (Cape Breton reserve)
369	Nancy	Googoo	24	Whycocomagh (Cape Breton reserve)
370	Patrick	Googoo	6	Whycocomagh (Cape Breton reserve)

Education	Housing	Occupation	Marital status	Notes
?	Shanty or wigwam	?	Single	
?	Shanty or wigwam	?	Single	
?	Shanty or wigwam	?	Single	
?	Shanty or wigwam	Cooper	Married	
?	Shanty or wigwam	?	Married	
?	Shanty or wigwam	?	Married	
?	Shanty or wigwam	?	Single	
?	Shanty or wigwam	?	Single	
School	Shanty or wigwam	?	Single	
?	Shanty or wigwam	?	Single	
?	Shanty or wigwam	?	Single	
?	House	?	Single	
School	House	?	Single	
?	Shanty or wigwam	Cooper	Single	
?	House	?	Married	
?	House	?	Single	
?	Shanty or wigwam	?	Single	
?	Shanty or wigwam	?	Single	
?	Shanty or wigwam	Farmer, cooper	Married	
?	Shanty or wigwam	?	Single	
?	Shanty or wigwam	Cooper	Married	
?	Shanty or wigwam	?	Single	
?	Shanty or wigwam	?	Single	
?	House	?	Married	
?	Shanty or wigwam	?	Single	
?	Shanty or wigwam	?	Single	
?	Shanty or wigwam	?	Married	
?	Shanty or wigwam	?	Married	
?	Shanty or wigwam	?	Single	
?	Shanty or wigwam	?	Single	
?	Shanty or wigwam	Cooper	Single	
School	House	?	Single	
?	House	Farmer, cooper	Married	
?	House	?	Single	
?	Shanty or wigwam	?	Married	
School	House	?	Single	
?	House	?	Single	
?	House	Cooper	Married	
?	Shanty or wigwam	Cooper	Married	
?	Shanty or wigwam	Cooper	Married	
?	Shanty or wigwam	?	Single	
?	Shanty or wigwam	?	Single	
School	House	?	Single	
?	Shanty or wigwam	?	Married	
?	Shanty or wigwam	?	Widowed	
School	House	?	Single	
?	Shanty or wigwam	?	Single	
?	House	?	Single	
?	Shanty or wigwam	?	Single	
?	House	?	Single	
?	House	?	Married	
?	Shanty or wigwam	?	Married	
School	House	?	Single	

1881 Census Data • Continued

ID no.	First name	Last name	Age in years	Location
371	Peter	Googoo	37	Antigonish Co., Antigonish
372	Peter	Googoo	33	Whycocomagh (Cape Breton reserve)
373	Peter	Googoo	17	Whycocomagh (Cape Breton reserve)
374	Samuel	Googoo	13	Whycocomagh (Cape Breton reserve)
375	Sarah	Googoo	68	Whycocomagh (Cape Breton reserve)
376	Simon	Googoo	50	Whycocomagh (Cape Breton reserve)
377	Stephen	Googoo	1	Antigonish Co., Antigonish
378	Steven	Googoo	15	North Sydney
379	Steven	Googoo	3	Waqamatkuk (Middle River, Cape Breton reserve)
380	Steven	Googoo	9	Whycocomagh (Cape Breton reserve)
381	Victor	Googoo	10	Waqamatkuk (Middle River, Cape Breton reserve)
382	Harry?	Gould	19	North Sydney
383	John	Gould	44	North Sydney
384	John	Gould	64	Cape Breton Co., North Side Mira
385	Joseph	Gould	16	North Sydney
386	Lizzie	Gould	19	Cape Breton Co., North Side Mira
387	Mary	Gould	25	North Sydney
388	Noel	Gould	4	North Sydney
389	Steven	Gould	14	North Sydney
390	Susan	Gould	1	North Sydney
391	Ann	Greguin	75	Potlotek, Chapel Island (Cape Breton reserve)
392	Joseph	Greguin	67	Eskasoni (Cape Breton reserve)
393	Mary	Greguin	70	Eskasoni (Cape Breton reserve)
394	Noel	Greguin	44	Potlotek, Chapel Island (Cape Breton reserve)
395	Ann	Herney	50	Sydney (King's Road reserve 1881/1891)
396	Christy	Herney	25	Eskasoni (Cape Breton reserve)
397	Ellen	Herney	17	North Sydney
398	Isabelle	Herney	13	North Sydney
399	Joe	Herney	20	Eskasoni (Cape Breton reserve)
400	John	Herney	3 mo	Eskasoni (Cape Breton reserve)
401	John	Herney	58	North Sydney
402	Magdalin	Herney	17	Eskasoni (Cape Breton reserve)
403	Mary	Herney	35	North Sydney
404	Noel	Herney	29	Eskasoni (Cape Breton reserve)
405	Peter	Herney	2	Eskasoni (Cape Breton reserve)
406	Peter	Herney	65	Sydney (King's Road reserve 1881/1891)
407	Susan	Herney	44	Eskasoni (Cape Breton reserve)
408	Thomas	Herney	12	Sydney (King's Road reserve 1881/1891)
409	Tom	Herney	68	Eskasoni (Cape Breton reserve)
410	Bridget	Humblewa	48	Guysborough Co., Sherbrooke
411	Gregwell	Humblewa	58	Guysborough Co., Sherbrooke
412	Maryann	Humblewa	3	Guysborough Co., Sherbrooke
413	Bella	Isaac	40	Sydney (King's Road reserve 1881/1891)
414	Jim	Isaac	11	Sydney (King's Road reserve 1881/1891)
415	John	Isaac	75	Sydney (King's Road reserve 1881/1891)
416	John	Isaac	3	Sydney (King's Road reserve 1881/1891)
417	Joseph	Isaac	5	Sydney (King's Road reserve 1881/1891)
418	Mary	Isaac	26	Sydney (King's Road reserve 1881/1891)
419	Noel	Isaac	30	Sydney (King's Road reserve 1881/1891)
420	Sally	Isaac	59	Sydney (King's Road reserve 1881/1891)
421	Sarah	Isaac	15	Sydney (King's Road reserve 1881/1891)
422	Susie	Isaac	1	Sydney (King's Road reserve 1881/1891)
423	Susan	James	60	Potlotek, Chapel Island (Cape Breton reserve)

Education	Housing	Occupation	Marital status	Notes
?	Shanty or wigwam	Cooper	Married	
?	House	Farmer	Married	
School	House	?	Single	
School	House	?	Single	
?	Shanty or wigwam	?	Widowed	
?	House	Farmer	Married	
?	Shanty or wigwam	?	Single	
?	Shanty or wigwam	Cooper	Married	
?	Shanty or wigwam	?	Single	
School	House	?	Single	
?	Shanty or wigwam	?	Single	
?	Shanty or wigwam	Cooper	Single	
?	Shanty or wigwam	Cooper	Married	
?	Shanty or wigwam	?	Widowed	
?	Shanty or wigwam	Cooper	Single	
?	Shanty or wigwam	?	Single	
?	Shanty or wigwam	Cooper	Married	
?	Shanty or wigwam	?	Single	
?	Shanty or wigwam	?	Single	
?	Shanty or wigwam	?	Single	
?	Shanty or wigwam	?	Widowed	
?	House	Cooper	Married	
?	House	?	Married	
?	Shanty or wigwam	Farmer	Widowed	
?	House	?	Married	
?	House	?	Married	
?	Shanty or wigwam	?	Single	
?	Shanty or wigwam	?	Single	
?	Shanty or wigwam	Cooper	Single	
?	House	?	Single	
?	Shanty or wigwam	Cooper	Married	
School	Shanty or wigwam	?	Single	
?	Shanty or wigwam	?	Married	
?	House	Cooper	Married	
?	House	?	Single	
?	House	Cooper	Married	
?	Shanty or wigwam	?	Widowed	
?	House	?	Single	
?	Shanty or wigwam	Cooper	Widowed	
?	Shanty or wigwam	?	Married	
?	Shanty or wigwam	?	Married	
?	Shanty or wigwam	?	Single	
?	House	?	Single	
?	House	?	Single	
?	House	Cooper	Married	
?	House	?	Single	
?	House	?	Single	
?	House	?	Married	
?	House	Laborer	Married	
?	House	?	Married	
?	House	?	Single	
?	House	?	Single	
?	Shanty or wigwam	?	Widowed	

1881 Census Data • Continued

ID no.	First name	Last name	Age in years	Location
424	Alex	Joe	56	Truro, Millbrook Reserve area
425	Francis	Joe	22	Potlotek, Chapel Island (Cape Breton reserve)
426	James	Joe	3	Waqamatkuk (Middle River, Cape Breton reserve)
427	John	Joe	2	Potlotek, Chapel Island (Cape Breton reserve)
428	John	Joe	39	Waqamatkuk (Middle River, Cape Breton reserve)
429	Louis	Joe	11	Truro, Millbrook Reserve area
430	Louis	Joe	27	Waqamatkuk (Middle River, Cape Breton reserve)
431	Margaret	Joe	25	Waqamatkuk (Middle River, Cape Breton reserve)
432	Mary	Joe	16	Truro, Millbrook Reserve area
433	Mary	Joe	65	River Inhabitants (Cape Breton Island)
434	Mary	Joe	5	Waqamatkuk (Middle River, Cape Breton reserve)
435	Michael	Joe	15	Waqamatkuk (Middle River, Cape Breton reserve)
436	Noeljoe	Joe	10 mo	Waqamatkuk (Middle River, Cape Breton reserve)
437	Paul	Joe	68	River Inhabitants (Cape Breton Island)
438	Sarah	Joe	29	Waqamatkuk (Middle River, Cape Breton reserve)
439	Steven	Joe	5	Potlotek, Chapel Island (Cape Breton reserve)
440	Susan	Joe	23	Potlotek, Chapel Island (Cape Breton reserve)
441	Susan	Joe	4	Waqamatkuk (Middle River, Cape Breton reserve)
442	Susan	Joe	1	Waqamatkuk (Middle River, Cape Breton reserve)
443	Tom	Joe	20	Potlotek, Chapel Island (Cape Breton reserve)
444	Benjamin	Johnson	12	Town of Guysborough (Subdistrict F)
445	Charles	Johnson	3	Town of Guysborough (Subdistrict F)
446	Elizabeth	Johnson	14	Town of Guysborough (Subdistrict F)
447	John	Johnson	20	Town of Guysborough (Subdistrict F)
448	Joseph	Johnson	18	Town of Guysborough (Subdistrict F)
449	Mary	Johnson	8	Town of Guysborough (Subdistrict F)
450	Richard	Johnson	2 mo	Town of Guysborough (Subdistrict F)
451	Sophia	Johnson	10	Town of Guysborough (Subdistrict F)
452	Susan	Johnson	50	Town of Guysborough (Subdistrict F)
453	Thomas	Johnson	50	Town of Guysborough (Subdistrict F)
454	Ann	Joseph	24	Tracadie (Paqtnkek Reserve Area)
455	James	Joseph	25	Guysborough Co., Sherbrooke
456	Mary	Joseph	49	Tracadie (Paqtnkek Reserve Area)
457	Mary	Joseph	12	Tracadie (Paqtnkek Reserve Area)
458	Mary	Joseph	9	Potlotek, Chapel Island (Cape Breton reserve)
459	Mary	Joseph	20	Guysborough Co., Sherbrooke
460	Peter	Joseph	50	Tracadie (Paqtnkek Reserve Area)
461	Steven	Joseph	20	Tracadie (Paqtnkek Reserve Area)
462	Edward	Julian	20	Potlotek, Chapel Island (Cape Breton reserve)
463	Isabella	Julian	19	Town of Guysborough (Subdistrict F)
464	Madeline	Julian	20	Potlotek, Chapel Island (Cape Breton reserve)
465	Maggie	Julian	6	Town of Guysborough (Subdistrict F)
466	Mary	Julian	15	Town of Guysborough (Subdistrict F)
467	Maryann	Julian	41	Potlotek, Chapel Island (Cape Breton reserve)
468	Maryann	Julian	28	Town of Guysborough (Subdistrict F)
469	Maryjane	Julian	4	Potlotek, Chapel Island (Cape Breton reserve)
470	Noel	Julian	34	Potlotek, Chapel Island (Cape Breton reserve)
471	Noel	Julian	2	Potlotek, Chapel Island (Cape Breton reserve)
472	Peter	Julian	14	Potlotek, Chapel Island (Cape Breton reserve)
473	Peter	Julian	72	Town of Guysborough (Subdistrict F)
474	Tilias	Julian	61	Town of Guysborough (Subdistrict F)
475	Tom	Julian	16	Potlotek, Chapel Island (Cape Breton reserve)
476	William	Julian	18	Town of Guysborough (Subdistrict F)

Education	Housing	Occupation	Marital status	Notes
?	Shanty or wigwam	Cooper	Widowed	
?	Shanty or wigwam	?	Single	
?	Shanty or wigwam	?	Single	
?	Shanty or wigwam	?	Single	
?	Shanty or wigwam	Cooper	Married	
?	Shanty or wigwam	?	Single	
?	Shanty or wigwam	Cooper	Married	
?	Shanty or wigwam	?	Married	
?	Shanty or wigwam	?	Single	
?	Shanty or wigwam	?	Married	
?	Shanty or wigwam	?	Single	
?	Shanty or wigwam	?	Single	
?	Shanty or wigwam	?	Single	
?	Shanty or wigwam	Cooper	Married	
?	Shanty or wigwam	?	Married	
?	Shanty or wigwam	?	Single	
?	Shanty or wigwam	?	Widowed	
?	Shanty or wigwam	?	Single	
?	Shanty or wigwam	?	Single	
?	Shanty or wigwam	?	Single	
?	House	?	Single	
?	House	?	Single	
?	House	?	Single	
?	House	Farmer	Single	
?	House	?	Single	
?	House	?	Single	
?	House	?	Single	
?	House	?	Single	
?	House	?	Married	
?	House	Farmer	Married	
?	Shanty or wigwam	?	Single	
?	Shanty or wigwam	?	Married	
?	Shanty or wigwam	?	Married	
?	Shanty or wigwam	?	Single	
?	House	?	Single	
?	Shanty or wigwam	?	Married	
?	Shanty or wigwam	Farmer	Married	
?	Shanty or wigwam	Hunter	Single	
?	House	Farmer, cooper	Married	
?	Shanty or wigwam	?	Single	
?	House	?	Married	
?	Shanty or wigwam	?	Single	
?	Shanty or wigwam	?	Single	
?	Shanty or wigwam	?	Married	
?	Shanty or wigwam	?	Single	
?	Shanty or wigwam	?	Single	
?	Shanty or wigwam	Cooper	Married	
?	Shanty or wigwam	?	Single	
?	Shanty or wigwam	?	Single	
?	Shanty or wigwam	Cooper	Married	
?	Shanty or wigwam	?	Married	Male
?	Shanty or wigwam	Cooper	Single	
?	Shanty or wigwam	?	Single	

1881 Census Data • Continued

ID no.	First name	Last name	Age in years	Location
477	Margaret	Knockwood	40	Pictou Co., Hardwood Hill
478	Maryann	Knockwood	13	Pictou Co., Hardwood Hill
479	Peter	Knockwood	40	Pictou Co., Hardwood Hill
480	Sarah	Knockwood	17	Pictou Co., Hardwood Hill
481	John	Labrado?	34	Amherst
482	Susan	Labrado?	32	Amherst
483	Jane	Lafford	11 mo	Tracadie (Paqtnkek Reserve Area)
484	Joseph	Lafford	44	Tracadie (Paqtnkek Reserve Area)
485	Mary	Lafford	20	Tracadie (Paqtnkek Reserve Area)
486	Thomas	Levi	30	Amherst
487	Cecile	Lewis	17	Potlotek, Chapel Island (Cape Breton reserve)
488	Isabel	Lewis	54	Heatherton (Paqtnkek Reserve Area)
489	Nancy	Lewis	67	Potlotek, Chapel Island (Cape Breton reserve)
490	Noel	Lewis	44	Potlotek, Chapel Island (Cape Breton reserve)
491	Peter	Lewis	56	Heatherton (Paqtnkek Reserve Area)
492	Susan	Lewis	36	Potlotek, Chapel Island (Cape Breton reserve)
493	Thomas	Lewis	9	Potlotek, Chapel Island (Cape Breton reserve)
494	Maryann	Luland?	14	Truro, Millbrook Reserve area
495	Noel	Luland?	39	Truro, Millbrook Reserve area
496	Angelic	Marble	16	Pictou Co., Pictou Landing (reserve)
497	Ellen	Marble	12	Heatherton (Paqtnkek Reserve Area)
498	Frances	Marble	46	Pictou Co., Pictou Landing (reserve)
499	Madelin	Marble	9	Pictou Co., Pictou Landing (reserve)
500	Maryann	Marble	32	Pictou Co., Pictou Landing (reserve)
501	Peter	Marble	17	Heatherton (Paqtnkek Reserve Area)
502	Rosalie	Marble	31	Pictou Co., Pictou Landing (reserve)
503	Susan	Marble	1	Pictou Co., Pictou Landing (reserve)
504	William	Marble	6	Pictou Co., Pictou Landing (reserve)
505	Andrew	Marshall	2	Eskasoni (Cape Breton reserve)
506	Benjamin	Marshall	3	Town of Guysborough (Subdistrict F)
507	Bridget	Marshall	1	Town of Guysborough (Subdistrict F)
508	Caroline	Marshall	11	Town of Guysborough (Subdistrict F)
509	Caroline	Marshall	1	Town of Guysborough (Subdistrict F)
510	Charles	Marshall	52	Eskasoni (Cape Breton reserve)
511	Esther	Marshall	42	Town of Guysborough (Subdistrict F)
512	Esther	Marshall	18	Town of Guysborough (Subdistrict F)
513	James	Marshall	57	Tracadie (Paqtnkek Reserve Area)
514	James	Marshall	23	Tracadie (Paqtnkek Reserve Area)
515	John	Marshall	28	Town of Guysborough (Subdistrict F)
516	Joseph	Marshall	45	Town of Guysborough (Subdistrict F)
517	Joseph	Marshall	4	Town of Guysborough (Subdistrict F)
518	Julia	Marshall	29	Town of Guysborough (Subdistrict F)
519	Mary	Marshall	15	Eskasoni (Cape Breton reserve)
520	Mary	Marshall	10	Town of Guysborough (Subdistrict F)
521	Maryann	Marshall	5	Town of Guysborough (Subdistrict F)
522	Maryann	Marshall	23	Town of Guysborough (Subdistrict F)
523	Mayann	Marshall	37	Eskasoni (Cape Breton reserve)
524	Michael	Marshall	6	Town of Guysborough (Subdistrict F)
525	Noel	Marshall	37	Town of Guysborough (Subdistrict F)
526	Peter	Marshall	4	Eskasoni (Cape Breton reserve)
527	Peter	Marshall	9	Town of Guysborough (Subdistrict F)
528	Sally	Marshall	55	Tracadie (Paqtnkek Reserve Area)
529	Steven	Marshall	16	Town of Guysborough (Subdistrict F)

Education	Housing	Occupation	Marital status	Notes
?	House	?	Married	
?	House	?	Single	
?	House	Basketmaker	Married	
?	House	?	Single	
?	Shanty or wigwam	?	Married	Born New Brunswick
?	Shanty or wigwam	?	Married	Born New Brunswick
?	Shanty or wigwam	?	Single	
?	Shanty or wigwam	Hunter	Married	
?	Shanty or wigwam	?	Married	
?	Shanty or wigwam	?	Widowed	Born New Brunswick
?	Shanty or wigwam	?	Single	
?	House	?	Married	
?	Shanty or wigwam	?	Widowed	
?	Shanty or wigwam	Farmer, cooper	Married	
?	House	Cooper, farmer	Married	
?	Shanty or wigwam	?	Married	
?	Shanty or wigwam	?	Single	
?	Shanty or wigwam	?	Single	
?	Shanty or wigwam	Basketmaker	Widowed	
?	Shanty or wigwam	?	Single	
?	House	?	Single	
?	Shanty or wigwam	Cooper	Married	
?	Shanty or wigwam	?	Single	
?	Shanty or wigwam	?	Married	
?	House	Cooper	Single	
?	Shanty or wigwam	?	Widowed	
?	Shanty or wigwam	?	Single	
?	Shanty or wigwam	?	Single	
?	Wigwam	?	Single	
?	Shanty or wigwam	?	Single	
?	Shanty or wigwam	?	Single	
?	Shanty or wigwam	?	Single	
?	Shanty or wigwam	?	Single	
?	Wigwam	Cooper	Married	
?	Shanty or wigwam	?	Married	
?	Shanty or wigwam	Cooper	Single	
?	Shanty or wigwam	Hunter	Married	
?	Shanty or wigwam	?	Single	
?	Shanty or wigwam	Cooper	Married	
?	Shanty or wigwam	Cooper	Married	
?	Shanty or wigwam	?	Single	
?	Shanty or wigwam	?	Married	
School	Wigwam	?	Single	
?	Shanty or wigwam	?	Single	
?	Shanty or wigwam	?	Single	
?	Shanty or wigwam	?	Married	
?	Wigwam	?	Married	
?	Shanty or wigwam	?	Single	
?	Shanty or wigwam	Cooper	Married	
?	Wigwam	?	Single	
?	Shanty or wigwam	Cooper	Single	
?	Shanty or wigwam	?	Married	
?	Shanty or wigwam	Cooper	Single	

1881 Census Data • Continued

ID no.	First name	Last name	Age in years	Location
530	Steven	Marshall	8	Town of Guysborough (Subdistrict F)
531	Susan	Marshall	75	Potlotek, Chapel Island (Cape Breton reserve)
532	Susan	Marshall	2	Town of Guysborough (Subdistrict F)
533	Thomas	Marshall	10	Eskasoni (Cape Breton reserve)
534	Annie	Martin	21	Pictou Co., Hardwood Hill
535	John	Martin	24	Pictou Co., Hardwood Hill
536	Mary	McDonald	26	Pictou Co., West Branch Rver John
537	Madeline	Medwith	60	Truro, Millbrook Reserve area
538	Anne	Michael	78	Eskasoni (Cape Breton reserve)
539	Bella	Michael	5	North Mountain (Cape Breton, 'Malakawe:j reserve)
540	Beloni	Michael	36	North Mountain (Cape Breton, 'Malakawe:j reserve)
541	John	Michael	2	North Mountain (Cape Breton, 'Malakawe:j reserve)
542	May	Michael	36	North Mountain (Cape Breton, 'Malakawe:j reserve)
543	Michael	Michael	88	New Glasgow
544	Noel	Michael	4	North Mountain (Cape Breton, 'Malakawe:j reserve)
545	Noel	Michael	23	Waqamatkuk (Middle River, Cape Breton reserve)
546	Sarah	Michael	7	North Mountain (Cape Breton, 'Malakawe:j reserve)
547	Allan	Mosier	11	Antigonish Co., Lochaber
548	Annie	Muse	22	Pictou Co., Little Harbour
549	Annie	Muse	6	Pictou Co., Little Harbour
550	Bridget	Muse	2	Antigonish Co., Antigonish
551	Charles	Muse	22	Pictou Co., Hardwood Hill
552	Clemmet	Muse	48	Town of Guysborough (Subdistrict F)
553	Eliza	Muse	3	Pictou Co., Hardwood Hill
554	Francis	Muse	22	St. Peters
555	Joe	Muse	28	Antigonish Co., Antigonish
556	John	Muse	28	Pictou Co., Little Harbour
557	Joseph	Muse	2	Town of Guysborough (Subdistrict F)
558	Libby	Muse	2	Pictou Co., Little Harbour
559	Magdelin	Muse	21	Pictou Co., Hardwood Hill
560	Margaret	Muse	16	Town of Guysborough (Subdistrict F)
561	Martha	Muse	23	Town of Guysborough (Subdistrict F)
562	Mary	Muse	2	Pictou Co., Hardwood Hill
563	Mary	Muse	19	Town of Guysborough (Subdistrict F)
564	Morris	Muse	4 mo	Antigonish Co., Antigonish
565	Nancy	Muse	24	Antigonish Co., Antigonish
566	Nancy	Muse	80	Town of Guysborough (Subdistrict F)
567	Noel	Muse	1	Town of Guysborough (Subdistrict F)
568	Amary	Nevin	77	Whycocomagh (Cape Breton reserve)
569	Ann	Nevin	36	Eskasoni (Cape Breton reserve)
570	Fmary	Nevin	4	Whycocomagh (Cape Breton reserve)
571	Jane	Nevin	30	Whycocomagh (Cape Breton reserve)
572	Joanna	Nevin	13	Whycocomagh (Cape Breton reserve)
573	John	Nevin	10	Eskasoni (Cape Breton reserve)
574	Maryann	Nevin	5	Eskasoni (Cape Breton reserve)
575	Noel	Nevin	47	Eskasoni (Cape Breton reserve)
576	Paul	Nevin	2	Eskasoni (Cape Breton reserve)
577	Peter	Nevin	2	Whycocomagh (Cape Breton reserve)
578	Steven	Nevin	12	Eskasoni (Cape Breton reserve)
579	Steven	Nevin	30	Whycocomagh (Cape Breton reserve)
580	Steven	Nevin	11	Whycocomagh (Cape Breton reserve)
581	Annie	Nicholas	19	Big Pond (Cape Breton)
582	Anthony	Nicholas	27	Potlotek, Chapel Island (Cape Breton reserve)

Education	Housing	Occupation	Marital status	Notes
?	Shanty or wigwam	?	Single	
?	Shanty or wigwam	?	Widowed	
?	Shanty or wigwam	?	Single	
School	Wigwam	?	Single	
?	Shanty or wigwam	?	Married	
?	Shanty or wigwam	Cooper	Married	
?	Shanty or wigwam	?	Married	
?	Shanty or wigwam	?	Widowed	
?	House	?	Widowed	
?	Shanty or wigwam	?	Single	
?	Shanty or wigwam	Hunter, fisherman	Married	Male
?	Shanty or wigwam	?	Single	
?	Shanty or wigwam	?	Married	
?	Shanty or wigwam	?	Widowed	
?	Shanty or wigwam	?	Single	
?	Shanty or wigwam	?	Single	
?	Shanty or wigwam	?	Single	
?	House	?	?	
?	Shanty or wigwam	?	Married	
?	Shanty or wigwam	?	Single	
?	Shanty or wigwam	?	Single	
?	House	?	Married	
?	Shanty or wigwam	Cooper	Married	
?	House	?	Single	
?	Shanty or wigwam	Hunter, fisherman	Single	
?	Shanty or wigwam	Cooper	Married	
?	Shanty or wigwam	Cooper	Married	
?	Shanty or wigwam	?	Single	
?	Shanty or wigwam	?	Single	
?	House	?	Married	
?	Shanty or wigwam	?	Single	
?	Shanty or wigwam	?	Married	
?	House	?	Single	
?	Shanty or wigwam	?	Single	
?	Shanty or wigwam	?	Single	
?	Shanty or wigwam	?	Married	
?	Shanty or wigwam	?	Single	
?	Shanty or wigwam	?	Single	
?	House	?	Widowed	
?	Shanty or wigwam	?	Married	
?	House	?	Single	
?	House	?	Married	
School	House	?	Single	
?	Shanty or wigwam	?	Single	
?	Shanty or wigwam	?	Single	
?	Shanty or wigwam	Cooper	Married	
?	Shanty or wigwam	?	Single	
?	House	?	Single	
School	Shanty or wigwam	?	Single	
?	House	Farmer, cooper	Married	
School	House	?	Single	
?	Shanty or wigwam	?	Single	
?	Shanty or wigwam	Farmer, cooper	Married	

1881 Census Data • Continued

ID no.	First name	Last name	Age in years	Location
583	Catharine	Nicholas	10	Pictou Co., Pictou Landing (reserve)
584	Charlot	Nicholas	8	Pictou Co., Pictou Landing (reserve)
585	Christy	Nicholas	56	Big Pond (Cape Breton)
586	Elizabeth	Nicholas	18	Antigonish Co., Antigonish, District 2
587	Joseph	Nicholas	57	Big Pond (Cape Breton)
588	Julia	Nicholas	8	Colchester Co., Salmon River (reserve)
589	Mary	Nicholas	20	Pictou Co., Pictou Landing (reserve)
590	Oliver	Nicholas	27	Pictou Co., Pictou Landing (reserve)
591	Sally	Nicholas	19	Potlotek, Chapel Island (Cape Breton reserve)
592	Samuel	Nicholas	1	Potlotek, Chapel Island (Cape Breton reserve)
593	Thomas	Nicholas	23	Antigonish Co., Antigonish, District 10
594	Abram	Noel	21	Truro, Millbrook Reserve area
595	Agnes	Noel	43	Pictou Co., Pictou Landing (reserve)
596	Amary	Noel	15	Whycocomagh (Cape Breton reserve)
597	Andrew	Noel	61	Whycocomagh (Cape Breton reserve)
598	Angelic	Noel	5	Waqamatkuk (Middle River, Cape Breton reserve)
599	Ann	Noel	13	Eskasoni (Cape Breton reserve)
600	Ann	Noel	2	Whycocomagh (Cape Breton reserve)
601	Anna	Noel	43	Pictou Co., Pictou Landing (reserve)
602	Annie	Noel	54	Waqamatkuk (Middle River, Cape Breton reserve)
603	Bella	Noel	8	Waqamatkuk (Middle River, Cape Breton reserve)
604	Bella	Noel	5	Whycocomagh (Cape Breton reserve)
605	Bernard	Noel	40	Amherst
606	Bridget	Noel	30	Waqamatkuk (Middle River, Cape Breton reserve)
607	Bridget	Noel	25	Guysborough Co., Sherbrooke
608	Caroline	Noel	3	Town of Guysborough (Subdistrict F)
609	Catharine	Noel	89	Waqamatkuk (Middle River, Cape Breton reserve)
610	Charlot	Noel	7	New Glasgow
611	Charlot	Noel	29	Waqamatkuk (Middle River, Cape Breton reserve)
612	Christy	Noel	15	Guysborough Co., Sherbrooke
613	Dennis	Noel	54	Antigonish Co., Lochaber
614	Elizabeth	Noel	11	Pictou Co., Pictou Landing (reserve)
615	Elizabeth	Noel	10	Whycocomagh (Cape Breton reserve)
616	Elizabeth	Noel	21	Town of Guysborough (Subdistrict F)
617	Ellen	Noel	17	Guysborough Co., Sherbrooke
618	Ellen	Noel	16	Town of Guysborough (Subdistrict F)
619	Freman	Noel	55	Town of Guysborough (Subdistrict F)
620	Gabriel	Noel	6	Whycocomagh (Cape Breton reserve)
621	Harriet	Noel	2	Waqamatkuk (Middle River, Cape Breton reserve)
622	Harriet	Noel	19	Guysborough Co., Sherbrooke
623	Janet	Noel	68	Waqamatkuk (Middle River, Cape Breton reserve)
624	Joe	Noel	79	Waqamatkuk (Middle River, Cape Breton reserve)
625	Joe	Noel	11	Waqamatkuk (Middle River, Cape Breton reserve)
626	Joe	Noel	27	Whycocomagh (Cape Breton reserve)
627	John	Noel	47	Pictou Co., Little Harbour
628	John	Noel	47	Pictou Co., Pictou Landing (reserve)
629	John	Noel	9	Pictou Co., Pictou Landing (reserve)
630	John	Noel	4	Whycocomagh (Cape Breton reserve)
631	Joseph	Noel	67	Antigonish Co., Antigonish, District 12
632	Joseph	Noel	19	Truro, Millbrook Reserve area
633	Joseph	Noel	48	Town of Guysborough (Subdistrict F)
634	Levi	Noel	9	Guysborough Co., Sherbrooke
635	Lewis	Noel	31	Town of Guysborough (Subdistrict F)

Education	Housing	Occupation	Marital status	Notes
?	Shanty or wigwam	?	Single	
?	Shanty or wigwam	?	Single	
?	Shanty or wigwam	?	Married	
?	Shanty or wigwam	?	Married	
?	Shanty or wigwam	Cooper	Married	
?	Shanty or wigwam	?	Single	
?	Shanty or wigwam	?	Married	
?	Shanty or wigwam	Cooper	Married	Born New Brunswick
?	Shanty or wigwam	?	Married	
?	Shanty or wigwam	?	Single	
?	Shanty or wigwam	Cooper	Married	
?	Shanty or wigwam	Cooper	Single	
?	Shanty or wigwam	?	Married	
?	House	?	Single	
?	Shanty or wigwam	?	Single	
?	Shanty or wigwam	?	Single	
?	Shanty or wigwam	?	Single	
?	House	?	Single	
?	Shanty or wigwam	?	Widowed	
?	House	?	Single	
?	Shanty or wigwam	?	Single	
School	House	?	Single	
?	Shanty or wigwam	Cooper, hunter	Married	Born New Brunswick
?	Shanty or wigwam	?	Married	
?	Shanty or wigwam	?	Single	
?	Shanty or wigwam	?	Single	
?	Shanty or wigwam	?	Single	
?	Shanty or wigwam	?	Single	
?	Shanty or wigwam	?	Married	
?	Shanty or wigwam	?	Single	
?	House	Cooper	Married	
?	Shanty or wigwam	?	Single	
School	House	?	Single	
?	Shanty or wigwam	?	Single	
?	Shanty or wigwam	?	Single	
?	Shanty or wigwam	Cooper	Married	
?	Shanty or wigwam	Cooper	Married	
School	House	?	Single	
?	Shanty or wigwam	?	Single	
?	Shanty or wigwam	?	Single	
?	House	?	Married	
?	House	Cooper	Married	
?	Shanty or wigwam	?	Single	
?	House	Farmer	Married	
?	Shanty or wigwam	Cooper	Married	
?	Shanty or wigwam	Cooper	Married	
?	Shanty or wigwam	?	Single	
?	House	?	Single	
?	Shanty or wigwam	Cooper	Married	
?	Shanty or wigwam	?	Single	
?	Shanty or wigwam	?	Married	
?	Shanty or wigwam	?	Single	
?	Shanty or wigwam	Cooper	Married	

1881 Census Data • Continued

ID no.	First name	Last name	Age in years	Location
636	Louis	Noel	30	Waqamatkuk (Middle River, Cape Breton reserve)
637	Madeline	Noel	41	Whycocomagh (Cape Breton reserve)
638	Margaret	Noel	23	Town of Guysborough (Subdistrict F)
639	Margaret	Noel	38	Town of Guysborough (Subdistrict F)
640	Mary	Noel	43	Pictou Co., Little Harbour
641	Mary	Noel	58	Antigonish Co., Lochaber
642	Mary	Noel	44	Antigonish Co., Antigonish, District 4
643	Mary	Noel	22	New Glasgow
644	Mary	Noel	63	Truro, Millbrook Reserve area
645	Mary	Noel	9	Eskasoni (Cape Breton reserve)
646	Mary	Noel	38	Whycocomagh (Cape Breton reserve)
647	Mary	Noel	73	Whycocomagh (Cape Breton reserve)
648	Mary	Noel	9	Whycocomagh (Cape Breton reserve)
649	Mary	Noel	8	Guysborough Co., Sherbrooke
650	Mary	Noel	1	Town of Guysborough (Subdistrict F)
651	Maryann	Noel	62	Guysborough Co., Sherbrooke
652	Mathew	Noel	9	New Glasgow
653	Michael	Noel	38	Waqamatkuk (Middle River, Cape Breton reserve)
654	Michael	Noel	1 mo	Waqamatkuk (Middle River, Cape Breton reserve)
655	Michael	Noel	34	Guysborough Co., Sherbrooke
656	Nancy	Noel	28	Guysborough Co., Sherbrooke
657	Nicholas	Noel	6	Guysborough Co., Sherbrooke
658	Noel	Noel	6	Waqamatkuk (Middle River, Cape Breton reserve)
659	Noel	Noel	18	Waqamatkuk (Middle River, Cape Breton reserve)
660	Noel	Noel	12	Town of Guysborough (Subdistrict F)
661	Paul	Noel	32	New Glasgow
662	Paul	Noel	2 mo	New Glasgow
663	Paul	Noel	1	Town of Guysborough (Subdistrict F)
664	Peter	Noel	3	Waqamatkuk (Middle River, Cape Breton reserve)
665	Peter	Noel	74	Whycocomagh (Cape Breton reserve)
666	Peter	Noel	24	Town of Guysborough (Subdistrict F)
667	Prosper	Noel	2	Pictou Co., Pictou Landing (reserve)
668	Sarah	Noel	10	Truro, Millbrook Reserve area
669	Sarah	Noel	33	Town of Guysborough (Subdistrict F)
670	Simon	Noel	29	Waqamatkuk (Middle River, Cape Breton reserve)
671	Sofie	Noel	32	Waqamatkuk (Middle River, Cape Breton reserve)
672	Steven	Noel	14	Pictou Co., Pictou Landing (reserve)
673	Steven	Noel	11	Eskasoni (Cape Breton reserve)
674	Steven	Noel	4	Waqamatkuk (Middle River, Cape Breton reserve)
675	Steven	Noel	9	Whycocomagh (Cape Breton reserve)
676	Susan	Noel	78	Whycocomagh (Cape Breton reserve)
677	Susan	Noel	24	Whycocomagh (Cape Breton reserve)
678	Thomas	Noel	11 mo	Town of Guysborough (Subdistrict F)
679	Victoria	Noel	13	Town of Guysborough (Subdistrict F)
680	William	Noel	25	Antigonish Co., St. Joseph's
681	Mary	Noel	18	Amherst
682	Abram	Paid?	13	Catalone
683	Frank	Paid?	12	Catalone
684	Lucy	Paid?	53	Catalone
685	Madelin	Paid?	50	Catalone
686	Maggie	Paid?	16	Catalone
687	Maryan	Paid?	7	Catalone
688	Steven	Paid?	3	Catalone

Education	Housing	Occupation	Marital status	Notes
?	Shanty or wigwam	Cooper	Married	
?	House	?	Single	
?	Shanty or wigwam	?	Married	
?	Shanty or wigwam	?	Married	
?	Shanty or wigwam	?	Married	
?	House	?	Married	
?	Shanty or wigwam	?	Married	
?	Shanty or wigwam	?	Married	
?	Shanty or wigwam	?	Widowed	
School	Shanty or wigwam	?	Single	
?	House	Farmer	Widowed	
?	House	?	Married	
School	House	?	Single	
?	Shanty or wigwam	?	Single	
?	Shanty or wigwam	?	Single	
?	Shanty or wigwam	?	Widowed	
?	Shanty or wigwam	?	Single	
?	Shanty or wigwam	Cooper	Married	
?	Shanty or wigwam	?	Single	
?	Shanty or wigwam	?	Married	
?	Shanty or wigwam	?	Married	
?	Shanty or wigwam	?	Single	
?	Shanty or wigwam	?	Single	
?	House	?	Single	
?	Shanty or wigwam	?	Single	
?	Shanty or wigwam	?	Married	
?	Shanty or wigwam	?	Single	
?	Shanty or wigwam	?	Single	
?	Shanty or wigwam	?	Single	
?	House	Farmer	Married	
?	Shanty or wigwam	Cooper	Married	
?	Shanty or wigwam	?	Single	
?	Shanty or wigwam	?	Single	
?	Shanty or wigwam	?	Married	
?	Shanty or wigwam	Cooper	Married	
?	Shanty or wigwam	?	Married	
?	Shanty or wigwam	?	Single	
School	Shanty or wigwam	?	Single	
?	Shanty or wigwam	?	Single	
School	House	?	Single	
?	House	?	Widowed	
?	House	?	Married	
?	Shanty or wigwam	?	Single	
?	Shanty or wigwam	?	Single	
?	Shanty or wigwam	?	Single	
?	Shanty or wigwam	?	Married	Born New Brunswick
?	Shanty or wigwam	?	Single	Born Prince Edward Island
?	Shanty or wigwam	?	Single	Born Prince Edward Island
?	Shanty or wigwam	Cooper	Married	Born Prince Edward Island; male?
?	Shanty or wigwam	?	Married	Born Prince Edward Island
?	Shanty or wigwam	?	Single	Born Prince Edward Island
?	Shanty or wigwam	?	Single	Born Prince Edward Island
?	Shanty or wigwam	?	Single	Born Prince Edward Island

1881 Census Data • Continued

ID no.	First name	Last name	Age in years	Location
689	Abram	Paul	3 mo	Pictou Co., Pictou Landing (reserve)
690	Alex	Paul	18	Amherst
691	Andrew	Paul	65	Potlotek, Chapel Island (Cape Breton reserve)
692	Angelic	Paul	9	Pictou Co., Pictou Landing (reserve)
693	Angelic	Paul	14	Pictou Co., Pictou Landing (reserve)
694	Ann	Paul	30	Potlotek, Chapel Island (Cape Breton reserve)
695	Betsy	Paul	45	Potlotek, Chapel Island (Cape Breton reserve)
696	Caroline	Paul	21	Potlotek, Chapel Island (Cape Breton reserve)
697	Catharine	Paul	25	Pictou Co., Little Harbour
698	Charlot	Paul	14	Pictou Co., Little Harbour
699	Charlot	Paul	7	Pictou Co., Pictou Landing (reserve)
700	Charlot	Paul	12	Pictou Co., Pictou Landing (reserve)
701	Charlot	Paul	12	Pictou Co., Pictou Landing (reserve)
702	Elizabe	Paul	1	Amherst
703	Fanny	Paul	21	Amherst
704	Frances	Paul	9 mo	Waqamatkuk (Middle River, Cape Breton reserve)
705	Francis	Paul	28	Pictou Co., Little Harbour
706	Francis	Paul	53	Pictou Co., Little Harbour
707	Francis	Paul	29	Antigonish Co., Antigonish, District 11
708	Francis	Paul	13	Pictou Co., Pictou Landing (reserve)
709	Francis	Paul	32	Judique
710	Frank	Paul	30	New Glasgow
711	James	Paul	33	Pictou Co., Pictou Landing (reserve)
712	James	Paul	4	Waqamatkuk (Middle River, Cape Breton reserve)
713	Jane	Paul	19	Pictou Co., Pictou Landing (reserve)
714	Jennie	Paul	19	Pictou Co., Little Harbour
715	Jenny	Paul	0	Amherst
716	Jessie	Paul	2	Waqamatkuk (Middle River, Cape Breton reserve)
717	Joe	Paul	14	Pictou Co., Pictou Landing (reserve)
718	Joe	Paul	53	Waqamatkuk (Middle River, Cape Breton reserve)
719	John	Paul	8	Pictou Co., Little Harbour
720	John	Paul	3	Antigonish Co., Antigonish, District 5
721	John	Paul	42	Pictou Co., Pictou Landing (reserve)
722	John	Paul	23	Truro, Millbrook Reserve area
723	John	Paul	7	Waqamatkuk (Middle River, Cape Breton reserve)
724	John	Paul	29	Amherst
725	Joseph	Paul	1	Pictou Co., Little Harbour
726	Joseph	Paul	30	Truro, Millbrook Reserve area
727	Julia	Paul	7 mo	Colchester Co., Salmon River (reserve)
728	Julia	Paul	16	Pictou Co., Pictou Landing (reserve)
729	Julie	Paul	23	Waqamatkuk (Middle River, Cape Breton reserve)
730	Larry	Paul	38	Colchester Co., Salmon River (reserve)
731	Larry	Paul	16	Pictou Co., Little Harbour
732	Levi	Paul	4	Waqamatkuk (Middle River, Cape Breton reserve)
733	Libby	Paul	40	Truro, Millbrook Reserve area
734	Louie	Paul	13	Amherst
735	Louis	Paul	26	Potlotek, Chapel Island (Cape Breton reserve)
736	Louisa	Paul	19	Pictou Co., Little Harbour
737	Louisa	Paul	18	Pictou Co., Pictou Landing (reserve)
738	Madeline	Paul	66	Pictou Co., Little Harbour
739	Madeline	Paul	7	Pictou Co., Little Harbour
740	Madeline	Paul	27	New Glasgow
741	Madeline	Paul	60	Pictou Co., Pictou Landing (reserve)

Education	Housing	Occupation	Marital status	Notes
?	Shanty or wigwam	?	Single	
?	Shanty or wigwam	?	Single	Born New Brunswick
?	Shanty or wigwam	Farmer, cooper	Married	
?	Shanty or wigwam	?	Single	
?	Shanty or wigwam	?	Single	
?	Shanty or wigwam	?	Married	
?	Shanty or wigwam	?	Married	
?	Shanty or wigwam	?	Married	
?	Shanty or wigwam	?	Married	
?	Shanty or wigwam	?	Single	
?	Shanty or wigwam	?	Single	
?	Shanty or wigwam	?	Single	
?	Shanty or wigwam	?	Single	
?	Shanty or wigwam	?	Single	Born New Brunswick
?	Shanty or wigwam	?	Married	Born New Brunswick
?	Shanty or wigwam	?	Single	
?	Shanty or wigwam	Cooper	Married	
?	Shanty or wigwam	Cooper	Married	
?	Shanty or wigwam	Cooper	Married	
?	Shanty or wigwam	?	Single	
?	Wigwam	Cooper	Married	
?	Shanty or wigwam	?	Single	
?	Shanty or wigwam	Cooper	Single	
?	Shanty or wigwam	?	Single	
?	Shanty or wigwam	?	Married	
?	Shanty or wigwam	?	Single	
?	Shanty or wigwam	?	Single	
?	Shanty or wigwam	?	Single	
?	Shanty or wigwam	?	Single	
?	Shanty or wigwam	Cooper	Married	
?	Shanty or wigwam	?	Single	
?	Shanty or wigwam	?	Single	
?	Shanty or wigwam	Cooper	Widowed	
?	Shanty or wigwam	Cooper	Married	
?	Shanty or wigwam	?	Single	
?	Shanty or wigwam	Cooper	Married	Born New Brunswick
?	Shanty or wigwam	?	Single	
?	Shanty or wigwam	Cooper	Married	
?	Shanty or wigwam	?	Single	
?	Shanty or wigwam	?	Single	
?	Shanty or wigwam	?	Married	
?	Shanty or wigwam	hunter	Married	
?	Shanty or wigwam	?	Single	
?	Shanty or wigwam	?	Single	
?	Shanty or wigwam	?	Married	
?	Shanty or wigwam	?	Single	Born New Brunswick
?	Shanty or wigwam	Farmer, cooper	Married	
?	Shanty or wigwam	?	Single	
?	Shanty or wigwam	?	Single	
?	Shanty or wigwam	?	Married	
?	Shanty or wigwam	?	Single	
?	Shanty or wigwam	?	Single	
?	Shanty or wigwam	?	Married	

1881 Census Data • Continued

ID no.	First name	Last name	Age in years	Location
742	Madeline	Paul	13	Waqamatkuk (Middle River, Cape Breton reserve)
743	Magdalin	Paul	33	Colchester Co., Salmon River (reserve)
744	Margare	Paul	33	Amherst
745	Margaret	Paul	28	Truro, Millbrook Reserve area
746	Maria	Paul	5	Truro, Millbrook Reserve area
747	Mary	Paul	42	Pictou Co., Little Harbour
748	Mary	Paul	11	Pictou Co., Little Harbour
749	Mary	Paul	31	Antigonish Co., Antigonish, District 3
750	Mary	Paul	16	Pictou Co., Pictou Landing (reserve)
751	Mary	Paul	1	Truro, Millbrook Reserve area
752	Mary	Paul	90	Potlotek, Chapel Island (Cape Breton reserve)
753	Mary	Paul	37	Judique
754	Mary	Paul	11	Waqamatkuk (Middle River, Cape Breton reserve)
755	Mary	Paul	48	Pictou Co., Pictou Landing (reserve)
756	Mary	Paul	38	North Sydney
757	Mary	Paul	18	Amherst
758	Maryann	Paul	24	Pictou Co., Little Harbour
759	Maryann	Paul	30	Truro, Millbrook Reserve area
760	Maryann	Paul	7	Waqamatkuk (Middle River, Cape Breton reserve)
761	Maryann	Paul	53	Waqamatkuk (Middle River, Cape Breton reserve)
762	Maryjane	Paul	23	Pictou Co., Pictou Landing (reserve)
763	Mathew	Paul	7	Pictou Co., Little Harbour
764	Mathew	Paul	49	Pictou Co., Pictou Landing (reserve)
765	Matthew	Paul	9	Pictou Co., Pictou Landing (reserve)
766	Matthew	Paul	10	Waqamatkuk (Middle River, Cape Breton reserve)
767	Michael	Paul	7 mo	Potlotek, Chapel Island (Cape Breton reserve)
768	Michael	Paul	13	Potlotek, Chapel Island (Cape Breton reserve)
769	Michael	Paul	8	Whycocomagh (Cape Breton reserve)
770	Nancy	Paul	18	Potlotek, Chapel Island (Cape Breton reserve)
771	Nancy	Paul	28	Whycocomagh (Cape Breton reserve)
772	Noel	Paul	26	Pictou Co., Little Harbour
773	Noel	Paul	13	Pictou Co., Little Harbour
774	Noel	Paul	33	Pictou Co., Pictou Landing (reserve)
775	Noel	Paul	49	Potlotek, Chapel Island (Cape Breton reserve)
776	Noel	Paul	33	Waqamatkuk (Middle River, Cape Breton reserve)
777	Noel	Paul	10	Whycocomagh (Cape Breton reserve)
778	Noname	Paul	2 mo	Pictou Co., Pictou Landing (reserve)
779	Paul	Paul	55	Pictou Co., Pictou Landing (reserve)
780	Peter	Paul	5	Pictou Co., Little Harbour
781	Peter	Paul	65	Pictou Co., Little Harbour
782	Peter	Paul	12	Pictou Co., Little Harbour
783	Peter	Paul	27	Pictou Co., Pictou Landing (reserve)
784	Peter	Paul	68	Pictou Co., Pictou Landing (reserve)
785	Peter	Paul	7	Truro, Millbrook Reserve area
786	Richard	Paul	13	Potlotek, Chapel Island (Cape Breton reserve)
787	Sally	Paul	4	Pictou Co., Little Harbour
788	Sally	Paul	16	Pictou Co., Little Harbour
789	Sally	Paul	67	Pictou Co., Little Harbour
790	Sally	Paul	11	Pictou Co., Pictou Landing (reserve)
791	Sally	Paul	65	Pictou Co., Pictou Landing (reserve)
792	Sam	Paul	6	Pictou Co., Little Harbour
793	Samuel	Paul	30	Pictou Co., Little Harbour
794	Simon	Paul	38	Waqamatkuk (Middle River, Cape Breton reserve)

Education	Housing	Occupation	Marital status	Notes
?	Shanty or wigwam	?	Single	
?	Shanty or wigwam	?	Married	
?	Shanty or wigwam	?	Married	Born New Brunswick
?	Shanty or wigwam	Basketmaker	Married	
?	Shanty or wigwam	?	Single	
?	Shanty or wigwam	?	Married	
?	Shanty or wigwam	?	Single	
?	Shanty or wigwam	?	Married	
?	Shanty or wigwam	?	Single	
?	Shanty or wigwam	?	Single	
?	Shanty or wigwam	?	Widowed	
?	Wigwam	?	Married	
?	Shanty or wigwam	?	Single	
?	Shanty or wigwam	?	Married	Born Prince Edward Island
?	Shanty or wigwam	?	Single	Born Newfoundland
?	Shanty or wigwam	?	Married	Born New Brunswick
?	Shanty or wigwam	?	Married	
?	Shanty or wigwam	?	Married	
?	Shanty or wigwam	?	Single	
?	Shanty or wigwam	?	Married	
?	Shanty or wigwam	?	Married	
?	Shanty or wigwam	?	Single	
?	Shanty or wigwam	Boat builder	Widowed	
?	Shanty or wigwam	?	Single	
?	Shanty or wigwam	?	Single	
?	Shanty or wigwam	?	Single	
?	Shanty or wigwam	?	Single	
School	House	?	Single	
?	Shanty or wigwam	?	Single	
?	House	?	Married	
?	Shanty or wigwam	Cooper	Married	
?	Shanty or wigwam	?	Single	
?	Shanty or wigwam	Cooper	Married	
?	Shanty or wigwam	Cooper	Married	
?	Shanty or wigwam	?	Single	
School	House	?	Single	
?	Shanty or wigwam	?	Single	
?	Shanty or wigwam	Cooper	Married	
?	Shanty or wigwam	?	Single	
?	Shanty or wigwam	Cooper	Married	
?	Shanty or wigwam	?	Single	
?	Shanty or wigwam	Cooper	Married	
?	Shanty or wigwam	Cooper	Married	
?	Shanty or wigwam	?	Single	
?	Shanty or wigwam	?	Single	
?	Shanty or wigwam	?	Single	
?	Shanty or wigwam	?	Single	
?	Shanty or wigwam	Cooper	Widowed	
?	Shanty or wigwam	?	Single	
?	Shanty or wigwam	?	Widowed	
?	Shanty or wigwam	?	Single	
?	Shanty or wigwam	Cooper	Widowed	
?	Shanty or wigwam	Cooper	Married	

1881 Census Data • Continued

ID no.	First name	Last name	Age in years	Location
795	Sophie	Paul	9	Antigonish Co., Antigonish, District 6
796	Stephen	Paul	24	Amherst
797	Steven	Paul	5	Potlotek, Chapel Island (Cape Breton reserve)
798	Steven	Paul	30	Whycocomagh (Cape Breton reserve)
799	Steven	Paul	17	Pictou Co., Pictou Landing (reserve)
800	Terry	Paul	10	Potlotek, Chapel Island (Cape Breton reserve)
801	Thomas	Paul	7	Truro, Millbrook Reserve area
802	Thomas	Paul	2	Potlotek, Chapel Island (Cape Breton reserve)
803	William	Paul	22	Potlotek, Chapel Island (Cape Breton reserve)
804	Bella	Peck	7 mo	Waqamatkuk (Middle River, Cape Breton reserve)
805	Ben	Peck	7	Waqamatkuk (Middle River, Cape Breton reserve)
806	Fannie	Peck	28	Waqamatkuk (Middle River, Cape Breton reserve)
807	Isaac	Peck	7	Whycocomagh (Cape Breton reserve)
808	Kate	Peck	2	Waqamatkuk (Middle River, Cape Breton reserve)
809	Louisa	Peck	18	Whycocomagh (Cape Breton reserve)
810	Mary	Peck	62	Whycocomagh (Cape Breton reserve)
811	Michael	Peck	34	Waqamatkuk (Middle River, Cape Breton reserve)
812	Peter	Peck	9	Waqamatkuk (Middle River, Cape Breton reserve)
813	Jennie	Peters	40	Pictou Co., Little Harbour
814	Louis	Peters	27	Town of Guysborough (Subdistrict F)
815	Mary	Peters	13	Town of Guysborough (Subdistrict F)
816	Moses	Peters	3	Pictou Co., Little Harbour
817	Paul	Peters	18	Pictou Co., Little Harbour
818	Sam	Peters	21	Pictou Co., Little Harbour
819	Sarah	Peters	57	Town of Guysborough (Subdistrict F)
820	Stephen	Peters	67	Town of Guysborough (Subdistrict F)
821	Alex	Philips	16	Antigonish Co., St. Joseph's
822	Anne	Philips	10	Antigonish Co., St. Joseph's
823	Annmagda	Philips	10	Colchester Co., Salmon River (reserve)
824	Frank	Philips	7	Antigonish Co., St. Joseph's
825	Jennie	Philips	20	New Glasgow
826	Joe	Philips	4	Antigonish Co., St. Joseph's
827	John	Philips	25	New Glasgow
828	Joseph	Philips	46	Colchester Co., Salmon River (reserve)
829	Levi	Philips	18	Antigonish Co., St. Joseph's
830	Magdalin	Philips	64	Colchester Co., Salmon River (reserve)
831	Maryann	Philips	35	Antigonish Co., St. Joseph's
832	Noel	Philips	47	Antigonish Co., St. Joseph's
833	Philip	Philips	5	New Glasgow
834	Sarah	Philips	12	Antigonish Co., St. Joseph's
835	Annie	Pictou	64	Heatherton (Paqtnkek Reserve Area)
836	Annie	Pictou	18	Heatherton (Paqtnkek Reserve Area)
837	James	Pictou	24	Heatherton (Paqtnkek Reserve Area)
838	Mary	Pictou	20	Heatherton (Paqtnkek Reserve Area)
839	Noel	Pictou	33	Heatherton (Paqtnkek Reserve Area)
840	Sarah	Pictou	33	Heatherton (Paqtnkek Reserve Area)
841	Angelic	Pierro	21	Waqamatkuk (Middle River, Cape Breton reserve)
842	Joe	Pierro	1	Waqamatkuk (Middle River, Cape Breton reserve)
843	Louis	Pierro	76	Waqamatkuk (Middle River, Cape Breton reserve)
844	Noel	Pierro	4	Waqamatkuk (Middle River, Cape Breton reserve)
845	Peter	Pierro	27	Waqamatkuk (Middle River, Cape Breton reserve)
846	Charles	Poulette	36	Heatherton (Paqtnkek Reserve Area)
847	Ellen	Poulette	26	Heatherton (Paqtnkek Reserve Area)

Education	Housing	Occupation	Marital status	Notes
?	Shanty or wigwam	?	Single	
?	Shanty or wigwam	Cooper	Married	Born New Brunswick
?	Shanty or wigwam	?	Single	
?	House	Farmer, cooper	Married	
?	Shanty or wigwam	Cooper	Single	Born New Brunswick
?	Shanty or wigwam	?	Single	Male
?	Shanty or wigwam	?	Single	
?	Shanty or wigwam	?	Single	
?	Shanty or wigwam	Cooper	Single	
?	House	?	Single	
?	House	?	Single	
?	House	?	Married	
?	House	?	Single	
?	House	?	Single	
?	House	?	Single	
?	House	?	Widowed	
?	House	Cooper	Married	
?	House	?	Single	
?	Shanty or wigwam	?	Widowed	
?	Shanty or wigwam	Cooper, hunter	Single	
?	Shanty or wigwam	Cooper, hunter	Single	
?	Shanty or wigwam	?	Single	
?	Shanty or wigwam	?	Single	
?	Shanty or wigwam	Cooper	Single	
?	Shanty or wigwam	Cooper	Married	
?	Shanty or wigwam	Cooper	Married	
?	Shanty or wigwam	?	Single	
?	Shanty or wigwam	?	Single	
?	Shanty or wigwam	?	Single	
?	Shanty or wigwam	?	Single	
?	Shanty or wigwam	?	Married	
?	Shanty or wigwam	?	Single	
?	Shanty or wigwam	?	Married	
?	Shanty or wigwam	hunter	Married	
?	Shanty or wigwam	?	Single	
?	Shanty or wigwam	?	Married	
?	Shanty or wigwam	?	Married	
?	Shanty or wigwam	Cooper	Married	
?	Shanty or wigwam	?	Single	
?	Shanty or wigwam	?	Single	
?	Shanty or wigwam	Basketmaker	Widowed	
School	Shanty or wigwam	?	Single	
?	Shanty or wigwam	Hunter, fisherman	Married	
?	Shanty or wigwam	Basketmaker	Married	
?	Shanty or wigwam	Cooper, farmer	Single	
?	Shanty or wigwam	?	Single	
?	Shanty or wigwam	?	Married	
?	Shanty or wigwam	?	Single	
?	Shanty or wigwam	?	Single	
?	Shanty or wigwam	?	Single	
?	Shanty or wigwam	Cooper	Married	
?	House	Miner	Married	
?	House	?	Married	

1881 Census Data • Continued

ID no.	First name	Last name	Age in years	Location
848	James	Poulette	55	Amherst
849	Louis	Poulette	13	Amherst
850	Mary	Poulette	19	Amherst
851	Michael	Poulette	16	Amherst
852	Noel	Poulette	3	Heatherton (Paqtnkek Reserve Area)
853	Tatima	Poulette	9	Amherst
854	Theresa	Poulette	11	Heatherton (Paqtnkek Reserve Area)
855	Adeline	Prosper	3	Truro, Millbrook Reserve area
856	Alex	Prosper	14	Truro, Millbrook Reserve area
857	Ann	Prosper	65	St. Peters
858	Ben	Prosper	5	Tracadie (Paqtnkek Reserve Area)
859	Caroline	Prosper	15	Antigonish Co., Antigonish
860	Caroline	Prosper	5	Guysborough Co., Larry's River
861	Catharine	Prosper	11 mo	Guysborough Co., Larry's River
862	Charles	Prosper	3	Tracadie (Paqtnkek Reserve Area)
863	Christopher	Prosper	67	Heatherton (Paqtnkek Reserve Area)
864	Christopher	Prosper	15	Eskasoni (Cape Breton reserve)
865	Elizabeth	Prosper	2	Heatherton (Paqtnkek Reserve Area)
866	Elizabeth	Prosper	11	Pictou Co., Hardwood Hill
867	Ellen	Prosper	44	Eskasoni (Cape Breton reserve)
868	Eunice	Prosper	29	Truro, Millbrook Reserve area
869	Flora	Prosper	40	Heatherton (Paqtnkek Reserve Area)
870	Frank	Prosper	34	Antigonish Co., St. Joseph's
871	Gabriel	Prosper	12	Heatherton (Paqtnkek Reserve Area)
872	Harriet	Prosper	23	Tracadie (Paqtnkek Reserve Area)
873	J?	Prosper	66	St. Peters
874	James	Prosper	44	Heatherton (Paqtnkek Reserve Area)
875	James	Prosper	11	Heatherton (Paqtnkek Reserve Area)
876	James	Prosper	18	Heatherton (Paqtnkek Reserve Area)
877	Joanna	Prosper	22	Tracadie (Paqtnkek Reserve Area)
878	Joe	Prosper	23	Whycocomagh (Cape Breton reserve)
879	John	Prosper	3	Pictou Co., Hardwood Hill
880	John	Prosper	33	Guysborough Co., Larry's River
881	Joseph	Prosper	1 mo	Heatherton (Paqtnkek Reserve Area)
882	Joseph	Prosper	40	Antigonish Co., Antigonish
883	Joseph	Prosper	2	Antigonish Co., Antigonish
884	Joseph	Prosper	7	Pictou Co., Hardwood Hill
885	Joseph	Prosper	38	Truro, Millbrook Reserve area
886	Joseph	Prosper	2	Guysborough Co., Larry's River
887	Julia	Prosper	5	Tracadie (Paqtnkek Reserve Area)
888	Levi	Prosper	25	Truro, Millbrook Reserve area
889	Lisa	Prosper	2 mo	Whycocomagh (Cape Breton reserve)
890	Madeline	Prosper	68	Heatherton (Paqtnkek Reserve Area)
891	Magdalin	Prosper	1	Eskasoni (Cape Breton reserve)
892	Magdelin	Prosper	35	Pictou Co., Hardwood Hill
893	Mary	Prosper	48	Tracadie (Paqtnkek Reserve Area)
894	Mary	Prosper	10 mo	Tracadie (Paqtnkek Reserve Area)
895	Mary	Prosper	15	Heatherton (Paqtnkek Reserve Area)
896	Mary	Prosper	33	Heatherton (Paqtnkek Reserve Area)
897	Mary	Prosper	36	Antigonish Co., Antigonish
898	Mary	Prosper	8	Antigonish Co., Antigonish
899	Mary	Prosper	6	Antigonish Co., Antigonish
900	Mary	Prosper	4	Eskasoni (Cape Breton reserve)

Education	Housing	Occupation	Marital status	Notes
?	Shanty or wigwam	?	Widowed	
?	Shanty or wigwam	?	Single	Born New Brunswick
?	Shanty or wigwam	?	Single	Born New Brunswick
?	Shanty or wigwam	?	Single	
?	House	?	Single	
?	Shanty or wigwam	?	Single	Born New Brunswick; female
?	House	?	Single	
?	Shanty or wigwam	?	Single	
?	Shanty or wigwam	?	Single	
?	Shanty or wigwam	?	Married	
?	Shanty or wigwam	?	Single	
?	Shanty or wigwam	?	Single	
?	Shanty or wigwam	?	Single	
?	Shanty or wigwam	?	Single	
?	Shanty or wigwam	?	Single	
?	House	Farmer, cooper	Married	
School	House	Cooper	Single	
?	House	?	Single	
?	Shanty or wigwam	?	Single	
?	House	?	Married	
?	Shanty or wigwam	?	Married	
?	House	?	Married	French woman
?	House	Cooper	Married	
?	House	?	Single	
?	Shanty or wigwam	?	Married	
?	Shanty or wigwam	Hunter, fisherman	Married	
?	House	Cooper	Married	
School	House	?	Single	
?	House	?	Single	
?	Shanty or wigwam	?	Single	
?	House	Farmer, cooper	Married	
?	Shanty or wigwam	?	Single	
?	Shanty or wigwam	Fisherman	Married	
?	House	?	Single	
?	Shanty or wigwam	Cooper	Married	
?	Shanty or wigwam	?	Single	
?	Shanty or wigwam	?	Single	
?	Shanty or wigwam	Cooper	Married	
?	Shanty or wigwam	?	Single	
?	Shanty or wigwam	?	Single	
?	Shanty or wigwam	?	Single	
?	House	?	Single	
?	House	?	Widowed	Blind
?	House	?	Single	
?	Shanty or wigwam	?	Married	
?	Shanty or wigwam	?	Widowed	
?	Shanty or wigwam	?	Single	
?	House	?	Single	
?	House	Basketmaker	Married	
?	Shanty or wigwam	?	Married	
?	Shanty or wigwam	?	Single	
?	Shanty or wigwam	?	Single	
?	House	?	Single	

1881 Census Data • Continued

ID no.	First name	Last name	Age in years	Location
901	Mary	Prosper	19	Whycocomagh (Cape Breton reserve)
902	Mary	Prosper	26	Guysborough Co., Larry's River
903	Maryann	Prosper	30	Antigonish Co., St. Joseph's
904	Maryann	Prosper	18	Eskasoni (Cape Breton reserve)
905	Michael	Prosper	33	Tracadie (Paqtnkek Reserve Area)
906	Nancy	Prosper	28	Tracadie (Paqtnkek Reserve Area)
907	Nancy	Prosper	8	Eskasoni (Cape Breton reserve)
908	Noel	Prosper	12	Heatherton (Paqtnkek Reserve Area)
909	Noel	Prosper	12	Antigonish Co., Antigonish
910	Noel	Prosper	10	Guysborough Co., Larry's River
911	Paul	Prosper	64	Eskasoni (Cape Breton reserve)
912	Peter	Prosper	35	Tracadie (Paqtnkek Reserve Area)
913	Peter	Prosper	22	Eskasoni (Cape Breton reserve)
914	Richard	Prosper	1	Tracadie (Paqtnkek Reserve Area)
915	Richard	Prosper	9	Heatherton (Paqtnkek Reserve Area)
916	Sarah	Prosper	7	Heatherton (Paqtnkek Reserve Area)
917	Stephen	Prosper	20	Eskasoni (Cape Breton reserve)
918	Steven	Prosper	25	Antigonish Co., St. Joseph's
919	Susan	Prosper	47	Heatherton (Paqtnkek Reserve Area)
920	Susan	Prosper	4	Heatherton (Paqtnkek Reserve Area)
921	Susan	Prosper	19	Truro, Millbrook Reserve area
922	Valentin	Prosper	32	Heatherton (Paqtnkek Reserve Area)
923	William	Prosper	45	Pictou Co., Hardwood Hill
924	Ben	Richard	5	Potlotek, Chapel Island (Cape Breton reserve)
925	Catharine	Richard	37	Potlotek, Chapel Island (Cape Breton reserve)
926	Janet	Richard	3	Potlotek, Chapel Island (Cape Breton reserve)
927	John	Richard	60	Waqamatkuk (Middle River, Cape Breton reserve)
928	Margaret	Richard	5 mo	Potlotek, Chapel Island (Cape Breton reserve)
929	Maryann	Richard	7	Potlotek, Chapel Island (Cape Breton reserve)
930	Maryann	Richard	59	Waqamatkuk (Middle River, Cape Breton reserve)
931	Nancy	Richard	14	Potlotek, Chapel Island (Cape Breton reserve)
932	Peter	Richard	40	Potlotek, Chapel Island (Cape Breton reserve)
933	Sarah	Richard	19	Potlotek, Chapel Island (Cape Breton reserve)
934	Anne	Salome	6	Antigonish Co., Antigonish
935	Elizabeth	Salome	17	Antigonish Co., St. Joseph's
936	Joe	Salome	62	Antigonish Co., St. Joseph's
937	Maggie	Salome	7	Antigonish Co., Antigonish
938	Maryann	Salome	34	Antigonish Co., Antigonish
939	Michael	Salome	2	Antigonish Co., Antigonish
940	Andrew	Sappier	55	Pictou Co., Little Harbour
941	Catharine	Sappier	1	Pictou Co., Pictou Landing (reserve)
942	Elizabeth	Sappier	23	Pictou Co., Pictou Landing (reserve)
943	Francis	Sappier	27	Pictou Co., Pictou Landing (reserve)
944	Jamie	Sappier	10	Pictou Co., Little Harbour
945	Larry	Sappier	6	Pictou Co., Little Harbour
946	Libby	Sappier	9	Pictou Co., Little Harbour
947	Liza	Sappier	11	Pictou Co., Little Harbour
948	Louis	Sappier	56	Pictou Co., Little Harbour
949	Louis	Sappier	4	Pictou Co., Pictou Landing (reserve)
950	Madelin	Sappier	78	Pictou Co., Little Harbour
951	Marcy	Sappier	52	Pictou Co., Little Harbour
952	Mary	Sappier	14	Pictou Co., Little Harbour
953	Nancy	Sappier	1 mo	Pictou Co., Little Harbour

Education	Housing	Occupation	Marital status	Notes
?	House	?	Married	
?	Shanty or wigwam	?	Married	
?	House	?	Married	
?	House	?	Married	
?	Shanty or wigwam	Hunter	Single	
?	Shanty or wigwam	?	Single	
?	House	?	Single	
?	House	?	Single	
?	Shanty or wigwam	?	Single	
?	Shanty or wigwam	?	Single	
?	House	Cooper	Married	
?	Shanty or wigwam	Hunter	Married	
?	House	Cooper	Married	
?	Shanty or wigwam	?	Single	
?	House	?	Single	
?	House	?	Single	
?	House	Cooper	Single	
?	House	Cooper	Single	
?	House	?	Married	
?	House	?	Single	
?	Shanty or wigwam	?	Single	
?	House	Cooper, farmer	Married	
?	Shanty or wigwam	Cooper	Married	
?	House	?	Single	
?	House	?	Married	
?	House	?	Single	
?	House	Cooper	Married	
?	House	?	Single	
?	House	?	Single	
?	House	?	Married	
?	House	?	Single	
?	House	Farmer, cooper	Married	
?	House	?	Single	
?	Shanty or wigwam	?	Single	
?	Shanty or wigwam	?	Single	
?	Shanty or wigwam	Cooper	Widowed	
?	Shanty or wigwam	?	Single	
?	Shanty or wigwam	?	Widowed	
?	Shanty or wigwam	?	Single	
?	Shanty or wigwam	Cooper	Married	
?	Shanty or wigwam	?	Single	
?	Shanty or wigwam	?	Married	
?	Shanty or wigwam	Cooper	Married	
?	Shanty or wigwam	?	Single	
?	Shanty or wigwam	?	Single	
?	Shanty or wigwam	?	Single	
?	Shanty or wigwam	?	Single	
?	Shanty or wigwam	Cooper	Married	
?	Shanty or wigwam	?	Single	
?	Shanty or wigwam	?	Widowed	Born Newfoundland
?	Shanty or wigwam	?	Married	
?	Shanty or wigwam	?	Single	
?	Shanty or wigwam	?	Single	

1881 Census Data • Continued

ID no.	First name	Last name	Age in years	Location
954	Noel	Sappier	21	Pictou Co., Little Harbour
955	Peter	Sappier	2	Pictou Co., Little Harbour
956	Sally	Sappier	41	Pictou Co., Little Harbour
957	Jennet	Selome	5	Antigonish Co., St. Joseph's
958	Michael	Selome	18	Antigonish Co., St. Joseph's
959	Annie	Sock	7	Pictou Co., Pictou Landing (reserve)
960	Annie	Sock	27	Pictou Co., Pictou Landing (reserve)
961	Annie	Sock	9	Pictou Co., Pictou Landing (reserve)
962	Charles	Sock	12	Pictou Co., Pictou Landing (reserve)
963	Francis	Sock	83	Pictou Co., Pictou Landing (reserve)
964	Frank	Sock	9	Amherst
965	John	Sock	4	Pictou Co., Pictou Landing (reserve)
966	John	Sock	38	Pictou Co., Pictou Landing (reserve)
967	Julia	Sock	18	Pictou Co., Pictou Landing (reserve)
968	Madeline	Sock	56	Amherst
969	Margaret	Sock	27	Pictou Co., Pictou Landing (reserve)
970	Maryann	Sock	35	Pictou Co., Pictou Landing (reserve)
971	Michael	Sock	20	Amherst
972	Nancy	Sock	78	Pictou Co., Pictou Landing (reserve)
973	Noel	Sock	9	Pictou Co., Pictou Landing (reserve)
974	Noel	Sock	38	Pictou Co., Pictou Landing (reserve)
975	Noel	Sock	60	Amherst
976	Noname	Sock	4 mo	Pictou Co., Pictou Landing (reserve)
977	Noname	Sock	1 mo	Pictou Co., Pictou Landing (reserve)
978	Thomas	Sock	6	Pictou Co., Pictou Landing (reserve)
979	Thomas	Sock	18	Amherst
980	Andrew	Stevens	9	River Inhabitants (Cape Breton Island)
981	Bridget	Stevens	3	Eskasoni (Cape Breton reserve)
982	Bridget	Stevens	3	Sydney (King's Road reserve 1881/1891)
983	Bridget	Stevens	11	River Inhabitants (Cape Breton Island)
984	Joe	Stevens	11	Eskasoni (Cape Breton reserve)
985	John	Stevens	28	Pictou Co., Little Harbour
986	John	Stevens	29	New Glasgow
987	John	Stevens	64	Eskasoni (Cape Breton reserve)
988	John	Stevens	60	Sydney (King's Road reserve 1881/1891)
989	John	Stevens	38	River Inhabitants (Cape Breton Island)
990	Madeline	Stevens	22	River Inhabitants (Cape Breton Island)
991	Magdelin	Stevens	22	Eskasoni (Cape Breton reserve)
992	Margret	Stevens	34	New Glasgow
993	Marjorie	Stevens	22	Sydney (King's Road reserve 1881/1891)
994	Martha	Stevens	10 mo	New Glasgow
995	Martin	Stevens	1	River Inhabitants (Cape Breton Island)
996	Morris	Stevens	13	River Inhabitants (Cape Breton Island)
997	Nancy	Stevens	4	New Glasgow
998	Noel	Stevens	1	Eskasoni (Cape Breton reserve)
999	Noel	Stevens	9 mo	Sydney (King's Road reserve 1881/1891)
1000	Paul	Stevens	28	Eskasoni (Cape Breton reserve)
1001	Paul	Stevens	25	Sydney (King's Road reserve 1881/1891)
1002	Victor	Stevens	4	River Inhabitants (Cape Breton Island)
1003	Amary	Sylliboy	3	Whycocomagh (Cape Breton reserve)
1004	Ben	Sylliboy	3	Whycocomagh (Cape Breton reserve)
1005	Caroline	Sylliboy	7	Whycocomagh (Cape Breton reserve)
1006	Catharine	Sylliboy	20	Whycocomagh (Cape Breton reserve)

Education	Housing	Occupation	Marital status	Notes
?	Shanty or wigwam	Cooper	Single	
?	Shanty or wigwam	?	Single	
?	Shanty or wigwam	?	Married	
?	Shanty or wigwam	?	Single	
?	Shanty or wigwam	Cooper	Single	
?	Shanty or wigwam	?	Single	
?	Shanty or wigwam	?	Married	
?	Shanty or wigwam	?	Single	
?	Shanty or wigwam	?	Single	
?	Shanty or wigwam	Cooper	Married	Born Prince Edward Island
?	Shanty or wigwam	?	Single	
?	Shanty or wigwam	?	Single	
?	Shanty or wigwam	Cooper	Married	Born Prince Edward Island
?	Shanty or wigwam	?	Single	
?	Shanty or wigwam	?	Married	Born New Brunswick
?	Shanty or wigwam	?	Single	
?	Shanty or wigwam	?	Married	Scottish woman
?	Shanty or wigwam	Cooper, hunter	Single	Born New Brunswick
?	Shanty or wigwam	?	Married	
?	Shanty or wigwam	?	Single	
?	Shanty or wigwam	?	Married	Born Prince Edward Island
?	Shanty or wigwam	Cooper	Married	Born New Brunswick
?	Shanty or wigwam	?	Single	
?	Shanty or wigwam	?	Single	
?	Shanty or wigwam	?	Single	
?	Shanty or wigwam	Cooper	Single	Born New Brunswick
?	Shanty or wigwam	?	Single	
?	Shanty or wigwam	?	Single	
?	House	?	Single	
?	Shanty or wigwam	?	Single	
School	House	?	Single	
?	Shanty or wigwam	Cooper	Married	
?	Shanty or wigwam	?	Married	
?	Shanty or wigwam	Cooper	Widowed	
?	House	Cooper	Married	
?	Shanty or wigwam	Cooper	Married	
?	Shanty or wigwam	?	Married	
?	Shanty or wigwam	?	Married	
?	Shanty or wigwam	?	Married	
?	House	?	Married	
?	Shanty or wigwam	?	Single	
?	Shanty or wigwam	?	Single	
?	Shanty or wigwam	?	Single	
?	Shanty or wigwam	?	Single	
?	Shanty or wigwam	?	Single	
?	House	?	Single	
?	Shanty or wigwam	Cooper	Married	
?	House	Cooper	Married	
?	Shanty or wigwam	?	Single	
?	House	?	Single	
?	House	?	Single	
School	House	?	Single	
?	House	?	Married	

1881 Census Data • Continued

ID no.	First name	Last name	Age in years	Location
1007	Catharine	Sylliboy	30	Whycocomagh (Cape Breton reserve)
1008	Christopher	Sylliboy	12	Whycocomagh (Cape Breton reserve)
1009	Elisabeth	Sylliboy	7	Whycocomagh (Cape Breton reserve)
1010	Ellen	Sylliboy	6	Whycocomagh (Cape Breton reserve)
1011	Esther	Sylliboy	30	Whycocomagh (Cape Breton reserve)
1012	Jennie	Sylliboy	13	Whycocomagh (Cape Breton reserve)
1013	Joe	Sylliboy	25	Whycocomagh (Cape Breton reserve)
1014	Joe	Sylliboy	7 mo	Whycocomagh (Cape Breton reserve)
1015	Madeline	Sylliboy	10	Whycocomagh (Cape Breton reserve)
1016	Mary	Sylliboy	20	Whycocomagh (Cape Breton reserve)
1017	Mary	Sylliboy	4 mo	Whycocomagh (Cape Breton reserve)
1018	Michael	Sylliboy	50	Whycocomagh (Cape Breton reserve)
1019	Noel	Sylliboy	22	Whycocomagh (Cape Breton reserve)
1020	Noel	Sylliboy	18	Whycocomagh (Cape Breton reserve)
1021	Sophia	Sylliboy	35	Whycocomagh (Cape Breton reserve)
1022	Steven	Sylliboy	35	Whycocomagh (Cape Breton reserve)
1023	Susan	Sylliboy	17	Whycocomagh (Cape Breton reserve)
1024	Susan	Sylliboy	10	Whycocomagh (Cape Breton reserve)
1025	William	Sylliboy	52	Whycocomagh (Cape Breton reserve)
1026	William	Sylliboy	1	Whycocomagh (Cape Breton reserve)
1027	William	Sylliboy	5	Whycocomagh (Cape Breton reserve)
1028	Mary	Thom	5	New Glasgow
1029	Mary	Thomas	37	Truro, Millbrook Reserve area
1030	James	Tom	13	Pictou Co., Merigomish, Pictou Landing Reserve area
1031	John	Tom	8	Pictou Co., Pictou Landing (reserve)
1032	Louis	Tom	58	Pictou Co., Merigomish, Pictou Landing Reserve area
1033	Louis	Tom	2	Pictou Co., Pictou Landing (reserve)
1034	Mary	Tom	42	Pictou Co., Merigomish, Pictou Landing Reserve area
1035	Maryann	Tom	46	Pictou Co., Pictou Landing (reserve)
1036	Matthew	Tom	17	Pictou Co., Pictou Landing (reserve)
1037	Michael	Tom	11	Pictou Co., Pictou Landing (reserve)
1038	Nancy	Tom	70	Pictou Co., Little Harbour
1039	Noel	Tom	?	Pictou Co., Pictou Landing (reserve)
1040	Peter	Tom	30	Pictou Co., Little Harbour
1041	Peter	Tom	49	Pictou Co., Pictou Landing (reserve)
1042	Stephen	Tom	14	Pictou Co., Pictou Landing (reserve)
1043	Tom	Tom	18	Pictou Co., Pictou Landing (reserve)
1044	Bridget	Tomah	45	Eskasoni (Cape Breton reserve)
1045	Annie	Toney	11	Pictou Co., Little Harbour
1046	Elizabeth	Toney	3	Pictou Co., Pictou Landing (reserve)
1047	John	Toney	46	Pictou Co., Little Harbour
1048	Joseph	Toney	67	Pictou Co., Little Harbour
1049	Louisa	Toney	3 mo	Pictou Co., Pictou Landing (reserve)
1050	Madeline	Toney	6	Pictou Co., Little Harbour
1051	Madeline	Toney	7	Pictou Co., Pictou Landing (reserve)
1052	Maggie	Toney	29	Pictou Co., Little Harbour
1053	Maggie	Toney	14	Pictou Co., Little Harbour
1054	Martin	Toney	8 mo	Pictou Co., Little Harbour
1055	Mary	Toney	19	Pictou Co., Pictou Landing (reserve)
1056	Maryann	Toney	80	Amherst
1057	Michael	Toney	28	Pictou Co., Pictou Landing (reserve)
1058	Nancy	Toney	3	Pictou Co., Little Harbour
1059	Nancy	Toney	33	Pictou Co., Pictou Landing (reserve)

Education	Housing	Occupation	Marital status	Notes
?	House	?	Married	
School	House	?	Single	
School	House	?	Single	
?	House	?	Single	
?	House	?	Married	
School	House	?	Single	
?	House	Cooper	Married	
?	House	?	Single	
School	House	?	Single	
School	House	?	Single	
?	House	?	Single	
?	House	Farmer	Married	
?	House	?	Single	
School	House	?	Single	
?	House	?	Married	
?	House	Farmer, cooper	Married	
?	House	?	Single	
School	House	?	Single	
?	House	Farmer	Married	
?	House	?	Single	
School	House	?	Single	
?	Shanty or wigwam	?	Single	
?	Shanty or wigwam	Cooper	Widowed	
?	Shanty or wigwam	?	Single	
?	Shanty or wigwam	?	Single	
?	Shanty or wigwam	Hunter, trapper	Married	
?	Shanty or wigwam	?	Single	
?	Shanty or wigwam	?	Married	
?	Shanty or wigwam	?	Married	
?	Shanty or wigwam	Cooper	Single	
?	Shanty or wigwam	?	Single	
?	Shanty or wigwam	?	Widowed	Born Newfoundland
?	Shanty or wigwam	Cooper	Single	
?	Shanty or wigwam	Cooper	Single	
?	Shanty or wigwam	Cooper	Married	
?	Shanty or wigwam	?	Single	
?	Shanty or wigwam	Cooper	Single	
?	Shanty or wigwam	?	Widowed	
?	Shanty or wigwam	?	Single	
?	Shanty or wigwam	?	Single	
?	Shanty or wigwam	Cooper	Widowed	
?	Shanty or wigwam	Cooper	Widowed	
?	Shanty or wigwam	?	Single	
?	Shanty or wigwam	?	Single	
?	Shanty or wigwam	?	Single	
?	Shanty or wigwam	?	Married	
?	Shanty or wigwam	?	Single	
?	Shanty or wigwam	?	Single	
?	Shanty or wigwam	?	Married	
?	Shanty or wigwam	?	Married	
?	Shanty or wigwam	Cooper	Married	
?	Shanty or wigwam	?	Single	
?	Shanty or wigwam	?	Married	

1881 Census Data • Continued

ID no.	First name	Last name	Age in years	Location
1060	Noel	Toney	34	Pictou Co., Little Harbour
1061	Noel	Toney	34	Pictou Co., Pictou Landing (reserve)
1062	Peter	Toney	33	Pictou Co., Pictou Landing (reserve)
1063	Sarah	Toney	33	Pictou Co., Little Harbour
1064	Sarah	Toney	25	Pictou Co., Pictou Landing (reserve)
1065	Steven	Toney	4	Pictou Co., Little Harbour
1066	Steven	Toney	5	Pictou Co., Pictou Landing (reserve)
1067	Tom	Welsh	11	Potlotek, Chapel Island (Cape Breton reserve)
1068	Alex	Wilmot	80	Potlotek, Chapel Island (Cape Breton reserve)
1069	Alexander	Wilmot	6	Colchester Co., Salmon River (reserve)
1070	Ann	Wilmot	17	Colchester Co., Salmon River (reserve)
1071	Ann	Wilmot	10	Pictou Co., Pictou Landing (reserve)
1072	Bella	Wilmot	18	Pictou Co., Pictou Landing (reserve)
1073	Charles	Wilmot	11	Colchester Co., Salmon River (reserve)
1074	Francis	Wilmot	67	Potlotek, Chapel Island (Cape Breton reserve)
1075	Isaac	Wilmot	2	Pictou Co., Pictou Landing (reserve)
1076	Joseph	Wilmot	18	Colchester Co., Salmon River (reserve)
1077	Joseph	Wilmot	26	Pictou Co., Pictou Landing (reserve)
1078	Lewis	Wilmot	28	Pictou Co., Pictou Landing (reserve)
1079	Margaret	Wilmot	4	Colchester Co., Salmon River (reserve)
1080	Mary	Wilmot	40	Colchester Co., Salmon River (reserve)
1081	Mary	Wilmot	7	Pictou Co., Pictou Landing (reserve)
1082	Mary	Wilmot	6 mo	Pictou Co., Pictou Landing (reserve)
1083	Mary	Wilmot	16	Potlotek, Chapel Island (Cape Breton reserve)
1084	Mary	Wilmot	73	Potlotek, Chapel Island (Cape Breton reserve)
1085	Maryann	Wilmot	22	Pictou Co., Pictou Landing (reserve)
1086	Maryann	Wilmot	24	Pictou Co., Pictou Landing (reserve)
1087	Maryann	Wilmot	39	Pictou Co., Pictou Landing (reserve)
1088	Nancy	Wilmot	58	Potlotek, Chapel Island (Cape Breton reserve)
1089	Natasha	Wilmot	4	Pictou Co., Pictou Landing (reserve)
1090	Peter	Wilmot	48	Colchester Co., Salmon River (reserve)
1091	Sarah	Wilmot	1	Pictou Co., Pictou Landing (reserve)
1092	Thomas	Wilmot	68	Pictou Co., Pictou Landing (reserve)
1093	Agnes	Young	19	Truro, Millbrook Reserve area
1094	Charles	Young	20	Truro, Millbrook Reserve area

Education	Housing	Occupation	Marital status	Notes
?	Shanty or wigwam	Cooper	Married	
?	Shanty or wigwam	?	Married	
?	Shanty or wigwam	Cooper	Married	
?	Shanty or wigwam	?	Married	
?	Shanty or wigwam	?	Married	
?	Shanty or wigwam	?	Single	
?	Shanty or wigwam	?	Single	
?	Shanty or wigwam	?	Single	
?	Shanty or wigwam	?	Married	Blind
?	Shanty or wigwam	?	Single	
?	Shanty or wigwam	?	Single	
?	Shanty or wigwam	?	Single	
?	Shanty or wigwam	?	Single	
?	Shanty or wigwam	?	Single	
?	House	Farmer, cooper	Married	
?	Shanty or wigwam	?	Single	
?	Shanty or wigwam	Hunter	Single	
?	Shanty or wigwam	Cooper	Married	
?	Shanty or wigwam	Cooper	Married	
?	Shanty or wigwam	?	Single	
?	Shanty or wigwam	?	Married	
?	Shanty or wigwam	?	Single	
?	Shanty or wigwam	?	Single	
?	House	?	Single	
?	Shanty or wigwam	?	Married	
?	Shanty or wigwam	?	Married	
?	Shanty or wigwam	?	Married	
?	Shanty or wigwam	?	Married	
?	House	?	Married	
?	Shanty or wigwam	?	Single	
?	Shanty or wigwam	Hunter	Married	
?	Shanty or wigwam	?	Single	
?	Shanty or wigwam	Cooper	Married	
?	Shanty or wigwam	?	Married	
?	Shanty or wigwam	Cooper	Married	

1881 Census Data • Continued

ID no.	First name	Last name	Age in years	Location
CENSUS DATA FOR 1891				
1	Bella	Addle	8	Waqamatkuk (Middle River, Cape Breton reserve)
2	Ben	Addle	18	Waqamatkuk (Middle River, Cape Breton reserve)
3	Jane	Addle	84	Waqamatkuk (Middle River, Cape Breton reserve)
4	Katie	Addle	33	Waqamatkuk (Middle River, Cape Breton reserve)
5	Madeline	Addle	5	Waqamatkuk (Middle River, Cape Breton reserve)
6	Mary	Addle	21	Waqamatkuk (Middle River, Cape Breton reserve)
7	Noel	Addle	62	Waqamatkuk (Middle River, Cape Breton reserve)
8	Simon	Addle	33	Waqamatkuk (Middle River, Cape Breton reserve)
9	Agnes	Alex	9 mo	Potlotek, Chapel Island (Cape Breton reserve)
10	John	Alex	50	Potlotek, Chapel Island (Cape Breton reserve)
11	Mary	Alex	58	Potlotek, Chapel Island (Cape Breton reserve)
12	Mary	Alex	36	Potlotek, Chapel Island (Cape Breton reserve)
13	Mary	Alex	17	Potlotek, Chapel Island (Cape Breton reserve)
14	Maryann	Alex	16	Potlotek, Chapel Island (Cape Breton reserve)
15	Nancy	Alex	11	Potlotek, Chapel Island (Cape Breton reserve)
16	Nancy	Alex	60	Potlotek, Chapel Island (Cape Breton reserve)
17	Peter	Alex	13	Potlotek, Chapel Island (Cape Breton reserve)
18	Tom	Alex	60	Potlotek, Chapel Island (Cape Breton reserve)
19	Kate	Andra	25	Sydney (King's Road reserve 1881/1891)
20	Madaline	Andra	7	Sydney (King's Road reserve 1881/1891)
21	Harvey	Andrews	2	Town of Guysborough (Subdistrict F)
22	John	Andrews	4	Town of Guysborough (Subdistrict F)
23	Mable	Andrews	13	Town of Guysborough (Subdistrict F)
24	Mary	Andrews	37	Town of Guysborough (Subdistrict F)
25	Mary	Andrews	7	Town of Guysborough (Subdistrict F)
26	Thomas	Andrews	39	Town of Guysborough (Subdistrict F)
27	Emeline	Bartlett	30	Yarmouth Co., Arcadia
28	Hannah	Bartlett	8	Yarmouth Co., Argyle
29	Henry	Bartlett	7	Yarmouth Co., Argyle
30	James	Bartlett	36	Yarmouth Co., Arcadia
31	John	Bartlett	6	Yarmouth Co., Argyle
32	Mary	Bartlett	10 mo	Yarmouth Co., Argyle
33	Simon	Bartlett	4	Yarmouth Co., Argyle
34	Steven	Bartlett	84	Yarmouth Co., Arcadia
35	Thomas	Bartlett	35	Yarmouth Co., Argyle
36	Andrew	Basque	38	Town of Guysborough (Subdistrict F)
37	John	Basque	7	Town of Guysborough (Subdistrict F)
38	June	Basque	23	Whycocomagh (Cape Breton reserve)
39	May	Basque	12	Town of Guysborough (Subdistrict F)
40	Michael	Basque	31	Pictou Co., Bailey's Brook
41	Nancy	Basque	2	Town of Guysborough (Subdistrict F)
42	Sarah	Basque	28	Pictou Co., Bailey's Brook
43	Simon	Basque	28	Whycocomagh (Cape Breton reserve)
44	Susan	Basque	27	Town of Guysborough (Subdistrict F)
45	William	Basque	5	Pictou Co., Bailey's Brook
46	Andrew	Battiste	37	Potlotek, Chapel Island (Cape Breton reserve)
47	Elizabeth	Battiste	28	Potlotek, Chapel Island (Cape Breton reserve)
48	Madlin	Battiste	11	Potlotek, Chapel Island (Cape Breton reserve)
49	Mary	Battiste	12	Heatherton (Paqtnkek Reserve Area)
50	Maryann	Battiste	71	Heatherton (Paqtnkek Reserve Area)
51	Nancy	Battiste	9	Potlotek, Chapel Island (Cape Breton reserve)
52	Stephen	Battiste	13	Potlotek, Chapel Island (Cape Breton reserve)

Education	Housing	Occupation	Marital status	Notes
Illiterate	House, wood (1 fl, 1 rm)	?	Single	
Literate	House, wood (1 fl, 1 rm)	Cooper	Single	
Illiterate	House, wood (1 fl, 1 rm)	?	Widowed	
Illiterate	House, wood (1 fl, 1 rm)	?	Married	
Illiterate	House, wood (1 fl, 1 rm)	?	Single	
Illiterate	House, wood (1 fl, 1 rm)	Basketmaker	Single	
Literate	House, wood (1 fl, 1 rm)	Carpenter	Widowed	
Illiterate	House, wood (1 fl, 1 rm)	Cooper	Married	
Illiterate	Shanty or wigwam	?	Single	
Illiterate	Shanty or wigwam	Farmer, cooper	Married	
Illiterate	Shanty or wigwam	?	Married	Away
Illiterate	Shanty or wigwam	?	Married	
Literate	Shanty or wigwam	?	Single	
Illiterate	Shanty or wigwam	?	Single	Away
Literate	Shanty or wigwam	?	Single	
Illiterate	Shanty or wigwam	?	Widowed	
Literate	Shanty or wigwam	?	Single	
Illiterate	Shanty or wigwam	Farmer, cooper	Married	Away
Illiterate	Shanty or wigwam	Basketmaker	Widowed	
Illiterate	Shanty or wigwam	?	Single	
Illiterate	Shanty or wigwam	?	Single	
Illiterate	Shanty or wigwam	?	Single	
Illiterate	Shanty or wigwam	?	Single	
Illiterate	Shanty or wigwam	?	Married	
Illiterate	Shanty or wigwam	?	Single	
Illiterate	Shanty or wigwam	Cooper, fisherman	Married	
Illiterate	Shanty or wigwam	?	Married	
Illiterate	Shanty or wigwam	?	Single	
Illiterate	Shanty or wigwam	?	Single	
Illiterate	House, wood (1 fl, 2 rm)	Basketmaker	Married	
Illiterate	Shanty or wigwam	?	Single	
Illiterate	Shanty or wigwam	?	Single	
Illiterate	Shanty or wigwam	?	Single	
Illiterate	House, wood (1 fl, 2 rm)	Basketmaker	Widowed	
Illiterate	Shanty or wigwam	?	Married	
Illiterate	Shanty or wigwam	Cooper, fisherman	Married	
Illiterate	Shanty or wigwam	?	Single	
Illiterate	House, wood (1 fl, 3 rm)	?	Single	
Illiterate	Shanty or wigwam	?	Single	
Illiterate	Shanty or wigwam	Cooper, fisherman	Married	
Illiterate	Shanty or wigwam	?	Single	
Illiterate	Shanty or wigwam	?	Married	
Illiterate	House, wood (1 fl, 3 rm)	Farmer	Married	
Illiterate	Shanty or wigwam	?	Married	
Illiterate	Shanty or wigwam	?	Single	
Illiterate	Shanty or wigwam	Farmer, cooper	Married	
Illiterate	Shanty or wigwam	?	Married	
Literate	Shanty or wigwam	?	Single	
Illiterate	Shanty or wigwam	Cooper	Single	
Illiterate	Shanty or wigwam	Cooper	Widowed	
Literate	Shanty or wigwam	?	Single	
Literate	Shanty or wigwam	?	Single	

1891 Census Data • Continued

ID no.	First name	Last name	Age in years	Location
53	Theresa	Battiste	7	Potlotek, Chapel Island (Cape Breton reserve)
54	Tom	Battiste	10 mo	Potlotek, Chapel Island (Cape Breton reserve)
55	William	Battiste	12	Heatherton (Paqtnkek Reserve Area)
56	Jennie	Beatle	56	Pictou Co., Little Harbour
57	Paul	Beatle	24	Pictou Co., Little Harbour
58	Annie	Bernard	6	North Sydney
59	Ben	Bernard	5	Whycocomagh (Cape Breton reserve)
60	Cicily	Bernard	20	Potlotek, Chapel Island (Cape Breton reserve)
61	Ellen	Bernard	2	Morland (Paqtnkek Reserve Area)
62	Francis	Bernard	14	North Sydney
63	Francis	Bernard	60	Whycocomagh (Cape Breton reserve)
64	Francis	Bernard	31	Whycocomagh (Cape Breton reserve)
65	Francis	Bernard	36	Morland (Paqtnkek Reserve Area)
66	Gabriel	Bernard	89	Sydney (King's Road reserve 1881/1891)
67	Harriet	Bernard	40	North Sydney
68	Hattie	Bernard	14	Queen's Co., Subdistrict Milton (1891)
69	Larry	Bernard	45	North Sydney
70	Madeline	Bernard	10	North Sydney
71	Madeline	Bernard	50	Whycocomagh (Cape Breton reserve)
72	Madeline	Bernard	30	Whycocomagh (Cape Breton reserve)
73	Mary	Bernard	45	North Sydney
74	Mary	Bernard	18	North Sydney
75	Mary	Bernard	14	North Sydney
76	Maryjane	Bernard	12	North Sydney
77	Michael	Bernard	25	Whycocomagh (Cape Breton reserve)
78	Noel	Bernard	16	North Sydney
79	Noel	Bernard	8	Whycocomagh (Cape Breton reserve)
80	Richard	Bernard	29	Potlotek, Chapel Island (Cape Breton reserve)
81	Sarah	Bernard	36	Morland (Paqtnkek Reserve Area)
82	Ann	Berris?	70	Potlotek, Chapel Island (Cape Breton reserve)
83	Dominic	Bradford	12	Queen's Co., Caledonia
84	Mary	Bradford	10	Queen's Co., Caledonia
85	Nancy	Bradford	32	Queen's Co., Caledonia
86	Rachel	Bradford	3	Queen's Co., Caledonia
87	Steven	Bradford	34	Queen's Co., Caledonia
88	William	Bradford	2 mo	Queen's Co., Caledonia
89	Ben	Brooks	21	Hants Co., Shubenacdie/Indian Brook Reserve area, St. Croix
90	Liza	Brooks	57	Hants Co., Shubenacdie/Indian Brook Reserve area, St. Croix
91	Lizzie	Brooks	22	Hants Co., Shubenacdie/Indian Brook Reserve area, St. Croix
92	Ben	Cabot	51	Whycocomagh (Cape Breton reserve)
93	Charles	Cabot	20	Whycocomagh (Cape Breton reserve)
94	Elizabeth	Cabot	37	Whycocomagh (Cape Breton reserve)
95	Isabella	Cabot	40	Whycocomagh (Cape Breton reserve)
96	Madeline	Cabot	5	Whycocomagh (Cape Breton reserve)
97	Peter	Cabot	48	Whycocomagh (Cape Breton reserve)
98	Steven	Cabot	11	Whycocomagh (Cape Breton reserve)
99	Maryann	Carty	32	Shelburne Co., Barrington Head
100	Williamj	Carty	22	Shelburne Co., Barrington Head
101	Florid	Christen	36	Town of Guysborough (Subdistrict F)
102	Benjam	Christmas	27	Sydney (King's Road reserve 1881/1891)
103	Bridget	Christmas	17	Eskasoni (Cape Breton reserve)
104	Bridget	Christmas	0	Sydney (King's Road reserve 1881/1891)
105	Cecily	Christmas	48	Eskasoni (Cape Breton reserve)

Education	Housing	Occupation	Marital status	Notes
Illiterate	Shanty or wigwam	?	Single	
Illiterate	Shanty or wigwam	?	Single	
Illiterate	Shanty or wigwam	Cooper	Single	
Illiterate	Shanty or wigwam	?	Widowed	
Illiterate	Shanty or wigwam	Cooper, fisherman	Single	
Illiterate	Wigwam	?	Single	
Illiterate	House, wood (1 fl, 3 rm)	?	Single	
Illiterate	Shanty or wigwam	?	Married	
Illiterate	House, wood (1 fl, 1 rm)	?	Single	
Literate	Wigwam	Basketmaker	Single	
Illiterate	House, wood (1 fl, 3 rm)	Farmer	Married	
Illiterate	House, wood (1 fl, 3 rm)	Cooper	Married	
Literate	House, wood (1 fl, 1 rm)	Farmer, fisherman	Married	
Illiterate	Shanty or wigwam	Cooper	Widowed	
Illiterate	Wigwam	Basketmaker	Widowed	
Illiterate	?	?	Single	
Illiterate	Wigwam	Basketmaker	Married	
Illiterate	Wigwam	?	Single	
Illiterate	House, wood (1 fl, 3 rm)	Farmer	Married	
Illiterate	House, wood (1 fl, 3 rm)	?	Married	
Illiterate	Wigwam	Basketmaker	Married	
Literate	Wigwam	Basketmaker	Single	
Literate	Wigwam	Basketmaker	Single	
Literate	Wigwam	?	Single	
Illiterate	House, wood (1 fl, 3 rm)	Cooper	Single	
Literate	Wigwam	Basketmaker	Single	
Illiterate	House, wood (1 fl, 3 rm)	?	Single	
Illiterate	Shanty or wigwam	Farmer, cooper	Married	
Literate	House, wood (1 fl, 1 rm)	?	Married	
Illiterate	Shanty or wigwam	?	Widowed	
Literate	House, wood (2 fl, 5 rm)	?	Single	
Illiterate	House, wood (2 fl, 5 rm)	?	Single	
Illiterate	House, wood (2 fl, 5 rm)	?	Married	
Illiterate	House, wood (2 fl, 5 rm)	?	Single	
Illiterate	House, wood (2 fl, 5 rm)	Hunter	Married	
Illiterate	House, wood (2 fl, 5 rm)	?	Single	
Literate	Shanty or wigwam	Laborer	Married	
Illiterate	Shanty or wigwam	Basketmaker	Single	
Literate	Shanty or wigwam	?	Married	
Illiterate	Shanty or wigwam	Farmer	Married	
Illiterate	Shanty or wigwam	?	Single	
Illiterate	Shanty or wigwam	?	Married	
Illiterate	Shanty or wigwam	?	Married	
Illiterate	Shanty or wigwam	?	Single	
Illiterate	Shanty or wigwam	Cooper	Married	
Illiterate	Shanty or wigwam	?	Single	
Literate	House, wood (1 fl, 2 rm)	?	Married	
Illiterate	House, wood (1 fl, 2 rm)	Hunter	Married	
Illiterate	Shanty or wigwam	?	Single	Female
Illiterate	Shanty or wigwam	Cooper	Married	
Literate	House, wood (2 fl, 7 rm)	?	Single	
Illiterate	Shanty or wigwam	?	Single	
Illiterate	House, wood (2 fl, 7 rm)	?	Married	

1891 Census Data • Continued

ID no.	First name	Last name	Age in years	Location
106	Elizabeth	Christmas	12	Sydney (King's Road reserve 1881/1891)
107	Ellen	Christmas	13	Eskasoni (Cape Breton reserve)
108	Elvira	Christmas	11	Waqamatkuk (Middle River, Cape Breton reserve)
109	Joe	Christmas	34	Waqamatkuk (Middle River, Cape Breton reserve)
110	Joe	Christmas	21	Potlotek, Chapel Island (Cape Breton reserve)
111	John	Christmas	51	Eskasoni (Cape Breton reserve)
112	John	Christmas	10	Sydney (King's Road reserve 1881/1891)
113	John	Christmas	12	Sydney (King's Road reserve 1881/1891)
114	John	Christmas	8 mo	Potlotek, Chapel Island (Cape Breton reserve)
115	Joseph	Christmas	7	Sydney (King's Road reserve 1881/1891)
116	Madeline	Christmas	36	Waqamatkuk (Middle River, Cape Breton reserve)
117	Maggie	Christmas	19	Sydney (King's Road reserve 1881/1891)
118	Maggie	Christmas	13	Sydney (King's Road reserve 1881/1891)
119	Maggie	Christmas	19	Potlotek, Chapel Island (Cape Breton reserve)
120	Margaret	Christmas	8	Waqamatkuk (Middle River, Cape Breton reserve)
121	Mary	Christmas	9	Eskasoni (Cape Breton reserve)
122	Mary	Christmas	5	Waqamatkuk (Middle River, Cape Breton reserve)
123	Maryann	Christmas	4	Sydney (King's Road reserve 1881/1891)
124	Marye	Christmas	2	Waqamatkuk (Middle River, Cape Breton reserve)
125	Michael	Christmas	8	Sydney (King's Road reserve 1881/1891)
126	Mick	Christmas	11	Eskasoni (Cape Breton reserve)
127	Noel	Christmas	19	Eskasoni (Cape Breton reserve)
128	Noel	Christmas	14	Sydney (King's Road reserve 1881/1891)
129	Noel	Christmas	23	Sydney (King's Road reserve 1881/1891)
130	Novel	Christmas	21	Sydney (King's Road reserve 1881/1891)
131	Paul	Christmas	44	Sydney (King's Road reserve 1881/1891)
132	Paul	Christmas	10	Sydney (King's Road reserve 1881/1891)
133	Sarah	Christmas	49	Sydney (King's Road reserve 1881/1891)
134	Susan	Christmas	46	Sydney (King's Road reserve 1881/1891)
135	Susan	Christmas	26	Sydney (King's Road reserve 1881/1891)
136	Thomas	Christmas	15	Eskasoni (Cape Breton reserve)
137	Victor	Christmas	4 mo	?
138	Victor	Christmas	18	Sydney (King's Road reserve 1881/1891)
139	Betsy	Christopher	44	Waqamatkuk (Middle River, Cape Breton reserve)
140	Christy	Christopher	32	Pictou Co., Bailey's Brook
141	Eunice	Christopher	2 mo	Pictou Co., Bailey's Brook
142	Francis	Christopher	18	Waqamatkuk (Middle River, Cape Breton reserve)
143	James	Christopher	10	Pictou Co., Bailey's Brook
144	Maryann	Christopher	9	Waqamatkuk (Middle River, Cape Breton reserve)
145	Steve	Christopher	45	Pictou Co., Bailey's Brook
146	James	Cope	60	Hants Co., Shubenacdie/Indian Brook Reserve area, Rawdon Church
147	Joseph	Cope	21	Hants Co., Shubenacdie/Indian Brook Reserve area, Rawdon Church
148	Mary	Cope	68	Hants Co., Shubenacdie/Indian Brook Reserve area, Rawdon Church
149	Alvin	Cremo	21	Potlotek, Chapel Island (Cape Breton reserve)
150	Anncath	Cremo	26	Waqamatkuk (Middle River, Cape Breton reserve)
151	Charles	Cremo	3	Waqamatkuk (Middle River, Cape Breton reserve)
152	Ellen	Cremo	25	Potlotek, Chapel Island (Cape Breton reserve)
153	Fran	Cremo	62	Potlotek, Chapel Island (Cape Breton reserve)
154	Frank	Cremo	8	Waqamatkuk (Middle River, Cape Breton reserve)
155	Freman	Cremo	62	West Bay, Division 1 ('Malakawe:j, Cape Breton reserve)

Education	Housing	Occupation	Marital status	Notes
Illiterate	Shanty or wigwam	Basketmaker	Single	
Literate	House, wood (2 fl, 7 rm)	?	Single	
Literate	Shanty or wigwam	?	Single	
Literate	Shanty or wigwam	Carpenter	Married	
Literate	Shanty or wigwam	?	Single	
Illiterate	House, wood (2 fl, 7 rm)	Cooper	Married	
Illiterate	Shanty or wigwam	?	Single	
Illiterate	Shanty or wigwam	Basketmaker	Single	
Illiterate	Shanty or wigwam	?	Single	
Illiterate	Shanty or wigwam	?	Single	
Literate	Shanty or wigwam	?	Married	
Illiterate	Shanty or wigwam	Basketmaker	Single	
Illiterate	Shanty or wigwam	Basketmaker	Single	
Literate	Shanty or wigwam	?	Single	
Literate	Shanty or wigwam	?	Single	
Literate	House, wood (2 fl, 7 rm)	?	Single	
Illiterate	Shanty or wigwam	?	Single	
Illiterate	Shanty or wigwam	?	Single	
Illiterate	Shanty or wigwam	?	Single	
Illiterate	Shanty or wigwam	?	Single	
Literate	House, wood (2 fl, 7 rm)	?	Single	
Literate	House, wood (2 fl, 7 rm)	Cooper	Single	
Illiterate	Shanty or wigwam	Cooper	Single	
Illiterate	Shanty or wigwam	Cooper	Single	
Illiterate	Shanty or wigwam	Cooper	Single	Male?
Illiterate	Shanty or wigwam	Cooper	Married	
Illiterate	Shanty or wigwam	Basketmaker	Single	
Illiterate	Shanty or wigwam	Basketmaker	Married	
Illiterate	Shanty or wigwam	?	Widowed	
Illiterate	Shanty or wigwam	Basketmaker	Married	
Literate	House, wood (2 fl, 7 rm)	?	Single	
Illiterate	Shanty or wigwam	?	?	
Illiterate	Shanty or wigwam	Cooper	Single	
Illiterate	House, wood (1 fl, 1 rm)	Basketmaker	Widowed	
Illiterate	Shanty or wigwam	?	Married	
Illiterate	Shanty or wigwam	?	Single	
Literate	House, wood (1 fl, 1 rm)	Cooper	Single	
Illiterate	Shanty or wigwam	?	Single	
Literate	House, wood (1 fl, 1 rm)	?	Single	
Illiterate	Shanty or wigwam	Cooper, fisherman	Married	Reversed?
Literate	Shanty or wigwam	?	Married	
Illiterate	Shanty or wigwam	?	Single	
Literate	Shanty or wigwam	?	Married	
Literate	Shanty or wigwam	?	Single	
Illiterate	House, wood (1 fl, 1 rm)	Basketmaker	Single	
Illiterate	House, wood (1 fl, 1 rm)	?	Single	
Illiterate	House, wood (1 fl, 1 rm)	?	Married	
Illiterate	Shanty or wigwam	?	Widowed	
Illiterate	House, wood (1 fl, 1 rm)	?	Single	
Illiterate	Shanty or wigwam	Cooper, fisherman	Married	

1891 Census Data • *Continued*

ID no.	First name	Last name	Age in years	Location
156	Harriet	Cremo	24	Potlotek, Chapel Island (Cape Breton reserve)
157	Isaac	Cremo	12	West Bay, Division 1 ('Malakawe:j, Cape Breton reserve)
158	Isadore	Cremo	25	Waqamatkuk (Middle River, Cape Breton reserve)
159	Joe	Cremo	54	West Bay, Division 1 ('Malakawe:j, Cape Breton reserve)
160	John	Cremo	18	Waqamatkuk (Middle River, Cape Breton reserve)
161	Mary	Cremo	48	West Bay, Division 1 ('Malakawe:j, Cape Breton reserve)
162	Mary	Cremo	35	West Bay, Division 1 ('Malakawe:j, Cape Breton reserve)
163	Moses	Cremo	23	Waqamatkuk (Middle River, Cape Breton reserve)
164	Noel	Cremo	?	Waqamatkuk (Middle River, Cape Breton reserve)
165	Peter	Cremo	31	Potlotek, Chapel Island (Cape Breton reserve)
166	Pierro	Cremo	55	Waqamatkuk (Middle River, Cape Breton reserve)
167	Susan	Cremo	44	Waqamatkuk (Middle River, Cape Breton reserve)
168	Theresa	Cremo	51	Waqamatkuk (Middle River, Cape Breton reserve)
169	Andrew	Dennis	16	Whycocomagh (Cape Breton reserve)
170	Isabella	Dennis	39	Whycocomagh (Cape Breton reserve)
171	Maggy	Dennis	12	Whycocomagh (Cape Breton reserve)
172	Maryann	Dennis	5	Whycocomagh (Cape Breton reserve)
173	Susan	Dennis	1 mo	Whycocomagh (Cape Breton reserve)
174	Anna	Denny	23	Eskasoni (Cape Breton reserve)
175	Bridget	Denny	5	Eskasoni (Cape Breton reserve)
176	Eliza	Denny	11	Eskasoni (Cape Breton reserve)
177	Elizabeth	Denny	40	Eskasoni (Cape Breton reserve)
178	Ellen	Denny	30	Eskasoni (Cape Breton reserve)
179	Ester	Denny	24	Sydney (King's Road reserve 1881/1891)
180	Eveline	Denny	9	Sydney (King's Road reserve 1881/1891)
181	Fanny	Denny	16	Eskasoni (Cape Breton reserve)
182	Francis	Denny	45	Sydney (King's Road reserve 1881/1891)
183	Jim	Denny	7	Eskasoni (Cape Breton reserve)
184	Joe	Denny	20	Eskasoni (Cape Breton reserve)
185	John	Denny	49	Eskasoni (Cape Breton reserve)
186	Joseph	Denny	6	Sydney (King's Road reserve 1881/1891)
187	Mary	Denny	19	Eskasoni (Cape Breton reserve)
188	Mary	Denny	14	Eskasoni (Cape Breton reserve)
189	Mary	Denny	5	Eskasoni (Cape Breton reserve)
190	Mary	Denny	12	Sydney (King's Road reserve 1881/1891)
191	Mick	Denny	17	Eskasoni (Cape Breton reserve)
192	Noel	Denny	49	Eskasoni (Cape Breton reserve)
193	Noel	Denny	52	Eskasoni (Cape Breton reserve)
194	Peter	Denny	22	Eskasoni (Cape Breton reserve)
195	Simon	Denny	2	Eskasoni (Cape Breton reserve)
196	Stephen	Denny	21	Eskasoni (Cape Breton reserve)
197	Susan	Denny	47	Eskasoni (Cape Breton reserve)
198	Susan	Denny	16	Eskasoni (Cape Breton reserve)
199	Susan	Denny	38	Sydney (King's Road reserve 1881/1891)
200	Thomas	Denny	9	Eskasoni (Cape Breton reserve)
201	Veronica	Denny	43	Eskasoni (Cape Breton reserve)
202	Angelica	Doucette	46	West Bay, Division 2 ('Malakawe:j, Cape Breton reserve)
203	Angelis	Doucette	40	Potlotek, Chapel Island (Cape Breton reserve)
204	Joe	Doucette	50	Potlotek, Chapel Island (Cape Breton reserve)
205	Joe	Doucette	5	Potlotek, Chapel Island (Cape Breton reserve)
206	Joseph	Doucette	50	West Bay, Division 2 ('Malakawe:j, Cape Breton reserve)
207	Joseph	Doucette	6	West Bay, Division 2 ('Malakawe:j, Cape Breton reserve)
208	Madeline	Doucette	8	Potlotek, Chapel Island (Cape Breton reserve)

Education	Housing	Occupation	Marital status	Notes
Illiterate	Shanty or wigwam	?	Single	
Illiterate	Shanty or wigwam	Cooper, fisherman	Single	
Illiterate	House, wood (1 fl, 1 rm)	Cooper	Single	
Illiterate	Shanty or wigwam	Cooper, fisherman	Married	
Illiterate	House, wood (1 fl, 1 rm)	Cooper	Single	
Illiterate	Shanty or wigwam	?	Married	
Illiterate	Shanty or wigwam	Cooper, fisherman	Married	
Illiterate	House, wood (1 fl, 1 rm)	Laborer	Single	
Illiterate	House, wood (1 fl, 1 rm)	Cooper	Married	
Illiterate	House, wood (1 fl, 1 rm)	Farmer, cooper	Married	
Illiterate	House, wood (1 fl, 1 rm)	Cooper	Married	
Illiterate	House, wood (1 fl, 1 rm)	Basketmaker	Married	
Illiterate	House, wood (1 fl, 1 rm)	?	Married	
Illiterate	Shanty or wigwam	?	Single	
Illiterate	Shanty or wigwam	?	Widowed	
Illiterate	Shanty or wigwam	?	Single	
Illiterate	Shanty or wigwam	?	Single	
Illiterate	Shanty or wigwam	?	Single	
Illiterate	Shanty or wigwam	Cooper	Single	
Illiterate	Shanty or wigwam	Cooper	Single	
Illiterate	House, wood (2 fl, 6 rm)	?	Single	
Illiterate	House, wood (2 fl, 6 rm)	?	Married	
Illiterate	Shanty or wigwam	Cooper	Married	
Illiterate	Shanty or wigwam	Basketmaker	Single	
Illiterate	Shanty or wigwam	?	Single	
Illiterate	Shanty or wigwam	Cooper	Single	
Illiterate	Shanty or wigwam	Cooper	Married	
Illiterate	Shanty or wigwam	Cooper	Single	
Illiterate	House, wood (2 fl, 6 rm)	Cooper	Single	
Illiterate	House, wood (2 fl, 6 rm)	Cooper	Married	
Illiterate	Shanty or wigwam	?	Single	
Illiterate	Shanty or wigwam	Cooper	Single	
Literate	Shanty or wigwam	Cooper	Single	
Illiterate	House, wood (2 fl, 6 rm)	?	Single	
Illiterate	Shanty or wigwam	Basketmaker	Single	
Illiterate	Shanty or wigwam	Cooper	Single	
Illiterate	Shanty or wigwam	Cooper	Married	
Illiterate	Shanty or wigwam	Cooper	Married	
Literate	Shanty or wigwam	?	Single	
Illiterate	House, wood (2 fl, 6 rm)	?	Single	
Illiterate	Shanty or wigwam	Cooper	Single	
Literate	Shanty or wigwam	servant	Widowed	
Illiterate	House, wood (2 fl, 6 rm)	?	Single	
Illiterate	Shanty or wigwam	Basketmaker	Married	
Literate	Shanty or wigwam	?	Single	
Illiterate	Shanty or wigwam	Cooper	Single	
Illiterate	Shanty or wigwam	?	Married	
Illiterate	Shanty or wigwam	?	Married	Away
Illiterate	Shanty or wigwam	Farmer, cooper	Married	Away
Illiterate	Shanty or wigwam	?	?	Away
Illiterate	Shanty or wigwam	Cooper, boat builder	Married	
Illiterate	Shanty or wigwam	?	Single	
Literate	Shanty or wigwam	?	Single	Away

1891 Census Data • *Continued*

ID no.	First name	Last name	Age in years	Location
209	Madeline	Doucette	9	West Bay, Division 2 ('Malakawe:j, Cape Breton reserve)
210	Noel	Doucette	19	Potlotek, Chapel Island (Cape Breton reserve)
211	Noel	Doucette	17	West Bay, Division 2 ('Malakawe:j, Cape Breton reserve)
212	Adelaide	Francis	3	Queen's Co., Subdistrict Milton (1891)
213	Andrew	Francis	11	Queen's Co., Subdistrict Milton (1891)
214	Andrew	Francis	?	Potlotek, Chapel Island (Cape Breton reserve)
215	Annie	Francis	30	Pictou Co., Pictou Landing (reserve)
216	Annie	Francis	2	Pictou Co., Pictou Landing (reserve)
217	Blair	Francis	45	Pictou Co., Pictou Landing (reserve)
218	Charles	Francis	30	Kings Co., Lakeville
219	Clem	Francis	4 mo	Whycocomagh (Cape Breton reserve)
220	Elizabeth	Francis	26	Potlotek, Chapel Island (Cape Breton reserve)
221	Elizabeth	Francis	25	Kings Co., Lakeville
222	Ellen	Francis	1	Pictou Co., Pictou Landing (reserve)
223	Ellen	Francis	35	Pictou Co., Pictou Landing (reserve)
224	Ellen	Francis	4	Sydney (King's Road reserve 1881/1891)
225	Jane	Francis	24	Pictou Co., Pictou Landing (reserve)
226	Jane	Francis	0	Kings Co., Lakeville
227	Jennie	Francis	3	Pictou Co., Pictou Landing (reserve)
228	Joe	Francis	29	Eskasoni (Cape Breton reserve)
229	John	Francis	13	Queen's Co., Subdistrict Milton (1891)
230	John	Francis	17	Pictou Co., Pictou Landing (reserve)
231	Joseph	Francis	15	Queen's Co., Subdistrict Milton (1891)
232	Joseph	Francis	70	Kings Co., Lakeville
233	Katie	Francis	43	Queen's Co., Subdistrict Milton (1891)
234	Lizzie	Francis	5	Pictou Co., Pictou Landing (reserve)
235	Lizzie	Francis	10	Pictou Co., Pictou Landing (reserve)
236	Louisa	Francis	6	Queen's Co., Subdistrict Milton (1891)
237	Madeline	Francis	21	Potlotek, Chapel Island (Cape Breton reserve)
238	Mary	Francis	25	Eskasoni (Cape Breton reserve)
239	Mary	Francis	9	Queen's Co., Subdistrict Milton (1891)
240	Mary	Francis	35	Pictou Co., Pictou Landing (reserve)
241	Mary	Francis	12	Potlotek, Chapel Island (Cape Breton reserve)
242	Mary	Francis	70	Kings Co., Lakeville
243	Maryann	Francis	60	Pictou Co., Pictou Landing (reserve)
244	Maryann	Francis	3	Pictou Co., Pictou Landing (reserve)
245	Maryann	Francis	30	Pictou Co., Pictou Landing (reserve)
246	Maryann	Francis	10	Pictou Co., Pictou Landing (reserve)
247	Maryann	Francis	76	Sydney (King's Road reserve 1881/1891)
248	Matteo	Francis	38	Pictou Co., Pictou Landing (reserve)
249	Mattie	Francis	8	Queen's Co., Subdistrict Milton (1891)
250	Michael	Francis	22	Pictou Co., Pictou Landing (reserve)
251	Michael	Francis	42	Potlotek, Chapel Island (Cape Breton reserve)
252	Mick	Francis	6	Eskasoni (Cape Breton reserve)
253	Noel	Francis	40	Pictou Co., Pictou Landing (reserve)
254	Peter	Francis	1	Pictou Co., Pictou Landing (reserve)
255	Peter	Francis	19	Potlotek, Chapel Island (Cape Breton reserve)
256	Peterjoe	Francis	14	Potlotek, Chapel Island (Cape Breton reserve)
257	Sally	Francis	3	Pictou Co., Pictou Landing (reserve)
258	Samuel	Francis	17	Yarmouth Co., Arcadia
259	Simon	Francis	4	Eskasoni (Cape Breton reserve)
260	Simon	Francis	2	Potlotek, Chapel Island (Cape Breton reserve)
261	Stephen	Francis	2	Eskasoni (Cape Breton reserve)

Education	Housing	Occupation	Marital status	Notes
Illiterate	Shanty or wigwam	?	Single	
Literate	Shanty or wigwam	Cooper	?	Away
Illiterate	Shanty or wigwam	Cooper	Single	
Illiterate	House, wood (1 fl, 3 rm)	?	Single	
Illiterate	House, wood (1 fl, 3 rm)	?	Single	
Illiterate	House, wood (1 fl, 1 rm)	?	Single	
Literate	House, wood (1 fl, 2 rm)	?	Married	
Illiterate	House, wood (1 fl, 2 rm)	?	Single	
Literate	House, wood (1 fl, 2 rm)	Cooper	Married	
Illiterate	Shanty or wigwam	Basketmaker	Married	
Illiterate	House, wood (1 fl, 4 rm)	?	Single	Male?
Illiterate	House, wood (1 fl, 1 rm)	?	Married	
Illiterate	Shanty or wigwam	?	Married	
Illiterate	House, wood (1 fl, 2 rm)	?	Single	
Illiterate	House, wood (1 fl, 1 rm)	?	Married	
Illiterate	Shanty or wigwam	?	Single	Male?
Literate	House, wood (1 fl, 2 rm)	?	Single	
Illiterate	Shanty or wigwam	?	Single	
Illiterate	House, wood (1 fl, 2 rm)	?	Single	
Illiterate	Shanty or wigwam	Cooper	Married	
Literate	House, wood (1 fl, 3 rm)	?	Single	
Literate	House, wood (1 fl, 2 rm)	Carpenter, cooper	Single	
Literate	House, wood (1 fl, 3 rm)	?	Single	
Illiterate	Shanty or wigwam	Basketmaker	Married	
Illiterate	House, wood (1 fl, 3 rm)	?	Married	
Illiterate	House, wood (1 fl, 2 rm)	?	Single	
Illiterate	House, wood (1 fl, 2 rm)	?	Single	
Illiterate	House, wood (1 fl, 3 rm)	?	Single	
Illiterate	House, wood (1 fl, 1 rm)	?	Single	
Illiterate	Shanty or wigwam	?	Married	
Illiterate	House, wood (1 fl, 3 rm)	?	Single	
Illiterate	House, wood (1 fl, 2 rm)	?	Married	
Literate	House, wood (1 fl, 1 rm)	?	Single	
Illiterate	Shanty or wigwam	?	Married	
Illiterate	House, wood (1 fl, 2 rm)	?	Widowed	
Illiterate	House, wood (1 fl, 2 rm)	?	Single	
Illiterate	House, wood (1 fl, 1 rm)	?	Married	
Illiterate	House, wood (1 fl, 1 rm)	?	Single	
Illiterate	Shanty or wigwam	Basketmaker	Widowed	
Literate	House, wood (1 fl, 1 rm)	Cooper	Married	
Illiterate	House, wood (1 fl, 3 rm)	?	Single	
Literate	House, wood (1 fl, 2 rm)	Carpenter, cooper	Single	
Illiterate	House, wood (1 fl, 1 rm)	Farmer, cooper	Married	
Illiterate	Shanty or wigwam	?	Single	
Literate	House, wood (1 fl, 1 rm)	Cooper	Married	
Illiterate	House, wood (1 fl, 1 rm)	?	Single	
Literate	House, wood (1 fl, 1 rm)	?	Single	
Literate	House, wood (1 fl, 1 rm)	?	Single	
Illiterate	House, wood (1 fl, 1 rm)	?	Single	
Illiterate	House, wood (1 fl, 2 rm)	Basketmaker	Single	
Illiterate	Shanty or wigwam	?	Single	
Illiterate	House, wood (1 fl, 1 rm)	?	Single	
Illiterate	Shanty or wigwam	?	Single	

1891 Census Data • Continued

ID no.	First name	Last name	Age in years	Location
262	Stephen	Francis	44	Queen's Co., Subdistrict Milton (1891)
263	Stephen	Francis	27	Pictou Co., Pictou Landing (reserve)
264	Stephen	Francis	5	Pictou Co., Pictou Landing (reserve)
265	Stephen	Francis	9	Potlotek, Chapel Island (Cape Breton reserve)
266	Susan	Francis	17	Queen's Co., Subdistrict Milton (1891)
267	Susie	Francis	12	Pictou Co., Pictou Landing (reserve)
268	Tom	Francis	30	Pictou Co., Pictou Landing (reserve)
269	Tom	Francis	12	Pictou Co., Pictou Landing (reserve)
270	Tom	Francis	17	Potlotek, Chapel Island (Cape Breton reserve)
271	Isabell	Frazer	9	Morland (Paqtnkek Reserve Area)
272	Kate	Frazer	60	Morland (Paqtnkek Reserve Area)
273	William	Frazer	60	Morland (Paqtnkek Reserve Area)
274	Maggie	Frio?	17	Potlotek, Chapel Island (Cape Breton reserve)
275	Bernard	Gabriel	87	Eskasoni (Cape Breton reserve)
276	Bridget	Gabriel	49	Eskasoni (Cape Breton reserve)
277	Charlot	Gabriel	24	Eskasoni (Cape Breton reserve)
278	Christy	Gabriel	53	Eskasoni (Cape Breton reserve)
279	Francis	Gabriel	16	Eskasoni (Cape Breton reserve)
280	Louis	Gabriel	66	Eskasoni (Cape Breton reserve)
281	Madelin	Gabriel	10	Eskasoni (Cape Breton reserve)
282	Mary	Gabriel	50	Eskasoni (Cape Breton reserve)
283	Sally	Gabriel	12	Eskasoni (Cape Breton reserve)
284	Susan	Gabriel	20	Eskasoni (Cape Breton reserve)
285	Charlot	Gilley	23	Pictou Co., Little Harbour
286	Peter	Gilley	4	Pictou Co., Little Harbour
287	Abram	Gloade	43	Queen's Co., Greenfield Subdistrict (1891)
288	Annie	Gloade	4	Kings Co., Canaan
289	Ben	Gloade	6	Queen's Co., Greenfield Subdistrict (1891)
290	Charlot	Gloade	11	Queen's Co., Greenfield Subdistrict (1891)
291	David	Gloade	15	Queen's Co., Greenfield Subdistrict (1891)
292	Esther	Gloade	13	Shelburne Co., Barrington Head
293	Fanny	Gloade	32	Queen's Co., Subdistrict Milton (1891)
294	Frank	Gloade	5	Shelburne Co., Shelburne
295	James	Gloade	1	Colchester Co., Acadia mines
296	James	Gloade	3	Shelburne Co., Shelburne
297	Joseph	Gloade	4	Queen's Co., Greenfield Subdistrict (1891)
298	Lewis	Gloade	28	Colchester Co., Acadia mines
299	Martha	Gloade	14	Kings Co., Canaan
300	Mary	Gloade	2	Queen's Co., Greenfield Subdistrict (1891)
301	Mary	Gloade	19	Colchester Co., Acadia mines
302	Mary	Gloade	27	Colchester Co., Acadia mines
303	Mary	Gloade	48	Queen's Co., Caledonia
304	Mary	Gloade	17	Kings Co., Canaan
305	Maryann	Gloade	26	Queen's Co., Greenfield Subdistrict (1891)
306	Maryann	Gloade	51	Queen's Co., Greenfield Subdistrict (1891)
307	Matthew	Gloade	64	Shelburne Co., Barrington Head
308	Michael	Gloade	11	Shelburne Co., Shelburne
309	Nancy	Gloade	47	Colchester Co., Acadia mines
310	Nancy	Gloade	60	Kings Co., Centreville
311	Noel	Gloade	55	Colchester Co., Acadia mines
312	Noel	Gloade	50	Queen's Co., Greenfield Subdistrict (1891)
313	Peter	Gloade	35	Queen's Co., Subdistrict Milton (1891)
314	Peter	Gloade	56	Kings Co., Canaan

Education	Housing	Occupation	Marital status	Notes
Illiterate	House, wood (1 fl, 3 rm)	Laborer	Married	
Literate	House, wood (1 fl, 2 rm)	Carpenter, cooper	Single	
Illiterate	House, wood (1 fl, 2 rm)	?	Single	
Illiterate	House, wood (1 fl, 1 rm)	?	Single	
Literate	House, wood (1 fl, 3 rm)	?	Single	
Illiterate	House, wood (1 fl, 2 rm)	?	Single	
Literate	House, wood (1 fl, 2 rm)	Carpenter, cooper	Married	
Illiterate	House, wood (1 fl, 1 rm)	?	Single	
Literate	House, wood (1 fl, 1 rm)	?	Single	
Illiterate	House, wood (1 fl, 1 rm)	?	Single	
Literate	House, wood (1 fl, 1 rm)	?	Married	
Literate	House, wood (1 fl, 1 rm)	Farmer, fisherman	Married	
Illiterate	Shanty or wigwam	?	Single	
Literate	Shanty or wigwam	Cooper	Married	
Illiterate	Shanty or wigwam	?	Married	
Literate	Shanty or wigwam	Cooper	Single	
Literate	Shanty or wigwam	Cooper	Single	
Illiterate	Shanty or wigwam	?	Single	
Literate	Shanty or wigwam	Cooper	Married	
Illiterate	Shanty or wigwam	?	Single	
Literate	Shanty or wigwam	Cooper	Single	
Illiterate	Shanty or wigwam	?	Single	
Illiterate	Shanty or wigwam	?	Single	
Illiterate	Shanty or wigwam	?	Widowed	
Illiterate	Shanty or wigwam	?	Single	
Literate	House, wood (1 fl, 3 rm)	Day laborer	Married	
Illiterate	Shanty or wigwam	?	Single	
Illiterate	House, wood (1 fl, 3 rm)	?	Single	
Literate	House, wood (1 fl, 5 rm)	?	Single	
Literate	House, wood (1 fl, 5 rm)	?	Single	
Literate	House, wood (1 fl, 2 rm)	?	Single	
Illiterate	Shanty or wigwam	Basketmaker	Married	
Illiterate	House, wood (1 fl, 2 rm)	?	Single	
Illiterate	Shanty or wigwam	?	Single	
Illiterate	House, wood (1 fl, 2 rm)	?	Single	
Illiterate	House, wood (1 fl, 3 rm)	?	Single	
Illiterate	Shanty or wigwam	Cooper	Married	
Illiterate	Shanty or wigwam	?	Single	
Illiterate	House, wood (1 fl, 3 rm)	?	Single	
Literate	Shanty or wigwam	Basketmaker	Married	
Illiterate	Shanty or wigwam	Basketmaker	Married	
Illiterate	Shanty or wigwam	Basketmaker	Widowed	
Illiterate	Shanty or wigwam	?	Single	
Literate	House, wood (1 fl, 3 rm)	?	Married	
Illiterate	House, wood (1 fl, 5 rm)	Basketmaker	Married	
Literate	House, wood (1 fl, 2 rm)	Hunter	Married	
Illiterate	House, wood (1 fl, 2 rm)	?	Single	
Literate	Shanty or wigwam	Basketmaker	Married	
Illiterate	Shanty or wigwam	Basketmaker	Widowed	
Illiterate	Shanty or wigwam	Basketmaker	Married	
Illiterate	House, wood (1 fl, 5 rm)	Hunter, fisherman	Married	
Literate	Shanty or wigwam	Laborer	Married	
Illiterate	Shanty or wigwam	Cooper	Widowed	Born Quebec

1891 Census Data • *Continued*

ID no.	First name	Last name	Age in years	Location
315	Samuel	Gloade	13	Shelburne Co., Shelburne
316	Sarah	Gloade	18	Colchester Co., Acadia mines
317	Sarah	Gloade	30	Shelburne Co., Shelburne
318	Steven	Gloade	44	Shelburne Co., Shelburne
319	Thomas	Gloade	23	Colchester Co., Acadia mines
320	Victoria	Gloade	53	Shelburne Co., Barrington Head
321	Alex	Gonley	38	Hants Co., Shubenacdie/Indian Brook Reserve area, St. Croix
322	Maryann	Gonley	58	Hants Co., Shubenacdie/Indian Brook Reserve area, St. Croix
323	Joe	Goodo	2	Town of Guysborough (Subdistrict F)
324	Mary	Goodo	38	Town of Guysborough (Subdistrict F)
325	Peter	Goodo	42	Town of Guysborough (Subdistrict F)
326	Peter	Googo	6	Waqamatkuk (Middle River, Cape Breton reserve)
327	Andrew	Googoo	35	Whycocomagh (Cape Breton reserve)
328	Andrew	Googoo	7	Whycocomagh (Cape Breton reserve)
329	Betty	Googoo	16	Waqamatkuk (Middle River, Cape Breton reserve)
330	Bridget	Googoo	7	Whycocomagh (Cape Breton reserve)
331	Catharine	Googoo	38	Whycocomagh (Cape Breton reserve)
332	Christy	Googoo	34	Eskasoni (Cape Breton reserve)
333	Flora	Googoo	22	Waqamatkuk (Middle River, Cape Breton reserve)
334	Francis	Googoo	58	Whycocomagh (Cape Breton reserve)
335	Frank	Googoo	19	Whycocomagh (Cape Breton reserve)
336	Gabriel	Googoo	12	Whycocomagh (Cape Breton reserve)
337	Isabell	Googoo	16	Whycocomagh (Cape Breton reserve)
338	James	Googoo	22	Whycocomagh (Cape Breton reserve)
339	Joe	Googoo	32	Eskasoni (Cape Breton reserve)
340	Joe	Googoo	1	Waqamatkuk (Middle River, Cape Breton reserve)
341	John	Googoo	50	Waqamatkuk (Middle River, Cape Breton reserve)
342	Linnie	Googoo	5	Waqamatkuk (Middle River, Cape Breton reserve)
343	Louis	Googoo	5	Whycocomagh (Cape Breton reserve)
344	Maggie	Googoo	21	Whycocomagh (Cape Breton reserve)
345	Marjess	Googoo	3	Whycocomagh (Cape Breton reserve)
346	Mary	Googoo	6	Eskasoni (Cape Breton reserve)
347	Maryann	Googoo	41	Waqamatkuk (Middle River, Cape Breton reserve)
348	Maryann	Googoo	25	Waqamatkuk (Middle River, Cape Breton reserve)
349	Maryann	Googoo	22	Whycocomagh (Cape Breton reserve)
350	Marys	Googoo	4	Eskasoni (Cape Breton reserve)
351	Michael	Googoo	10	Whycocomagh (Cape Breton reserve)
352	Mutgni	Googoo	17	Whycocomagh (Cape Breton reserve)
353	Nancy	Googoo	23	Whycocomagh (Cape Breton reserve)
354	Nancy	Googoo	38	Whycocomagh (Cape Breton reserve)
355	Noel	Googoo	37	Eskasoni (Cape Breton reserve)
356	Patrick	Googoo	16	Whycocomagh (Cape Breton reserve)
357	Peter	Googoo	12	Eskasoni (Cape Breton reserve)
358	Peter	Googoo	7	Waqamatkuk (Middle River, Cape Breton reserve)
359	Peter	Googoo	41	Whycocomagh (Cape Breton reserve)
360	Peter	Googoo	27	Whycocomagh (Cape Breton reserve)
361	Rjohn	Googoo	10	Eskasoni (Cape Breton reserve)
362	Sagnes	Googoo	58	Whycocomagh (Cape Breton reserve)
363	Sam	Googoo	23	Whycocomagh (Cape Breton reserve)
364	Simon	Googoo	63	Whycocomagh (Cape Breton reserve)
365	Stephen	Googoo	13	Waqamatkuk (Middle River, Cape Breton reserve)
366	Stephen	Googoo	19	Whycocomagh (Cape Breton reserve)
367	Susan	Googoo	7	Whycocomagh (Cape Breton reserve)

Education	Housing	Occupation	Marital status	Notes
Illiterate	House, wood (1 fl, 2 rm)	?	Single	
Illiterate	Shanty or wigwam	Basketmaker	Married	
Literate	House, wood (1 fl, 2 rm)	Basketmaker	Married	
Literate	House, wood (1 fl, 2 rm)	Hunter	Married	
Literate	Shanty or wigwam	Mason	Married	
Literate	House, wood (1 fl, 2 rm)	?	Married	
Illiterate	Shanty or wigwam	Basketmaker	Married	
Illiterate	Shanty or wigwam	Basketmaker	Married	
Illiterate	Shanty or wigwam	?	Single	
Illiterate	Shanty or wigwam	?	Married	
Illiterate	Shanty or wigwam	Fisherman, cooper	Married	
Literate	House, wood (1 fl, 1 rm)	?	Single	
Literate	Shanty or wigwam	Cooper	Married	
Illiterate	Shanty or wigwam	?	Single	
Literate	House, wood (1 fl, 1 rm)	Basketmaker	Single	
Literate	House, wood (1 fl, 3 rm)	?	Single	
Illiterate	Shanty or wigwam	?	Married	
Illiterate	Shanty or wigwam	?	Married	
Illiterate	House, wood (1 fl, 1 rm)	Basketmaker	Single	
Literate	House, wood (1 fl, 4 rm)	Farmer	Married	
Illiterate	Shanty or wigwam	Cooper	Single	
Illiterate	Shanty or wigwam	?	Single	
Illiterate	House, wood (1 fl, 3 rm)	?	Single	
Illiterate	Shanty or wigwam	Cooper	Single	
Illiterate	Shanty or wigwam	Cooper	Single	
Illiterate	House, wood (1 fl, 1 rm)	?	Single	
Literate	House, wood (1 fl, 1 rm)	Cooper	Married	
Illiterate	House, wood (1 fl, 1 rm)	?	Single	
Illiterate	Shanty or wigwam	?	Single	
Literate	House, wood (1 fl, 4 rm)	?	Married	
Illiterate	House, wood (1 fl, 3 rm)	?	Single	
Illiterate	Shanty or wigwam	?	Single	
Illiterate	House, wood (1 fl, 1 rm)	?	Married	
Literate	House, wood (1 fl, 1 rm)	?	Married	
Literate	House, wood (1 fl, 3 rm)	?	Single	
Illiterate	Shanty or wigwam	?	Single	
Illiterate	Shanty or wigwam	?	Single	
Illiterate	Shanty or wigwam	?	Single	Female?
Illiterate	House, wood (1 fl, 3 rm)	?	Married	
Literate	Shanty or wigwam	?	Married	
Illiterate	Shanty or wigwam	Cooper	Married	
Literate	House, wood (1 fl, 3 rm)	?	Single	
Literate	Shanty or wigwam	?	Single	
Literate	House, wood (1 fl, 1 rm)	?	Single	
Illiterate	House, wood (1 fl, 3 rm)	Farmer	Married	
Literate	House, wood (1 fl, 4 rm)	Carpenter	Single	
Literate	Shanty or wigwam	?	Single	
Illiterate	House, wood (1 fl, 4 rm)	Farmer	Married	
Literate	House, wood (1 fl, 4 rm)	Farmer	Single	
Illiterate	Shanty or wigwam	Cooper	Married	
Literate	House, wood (1 fl, 1 rm)	?	Single	
Literate	House, wood (1 fl, 3 rm)	?	Single	
Illiterate	Shanty or wigwam	?	Single	

1891 Census Data • Continued

ID no.	First name	Last name	Age in years	Location
368	Victor	Googoo	19	Waqamatkuk (Middle River, Cape Breton reserve)
369	William	Googoo	2	Eskasoni (Cape Breton reserve)
370	Albert	Gould	30	Whycocomagh (Cape Breton reserve)
371	Andrew	Gould	34	Whycocomagh (Cape Breton reserve)
372	John	Gould	53	Whycocomagh (Cape Breton reserve)
373	Joseph	Gould	27	Whycocomagh (Cape Breton reserve)
374	Joseph	Gould	6	Whycocomagh (Cape Breton reserve)
375	Mary	Gould	28	Whycocomagh (Cape Breton reserve)
376	Maryann	Gould	83	Whycocomagh (Cape Breton reserve)
377	Noel	Gould	13	Whycocomagh (Cape Breton reserve)
378	Susan	Gould	11	Whycocomagh (Cape Breton reserve)
379	Noel	Gregwar?	50	Potlotek, Chapel Island (Cape Breton reserve)
380	Bella	Isaac	51	Sydney (King's Road reserve 1881/1891)
381	John	Isaac	13	Sydney (King's Road reserve 1881/1891)
382	Joseph	Isaac	15	Sydney (King's Road reserve 1881/1891)
383	Nancy	Isaac	29	Sydney (King's Road reserve 1881/1891)
384	Noel	Isaac	40	Sydney (King's Road reserve 1881/1891)
385	Peter	Isaac	9	Sydney (King's Road reserve 1881/1891)
386	Sally	Isaac	71	Sydney (King's Road reserve 1881/1891)
387	Susie	Isaac	11	Sydney (King's Road reserve 1881/1891)
388	Nancy	Jeddore	77	Hants Co., Shubenacdie/Indian Brook Reserve area, St. Croix
389	Mattio	Jeremy	57	Queen's Co., Caledonia
390	John	Jeremy?	33	Queen's Co., Subdistrict Milton (1891)
391	John	Jeremy?	0	Queen's Co., Subdistrict Milton (1891)
392	Katie	Jeremy?	3	Queen's Co., Subdistrict Milton (1891)
393	Maggie	Jeremy?	34	Queen's Co., Subdistrict Milton (1891)
394	Mary	Jeremy?	6	Queen's Co., Subdistrict Milton (1891)
395	Jane	Jim	44	Waqamatkuk (Middle River, Cape Breton reserve)
396	John	Jim	44	Waqamatkuk (Middle River, Cape Breton reserve)
397	Mary	Jim	6	Waqamatkuk (Middle River, Cape Breton reserve)
398	Noel	Jim	12	Waqamatkuk (Middle River, Cape Breton reserve)
399	Susan	Jim	14	Waqamatkuk (Middle River, Cape Breton reserve)
400	Elvira	Joe	4	Waqamatkuk (Middle River, Cape Breton reserve)
401	Hannah	Joe	53	Pictou Co., Pictou Landing (reserve)
402	Harriet	Joe	2	Waqamatkuk (Middle River, Cape Breton reserve)
403	James	Joe	39	Potlotek, Chapel Island (Cape Breton reserve)
404	James	Joe	13	Town of Guysborough (Subdistrict F)
405	Jane	Joe	18	Waqamatkuk (Middle River, Cape Breton reserve)
406	John	Joe	18	Pictou Co., Pictou Landing (reserve)
407	Ledger	Joe	9	Waqamatkuk (Middle River, Cape Breton reserve)
408	Lewis	Joe	39	Town of Guysborough (Subdistrict F)
409	Louise	Joe	73	Potlotek, Chapel Island (Cape Breton reserve)
410	Madeline	Joe	15	Waqamatkuk (Middle River, Cape Breton reserve)
411	Mag	Joe	37	Town of Guysborough (Subdistrict F)
412	Margaret	Joe	7	Town of Guysborough (Subdistrict F)
413	Mary	Joe	1 mo	Waqamatkuk (Middle River, Cape Breton reserve)
414	Mary	Joe	28	Potlotek, Chapel Island (Cape Breton reserve)
415	Mary	Joe	72	Morland (Paqtnkek Reserve Area)
416	Mary	Joe	16	Town of Guysborough (Subdistrict F)
417	Maze	Joe	3 mo	Town of Guysborough (Subdistrict F)
418	Michael	Joe	26	Waqamatkuk (Middle River, Cape Breton reserve)
419	Michael	Joe	4	Town of Guysborough (Subdistrict F)
420	Paul	Joe	81	Potlotek, Chapel Island (Cape Breton reserve)

Education	Housing	Occupation	Marital status	Notes
Literate	House, wood (1 fl, 1 rm)	Cooper	Single	
Illiterate	Shanty or wigwam	?	Single	
Illiterate	Shanty or wigwam	Cooper	Single	
Illiterate	Shanty or wigwam	Cooper	Married	
Illiterate	Shanty or wigwam	Farmer	Widowed	
Illiterate	Shanty or wigwam	Cooper	Single	
Illiterate	Shanty or wigwam	?	Single	
Illiterate	Shanty or wigwam	?	Married	
Illiterate	Shanty or wigwam	?	Widowed	
Illiterate	Shanty or wigwam	?	Single	
Illiterate	Shanty or wigwam	?	Single	
Illiterate	House, wood (1 fl, 1 rm)	Cooper	Widowed	
Illiterate	Shanty or wigwam	Basketmaker	Widowed	
Illiterate	Shanty or wigwam	Cooper	Single	
Illiterate	Shanty or wigwam	?	Single	
Illiterate	Shanty or wigwam	Cooper	Married	
Illiterate	Shanty or wigwam	Cooper	Married	
Illiterate	Shanty or wigwam	?	Single	
Illiterate	Shanty or wigwam	?	Widowed	
Illiterate	Shanty or wigwam	?	Single	
Illiterate	Shanty or wigwam	?	?	
Illiterate	House, wood (2 fl, 5 rm)	Hunter	Widowed	
Illiterate	House, wood (1 fl, 3 rm)	Hunter, fisherman	Married	
Illiterate	House, wood (1 fl, 3 rm)	?	Single	
Illiterate	House, wood (1 fl, 3 rm)	?	Single	
Illiterate	House, wood (1 fl, 3 rm)	Basketmaker	Married	
Illiterate	House, wood (1 fl, 3 rm)	?	Single	
Illiterate	House, wood (1 fl, 1 rm)	?	Married	
Illiterate	House, wood (1 fl, 1 rm)	Cooper	Married	
Illiterate	House, wood (1 fl, 1 rm)	?	Single	
Literate	House, wood (1 fl, 1 rm)	?	Single	
Illiterate	House, wood (1 fl, 1 rm)	?	Single	
Illiterate	Shanty or wigwam	?	Single	
Illiterate	Shanty or wigwam	?	Widowed	
Illiterate	Shanty or wigwam	?	Single	
Illiterate	Shanty or wigwam	?	Married	
Illiterate	Shanty or wigwam	?	Single	
Illiterate	Shanty or wigwam	?	Married	
Illiterate	Shanty or wigwam	?	Single	
Illiterate	Shanty or wigwam	?	Single	Female
Illiterate	Shanty or wigwam	Cooper, fisherman	Married	
Illiterate	House, wood (1 fl, 1 rm)	?	Married	
Illiterate	Shanty or wigwam	?	Single	
Illiterate	Shanty or wigwam	?	Married	
Illiterate	Shanty or wigwam	?	Single	
Illiterate	Shanty or wigwam	?	Single	
Illiterate	Shanty or wigwam	?	Married	
Literate	House, wood (1 fl, 1 rm)	Farmer	Widowed	
Illiterate	Shanty or wigwam	?	Single	
Illiterate	Shanty or wigwam	?	Single	Female
Illiterate	Shanty or wigwam	Cooper	Married	
Illiterate	Shanty or wigwam	?	Single	
Illiterate	House, wood (1 fl, 1 rm)	Cooper	Married	

1891 Census Data • Continued

ID no.	First name	Last name	Age in years	Location
421	Susan	Joe	32	Waqamatkuk (Middle River, Cape Breton reserve)
422	Maggie	John	3	Waqamatkuk (Middle River, Cape Breton reserve)
423	Minnie	John	25	Waqamatkuk (Middle River, Cape Breton reserve)
424	Sarah	John	8 mo	Waqamatkuk (Middle River, Cape Breton reserve)
425	Stephen	John	37	Waqamatkuk (Middle River, Cape Breton reserve)
426	Amy	Johnson	21	Town of Guysborough (Subdistrict F)
427	Ben	Johnson	20	Town of Guysborough (Subdistrict F)
428	Charles	Johnson	13	Town of Guysborough (Subdistrict F)
429	Elizabeth	Johnson	18	Town of Guysborough (Subdistrict F)
430	Ellen	Johnson	4	Potlotek, Chapel Island (Cape Breton reserve)
431	John	Johnson	30	Potlotek, Chapel Island (Cape Breton reserve)
432	Joseph	Johnson	25	Town of Guysborough (Subdistrict F)
433	Mary	Johnson	17	Potlotek, Chapel Island (Cape Breton reserve)
434	Mary	Johnson	16	Town of Guysborough (Subdistrict F)
435	Noel	Johnson	2	Potlotek, Chapel Island (Cape Breton reserve)
436	Richard	Johnson	10	Town of Guysborough (Subdistrict F)
437	Sophie	Johnson	18	Potlotek, Chapel Island (Cape Breton reserve)
438	Sophie	Johnson	18	Town of Guysborough (Subdistrict F)
439	Susan	Johnson	63	Town of Guysborough (Subdistrict F)
440	Thomas	Johnson	70	Town of Guysborough (Subdistrict F)
441	Ellen	Joseph	3 mo	Pictou Co., Little Harbour
442	Lewis	Joseph	40	Pictou Co., Subdistrict Barney's River
443	Lissie	Joseph	22	Pictou Co., Little Harbour
444	Marie	Joseph	2	Pictou Co., Little Harbour
445	Morris	Joseph	10	Pictou Co., Subdistrict Barney's River
446	Peter	Joseph	28	Pictou Co., Little Harbour
447	Bridget	Julian	20	Potlotek, Chapel Island (Cape Breton reserve)
448	Francis	Julian	3 mo	Potlotek, Chapel Island (Cape Breton reserve)
449	William	Julian	30	Potlotek, Chapel Island (Cape Breton reserve)
450	Betsy	Kennedy	21	Heatherton (Paqtnkek Reserve Area)
451	Caroline	Kennedy	4	Pictou Co., Bailey's Brook
452	Caroline	Kennedy	4	Heatherton (Paqtnkek Reserve Area)
453	Sarah	Kennedy	25	Pictou Co., Bailey's Brook
454	Thomas	Kennedy	40	Pictou Co., Bailey's Brook
455	Thomas	Kennedy	44	Heatherton (Paqtnkek Reserve Area)
456	Annie	Knockwood	7	Pictou Co., Pictou Landing (reserve)
457	Ben	Knockwood	18	Kings Co., Centreville
458	Henry	Knockwood	5	Kings Co., Centreville
459	John	Knockwood	12	Kings Co., Centreville
460	Joseph	Knockwood	14	Kings Co., Centreville
461	Lizzie	Knockwood	14	Pictou Co., Pictou Landing (reserve)
462	Madeline	Knockwood	1	Kings Co., Lakeville
463	Maggie	Knockwood	58	Pictou Co., Pictou Landing (reserve)
464	Marian	Knockwood	25	Kings Co., Lakeville
465	Mary	Knockwood	12	Pictou Co., Pictou Landing (reserve)
466	May	Knockwood	17	Kings Co., Centreville
467	Peter	Knockwood	63	Pictou Co., Pictou Landing (reserve)
468	Rachel	Knockwood	7	Kings Co., Centreville
469	Rosa	Knockwood	14	Kings Co., Lakeville
470	Sarah	Knockwood	24	Pictou Co., Pictou Landing (reserve)
471	Sarah	Knockwood	45	Kings Co., Centreville
472	Stephen	Knockwood	42	Kings Co., Centreville
473	Steven	Knockwood	44	Kings Co., Lakeville

Education	Housing	Occupation	Marital status	Notes
Illiterate	Shanty or wigwam	Basketmaker	Single	
Illiterate	Shanty or wigwam	?	Single	
Illiterate	Shanty or wigwam	?	Married	
Illiterate	Shanty or wigwam	?	Single	
Literate	Shanty or wigwam	Cooper	Married	
Illiterate	House, wood (1 fl, 2 rm)	?	Single	
Illiterate	House, wood (1 fl, 2 rm)	?	Single	
Illiterate	House, wood (1 fl, 2 rm)	?	Single	
Illiterate	House, wood (1 fl, 2 rm)	?	Married	
Illiterate	House, wood (1 fl, 1 rm)	?	Single	
Illiterate	House, wood (1 fl, 1 rm)	Farmer, cooper	Widowed	
Illiterate	House, wood (1 fl, 2 rm)	?	Married	
Illiterate	House, wood (1 fl, 1 rm)	?	Single	
Illiterate	House, wood (1 fl, 2 rm)	?	Single	
Illiterate	House, wood (1 fl, 1 rm)	?	Single	
Illiterate	House, wood (1 fl, 2 rm)	?	Single	
Illiterate	House, wood (1 fl, 1 rm)	?	Single	
Illiterate	House, wood (1 fl, 2 rm)	?	Single	
Illiterate	House, wood (1 fl, 2 rm)	?	Married	Born Newfoundland
Illiterate	House, wood (1 fl, 2 rm)	Farmer	Married	
Illiterate	Shanty or wigwam	?	Single	
Illiterate	Shanty or wigwam	Cooper	Widowed	
Illiterate	Shanty or wigwam	?	Married	
Illiterate	Shanty or wigwam	?	Single	
Illiterate	Shanty or wigwam	?	Single	
Illiterate	Shanty or wigwam	Cooper, fisherman	Married	Reversed?
Illiterate	Shanty or wigwam	?	Married	
Illiterate	Shanty or wigwam	?	Single	
Literate	Shanty or wigwam	Farmer, cooper	Married	
Illiterate	House, wood (1 fl, 3 rm)	Farmer, cooper	Married	
Illiterate	Shanty or wigwam	?	Single	
Illiterate	House, wood (1 fl, 3 rm)	?	Single	
Illiterate	Shanty or wigwam	?	Married	
Illiterate	Shanty or wigwam	Cooper, fisherman	Married	
Literate	House, wood (1 fl, 3 rm)	Farmer, cooper	Married	
Illiterate	House, wood (1 fl, 2 rm)	?	Single	
Literate	Shanty or wigwam	Farmer, laborer	Single	
Illiterate	Shanty or wigwam	?	Single	
Literate	Shanty or wigwam	?	Single	
Literate	Shanty or wigwam	Farmer, laborer	Single	
Illiterate	House, wood (1 fl, 2 rm)	?	Single	
Illiterate	House, wood (1 fl, 2 rm)	?	Single	
Illiterate	House, wood (1 fl, 2 rm)	Cooper	Married	
Illiterate	House, wood (1 fl, 2 rm)	?	Married	
Illiterate	House, wood (1 fl, 2 rm)	?	Single	
Literate	Shanty or wigwam	?	Single	
Literate	House, wood (1 fl, 2 rm)	Cooper	Married	
Illiterate	Shanty or wigwam	?	Single	
Literate	House, wood (1 fl, 2 rm)	?	Single	
Literate	House, wood (1 fl, 2 rm)	?	Single	
Illiterate	Shanty or wigwam	?	Married	
Illiterate	Shanty or wigwam	Farmer, laborer	Married	
Literate	House, wood (1 fl, 2 rm)	Basketmaker	Married	

1891 Census Data • Continued

ID no.	First name	Last name	Age in years	Location
474	Thom	Knockwood	16	Pictou Co., Pictou Landing (reserve)
475	Dominic	Labrador	22	Queen's Co., Subdistrict Milton (1891)
476	Fanny	Labrador	53	Shelburne Co., Port Clyde
477	Frank	Labrador	2	Yarmouth Co., Arcadia
478	Frank	Labrador	38	Shelburne Co., Jordan Falls
479	Harriet	Labrador	25	Yarmouth Co., Arcadia
480	John	Labrador	19	Queen's Co., Subdistrict Milton (1891)
481	Julia	Labrador	3	Shelburne Co., Jordan Falls
482	Libby	Labrador	15	Shelburne Co., Jordan Falls
483	Louis	Labrador	42	Queen's Co., Subdistrict Milton (1891)
484	Luke?	Labrador	13	Shelburne Co., Jordan Falls
485	Maggie	Labrador	4	Yarmouth Co., Arcadia
486	Mary	Labrador	40	Queen's Co., Subdistrict Milton (1891)
487	Mary	Labrador	16	Queen's Co., Subdistrict Milton (1891)
488	Mary	Labrador	37	Shelburne Co., Jordan Falls
489	Mary	Labrador	70	Shelburne Co., Shelburne
490	Noel	Labrador	56	Queen's Co., Subdistrict Milton (1891)
491	Samuel	Labrador	26	Yarmouth Co., Arcadia
492	Stephen	Labrador	8	Queen's Co., Subdistrict Milton (1891)
493	Elizabeth	Lafford	6	Morland (Paqtnkek Reserve Area)
494	Joe	Lafford	20	Heatherton (Paqtnkek Reserve Area)
495	John	Lafford	2	Morland (Paqtnkek Reserve Area)
496	Joseph	Lafford	60	Morland (Paqtnkek Reserve Area)
497	Mary	Lafford	26	Morland (Paqtnkek Reserve Area)
498	Mary	Lafford	11	Morland (Paqtnkek Reserve Area)
499	Abraham	Lewis	16	Heatherton (Paqtnkek Reserve Area)
500	Ben	Lewis	15	Whycocomagh (Cape Breton reserve)
501	Bessie	Lewis	19	Queen's Co., Subdistrict Mill Village (1891)
502	Elizabeth	Lewis	65	Heatherton (Paqtnkek Reserve Area)
503	John	Lewis	2	Whycocomagh (Cape Breton reserve)
504	John	Lewis	10 mo	Potlotek, Chapel Island (Cape Breton reserve)
505	John	Lewis	30	Morland (Paqtnkek Reserve Area)
506	Noel	Lewis	25	Queen's Co., Subdistrict Mill Village (1891)
507	Noel	Lewis	56	Potlotek, Chapel Island (Cape Breton reserve)
508	Peter	Lewis	65	Heatherton (Paqtnkek Reserve Area)
509	Peterjoe	Lewis	26	Heatherton (Paqtnkek Reserve Area)
510	Susan	Lewis	47	Potlotek, Chapel Island (Cape Breton reserve)
511	Francis	Luxly	74	Queen's Co., Subdistrict Milton (1891)
512	Margaret	Luxly	70	Queen's Co., Subdistrict Mill Village (1891)
513	Maryann	Luxly	63	Queen's Co., Subdistrict Milton (1891)
514	Thomas	Maloney	19	Hants Co., Shubenacdie/Indian Brook Reserve area, St. Croix
515	Agnes	Marshall	4 mo	Potlotek, Chapel Island (Cape Breton reserve)
516	Agnes	Marshall	2 mo	Town of Guysborough (Subdistrict F)
517	Andrew	Marshall	13	Potlotek, Chapel Island (Cape Breton reserve)
518	Ben	Marshall	13	Potlotek, Chapel Island (Cape Breton reserve)
519	Bridget	Marshall	11	Town of Guysborough (Subdistrict F)
520	Caroline	Marshall	21	Town of Guysborough (Subdistrict F)
521	Charles	Marshall	60	?
522	Eleanor	Marshall	9	Town of Guysborough (Subdistrict F)
523	Eleanor	Marshall	10	Town of Guysborough (Subdistrict F)
524	Ellen	Marshall	8	Potlotek, Chapel Island (Cape Breton reserve)
525	Ellen	Marshall	8	Potlotek, Chapel Island (Cape Breton reserve)
526	Ester	Marshall	51	Town of Guysborough (Subdistrict F)

Education	Housing	Occupation	Marital status	Notes
Literate	House, wood (1 fl, 2 rm)	?	Single	
Illiterate	Shanty or wigwam	Basketmaker	Married	
Illiterate	House, wood (2 fl, 4 rm)	?	Widowed	
Illiterate	House, wood (1 fl, 2 rm)	?	Single	
Illiterate	Shanty or wigwam	?	Married	
Literate	House, wood (1 fl, 2 rm)	Basketmaker	Married	
Illiterate	Shanty or wigwam	Basketmaker	Single	
Illiterate	Shanty or wigwam	?	Single	
Illiterate	Shanty or wigwam	?	Single	
Illiterate	Shanty or wigwam	Basketmaker	Married	
Illiterate	Shanty or wigwam	?	Single	
Illiterate	House, wood (1 fl, 2 rm)	?	Single	
Illiterate	Shanty or wigwam	Basketmaker	Married	
Illiterate	Shanty or wigwam	Basketmaker	Married	
Illiterate	Shanty or wigwam	?	Married	
Illiterate	House, wood (1 fl, 2 rm)	?	Widowed	
Illiterate	House, wood (2 fl, 5 rm)	Cooper	Widowed	
Illiterate	House, wood (1 fl, 2 rm)	Basketmaker	Married	
Illiterate	Shanty or wigwam	Basketmaker	Single	
Illiterate	House, wood (1 fl, 1 rm)	?	Single	
Literate	House, wood (1 fl, 1 rm)	Cooper	Single	
Illiterate	House, wood (1 fl, 1 rm)	?	Single	
Illiterate	House, wood (1 fl, 1 rm)	Farmer, fisherman	Married	
Illiterate	House, wood (1 fl, 1 rm)	?	Married	
Illiterate	House, wood (1 fl, 1 rm)	?	Single	
Illiterate	Shanty or wigwam	Farmer, cooper	Single	
Literate	Shanty or wigwam	?	Single	
Literate	House, wood (1 fl, 2 rm)	?	Married	
Illiterate	Shanty or wigwam	Farmer, cooper	Married	
Illiterate	Shanty or wigwam	?	Single	
Illiterate	Shanty or wigwam	?	Single	
Literate	House, wood (1 fl, 1 rm)	?	Single	
Literate	House, wood (1 fl, 2 rm)	Hunter	Married	
Illiterate	Shanty or wigwam	Farmer, cooper	Married	
Illiterate	Shanty or wigwam	Farmer, cooper	Married	Born Prince Edward Island
Literate	Shanty or wigwam	Farmer, cooper	Single	
Illiterate	Shanty or wigwam	?	Married	
Illiterate	Shanty or wigwam	?	Married	
Illiterate	House, wood (1 fl, 3 rm)	Midwife	Widowed	
Illiterate	Shanty or wigwam	Basketmaker	Married	
Illiterate	Shanty or wigwam	Laborer	Married	
Illiterate	Shanty or wigwam	?	Single	Away
Illiterate	Shanty or wigwam	?	Single	
Literate	Shanty or wigwam	?	Single	
Illiterate	Shanty or wigwam	?	Single	
Illiterate	House, wood (1 fl, 1 rm)	?	Single	
Illiterate	House, wood (1 fl, 1 rm)	?	Single	
Illiterate	Shanty or wigwam	Farmer, cooper	Married	
Illiterate	House, wood (1 fl, 1 rm)	?	Single	
Illiterate	Shanty or wigwam	?	Single	
Literate	Shanty or wigwam	?	Single	Away
Illiterate	Shanty or wigwam	?	Single	
Illiterate	House, wood (1 fl, 1 rm)	?	Married	

1891 Census Data • Continued

ID no.	First name	Last name	Age in years	Location
527	Harriet	Marshall	6	Potlotek, Chapel Island (Cape Breton reserve)
528	Jim	Marshall	70	Morland (Paqtnkek Reserve Area)
529	Joe	Marshall	10	Potlotek, Chapel Island (Cape Breton reserve)
530	John	Marshall	3	Potlotek, Chapel Island (Cape Breton reserve)
531	John	Marshall	42	Potlotek, Chapel Island (Cape Breton reserve)
532	Joseph	Marshall	12	Potlotek, Chapel Island (Cape Breton reserve)
533	Joseph	Marshall	14	Town of Guysborough (Subdistrict F)
534	Joseph	Marshall	58	Town of Guysborough (Subdistrict F)
535	Julia	Marshall	40	Potlotek, Chapel Island (Cape Breton reserve)
536	Julie	Marshall	39	Town of Guysborough (Subdistrict F)
537	Maggie	Marshall	4	Town of Guysborough (Subdistrict F)
538	Mary	Marshall	20	Potlotek, Chapel Island (Cape Breton reserve)
539	Mary	Marshall	20	Town of Guysborough (Subdistrict F)
540	Maryann	Marshall	37	Potlotek, Chapel Island (Cape Breton reserve)
541	Maryann	Marshall	17	Town of Guysborough (Subdistrict F)
542	Michael	Marshall	16	Potlotek, Chapel Island (Cape Breton reserve)
543	Michael	Marshall	16	Town of Guysborough (Subdistrict F)
544	Nancy	Marshall	3	Potlotek, Chapel Island (Cape Breton reserve)
545	Noel	Marshall	47	Potlotek, Chapel Island (Cape Breton reserve)
546	Noel	Marshall	40	Morland (Paqtnkek Reserve Area)
547	Noel	Marshall	43	Town of Guysborough (Subdistrict F)
548	Peter	Marshall	16	Potlotek, Chapel Island (Cape Breton reserve)
549	Peter	Marshall	19	Town of Guysborough (Subdistrict F)
550	Stephen	Marshall	18	Potlotek, Chapel Island (Cape Breton reserve)
551	Stephen	Marshall	25	Town of Guysborough (Subdistrict F)
552	Stephen	Marshall	18	Town of Guysborough (Subdistrict F)
553	Susan	Marshall	10	Potlotek, Chapel Island (Cape Breton reserve)
554	Susan	Marshall	89	Potlotek, Chapel Island (Cape Breton reserve)
555	Susan	Marshall	12	Town of Guysborough (Subdistrict F)
556	Susie	Marshall	21	Morland (Paqtnkek Reserve Area)
557	Tom	Marshall	20	Potlotek, Chapel Island (Cape Breton reserve)
558	Amy	Martin	28	Heatherton (Paqtnkek Reserve Area)
559	Ann	Martin	10	Heatherton (Paqtnkek Reserve Area)
560	John	Martin	36	Heatherton (Paqtnkek Reserve Area)
561	Mary	Martin	61	Potlotek, Chapel Island (Cape Breton reserve)
562	Rose	Martin	2	Heatherton (Paqtnkek Reserve Area)
563	Alex	Michael	42	Queen's Co., Subdistrict Milton (1891)
564	Andrew	Michael	4	Eskasoni (Cape Breton reserve)
565	Angeline	Michael	27	North Sydney
566	Anna	Michael	89	Eskasoni (Cape Breton reserve)
567	Annie	Michael	25	North Sydney
568	Bridget	Michael	13	Eskasoni (Cape Breton reserve)
569	Bridget	Michael	10	North Sydney
570	Bridget	Michael	35	North Sydney
571	Elizabeth	Michael	20	Queen's Co., Subdistrict Milton (1891)
572	James	Michael	43	Eskasoni (Cape Breton reserve)
573	John	Michael	29	North Sydney
574	Madeline	Michael	8	North Sydney
575	Mary	Michael	9	Eskasoni (Cape Breton reserve)
576	Mary	Michael	54	Queen's Co., Subdistrict Milton (1891)
577	Mary	Michael	6 mo	North Sydney
578	Mary	Michael	50	North Sydney
579	Mary	Michael	12	North Sydney

Education	Housing	Occupation	Marital status	Notes
Illiterate	Shanty or wigwam	?	Single	
Literate	House, wood (1 fl, 1 rm)	Farmer	Widowed	
Literate	Shanty or wigwam	?	Single	
Illiterate	Shanty or wigwam	?	Single	
Illiterate	Shanty or wigwam	Cooper	Married	
Literate	Shanty or wigwam	?	Single	Away
Illiterate	Shanty or wigwam	?	Single	
Illiterate	House, wood (1 fl, 1 rm)	Farmer	Married	Born Newfoundland
Illiterate	Shanty or wigwam	?	Married	Away
Illiterate	Shanty or wigwam	?	Married	
Illiterate	Shanty or wigwam	?	Single	
Illiterate	Shanty or wigwam	?	Single	Away
Illiterate	Shanty or wigwam	?	Single	
Illiterate	Shanty or wigwam	?	Married	
Illiterate	House, wood (1 fl, 1 rm)	?	Single	
Literate	Shanty or wigwam	?	Single	Away
Illiterate	Shanty or wigwam	?	Single	
Illiterate	Shanty or wigwam	?	Single	Away
Illiterate	Shanty or wigwam	Farmer, cooper	Married	Away
Literate	House, wood (1 fl, 1 rm)	Farmer	Married	
Illiterate	Shanty or wigwam	Fisherman	Married	
Literate	Shanty or wigwam	Cooper	Single	
Illiterate	House, wood (1 fl, 1 rm)	?	Single	
Illiterate	Shanty or wigwam	Cooper	Single	Away
Illiterate	House, wood (1 fl, 1 rm)	?	Single	
Illiterate	Shanty or wigwam	?	Single	
Literate	Shanty or wigwam	?	Single	Away
Illiterate	Shanty or wigwam	?	Widowed	
Illiterate	Shanty or wigwam	?	Single	
Literate	House, wood (1 fl, 1 rm)	Farmer	Married	
Illiterate	Shanty or wigwam	Cooper	Single	
Literate	Shanty or wigwam	Fisherman, cooper	Married	
Illiterate	Shanty or wigwam	Fisherman, cooper	Single	
Literate	Shanty or wigwam	Fisherman, cooper	Married	
Illiterate	House, wood (1 fl, 1 rm)	Cooper	Widowed	
Illiterate	Shanty or wigwam	?	Single	
Illiterate	?	Cooper	Married	
Literate	Shanty or wigwam	?	Single	
Literate	Wigwam	Basketmaker	Married	
Illiterate	Shanty or wigwam	?	Widowed	
Literate	Wigwam	Basketmaker	Married	
Illiterate	Shanty or wigwam	?	Single	
Illiterate	Wigwam	Basketmaker	Single	
Illiterate	Wigwam	Basketmaker	Widowed	
Illiterate	?	Basketmaker	Single	
Illiterate	Shanty or wigwam	Cooper	Widowed	
Literate	Wigwam	Cooper	Married	
Illiterate	Wigwam	?	Single	
Literate	Shanty or wigwam	?	Single	
Illiterate	?	Basketmaker	Married	
Illiterate	Wigwam	?	Single	
Illiterate	Wigwam	Basketmaker	Single	
Illiterate	Wigwam	Basketmaker	Single	

1891 Census Data • Continued

ID no.	First name	Last name	Age in years	Location
580	Marycath	Michael	5 mo	Potlotek, Chapel Island (Cape Breton reserve)
581	Maryjane	Michael	8	North Sydney
582	Michael	Michael	13	North Sydney
583	Nancy	Michael	25	Potlotek, Chapel Island (Cape Breton reserve)
584	Noel	Michael	27	Sydney (King's Road reserve 1881/1891)
585	Noel	Michael	25	Town of Guysborough (Subdistrict F)
586	Peter	Michael	36	Shelburne Co., Port Clyde
587	Steven	Michael	26	North Sydney
588	Steven	Michael	26	Potlotek, Chapel Island (Cape Breton reserve)
589	William	Michael	4 mo	North Sydney
590	Beatrice	Mooney	8	Shelburne Co., Port Clyde
591	Rosie	Mooney	16	Shelburne Co., Port Clyde
592	Ann	Morris	65	Potlotek, Chapel Island (Cape Breton reserve)
593	Betsy	Morris	28	Sydney (King's Road reserve 1881/1891)
594	Christopher	Morris	24	Eskasoni (Cape Breton reserve)
595	Ellen	Morris	53	Eskasoni (Cape Breton reserve)
596	Isabella	Morris	33	Pictou Co., Bailey's Brook
597	Joe	Morris	2	Eskasoni (Cape Breton reserve)
598	Joseph	Morris	5	Sydney (King's Road reserve 1881/1891)
599	Kate	Morris	2	Sydney (King's Road reserve 1881/1891)
600	Madelin	Morris	11	Eskasoni (Cape Breton reserve)
601	Mary	Morris	23	Eskasoni (Cape Breton reserve)
602	Maryann	Morris	13	Eskasoni (Cape Breton reserve)
603	Mathew	Morris	3	Sydney (King's Road reserve 1881/1891)
604	Mattie	Morris	4	Eskasoni (Cape Breton reserve)
605	Morris	Morris	11	Sydney (King's Road reserve 1881/1891)
606	Nancy	Morris	19	Eskasoni (Cape Breton reserve)
607	Nancy	Morris	7	Sydney (King's Road reserve 1881/1891)
608	Peter	Morris	5 mo	Pictou Co., Bailey's Brook
609	Solomon	Morris	31	Sydney (King's Road reserve 1881/1891)
610	Stephen	Morris	34	Pictou Co., Bailey's Brook
611	Susie	Morris	52	Sydney (King's Road reserve 1881/1891)
612	Sylvester	Morris	12	Sydney (King's Road reserve 1881/1891)
613	Caroline	Muse	4	Potlotek, Chapel Island (Cape Breton reserve)
614	Fred	Muse	14	Guysborough Co., Cape Canso
615	Freman	Muse	55	Potlotek, Chapel Island (Cape Breton reserve)
616	James	Muse	45	Queen's Co., Subdistrict Milton (1891)
617	Joseph	Muse	13	Potlotek, Chapel Island (Cape Breton reserve)
618	Joseph	Muse	28	Kings Co., Gaspereaux
619	Judith	Muse	33	Potlotek, Chapel Island (Cape Breton reserve)
620	Kate	Muse	21	Kings Co., Gaspereaux
621	Lizzie	Muse	6	Guysborough Co., Cape Canso
622	Maggie	Muse	9	Queen's Co., Subdistrict Mill Village (1891)
623	Mary	Muse	10	Guysborough Co., Cape Canso
624	Maryjane	Muse	9	Potlotek, Chapel Island (Cape Breton reserve)
625	Nancy	Muse	7	Potlotek, Chapel Island (Cape Breton reserve)
626	Nancy	Muse	97	Potlotek, Chapel Island (Cape Breton reserve)
627	Oliver	Muse	1	Potlotek, Chapel Island (Cape Breton reserve)
628	Rachel	Muse	9 mo	Kings Co., Gaspereaux
629	Selina	Muse	38	Guysborough Co., Cape Canso
630	Ann	Nevin	46	Sydney (King's Road reserve 1881/1891)
631	Francis	Nevin	5	Whycocomagh (Cape Breton reserve)
632	Joanna	Nevin	22	Whycocomagh (Cape Breton reserve)

Education	Housing	Occupation	Marital status	Notes
Illiterate	Shanty or wigwam	?	Single	
Illiterate	Wigwam	Basketmaker	Single	
Literate	Wigwam	Cooper	Single	
Illiterate	Shanty or wigwam	?	Married	
Illiterate	Shanty or wigwam	Cooper	Single	
Illiterate	House, wood (1 fl, 1 rm)	?	Single	
Illiterate	House, wood (2 fl, 4 rm)	Lumberjack	Married	
Literate	Wigwam	Cooper	Married	
Illiterate	Shanty or wigwam	Farmer, cooper	Married	
Illiterate	Wigwam	?	Single	
Illiterate	House, wood (2 fl, 4 rm)	?	Single	
Illiterate	House, wood (2 fl, 4 rm)	?	Single	
Illiterate	House, wood (1 fl, 1 rm)	?	Widowed	
Illiterate	Shanty or wigwam	Basketmaker	Married	
Literate	Shanty or wigwam	Cooper	Married	
Literate	Shanty or wigwam	Farmer	Widowed	
Illiterate	Shanty or wigwam	?	Married	
Illiterate	Shanty or wigwam	?	Single	
Illiterate	Shanty or wigwam	?	Single	
Illiterate	Shanty or wigwam	?	Single	
Illiterate	Shanty or wigwam	?	Single	
Illiterate	Shanty or wigwam	?	Married	
Illiterate	Shanty or wigwam	?	Single	
Illiterate	Shanty or wigwam	?	Single	
Illiterate	Shanty or wigwam	?	Single	
Illiterate	Shanty or wigwam	?	Single	
Illiterate	Shanty or wigwam	?	Widowed	
Illiterate	Shanty or wigwam	?	Single	
Illiterate	Shanty or wigwam	?	Single	
Illiterate	Shanty or wigwam	Cooper	Married	
Illiterate	Shanty or wigwam	Cooper, fisherman	Married	
Illiterate	Shanty or wigwam	?	Widowed	
Illiterate	Shanty or wigwam	Cooper	Single	
Illiterate	Shanty or wigwam	?	Single	
Illiterate	Shanty or wigwam	Laborer	Single	
Illiterate	Shanty or wigwam	Farmer, cooper	Married	
Illiterate	Shanty or wigwam	Basketmaker	Widowed	
Literate	Shanty or wigwam	?	Single	
Illiterate	Shanty or wigwam	Steamdrier	Married	
Illiterate	Shanty or wigwam	?	Married	
Literate	Shanty or wigwam	?	Married	Born New Brunswick; female
Illiterate	Shanty or wigwam	?	Single	
Illiterate	House, wood (1 fl, 3 rm)	?	Single	
Illiterate	Shanty or wigwam	?	Single	
Literate	Shanty or wigwam	?	Single	
Illiterate	Shanty or wigwam	?	Single	
Illiterate	Shanty or wigwam	?	Widowed	
Illiterate	Shanty or wigwam	?	Single	
Illiterate	Shanty or wigwam	?	Single	
Illiterate	Shanty or wigwam	Laborer	Widowed	
Illiterate	Shanty or wigwam	Basketmaker	Married	
Illiterate	House, wood (1 fl, 2 rm)	?	Single	
Literate	House, wood (1 fl, 2 rm)	?	Single	

1891 Census Data • Continued

ID no.	First name	Last name	Age in years	Location
633	Julie	Nevin	12	Whycocomagh (Cape Breton reserve)
634	June	Nevin	40	Whycocomagh (Cape Breton reserve)
635	Maryann	Nevin	16	Sydney (King's Road reserve 1881/1891)
636	Noeljohn	Nevin	58	Sydney (King's Road reserve 1881/1891)
637	Peter	Nevin	10	Whycocomagh (Cape Breton reserve)
638	Simon	Nevin	7	Whycocomagh (Cape Breton reserve)
639	Stephen	Nevin	35	Whycocomagh (Cape Breton reserve)
640	Steven	Nevin	20	Whycocomagh (Cape Breton reserve)
641	Andrew	Nicholas	6	Potlotek, Chapel Island (Cape Breton reserve)
642	Anthony	Nicholas	37	Potlotek, Chapel Island (Cape Breton reserve)
643	Christy	Nicholas	60	Potlotek, Chapel Island (Cape Breton reserve)
644	Fannie	Nicholas	3	Potlotek, Chapel Island (Cape Breton reserve)
645	John	Nicholas	12	Potlotek, Chapel Island (Cape Breton reserve)
646	Joseph	Nicholas	65	Potlotek, Chapel Island (Cape Breton reserve)
647	Louis	Nicholas	21	Pictou Co., Little Harbour
648	Maryann	Nicholas	28	Potlotek, Chapel Island (Cape Breton reserve)
649	Michael	Nicholas	?	Potlotek, Chapel Island (Cape Breton reserve)
650	Moses	Nicholas	12	Pictou Co., Little Harbour
651	Paul	Nicholas	4	Potlotek, Chapel Island (Cape Breton reserve)
652	Peter	Nicholas	8	Potlotek, Chapel Island (Cape Breton reserve)
653	Agnes	Noel	35	Guysborough Co., Cape Canso
654	Alice	Noel	7	Guysborough Co., Cape Canso
655	Ann	Noel	14	Waqamatkuk (Middle River, Cape Breton reserve)
656	Ann	Noel	64	Waqamatkuk (Middle River, Cape Breton reserve)
657	Annabell	Noel	3	Whycocomagh (Cape Breton reserve)
658	Bella	Noel	18	Waqamatkuk (Middle River, Cape Breton reserve)
659	Ben	Noel	12	Whycocomagh (Cape Breton reserve)
660	Bridget	Noel	40	Waqamatkuk (Middle River, Cape Breton reserve)
661	Caroline	Noel	3 mo	Whycocomagh (Cape Breton reserve)
662	Catharine	Noel	45	Whycocomagh (Cape Breton reserve)
663	Catharine	Noel	27	Whycocomagh (Cape Breton reserve)
664	Charles	Noel	4	Guysborough Co., Cape Canso
665	Christopher	Noel	21	Whycocomagh (Cape Breton reserve)
666	Dennis	Noel	60	Heatherton (Paqtnkek Reserve Area)
667	Eddy	Noel	8	Whycocomagh (Cape Breton reserve)
668	Eliza	Noel	13	Guysborough Co., Cape Canso
669	Elizabeth	Noel	18	Whycocomagh (Cape Breton reserve)
670	Elizabeth	Noel	20	Whycocomagh (Cape Breton reserve)
671	Ellen	Noel	16	Whycocomagh (Cape Breton reserve)
672	Ellen	Noel	12	Potlotek, Chapel Island (Cape Breton reserve)
673	Ellen	Noel	20	Whycocomagh (Cape Breton reserve)
674	Elsie	Noel	2	Guysborough Co., Cape Canso
675	Elzabet	Noel	4	Whycocomagh (Cape Breton reserve)
676	Ester	Noel	41	Whycocomagh (Cape Breton reserve)
677	Esther	Noel	10	Whycocomagh (Cape Breton reserve)
678	Gabriel	Noel	16	Whycocomagh (Cape Breton reserve)
679	Hannah	Noel	14	Pictou Co., Pictou Landing (reserve)
680	James	Noel	44	Guysborough Co., Cape Canso
681	Janet	Noel	84	Waqamatkuk (Middle River, Cape Breton reserve)
682	Jannet	Noel	24	Whycocomagh (Cape Breton reserve)
683	John	Noel	3	Queen's Co., Subdistrict Mill Village (1891)
684	John	Noel	62	Hants Co., Shubenacadie/Indian Brook Reserve area, South Rawdon and Uniacke

Education	Housing	Occupation	Marital status	Notes
Illiterate	House, wood (1 fl, 2 rm)	?	Single	
Illiterate	House, wood (1 fl, 2 rm)	?	Married	
Illiterate	Shanty or wigwam	Basketmaker	Married	
Illiterate	Shanty or wigwam	Cooper	Married	
Illiterate	House, wood (1 fl, 2 rm)	?	Single	
Illiterate	House, wood (1 fl, 2 rm)	?	Single	
Literate	House, wood (1 fl, 2 rm)	Cooper	Married	
Illiterate	House, wood (1 fl, 2 rm)	Cooper	Single	
Illiterate	House, wood (1 fl, 1 rm)	?	Single	
Illiterate	House, wood (1 fl, 1 rm)	Farmer, cooper	Married	
Illiterate	Shanty or wigwam	?	Married	
Illiterate	House, wood (1 fl, 1 rm)	?	Single	
Illiterate	Shanty or wigwam	?	Single	
Illiterate	Shanty or wigwam	Cooper	Married	
Illiterate	Shanty or wigwam	?	Single	
Illiterate	House, wood (1 fl, 1 rm)	?	Married	
Illiterate	House, wood (1 fl, 1 rm)	?	Single	
Illiterate	Shanty or wigwam	?	Single	
Illiterate	House, wood (1 fl, 1 rm)	?	Single	
Illiterate	Shanty or wigwam	?	Single	
Illiterate	House, wood (1 fl, 3 rm)	?	Married	
Illiterate	House, wood (1 fl, 3 rm)	?	Single	
Illiterate	House, wood (1 fl, 1 rm)	Basketmaker	Single	
Illiterate	House, wood (1 fl, 1 rm)	?	Single	
Illiterate	Shanty or wigwam	?	Single	
Literate	Shanty or wigwam	?	Single	
Literate	House, wood (1 fl, 3 rm)	?	Single	
Literate	Shanty or wigwam	?	Married	
Illiterate	Shanty or wigwam	?	Single	
Illiterate	Shanty or wigwam	?	Widowed	
Illiterate	Shanty or wigwam	?	Married	
Illiterate	House, wood (1 fl, 3 rm)	?	Single	
Literate	House, wood (1 fl, 3 rm)	Cooper	Single	
Illiterate	House, wood (1 fl, 1 rm)	Farmer, cooper	Married	
Illiterate	Shanty or wigwam	?	Single	
Literate	House, wood (1 fl, 3 rm)	?	Single	
Illiterate	Shanty or wigwam	?	Single	
Illiterate	House, wood (1 fl, 3 rm)	?	Single	
Illiterate	Shanty or wigwam	?	Single	
Literate	Shanty or wigwam	?	Single	
Illiterate	House, wood (1 fl, 1 rm)	?	Married	
Illiterate	House, wood (1 fl, 3 rm)	?	Single	
Illiterate	House, wood (1 fl, 3 rm)	?	Single	
Illiterate	House, wood (1 fl, 1 rm)	Farmer	Married	
Illiterate	Shanty or wigwam	?	Single	
Illiterate	House, wood (1 fl, 3 rm)	Cooper	Single	
Illiterate	House, wood (1 fl, 1 rm)	?	Single	
Literate	House, wood (1 fl, 3 rm)	Teamster	Married	
Literate	House, wood (1 fl, 1 rm)	?	Widowed	
Illiterate	Shanty or wigwam	?	Single	
Illiterate	House, wood (1 fl, 2 rm)	?	Single	
Literate	House, wood (2 fl, 4 rm)	Cooper	Married	

1891 Census Data • Continued

ID no.	First name	Last name	Age in years	Location
685	John	Noel	60	Pictou Co., Pictou Landing (reserve)
686	Joseph	Noel	37	Whycocomagh (Cape Breton reserve)
687	Joseph	Noel	35	Whycocomagh (Cape Breton reserve)
688	Joseph	Noel	10	Whycocomagh (Cape Breton reserve)
689	Kate	Noel	10	Guysborough Co., Cape Canso
690	Louis	Noel	40	Waqamatkuk (Middle River, Cape Breton reserve)
691	Lydia	Noel	47	Queen's Co., Subdistrict Mill Village (1891)
692	Madaline	Noel	14	Whycocomagh (Cape Breton reserve)
693	Mary	Noel	48	Whycocomagh (Cape Breton reserve)
694	Mary	Noel	81	Whycocomagh (Cape Breton reserve)
695	Mary	Noel	50	Pictou Co., Pictou Landing (reserve)
696	Mary	Noel	4	Whycocomagh (Cape Breton reserve)
697	Mary	Noel	67	Heatherton (Paqtnkek Reserve Area)
698	Mary	Noel	17	Hants Co., Shubenacdie/Indian Brook Reserve area, South Rawdon and Uniacke
699	Maryann	Noel	13	Whycocomagh (Cape Breton reserve)
700	Maryann	Noel	29	Pictou Co., Pictou Landing (reserve)
701	Maryann	Noel	66	Hants Co., Shubenacdie/Indian Brook Reserve area, South Rawdon and Uniacke
702	Maurice	Noel	30	Pictou Co., Pictou Landing (reserve)
703	Michael	Noel	50	Waqamatkuk (Middle River, Cape Breton reserve)
704	Noel	Noel	17	Waqamatkuk (Middle River, Cape Breton reserve)
705	Noel	Noel	10	Waqamatkuk (Middle River, Cape Breton reserve)
706	Noel	Noel	30	Whycocomagh (Cape Breton reserve)
707	Peter	Noel	9	Queen's Co., Subdistrict Mill Village (1891)
708	Rachel	Noel	7	Whycocomagh (Cape Breton reserve)
709	Sarah	Noel	5	Waqamatkuk (Middle River, Cape Breton reserve)
710	Solomon	Noel	58	Queen's Co., Subdistrict Mill Village (1891)
711	Sophia	Noel	41	Waqamatkuk (Middle River, Cape Breton reserve)
712	Sophie	Noel	40	Whycocomagh (Cape Breton reserve)
713	Stephen	Noel	18	Whycocomagh (Cape Breton reserve)
714	Stephen	Noel	6	Whycocomagh (Cape Breton reserve)
715	Stephen	Noel	7	Waqamatkuk (Middle River, Cape Breton reserve)
716	Steven	Noel	42	Whycocomagh (Cape Breton reserve)
717	Susan	Noel	20	Whycocomagh (Cape Breton reserve)
718	Susan	Noel	85	Whycocomagh (Cape Breton reserve)
719	Susan	Noel	30	Whycocomagh (Cape Breton reserve)
720	Theresa	Noel	5	Guysborough Co., Cape Canso
721	William	Noel	11	Whycocomagh (Cape Breton reserve)
722	William	Noel	61	Whycocomagh (Cape Breton reserve)
723	William	Noel	6 mo	Whycocomagh (Cape Breton reserve)
724	Willie	Noel	16	Pictou Co., Pictou Landing (reserve)
725	Alvin	Paul	3 mo	Heatherton (Paqtnkek Reserve Area)
726	Anata	Paul	3	Colchester Co., Acadia mines
727	Andrew	Paul	7	Colchester Co., Acadia mines
728	Andrewp	Paul	9	Heatherton (Paqtnkek Reserve Area)
729	Angeline	Paul	26	Potlotek, Chapel Island (Cape Breton reserve)
730	Ann	Paul	2	Potlotek, Chapel Island (Cape Breton reserve)
731	Anne	Paul	3	Heatherton (Paqtnkek Reserve Area)
732	Annie	Paul	10	Potlotek, Chapel Island (Cape Breton reserve)
733	Annie	Paul	21	Kings Co., Centreville
734	Annmary	Paul	9	Pictou Co., Little Harbour
735	Bella	Paul	38	Waqamatkuk (Middle River, Cape Breton reserve)

Education	Housing	Occupation	Marital status	Notes
Literate	House, wood (1 fl, 1 rm)	Carpenter, cooper	Married	Born New Brunswick
Illiterate	House, wood (1 fl, 3 rm)	Farmer	Married	
Illiterate	Shanty or wigwam	Cooper	Married	
Illiterate	Shanty or wigwam	?	Single	
Literate	House, wood (1 fl, 3 rm)	?	Single	
Literate	Shanty or wigwam	Cooper	Married	
Illiterate	House, wood (1 fl, 2 rm)	?	Married	
Illiterate	House, wood (1 fl, 3 rm)	?	Single	
Illiterate	House, wood (1 fl, 3 rm)	Farmer	Widowed	
Illiterate	House, wood (1 fl, 3 rm)	Farmer	Widowed	
Literate	House, wood (1 fl, 1 rm)	?	Married	
Illiterate	House, wood (1 fl, 1 rm)	?	Single	
Illiterate	House, wood (1 fl, 1 rm)	Farmer, cooper	Married	
Illiterate	House, wood (2 fl, 4 rm)	?	Single	
Illiterate	Shanty or wigwam	?	Single	
Literate	House, wood (1 fl, 1 rm)	?	Single	
Literate	House, wood (2 fl, 4 rm)	?	Married	
Literate	House, wood (1 fl, 1 rm)	Carpenter, cooper	Single	
Illiterate	House, wood (1 fl, 1 rm)	Cooper	Married	
Literate	Shanty or wigwam	?	Single	
Illiterate	House, wood (1 fl, 1 rm)	?	Single	
Illiterate	House, wood (1 fl, 1 rm)	Cooper	Married	
Illiterate	House, wood (1 fl, 2 rm)	?	Single	
Illiterate	House, wood (1 fl, 3 rm)	?	Single	
Illiterate	Shanty or wigwam	?	Single	
Illiterate	House, wood (1 fl, 2 rm)	Fisherman	Married	
Illiterate	House, wood (1 fl, 1 rm)	?	Married	
Literate	House, wood (1 fl, 3 rm)	Farmer	Married	
Illiterate	House, wood (1 fl, 3 rm)	Cooper	Single	
Illiterate	Shanty or wigwam	?	Single	
Illiterate	House, wood (1 fl, 1 rm)	?	Single	
Illiterate	House, wood (1 fl, 3 rm)	Farmer	Married	
Illiterate	Shanty or wigwam	?	Single	
Illiterate	House, wood (1 fl, 3 rm)	?	Widowed	
Illiterate	House, wood (1 fl, 3 rm)	?	Married	
Illiterate	House, wood (1 fl, 3 rm)	?	Single	
Illiterate	Shanty or wigwam	?	Single	
Illiterate	House, wood (1 fl, 1 rm)	Farmer	Married	
Illiterate	House, wood (1 fl, 1 rm)	?	Single	
Illiterate	House, wood (1 fl, 1 rm)	Carpenter, cooper	Single	
Illiterate	House, wood (1 fl, 1 rm)	?	Single	
Illiterate	Shanty or wigwam	?	Single	Female
Illiterate	Shanty or wigwam	?	Single	
Illiterate	House, wood (1 fl, 1 rm)	Farmer, cooper	Single	
Literate	Shanty or wigwam	?	Married	
Illiterate	Shanty or wigwam	?	Single	
Illiterate	House, wood (1 fl, 1 rm)	?	Single	
Literate	House, wood (1 fl, 1 rm)	?	Single	
Illiterate	Shanty or wigwam	?	Married	
Illiterate	Shanty or wigwam	?	Single	
Illiterate	Shanty or wigwam	?	Married	

1891 Census Data • Continued

ID no.	First name	Last name	Age in years	Location
736	Betsy	Paul	55	Potlotek, Chapel Island (Cape Breton reserve)
737	Caroline	Paul	31	Potlotek, Chapel Island (Cape Breton reserve)
738	Charlie	Paul	7	Heatherton (Paqtnkek Reserve Area)
739	Charlie	Paul	5	Colchester Co., Acadia mines
740	Charlot	Paul	25	Pictou Co., Pictou Landing (reserve)
741	Charlot	Paul	4	Potlotek, Chapel Island (Cape Breton reserve)
742	Christy	Paul	22	Pictou Co., Subdistrict Barney's River
743	Dennis	Paul	38	Hants Co., Shubenacdie/Indian Brook Reserve area, St. Croix
744	Elizabeth	Paul	26	Queen's Co., Subdistrict Milton (1891)
745	Elizabeth	Paul	15	Pictou Co., Subdistrict Barney's River
746	Francis	Paul	33	Eskasoni (Cape Breton reserve)
747	Francis	Paul	42	Heatherton (Paqtnkek Reserve Area)
748	Francis	Paul	45	Colchester Co., Acadia mines
749	Frank	Paul	67	Pictou Co., Little Harbour
750	Frank	Paul	39	Pictou Co., Subdistrict Barney's River
751	Frank	Paul	68	Hants Co., Shubenacdie/Indian Brook Reserve area, St. Croix
752	Harriet	Paul	24	Queen's Co., Subdistrict Milton (1891)
753	Harry	Paul	9	Pictou Co., Subdistrict Barney's River
754	Jane	Paul	15	Waqamatkuk (Middle River, Cape Breton reserve)
755	Jessie	Paul	4	Waqamatkuk (Middle River, Cape Breton reserve)
756	Joe	Paul	67	Waqamatkuk (Middle River, Cape Breton reserve)
757	Joe	Paul	13	Waqamatkuk (Middle River, Cape Breton reserve)
758	John	Paul	2	Eskasoni (Cape Breton reserve)
759	John	Paul	62	Pictou Co., Little Harbour
760	John	Paul	17	Waqamatkuk (Middle River, Cape Breton reserve)
761	John	Paul	5	Potlotek, Chapel Island (Cape Breton reserve)
762	John	Paul	15	Colchester Co., Acadia mines
763	John	Paul	19	Kings Co., Lakeville
764	Johnp	Paul	16	Pictou Co., Subdistrict Barney's River
765	Johnp	Paul	15	Heatherton (Paqtnkek Reserve Area)
766	Julie	Paul	54	Waqamatkuk (Middle River, Cape Breton reserve)
767	Julie	Paul	9 mo	Waqamatkuk (Middle River, Cape Breton reserve)
768	Levi	Paul	14	Waqamatkuk (Middle River, Cape Breton reserve)
769	Louis	Paul	37	Potlotek, Chapel Island (Cape Breton reserve)
770	Louisa	Paul	1	Pictou Co., Subdistrict Barney's River
771	Madeline	Paul	18	Pictou Co., Little Harbour
772	Maggie	Paul	6	Waqamatkuk (Middle River, Cape Breton reserve)
773	Mary	Paul	44	Pictou Co., Pictou Landing (reserve)
774	Mary	Paul	23	Waqamatkuk (Middle River, Cape Breton reserve)
775	Mary	Paul	7	Potlotek, Chapel Island (Cape Breton reserve)
776	Mary	Paul	47	Heatherton (Paqtnkek Reserve Area)
777	Mary	Paul	45	Colchester Co., Acadia mines
778	Mary	Paul	15	Hants Co., Shubenacdie/Indian Brook Reserve area, St. Croix
779	Maryann	Paul	17	Waqamatkuk (Middle River, Cape Breton reserve)
780	Maryann	Paul	6	Waqamatkuk (Middle River, Cape Breton reserve)
781	Maryann	Paul	37	Waqamatkuk (Middle River, Cape Breton reserve)
782	Maryann	Paul	14	Hants Co., Shubenacdie/Indian Brook Reserve area, St. Croix
783	Marysusi	Paul	9	Eskasoni (Cape Breton reserve)
784	Mathew	Paul	17	Pictou Co., Subdistrict Barney's River
785	Mathew	Paul	20	Waqamatkuk (Middle River, Cape Breton reserve)
786	Matteo	Paul	60	Pictou Co., Pictou Landing (reserve)
787	Michael	Paul	10	Potlotek, Chapel Island (Cape Breton reserve)
788	Michael	Paul	23	Potlotek, Chapel Island (Cape Breton reserve)

Education	Housing	Occupation	Marital status	Notes
Illiterate	House, wood (1 fl, 1 rm)	?	Married	
Illiterate	Shanty or wigwam	?	Married	
Illiterate	House, wood (1 fl, 1 rm)	Farmer, cooper	Single	
Illiterate	Shanty or wigwam	?	Single	
Illiterate	House, wood (1 fl, 1 rm)	?	Single	
Illiterate	Shanty or wigwam	?	Single	
Literate	Shanty or wigwam	?	Single	
Literate	House, wood (1 fl, 3 rm)	Hunter	Single	
Illiterate	House, wood (1 fl, 7 rm)	Basketmaker	Single	
Literate	Shanty or wigwam	?	Single	
Literate	Shanty or wigwam	Cooper	Married	
Illiterate	House, wood (1 fl, 1 rm)	Farmer, cooper	Married	
Illiterate	Shanty or wigwam	Cooper	Married	
Illiterate	Shanty or wigwam	?	Widowed	
Literate	Shanty or wigwam	Cooper	Married	
Literate	House, wood (1 fl, 3 rm)	Hunter	Widowed	
Literate	House, wood (1 fl, 7 rm)	Basketmaker	Single	
Literate	Shanty or wigwam	?	Single	
Literate	Shanty or wigwam	Basketmaker	Single	
Illiterate	Shanty or wigwam	?	Single	
Illiterate	Shanty or wigwam	Cooper	Married	
Literate	Shanty or wigwam	?	Single	
Illiterate	Shanty or wigwam	?	Single	
Illiterate	Shanty or wigwam	Hunter	Married	
Illiterate	Shanty or wigwam	Cooper	Single	
Illiterate	Shanty or wigwam	?	Single	
Illiterate	Shanty or wigwam	Basketmaker	Single	
Illiterate	House, wood (1 fl, 2 rm)	Lumberjack	Single	
Literate	Shanty or wigwam	?	Single	
Illiterate	House, wood (1 fl, 1 rm)	Farmer, cooper	Single	
Illiterate	House, wood (1 fl, 1 rm)	Basketmaker	Married	
Illiterate	Shanty or wigwam	?	Single	
Literate	House, wood (1 fl, 1 rm)	?	Single	
Illiterate	Shanty or wigwam	Farmer, cooper	Married	
Illiterate	Shanty or wigwam	?	Single	
Illiterate	Shanty or wigwam	?	Single	
Illiterate	Shanty or wigwam	?	Single	
Illiterate	House, wood (1 fl, 2 rm)	?	Married	
Illiterate	Shanty or wigwam	Basketmaker	Single	
Literate	Shanty or wigwam	?	Single	
Illiterate	House, wood (1 fl, 1 rm)	Farmer, cooper	Married	
Illiterate	Shanty or wigwam	?	Married	
Illiterate	Shanty or wigwam	Servant	Single	
Literate	House, wood (1 fl, 1 rm)	Basketmaker	Single	
Illiterate	Shanty or wigwam	?	Single	
Illiterate	Shanty or wigwam	?	Married	
Literate	House, wood (1 fl, 3 rm)	?	Single	
Literate	Shanty or wigwam	?	Single	
Literate	Shanty or wigwam	?	Single	
Literate	House, wood (1 fl, 1 rm)	Cooper	Single	
Illiterate	House, wood (1 fl, 1 rm)	Cooper	Widowed	
Literate	Shanty or wigwam	?	Single	
Illiterate	House, wood (1 fl, 1 rm)	Cooper	Single	

1891 Census Data • Continued

ID no.	First name	Last name	Age in years	Location
789	Michael	Paul	18	West Bay, Division 1 ('Malakawe:j, Cape Breton reserve)
790	Nancy	Paul	26	Potlotek, Chapel Island (Cape Breton reserve)
791	Noel	Paul	56	Queen's Co., Subdistrict Milton (1891)
792	Noel	Paul	46	Pictou Co., Subdistrict Barney's River
793	Noel	Paul	47	Waqamatkuk (Middle River, Cape Breton reserve)
794	Noel	Paul	63	Potlotek, Chapel Island (Cape Breton reserve)
795	Noel	Paul	2 mo	Potlotek, Chapel Island (Cape Breton reserve)
796	Noel	Paul	19	West Bay, Division 1 ('Malakawe:j, Cape Breton reserve)
797	Oliver	Paul	3 mo	Colchester Co., Acadia mines
798	Paul	Paul	7	Eskasoni (Cape Breton reserve)
799	Paul	Paul	63	Pictou Co., Pictou Landing (reserve)
800	Peter	Paul	14	Queen's Co., Subdistrict Milton (1891)
801	Peter	Paul	77	Pictou Co., Little Harbour
802	Peter	Paul	15	Pictou Co., Subdistrict Barney's River
803	Peter	Paul	9	Yarmouth Co., Arcadia
804	Philip	Paul	42	Queen's Co., Subdistrict Milton (1891)
805	Rosy	Paul	53	Queen's Co., Subdistrict Milton (1891)
806	Sally	Paul	50	Pictou Co., Subdistrict Barney's River
807	Sarah	Paul	18	Pictou Co., Pictou Landing (reserve)
808	Simon	Paul	43	Waqamatkuk (Middle River, Cape Breton reserve)
809	Solomon	Paul	9	Waqamatkuk (Middle River, Cape Breton reserve)
810	Sophia	Paul	20	Colchester Co., Acadia mines
811	Sophie	Paul	18	Heatherton (Paqtnkek Reserve Area)
812	Stephen	Paul	15	Potlotek, Chapel Island (Cape Breton reserve)
813	Susie	Paul	36	Pictou Co., Subdistrict Barney's River
814	Sylvester	Paul	9	Pictou Co., Subdistrict Barney's River
815	Sylvester	Paul	4	Pictou Co., Subdistrict Barney's River
816	Terry	Paul	20	Potlotek, Chapel Island (Cape Breton reserve)
817	Theresa	Paul	7	Potlotek, Chapel Island (Cape Breton reserve)
818	Thomas	Paul	16	Pictou Co., Pictou Landing (reserve)
819	Tom	Paul	12	Potlotek, Chapel Island (Cape Breton reserve)
820	Veronica	Paul	28	Eskasoni (Cape Breton reserve)
821	William	Paul	30	Potlotek, Chapel Island (Cape Breton reserve)
822	Susan	Paul	22	Pictou Co., Little Harbour
823	Bella	Peck	10	Town of Guysborough (Subdistrict F)
824	Ben	Peck	19	Town of Guysborough (Subdistrict F)
825	Charles	Peck	2	Town of Guysborough (Subdistrict F)
826	Isaac	Peck	16	Whycocomagh (Cape Breton reserve)
827	Jane	Peck	12	Town of Guysborough (Subdistrict F)
828	Mary	Peck	7	Waqamatkuk (Middle River, Cape Breton reserve)
829	Mary	Peck	27	Town of Guysborough (Subdistrict F)
830	Mary	Peck	75	Whycocomagh (Cape Breton reserve)
831	Michael	Peck	42	Town of Guysborough (Subdistrict F)
832	Peter	Peck	21	Town of Guysborough (Subdistrict F)
833	Victoria	Perry	13	West Bay, Division 1 ('Malakawe:j, Cape Breton reserve)
834	Alex	Philips	12	Pictou Co., Pictou Landing (reserve)
835	Annie	Philips	22	North Sydney
836	Hannah	Philips	10	Pictou Co., Pictou Landing (reserve)
837	James	Philips	2	Pictou Co., Pictou Landing (reserve)
838	Jennie	Philips	25	Pictou Co., Pictou Landing (reserve)
839	Jenny	Philips	30	Pictou Co., Pictou Landing (reserve)
840	Joe	Philips	27	Pictou Co., Pictou Landing (reserve)
841	John	Philips	35	Pictou Co., Pictou Landing (reserve)

Education	Housing	Occupation	Marital status	Notes
Illiterate	Shanty or wigwam	Cooper, fisherman	Single	
Illiterate	House, wood (1 fl, 1 rm)	?	Single	
Literate	House, wood (1 fl, 7 rm)	Carpenter	Married	
Literate	Shanty or wigwam	Cooper	Married	
Illiterate	Shanty or wigwam	Cooper	Married	
Illiterate	House, wood (1 fl, 1 rm)	Farmer, cooper	Married	
Illiterate	Shanty or wigwam	?	Single	
Illiterate	Shanty or wigwam	Cooper, fisherman	Single	
Illiterate	Shanty or wigwam	?	Single	
Literate	Shanty or wigwam	?	Single	
Illiterate	House, wood (1 fl, 2 rm)	Cooper	Married	
Illiterate	House, wood (1 fl, 7 rm)	?	Single	
Illiterate	Shanty or wigwam	?	Widowed	
Literate	Shanty or wigwam	?	Single	
Illiterate	House, wood (2 fl, 3 rm)	?	Single	
Illiterate	House, wood (1 fl, 7 rm)	?	Widowed	
Illiterate	House, wood (1 fl, 7 rm)	Basketmaker	Married	
Literate	Shanty or wigwam	?	Married	
Literate	House, wood (1 fl, 2 rm)	?	Single	
Illiterate	House, wood (1 fl, 1 rm)	Cooper	Married	
Literate	Shanty or wigwam	?	Single	
Illiterate	Shanty or wigwam	Basketmaker	Single	
Illiterate	House, wood (1 fl, 1 rm)	Farmer, cooper	Single	
Literate	House, wood (1 fl, 1 rm)	?	Single	
Literate	Shanty or wigwam	?	Married	
Literate	Shanty or wigwam	?	Single	
Illiterate	Shanty or wigwam	?	Single	
Illiterate	House, wood (1 fl, 1 rm)	Cooper	Single	Male
Literate	Shanty or wigwam	?	Single	
Literate	House, wood (1 fl, 2 rm)	?	Single	
Literate	Shanty or wigwam	?	Single	
Literate	Shanty or wigwam	?	Married	
Illiterate	Shanty or wigwam	Farmer, cooper	Married	
Illiterate	Shanty or wigwam	?	Married	Born New Brunswick
Illiterate	Shanty or wigwam	?	Single	
Illiterate	Shanty or wigwam	?	Single	
Illiterate	Shanty or wigwam	?	Single	
Illiterate	Shanty or wigwam	?	Single	Born Newfoundland
Illiterate	Shanty or wigwam	?	Single	
Literate	House, wood (1 fl, 1 rm)	?	Single	
Illiterate	Shanty or wigwam	?	Married	
Illiterate	Shanty or wigwam	?	Widowed	Born Newfoundland
Illiterate	Shanty or wigwam	Cooper, fisherman	Married	
Illiterate	Shanty or wigwam	?	Single	
Illiterate	Shanty or wigwam	?	Single	
Illiterate	House, wood (1 fl, 1 rm)	?	Single	
Illiterate	Wigwam	Basketmaker	Married	
Illiterate	House, wood (1 fl, 1 rm)	?	Single	
Illiterate	House, wood (1 fl, 1 rm)	?	Single	
Literate	House, wood (1 fl, 1 rm)	?	Married	
Illiterate	House, wood (1 fl, 1 rm)	?	Married	
Literate	House, wood (1 fl, 1 rm)	Cooper	Married	
Illiterate	House, wood (1 fl, 1 rm)	Cooper	Married	

1891 Census Data • Continued

ID no.	First name	Last name	Age in years	Location
842	John	Philips	3	Pictou Co., Pictou Landing (reserve)
843	Mary	Philips	5	Pictou Co., Pictou Landing (reserve)
844	Noel	Philips	27	North Sydney
845	Peter	Philips	7 mo	North Sydney
846	Ann	Pictou	27	Heatherton (Paqtnkek Reserve Area)
847	Annmary	Pictou	27	Guysborough Co., Fork St. Mary's
848	James	Pictou	35	Guysborough Co., Fork St. Mary's
849	Jim	Pictou	32	Heatherton (Paqtnkek Reserve Area)
850	John	Pictou	14	Queen's Co., Subdistrict Milton (1891)
851	John	Pictou	36	Yarmouth Co., Argyle
852	Joseph	Pictou	6	Yarmouth Co., Arcadia
853	Margaret	Pictou	36	Yarmouth Co., Argyle
854	Maryf	Pictou	3	Yarmouth Co., Argyle
855	Simonp	Pictou	1	Yarmouth Co., Argyle
856	Williamj	Pictou	6	Yarmouth Co., Argyle
857	Frank	Pitchcoc	44	Yarmouth Co., Arcadia
858	John	Pitchcoc	2	Yarmouth Co., Arcadia
859	Mary	Pitchcoc	34	Yarmouth Co., Arcadia
860	Thomas	Pitchcoc	14	Yarmouth Co., Arcadia
861	Noel	Poulete	15	Morland (Paqtnkek Reserve Area)
862	Charles	Poulette	56	Morland (Paqtnkek Reserve Area)
863	Jane	Poulette	6	Morland (Paqtnkek Reserve Area)
864	Julia	Poulette	46	Morland (Paqtnkek Reserve Area)
865	Abraham	Prosper	19	Heatherton (Paqtnkek Reserve Area)
866	Ann	Prosper	?	Eskasoni (Cape Breton reserve)
867	Anne	Prosper	80	St. Peters
868	Bridget	Prosper	3 mo	Potlotek, Chapel Island (Cape Breton reserve)
869	Caroline	Prosper	10	St. Peters
870	Caroline	Prosper	14	Potlotek, Chapel Island (Cape Breton reserve)
871	Charles	Prosper	13	Potlotek, Chapel Island (Cape Breton reserve)
872	Eliza	Prosper	7	Eskasoni (Cape Breton reserve)
873	Eliza	Prosper	15	Eskasoni (Cape Breton reserve)
874	Elizabeth	Prosper	12	Heatherton (Paqtnkek Reserve Area)
875	Ester	Prosper	28	Potlotek, Chapel Island (Cape Breton reserve)
876	Flora	Prosper	53	Heatherton (Paqtnkek Reserve Area)
877	Harriet	Prosper	36	Potlotek, Chapel Island (Cape Breton reserve)
878	J	Prosper	80	St. Peters
879	James	Prosper	14	Morland (Paqtnkek Reserve Area)
880	James	Prosper	56	Heatherton (Paqtnkek Reserve Area)
881	James	Prosper	21	Heatherton (Paqtnkek Reserve Area)
882	Jane	Prosper	38	Morland (Paqtnkek Reserve Area)
883	Joe	Prosper	4	Heatherton (Paqtnkek Reserve Area)
884	John	Prosper	8	St. Peters
885	John	Prosper	44	Potlotek, Chapel Island (Cape Breton reserve)
886	John	Prosper	7	Potlotek, Chapel Island (Cape Breton reserve)
887	Joseph	Prosper	30	St. Peters
888	Joseph	Prosper	5	Potlotek, Chapel Island (Cape Breton reserve)
889	Joseph	Prosper	56	Morland (Paqtnkek Reserve Area)
890	Julia	Prosper	15	Potlotek, Chapel Island (Cape Breton reserve)
891	Julia	Prosper	50	Morland (Paqtnkek Reserve Area)
892	Julie	Prosper	17	Heatherton (Paqtnkek Reserve Area)
893	Kathleen	Prosper	9	St. Peters
894	Louisa	Prosper	6	Morland (Paqtnkek Reserve Area)

Education	Housing	Occupation	Marital status	Notes
Illiterate	House, wood (1 fl, 1 rm)	?	Single	
Illiterate	House, wood (1 fl, 1 rm)	?	Single	
Literate	Wigwam	Buttertub manufacturer	Married	
Illiterate	Wigwam	?	Single	
Illiterate	House, wood (1 fl, 1 rm)	Farmer, cooper	Married	
Literate	Wigwam	?	Married	
Illiterate	Wigwam	Cooper	Married	
Literate	House, wood (1 fl, 1 rm)	Farmer, cooper	Married	
Illiterate	Shanty or wigwam	Basketmaker	Single	
Illiterate	House, wood (2 fl, 4 rm)	Farmer	Married	Born New Brunswick
Illiterate	House, wood (1 fl, 2 rm)	?	Single	
Illiterate	House, wood (2 fl, 4 rm)	?	Married	
Illiterate	House, wood (2 fl, 4 rm)	?	Single	
Illiterate	House, wood (2 fl, 4 rm)	?	Single	
Illiterate	House, wood (2 fl, 4 rm)	?	Single	
Illiterate	House, wood (1 fl, 2 rm)	Basketmaker	Married	
Illiterate	House, wood (1 fl, 2 rm)	?	Single	
Literate	House, wood (1 fl, 2 rm)	Basketmaker	Married	
Illiterate	House, wood (1 fl, 2 rm)	Basketmaker	Single	
Literate	House, wood (1 fl, 1 rm)	?	Single	
Illiterate	House, wood (1 fl, 1 rm)	Farmer, fisherman	Married	
Illiterate	House, wood (1 fl, 1 rm)	?	Single	
Literate	House, wood (1 fl, 1 rm)	?	Married	
Literate	House, wood (1 fl, 1 rm)	Cooper	Single	
Illiterate	Shanty or wigwam	Cooper	Single	
Illiterate	Shanty or wigwam	?	Married	
Illiterate	Shanty or wigwam	?	Single	
Illiterate	Shanty or wigwam	?	Single	
Illiterate	Shanty or wigwam	?	Single	
Illiterate	House, wood (1 fl, 1 rm)	?	Single	
Illiterate	Shanty or wigwam	?	Single	
Illiterate	Shanty or wigwam	Cooper	Single	
Illiterate	House, wood (1 fl, 1 rm)	Farmer, cooper	Single	
Illiterate	Shanty or wigwam	?	Married	
Illiterate	House, wood (1 fl, 2 rm)	Cooper	Married	
Illiterate	House, wood (1 fl, 1 rm)	?	Married	
Illiterate	Shanty or wigwam	Fisherman	Married	Male
Illiterate	House, wood (1 fl, 1 rm)	?	Single	
Illiterate	House, wood (1 fl, 2 rm)	Cooper	Married	
Literate	House, wood (1 fl, 2 rm)	Cooper	Single	
Literate	House, wood (1 fl, 1 rm)	?	Married	
Illiterate	House, wood (1 fl, 1 rm)	?	Single	
Illiterate	Shanty or wigwam	?	Single	
Illiterate	Shanty or wigwam	Farmer, cooper	Married	
Illiterate	Shanty or wigwam	?	Single	
Illiterate	Shanty or wigwam	Fisherman	Married	
Illiterate	Shanty or wigwam	?	Single	
Illiterate	House, wood (1 fl, 1 rm)	Farmer, fisherman	Married	
Literate	House, wood (1 fl, 1 rm)	?	Single	
Illiterate	House, wood (1 fl, 1 rm)	?	Married	
Illiterate	House, wood (1 fl, 1 rm)	Farmer, cooper	Single	
Illiterate	Shanty or wigwam	?	Single	
Illiterate	House, wood (1 fl, 1 rm)	?	Single	

1891 Census Data • Continued

ID no.	First name	Last name	Age in years	Location
895	Louise	Prosper	29	Pictou Co., Little Harbour
896	Martin	Prosper	48	Heatherton (Paqtnkek Reserve Area)
897	Mary	Prosper	20	Eskasoni (Cape Breton reserve)
898	Mary	Prosper	25	St. Peters
899	Mary	Prosper	1	Potlotek, Chapel Island (Cape Breton reserve)
900	Mary	Prosper	10	Morland (Paqtnkek Reserve Area)
901	Mary	Prosper	47	Heatherton (Paqtnkek Reserve Area)
902	Maryann	Prosper	30	Eskasoni (Cape Breton reserve)
903	Michael	Prosper	6	St. Peters
904	Moriah	Prosper	73	Heatherton (Paqtnkek Reserve Area)
905	Noel	Prosper	22	Heatherton (Paqtnkek Reserve Area)
906	Peter	Prosper	54	Morland (Paqtnkek Reserve Area)
907	Stephen	Prosper	8	Pictou Co., Little Harbour
908	Stephen	Prosper	40	Potlotek, Chapel Island (Cape Breton reserve)
909	Susan	Prosper	2	Morland (Paqtnkek Reserve Area)
910	Susie	Prosper	49	Heatherton (Paqtnkek Reserve Area)
911	Ben	Richard	15	Potlotek, Chapel Island (Cape Breton reserve)
912	Charles	Richard	6	Potlotek, Chapel Island (Cape Breton reserve)
913	Jane	Richard	13	Potlotek, Chapel Island (Cape Breton reserve)
914	John	Richard	73	Waqamatkuk (Middle River, Cape Breton reserve)
915	Katie	Richard	47	Potlotek, Chapel Island (Cape Breton reserve)
916	Maggie	Richard	11	Potlotek, Chapel Island (Cape Breton reserve)
917	Maryann	Richard	17	Potlotek, Chapel Island (Cape Breton reserve)
918	Peter	Richard	50	Potlotek, Chapel Island (Cape Breton reserve)
919	Sarah	Richard	29	Potlotek, Chapel Island (Cape Breton reserve)
920	Stephen	Richard	2	Potlotek, Chapel Island (Cape Breton reserve)
921	Ann	Sack	29	Hants Co., Shubenacdie/Indian Brook Reserve area, South Rawdon and Uniacke
922	Bridget	Sack	4	Hants Co., Shubenacdie/Indian Brook Reserve area, South Rawdon and Uniacke
923	Henry	Sack	10	Hants Co., Shubenacdie/Indian Brook Reserve area, South Rawdon and Uniacke
924	Isaac	Sack	35	Hants Co., Shubenacdie/Indian Brook Reserve area, South Rawdon and Uniacke
925	Joseph	Sack	12	Hants Co., Shubenacdie/Indian Brook Reserve area, South Rawdon and Uniacke
926	Ledham	Sack	14	Hants Co., Shubenacdie/Indian Brook Reserve area, South Rawdon and Uniacke
927	Matilda	Sack	46	Hants Co., Shubenacdie/Indian Brook Reserve area, South Rawdon and Uniacke
928	Matthew	Sack	14	Hants Co., Shubenacdie/Indian Brook Reserve area, South Rawdon and Uniacke
929	Richard	Sack	3	Hants Co., Shubenacdie/Indian Brook Reserve area, South Rawdon and Uniacke
930	Ben	Salome	30	Morland (Paqtnkek Reserve Area)
931	Joseph	Salome	80	Morland (Paqtnkek Reserve Area)
932	Joseph	Sappier	1	Pictou Co., Pictou Landing (reserve)
933	Joseph	Sappier	10	Pictou Co., Subdistrict Lome
934	Kate	Sappier	13	Pictou Co., Pictou Landing (reserve)
935	Maryann	Sappier	10	Pictou Co., Pictou Landing (reserve)
936	Mathew	Sappier	5	Pictou Co., Subdistrict Lome
937	Matty	Sappier	41	Pictou Co., Subdistrict Lome
938	Matty	Sappier	1	Pictou Co., Subdistrict Lome

Education	Housing	Occupation	Marital status	Notes
Illiterate	Shanty or wigwam	?	Widowed	
Illiterate	House, wood (1 fl, 1 rm)	Farmer, cooper	Married	
Illiterate	Shanty or wigwam	Cooper	Single	
Illiterate	Shanty or wigwam	?	Married	
Illiterate	Shanty or wigwam	?	Single	
Illiterate	House, wood (1 fl, 1 rm)	?	Single	
Illiterate	House, wood (1 fl, 1 rm)	Farmer, cooper	Married	
Literate	Shanty or wigwam	Cooper	Widowed	
Illiterate	Shanty or wigwam	?	Single	
Illiterate	Shanty or wigwam	Fisherman, cooper	Widowed	
Illiterate	House, wood (1 fl, 1 rm)	Cooper	Single	
Literate	House, wood (1 fl, 1 rm)	Farmer, fisherman	Married	
Illiterate	Shanty or wigwam	?	Single	
Illiterate	House, wood (1 fl, 1 rm)	Cooper	Married	
Illiterate	House, wood (1 fl, 1 rm)	?	Single	
Illiterate	House, wood (1 fl, 1 rm)	Cooper	Widowed	
Literate	Shanty or wigwam	?	Single	
Illiterate	Shanty or wigwam	?	Single	
Literate	Shanty or wigwam	?	Single	
Literate	House, wood (1 fl, 1 rm)	Cooper	Widowed	
Illiterate	Shanty or wigwam	?	Married	
Literate	Shanty or wigwam	?	Single	
Illiterate	Shanty or wigwam	?	Single	
Illiterate	Shanty or wigwam	Farmer, cooper	Married	
Illiterate	Shanty or wigwam	?	Single	
Illiterate	Shanty or wigwam	?	Single	
Illiterate	House, wood (2 fl, 4 rm)	?	Married	
Illiterate	House, wood (2 fl, 4 rm)	?	Single	
Illiterate	House, wood (2 fl, 4 rm)	?	Single	
Illiterate	House, wood (2 fl, 4 rm)	Cooper	Married	
Illiterate	House, wood (2 fl, 4 rm)	?	Single	
Illiterate	House, wood (2 fl, 4 rm)	?	Single	Male
Literate	House, wood (2 fl, 4 rm)	?	Widowed	
Illiterate	House, wood (2 fl, 4 rm)	Cooper	Single	
Illiterate	House, wood (2 fl, 4 rm)	?	Single	
Literate	House, wood (1 fl, 1 rm)	Farmer	Single	
Literate	House, wood (1 fl, 1 rm)	Farmer	Widowed	
Illiterate	House, wood (1 fl, 2 rm)	?	Single	
Illiterate	Shanty or wigwam	?	Single	
Illiterate	House, wood (1 fl, 2 rm)	?	Single	
Illiterate	House, wood (1 fl, 2 rm)	?	Single	
Illiterate	Shanty or wigwam	?	Single	
Illiterate	Shanty or wigwam	?	Married	Female
Illiterate	Shanty or wigwam	?	Single	Female

1891 Census Data • Continued

ID no.	First name	Last name	Age in years	Location
939	Noel	Sappier	3	Pictou Co., Subdistrict Lome
940	Paul	Sappier	42	Pictou Co., Subdistrict Lome
941	Peter	Sappier	45	Pictou Co., Subdistrict Lome
942	Sue	Sappier	8	Pictou Co., Subdistrict Lome
943	Tom	Sappier	8	Pictou Co., Pictou Landing (reserve)
944	Harriet	Simon	11	Eskasoni (Cape Breton reserve)
945	Judith	Simon	25	Pictou Co., Pictou Landing (reserve)
946	Mary	Simon	5	Pictou Co., Pictou Landing (reserve)
947	Maryann	Simon	27	Eskasoni (Cape Breton reserve)
948	Michael	Simon	35	Pictou Co., Pictou Landing (reserve)
949	Nancy	Simon	9	Eskasoni (Cape Breton reserve)
950	Noel	Simon	40	Eskasoni (Cape Breton reserve)
951	Charlie	Sock	25	Pictou Co., Pictou Landing (reserve)
952	Frank	Sock	28	Pictou Co., Pictou Landing (reserve)
953	Henry	Sock	6	Pictou Co., Pictou Landing (reserve)
954	Jane	Sock	7	Pictou Co., Pictou Landing (reserve)
955	Jennie	Sock	25	Pictou Co., Pictou Landing (reserve)
956	Jennie	Sock	22	Pictou Co., Pictou Landing (reserve)
957	John	Sock	38	Pictou Co., Pictou Landing (reserve)
958	Judy	Sock	25	Pictou Co., Pictou Landing (reserve)
959	Liza	Sock	2	Pictou Co., Pictou Landing (reserve)
960	Madeline	Sock	30	Pictou Co., Pictou Landing (reserve)
961	Mary	Sock	70	Pictou Co., Pictou Landing (reserve)
962	Maryann	Sock	45	Pictou Co., Pictou Landing (reserve)
963	Michael	Sock	21	Pictou Co., Pictou Landing (reserve)
964	Nancy	Sock	12	Pictou Co., Pictou Landing (reserve)
965	Noel	Sock	50	Pictou Co., Pictou Landing (reserve)
966	Susie	Sock	5	Pictou Co., Pictou Landing (reserve)
967	Andrew	Stevens	3	Waqamatkuk (Middle River, Cape Breton reserve)
968	Bridget	Stevens	21	Town of Guysborough (Subdistrict F)
969	Elizabeth	Stevens	1	Waqamatkuk (Middle River, Cape Breton reserve)
970	John	Stevens	67	Waqamatkuk (Middle River, Cape Breton reserve)
971	John	Stevens	34	Heatherton (Paqtnkek Reserve Area)
972	Joseph	Stevens	5	Town of Guysborough (Subdistrict F)
973	Levi	Stevens	6	Heatherton (Paqtnkek Reserve Area)
974	Madelin	Stevens	32	Waqamatkuk (Middle River, Cape Breton reserve)
975	Martin	Stevens	13	Heatherton (Paqtnkek Reserve Area)
976	Mary	Stevens	9	Waqamatkuk (Middle River, Cape Breton reserve)
977	Michael	Stevens	5	Waqamatkuk (Middle River, Cape Breton reserve)
978	Morris	Stevens	24	Town of Guysborough (Subdistrict F)
979	Nancy	Stevens	14	Heatherton (Paqtnkek Reserve Area)
980	Noel	Stevens	11	Waqamatkuk (Middle River, Cape Breton reserve)
981	Paul	Stevens	35	Waqamatkuk (Middle River, Cape Breton reserve)
982	Peter	Stevens	65	Hants Co., Shubenacdie/Indian Brook Reserve area, Noel
983	Picto	Stevens	15	Town of Guysborough (Subdistrict F)
984	Sally	Stevens	27	Town of Guysborough (Subdistrict F)
985	Sally	Stevens	65	Hants Co., Shubenacdie/Indian Brook Reserve area, Noel
986	Sam	Stevens	44	Town of Guysborough (Subdistrict F)
987	Sarah	Stevens	47	Heatherton (Paqtnkek Reserve Area)
988	Anabel	Sulean	3	Town of Guysborough (Subdistrict F)
989	Carmel	Sulean	4 mo	Town of Guysborough (Subdistrict F)
990	Joseph	Sulean	32	Town of Guysborough (Subdistrict F)
991	Joseph	Sulean	9	Town of Guysborough (Subdistrict F)

Education	Housing	Occupation	Marital status	Notes
Illiterate	Shanty or wigwam	?	Single	
Illiterate	Shanty or wigwam	?	Married	
Illiterate	Shanty or wigwam	Cooper	Married	
Illiterate	Shanty or wigwam	?	Single	
Illiterate	House, wood (1 fl, 2 rm)	?	Single	
Literate	?	Cooper	Single	
Illiterate	House, wood (1 fl, 1 rm)	?	Married	
Illiterate	House, wood (1 fl, 1 rm)	?	Single	
Literate	?	Cooper	Married	
Literate	House, wood (1 fl, 1 rm)	Cooper	Married	
Literate	?	Cooper	Single	
Literate	?	Cooper	Married	
Literate	House, wood (1 fl, 1 rm)	Cooper	Married	
Illiterate	House, wood (1 fl, 1 rm)	Cooper	Single	
Illiterate	House, wood (1 fl, 1 rm)	?	Single	
Illiterate	House, wood (1 fl, 1 rm)	?	Single	
Illiterate	House, wood (1 fl, 1 rm)	?	Married	
Illiterate	House, wood (1 fl, 1 rm)	?	Married	
Literate	House, wood (1 fl, 1 rm)	Cooper	Married	
Illiterate	House, wood (1 fl, 1 rm)	?	Single	
Illiterate	House, wood (1 fl, 1 rm)	?	Single	
Illiterate	House, wood (1 fl, 1 rm)	?	Single	
Illiterate	House, wood (1 fl, 1 rm)	?	Widowed	
Illiterate	House, wood (1 fl, 1 rm)	?	Married	
Literate	House, wood (1 fl, 1 rm)	Cooper	Single	
Illiterate	House, wood (1 fl, 1 rm)	?	Single	
Illiterate	House, wood (1 fl, 1 rm)	Cooper	Married	
Illiterate	House, wood (1 fl, 1 rm)	?	Single	
Illiterate	Shanty or wigwam	?	Single	
Illiterate	Shanty or wigwam	?	Single	
Illiterate	Shanty or wigwam	?	Single	
Illiterate	Shanty or wigwam	?	Single	
Literate	Shanty or wigwam	Farmer, cooper	Married	
Illiterate	Shanty or wigwam	?	Single	
Illiterate	Shanty or wigwam	?	Single	
Illiterate	Shanty or wigwam	?	Married	
Illiterate	Shanty or wigwam	Farmer, cooper	Single	
Literate	Shanty or wigwam	?	Single	
Illiterate	Shanty or wigwam	?	Single	
Illiterate	Shanty or wigwam	?	Single	
Illiterate	Shanty or wigwam	Farmer, cooper	Single	
Literate	Shanty or wigwam	?	Single	
Literate	Shanty or wigwam	Cooper	Married	
Illiterate	Shanty or wigwam	Cooper	Married	
Illiterate	Shanty or wigwam	?	Single	Male
Illiterate	Shanty or wigwam	?	Married	
Illiterate	Shanty or wigwam	?	Married	
Illiterate	Shanty or wigwam	Cooper, fisherman	Married	
Illiterate	Shanty or wigwam	Farmer, cooper	Married	
Illiterate	Shanty or wigwam	?	Single	
Illiterate	Shanty or wigwam	?	Single	
Illiterate	Shanty or wigwam	Farmer	Married	
Illiterate	Shanty or wigwam	?	Single	

1891 Census Data • Continued

ID no.	First name	Last name	Age in years	Location
992	Kate	Sulean	30	Town of Guysborough (Subdistrict F)
993	Levi	Sulean	7	Town of Guysborough (Subdistrict F)
994	Steven	Sulean	4	Town of Guysborough (Subdistrict F)
995	Sulian	Sulean	11	Town of Guysborough (Subdistrict F)
996	Annmary	Suprine?	10	Pictou Co., Little Harbour
997	Cateline	Suprine?	12	Pictou Co., Little Harbour
998	Charlie	Suprine?	5	Pictou Co., Little Harbour
999	Elizabeth	Suprine?	22	Pictou Co., Little Harbour
1000	Frank	Suprine?	38	Pictou Co., Little Harbour
1001	Joseph	Suprine?	1	Pictou Co., Little Harbour
1002	Lewis	Suprine?	67	Pictou Co., Little Harbour
1003	Louis	Suprine?	14	Pictou Co., Little Harbour
1004	Mary	Suprine?	65	Pictou Co., Little Harbour
1005	Mary	Suprine?	4	Pictou Co., Little Harbour
1006	Mathew	Suprine?	8 mo	?
1007	Michael	Suprine?	2	Pictou Co., Little Harbour
1008	Noel	Suprine?	32	Pictou Co., Little Harbour
1009	Peter	Suprine?	40	Pictou Co., Little Harbour
1010	Sally	Suprine?	24	Pictou Co., Little Harbour
1011	Thomas	Suprine?	4	Pictou Co., Little Harbour
1012	Frank	Thom	39	Pictou Co., Little Harbour
1013	Jim	Thom	37	Pictou Co., Little Harbour
1014	Jim	Thom	22	Pictou Co., Little Harbour
1015	Lewis	Thom	70	Pictou Co., Little Harbour
1016	Mary	Thom	44	Pictou Co., Little Harbour
1017	Mary	Thom	35	Pictou Co., Little Harbour
1018	Mike	Thom	6	Pictou Co., Little Harbour
1019	Susan	Thom	9	Pictou Co., Little Harbour
1020	Andrew	Tom	37	Potlotek, Chapel Island (Cape Breton reserve)
1021	Isaac	Tom	1	Potlotek, Chapel Island (Cape Breton reserve)
1022	John	Tom	3	Potlotek, Chapel Island (Cape Breton reserve)
1023	Martin	Tom	10	Potlotek, Chapel Island (Cape Breton reserve)
1024	Maryann	Tom	37	Potlotek, Chapel Island (Cape Breton reserve)
1025	Susan	Tom	5	Potlotek, Chapel Island (Cape Breton reserve)
1026	Amyalia	Toney	33	Waqamatkuk (Middle River, Cape Breton reserve)
1027	Annie	Toney	2	Waqamatkuk (Middle River, Cape Breton reserve)
1028	Ben	Toney	2 mo	Pictou Co., Pictou Landing (reserve)
1029	Charles	Toney	9	Waqamatkuk (Middle River, Cape Breton reserve)
1030	Francis	Toney	41	Yarmouth Co., Arcadia
1031	James	Toney	18	Yarmouth Co., Arcadia
1032	Joe	Toney	12	Waqamatkuk (Middle River, Cape Breton reserve)
1033	John	Toney	51	Waqamatkuk (Middle River, Cape Breton reserve)
1034	Joseph	Toney	68	Pictou Co., Subdistrict Lome
1035	Julia	Toney	25	Pictou Co., Pictou Landing (reserve)
1036	Julia	Toney	47	Yarmouth Co., Arcadia
1037	Liza	Toney	5	Pictou Co., Pictou Landing (reserve)
1038	Louis	Toney	19	Waqamatkuk (Middle River, Cape Breton reserve)
1039	Louis	Toney	84	Waqamatkuk (Middle River, Cape Breton reserve)
1040	Louis	Toney	9	Hants Co., Shubenacdie/Indian Brook Reserve area, South Rawdon and Uniacke
1041	Maggie	Toney	7	Waqamatkuk (Middle River, Cape Breton reserve)
1042	Mary	Toney	23	Hants Co., Shubenacdie/Indian Brook Reserve area, South Rawdon and Uniacke

Education	Housing	Occupation	Marital status	Notes
Illiterate	Shanty or wigwam	?	Married	
Illiterate	Shanty or wigwam	?	Single	
Illiterate	Shanty or wigwam	?	Single	
Illiterate	Shanty or wigwam	?	Single	Female
Literate	Shanty or wigwam	?	Single	
Illiterate	Shanty or wigwam	?	Single	
Illiterate	Shanty or wigwam	?	Single	
Illiterate	Shanty or wigwam	?	Married	
Illiterate	Shanty or wigwam	Cooper, fisherman	Widowed	
Illiterate	Shanty or wigwam	?	Single	
Illiterate	Shanty or wigwam	Cooper, fisherman	Married	
Literate	Shanty or wigwam	?	Single	
Illiterate	Shanty or wigwam	?	Married	
Illiterate	Shanty or wigwam	?	Single	
Illiterate	Shanty or wigwam	?	?	
Illiterate	Shanty or wigwam	?	Single	
Illiterate	Shanty or wigwam	Cooper, fisherman	Married	
Illiterate	Shanty or wigwam	Cooper, fisherman	Married	
Illiterate	Shanty or wigwam	?	Married	
Illiterate	Shanty or wigwam	?	Single	
Literate	Shanty or wigwam	Cooper, fisherman	Married	
Literate	Shanty or wigwam	Cooper, fisherman	Widowed	
Literate	Shanty or wigwam	Cooper, fisherman	Single	
Literate	Shanty or wigwam	Cooper, fisherman	Married	
Literate	Shanty or wigwam	?	Married	
Illiterate	Shanty or wigwam	?	Married	
Illiterate	Shanty or wigwam	?	Single	
Illiterate	Shanty or wigwam	?	Single	
Illiterate	Shanty or wigwam	Farmer, cooper	Married	Away
Illiterate	Shanty or wigwam	?	Single	Away
Illiterate	Shanty or wigwam	?	Single	Away
Illiterate	Shanty or wigwam	?	Single	Away
Illiterate	Shanty or wigwam	?	Married	Away
Illiterate	Shanty or wigwam	?	Single	Away
Illiterate	Shanty or wigwam	?	Married	
Illiterate	Shanty or wigwam	?	Single	
Illiterate	House, wood (1 fl, 1 rm)	?	Single	
Literate	Shanty or wigwam	?	Single	
Illiterate	House, wood (2 fl, 3 rm)	Basketmaker	Married	
Illiterate	House, wood (2 fl, 3 rm)	Basketmaker	Married	
Literate	Shanty or wigwam	?	Single	
Illiterate	Shanty or wigwam	Cooper	Married	
Illiterate	Shanty or wigwam	?	Widowed	
Literate	House, wood (1 fl, 1 rm)	?	Married	
Illiterate	House, wood (2 fl, 3 rm)	Basketmaker	Married	
Illiterate	House, wood (1 fl, 1 rm)	?	Single	
Literate	Shanty or wigwam	Cooper	Single	
Illiterate	Shanty or wigwam	?	Widowed	
Illiterate	House, wood (2 fl, 4 rm)	?	Single	
Illiterate	Shanty or wigwam	?	Single	
Illiterate	House, wood (2 fl, 4 rm)	?	Married	

1891 Census Data • Continued

ID no.	First name	Last name	Age in years	Location
1043	Moses	Toney	13	Hants Co., Shubenacdie/Indian Brook Reserve area, St. Croix
1044	Moses	Toney	14	Kings Co., Centreville
1045	Noel	Toney	13	Waqamatkuk (Middle River, Cape Breton reserve)
1046	Peter	Toney	35	Pictou Co., Pictou Landing (reserve)
1047	Peter	Toney	38	Waqamatkuk (Middle River, Cape Breton reserve)
1048	Philip	Toney	31	Hants Co., Shubenacdie/Indian Brook Reserve area, South Rawdon and Uniacke
1049	Telis	Toney	41	Waqamatkuk (Middle River, Cape Breton reserve)
1050	Belle	Wilmot	28	Pictou Co., Pictou Landing (reserve)
1051	Francis	Wilmot	78	Potlotek, Chapel Island (Cape Breton reserve)
1052	Hannah	Wilmot	16	Pictou Co., Pictou Landing (reserve)
1053	Jennie	Wilmot	11	Pictou Co., Pictou Landing (reserve)
1054	Louie	Wilmot	60	Pictou Co., Pictou Landing (reserve)
1055	Madlean	Wilmot	29	Potlotek, Chapel Island (Cape Breton reserve)
1056	Mary	Wilmot	56	Pictou Co., Pictou Landing (reserve)
1057	Maryann	Wilmot	27	Pictou Co., Pictou Landing (reserve)
1058	Noel	Wilmot	13	Pictou Co., Pictou Landing (reserve)
1059	Polly	Wilmot	32	Pictou Co., Pictou Landing (reserve)
1060	Sally	Wilmot	10	Pictou Co., Pictou Landing (reserve)
1061	Simon	Wilmot	6	Potlotek, Chapel Island (Cape Breton reserve)
1062	Stephen	Wilmot	9	Potlotek, Chapel Island (Cape Breton reserve)
1063	Thom	Wilmot	85	Pictou Co., Pictou Landing (reserve)
1064	Tom	Wilmot	8	Pictou Co., Pictou Landing (reserve)

Education	Housing	Occupation	Marital status	Notes
Illiterate	Shanty or wigwam	?	Single	
Illiterate	Shanty or wigwam	?	Single	
Illiterate	Shanty or wigwam	?	Single	
Literate	House, wood (1 fl, 1 rm)	Cooper	Married	
Illiterate	Shanty or wigwam	Cooper	Married	
Literate	House, wood (2 fl, 4 rm)	Cooper	Married	
Illiterate	Shanty or wigwam	?	Married	Female
Illiterate	House, wood (1 fl, 2 rm)	?	Single	
Illiterate	House, wood (1 fl, 1 rm)	Farmer, cooper	Widowed	
Literate	House, wood (1 fl, 1 rm)	?	Single	
Illiterate	House, wood (1 fl, 2 rm)	?	Single	
Illiterate	House, wood (1 fl, 1 rm)	Cooper	Widowed	
Illiterate	House, wood (1 fl, 1 rm)	?	Widowed	
Illiterate	House, wood (1 fl, 2 rm)	Cooper	Married	
Illiterate	House, wood (1 fl, 1 rm)	?	Single	
Illiterate	House, wood (1 fl, 2 rm)	?	Single	
Illiterate	House, wood (1 fl, 1 rm)	?	Single	
Illiterate	House, wood (1 fl, 1 rm)	?	Single	
Illiterate	House, wood (1 fl, 1 rm)	?	Single	
Literate	House, wood (1 fl, 1 rm)	?	Single	
Illiterate	House, wood (1 fl, 2 rm)	?	Married	
Illiterate	House, wood (1 fl, 1 rm)	?	Single	

Treaty of 1752

Enclosure in letter of
Governor Hopson

to the

Right Honourable, The Earl of Holdernesse

6th of Dec. 1752

Treaty or
Articles of Peace and Friendship Renewed

Between

His Excellency Thomas Hopson Esquire Captain General and Governor in Chief in and over His Majesty's Province of Nova Scotia or Acadie Vice Admiral of the same & Colonel of One of His Majesty's Regiments of Foot, and His Majesty's Council on behalf of His Majesty.

AND

Major Jean Baptist Cope chief Sachem of the Tribe of Mick Mack Indians, Inhabiting the Eastern Coast of the said Province, and Andrew Hadley Martin, Gabriel Martin and Francis Jeremiah members & Delegates of the said Tribe, for themselves and their said Tribe their heirs and the heirs of their heirs forever. Begun made and Concluded in the manner form & Tenor following, viz.

1. It is agreed that the Articles of Submission & Agreement made at Boston in New England by the Delegates of the Penobscot Norridgwolk & St John's Indians in the Year 1725 Ratifyed and Confirmed by all the Nova Scotia Tribes at Annapolis Royal in the Month of June 1726 and lately Renewed with Governor Cornwallis at Halifax and Ratifyed at St John's River, now read over Explained & Interpreted shall be and are from hereby from this time forward renewed, reiterated and forever Confirmed by them and their Tribe, and the said Indians for themselves and their Tribe and their Heirs aforesaid do make and renew the same Solemn Submissions and promises for the strict Observance of all the Articles therein Contained as at any time heretofore hath been done.

2. That all Transactions during the late War shall on both sides be buried in Oblivion with the Hatchet, And that the said Indians shall have all favour, Friendship & Protection shewn them from His Majesty's Government.

3. That the said Tribe shall use their utmost Endeavours to bring in the other Indians to Renew and Ratify this Peace, and shall discover and make known any attempts or designs of any other Indians or any Enemy whatever against his Majesty's Subjects within this Province so soon as they shall know thereof and shall also hinder and Obstruct the same to the utmost of their Power, and on the other hand if any of the Indians refusing to ratify this Peace shall make War upon the Tribe who have now Confirmed the same; they shall upon Application have such aid and Assistance from the Government for their defence as the Case may require.

4. It is agreed that the said Tribe of Indians shall not be hindered from, but have free liberty of hunting and Fishing as usual and that if they shall think a Truck house needful at the River Chibenaccadie, or any other place of their resort they shall have the same built and proper Merchandize, lodged therein to be exchanged for what the Indians shall have to dispose of and that in the mean time the Indians shall have free liberty to bring to Sale to Halifax or any other Settlement within this Province, Skins, feathers, fowl, fish or any other thing that they shall have to sell, where they shall have liberty to dispose thereof to the best Advantage.

5. That a Quantity of bread, flour, and such other Provisions, as can be procured, necessary for the Familys and proportionable to the Numbers of the said Indians, shall be given to the half Yearly for the time to come; and the same regard shall be had to the other Tribes that shall hereafter Agree to Renew and Ratify the Peace upon the Terms and Conditions now Stipulated.

6. That to Cherish a good harmony and mutual Correspondence between the said Indians and this Government His Excellency Peregrine Thomas Hopson Esq. Capt. General & Governor in Chief in & over His Majesty's Province of Nova Scotia or Accadie Vice Admiral of the same & Colonel of One of His Majesty's Regiments of Foot hereby promises on the part of His Majesty that the said Indians shall upon the first day of October Yearly, so long as they shall Continue in Friendship, Receive Presents of Blankets, Tobacco, some Powder & Shott, and the said Indians promise once every year, upon the said first of October, to come by themselves or their Delegates and Receive the said Presents and Renew their Frienship and Submissions.

7. That the Indians shall use their best Endeavors to save the Lives & Goods of any People Shipwrecked on this Coast where they resort and shall Conduct the People saved to Halifax with their Goods, and a Reward adequate to the Salvage shall be given them.

8. That all Disputes whatsoever that may happen to arise between the Indians now at Peace and others His Majesty's Subjects in this Province shall be tryed in His Majesty's Courts of Civil Judicature, where the Indians shall have the same benefits, Advantages & Privileges as any others of His Majesty's Subjects.

In Faith & Testimony whereof the Great Seal of the Province is hereunto appended, and the Partys to these Presents have hereunto interchangeably Set their Hands in the Council Chamber at Halifax this 22nd day of Nov. 1752 in the 26th Year of His Majesty's Reign.

P.T. Hopson	Jean Baptiste Cope	His
Chas Lawrence	Andrew Hadley	Mark
Benj. Green	Francois	
Jno. Salusbury	Gabriel	
Willm. Steele		
Jno. Collier		

Reprinted from Wildsmith 1985:189–191

Section 81 of the *Indian Act* (Band Council Powers)

Section 81, R.S.C. 1970, c. 10: (1) The council of a band may make by-laws not inconsistent with this Act or with any regulation made by the Governor in Council or the Minister, for any or all of the following purposes, namely:

(a) to provide for the health of residents on the reserve and to prevent the spreading of contagious and infectious diseases;

(b) the regulation of traffic;

(c) the observance of law and order;

(d) the prevention of disorderly conduct and nuisances;

(e) the protection against and prevention of trespass by cattle and other domestic animals, the establishment of pounds, the appointment of pound-keepers, the regulation of their duties and the for fees and charges for their services;

(f) the construction and maintenance of water courses, roads, bridges, ditches, fences and other local works;

(g) the dividing of the reserve or a portion thereof into zones and the prohibition of the construction or maintenance of any class of buildings or the carrying on of any class of business, trade or calling in any such zone;

(h) the regulation of the construction, repair and use of buildings, whether owned by the band or by individual members of the band;

(i) the survey and allotment of reserve lands among the members of the band and the establishment of a register of Certificates of Possession and Certificates of Occupation relating to allotments and the setting apart of reserve lands for common use, if authority therefor has been granted under section 60;

(j) the destruction and control of noxious weeds;

(k) the regulation of bee-keeping and poultry raising;

(l) the construction and regulation of the use of public wells, cisterns, reservoirs and other water supplies;

(m) the control and prohibition of public games, sports, races, athletic contests and other amusements;

(n) the regulation of the conduct and activity of hawkers, peddlers or others who enter the reserve to buy, sell or otherwise deal in wares or merchandise;

(o) the preservation, protection and management of fur-bearing animals, fish and other game on the reserve;

(p) the removal and punishment of persons trespassing upon the reserve or frequenting the reserve for prohibited purposes;

(p. 1) the residence of band members and other persons on the reserve;

(p. 2) to provide for the rights of spouses and children who reside with members of the band on the reserve with respect to any matter in relation to which the council may make by-laws in respect of members of the band;

(p. 3) to authorize the Minister to make payments out of capital or revenue moneys to persons whose names were deleted from the Band List of the band;

(p. 4) to bring subsection 10(3) or 64.1(2) into effect in respect of the band;

(q) with respect to any matter arising out of or ancillary to the exercise of powers under this section;

(r) the imposition on summary conviction of a fine not exceeding one thousand dollars or imprisonment for a term not exceeding thirty days, or both, for violation of a by-law made under this section.

(2) Where any by-law of a band is contravened and a conviction entered, in addition to any other remedy and to any penalty imposed by the by-law, the court in which the conviction has been entered, and any court of competent jurisdiction thereafter, may make an order prohibiting the continuation or repetition of the offence by the person convicted.

(3) Where any by-law of a band passed is contravened, in addition to any other remedy and to any penalty imposed by the by-law, such contravention may be restrained by court action at the instance of the band council.

R.S., c. I-6, s. 81;
1980, 1981, 1982, 1983, c. 47, s. 53;
1985, c. 27, ss. 15, 15.1

Treaty of Watertown, 1776

Treaty of Watertown, 1776

A treaty of Alliance and Friendship entered into and concluded by and between the Governors of the State of Massachusetts Bay, and the Delegates of the St. John's & Mickmac Tribes of Indians.

Whereas the United States of America in General Congress Assembled have in the name, and by the Authority of the Good people of these Colonies Solemnly published and declared, that these United Colonies are, and of Right ought to be free and Independent States; that they are absolved from all Alliegances to the British Crown; and that all political connection between them, and the State of Great Britain is and ought to be dissolved; and that as Free and Independent States they have full power to Levy War, conclude Peace, contract Alliances establishe Commerce, and to do all other Acts and things which Independent States may of Right do;

We the Governors of the State of Massachusetts Bay do by virtue hereof, and by the powers vested in us enter into and conclude the following Treaty of Friendship and Alliance, viz.,

1st. We the Governors of the said State of Massachusetts Bay on behalf of said States, and the other United States of America on the one part, and Ambrose Var, Newell Wallis, and Francis, Delegates of the St. John's Tribe, John Denaquara, Charles, Mattahu Ontrane, Nicholas, John Battis, Peter Andre, and Sabbatis Netobcobwit Delegates of the Mickmac Tribes of Indians, inhabiting within the Province of Nova Scotia for themselves and in behalf of the said Tribes on the other part do solemnly agree that the people of the said State of Massachusetts Bay and of the other United States of America, and of the said Tribes of Indians shall hence forth be at peace with each other and be considered as Friends and Brothers united and allied together for their mutual defence Safety and Happiness.

2nd. That each party to this Treaty shall, and will consider the Enemies of the other as Enemies to themselves, and do hereby solemnly promise and engage to, and with each other when called upon for that purpose, they shall, and will to the utmost of their abilities, aid and assist each other against their public Enemies; and particularly, that the people of the said Tribes of Indians shall and will afford, and give to the people of the said State of Massachusetts Bay and the people of the other United States of America during their present War with the King of Britain, all the aid and assistance within their power. And that they the people of said Tribes of Indians shall not, and will not directly or indirectly give any aid, or assistance to the Troops or Subjects of the said King of Great Britain, or others adhering to him or hold any correspondence or carry on any Commerce with them during the present War.

3rd. That if any Robbery, or Outrage happens to be committed by any of the Subjects of said State of Massachusetts Bay, or of any other of the United States of America upon any of the people of the said Tribes, and said State shall be upon proper application being made, cause satisfaction and restitution speedily to be made to the party injured.

4th. That if any Robbery or Outrage happens to be committed by any of the said Tribes of Indians upon any of the Subjects of said State or of any other of the United States of America the Tribe to which the Offender or Offenders shall belong, shall upon proper application being made, cause satisfaction and Restitution speedily to be made to the Party injured.

5th. That in case any Misunderstanding, Quarrel, or injury shall happen between the said State of Massachusetts Bay, or of any other of the United States of America and the said Tribes of Indians, or either of them, no private revenge shall be taken but a peaceable application shall be made for Redress.

6th. That the said Tribes of Indians shall and will furnish and supply 600 Strong Men out of the said Tribes, or as many as may be, who shall without delay proceed from their several homes up to the Town of Boston within this State, and from thence shall march to join the Army of the United States of America now at New York under the immediate command of his Excellency General Washington, there to take his Orders.

7th. That each of the Indians who shall by their respective Tribes be appointed to join the Army of the United States of America shall bring with him a good Gun, and shall be allowed one Dollar for the use of it; and in case the Gun shall be lost in the service, shall be paid the Value of it. And the pay of each Man shall begin from the time the sail from Machias for Boston, and they shall be supplied with provisions and a Vessel or Vessels for their passage up to Boston. Each private Man shall receive the like pay as given to our own private Men. The Indians shall be formed into Companies when they arrive at Boston, and shall engage, or enlist for so long a time as General Washington shall want them, not exceeding the term of three years, unless General Washington and they shall agree for a longer time. And as Joseph Denaquara, Peter Andre, and Sabbatis Netobcobwit have manfully and Generously offered to enter immediately into the War they shall be sent as soon as may be to General Washington to join the Army, and shall be considered as entering into our pay at the time of arrival at New York.

8th. The Delegates above named, who may return to their Homes, do promise and engage, to use their utmost influence with the Passamaquoddy and other Neighbouring Tribes of Indians to persuade them to furnish, and supply for the said service as many strong men of their respective Tribes as possible, and that they come along with those of the Tribes of St. John's (and) Mickmac. And the said Governor of the said State of Massachusetts Bay do hereby engage to give to such of the Passamaquoddy or other Neighbouring Indians, who shall enter into the Service of the United States of America, the same pay and encouragement, in every particular, as above agreed to be given to the St. John's, or Mickmac Indians, and to consider them as our friends, and Brothers.

9th. That the said State of Massachusetts Bay shall, and will furnish their Truckmaster at Machias as soon as may be with proper articles for the purpose of supplying the Indians of said Tribes with the necessities and conveniences of life.

10th. And the said Delegates do hereby annul and make void all former Treaties by them or by others in behalf of their respective Tribes made with any other power, State or person so far forth as the same shall be repugnant to any of the Articles contained in this Treaty.

In Faith & Testimony whereof we the said Governors of the said State of Massachusetts Bay have signed these presents, and caused the Seal of said State to be hereunto affixed, and the said Ambrose Var, Newell Wallis and Francis, Delegates of the St. John's Tribe, Joseph Denaquara, Charles, Mattahu Ontrane, Nicholas, John Battis, Peter Andre, and Sabbatis Netobcobwit, Delegates of the Mickmac Tribes of Indians have hereunto put their Marks, and Seals in the Council Chamber at Watertown in the State aforesaid the Nineteenth day July in the year of our Lord One Thousand and Seven Hundred, and seventy six.

Source: Treaty of Watertown 1987

The Commonwealth of Massachusetts

In the Year One Thousand Nine Hundred and Eighty-seven

Resolutions Commending the Mikmaq Nation on the Occasion of the Reenactment of the Treaty of Watertown, July 19, 1776

WHEREAS. The United States owes a great deal to the Mikmaqs for their friendship and military support during the American Revolution. They protected America's claim to all of Northern and Eastern Maine; and

WHEREAS. The Mikmaq Nation was the largest and most powerful of the Wabanaki Tribes, and could have defeated the Americans in the Region had they sided with the British. Yet, the Mikmaq Nation remained faithful to their commitments to the Americans; and

WHEREAS. As recorded in the "Minutes of the Meeting" relative to the Treaty of Watertown, 1776, The Mikmaq delegates responded to an invitation from General Washington, who at that time was Commander of all Continental Forces to attend a conference held at Watertown "in the Colony of Massachusetts Bay, between the Honourable Council of the said colony in behalf of all the United Colonies"; and

WHEREAS. In his opening address to the Conference, the President of the Council said, "We the Governor of the Colony of Massachusetts Bay, in behalf of this colony and of all the United Colonies in North America receive you to our Friendship." Likewise the first article of the Treaty itself refers to the Colony or State of Massachusetts acting on behalf of all the States; and

WHEREAS. At Watertown, Mikmakik became the first government to recognize the United States as "Free and Independent States (with) full power to levy war, conclude peace (and) contract alliances," and the Watertown Treaty is still today a legally recognized document and thus is one of the First International Treaties in United States History; and

WHEREAS. The Mikmaq Nation is and always has been a distinct people, speaking its own language, free in the enjoyment of its own culture and religion, governed by its own officers and laws in its own territory, and recognized, until limited by its free association with Great Britain and the United States, as capable of engaging in Treaties with other States, both States native to this continent and States of Europe; and

WHEREAS. The authority of the Mikmaq Government always has been spiritual, persuasive and non-coercive. The continuity and authority of the Mikmaq States exists in its culture, in a common bond and vision that transcends temporary interest; and

WHEREAS. The Mikmaq Nation embraces the concept expressed in the United States of America Declaration of Independence "We hold these truths to be self-evident: that all men are endowed by their creator with inherent and inalienable rights; that among these are life, liberty, and the pursuit of happiness; that to secure these rights, governments are instituted among men, deriving their just powers from the consent of the governed...and organizing its powers in such form as to them shall seem mostly likely to effect their safety and happiness"; and

WHEREAS. As keepers of the chain of union between the United States and the Mikmaq Nation, the Santeoi Mawa'iomi have long desired to renew the Treaty relationship with Massachusetts and the other United States; therefore be it

RESOLVED. That the Massachusetts House of Representatives commends the Mikmaq Nation on the occasion of the reenactment of the Treaty of Watertown of July 19, 1776: and be it further

RESOLVED. That a copy of these resolutions be forwarded by the Clerk of the House of Representatives to the Mikmaq Nation.

House of Representatives
Adopted, June 22, 1987
Speaker of the House
Clerk of the House
Offered by: George Keverian,
Speaker of the House

Source: Resolutions Commending the Mikmq Nation 1987

Speech by Micmac Grand Captain Alex Denny to Massachusetts House of Representatives in Boston, June 24, 1987, during the 1776 Treaty Renewal Ceremonies

The delegation from the Grand Council is here to honor our forefather's [*sic*] vision of America — a land of liberty, a land of freedoms, a land where human rights prevail over other values. We believe that these values are unique to Mikmaq culture and soul and other tribal nations of America, values which we shared with the new peoples who came to our land.

The Treaty of 1776 reflects our ancient Mikmaq truths. Truths which were reaffirmed and expressed by the drafters of the Declaration of Independence against the British Sovereign: that all men are created equal, all are endowed with inherent rights under the laws of nature and nature's God and that unjust government intrusion or infringement of these rights cannot be tolerated. That true men must oppose any law which conflicts with these universal truths.

For the last five generations, the eternal truths of the American Revolution has [*sic*] been continually affirmed to the Mikmaq. Through the dark tunnel which brought European violence to our beloved forest, enshrouded our dignity, occupied our land and the oppression of our ancient governmental system — the Grand Council has struggled to maintain these truths and teach the British immigrant their values. Through hunger, malnutrition, disease, alcoholism and despair, our struggles for human existence and dignity, we have continually argued these truths to our oppressors. As the keepers of the Chain [*sic*] of union with the Vatican, the British Crown, and the United States, the Grand Council has repeatedly pointed out that they are the inherent in our aboriginal and treaty rights.

At any time, we could have turned to violence as a solution to our Oppres sion [*sic*]. The fact that we did not demonstrates our continuing commitment to our treaty with the Holy See in 1610 and to our Catholic Faith. In an age of rule by brute force, we followed the teachings of Jesus Christ, we have used the law of nature and nature's God to assert our truths, our culture values, and our Faith [*sic*] in the indomitable will of justice and liberty. This path we see as the dignity of man, the strength of the Mikmaq spirit.

Recently we have affirmed the universal truths which stand behind our treaties — the principles of equality between peoples, self-determination, and human rights. We have convinced the Canadian people that our aboriginal and treaties right [*sic*] should be enshrined in the constitution of Canada and protected against governmental excesses. In the process, we have pushed back the idea that our race determines our legal rights, pushed back the racially based exclusion which justifies government violations of our human rights and fundamental freedoms, and exposed the fiction that we were a savage people not entitled to the equal protection of the King's prerogative and laws.

Under the new Canadian constitution, no longer can federal, provincial or local government ignore the Grand Council's aboriginal and treaty rights. No longer can they discriminate against the traditional government of the Mikmaq. No longer can the federal government modify our cultural heritage and values with the stroke of a law or classify the Mikmaq as a racial minority without governmental rights — probably the grossest form of racism ever disguised by law. The era of racial superiority of the white man over the natives is over.

The Mikmaq have been demeaned for many generations under different governments. No law, no reparation can reverse the loss of our self-esteem or the affects [*sic*] of their brain washing of young Mikmaq about their culture or language or dispel the great darkness of self-doubt left by our oppression by the white people. We can do little about past injustices, the psychological traumas of the Mikmaqs. All the Grand Council can do is to attempt to take the spiritual and political lead in rebuilding the spirit and aspiration of our people and spark, again, the genius that has made such a unique and irreplaceable contribution to human achievement.

Our old treaties are a living process. Our promises are as valid now as in the past. Today, we realize that the same is true for Massachusetts and the other United States. The 1776 Treaty is a moral and legal compass to guide our reconstruction of Mikmaq society and our children's destiny. We are honored that our forefathers had the wisdom and cultural values to build on the same foundation as the United States. We are honored that they fought and died for these truths, and are proud of our ancestor's [*sic*] legacy which guided the Grand Council through the great darkness of the age of racial superiority. And we are proud to say that we will build a better Mikmaq society upon our legacy and with the active participation of our allies who also deeply believe in the eternal truths of America's birth.

Source: Denny 1987

Mi'kmaq Treaty Day Proclamation

Mi'kmaq Treaty Day Proclamation of Grand Chief Donald Marshall

When the English began to make their new homes in our land our forefathers protected the livelihood and survival of the Mi'kmaq by signing treaties with their Kings. Throughout the seasons the treaties have remained.

On November 21, 1985, the Supreme Court of Canada affirmed that the Treaty of 1752 is still strong. The Mi'kmaq are still protected by its articles and we call upon Her Majesty to honour this Treaty and others made with the Mi'kmaq Nation.

On this 234th year of the Treaty of 1752, I, as Grand Chief of the Mi'kmaq invite every Mi'kmaq to observe October 1 this year and every year thereafter, as "Treaty Day" to commemorate the unique and special relationship that exists between the Mi'kmaq and Her Majesty.

PROCLAIMED at HALIFAX, NOVA SCOTIA, this 1st day of October, A.D., 1986

Source: Marshall 1988

A Petition for Police Protection

January 3, 1970

Dear Sir:

As you will note from the enclosed petition, a large number of citizens of Membertou Indian Reserve located in the City of Sydney are very much dissatisfied with the degree of police protection afforded the Reserve by the City of Sydney Police and the R.C.M.P.

First of all we acknowledge the slackness of our Band Council in failing to meet this problem which stems in large measure from weakness in the administration of the Reserve, particularly in regard to by-laws respecting law and order. One area in which they have fallen down very badly is in the failure to provide street lighting, resulting in dark streets which encourage a degree of vandalism and more serious crime that has many of our citizens staying up nights to protect their property. We realize vandalism and minor crime are not exclusive to Membertou but we do say that our close-knit, little community should make it much easier to stamp out this kind of thing in the bud.

For their part the R.C.M.P. could take very stern action against increasing making and sale of home brew which is being sold to young people and making its contribution to the disorder problem. Possibly our Band Council has not brought this to the attention of the R.C.M.P., in which case you could consider this letter as such notification. The City Police, on the other hand, has shown a lack of serious concern for the problems we face, and indeed some of our citizens would say that the local police tend to treat us and our problems as being not very important. There is no reason why both R.C.M.P. and City Police cannot do a great deal more in the way of patrols to prevent crime and investigation to solve it.

As for our band Council they have very wide power under the Indian Act to protect and preserve order on the reserve and indeed to promote and encourage citizenship and good behavior. The act also seems to give Council very wide discretion as to the frequency of its meetings, with the result that our Council has found it unnecessary to meet for approximately eighteen months. With due respect for the Chief and two councillors, it seems fair to say that this does not constitute proper attention to the needs of the Reserve.

We might note that the situation has come to the point where many good and law-abiding citizens are considering some type of vigilante action to prevent vandalism, etc. We would not want to take this step unless it is absolutely necessary. We would appreciate it very much if you would look into this matter at once, with a view to early and effective action to improve police protection and encourage, if possible, more effective administration by our Band Council.

Citizens of Membertou
103 Membertou Street
Sydney, Nova Scotia

cc: Sydney Police Commission

Source: Public Archives of Canada, RG 10, vol. 8506, file 50/18-1, part 3

Micmac Surnames

The following are most of the surnames traditional among the Micmac. Those uncommon to Cape Breton Island have the location of the area or areas where they are usually found in parentheses.

Alex
Augustine (New Brunswick)
Basque (especially mainland Nova Scotia)
Battiste
Beadle (mainland Nova Scotia)
Bernard
Brooks (mainland Nova Scotia)
Cabot
Christmas
Clair (New Brunswick)
Clement (New Brunswick and Quebec)
Copage (New Brunswick)
Cope (mainland Nova Scotia)
Cremo
Dedam (New Brunswick and Quebec)
Dennis
Denny
Doucette
Francis
Gabriel
Gehue (mainland Nova Scotia)
Ginnish (New Brunswick)
Gloade (mainland Nova Scotia)
Googoo (from the Micmac *'kukukwes,* or "owl")
Gould
Herney
Isaac
Isadore (mainland Nova Scotia)
Jeddore (especially Newfoundland)
Joe
Johnson
Joseph (mainland Nova Scotia)
Julian
Julien
Knockwood (especially mainland Nova Scotia)
Labrador (mainland Nova Scotia)
Lafford
Levi (New Brunswick)
Lewis
Maloney (mainland Nova Scotia)
Marble (mainland Nova Scotia)
Marr (mainland Nova Scotia)
Marshall
Martin (Restigouche)
McEwan (mainland Nova Scotia)
Metallic (Quebec)
Meuse (mainland Nova Scotia)
Michael
Milliea (New Brunswick)
Moore
Morris
Morrison
Muise (mainland Nova Scotia)
Nevin
Nicholas
Noel
Patles (especially New Brunswick)
Paul
Peck
Peters (New Brunswick, mainland Nova Scotia)
Phillips (mainland Nova Scotia)
Pictou (from the Micmac *'piktuk,* or "something which gives gaseous explosions") (mainland Nova Scotia)
Pierro
Poulette
Prosper
Richard (mainland Nova Scotia)
Sack (mainland Nova Scotia)
Sanipass (New Brunswick)
Sappier (New Brunswick)
Simon
Smith
Sock (mainland Nova Scotia)
Stevens (especially mainland Nova Scotia)
Sylliboy (Micmac for "Levi")
Tomah (Micmac for "Tom")
Toney
Ward
Wilmot
Young

Micmac Migration at the End of the 19th Century

This appendix uses the Canadian censuses of 1871, 1881, and 1891 to determine the degree of mobility among the Micmac people of Cape Breton Island, Nova Scotia from 1871 to 1891. The methodology was to find the names of Indians in the three censuses and compare the locations for each individual and nuclear family, the two largest identifiable units of people who moved. The 1871 census is compared to the 1881 census and the 1881 census with the 1891 census.

There are difficulties in the use of census data for this purpose. First is the frequency of the census data per se — there are only three observations available, and they are 10 years apart. It is difficult, for example, to use the census to determine the mobility of a family or individual who was recorded as living at one place in 1871, subsequently left the area, but returned in time to be recorded in the 1881 census. Given the Micmac propensity to travel between relatively few accustomed places, in addition to the multitude of infrequently visited places, the number of people who were mobile between censuses could be considerable; yet because the censuses recorded them in the same place, they cannot be counted as having migrated.

For example, consider four brothers who spent at least part of their childhood growing up in Eskasoni, as shown in the 1871 census (see Appendix A, 1871, ID nos. 351–354). The 1881 census does not mention them at all, meaning, as discussed below, that they were living in some place inaccessible to the census officers, probably deep in the woods. The 1891 census shows one of the brothers in the city of Sydney, newly colonized by the Micmac but not yet a reserve, and another in a place on the mainland known for good hunting (he would later join his brother in Sydney). A third brother had returned to Eskasoni and the fourth had died, according to informants. Census and other data show this sort of pattern repeatedly. Similarly, someone who moves away from a particular region for only a few weeks when the census is taken could be counted as mobile. Hence, the census data provides an unsophisticated measurement of mobility. All the censuses were taken in the month of April. This has the advantage of controlling for the importance of purely seasonal migration, but says little about movements between summer and winter habitats.

While these problems made identification difficult, by checking the data for the same location 10 years later it was possible in all cases to determine whether a family had stayed or moved (or, conversely, had recently come to the locality). This was achieved by lisiting nuclear family groups, which usually remained largely intact for 10 years or more, and looking at Christian names, ages, marital status, and number of children. This analysis was aided by the small size of the group populations involved.

Two events can insert some small degree of inaccuracy into the analysis. The first is the death of an entire family. While infant and child mortality was indeed high, it seems unlikely that a disease that killed an entire family would not have affected more people as well; however, there is no evidence of epidemic or endemic diseases at that time (the major communicable disease was tuberculosis, which was selectively fatal).

The second is enfranchisement. From 1868 through 1985, a Canadian Indian had the opportunity to change his or her legal status from "Indian" to that of full-fledged Canadian citizen. (The distinction really later was between having the legal status of "Indian" and not having it.) In the late 1950s and early 1960s Indians in various parts of the country received all of the rights that other citizens of Canada enjoyed. Indians still have other specific rights in addition and are administered separately by the federal government. From 1871 through 1891 (as well as before and after) an Indian man's decision to enfranchise meant that his wife and minor children also changed their legal status at the same time. Examination of old Indian Affairs records, although incomplete, shows that an insignificant number of families became enfranchised during this period, and later. Moreover, older informants disclose that in the early part of this century, until the present, only rarely have people ever decided to enfranchise voluntarily. In any event, enfranchisement, and the resultant departure from the Micmac community and forced exclusion from the reserves (for those living there), should be considered as instances of mobility.

The biggest reason for the disappearance of significant numbers of people from census rolls (majorities in some localities) is that Micmac traveled to, and lived in, areas that were not easily accessible. In other words, the census takers did not find them to count them. Though this work focuses on the mobility of the Cape Breton Micmac, I compiled data on all the Nova Scotia Indians recorded by the census for 1871, 1881, and 1891. Thus, it was possible to place all of those recorded by the census who moved from one place to another within the province. Of course, some undoubtedly emigrated from the province to New Brunswick, Quebec, Prince Edward Island, and Newfoundland, as well as possibly to Maine and Boston, since a few Indian people listed in the Nova Scotia census were recorded as having been born in the other Atlantic provinces and Newfoundland. The number of people who left the province was also probably quite small, since travel was difficult, slow, and expensive.

In most cases those who appeared in the census in one decade, but not in the next, were counted as having emigrated, on the assumption that those who were listed and did not move would be on the census rolls 10 years later as well. Because the major Micmac meeting areas were always counted, whether they were reserves or not, and because census takers were paid by the number of names they collected, there can be no confusion that all Indians who were at those places at the time of the census were counted.

The individuals and groups discussed thus far have been amenable to identification; either they were included in the census records and their new locations were identified, or they were not found and can be considered to have emigrated because they no longer occupied their prior addresses. Those considered unidentifiable, and who were not counted as either mobile or as settled, are those of the elderly, unmarried women of marriageable age, and unmarried men who also did not appear in the next census; in short, the elderly and those unattached to a nuclear family were discounted.

The elderly could have died or moved, but no sure determination of either can be made. Single women of marriageable age were likely to marry and change their family names; although they may have stayed in the same community, even a rigorous search of the married women in the area would not yield results of any certainty. In many cases, women and men living in separate groups married; in not a few cases, young people met and married during the two weeks of the St. Anne's Mission at Chapel Island, because that was the only time each year that many Micmac people saw a priest. In such cases, a woman usually left to live with her husband, no matter where he decided to live.

Also not considered were nearly all single or recently married men. Because of the relatively few Micmac family names and the fashions in giving Christian names, there were many cases of two or more men of the same name who were also close in age. Without being able to associate a male with an unusual name or with a single nuclear family from one census to the next, it was impossible to be sure whether he was living or dead in the following census. These men were discounted, although many single men leave their natal families and travel around alone, or with other men. In other words, far more single men stayed alive and moved around than stayed put and died.

Finally, children under the age of 10 years were not counted as immigrants, because they could have been born in the place to which their parents had moved.

In these last three cases, the likelihood of movement is regarded as more likely than the likelihood of staying in place. Thus, results are greatly skewed in favor of settlement and the actual mobility rates must be greater than those indicated below.

The following is a compilation of migration information and rates for all Cape Breton localities where census takers found Micmac Indians in 1871, 1881, and 1891. "People" refers to Micmac Indian persons. "Disappeared" refers to individuals who were not included in the next census. The average rate of migration of Cape Breton Micmac was 104.8% between 1871 and 1881, and 87.0% between 1881 and 1891. Migration rates were computed according to the following formula (Beale and Fuguitt 1978:161):

$$\text{Rate of migration} = \frac{\text{Number of migrants}}{1/2\ (\text{Population 1} + \text{Population 2})}$$

Big Pond
- 1871
  - Enumeration
    - People: 6
    - Domiciles: 1
- 1881
  - Enumeration
    - People: 3
    - Domiciles: 1
  - Migration (1871–1881)
    - Emigrants: 3
      - Disappeared: 2
      - Moved: 1 (Potlotek)
    - Immigrants: 0
  - Rate of migration: 66.7% over a 10-year period
- 1891
  - Enumeration
    - People: 0
  - Migration (1881–1891)
    - Emigrants: 3
      - Moved: 3 (Potlotek)
    - Immigrants: 0
  - Rate of migration: 200.0% over a 10-year period

Catalone
- 1871
  - Enumeration
    - People: 0
- 1881
  - Enumeration
    - People: 7
    - Domiciles: 1
  - Migration (1871–1881)
    - Emigrants: 0
    - Immigrants: 5
  - Rate of migration: 142.9% over a 10-year period
- 1891
  - Enumeration
    - People: 0
  - Migration (1881–1891)
    - Emigrants: 7
      - Disappeared: 7
  - Rate of migration: 200.0% over a 10-year period

Continued

Cheticamp
1871
Enumeration
People: 1
Domiciles: 1

1881
Enumeration
People: 0
Migration (1871–1881)
Emigrants: 1
Disappeared: 1
Immigrants: 0
Rate of migration: 200.0% over a 10-year period

1891
Enumeration
People: 0

Eskasoni
1871
Enumeration
People: 127
Nuclear families: 27
Domiciles: 20

1881
Enumeration
People: 120
Nuclear families: 31
Domiciles: 29
Migration (1871–1881)
Remained: 43
Emigrants: 69
Disappeared: 50
Moved: 19
North Sydney: 8
Sydney: 11
Immigrants: 46
Rate of migration: 93.1% over a 10-year period

1891
Enumeration
People: 85
Domiciles: 15
Migration (1881–1891)
Remained: 25
Emigrants: 67
Disappeared: 49
Moved: 18
Sydney: 9
Waqamatkuk: 4
Potlotek: 5
Immigrants: 32
Rate of migration: 96.6% over a 10-year period

Howley's Ferry
1871
Enumeration
People: 8
Domiciles: 1

1881
Enumeration
People: 0
Migration (1871–1881)
Emigrants: 8
Disappeared: 8
Immigrants: 0
Rate of migration: 200.0% over a 10-year period

1891
Enumeration
People: 0

Judique
1871
Enumeration
People: 0

1881
Enumeration
People: 2
Domiciles: 1
Migration (1871–1881)
Immigrants: 2
Rate of migration: 200.0% over a 10-year period

1891
Enumeration
People: 0
Migration (1881–1891)
Emigrants: 2
Moved: 2 (Heatherton)
Rate of migration: 200.0% over a 10-year period

Continued

***Ma'lakawe:j* (North Mountain, Plaister Cove and West Bay combined)**
1871
Enumeration
People: 50
Domiciles: 10

1881
Enumeration
People: 8
Domiciles: 2
Migration (1871–1881)
Remained: 0
Emigrants: 50
Disappeared: 36
Moved: 14
Antigonish Co., Lochaber: 2
Waqamatkuk: 2
Potlotek: 1
Guysborough: 9
Immigrants: 4
Rate of migration: 186.2% over a 10-year period

1891
Enumeration
People: 13
Domiciles: 3
Migration (1881–1891)
Remained: 0
Emigrants: 8
Disappeared: 8
Immigrants: 11
Rate of migration: 181.0% over a 10-year period

Mabou
1871
Enumeration
People: 27
Domiciles: 7

1881
Enumeration
People: 0
Migration (1871–1881)
Emigrants: 27
Disappeared: 15
Moved: 12
Guysborough Co., Larry's River: 2
Potlotek: 8
Pictou Landing: 2
Immigrants: 0
Rate of migration: 200.0% over a 10-year period

1891
Enumeration
People: 0

North Sydney
1871
Enumeration
People: 44
Domiciles: 12

1881
Enumeration
People: 52
Domiciles: 10
Migration (1871–1881)
Remained: 8
Emigrants: 29
Disappeared: 22
Moved: 7
Pictou County, Hardwood Hill: 5
North Side Mira: 2
Immigrants: 23
Rate of migration: 108.3% over a 10-year period

1891
Enumeration
People: 26
Domiciles: 5
Migration (1881–1891)
Remained: 6
Emigrants: 31
Disappeared: 23
Moved: 8 (Whycocomagh)
Immigrants: 16
Rate of migration: 120.5% over a 10-year period

North Side Mira
1871
Enumeration
People: 0

1881
Enumeration
People: 9
Domiciles: 2

Continued

Migration (1871–1881)
Emigrants: 0
Immigrants: 7
Rate of migration: 155.6% over a 10-year period

1891
Enumeration
People: 0
Migration (1881–1891)
Emigrants: 9
Disappeared: 2
Moved: 7 (Sydney)
Immigrants: 0
Rate of migration 200.0% over a 10-year period

Potlotek
1871
Enumeration
People: 66
Nuclear families: 15
Domiciles: 14

1881
Enumeration
People: 94
Nuclear families: 24
Domiciles: 17
Migration (1871–1881)
Remained: 29
Emigrants: 24
Disappeared: 21
Moved: 3 (Eskasoni)
Immigrants: 38
Rate of migration: 77.5% over a 10-year period

1891
Enumeration
People: 132
Domiciles: 28
Migration (1881–1891)
Remained: 46
Emigrants: 45
Disappeared: 29
Moved: 16
Waqamatkuk: 1
Guysborough: 10
Ma'lakawe:j: 5
Immigrants: 55
Rate of migration: 88.5% over a 10-year period

River inhabitants, Division 2
1871
Enumeration
People: 8
Domiciles: 1

1881
Enumeration
People: 0
Migration (1871–1881)
Remained: 0
Emigrants: 8
Immigrants: 0
Rate of migration: 200.0% over a 10-year period

1891
Enumeration
People: 0

River inhabitants, Division 4
1871
Enumeration
People: 11
Domiciles: 3

1881
Enumeration
People: 9
Domiciles: 2
Migration (1871–1881)
Remained: 2
Emigrants: 7
Disappeared: 7
Immigrants: 4
Rate of migration: 110.0% over a 10-year period

1891
Enumeration
People: 0
Migration (1881–1891)
Remained: 0
Emigrants: 8
Disappeared: 3
Moved: 5
Heatherton: 3
Guysborough: 1
Morland: 1
Immigrants: 0
Rate of migration: 177.8% over a 10-year period

Continued

St. Peter's
1871
Enumeration: 0

1881
Enumeration
People: 3
Domiciles: 1
Migration (1871–1881)
Emigrants: 0
Immigrants: 3
Rate of migration: 200.0% over a 10-year period

1891
Enumeration
People: 8
Domiciles: 2
Migration (1881–1891)
Emigrants: 1
Disappeared: 1
Immigrants: 3
Rate of migration: 72.7% over a 10-year period

Sydney
1871
Enumeration
People: 3
Domiciles: 1

1881
Enumeration
People: 44
Domiciles: 9
Migration (1871–1891)
Remained: 0
Emigrants: 3
Disappeared: 3
Immigrants: 44
Rate of migration: 200.0% over a 10-year period

1891
Enumeration
People: 51
Domiciles: 9
Migration (1881–1891)
Remained: 12
Emigrants: 22
Disappeared: 16
Moved: 6 (Waqamatkuk)
Immigrants: 23
Rate of migration: 94.7% over a 10-year period

Waqamatkuk
1871
Enumeration
People: 69
Domiciles: 14

1881
Enumeration
People: 89
Domiciles: 15
Migration (1871–1881)
Remained: 24
Emigrants: 25
Disappeared: 22
Moved: 3 (Pictou Landing)
Immigrants: 30
Rate of migration: 69.6% over a 10-year period

1891
Enumeration
People: 108
Domiciles: 19
Migration (1881–1891)
Remained: 45
Emigrants: 28
Disappeared: 13
Moved: 15
Whycocomagh: 1
Sydney: 1
Guysborough: 13
Immigrants: 27
Rate of migration: 55.8% over a 10-year period

Whycocomagh
1871
Enumeration
People: 52
Domiciles: 8

1881
Enumeration
People: 88
Domiciles: 13
Migration (1871–1881)
Remained: 19
Emigrants:26
Disappeared: 20

Continued

Moved: 6 (Eskasoni)
Immigrants: 38
Rate of migration: 91.4% over a 10-year period

1891
Enumeration
People: 104
Domiciles: 18
Migration (1881–1891)
Remained: 40
Emigrants: 33
Disappeared: 28
Moved: 5
St. Peter's: 3
Ma'lakawe:j: 2
Immigrants: 38
Rate of migration: 74.0% over a 10-year period

Demographic Data

This appendix provides a demographic portrait of the Eskasoni Micmac as they were in 1981, with selected information on other Micmac communities for comparison (Statistics Canada 1983:1-9 through 1-14, 1-17 through 1-23, 1-50 through 1-56, and 1-58 through 1-64). In September 1985, the population of Nova Scotia's bands was as follows:

Eskasoni	2,043
Membertou	528
Whycocomagh	493
Shubenacadie (a mainland Nova Scotia band)	1,182
Total for all bands	6,781

Source: Indian Affairs Branch band lists (IAB 1986:18)

These figures are undoubtedly somewhat inflated. Bands receive money on a per capita basis and band offices are sometimes tardy in removing the names of the deceased from the band lists.

The Eskasoni Population in 1949

Age	Male	Female	Combined	Percentage of total population
0–5	94	86	180	26
6–10	48	42	90	13
11–15	42	34	76	11
16–20	25	26	51	7
21–30	37	45	82	12
31–40	42	45	87	13
41–50	29	20	49	7
51–60	15	17	32	5
61–80	26	19	45	6
Total	358	334	692	100

After Steen 1951:43

Continued

Band	**Eskasoni**	**Membertou**	**Whycocomagh**
Situation	Rural	Urban	Near a town
Population in 1976	1,497	318	398
Population in 1981	1,704	338	455
Reserve size (in sq. km.)	12.38	0.60	6.86
Population density (per sq. km.)	137.6	563.3	360.7
Born in Canada	1,590	380	400
Born in U.S.A.	95	15	55
Population older than 14 years	930	205	255
Schooling:			
Below grade 9	345	60	75
Grades 9 to 13	270	45	105
High school graduate	25	5	5
University	115	20	10
University graduate	5	0	0
Private dwellings	315	70	95
Built before 1946	50	25	0
Built from 1971 to 1981	130	35	70
Labor force:			
Men older than 14 years	455	110	95
Employed men	130	55	55
Women older than 14 years	470	100	130
Employed women	110	35	30

Male employment	**Eskasoni**	**Membertou**	**Whycocomagh**
Administrative	20	5	0
Technical	20	10	0
Sales	0	0	5
Service	20	5	10
Primary	35	5	0
Processing	10	0	0
Manufacturing	20	0	45
Construction	30	45	0
Transport	5	5	0
Other	10	5	0
Self-employed (of total)	15	0	5

Continued

Female employment	**Eskasoni**	**Membertou**	**Whycocomagh**
Administrative	10	10	0
Teaching	20	0	5
Technical	20	0	5
Clerical	35	15	10
Sales	0	0	10
Service	20	0	10
Manufacturing	5	0	0
Other	10	0	0
Self-employed (of total)	0	0	0

Annual income (in Canadian dollars)	**Eskasoni**	**Membertou**	**Whycocomagh**
Men over 14 years of age:	385	95	95
Less than $2,000	85	30	20
$2,000–3,999	65	10	15
$4,000–5,999	75	10	15
$6,000–9,999	70	5	20
$10,000–14,999	65	5	20
$15,000–19,999	10	5	5
$20,000–24,999	20	15	0
Over $25,000	0	0	0
Women over 14 years of age:	285	60	100
Less than $1,000	20	5	5
$1,000–1,999	75	5	10
$2,000–2,999	40	0	0
$3,000–3,999	20	10	20
$4,000–5,999	55	25	20
$6,000–7,999	15	0	15
$8,000–9,999	15	5	10
$10,000–14,999	20	10	0
Over $15,000	10	5	15

THE "NEW RULES" 2005

Eskasoni Band Council

Housing Policies

MISSION STATEMENT FOR THE ESKASONI HOUSING PROGRAM

To provide Eskasoni Band Members with shelter that meets National Building Codes minimum standards, through a process that is fair and beneficial to the community as a whole.

COMMUNITY AWARENESS & PARTICIPATION

With the development of our housing program it is very important that band members are aware and participate in this process. The community members must be informed of changes and developments that will ultimately affect them.

The community's housing needs and administration are changing dramatically. The transformation will not be easy but is necessary to reassert control over our own lives and community. The complementary contributions from the community members are also described in this policy. Council issues this new housing policy to:

- map out a path for the future;
- bring clarity to changing housing objectives;
- provide direction to employees;
- ensure transparency in managing community assets;
- allow the community to hold Council accountable for its actions,
- allow the housing department to hold tenants accountable for their actions

Good homes, strong families and a sustainable community are not just the responsibility of government. Eskasoni members must act to ensure these things happen.

"TOGETHER, WE WILL ENSURE THAT THESE OPPORTUNITIES CONTRIBUTE TO A SUSTAINABLE ENVIRONMENT WHICH OUR CHILDREN AND THEIR CHILDREN WILL INHERIT."

AUTHORITY

The Chief and Council are responsible for the approval of the housing policy and delegates responsibility for delivery of the Housing program to the Eskasoni Housing Department.

The Chief and Council will not have direct day to day responsibility for operations and program management.

The Housing Department is responsible for the development and any recommendations to Council on policy implementation and changes.

The Housing Department is expected at all times to act in the best interest of the community as a whole. Each employee shall be expected to abide by the Band code of ethics.

Source: Eskasoni Band Council

The Eskasoni Housing Department is responsible for drafting and implementing housing policies and programs regarding new construction, maintenance, repairs, rental units, tenants selection and sewage and water. It also recommends budgets and changes for the Eskasoni housing program.

ADMINISTRATIVE STRUCTURE

The Housing Director will report directly to the Band Manager and manage the day to day operations of the Housing program.

The Housing Director shall be responsible for the planning and co-ordination of all housing activities and for the application of all housing policies and regulations that may be established from time to time by the Band Council.

The Housing Director will submit written and / or verbal reports on a regular basis and as required to the Band Council concerning the operation and delivery of the housing program.

STANDARDS OF CONSTRUCTION AND / OR RENOVATIONS

Acceptable standards shall be applied to the construction and renovation of all buildings in the community, and the installation of all water delivery, waste disposal and electrical systems.

The National Building code shall be the minimum standard of construction and renovation of all buildings within the boundaries of the community.

The National Fire Code shall be applied as the minimum standard of construction with regard to fire retardation.

If construction or renovation is carried out with the assistance of Canada Mortgage and Housing Corporation (CMHC), CMHC standards will apply, and housing units must be completed and final inspection have been performed to meet these standards before occupancy is permitted.

All water delivery and waste disposal installations must meet standards set by Health and Welfare Canada, and meet the requirements of the federal Environment Protection Act.

Installation of all electrical wiring and equipment must comply with standards in effect in the surrounding area.

INSPECTIONS

Inspection of all building construction and renovation, water, waste and electrical installations must be carried out by certified personnel at appropriate stages of construction, renovation or installation to ensure compliance with Standards of Construction/Renovations referred to in the above section.

Inspectors employed by or working on behalf of CMHC shall inspect all housing units being constructed or renovated under CMHC programs.

Inspection of water and plumbing installations within a unit shall be carried out as part of the normal compliance inspection.

Inspection of central water supply and waste disposal systems, or waste disposal installations attached to, but outside of the unit e.g.: septic holding tanks and weeping fields, must be inspected by inspectors working on behalf of Health Canada/or Environment Canada.

Electrical installations must be inspected and approved by qualified and duly authorized personnel only.

DISPOSAL OF DILAPITATED BUILDINGS

Residential buildings that are no longer fit for habitation must be demolished or dismantled as soon as possible or immediately at the discretion of the Housing Department. If unit is privately owned the owner must reply within 7 days of notice being given of their intentions for those units which may cause health and safety threats to community members because of the physical condition of unit.

Non-residential buildings, which because of their physical condition constitute threat to the health and safety of community residents or detract from the community must be demolished or dismantled within 90 days of notice being given to owner.

ENVIRONMENTAL PROTECTION

All plans for new construction, renovation or waste disposal installation must be reviewed to ensure that there is no threat to the environment, and that applicable legislation is respected. Environmental assessment will be conducted where and when applicable.

MAINTENANCE OF HOUSING UNITS

It shall be the responsibility of the occupant of a dwelling or housing unit to take preventive measures to maintain the unit and all integrated equipment in good condition.

If the unit is owned by the Eskasoni Band, the Eskasoni Housing Department is responsible to ensure that any required maintenance and repairs carried out are done so according to housing policy, keeping in mind that the total costs all housing repairs must be consistent with the annual approved budget.

If an individual holds a dwelling unit by way of Certificate of Possession or owns the units outright and is renting the unit to the Band Council, the owner is responsible for all necessary maintenance and repairs (no exceptions).

The occupant, regardless of who owns the unit, is responsible for maintaining the grounds of the unit in reasonable condition.

INSURANCE

The Eskasoni First Nation owns many of the homes in the community and act as manager of most debt financing. The Band will make reasonable efforts to ensure that homes for which it is responsible are covered by adequate replacement insurance. The individual homeowners are responsible for their own insurance coverage on personal contents. Tenants are responsible for insuring their home contents.

The Housing Department shall work in co-operation with organizations whose purpose is to prevent, reduce and protect against loss due to fire.

TENANT AND OWNERSHIP

As of April 1, 1997 lands and homes within the boundaries of the reserve are held in common by the members of the Eskasoni First Nation and are not subject to sale by an individual or group (unencumbered band land).

Land within the boundaries of the reserve, held by individuals through such instruments as Certificates of Possession, shall not be sold, transferred or otherwise conveyed to anyone who is not a member of the Eskasoni First Nation.

The Band Council shall determine the way in which land is to be occupied. The Eskasoni Housing Department shall develop regulations concerning ownership of houses in the community. The Chief and Council must first approve these regulations.

No person who already occupies a house which is in good repair shall be entitled to receive a new housing unit, unless it can be demonstrated that the requirement for a new home is considered justified by changes in family size or other factors deemed relevant by the Eskasoni New Housing Selection Policy.

If a person who already has a Band owned house demonstrates to the satisfaction of Council that they are in need a new unit, he or she must undertake in releasing by Quit Claim the unit currently occupied without reimbursement from the Eskasoni Housing Department and without monetary gain from any source. Unit will then be reallocated by the Housing Department with approval of the Chief & Council.

No person shall sell or otherwise dispose of a Band owned housing unit. (BCM Sept. 30/91)

The Eskasoni Band Council recognizes after 1 (one) year a couple living together is considered common-law.

In case of dispute following break-up of marriage/family between two Aboriginal persons, continued occupancy shall be consistent with direction that may be handed downed by a court of law, but in no case shall occupancy be granted to a non-aboriginal person to the exclusion of the aboriginal person. (Parent with custody receives the home.)(By-Law 6-81) June 17, 1981

Only a resident band member may be eligible for allocation of a recently vacated house. The Housing Department & Chief and Council will decide the allocation.

PURCHASE OF MATERIALS AND CONTRACT MANAGEMENT

Any person(s) given repair material and who is capable of completing the repair work in the unit, will be required to do so free of charge.

All repairs require purchase orders to be eligible for payment.

Purchase orders are only to be issued in the homeowner or tenant name.

The Housing Department will no longer be issuing purchase orders for carpets due to the high number of health issues relating to carpets.

The Housing Department is only responsible for basic material issued, the recipient is responsible for any cost above the approved material cost.

The Housing Department is directed to give all contracts to local tradesmen, (electrical, heating, cabinets & plumbing). If unable to contract or if tradesman is unavailable the Housing Department may then use an alternative tradesperson (BCM March 27, 1996).

The Housing Department will not approve any repairs to any Section 95 or Section 10 unit in the first 5 years unless there are exceptional circumstances. The Housing Department may consider routine maintenance (ex. heating, plumbing and electrical repairs).

The Housing Department will not reimburse homeowners for material purchased for unit.

Any damage done to homes due to neglect/vandalism (ex: broken windows) will not be the responsibility of the Housing Department. The onus will be upon the homeowner to repair and report to the proper authorities for restitution for damages. If the responsibility is taken by the homeowner the Housing Department may consider assisting in repairing the unit depending on the circumstances.

The Eskasoni Housing Department shall make reasonable efforts to ensure that the best possible prices are obtained for building materials used in the houses built or renovated in the community, and that the terms of agreements are respected by contractors.

The 21 days invalidation on a purchase order will be strictly enforced (past 21 day period it would become null and void).

AMENDMENTS TO HOUSING POLICIES

The Housing Policies may be amended only by a majority vote of the incumbent Band Council.

FINANCIAL RESPONSIBILITIES

The Housing Department will monitor the operations and make reasonable efforts to ensure that the Band's financial policies are being followed.

Chief and Council will be responsible for approving and directing the Housing Department on all budgets and finances but at no time shall direct the Housing Department to incur deficits in the housing program as funds must be reallocated from other Band programs to cover funding shortfalls in housing.

ENFORCEMENT REGULATIONS

These regulations are agreed to and signed by proper documentation by Chief and Council.

REPAIR RENOVATION ASSISTANCE PROGRAM (RRAP)

CMHC's RRAP grants will be accessed for those individuals who qualify under CMHC's guidelines.

Priority Process

Repairs will be done on a priority basis. The Housing Department will review information on all units to determine which units are in need of repairs. Repairs will be indicated on an inspection report.

The following is the criteria that will be used to determine the priority for major repairs (over $5000)

a) Five points if the applicant's present living conditions are a hazard to their health as indicated by documentation from an appropriate inspector.

b) Five points if the applicant living conditions are a fire and safety hazard as indicated by an inspection report.

c) Two points if the foundation system has a structural deficiency that does not meet minimum standards as indicated by an inspection report.

d) Two points if the flooring system has a structural deficiency that does not meet minimum standards as indicated by an inspection report.

e) Two points if the wall system has a structural deficiency that does not meet minimum standards as indicated by an inspection report.

f) Two points if the roof system has a structural deficiency that does not meet minimum standards as indicated by an inspection report.

g) Two points if the applicant's present dwelling has an inadequate or defective heating system.

h) Two points if the applicant's present dwelling has an inadequate electrical service.

i) Two points if the applicant's present dwelling has an inadequate or defective plumbing system.

j) Two points for each band member or dependant that results in an overcrowding situation in their current residence.

DEFINITION OF OVERCROWDING

Consideration is granted to families where overcrowding situations exist in the current living arrangements. To determine overcrowding for point allocation, a guideline for a minimum number of bedrooms required can be as follows:

- One bedroom for each adult or couple.
- One bedroom for children 16 years of age or older.
- One bedroom for 2 children of the same sex up to 16 years of age.
- One bedroom for 2 children of opposite sex up to 5 years of age.

MINIMUM CRITERIA FOR RRAP ELIGIBILITY

The following criteria must be met before an individual is considered for RRAP:

1. A resident band member must be 18 years of age or older in order to be considered for any housing program.
2. A band member will be responsible to have an updated application on file with the Housing Department for major repairs. (over $5,000)
3. Band member will have the responsibility to ensure that their application is updated on an annual basis.
4. Applications will only kept on file for a maximum of one year. An application that has not been updated within the year will be considered inactive and removed from the housing files.
5. CMHC's RRAP grants will be accessed for those individuals who qualify under CHMC guidelines.
6. Mandatory Homeowner Training sessions will be set and must be attended by the homeowners prior to being accepted for any program. This session will provide them with the information on policies such as estimate requirements, inspection requirements, financial responsibilities, procedures for construction, recommended products and general policies. Maintenance requirements to extend the life of the unit will also be explained and identified to homeowners. Information on items such as ventilation, maximizing energy efficiency savings, general problem areas and probable causes will also be explained. The Housing Director will coordinate this session.

JOB CREATION AND TRAINING

Where the band members are responsible for hiring their own contractors they will provide names to the Housing Department and they are encouraged to hire band members who qualify as contractors and labourers.

RE-ALLOCATION OF UNITS

Once a unit is vacated the unit will be inspected, necessary repairs done and allocated to the next band member on the priority list with an application on file for that size of unit. The Housing Department will immediately make a recommendation to the **Chief & Council** based on eligibility, as set by the pre – determined criteria for unit allocation.

Prior to vacating a unit is the tenant's responsibility to inform the Housing Department the tentative date on vacating the unit. This will start the reallocation process according to the policy noted in the previous paragraph.

TENANT TRAINING SESSIONS

Mandatory sessions will be provided to tenants prior to being accepted for a rental unit. This session will identify all the responsibilities and terms and conditions that the tenant must comply with. Maintenance responsibilities will be explained and demonstrate what is required by the tenant in order to extent the life to the unit. Information on items such as ventilation, general problem areas and probable causes and maximizing energy efficiency savings will be provided. It should be clearly indicated that minor items that are left not corrected do often lead to major repairs.

Mandatory sessions will be provided to identified units that have high repair and maintenance costs. These units will be prioritized for a tenant training session.

CRITERIA FOR NON - EMERGENCY REPAIRS

Homeowners or tenants who access the repair program frequently will be a priority for the home maintenance-counseling program.

The criteria for non – emergency housing repairs is as follows:

1. The resident must be 18 years or older.
2. The resident must be a Band Member.
3. The resident must be a homeowner.
4. The resident must complete a written request for non - emergency repairs.
5. The resident must provide verification of household income.
6. The resident must occupy a band owned home as a tenant (private rentals are not eligible to access program).
7. The approval amount will be based on a written request and the income of the household.

PROCEDURES TO ACCESS NON-EMERGENCY REPAIRS

The procedure to access non – emergency repairs is as follows:

1. A written request must be submitted to Band Technician by the homeowner. (see page 11)
2. The Band Housing Technician will inspect the unit upon receiving the written request and make application for repairs to determine eligibility based on income level of applicant.
3. The Band Technician will prepare a written inspection report based on the non-emergency request and will do an estimate of cost and program eligibility.
4. Upon reviewing non-emergency request a unit file of prior material received for unit will be reviewed by the Housing Director for recommendations to be submitted to Council for approval at the designated time.
5. Upon Council approval, the Housing Technician will issue a purchase order for material to homeowner or directly to the supplier.
6. The approved purchase order must be signed out by homeowner.

PROCEDURE FOR REQUEST OF LABOUR CONTRACTS

*******There will be no advances for labour contracts.**

1. Contractor must provide quote to band technician.
2. Work order issued by purchase order by Band Housing Technician upon approval of quote.
3. Upon submitting invoice for payment, the band technician will do an inspection for approval of payment.
4. Once inspected, the invoice will then be submitted to the housing clerk for payment to be issued no earlier than the following Thursday at 3 p.m..

HOMEOWNER OR TENANT RESPONSIBILITY

The following will be the responsibility of the homeowner or tenant:

1. Ordinary cleanliness of the premises.
2. To repair within a reasonable time after it occurs, any damage to the premises caused by the tenant's own willful or negligent conduct or by such conduct of persons who are permitted on the premises by the tenant.
3. To inform the Housing Department of any damage that may have been done by individuals not invited by tenants.
4. Trading or switching of units will not be allowed without the consent of the Chief and Council.
5. To inform the housing department of any leaks (ex. Plumbing, roof & foundation) to avoid any additional damage.

NEW HOUSING SELECTION POLICY

CRITERIA

A Band member must be 18 years of age or older in order to be considered for the new housing program.

Band members will be responsible to have an updated application on file with the Housing Department at the Band Administration Office.

Band members will have the responsibility to ensure that their application is updated on the annual basis. Points will be allocated to the application on file.

All applications will only be kept on file for a maximum of one year. An application that has not been updated within the year will be considered inactive and removed from the priority list. This process will be done on the last day of fiscal year (March 31). This process will eliminate a long waiting list that may have more needy people at the bottom of a list and will ensure that the Band member is still interested in a home, and that their circumstances have not changed from the previous year.

All applications must be fully completed or will not be accepted for evaluation because of the lack of information.

BAND COUNCIL ISSUES

Once the band member has completed their application for new housing the application will be awarded points based on a pre-determined point allocation system.

Band members will be awarded points for the set criteria which will be calculated from the information on the application form and references stated on the application.

Band members can only access the new housing program once with the exception of emergency situations. (Ex. Fire)

Mandatory Homeowner Training Session (Client Counseling) will be set and must be attended by the home owner prior to being accepted for new housing.

Once allocated a new unit, the homeowner will be responsible for all extra cost up above allocated funds for the unit. Prior to construction of unit the homeowner must have finance arrangements in place and must be identified and approved by the Housing Department.

Homeowner will not interfere with construction of the new unit (ex. Structure changes) This allows the unit to completed on schedule and within the budget costs.

Upon allocation of new unit the homeowner is required to relinquish present dwelling by quit claim to the Band Council without monetary gain. The unit will be reallocated as explained on page four (4) of the Housing Policies under Tenant & Ownership.

If a special circumstance is identified on housing application, a Housing Department representative will inspect your present dwelling upon receiving application to determine the severity of the circumstance.

Tenant training sessions are mandatory upon allocation of new unit.

CONTRACTS

The Housing Department will allocate contracts for construction of unit based on a system that is fair and cost efficient.

Contractors will sign a contract with the Eskasoni Housing Department to commence work on the unit.

Contractors will not be advanced any labor money. Payments will only be disbursed upon inspection of unit.

A construction schedule will be issued to each contractor in order to complete unit(s) within designated time.

The Housing Department will be utilizing other job development programs to lessen labor costs. If the contractor wishes to use labor job development project from the Band, the Housing Department must be contacted to determine adjustments to the cost of constructing the unit.

DEFINITION OF OVERCROWDING

Consideration is granted to families where overcrowding situations exist in the current living arrangements. To determine overcrowding for point allocation, a guideline for a minimum number of bedrooms required can be used as follows:

* One bedroom for each adult or couple.
* One bedroom for children 16 years of age or older.
* One bedroom for 2 children of the same sex up to 16 years of age.
* One bedroom for 2 children of opposite sex up to 5 years of age.

INSURANCE

The First Nation will be responsible for full structural replacement coverage. The tenant is responsible for tenant content insurance.

RE-ALLOCATING VACANT/ABANDONED UNITS

Once a unit is vacated, inspected and necessary repairs are completed the unit will be reallocated to a band member on the priority list with an application on file. The housing department will submit make a recommendation for reallocation based on criteria.

TENANT TRAINING SESSIONS

Mandatory sessions will be provided to tenants prior to being accepted for a rental unit. This session will identify all the responsibilities and terms and conditions that the tenant must comply with. Maintenance responsibilities will be explained and demonstrate what is required by the tenant in order to extend the life of the unit. Information on items such as ventilation, general problem areas and probable causes and maximizing energy efficiency saving will be provided. It should be clearly indicated that minor items that are left not corrected do often lead to major repairs.

OTHER FUNDING RESOURCE

Section 10 loans are available for those who are considering constructing a new home on their own. The Eskasoni Band Council will assist band members with ministerial guarantee that is capped. Inquire at the Housing Department for more information.

References

Appadurai, Arjun.

1996a. Sovereignty without territoriality: notes for a post-national geography. In: Patricia Yeager, editor. *The Geography of Identity.* Ann Arbor: University of Michigan Press. pp. 40–58.

1996b. *Modernity at Large: Cultural Dimensions of Globalization.* Minneapolis: University of Minnesota Press. 229 pp.

2001. *Globalization.* Durham, NC: Duke University Press. 344 pp.

Applbaum, Kalman.

2000. Crossing borders: globalization as myth and charter and American transnational consumer marketing. *America Ethnologist* 27(2):257–282.

Bakker, Peter.

1989. Two Basque loanwords in Micmac. *International Journal of American Linguistics* 55(2): 258–261.

Barnouw, Victor.

1950. *Acculturation and Personality among the Wisconsin Chippewa.* [Menasha, WI]: American Anthropological Association. 152 pp. (American Anthropological Association Memoir 72.)

1961. Chippewa social atomism. *American Anthropologist* 63:1006–1013.

Beale, Calvin L. and Glenn V. Fuguitt.

1978. The new pattern of nonmetropolitan population change. In: Karl E. Taeuber, Larry L. Bumpass and James A. Sweet, editors. *Social Demography.* New York: Academic Press. pp. 157–177.

Bestor, Theodor C.

2001. Supply-side sushi: commodity, market, and the global city. *American Anthropologist* 103(1):76–95.

Black-Michaud, Jacob.

1986. *Sheep and Land: The Economics of Power in a Tribal Society.* Cambridge: Cambridge University Press. 231 pp.

Bock, Philip K.

1966. *The Micmac Indians of Restigouche: History and Contemporary Description.* Ottawa: [Department of the Secretary of State]. 95 pp. (National Museum of Canada, Bulletin 213.)

Brown, Richard.

1869. *A History of the Island of Cape Breton with Some Account of the Discovery and Settlement of Canada, Nova Scotia, and Newfoundland.* London: Sampson Low, Son, and Marston. 464 pp.

[CHRT] Canadian Human Rights Tribunal.

2003. Dawson v. Eskasoni Indian Band [internet]. Ottawa: CHRT. [accessed 2006 May 4]. Available from: http://www.chrt-tcdp.gc.ca/search/files/t756_0603de.pdf

Cashdan, Elizabeth A.

1983. Territoriality among human foragers: ecological models and an application to four Bushman groups. *Current Anthropology* 24:47–66.

CBC NEWS.

1999. Mi'kmaq claims parcel of Eskasoni land is his [online news service]. Toronto: Canadian Broadcasting Corporation. [updated 1999 August 3; accessed 23 June 2005]. Available from: http://www.cbc.ca/news/story/1999/08/03 /nsdenny030899.html

2000. Mi'kmaq band split rejected [online news service]. Toronto: Canadian Broadcasting Corporation. [updated 2000 April 4; accessed 6 December 2000]. Available from: http://www.cbc.ca/news/story/2000/04/04 /peiSark04Apr00.html

CHUTE, JANET E.

1999. Frank G. Speck's contributions to the understanding of Mi'kmaq land use, leadership, and land management. *Ethnohistory* 46(3):481–540.

COLLINS, JANE L.

2002. Deterritorialization and workplace culture. *American Ethnologist* 29(1):151–171.

DENYS, NICOLAS.

1908. *The Description and Natural History of the Coasts of North America (Acadia).* William F. Ganong, translator and editor. Toronto: Champlain Society. 625 pp.

DENNY, ALEX.

1987 Aug. Special Report: Denny's bold quest. *Micmac News* 17(8):29. Sydney, NS: Native Communications Society of Nova Scotia. Available from: Mi'kmaq Holdings Resource Guide, Nova Scotia Archives and Records Management Library, Halifax, NS; http://www.gov.ns.ca/nsarm/library/

[DIAND] DEPARTMENT OF INDIAN AFFAIRS AND NORTHERN DEVELOPMENT.

1997–2004. First Nation Detail: Eskasoni. First Nation Profiles [internet database]. [Ottawa]: DIAND. [accessed 2001 January 18]. Available from: http://sdiprod2.inac.gc.ca/FNProfiles/FNProfiles_home.htm

DINERO, STEVEN C.

1997. Female role change and male response in the post-nomadic urban environment: the case of the Israeli Negev Bedouin. *Journal of Comparative Family Studies* 28:248–261.

DRAPER, PATRICIA.

1975. !Kung women: contrasts in sexual egalitarianism in foraging and sedentary contexts. In: Rayna Reiter, editor. *Toward an Anthropology of Women.* New York: Monthly Review Press. pp. 77–109.

DYSON-HUDSON, RADA AND ERIC ALDEN SMITH.

1978. Human territoriality: an ecological reassessment. *American Anthropologist* 80(1):21–41.

ELLEN, ROY F.

1978. *Nualu Settlement and Ecology: An Approach to the Environmental Relations of an Eastern Indonesian Community.* The Hague: Martinus Nijhoff. 265 pp.

ELLIOTT, DAVID W.

2000. *Law and Aboriginal Peoples in Canada.* 4th ed. North York, ON: Captus Press. 392 pp.

ELLIOTT, MICHAEL.

2003 Jul 7. The war that never ends. *Time* 162(1):28–31.

EMBER, CAROL R. AND MELVIN EMBER.

1996. *Cultural Anthropology.* 8th ed. Upper Saddle River, NJ: Prentice Hall. 433 pp.

ESMER, YILMAZ.

2006. Globalization, "McDonaldization" and values: quo vadis? *Comparative Sociology* 5(2–3):183–202.

FAHIM, HUSSEIN M.

1980. Nubian resettlement and nomadic sedentarization in Khasm el-Girba Scheme, Eastern

Sudan. In: Philip Carl Salzman, editor. *When Nomads Settle: Processes of Sedentarization as Adaptation and Response.* New York: Praeger Publishers. pp. 140–156.

FRANTZ, CHARLES.
1980. The open niche, pastoralism, and sedentarization in the Mambila grasslands of Nigeria. In: Philip Carl Salzman, editor. *When Nomads Settle: Processes of Sedentarization as Adaptation and Response.* New York: Praeger Publishers. pp. 62–79.

FRATKIN, ELLIOT M., ERIC ABELLA ROTH AND MARTHA A. NATHAN.
1999. When nomads settle: the effects of commoditization, nutritional change, and formal education on Ariaal and Rendille pastoralists. Current Anthropology 40(5):729–735.

FRIEDMAN, THOMAS L.
2006. *The World Is Flat: A Brief History of the Twenty-first Century.* 1st updated and expanded edition. New York: Farrar, Straus and Giroux. 593 pp.

GALATY, JOHN G.
1980. The Maasai group-ranch: politics and development in an African pastoral society. In: Philip Carl Salzman, editor. *When Nomads Settle: Processes of Sedentarization as Adaptation and Response.* New York: Praeger Publishers. pp. 157–172.

GLOADE, HAROLD.
1989. Oct. Our life on Horton Reserve. *Micmac News* 19(10):30. Sydney, NS: Native Communications Society of Nova Scotia. Available from: Mi'kmaq Holdings Resource Guide, Nova Scotia Archives and Records Management Library, Halifax, NS; http://www.gov.ns.ca/nsarm/ library/

GOLDSCHMIDT, WALTER R.
1980. Career reorientation and institutional adaptation in the process of natural sedentarization. In: Philip Carl Salzman, editor. *When Nomads Settle: Processes of Sedentarization as Adaptation and Response.* New York: Praeger Publishers. pp. 48–61.

HALLIDAY, MICHAEL.
1989 Nov. Life on Horton Reserve—sequel. *Micmac News* 19(11):20. Sydney, NS: Native Communications Society of Nova Scotia. Available from: Mi'kmaq Holdings Resource Guide, Nova Scotia Archives and Records Management Library, Halifax, NS; http://www.gov.ns.ca/nsarm/library/

HAMILTON, W. D.
1984. *The Julian Tribe.* Fredericton, NB: University of New Brunswick, Micmac-Maliseet Institute. 108 pp.

HAWLEY, DONNA LEA.
1986. *The Indian Act Annotated.* 2nd ed. Toronto: Carswell. 210 pp.

HOFFMAN, BERNARD G.
1955. *The Historical Ethnography of the Micmac of the Sixteenth and Seventeenth Centuries* [dissertation]. Berkeley: University of California, Berkeley, Department of Anthropology. 839 pp. Available from: Mi'kmaq Holdings Resource Guide, Nova Scotia Archives and Records Management Library, Halifax, NS; http://www.gov.ns.ca/nsarm/library/

HOWARD, JAMES H.
1965. The St. Anne's Day celebration of the Micmac Indians, 1962. *Museum News, South Dakota Museum* 26(2):5–20.

[IAB] INDIAN AFFAIRS BRANCH.
1986 Dec. [Band lists]. *Micmac News* 16(12)(Christmas Suppl):18. Available from: Mi'kmaq Holdings Resource Guide, Nova Scotia Archives and Records Management Library, Halifax, NS; http://www.gov.ns.ca/nsarm/library/

INGLEHART, RONALD AND WAYNE E. BAKER.

2000. Modernization, cultural change, and the persistence of traditional values. *American Sociological Review* 65(1):19–51.

JOHNSON, JOAN.

1982 May. Grand Council member speaks. *Micmac News* 12(5):B3. Sydney, NS: Native Communications Society of Nova Scotia. Available from: Mi'kmaq Holdings Resource Guide, Nova Scotia Archives and Records Management Library, Halifax, NS; http://www.gov.ns.ca/nsarm/library/

JOURNAL OF LEGAL PLURALISM AND UNOFFICIAL LAW.

Birmingham, UK: Foundation for the Journal of Legal Pluralism, in association with the African Studies Center, University of California, Los Angeles. Vol. 1, 1969–. Available from: http://www.jlp.bham.ac.uk/

KENT, SUSAN.

1989. And justice for all: the development of political centralization among newly sedentary foragers. *American Anthropologist* 91:703–712.

1995a. Unstable households in a stable Kalahari community in Botswana. *American Anthropologist* 97:297–312.

1995b. Does sedentarization promote gender inequality? A case study from the Kalahari. *Journal of the Royal Anthropological Institute* 1(3):513–536.

KOSANSKY, OREN.

2002. Tourism, charity, and profit: the movement of money in Moroccan Jewish pilgrimage. *Cultural Anthropology* 17(3):359–400.

LEACOCK, ELEANOR.

1954. *The Montagnais "Hunting Territory" and the Fur Trade.* [Menasha, WI]: American Anthropological Association. 59 pp. (American Anthropological Association Memoir 78.)

LE CLERCQ, FATHER CHRESTIEN.

1910. *New Relation of Gaspesia.* W. F. Ganong, editor. Toronto: Champlain Society. 452 pp.

LEE, RICHARD B.

1979. *The !Kung San: Men, Women, and Work in a Foraging Society.* Cambridge: Cambridge University Press. 526 pp.

1988. Reflections on primitive communism. In: Tim Ingold, David Riches and James Woodburn, editors. *Hunters and Gatherers.* Volume 1, History, Evolution, and Social Change. Papers from the Fourth International Conference on Hunting and Gathering Societies; 1986 Sept 8–13; London. Oxford: Berg Publishers. pp. 252–268.

LESCARBOT, MARC.

1928. *Nova Francia: A Description of Acadia, 1606.* P. Erondelle, translator, 1609. Introduction by H. P. Biggar. London: George Routledge & Sons, Ltd. 346 pp.

LLEWELLYN, K. N. AND E. ADAMSON HOEBEL.

1941. *The Cheyenne Way: Conflict and Case Law in Primitive Jurisprudence.* Norman: University of Oklahoma Press. 360 pp.

MARSHALL, DONALD.

1988a Jul. Notice. *Micmac News* 18(7):44. Sydney, NS: Native Communications Society of Nova Scotia. Available from: Mi'kmaq Holdings Resource Guide, Nova Scotia Archives and Records Management Library, Halifax, NS; http://www.gov.ns.ca/nsarm/library/

1988b Aug. Mi'kmaq Treaty Day Proclamation. *Micmac News* 18(8):2. Sydney, NS: Native Communications Society of Nova Scotia. Available from: Mi'kmaq Holdings Resource Guide, Nova Scotia Archives and Records Management Library, Halifax, NS; http://www.gov.ns.ca/nsarm/library/

Marx, Emanuel.

1980. Wage labor and tribal economy of the Bedouin in South Sinai. In: Philip Carl Salzman, editor. *When Nomads Settle: Processes of Sedentarization as Adaptation and Response.* New York: Praeger Publishers. pp. 111–123.

Mbembe, Achille.

2001. At the edge of the world: boundaries, territoriality, and sovereignty in Africa. In: Arjun Appadurai, editor. *Globalization.* Durham, NC: Duke University Press. pp. 22–51.

Meir, Avinoam and Yosef Ben-David.

1995. From latent surplus to changing norms: fertility behavior of the Israeli Bedouin along the nomadism-sedentarism continuum. *Journal of Comparative Family Studies* 26:389–408.

Mi'kmaq Resource Centre.

1998. Ethnographies [internet]. Sydney, NS: University College of Cape Breton. [updated 1998 Oct 27; accessed 2000 Dec 6]. Available from: http:// www.uccb.ns.ca/mikmaq/ethnog.html

Moore, Erin P.

1998. *Gender, Law, and Resistance in India.* Tucson: University of Arizona Press. 205 pp.

Morse, Bradford W., editor.

1985. *Aboriginal Peoples and the Law: Indian, Metis and Inuit Rights in Canada.* Ottawa: Carleton University Press. 800 pp.

New Factfinder to Advise on First Nations Matrimonial Property Rights.

1998 Sept. *Mi'kmaq-Maliseet Nations News* 9(9):5. Truro, NS: The Confederacy of Mainland Mi'kmaq/Eastern Woodlands Publishing. http://www.cmmns.com/ EWP.php

Pastore, Ralph T.

1977. The Mic-Mac colonization of Newfoundland; paper presented at the annual meeting of the Canadian Historical Association, 1977. 21 pp. Available from: Mi'kmaq Holdings Resource Guide, Nova Scotia Archives and Records Management Library, Halifax, NS; http://www.gov.ns.ca/nsarm/library/

Pospisil, Leopold.

1958a. *Kapauku Papuans and Their Law.* New Haven: Yale University, Department of Anthropology. 296 pp. (Yale University Publications in Anthropology 54.)

1958b. Social change and primitive law: consequences of a Papuan legal case. American Anthropologist 60:832–837.

1971. *Anthropology of Law: A Comparative Theory.* New York: Harper and Row. 385 pp.

Prins, Harald E. L.

1988. *Tribulations of a Border Tribe: A Discourse on the Political Ecology of the Aroostook Band of the Micmacs (Sixteenth–Twentieth Centuries)* [dissertation]. New York: New School for Social Research. 368 pp. Available from: Dissertations & Theses: Full Text [online database]; http://www.proquest.com/ (publication no. AAT 8827013).

Public Archives of Canada.

Record Group 10 (Department of Indian Affairs). Library and Archives Canada, Ottawa; http://collectionscanada.gc.ca

Pufendorf, Samuel von.

1927. *De Officio Hominus et Civis Juxta Legem Naturalem Libri Duo,* 1682. Volume 1, Facsimile. Volume 2, Translation of 1682 edition. Frank Gardner Moore, translator. New York: Oxford University Press. (Classics of International Law 10.)

Rand, Silas Tertius.

1888. *Dictionary of the Language of the Micmac Indians, who reside in Nova Scotia, New Brunswick, Prince Edward Island, Cape Breton and Newfoundland.* Halifax, NS: Nova Scotia Printing Company. 286 pp.

1902. *Rand's Micmac Dictionary: From Phonographic Word-Lists.* Charlottetown, PEI: Patriot Pub. 192 pp.

RENTELN, ALISON DUNDES AND ALAN DUNDES, EDITORS.

1995. F*olk Law: Essays in the Theory and Practice of Lex Non Scripta.* Madison: University of Wisconsin Press. 1037 pp.

RESOLUTIONS COMMENDING THE MIKMAQ NATION ON THE OCCASION OF THE REENACTMENT OF THE TREATY OF WATERTOWN, JULY 19, 1776

1987 Aug. *Micmac News* 17(8):32. Sydney, NS: Native Communications Society of Nova Scotia. Available from: Mi'kmaq Holdings Resource Guide, Nova Scotia Archives and Records Management Library, Halifax, NS; http://www.gov.ns.ca/ nsarm/library/

REYNOLDS, BARRIE.

1978. Beothuk. In: Bruce Trigger, editor. William Sturtevant, general editor. *Handbook of North American Indians.* Volume 15, Northeast. Washington, DC: Smithsonian Institution. pp. 101–108.

RODMAN, WILLIAM L.

1985. "A law unto themselves": legal innovation in Ambae, Vanuatu. *American Ethnologist* 12(4):603–624.

SALZMAN, PHILIP CARL.

1980a. Introduction: processes of sedentarization as adaptation and response. In: Philip Carl Salzman, editor. *When Nomads Settle: Processes of Sedentarization as Adaptation and Response.* New York: Praeger Publishers. pp. 1–19.

1980b. Processes of sedentarization among the nomads of Baluchistan. In: Philip Carl Salzman, editor. *When Nomads Settle: Processes of Sedentarization as Adaptation and Response.* New York: Praeger Publishers. pp. 95–110.

SANDERS, TODD.

2003. Reconsidering witchcraft: postcolonial Africa and analytic (un)certainties. *American Anthropologist* 105:338–352.

SEIDLER, MICHAEL, TRANSLATOR.

1990. *Samuel Pufendorf's On the Natural State of Men: The 1687 Latin Edition and English Translation.* Lewiston, NY: Edwin Mellen Press. 140 pp. (Studies in the History of Philosophy 13.)

SMITH, MELVIN.

1995. *Our Home or Native Land?: What Governments Aboriginal Policy Is Doing to Canada.* Toronto: Stoddart Publishing. 287 pp.

SPECK, FRANK G.

1922. *Beothuk and Micmac.* New York: Museum of the American Indian, Heye Foundation. 187 pp. (Indian Notes and Monographs, Miscellaneous Series 22.)

STATISTICS CANADA.

1983. *1981 Census of Canada: Selected Social and Economic Characteristics: Nova Scotia.* Ottawa: Minister of Supply and Services. PAGES?

STEEN, SHEILA CRAIG.

1951. *The Psychological Consequences of Acculturation Among the Cape Breton Micmac* [master's thesis]. Philadelphia: University of Pennsylvania, Department of Anthropology. 140 pp.

STOLLER, PAUL.

2003. Circuits of African art/paths of wood: exploring an anthropological trail. *Anthropological Quarterly* 76(2):207–234.

THWAITES, REUBEN GOLD, EDITOR.

1896a. *The Jesuit relations and allied documents: travels and explorations of the Jesuit missionaries in New France, 1610–1791; the original French, Latin, and Italian texts, with English translations and notes.* Volume 1, Acadia: 1610–1613. Cleveland: Burrows Brothers. 319 pp. Available from: http:// www.alexanderstreet2.com/eenalive/index.html

1896b. *The Jesuit relations and allied documents: travels and explorations of the Jesuit missionaries in New France, 1610–1791; the original French, Latin, and Italian texts, with English translations and notes.* Volume 2, Acadia: 1612–1614. Cleveland: Burrows Brothers. 307 pp. Available from: http:// www.alexanderstreet2.com/eenalive/index.html

1897. *The Jesuit relations and allied documents: travels and explorations of the Jesuit missionaries in New France, 1610–1791; the original French, Latin, and Italian texts, with English translations and notes.* Volume 3, Acadia: 1611–1616. Cleveland: Burrows Brothers. 301 pp. Available from: http:// www.alexanderstreet2.com/eenalive/index.html

TREATY OF WATERTOWN, 1776

1987 Aug. *Micmac News* 17(8):28. Sydney, NS: Native Communications Society of Nova Scotia. Available from: Mi'kmaq Holdings Resource Guide, Nova Scotia Archives and Records Management Library, Halifax, NS; http://www.gov.ns.ca/ nsarm/library/

TSING, ANNA.

2000. The global situation. *Cultural Anthropology* 15(3):327–360.

TUCK, JAMES A.

1978. Regional cultural development, 3000 to 300 B.C. In: Bruce Trigger, editor. William Sturtevant, general editor. *Handbook of North American Indians.* Volume 15, Northeast. Washington, DC: Smithsonian Institution. pp. 28–43.

UPTON, LESLIE F. S.

1979. *Micmacs and Colonists: Indian–White Relations in the Maritimes, 1713–1867.* Vancouver: University of British Columbia Press. 243 pp.

WALLIS, WILSON D. AND R. S. WALLIS.

1955. *The Micmac Indians of Eastern Canada.* Minneapolis: University of Minnesota Press. 515 pp.

WHEWELL, WILLIAM, TRANSLATOR.

1853. *Grotius on the Rights of War and Peace: An Abridged Translation.* Volume 1. London: John W. Parker. 416 pp.

WILDSMITH, BRUCE H.

1985. Pre Confederation treaties. In: Bradford W. Morse, editor. *Aboriginal Peoples and the Law: Indian, Metis and Inuit rights in Canada.* Ottawa: Carleton University Press. pp. 122–271.

WOODWARD, JACK.

1990. *Native Law.* Toronto: Carswell. 626 pp.

Index

Entries referring to figures (*f*) and tables (*t*) are in italics.

M

S